Relationships Between Industry and Bank in Germany

Toshio Yamazaki

Relationships Between Industry and Bank in Germany

A Historical Study of Personnel Connection Built Through Interlocking Directorate and Bank's Advisory Council System

Springer

Toshio Yamazaki
College of Business Administration
Ritsumeikan University
Ibaraki, Osaka, Japan

ISBN 978-981-97-4995-9 ISBN 978-981-97-4996-6 (eBook)
https://doi.org/10.1007/978-981-97-4996-6

This Springer imprint is published by the registered company Springer Nature Singapore Pte Ltd.
The registered company address is: 152 Beach Road, #21-01/04 Gateway East, Singapore 189721, Singapore

For my wife, Naomi

Preface

This book elucidates the foundational characteristics and significance of industry–bank relationships in Germany by examining the structures and functions of personnel connections of three large banks with other enterprises historically. Given that the research by Otto Jeidels published in 1905 (Jeidels 1905) is considered a classical work, numerous research results have been published. Such a system of industrial concentration based on the industry–bank relationships is an important element that determines the characteristics and a cornerstone of the accumulation structure of German capitalism.

The personnel connections of big banks with many companies in various industries form the foundation of an industry–bank relationship. An individual enterprise as an independent behavioral agent does not always perform decision-making alone but develops businesses using the relationships of interaction and interdependence between companies, including competing enterprises. Such interactive and interdependent relations are typically developed through various contacts and exchanges of information based on personnel connections between enterprises. Moreover, personnel connections established by large banks with several firms are more robust than those built by industrial enterprises. There are numerous instances in which personnel connections are established through interlocking directorates with a mandate of an important position, such as chairman or vice-chairman of the supervisory board.

When considering a system of interfirm relationships from the international perspective, it can be observed that the interactive relationships between enterprises in Germany differ from those in other countries. A typical pattern can be observed. This includes personnel connection through assignment and interlocking directorates of members of the supervisory board and the board of directors on the supervisory board of other enterprises, as well as an advisory council system as a special committee to build and strengthen relationships between a bank and industrial enterprises in various industrial sectors. This is an important element of the industry–bank relationship. In contrast to the limited personnel connections between enterprises that are typical of industrial enterprises, large banks have established more extensive and effective personnel connections. These connections facilitate the exchange and sharing of information, coordination of interests, and the management of conflicts between banks and industrial companies and between corporations. This system is related to the German characteristics of business management and corporate behavior and is linked to the social and economic system called "cooperative capitalism." Consequently, the structure and function of the personnel connections between banks and industrial enterprises, as well as their evolution throughout the historical process from the shift to monopolistic capitalism in the early twentieth century to the present, represent significant research topics that require further clarification.

This book addresses these issues by examining the structure and function of personnel connections through interlocking directorates of the members of top management. These include the supervisory and managing boards of the three largest banks, namely Deutsche Bank, Dresdner Bank, and Commerzbank, on the supervisory board of other enterprises, as well as personnel relations through advisory council organizations. This book also considers personnel ties through bank's advisory council organizations. It asks what companies and industries the three banks built personnel connections through such means. What differences can be observed between the direct interlocking directorates of each bank and indirect interlocking directorates built among the three banks and between two on the supervisory board of other enterprises? What were the conditions for members of each advisory council and top management? What are the functions exhibited by such personnel connection? This book examines the German-style mechanism of cooperation between enterprises by exploring these issues.

First, this book employs a case study approach to analyze the personnel connections of three major banks with industrial enterprises. It posits that the quality of these connections is contingent upon the purpose of obtaining information. To illustrate this point, the book presents concrete examples of personnel connections between the banks and industrial enterprises, including the structures of personnel connections established through direct and indirect interlocking directorates and advisory councils. This book is concerned with the analysis of concrete situations of personnel connections built by three representative banks through interlocking directorates of their top management and specific organizations such as the advisory council system.

Second, this book explores the structure of personnel connections during some periods regarded as important in historical analysis. The actual conditions during the establishment of monopolistic capitalism in the early twentieth century, inflation after World War I, the mid-1930s during National Socialism, the late 1950s as the period before the 1965 Corporations Law, which regulated the number of supervisory board members, is considered alongside the late 1960s, the period after this law was enacted, and the recent period of the latter half of the 2010s.

Third, the text elucidates the function of personnel connections between banks and industrial enterprises, as well as between industrial enterprises themselves, with regard to the structure of such interfirm relationships. The structure of personnel connections represents an essential foundation for the display of function. Through a comprehensive analysis of both the structure and function of personnel ties, this book endeavors to elucidate the mechanism of cooperative interfirm relationships in Germany and its significance from the standpoint of historical comparison and comparison among the three largest German banks. The originality and significance of this book lie in its combined analysis of the structure and function of personnel connections between enterprises through interlocking directorates and banks' advisory councils.

Fourth, this book employs social network analysis to examine the structure of personnel networks between enterprises. This research method allows for the quantitative understanding of the "cohesiveness" of the network and the identification of which company is at a central position in the network. Whereas the former is measured by an indicator "density," the latter is grasped by another indicator "centrality." This book compares the networks of three large banks using these two key concepts.

Fifth, the aforementioned research topics are considered using a multitude of historical original materials from the archives of major banks and representative enterprises of major industries. The analysis in this book is based on a plethora of internal documents of banks and industrial companies regarding important persons, such as interlocking supervisory board members and key figures in the relevant sector, as well as advisory council organizations. The analysis also encompasses a number of studies provided by books, articles, reports, and various materials.

Sixth, with regard to the influence of banks on industrial enterprises and the power of banks, this book examines the relationships between industry and banks based on the distinction of two key issues: (1) "the power to determine the member composition of the board of directors or supervisory board" ("corporate control") and (2) "control over business and assets of enterprise" ("corporate rule") (Scott 1990). Prior studies have not differentiated these two phenomena as distinct concepts, and both were interpreted as a single concept of "control." This book examines the personnel connection created by interlocks, distinguishing banks' involvement in or their influence on other enterprises' management and business policy, as well as bank restrictions in decision-making in individual companies through interlocking directorates and personnel networks.

The book is structured as follows: Chap. 1 introduces the purpose and significance of the book by explaining the various issues that are covered. Furthermore, the analytical framework is elucidated.

Part I considers the structure of the interlocking directorates of the members of large banks belonging to the supervisory or managing board on the supervisory board of other enterprises. It discusses the direct and indirect interlocking directorates developed among the three large banks and between two banks on the supervisory board of another company. Chapter 2 examines the interlocking directorates in the early twentieth century as the period of the shift to monopolistic capitalism in Germany when "finance capital" developed by Lenin (Ленин 1962) was created through unity and adhesion of industrial and bank capital. Chapter 3 analyzes the actual conditions of interlocking directorates in the period of inflation after World War I. In earlier studies, the influence of banks on industrial enterprises became weaker and industrial companies became more independent from a bank with a big change in funds demand for these enterprises, movement to avoid possession of money capital, and pursue securing of assets with the real value under the extremely progressive extensive inflation. In this chapter, the condition of personnel connection of three large banks through both direct and indirect interlocking directorates is explained compared with the situation in beginning of the early twentieth century. Chapter 4 discusses the interlocking directorates in the Nazi era compared with the condition during the inflationary period in the Weimar era. Regarding the periods after World War II, three periods are analyzed. Chapter 5 examines the circumstances that led to the establishment of the oligopolistic competitive system of three major banks as a cornerstone of the industrial concentration system during the late 1950s. This was achieved through the reconcentration of dissolved banks following the war, with no influence of the 1965 Corporations Law that regulated the number of mandates one person could hold on the supervisory board. Chapter 6 compares the interlocking directorates in the late 1960s, a period following the enactment of the aforementioned legislation, with the period in the late 1950s. Furthermore, in Chap. 7, the author considers changes observed since the 1990s, specifically the recent condition of the interlocking directorates. The author examines the cases of two of the largest banks, namely Deutsche Bank and Commerzbank, in the latter half of the 2010s.

In Part II, the personnel networks of three large banks are analyzed using the methodology of social network analysis. This is done by examining the interlocking directorates of members of the supervisory board on the same top management of other companies, including second- and third-party enterprises. Three chapters in Part II present a quantitative analysis of the characteristics of the network as a whole and the importance of each company in the network. This is done by analyzing the key indicators of social network analysis, such as "density" and "centrality." Chapter 8 considers the conditions in the mid-1930s during National Socialism before World War II. Chapter 9 investigates the situation during the late 1960s concerning the period after the war. The establishment of the basic system of interlocking directorates in postwar Germany under the 1965 Corporations Law, which greatly influenced the conditions of the interlocking directorates on the supervisory board of other enterprises, is the main reason why this period is considered in this chapter. In addition to these two periods, Chap. 10 analyzes personnel networks of two of the largest banks in Germany (Deutsche Bank and Commerzbank) in the latter half of the 2010s.

Part III examines the function of interlocking directorates on the supervisory board before and after World War II using the original materials possessed in the archives of representative enterprises in banking and major industries. In general, such functions can be observed in exchanging and sharing information and coordinating interests and conflicts between enterprises. Chapter 11 analyzes the function of direct interlocking directorates before World War II. The text considers the election of directors of the managing board in industrial enterprises in which a bank's representative had the mandate of the supervisory board and the influence of this bank in such matters. It also examines the selection of candidates as members of the supervisory board of the large bank itself, who were to be suggested at the general meeting. Furthermore, it elucidates roles of interlocking supervisory board members from bank in management. Chapter 12 examines the functions and roles of interlocking supervisory board members in the context of personnel issues of a member of the supervisory board in both industrial enterprises and banks, as well as the coordination function of the interlocking supervisory board member between enterprises.

In Part IV, the structure and function of personnel connections between the bank and industrial enterprises and among corporations through the bank's advisory council system are analyzed using primary materials owned in the archives of large banks. This analysis reveals the important role of the council system as an important means of complementing personnel relations formed through interlocking directorates. The period preceding the World War II, specifically the mid-1930s, is of interest due to the availability of a substantial number of original historical materials related to this era. Chapter 13 examines the conditions of personnel connections through regional advisory councils during National Socialism. Chapter 14 analyzes the functions of such personnel connections prior to the outbreak of war. With regard to the period following the World War II, Chap. 15 analyzes the conditions of personnel connections through central and regional advisory councils in the late 1960s, at a time when the 1965 Corporations Law, which regulated the number of supervisory board posts that one person could hold, had already been enacted. Chapter 16 investigates the functions of personnel connections through such systems by examining the activities of advisory councils following the World War II.

Chapter 17 builds upon the preceding sections by elucidating the structure and characteristics of a cooperative system between enterprises based on industry–bank relationships and the roles of such a system in German cooperative capitalism. Moreover, this chapter elucidates the historical changes in industry–bank relationships that are based on personnel connections. This is achieved by understanding the structure and function of personnel connections of large banks established with several enterprises across various industries. Furthermore, the German form of "finance capital," which is based on the uniting and knitting of monopolistic capital in industries and the banking industry, is examined. Additionally, this book attempts to grasp the changes in personnel ties in relation to historical conditions in each period. It examines how changes in the personnel connections of big banks during each significant period were shaped by the historical situations of both global and German capitalism in terms of economic and industrial factors, without limiting the factors specific to the enterprise level.

I am grateful to those who have supported and encouraged me to complete this book. Professor Masaki Nakata, my esteemed researcher and emeritus professor at Ritsumeikan University in Japan, who has provided valuable insight and enlightening perspectives over a long period of more than forty years, provided me with many important instructions and advice in writing this book. This book would not have been possible without them. I express my gratitude to Professor Werner Plumpe, emeritus professor at the Goethe University Frankfurt and Professor Alexander Nützenadel at the Humboldt University of Berlin. They accepted me as a visiting scholar at their universities. I am also grateful to my wife, Naomi, who has provided invaluable assistance in maintaining my study. Without her constant encouragement and support, it would not have been possible to complete this book. I dedicate this book to her.

Ibaraki, Osaka, Japan Toshio Yamazaki

References

Jeidels O (1905) Das Verhältnis der deutschen Groβbanken zur Industrie mit besonderer Berücksichtigung der Eisenindustrie. Duncker & Humblot, Leipzig

Ленин ВИ (1962) Империализм, как высшая стадия капитализма: популярный очерк. In: Полное собрание сочинений. Tom 27, ос. изд-во полит. лит-ры, Москва, pp. 299–426

Scott J (1990) Corporate control and corporate rule: Britain in an international perspective. Br J Sociol 41(3):351–373

Contents

About the Author

Toshio Yamazaki Dr. in Business Administration, Ritsumeikan University, is Professor at the College of Business Administration, Ritsumeikan University. He previously held the positions of Assistant Professor, Lecturer, and Associate Professor at the Faculty of Humanities and Economics, Kochi University; Associate Professor at the College of Business Administration, Ritsumeikan University; and Visiting Scholar at the Free University of Berlin, University of Cologne, University of Marburg, Goethe University Frankfurt, and Humboldt University of Berlin.

His areas of expertise include management studies and comparative business history. His main research field is the history of business management and interfirm relationships. He served as director of the Japan Association for the Comparative Studies of Management of Japan from 2011 to 2017. He is the editor of the *Journal of Business Management* (edited by the Japan Association of Business Management, language: Japanese).

He has published numerous monographs and articles, including the book *German Business Management: A Japanese Perspective on Regional Development Factors* (Springer, 2013), which was awarded the Japan Association for the Comparative Studies of Management Academic Prize.

List of Figures

List of Tables

Chapter 1
Introduction: Research Topics and Analytical Framework

Abstract This chapter elaborates on the book's purpose and significance using findings from previous research on related topics. It begins by explaining changes in German interfirm relationships due to globalization and Americanization after the 1990s. Subsequently, building and developing relationships between industry and banks are considered in terms of their historical context, universal banking system, principal forms and fundamental characteristics of personal unions, corporate governance systems, and changes in personnel connections. Based on these examinations, four research topics will be identified: (1) the structure of personnel ties built through interlocking directorates, (2) the functions of such personnel connections, (3) the structure of functions of personnel connections through the bank advisory council system, and (4) the German form of "finance capital" based on the uniting and knitting of monopolistic capitals in industries and banking. Furthermore, the analytical framework used in this book is described from the perspective of industry–bank relationships, including business management issues concerning behavioral mode, mutual relationships among political, industrial, and business economies, accumulation structure of German enterprises, and the methodology of social network analysis.

Keywords Advisory council · Corporate control · Corporate rule · Germany Inc. · Industry–bank relationships · Interlocking directorate · Personnel connection · Social network analysis

1.1 German Interfirm Relationships Under Globalization and Americanization

Today, the foundations of capitalism are being challenged. Economic globalization, which began in the 1990s, clarified the "American standard" as a model capitalistic system and strengthened US influence. The phenomenon of Americanization resurfaced as globalization progressed. Against the backdrop of relatively long-term US economic development known as the "new economy," a corporate perspective

T. Yamazaki, *Relationships Between Industry and Bank in Germany*,
https://doi.org/10.1007/978-981-97-4996-6_1

oriented toward shareholder value, increased capital market pressures on corporations, and further financial expansion based on the rapid development of financial globalization have emerged. Although various nations are in the process of settling while their versions of capitalism share some similarities, they have not yet fully adapted to Americanization, and significant differences in such processes have been observed between countries. Discussing the "varieties of capitalism" has resulted in important research topics. With the US-led financial crisis of 2008 increasing global impact and economic severity, US-style capitalism and management model encountered marked limitations and failures.

In such cases, the "Rheinland model of capitalism" (Rhenish capitalism) (Albert 1991) or a "coordinated market economy" (Hall and Soskice 2001) best represents capitalism in Germany. This market economy model differs from the US model in that the latter views the entire spectrum of market principles as the greatest good, whether in the commodity, financial, or labor markets. Industrial systems based on interfirm relationships are closely related to the cooperative characteristics of German capitalism. Such a company constitution has been dubbed "die Deutschland AG" ("Germany Inc.") (Streeck and Höpner 2003; Zugehör 2003; Cromme 2005; Adams 1994). Capital connections based on shareholdings and personnel connections formed through interlocking directorates between industrial enterprises and banks, as well as between industrial enterprises themselves, have been central components of such interfirm relationships. In addition to the codetermination system, which reduced the number of shareholder representatives on the supervisory board, this type of interfirm relationship has laid a solid foundation for Germany's unique corporate behavioral mode and provided opportunities for autonomous corporate management even as capital market pressures increase. Following World War II, Germany pursued long-term business expansion, emphasizing product differentiation based on technology, quality, and functionality. Given that a large portion of sales were made in Europe and Germany, this management style is better suited to the market's structure and conditions. Even as country companies continued to accept American-style methods, the German method provided an alternative. Product differentiation is built on the post-World War II, diversified, high-quality production system (Abelshauser 2003; Streeck 1992), focusing on product and pricing policies rather than marketing methods. The development of management that emphasizes production, technique, and quality based on functionality to enable product differentiation has been significant for establishing competitive advantage (Yamazaki 2013a, b, 2017). Many German companies specialize in niche markets geared toward exports. The characteristic of the German system can be seen in the mutual close connections of many enterprises on the one hand and the thorough evasion of price competition on the other hand (Furch 2012, S. 91). Establishing cooperative relationships based on personnel connections between industry and banks, as well as among industrial enterprises, has laid the groundwork for such corporate behavior.

The social economic system known as "Rhenish capitalism" is a model of capitalism defined by a financial system centered on banks, close economic relationships between banks and industry, a balance of power between shareholders and management, and social partnerships between labor unions and employers (Marx and Leitmeyer 2022a). Banks are interested in not only individual enterprise but also the success of national economic sectors as a whole, thus ensuring the entire system's stability (Ringe 2015, p. 501). An important aspect of "Germany Inc." is the effect of risk decrease in connection relationships for banks (Beyer 2006, S. 103). Karoline Krenn points out that the essential feature of "Germany Inc." was already observed during the Weimar Republic (Krenn 2013, S. 108). Germany Inc., as a close network of mutual connections in which Deutsche Bank and Dresdner Bank on the one hand and Allianz and Münchener Rückversicheungs-Gesellschaft on the other hand are core actors, reached its peak after World War II and was not fundamentally eroded until the 1990s (Plumpe et al. 2020, S.XVI; Furch 2012, S. 67; Eggenkämper et al. 2015, S. 248; Beyer 2006, S. 107). Ralf Ahrens emphasizes that representatives of large banks in the "Germany Inc." system tended to largely balance competition and cooperation, particularly long-term securing and expanding relationships as house banks (Ahrens 2013, S. 211). Industrial enterprises also build their capital and personnel connections, and as a result, the close networks of Germany Inc. make hostile acquisitions impossible (Furch 2012, S. 65).

In many cases, individual entrepreneurs make decisions and behave not alone, but develop management by establishing cooperative relationships between firms based on business relations, capital, and personnel connections between enterprises. In terms of international comparison, Germany's mode of mutual interaction between companies differs from that of other countries. In Germany, top management consists of a board of directors and a supervisory board. The institutional characteristics of such a two-layer system resulted in a German-specific structure of interlocking directorates that differs from that of other nations. Based on the functions and powers of the supervisory board that differ from those of the managing board (election and dismissal of management board members, supervision and monitoring of their administration, discussion functions, and preservation of agreement rights on important management issues) (Abshagen 2007, SS. 55–56, 58, 60–61, 64–65), this determines special significance in terms of personnel connection roles and functions.

However, it has been noted that supervisory boards can indirectly influence business management by appointing and dismissing directors (Bleicher et al. 1984, SS. 28–29) and are involved in deliberative corporate policy decision-making (Gutenberg 1970, S. 3, SS. 5–6). Interlocks on supervisory board posts by bank may have special meaning in cases where the supervisory board served as a second decision-making body in addition to the board of directors (Bleicher et al. 1989, S. 55; Gutenberg 1970, S. 6) and there was a significant gap between the law and actual practice.

The unique system of industry–bank relationships is one of the central components of such collaborative relationships. Such institutions are not only deeply concerned with the characteristics of the corporate behavioral mode and industrial economy in Germany, but also an important element determining the unique character of the social economic system known as "cooperative capitalism" (see Chandler 1990). It has also served as the foundation of German capitalism's accumulation structure and played an important process in postwar German corporate development.

Relationships between industries and banks have been established through a variety of means. Except for financing, Otto Jeidels identified four types: (1) account current transactions, (2) providing services for issuing securities, (3) assigning bank members to the supervisory boards of other enterprises, and (4) direct capital participation (Jeidels 1905, S. 109). Because of the universal characteristics of financial institutions that play an active role in industry, large banks have established as many connections with industrial enterprises as possible while eliminating unbalanced regional and industrial distributions. They also attempted to place relations with industrial enterprises on regular continuous business relations and give the possibility of enlarging and deepening relationships with industry through holding mandates on supervisory boards (Jeidels 1905, S. 180).

Personnel ties with numerous firms in various industrial sectors serve as an important foundation for close relationships between industry and banks. Albach (1993, S.III) found a correlation between capital participation and personnel connections. Therefore, it is important to understand the structure of interlocking directorates in the context of the capital network (Windolf 2002, p. 75). Banks' personnel connections with many companies, including industrial companies, were generally more intensive than those formed by industrial companies (Jeidels 1905, SS. 95, 105–108; Krenn 2013, SS. 95–96; Yamazaki 2019).

1.2 Establishment and Development of Relationships Between Industry and Bank in Germany

Following that, based on previous research, the establishment and development of special relationships between industry and banks are explored. This section looks at industry–bank relationships in the context of the universal banking system and the characteristics and changes in personnel connections.

1.2.1 Birth of Relationships Between Industry and Bank

The establishment of industry–bank relationships unique to Germany occurred at the end of the nineteenth century and the beginning of the twentieth century. According to W. Feldenkirchen, there was no unified model between industry and banks until 1895 (Feldenkirchen 1991, p. 127). This also applied to relationships between banks and heavy industries (Feldenkirchen 1979, S. 33). Fohlin clarifies that, while formal involvement of banks through interlocking directorates was relatively rare among Berlin-listed joint-stock companies until the end of the nineteenth century (Fohlin 1999, p. 308), such personnel connections rapidly increased with the development of industries and prevailed during the industrialization stage among Berlin-listed joint-stock companies. The interlocking directorate became a general institutional means until the industrial economy entered a new growth stage in the middle of the 1890s (Fohlin 1999, p. 309, 2007, p. 134). The arrangement of directors from banks on the supervisory boards of non-financial companies appeared at the end of industrialization, owing primarily to the pattern of institutional development in the form of universal banks, and the practice expanded toward the end of the nineteenth century (Fohlin 2007, p. 335). Jeidels pointed out that the period in 1897 or after the crisis in 1900 could be considered the starting point of the centrally and locally decentralized relationships among industrial enterprises (Jeidels 1905, S. 181).

In the assignment of persons from banks to the supervisory board of industrial enterprises, after such an organ of joint-stock companies became a more effective institution of supervision by the alternation of the Corporation Law in 1894, banks placed greater value on attending this committee (Feldenkirchen 1979, S. 32). At this point, the significance of the supervisory board as a place for banks to monitor the management of companies that have received credit becomes clear. The significant importance of a bank's representative on the supervisory board of German industrial corporations was first recognized at the end of the nineteenth century. Bank representatives frequently served as chairman of supervisory boards, especially in larger and more profitable companies (Burhop 2006, S. 25).

The development of special relationships between industry and banks was inextricably linked to enterprise mergers and acquisitions and cartelization progress. The involvement and attitude of banks in cartels most clearly demonstrated the premise of banks' industrial policy (Jeidels 1905, S. 253). Jeidels emphasized that a bank's deliberate involvement could significantly impact industrial concentration (Jeidels 1905, S. 270). A bank's representatives on the supervisory board cited an important assumption to understand which company would be a candidate for merger and takeover (Feldenkirchen 1991, p. 134). The expansion of the interlocking directorate can be considered a result of the movement toward concentration and cartelization (Fohlin 1999, p. 328). Banks were interested in industrial sectors where opportunities to cartelize were spreading and had tried to support concentration (Gerschenkron 1962, pp. 15–16). As Marx Dahlem points out, the supervisory board of a company can be considered an essential characteristic of the Second Reich's economic system (Dahlem 2009, SS. 195, 199). The early twentieth century marked a shift from general capital control to finance capital control (Ленин 1962, p. 343). Interlocking directorates were a unique feature of monopolistic capitalism.

The relationships between industry and bank varied significantly depending on market conditions and stockholder composition. Even before World War I, banks had a greater influence in the heavy and electrical industries than the machine and chemical industries (Feldenkirchen 1991, p. 135). However, personnel connections formed on the supervisory board between banks and industrial enterprises became widespread across all industries. This point was determined by the characteristics of the large bank business as universal banks providing commodities and services with the universal feature of money dealing, such as those seen in the credit, account current, and securities businesses.

1.2.2 The Universal Banking System and Its Relationships with Industry and Banks

The following subsection examines industry–bank relationships concerning the universal banking system, which serves as an important institutional foundation. In terms of corporate finance, while stock capital was the dominant financial source outside the company for US enterprises, the primary source of financial resources for German enterprises was bank credit, due to the undeveloped and non-liquid stock market (Windolf 2002, pp. 29, 48; Heinze 2001, SS. 650–651). Until the 1990s, stock markets played only a secondary role in German corporate finance (Furch 2012, S. 87). Unlike UK companies that had flexibly relied on different financial sources due to developed capital markets, German companies had raised funds through long-term bank credits (Heinze 2001, SS. 650–651). Therefore, personnel connections were critical for banks in terms of monitoring the management of companies in which they had an interest and maintaining and strengthening business relationships through financing and accounting for current business.

Rudolf Hilferding defined "bank capital transformed to industrial capital," namely "capital controlled by bank and used by industrial capital" as "finance capital" ("Finanzlkapital") (Hilferding 1923, S. 283). Because of characteristics such as fixed bank capital in industry via credit for fixed capital and the acceptance and possession of shares, banks had found it difficult to monitor the use of fixed capital in industrial enterprises. As a result, banks attempted to cooperate with as many enterprises as possible, sending their representatives to the supervisory boards of these enterprises in order to disperse risks and expand their business fields (Hilferding 1923, S. 134). As a common interest relationship in terms of ownership among various companies was built, personnel connections were forced to significantly influence policy in the company concerned (Hilferding 1923, SS. 132–133). Before World War I, German banks had already established a comprehensive system for gathering information and control to reduce risks in conjunction with fund lending (Windolf 2002, p. 44), as well as personnel ties based on director assignments and interlocking directorates.

Monitoring corporations with which banks have interest relations becomes an important issue because of the stable collection of credit by banks and the interest of improved efficiency of investment in companies (security investments). Such efforts can be best realized by sending bank representatives to the supervisory board. Hermann Josef Abs of Deutsche Bank emphasized that the financial institution's responsibility justified deeper involvement in the management of other companies, and that those who lend funds should at least know for what purpose they were used and where interest and repayment could come from. On November 3, 1965, the journal *Der Spiegel* stated that Abs was a banker and an industrialist for this reason (Der Spiegel 1965, S. 67).

Capital participation in industrial enterprises by banks is generally a result of financial and industrial policies, among other primary financing methods such as current account credit, the issue and acceptance of securities, capital participation, and personnel connection. In cases where large banks were satisfied with capital participation promising only very low-interest rates, this participation was undoubtedly done from the standpoint of industrial policy (Hagemann 1931, SS. 70, 166). Capital participation was frequently implemented due to business interests arising from collaboration in the company's formation and a capital increase. Its purpose was not control, but rather the accumulation of value (Dahlem 2009, S. 176). Capital participation acquires new customers, strengthens existing house bank relationships, and makes it difficult for companies to switch transactions to other banks (Plumpe et al. 2020, S. 47). It is an important basis for creating personnel ties through assigning of directors and interlocking directorates.

The interlocking directorate system, which serves as the central hub of personnel connections, is inextricably linked to the universal banking system. Except for the possibility of credit, the economic powers of banks are based on four measurements: (1) capital participation in industrial and commercial enterprises, (2) proxy execution of voting rights of customers, (3) mandates in other companies held by bank members of the managing and supervisory boards, and (4) information obtained from such posts (Arndt 1974, SS. 14–15). The primary business of German big banks is to provide short-term credit. However, credits were combined with long-term credits as they were forced to be renewed, and these long-term credits in exchange were developed to issue stocks and bonds (Marshall 1970, p. 342). Under the rapid expansion of German capitalism, with heavy industries playing significant roles and an underdeveloped capital market, the development of banks' business organically combined three credit, securities, and account current businesses to collect funds provided by credits and account current credit was an important foundation for special relationships between industry and banks. The regal form of enterprise as a joint-stock company provided banks with a basis for profitable capital market business (issue of shares and debentures) on the one hand, and created the possibility of systematized relationships between bank and company through the supervisory board on the other (Dahlem 2009, S. 277). Personnel ties based on the sending of directors and interlocking directorates on the supervisory board were interpreted as "personal guarantees" to form, maintain, and strengthen business relationships between banks and industrial enterprises.

Among three practices, such as stockholding typically combined with the German universal bank, proxy voting rights of shares owned by customers, and mandates on the supervisory boards of industrial enterprises (Fohlin 2007, p. 106), proxy voting rights by banks, particularly the largest bank, have been a key characteristic of banks' connection with company ownerships since the period of industrialization (Fohlin 2007, p. 328). Banks obtained mandates on boards through endorsement and intermediate businesses, more patient stockholding, regal execution of voting rights by deposited stocks, and an active security market between the nineteenth and twentieth centuries (Fohlin 2007, p. 336). Before World War I, German enterprises constructed more complex networks in addition to alliances, joint ventures, cartels, and communities of interests, rather than the complete fusion that prevailed in the 1920s (Fear and Kobrak 2010, p. 713). In Germany, where voting rights of deposited stocks are typically executed, personnel connections formed through supervisory board posts occurred even more frequently than capital connections (Schiffels 1981, S. 97). Proxy voting rights based on deposited stocks are of great significance in the distribution of the rate of acceptance within consortium banks for issuing debentures, and the share composition of acceptance tended to be fixed in leading companies (Eglau 1990, S. 182). Such business relationships between banks and industrial enterprises rely heavily on personnel ties formed by assigning directors and interlocking directorates.

In Germany, the structure of interlocking directorates has been systematized and built, as well as a system of personnel connections based on interlocking directorates led by banks. Unlike Japanese large banks, which played significant roles within industrial groups spread across various industrial sectors, banks in Germany are broadly associated with large corporate groups rather than a specific corporate group (Maekawa 1997, p. 58). These ties were significant for information sharing and coordination mechanisms and functions, particularly in industrial-banking relationships. This point highlights the significance of the German interfirm relationship system. Big banks have played an important role in developing collaborative relationships with many leading companies and corporate groups across various industries. Banks played an important role in establishing and strengthening the stable and more advantageous management foundations of the companies they provide financing and investment. Such a system was the foundation of German capitalism's accumulation structure, with significant implications for corporate expansion.

1.2.3 Primary Forms of Personnel Connection and Relationships Between Industry and Bank

Next, some types of personnel connections exist in Germany, including between enterprises and industrial enterprises. There are two distinct types: (1) personnel connections established through appointing directors or interlocking directorates, and (2) through the bank's advisory council system.

Such a system includes both direct and indirect interlocking directorates. A direct interlocking directorate is formed when members of a company's supervisory and managing boards hold mandates from other enterprises' top management organs. If companies A and B establish personnel connections in the top management organ of another company C via direct interlocking directorates, an indirect interlocking directorate is formed between companies A and B. Between these companies, an information transmission system is established, which significantly impacts information exchange and sharing, as well as coordinating corporate interests and conflicts. When companies A and B in the same industry establish direct personnel connections in another company C or they are in the same industrial sector as company C, such a system has significant meaning in coordinating interests, conflicts, and cooperation among enterprises (Schönwitz and Weber 1982, SS. 21–22, 72–73; Schönwitz and Weber 1981, SS. 12–13, 33–34). Schönwitz and Weber, who analyzed the German largest hundred enterprises measured by sales amount in 1978, clarified that although the horizontal and vertical indirect interlocking directorates between these enterprises were never exceptional phenomena (Schönwitz and Weber 1982, SS. 80–81, S. 103), cases of indirect interlocking directorates formed in the board of directors were rare, and the majority of such personnel ties were observed in the supervisory board (Schönwitz and Weber 1982, SS. 80–81, S. 103). They also noted that, whereas direct personnel ties between mutually competing companies were uncommon, horizontal indirect personnel connections allowed for much more communication, and there were significant differences in the degree of horizontal indirect personnel connections between the national economically important sectors (Schönwitz and Weber 1981, S. 33).

Another type of interfirm relationship can be observed in interlocking directorates. In many cases, members of the supervisory boards of several other enterprises, where the supervisory board members of a company have interlocking mandates, also hold many positions in third-party enterprises. When multiple companies are linked by personnel ties, such as interlocking directorates, the concept of "distance" is created (Hannemann and Riddle 2011, pp. 342–343; Nakata et al. 1997, p. 40). Considering the interlocking directorate between a company and another company as a second-party enterprise, as in "distance 1," "distance 2" can be considered between second and third parties, where the former has the mandate of the top management organ (Fig. 1.1). Thus, a personnel network is formed via interlocking directorates in "distant 2," which includes second and third parties. If such connections between enterprises are expanded, the network can grow to nearly infinite. Such a network can potentially increase the possibilities for exchanging and sharing information, coordinating interests, and resolving conflicts between industry and banks and among corporations.

Furthermore, in Germany, a bank's advisory council system serves as an important means of personnel connection between the bank and its member companies and among member companies. The connection between personnel is important in collecting, exchanging, and sharing information among enterprises. A central advisory council, established for bank headquarters following World War II, serves as the foundation of a special committee that manages information exchange between enterprises and between banks and industrial enterprises. The Dresdner Bank central advisory council, which served as a liaison between banks and industrial corporations, was established in 1957 (Meyen 1992, S. 331), despite the 1965 Corporations Law, which limited the number of supervisory board mandates a single individual could hold. Other large German banks, such as Deutsche Bank and Commerzbank, established central advisory councils in response to the limitation imposed by this law on the number of supervisory board mandates that one person could hold to maintain a level of personnel connection between a bank and industrial enterprises (Pfeiffer 1993, SS. 158–159; Pfeiffer 1986a, S. 164, 1986b, S. 477; Stanzick 1969, S. 72; Eglau 1990, S. 128; Der Spiegel, 1965, S. 50). The mission of the central advisory council comprised of representatives of leading companies in Germany was to provide advice to management on fundamental problems of important business policies and (Eglau 1990, SS. 192–193, 244; Aizawa 1994, p. 95; Aizawa 1988, p. 246). This organizational system was important in supplementing the function of personnel connections via direct and indirect interlocking directorates and top

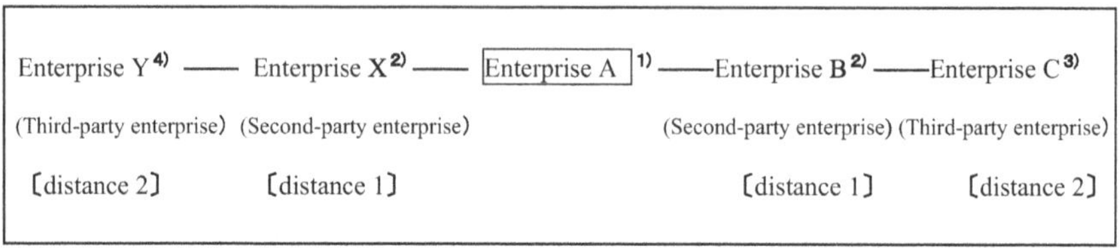

Note: 1) "Enterprise A" enclosed in square is enterprise that is at starting point of this network.

2) "Enterprise B" and "Enterprise X" are second-party enterprise in the extent of "distance 1" which are directly connected with "Enterprise A."

3) "Enterprise C" is third-party enterprise in the extent of "distance 2" which directly connected with "Enterprise B" and with which "Enterprise A" is connected indirectly through "Enterprise B."

4) "Enterprise Y" is third-party enterprise in the extent of "distance 2" which directly connected with "Enterprise X" and with which "Enterprise A" is connected indirectly through "Enterprise B."

Source: This figure was made by the author.

Fig. 1.1 Image figure of personnel network in the extent of "distant 2" including second-party and third-party enterprises

management organs. Before World War II, regional banking advisory councils were established in major districts. They also contributed significantly to the exchange of information between banks and industrial enterprises. Following World War II, the regional advisory council system was expanded, and the number of members of such organizations increased in comparison to prewar levels. The regional advisory council served as a coordination committee (Pfeiffer 1986b, S. 165). The central and regional advisory councils played an important role in collaborating with banks and industrial enterprises.

1.2.4 Personnel Connection Built Through Interlocking Directorate

1.2.4.1 Personnel Connection on the Supervisory Board

Although holding the mandate of the supervisory board was one of many alternatives for forming relationships between industry and banks. Such an organ was an important level of mutual interaction (Dahlem 2009, S. 318). The composition of the supervisory board is a significant indicator regarding the influence of the external exerting a company (Joly 1998, S. 241). The supervisory board of the enterprise in question is the channel through which a bank affects other enterprises (Shonfield 1965, p. 247), and an enterprise sends a representative to such an organ of another enterprise and invites the second enterprise's representative as an important customer. Thus, friendly relationships between enterprises in related industries that are not competitive can be strengthened by associating each party with the other's investment decisions. The membership of the supervisory board is to be considered as an additional source of information and influence in an enterprise in which a bank is interested (Shonfield 1965, pp. 250–252). Bank personnel ties with companies other than banks are the most important source that banks have in terms of providing and sharing useful information (Volkmann and Kronenberg 1994, S. 481). In general, whereas banks had the possibility of exerting extensive influence on industrial enterprises through the institution of the supervisory board based on shareholding and credit provision, representatives from industry could not exercise such power through banks (Hagemann 1931, SS. 77–78). Until the 1930s, the strong presence of banks on the supervisory boards of German enterprises was not only a characteristic of the industry, but also spread throughout the financial sector (Bol 2021, S. 128). Because their banks not only held stocks or provided credits, but also could build and maintain business contacts and accumulate information, bankers frequently had some positions on the supervisory boards of other companies (Ahrens 2022, p. 122).

In terms of personnel connection, not only the quantity but also the quality of bank mandates are important. Bank representatives frequently served as chairman and vice-chairman of the supervisory boards. The holding of chairman mandates on supervisory boards was much more concentrated on a small number of financial institutions than in cases where all enterprises held chairman mandates. By adding the post of vice-chairman, the dominant position of Deutsche Bank became even more prominent (Joly 1998, SS. 201–202). The chairman and vice-chairman mandates were typically endowed with additional responsibilities for specific management decisions. Before acting on certain matters, the management, which consisted of members of the managing board, had to consult with and obtain approval from the chairman or vice-chairman of the supervisory board. The most important issue was the timing and scale of investment expenditure (Shonfield, 1965, p. 251).

Among these powerful positions, the interlocking chairmanship on the supervisory board holds special significance. There are cases in which chairpersons or common representatives of directorial meetings, if established, informally meet with the board of directors beforehand or lead decision-making due to the advantage of information obtained from the core position within the corporate network (Gehlen 2022, pp. 75–76). The chairman of the supervisory board could quickly obtain all valuable and internal information through reports on important matters from the management board (Bundesministerium der Finanzen 1979, S. 116). The chairperson of the supervisory board can secure contact points between members of the supervisory board and the managing board (Eglau 1990, S. 297). Unlike other members of the supervisory board, the chairman can greatly influence the decision-making of the concerned company, and particularly in cases where his job is combined with capital participation, a powerful position that cannot be ignored can be created (Eglau 1990, S. 176). The mandates of the chairman of the supervisory board in the upper industrial enterprises revealed Deutsche Bank's overwhelming predominance among the three largest German banks (Eglau 1990, SS. 85, 136, 180). Dresdner Bank and

Commerzbank could not have a strong qualitatively and quantitatively connection with industrial firms comparable to those of Deutsche Bank (Eglau 1990, S. 242).

Holding a supervisory board mandate in industrial enterprises is important for banks because it influences their industrial policy. Jeidels pointed out that the emergence of clear industrial policies by banks since the 1890s began for the first time after the crisis (Jeidels 1905, S. 107). Holding a supervisory board mandate allows banks to gain direct access to customers in industries (Dahlem 2009, S. 199). As a house bank, the bank's supervisory board positions were almost always based on long-term relationships with the company in question (Eglau, 1990, S. 181). The primary advantage of assigning representatives to the supervisory boards of industrial firms for banks lies in reinforcing and opening up business connections with customers, expanding international networks, and managing appropriate relationships (Prambeck 2001, SS. 17–18). The possibility of reducing credit risks induces a company's strategic interests in personnel connection and capital participation, which the universal bank develops (Beyer 2013, S. 34). The interests of bank representatives on supervisory boards ultimately lay in the bank itself, and as bank directors, they were responsible for lending policy (Shonfield 1965, p. 255).

V. Wellhöner emphasized that one of the most important functions of bankers was to coordinate the diverse interests of each industrial capital with their banks and implement a common behavioral strategy. In principle, common interests between industry and banks emerged from the fact that the smooth return of capital invested in industrial companies by banks was dependent on the possibility of consecutive increases in value without hindrance (Wellhöner 1989, S. 241). Otto Eglau emphasizes that members of the enterprise board of Deutsche Bank played significant roles as the first-class center examining and deciding industrial policy, and was forced to regularly involve in individual enterprises and industrial sectors through capital dispersion into key industries (Eglau 1990, S. 125). Thus, holding supervisory board mandates of companies in various major industries by directors of this bank had a significant meaning in this regard (Eglau 1990, S. 131).

The appointment of members of the board of directors by the supervisory board of an industrial enterprise to which a bank sends one of its members, as well as the election of candidates to a bank's supervisory board from outside companies, occurred due to the importance of obtaining useful information for the bank's business, such as providing financing to companies and investing in other enterprises. Obtaining this information is important for banks' consistent collection of financing funds for enterprises and ensuring greater efficiency of investments in industrial companies.

Meanwhile, the possibility of obtaining a position that allows preferential access to reliable information from the best source can be quickly highlighted as a benefit for enterprises that accept bank representatives as members of their supervisory boards. This is a foundation for building close relationships by accepting individuals from banks as members of the supervisory board of industrial enterprises (Eglau 1990, S. 193). Eglau insists that companies could establish a basis for exchanging information and experience of specialists directly involved in management, particularly in law and finance, by forming intimate relationships with Deutsche Bank (Eglau 1990, S. 243). According to Paul Windolf, executives in industrial enterprises with a mandate on the supervisory board can obtain credits on favorable terms (Windolf 2014, p. 75). Thus, in industrial enterprises, obtaining valuable information from banks and developing cooperative interfirm relationships with banks through interlocking directorates at the supervisory board level are important.

1.2.4.2 Assignment of Directors to the Supervisory Board, Interlocking Directorates, and Personnel Networks

Next, when considering studies on the assignment of directors to supervisory boards, Wixforth and Ziegler clarified that the increase in supervisory board members in 40 industrial enterprises after World War I revealed seemingly contradictory phenomena. Such phenomena occurred from successful attempts by industrial enterprises to strengthen competition among banks by providing interlocking supervisory board members from banks with inside information to decrease risks resulting from information asymmetry between competitors (Wixforth and Ziegler 1995, p. 261). Hagemann compared the number of supervisory board positions in industrial enterprises held by banks between 1912 and 1927. According to it, while such numbers regarding Deutsche Bank, Dresdner Bank, and Disconto-Gesellschaft greatly increased from 159 to 530, 120 to 452, and 143 to 490, respectively, those concerning Berliner Handesgesellschaft were almost the same (123 in 1912 and 127 in. 1927). The significant increase in the number of mandates of supervisory boards held by banks resulted in a greatly increasing connection between banks and industry, harmony of intentions and goals, or at least coordination (Hagemann 1931, S. 81). Fear and Kobrak (2010) clarify that the level of existence of bank representatives on the boards in Germany was higher than that in other countries. The number of German enterprises in which bankers held chairman mandates on the supervisory board increased, reaching approximately one-fourth of the largest enterprises (Fear and Kobrak 2010, p. 714).

In examining the assignment of directors between banks and industries after World War II, we find that, according to a Monopoly Commission 1976/1977 report, 137 supervisory board members were selected from financial institutions, with 57 financial institution assignees serving as chairmen or vice-chairpersons among 51 surveyed corporations. The top three banks had 76 board members and 35 chairmen or vice-chairmen, accounting for more than 55.5% and 61.4%, respectively, of the total assignees from financial institutions (Monopolkommission 1978, SS. 574–577). According to the Gessler Committee, of the 74 publicly traded corporations surveyed in 1974 and 1975, 182 had supervisory board members from financial institutions, and 37 had supervisory board chairmen from financial institutions. The top three banks assigned 101 supervisory board members and 25 chairmen, accounting for 55.5% and 67.6% of those assigned from financial institutions, respectively (Bundesministerium der Finanzen 1979, SS. 438–439, S. 443).

Regarding subsequent periods, the Gottschalk survey revealed that in 1986, bankers or former bankers held 69 (27%) of the 256 supervisory positions in 27 non-bank corporations. Representatives from the top three banks filled 50 positions, or roughly three-fourths of them (Gottschalk 1988, S. 300). According to Ziegler et al. (1985), because larger production enterprises were able to attract executives from Deutsche Bank and Dresdner Bank, Germany's two largest banks, and did not limit their primary interlocking directorates to companies that belonged to the same domains, their domains overlapped to a high degree, and "banks acted more like integrators cross-connecting industrial enterprises from various economic sectors" (Ziegler et al. 1985, p. 109; Ziegler 1985, p. 271). In terms of differences between the three largest banks, they observed that "while the average size of companies assigning or receiving executives from Deutsche Bank and Dresdner Bank was about equal, the smaller Commerzbank showed a different pattern of primary interlocks" (Ziegler et al. 1985, p. 109). According to Rolf Ziegler, two, if not all, of the top three banks had representatives serving as supervisory board members among larger manufacturers, and one decisive factor in the banks having so many representatives was the economic importance of the firms accepting the representatives (Ziegler 1984, S. 597).

Taking into account the conditions in the former half of the 1990s, Pfeiffer (1993) clarified that the top three banks had assigned 1,053 directors to other corporations' supervisory boards in the 1990s, with 170 serving as supervisory board (or other management) chairs and 92 as vice-chairmen (Pfeiffer 1993, SS. 152–152, 172, 182–183). At least one bank representative served on the supervisory boards of the 261 publicly traded corporations surveyed by H. Hansen in 1993, and financial institutions appointed 372 supervisory board members. Of these, 192 (51.6%) came from the top three banks, and 59 companies had bank representatives on their supervisory boards as chairmen. The top three banks held 56 supervisory positions in the DAX 30 corporations, or 76.7% of the total (Hansen 1994, R. 78).

Many outstanding research results have been gathered from personnel networks. Some prominent studies have clarified personnel networks established through interlocking directorates, their historical changes, and the factors influencing such changes using large data sets. Researchers including P. Windolf, K. Krenn, and R. Ziegler have conducted notable studies. Furthermore, Windolf (2014) analyzes the structures of corporate networks from the end of the nineteenth century to the 2000s. Windolf (2002) compares corporate networks based on capital and personnel connections in five European countries (Germany, the UK, France, Switzerland, and the Netherlands) and the USA. Ziegler et al. (1985) presented important research results that attempted to understand corporate groups and analyze corporate networks through mass observation of 325 German enterprises. Krenn (2012) explores the structures of personnel networks in some pre-World War II periods through the lens of bank powers.

Germany's networks, like those in Italy, France, and Spain, are cohesive and can be explained by a combination of bank-based financial structure, interfering state, enterprises with block holders, and low economic internationalization (David and Weserhuis 2014, p. 7). Windolf pointed out that unlike networks in the USA and UK, which are relatively low-density and decentralized, networks in Germany, Switzerland, and the Netherlands are relatively highly concentrated and indicate high density (Windolf 2002, pp. 36–37, 49). According to Ziegler et al. (1985), "the

German network showed a densely connected center to which the largest commercial banks, the biggest insurance companies and the most important domestic production corporations (predominantly active in the capital-intensive basis and investment goods industries) belonged." Companies in a central position focused on the Rhein-Main as the primary economic region. Although the spheres of influence were built by bank executives holding mandates on the industrial boards, they overlapped to a high degree. In these common domains, big corporations primarily did not confine their interlocking directorates to other firms within the same spheres (Ziegler et al. 1985, p. 110). The large German banks played a very central role in the network of common directorships (Ziegler et al. 1985, p. 105, Ziegler 1985, p. 271).

When considering the historical process of networks until the end of the 1980s, Windolf pointed out that the period from the nineteenth century to World War I was a takeoff period for corporate networks (Windolf 2014, pp. 72, 80). Industrialization had an important impact on the development of corporate networks (David and Weserhuis 2014, p. 13). In contrast to the USA, where the Sherman Antitrust Act in 1890 and the Clayton Antitrust Act in 1914 prohibited cartels and regulated direct interlocking directorates as illegal, cartels were regarded as lawful in Germany before World War II, and the density and level of concentration in the network increased along with the increasing degree of cartelization (David and Weserhuis 2014, p. 14).

In the 1920s, the network's density increased substantially and peaked. Windolf cited two factors as the reason. First, "the network became concentrated on a small group of German managers who were repeatedly nominated to sit on the supervisory boards of large German firms." The other is concerned with specific historical circumstances, such as "a protective device against an external enemy (the French army) and an internal one (the communist party)" (Windolf 2014, pp. 73, 79). Krenn points out that the scale of the supervisory board was an important factor for the number of mandates in the network (Krenn 2013, S. 243), and the dense connection was a phenomenon defining economic organization in the Weimar period in comparison to other countries (Krenn 2013, S. 98). Windolf explains that "the density of network decreased thereafter but remained at a relatively high level during the 1930s, at least in comparison with the US" (Windolf 2014, p. 80). The decline in network density was caused by the legal limitation of the number of supervisory board members as a countermeasure to the bank crisis in 1930/1931 (the corporate law in 1931 prohibited holding more than 20 posts of the boards) and the expulsion of Jewish executives under the Nazi state (Windolf 2014, p. 73; David and Weserhuis 2014, p. 16). In addition to Italy, Portugal, and the USA, Germany is where laws played a beneficial role in the decline of corporate networks (David and Weserhuis 2014, p. 16). Changes in the characteristics of the existing network occurred most recently following Nazi economic policy. The trust network between directors of industry and banks came to have no longer decisive meaning for obtaining information and planning strategy due to the situation where network with persons in charge of political decisions and closeness with government became an important element for coordination and realizing interests under the stronger control of the state (Wixforth 2006, S. 893).

After World War II, a significant decrease in network density occurred due to a spillover effect of the deconcentration process in the 1950s and the regulation against cartels (Windolf 2014, pp. 74, 80). As in Japan, occupation by the USA resulted in implementing laws affecting networks in Germany (David and Weserhuis 2014, p. 17). Consequently, networks were maintained for a long time, and even in the 1980s, corporate networks experienced only a minor degree of erosion (David and Weserhuis 2014, p. 20).

Furthermore, regarding the centrality of bank in the network, German banks tended to assign many more executives to the supervisory boards of non-financial enterprises than they received industrial managers as members of their own supervisory boards (Windolf 2014, p. 76). According to Krenn (2012), although large banks were part of the network's structural core from the end of the nineteenth century to the Weimar Republic, they were not always in this position (Krenn 2012, S. 243). Meanwhile, network specialists who held many mandates in the corporate network comprised members of large banks' managing and supervisory boards to an above-average degree (Krenn 2012, S. 238). Krenn emphasizes that the relationship between industry and banks was not one-sided control by banks, but rather the structure of mutual personnel connections (Krenn 2012, S. 242). According to Windolf (2002, p. 70), although "German banks still hold a central position in the corporate network" and "send managers to other sectors," "the core of the network which contains the most central firms includes not only banks and financial institutions, but also large and prestigious industrial firms" (Windolf 2002, p. 74).

1.2.4.3 Changes in Personnel Connections After the 1990s

The interlocking directorate system and personnel networks underwent significant changes following the 1990s. As Wolfgang Streeck points out, Deutsche Bank's decisions to abandon its quasi-public position as a protector of German industry and orient toward more profitable international capital markets were made under political circumstances in which liberalization of the economy in this country had already become a dominant theme (Streeck 2009, p. 84). As primary factors determining changes in personnel ties, the following can be mentioned: globalization of the economy and enterprise, internationalization of the financial market and the corresponding change in conditions of company financing, changes in risks for banks with the development of new financial technologies (dispersion and avoidance of credit risks by securitization and the credit insurance system), trend toward the Anglo-American more transparent based on the US-GAAP or the International Accounting Standard, and transformation of bank behavior represented by movement from credit bank toward investment bank business, reforms in laws, and influences of the German Corporate Governance Code (Windolf 2014, p. 80; Beyer 2006, S. 104).

Globalization and financial deregulation have significantly impacted bank activities (David and Weserhuis 2014, p. 20). Corporate strategy oriented toward capital markets gained importance as the progress of globalization of financial markets (Furch 2012, S. 132), and actors in financial markets, such as investment fund as new owner of stocks, exerted considerable influence on the structures and strategies of enterprises (Windolf 2005a, pp. 8–9, 12, 14, 17, 2005b, pp. 25, 40, 52). Industrial enterprises also faced increased competition, innovation, and the need for risk-taking capital providers. As a result, external financing is less suitable than equity capital financing (Ifrim 2007, S. 36). Ringe (2015) emphasizes the decline of the traditional network of German companies known as "Germany Inc." (Ringe 2015, p. 494). He points out that Corporate Germany faced three factors: (1) decline in concentration of ownership, (2) decrease in banks' roles in stockholdings, and (3) progress in shareholder internationalization (Ringe 2015, pp. 526, 537). After the 1990s, Deutsche Bank no longer considered capital participation as a means of positive industrial policy to acquire and retain new customers and strengthen existing house bank-like relationships (Plumpe et al. 2020, SS. 474, 481). From 1996 to 2000, Deutsche Bank sold half of its capital ownership in Germany's 100 largest enterprises, and Dresdner Bank also sold some of its shares. The significance of the function of internal control exerted through personnel connections declined with the sale of stocks (Klages 2006, S. 45).

The shift in bank behavior from credit to investment business significantly impacts personnel ties. Under the increase in the significance of mergers and acquisitions (M&A) in corporate development (Beyer 2006, SS. 105–106) and the intensification of competition in the credit business (Beyer 2006, S. 103), banks came to have a worldwide scale, and M&A activities promised high profit in the globalized markets where the range of profit can be compared (Ringe 2015, p. 517; Furch 2012, S. 155, 235; Marx and Leitmeyer 2022b, p. 25). Under the condition that the global financial market is controlled by a few financial companies with high profit and competitiveness, in particular US investment banks, after the 1980s, Deutsche Bank succeeded in becoming an investment bank, particularly a leading actor in security and derivative business, and exchange transactions in Europe, with strong international expansion through acquisitions of firms (Plumpe et al. 2020, S. XVII-XVIII). Only Deutsche Bank is among the internationally important investment banks (Plumpe et al. 2020, S. 629, Furch 2012, S. 158; Berghoff 2016, p. 91).

With the transformation of corporate finance to direct financing through the issue of stocks and bonds, as risks are borne not by banks but by shareholders or bond owners, close relationships with industrial enterprises have no significance in terms of corporate strategy for pure investment banks, and such banks have no interest in integration into the corporate network (Beyer 2006, S. 102; Furch 2012, S. 155). Banks have left a large part of their involvement in industries in the process of moving toward investment banks (Klages 2006, S. 50). German large banks, particularly Deutsche Bank, have left the model of cooperative, long-term, and safety-oriented Germany Inc. and have coped with competition from global competitors because of a reorientation to their business model (Ringe 2015, p. 526). However, as David Furch pointed out in 2012, Commerzbank and Dresdner Bank had once again focused heavily on their traditional businesses. This can be interpreted as a shift in direction toward strong monitoring by banks (Furch 2012, S. 231). Ralf Ahrens also clarifies that "despite spectacular turns by some big banks toward international investment banking and loosing of their network ties, the vast majority remained engaged in relational banking" (Ahrens 2022, p. 130). As a result, it is important to understand how differences in managerial behaviors between large banks relate to changes in personnel connections.

In considering changes in interlocking directorates, Heinze (2002) and Heinze (2004) pointed out that personnel connections decreased during the period from 1989 to 2001, and the decline of such ties was stronger in the network of interlocking directorates by members of the management boards on the supervisory boards of other companies than by members of the supervisory boards (Heinze 2002, S. 403; Heinze 2004, pp. 228–230). Heinze emphasizes that despite this decrease, the impacts on interlocking directorates were quantitative rather than structural (Heinze 2004, p. 232). According to the Monopolkommission (2022), among the largest 100 companies, the number of personnel connections through sending members of the managing boards decreased dramatically from 235 to 186, 84, and 32, respectively, whereas similar figures for banking and insurance companies declined from 106 to 76, 24, and seven. Similar figures for only non-financial sectors decreased from 129 to 76, 60, and 25. Meanwhile, the number of personnel connections by members of the control organs has significantly decreased from 471 to 420, 234, and 71. (Monopolkommission 2022, SS. 6, 34–35). The Monopolkommission (2010) clarified that among the largest 100 firms, the rate of personnel ties by members of the managing boards of banking and insurance firms to all such connections had already significantly decreased from 54.3 to 27.6% from 1996 to 2008 (Monopolkommission 2010, S. 160). Examining the conditions by sector, while the decrease in the holding of posts in the control organs of other companies by members of the management boards of companies in the financial sector reached 79.2% in the same period, the figure for companies in industry, commerce, transportation, and services was 35.3%. Following 1996, there was a significant decrease in the importance of banks and insurance companies in personnel networks among the largest 100 companies (Monopolkommission 2010, SS. 160–161). According to Brullebaut et al. (2021), the withdrawal of key actors like Allianz and Deutsche Bank contributed to the network's overall thinness and density (Brullebaut et al. 2011, p. 1771).

Deutsche Bank and Allianz changed their strategies despite the comparative advantage of the German "coordinated" economic order and retreated from the networks of connection for corporate strategic reasons (Beyer 2006, S. 113). Jürgen Beyer emphasizes that despite Deutsche Bank and Allianz's approach to the Anglo-American type of capitalism, as seen in the codetermination system, impatient conclusions regarding changes in corporate networks should be avoided (Beyer 2006, S. 114). The dissolution of personnel connections resulted from the core of German Inc. rather than the network's periphery (Beyer 2006, S. 130). Prior studies have shown various indications of the hybrid adaptation process (Beyer 2006, S. 115). In the 1990s, the closed corporate network and cross-stockholdings of large enterprises were viewed as causes of poor economic performance and high unemployment. Furthermore, the German Corporate Governance Code served as a final blow to the network (Windolf 2014, p. 80). Big linkers with over ten mandates disappeared (Windolf 2014, pp. 74, 80). According to Windolf (2002, p. 50), as far as network structures at the time are concerned, financial firms no longer play a central role in the interlocking directorate network. He emphasizes that the network had almost completely collapsed by 2010 (Windolf 2014, pp. 80–81).

David Furch insists in 2012 that regarding reducing the broad part of capital participation and the supervisory board posts in the process of putting through strategic direction of German financial companies and reinforcing concentration on investment banking (Furch 2012, S. 155), while the network of capital participation had been dramatically dissolved, a relatively slight decrease of personnel connections was observed (Furch 2012, S. 175). Indeed, non-financial firms are left from much capital participation by eliminating capital gain taxation on selling shares, but there are many personnel connections simultaneously (Furch 2012, SS. 110, 153, 230). Concerning networks based on personnel ties, two competitive logic exist: (1) a dramatic decrease in the acceptance of supervisory board mandates by financial firms and the strengthening of market mechanisms with it, and (2) the promotion of a close personnel network fundamentally contributing to the restriction of competition or internal coordination in non-financial firms (Furch 2012, SS. 230–231). Furthermore, supervisory boards with labor representatives experience no fundamental change (Furch 2012, S. 175). Investment bankers and executives from the fields of finance and control in companies have served as catalysts for the diffusion and implementation of new shareholder control concepts (Beyer 2006, S. 142). However, despite a significant decrease in the decade following 2000, managing board members of large German corporations were more technologically oriented than their counterparts in the USA. Furthermore, top managers show much lower liquidity than expected and tend to stay in one company for a very long time (Furch 2012, S. 172). German executives' clear orientation toward production and technology contrasts with the results paradigm of Anglo-American managers based on their orientation toward the stock market (Heiber 2010, SS. 394–395). According to Berghoff (2016), "financialization changed German capitalism but not enough to dissolve Germany Inc." "despite dramatic changes in some of its parts, the most important pillars of Germany Inc. remained intact." He emphasizes "deviations from financialization" (Berghoff 2016, p. 106).

Concerning the decline of significances of interlocks and personnel networks, Windolf points out that, although corporate networks were at the national level in the twentieth century, they are no longer effective for coordination in the market under changes of stable circumstances with globalization (Windolf 2014, p. 74). Beyer observes that the general trend toward more transparency in the Anglo-American fields (strict rules for transparency of the US security exchange, market activities for corporate control, and the concept of shareholder value) and the advantages of internal monitoring became smaller (Beyer 2006, S. 104). However, it is pointed out that in Germany, despite the increasing pressure of the capital market, the market for corporate control has not developed as in the USA and the UK (Furch 2012, SS. 65, 153, 231; Velte and Weber 2011, S. 478; Beyer 2006, S. 104; Heinze 2004, pp. 218, 226, 228, 230). Brullebaut et al. (2021) examine global personnel ties and state that the presence of superseding effects of cross-border connections of directors that function to replace domestic networks cannot be observed (Brullebaut et al. 2021, pp. 1773, 1779).

Such changes after the 1990s can be interpreted as German corporations gaining access to the Anglo-American system and its overall influence. However, rebuilding the institutional architecture of corporate control was a hybrid process (Klages 2006, SS. 50–51), consisting of continuity and reform (Klages 2006, SS. 37–38). Thomas Heinze also emphasized that, despite changes after the 1990s, the continuation of ownership structure, strengthening of the supervisory board, and reproduction of codetermination indicated the possibility of an unchanged internal governance mechanism and partial continuity of the strategic coordination mechanism (Heinze 2001, S. 641, 2004, p. 218). The tendency of the German corporate governance system to be stakeholder-oriented has been maintained due to factors such as the characteristics of two-layer top management organs, the influence of codetermination, and the special field that executives are originally from (Marx and Leitmeyer 2022b, p. 25; Goutas and Lane 2009, SS. 340, 342; Aglietta 2009, pp. 203, 220; Goergen et al. 2008, p. 190; Pönisch 2007, S. 111).

1.2.4.4 Functions of the Interlocking Directorate and Personnel Network

German enterprises tended to cope with uncertainty caused by circumstances through the appropriate composition of the supervisory board (Schiffels 1981, S. 97). As Markus Dahlem points out, although access to company information that could not be obtained otherwise was only a side of the close relationships between bank and company through systematization by the supervisory board (Dahlem 2009, S. 279), the system of sharing information between companies through sending person as supervisory board member can be further expanded by enabling contact through such organ (Hopt 1979, SS. 235–238). Members of the board of directors can gain direct access to information about other firms' business policies and market strategies by serving on their control boards (Schönwitz and Weber 1982, S. 20). Interlocks establish a pattern of meetings among directors. The significance of interlocking directorates lies in increasing the quantity and quality of communication and enriching communication channels between enterprises (Sato 1986, pp. 27–28). Trust is a fundamental condition for the function of a network (Fiedler 2005, S. 96), and the trust network between industry and bank had decisive significance for obtaining information and planning strategy (Wixforth 2006, S. 893). People who have many posts on the supervisory boards not only influence the monitoring of control organs but also contribute to better advice for members of the managing boards in the context of the development of corporate strategy (Prinz 2012, S. 903).

Interlocking directorates have built reciprocal social and personnel networks that lower economic transaction costs between companies (Fear and Kobrak 2010, p. 714). Networks only provide additional options (Gehlen 2022, p. 76), but joint-stock companies combined with financial and personnel networks have more options to overcome crises than the possibility of acquiring from outside companies (Tilly 2005). Although personnel connections initially indicate the possibility of high-level information and communication within the company, the ability to exchange regulated information expands the room for activities under the competition. Enterprises can reduce market risks by cooperating based on the discussion route between competing enterprises, and their market position can be improved. Large firms have both direct and indirect collaboration opportunities. When such a possibility of cooperation is used, personnel connections result in a coordinated behavioral mode and broad harmony of large firms' interests (Schönwitz and Weber 1982, SS. 24–25). Above all, when members of the managing board hold mandates on the control organs of companies with transaction relations, the effects of limiting competition become apparent. Such effects result from coordinating with company activities, which are monitored so that members of the managing board are aware of business policy decisions (Schönwitz and Weber 1982, S. 20). As long as a channel of discussion between competing companies is established and maintained in a manner-like quasi-system, companies will have a high likelihood of relying on how conflicts between parties involved are coordinated through discussion rather than the market. Companies can reduce market risks and improve their market position by cooperating (Schönwitz and Weber 1982, S. 34). Interlocking creates and measures opportunities.

Personnel networks' function lies in decreasing risks and allocating risks between industrialists and banks (Windolf 2002, p. 30). Enterprises that play a relatively central role in the network, specifically those that maintain stable relationships with a large number of other enterprises, can decrease risk. These connections offer companies valuable information (Windolf 2002, p. 43). As a result, the close networks between the largest companies acted as a limiting function of competition among domestic competing companies (Beyer 2013, SS. 31, 50). Windolf emphasizes that corporate networks were used in Germany to coordinate markets, as well as cartels (Windolf 2014, p. 79). Interlocking directorates serve two contradictory functions: (1) monitoring company directors by supervisory board members and (2) preventing erroneous use of their powers (Windolf 2002, p. 76). According to Rolf Ziegler, the combining post is not only the result of corporate players' decisions, but also of individuals' behavior in pursuit of their personal interests (Ziegler 1984, S. 610). As personnel connections are appropriate for reinforcing the influence of an individual enterprise on certain cross-border purchasing and sales markets, international markets can have meaning in terms of competition policy (Monopolkommission 2010, S. 177).

Regarding the possibility of limiting competition among companies through personnel ties, according to Beyer, the strategic orientation that is advantageous for coordination and restraint of competition between industrial enterprises developed from a desire to secure bank credits. The continuation of restricted competition can be observed, particularly in the involvement of private banks in industrial policy (Beyer 2006, SS. 100–101). Banks could gain insider knowledge, limiting competition in both the non-financial and financial sectors, by holding multiple positions on non-bank sector control organs. Banks with mandates from such competing companies can use company information to benefit companies in which each bank has an interest by providing information and to disadvantage other companies by restricting the provision of information (Schönwitz and Weber 1982, S. 28; Arndt 1974, S. 21). Furthermore, financial institutions can appoint their posts on the basis of their influence over companies' means of raising funds for the purpose of potentially or actually obstructing offensive competition strategies of enterprises as objects of competition for achieving their goals, or completely excluding competition between certain companies by introducing the coordinated behavioral mode (Schönwitz and Weber 1982, S. 29). Bank representatives frequently hold mandates on the supervisory boards of mutually competing (or should mutually compete in the market economy) firms, and a quasi-cartel can be created by detouring through supervisory board positions (Arndt 1974, SS. 20–21). Acceptance of mandates on control organs and personnel connections resulting from them can also ease competition between banks, and indirect interlocks created between banks on the supervisory boards of other firms can be an important means of mitigating competition (Schönwitz and Weber 1982, S. 29). Banks do not create another corporate group composed of mutually coordinated enterprises in their vicinity, but rather have adjacent and overlapped enterprises. Banks are fundamentally competing and, despite no direct connection, frequently develop coordinated behaviors to relevant companies or join the reorganization of the entire industry (Ziegler 1985, p. 280).

Many points have been raised about the importance of interlocking directorates in banks. Hagemann emphasized that bank representatives could obtain a detailed outline of companies' financial, economic, and production technological conditions (Hagemann 1931, S. 77). Dahlem emphasizes that each bank group attempted to improve the market condition of the industrial enterprises it manages. Contact on the supervisory board was critical (Dahlem 2009, S. 299). Jacob Riesser found that bank representatives on the supervisory boards of industrial enterprises always took the trouble on a large scale to find a suitable industrial firm on which the bank could exert influence (Riesser 1971, S. 309). Fear and Kobrak point out that banks' mandates on boards have the potential to overcome information asymmetry and reduce capital costs as much as possible (Fear and Kobrak 2010, p. 715).

Supervisory board positions that provide direct access to internal information are the most beneficial to the bank regarding financial information, strategy development, and organizational structure (Dahlem 2009, S. 303). Dahlem points out that an essential weakness of bankers against industry customers lay in their insufficient knowledge concerning technical issues; thus, bankers were forced to obtain knowledge that specialists have to secure the basis for their decision-making (Dahlem 2009, S. 291). Interlocks of banks in companies in various industries and the invitation of persons from other companies as supervisory board members are deeply concerned with banks' goal to achieve stable collection of funds lent in the credit business and secure a higher return on investment in industrial enterprises (Beyer 2013, S. 34; Feldenkirchen 1991, pp. 126–127, 134). According to the annual report of Deutsche Bank, the situation that banks had financial specialized knowledge and economic experience necessary for proactively avoiding erroneous actions or measures of the managing board was an important factor of increased significance supervisory board post that the bank held (Deutsche Bank AG 1986, S. 17). According to Fiedler, the long-term existence of personnel connections between bank and non-bank companies can be regarded as an institutional measure to cope with the asymmetry of information and the risk of providing credits; thus, it is a product of the capital market's economic logic (Fiedler 2005, S. 97). Engenhardt emphasized that acceptance of supervisory board mandate by bank representatives decreased risks concerning banks' holding shares and provision of credits on the one hand and sales market on the other (Engenhardt 1995, S. 49). Fear and Kobrak emphasize methods for building trust and reducing risks over "control." Banks act as special intermediaries and gatekeepers who issue and deal with securities, owing to their close relationships with leading companies (Fear and Kobrak 2010, p. 706).

The Germans tend to regard banks' board mandates as an institutional safety system (Fear and Kobrak 2010, p. 735). Bankers frequently intermediated in ways contradicting industry interests (Krenn 2013, S. 108). Banks played an important role as advisors to companies in securing the interests of banks and industrial companies (Dahlem 2009, S. 279). Banks considered it a duty to provide financial advice to industrial enterprises with whom they had friendly relationships and those with no direct influence. This was typically performed by bank representatives holding supervisory board positions in other companies (Hagemann 1931, S. 168). Wellhöner also points out that the role of a bank representative on the supervisory board is to provide advice on financial support for an investment plan and to facilitate the intermediation of external monetary capital required to carry out such a plan. As Shonfield pointed out, the supervisory board's function as a device for systematic consultation between enterprises with intertwined interests was most clear concerning the bank (Shonfield 1965, p. 251). The listed companies that acted internationally had connections with the banking industry, ranging from capital increases to foreign investment, and their interest in inviting bank representatives to the supervisory board stemmed from business policy decisions in which banks played a significant role. As a result, Eglau emphasized that the power factor seen in the exercise of proxy voting rights was not a necessary means of obtaining supervisory board mandates (Eglau 1990, SS. 180–181).

Meanwhile, some studies deny the strong influence of personnel connections by banks on the supervisory board of other enterprises. According to Edwards and Fischer (1994), supervisory board representatives are generally insignificant sources of information used by banks to make loan decisions. According to them, one reason for this was that bank supervisory board representatives were legally required to maintain confidentiality regarding information obtained through such an organ and were prohibited from disclosing such information to others. The evidence presented in their study did not support "the view that representation of banks on supervisory boards in Germany enables them to provide a large proportion of firm's investment finance in the form of loans" (Edwards and Fischer 1994, pp. 129–130). According to Edwards and Fischer (1994, p. 212), the number of bank representatives on the supervisory board is not "a perfect indicator of bank's ability to determine supervisor board decisions" (Edwards and Fischer 1994, p. 212).

Significant research findings concern influential individuals who also serve as interlocking supervisory board members. Schwein and Krosigk (1958), James (2003), and Wixforth (1995) are examples of representative studies from the pre-World War II period. Gall (2004) on Hermann Josef Abs (Deutsche Bank), Sattler (2009) on Ernst Matthiensen (Dresdner Bank), and Ahrens and Bähr (2013) Ahrens (2013), and Ahrens (2022) on Jürgen Ponto (Dresdner Bank) are notable research results in the postwar period.

Schwein and Krosigk (1958) clarify that Oskar Schlitter, who held mandates on the supervisory boards of various corporate groups, played significant roles as advisor to Mannesmann and Essener Bergverein König Wilhelm (Schwein and Krosigk 1958, SS. 649–650). James (2003) notes that E. G. von Stauss, who had supervisory board mandates in Daimler-Benz and BMW, made efforts to conclude an agreement for consignment of production of aircraft engines and pursue effective division of labor as both firms' survival strategies (James 2003, SS. 93, 95).

Sattler (2009) emphasizes Matthienssen, who had many mandates of supervisory boards of other enterprises and was typical of "Rhenish Capitalism," which demonstrated the function of cooperative coordination between companies (Sattler 2009, S. 334). She clarifies that Matthienssen played a significant role in improving the atmosphere, providing advice on investment decisions by this industrial enterprise, and being an interlocking supervisory board member in Metallgesellschaft AG (Sattler 2009, S. 244). Ralf Ahrens characterizes Jürgen Ponto's role as an interlocking supervisory board member in Krupp as a "moderate supervisor" (Ahrens 2022, p. 125). He clarifies that Ponto considered business affairs from the perspective of not only the bank category, but also the entire industry, which had characteristics similar to the entire economy and social policy (Ahrens and Bähr 2013, SS. 153–155; Ahrens 2013, S. 212). Ahrens and Bähr (2013) noted that Ponto's role as a "moderator" can be seen in other cases, citing one instance in which he coordinated conflicts between Allianz and Bayern-Hypo by acting as a moderator of the discussion (Ahrens and Bähr 2013, S. 133).

1.2.4.5 Relationships Between Industry and Banks and Corporate Governance

Bank monitoring has played an important role in addressing the corporate governance relationships between industry and banks in Germany. Regarding large enterprises, this appears because financial enterprises have many shares and mandates on supervisory boards (Furch 2012, S. 65). Holding stocks of companies for which banks provide credits, as well as having voting rights on deposited stocks and supervisory board posts, improves the flow of information and helps banks monitor corporations (Ringe 2015, p. 501). Interlocking directors provide access to secret information and vote on many corporate governance issues (Windolf 2014, p. 67). Bank directors who hold positions on the boards of many industrial companies have the opportunity to influence their strategies and monitor the level of risk that these companies take (Windolf 2014, p. 75).

Different socioeconomic factors determine whether a corporate governance system is internal or external (Velte and Weber 2011, S. 473). The German corporate governance system is an insider one. As in this system, monitoring cost is small in comparison to the profit to be achieved; in particular, block holders have strong incentives to monitor the management of a company (Velte and Weber 2011, S. 475) and rely on a legal framework characterized by high creditor protection (Velte and Weber 2011, S. 477). In the internal corporate governance system, large shareholders are the predominant type of owner, and relations are harmonized through strategic coordination mechanisms (Klages 2006, SS.40–41). The primary elements of the German corporate governance system are bank control, supervisory boards with codetermination, and enterprise connection. Meanwhile, dispersed ownership stockholders with a return orientation dominate in the external corporate governance system, and coordination is carried out through external governance mechanisms. Many joint-stock companies in Anglo-Saxon countries have dispersed ownership, and the Anglo-American corporate governance system is based on minority shareholder protection, an intense competitive product market, and a large-scale market for acquisition (Klages 2006, SS. 43–44). Since the 1990s, Germany has attempted to reform corporate governance in line with the European Union (Cioffi 2010; Seibert 2004; Cioffi and Höpner 2006; Armor and McCahery 2006, Part IV). According to S. Vitols, in the 1980s, the bank-based system was widely thought to be superior to the market-based system in terms of providing long-term patient capital (Vitols 2003, p. 240).

1.2.4.6 Bank Power and Its Impact on Industrial Enterprises

Next, this section considers arguments about the influence of banks on industrial enterprises, which has become an important issue following Otto Jeidels' study emphasizing bank control over industry. According to Jeidels (1905, S.145), large banks' power was exercised through the legal institution of the supervisory board rather than through direct influence by financial strength (Jeidels 1905, S. 145). Eglau emphasizes that there were many cases where, despite no special justice of capital participation, the chairman mandate of the supervisory board of Deutsche Bank affected the decision of business policies of companies that trusted in the chairman's control (Eglau 1990, S. 178). Gerschenkron stated that "through the device of formally short-term but in reality long-term current account credits and through the development of the institution of the supervisory boards to the position of most powerful organs within corporate organizations, the banks acquired a formidable degree of ascendancy over industrial enterprises" (Gerschenkron 1962, p. 15). Feldenkirchen insists that banks' roles in mergers and amalgamations can be clearly demonstrated (Feldenkirchen 1979, S. 38, 1991, p. 134), and bank representatives holding supervisory board positions in other companies were able to determine which company would be the target of such concentrations on the basis of various business relationships. Regarding the merger of Phönix and Düsseldorfer Röhlen- und Eisenwalzwerke AG implemented in 1920 under the initiative of Schaaffhausenscher Banksverein, he indicated a case in which this bank admitted new credit only after Phönix agreed to this merger (Feldenkirchen 1979, S. 38). Gossweiler pointed out that the relationships between banking capital and industrial capital described by Lenin did not fundamentally change. Changes in the manner of driving away banks by heavy industry did not occur in the ten years from 1926 to 1936. The predominance of banking capital over heavy industry had appeared additionally and more strongly as influences of large banks on state decision concerning the fate of industrial monopoly (Gossweiler 1965, SS. 36–37, 51).

While such views exist, studies have been published denying banks' involvement and influence in industrial enterprises' management and business policy. Wellhöner (1989) refuted Hilferding's claim that banks exercised excessive control over industrial enterprises before World War II. According to him, although the relationship between the reproduction process of banking capital and industrial capital found corresponding relations in institutional tie through the supervisory board, such an institutional connection was neither expression of bank control nor fusion of both in the sense of loss of identity of banking capital or industrial capital as finance capital united in all capital groups. According to Wellhöner (1989, S. 245), such an institutional connection was more likely the result of close business relationships and mutual interests.

Furthermore, Wixforth, who investigated relationships between banks and heavy industry during the Weimar period, emphasizes that, as bank directors frequently functioned as advisors for the board of directors and the entire supervisory board in decisions in terms of financial technology, economic law, or company organization on the basis of their special abilities, even in cases where bankers attended to advice and decisions in the supervisory board, the influence of banks cannot be observed. Wixforth emphasized that the presence of bank directors on the supervisory board of industrial firms should not be regarded as "the power mechanism" in the hands of banks (Wixforth 1995, S. 40).

Wixforth (1995) clarified that cases in which supervisory board mandates members from banks held were used as a means of achieving interests and influencing business policy were rare, and banks could not generally realize such behaviors, while cases in which bank representatives on supervisory boards were in charge of functions as advisors, intermediaries, and information providers were numerous. There were many cases where the purpose of holding a supervisory board position by a bank was to build and maintain business relationships with the concerned company, as well as cases where banks intended to exert strong influence on the business policies of other companies (Wixforth 1995, SS. 93–96, 114, 170, 193, 195, 198, 207, 325, 330, 356, 380, 384, 430–431, 434, 451, 489, 498, 502–503, 507–550).

In particular, in family businesses, autonomy and the degree of freedom of management behavior were high (Wixforth 1995, S. 239, 505). Of the enterprises in the heavy industry Wixforth analyzed, only Mannesmann, in which Deutsche Bank played a decisive role as a large shareholder (Wixforth 1995, SS. 273, 304), was exceptional. In this company, Deutsche Bank could make important business policy decisions jointly with the managing board of this industrial company in the form of cooperative conversation (Wixforth 1995, S. 275). Meanwhile, in enterprises where stock capital was widely dispersed and salaried managers took charge of management, banks had a large possibility of exerting great influence, and of the sample of ten enterprises, Wixforth investigated Rheinische Stahlwerke as the best example of such a phenomenon (Wixforth 1995, S. 506). However, even in the case of Mannesmann, bankers had no ambition to use their supervisory board mandates as a means of exerting influence on business policy (Wixforth 1995, S. 278), and the chairman of the supervisory board of the bank and the board of directors attempted to find a solution suitable for both companies' interests (Wixforth 1995, SS. 284, 302–303).

Wixforth emphasized that most sample firms could use competition among banks on a domestic and international scale, which was crucial to their high independence from financial institutions (Wixforth 1995, SS. 424, 502, 508). He also emphasized that the results of his case studies regarding the Weimar period generally supported the evaluation of the loosening of relationships between banks and industries and the further independence of industries from banks (Wixforth 1995, S. 508).

Wixforth and Ziegler's (1995) study of bank-industry relationships prior to 1933 clarified the hypothesis that banks' general dominance over industrial enterprises had also been denied (Wixforth and Ziegler 1995, p. 261). Fohlin (1999) and Ziegler (1998) emphasized that in studies concerning the periods of the Second Reich, the interwar period, and the Federal Republic of Germany, interpreting the connection of German large firms as bank hegemony was negated with sufficient reason (Fohlin 1999; Ziegler 1998). Fohlin stated that the board assignment was made in both directions, from the bank to the industrial enterprise and from the latter to the former. Contrary to Rudolf Hilferding's and his followers' beliefs, interlocking directorates generally appeared to be unrelated to bank power (Fohlin 1999, p. 329). She also emphasizes that although banks had substantial interests in the heavy industry, this fact did not support any bank control theory (Fohlin 2007, p. 140), and the predominance of banks in the ownership and control of companies is a myth about current Germany as well as the period of industrialization (Fohlin 2007, p. 140). In his study on the 1920s, Dieter Ziegler also negatively evaluated the existence of bank power (Ziegler 1998).

During the period until the 1930s, Hagemann (1931) emphasized that big banks exerted a general influence in excluding competition or at least making efforts to pursue peaceful agreement (Hagemann 1931, SS. 74–75). He insisted that it is very dangerous to evaluate the influence power of a bank on an industrial enterprise only through the condition of the assignment of members from the bank to the supervisory board (Hagemann 1931, SS. 74–75). Krenn (2012) also points out that, although the model of financial control can explain a part of the structure of a network, in all periods before World War II analyzed by her, networks did not indicate a structure that provided an opportunity for the one-sided control relationship over industry by banks (Krenn 2012, S. 245). She emphasizes that the structural premise for one-sided pursuit of interests on the side of industry or bank was only rarely given at the level of personnel connection (Krenn 2012, S. 239). Feldenkirchen (1979) pointed out that although banks were strongly involved in the supervisory boards of all enterprises in the years from the nineteenth century to the twentieth century, it seemed unjustified to conclude that enterprises became dependent on banks as a whole from this fact (Feldenkirchen 1979, S. 34).

When considering the period after World War II, David and Weserhuis (2014) clarified that relationships between industry and banks were not often bank control, but a reciprocal coordination (David and Weserhuis 2014, p. 22). Ahrens (2016) points out that if we realize its own interests by bank against management of the company as bank power, even in cases of Hermann Josef Abs and Ernst Matthiensen, as two representative bankers during the Adenauer period after World War II, that bankers truly exerted power through their posts cannot be recognized (Ahrens 2016,

S. 136). Ahrens (2022) and Marx and Leitmeyer (2022b) emphasize that the German economy after 1945 was not characterized by bank hegemony (Ahrens 2022; Marx and Leitmeyer 2022b, p. 23).

In his 1994 and 1995 study of the 100 largest German companies, Brendel emphasized the importance of distinguishing the potential for banks to exert influence and power. He noted that, while the potential possibility of a bank's influence on companies could generally be proven, concerning voting rights factors based on deposited stocks, capital participation, and holding of supervisory board posts, evidence of banks maximizing direct effect could not be confirmed (Brendel 2001, SS. 176–177). Furthermore, in a robust examination of strategy decisions at Thyssen, Hoesch, and Mannesmann from 1955 to 1975, Rennert contends that each corporate group's fundamental and long-term strategy was almost entirely built by the board of directors and its members at the time. As studies in business history frequently recognize the significant role of bank representatives on the supervisory board in building strategy, her research result is an unexpected consequence (Rennert 2015, S. 347).

There are also claims that the current state of competition among banks and its promotion by industrial enterprises has prevented banks from exerting a strong influence on the management of these enterprises and business policy decisions. Tilly pointed out that, because banks were in intense competition during the period from 1900 to 1911, an increase in the number of bank representatives on the supervisory boards of industrial enterprises implied the negotiation power of the company against the bank and capital market, and it was impossible to mention the one-sided influence of banks on these enterprises (Tilly 1980, S. 184). Ziegler (1985) also emphasized that, while large banks were linked to enterprises via primary interlocks, particularly larger ones in various industrial sectors, the high degree of overlap in their spheres of influence did not indicate one-sided bank control. This was because "large industrial corporations were obviously able to attract directors from several banks or to send their executives to the boards of more than one of the very big banks" (Ziegler 1985, p. 278).

Bank involvement and influence on industrial firm management and business policy can be seen primarily when the firm is experiencing a management crisis. Gehlen points out that although business history indicates some evidence of "bank power," the majority of cases have occurred in the case of a management crisis (Gehlen 2022, p. 80). Tilly also emphasized that many strong involvements of banks in managing industrial enterprises occurred in the context of an enterprise in which finance was a key problem (Tilly 2005, p. 109). Ahrens clarifies that although banks' influence was primarily exerted through the election of members of management (managing board) and admission or denial of larger investment projects, cases where banks intend to truly govern industrial enterprises in terms of determining managerial decision-making can only be observed in cases of serious management crises (Ahrens 2022, p. 129). Joly also insisted that involvement of banks occurred in cases where the financial condition of the concerned company was very bad and sufficient profit was not achieved, and that the influence of banks was, in fact, decisive only in corporate groups suffering from strict financial conditions (Joly 1998, S. 204).

According to Wixforth and Ziegler (1995), the power of banks had a very different dimension, partly because critics and protectors of the close relationships between banks and industry looked at different dimensions of power. Whereas critics emphasized bank control in the microdimension, defenders stressed the much more harmonious macrodimension of the bank (Wixforth and Ziegler, 1995, p. 264).

1.3 Study Fields of Personnel Connections Between Enterprises and Research Topics in This Book

Based on the preceding considerations, this section presents the central theme of this book's analysis in relation to each of the study fields of personnel connections between companies.

This book explores the personnel connections of the three largest German banks, namely Deutsche Bank, Dresdner Bank, and Commerzbank, from the beginning of the twentieth century to the present from comparative viewpoint of these banks [(1)]. It examines three major fields: (1) structures of personnel ties built through direct and indirect interlocking directorates and interlock-based personnel networks, (2) functions of interlocking directorates, and (3) structures and functions of personnel connections through the Bank's advisory council system, which consists of central and regional advisory councils. This section presents the main points in question. This book attempts to clarify the structure and functions of personnel connections using interlocking directorate and bank advisory council systems to better understand the characteristics and significance of industry–bank relationships in Germany. These research topics are analyzed historically in this book, and the historical changes in some important periods and the factors influencing them are understood.

1.3.1 Primary Points in Question Regarding Structures of Interlocking Directorates

Interlocking directorate: First, in terms of personnel connections built through indirect interlocking directorates, this book examines how three large banks established personnel connections through the interlocking of members of supervisory and managing boards on the supervisory boards of other companies. The actual conditions under which members of the board of directors and the supervisory board, which is made up of people from each bank and invited people from other companies, have formed personnel ties are examined, with a focus on the industrial distribution of enterprises where interlocking directorates are established, the types of mandates such as chairman and vice-chairman on the supervisory board, and cases of personnel ties formed through plural mandates. Such an analysis will be developed not only for direct interlocks, but also for indirect interlocks in which personnel ties are formed among the three largest banks or between two of them on the supervisory boards of other enterprises. In terms of indirect interlocking directorates formed by enterprises in the same industry on the supervisory boards of other companies, considering it in relation to the number of interlocking posts allows us to understand which enterprise with multiple mandates is in the lead and to clarify the industrial sector to which such an enterprise belongs.

Interlocking directorates of members of top management organs, such as the supervisory and managing boards of large representative banks and the supervisory boards of other enterprises, are examined for six periods. In the period preceding World War II, three periods of the transition to monopolistic capitalism in Germany in the early twentieth century, the inflation period following World War I, and the mid-1930s during National Socialism are examined. Three post-World War II periods are considered recent: the late 1950s, the late 1960s, and the latter half of the 2010s. However, in the analysis of the latter half of the 2010s, only the cases of two banks are examined, as Dresdner Bank no longer exists. An attempt to historically analyze the structure of personnel connections built through both direct and indirect interlocks on the basis of concrete cases of the most leading enterprises in the banking industry as a core sector of German capitalism, such as the three largest banks, has not been completed adequately.

Personnel network: Next, as another type of personnel ties between enterprises, it is important to clarify the structure of networks using social network analysis methodology. Many previous studies tended to examine the structure of networks that spread over a limitless number of personnel ties. Such studies have produced valuable research results. However, given the significance of personnel networks as information flows and media available for decision-making in a company and the coordination of conflicts and interests between companies, a personnel network through interlocking directorates in "distant 2," including second- and third-party enterprises, has significant meaning. This is because, for the company involved at the network's inception, this network can form a valuable information bank system, allowing for the exchange and sharing of information, coordination of interests, and resolution of conflicts between industry and banks and among corporations. As a result, it is important to analyze personnel networks, which include second- and third-party companies established by large banks and representative large enterprises in key industrial sectors. Few studies have analyzed the actual conditions of personnel connections and networks formed through interlocking directorates using concrete examples of representative enterprises in the banking sector. The structures of personnel networks built in "distant 2" of the three largest German banks were not considered. This book examines the personnel networks formed between supervisory board members using the three banks as examples. Because of the importance of personnel networks as valuable information flows and media, the network's extent in this book is limited to distance 2. The reason for such limitation of object is that in the case of the network of more than "distance 3" character as the interfirm relationship of the concerned individual enterprise is weaker, the network of "distance

1" is only a mere direct personnel connection of the individual company concerned (Nakata et al. 1997, p. 40).

Three time periods will be considered in network analysis: (1) the mid-1930s during the Nazi era, (2) the end of the 1960s when the 1965 Corporations Law was enacted, and (3) the latter half of the 2010s as the destination in tremendous changes following the 1990s. As previously mentioned, the density of network established in Germany from the end of the nineteenth century to the beginning of the twentieth century reached its peak in 1928 and then declined, but it remained relatively thick in the 1930s (Windolf 2014, SS. 79–80). As a result, grasping the conditions in the 1930s is crucial for comparison with the conditions after World War II. In the period following World War II, due to the tendency of big banks to select enterprises to be regarded as important objects of personnel tie, the decrease of the number of joint-stock companies with the progress of enterprise concentration, the structure of interlocking directorates changed, and personnel connection in the late 1960s became a basic system of interlocking directorates in postwar Germany and was maintained for quite some time. This is why the late 1960s are referred to as the post-World War II era.

As examined in Sect. 1.4, "density" and "centrality" are key concepts in the methodology of social network analysis (Hannemann and Riddle 2011, pp. 341–342, 362–367; Nakata et al. 1997, Chap. 2). It is an important research topic to analyze the structure of the personnel network using these two concepts to understand cohesiveness as a characteristic of the network as a whole and which enterprise holds a central position among the companies that make up the network in question. Such an analysis will help to clarify how the network has changed.

Furthermore, it is important to examine the clique of interlocking supervisory board members who have multiple mandates on the supervisory boards of multiple companies and play a significant role in the network in significance to understand personnel ties in each company's network. This book examines the interlocking of supervisory board members in banks and industrial enterprises and the combination of those two. Clique refers to "the largest possible collection of nodes (more than two) in which all actors are directly connected to all others" (Hannemann and Riddle 2011, p. 350). As a result, by grasping cliques, it is possible to identify major linkers who play an important role in the network of each firm, enterprise to which they belong, industrial sector to which such enterprises belong, and individual who can act as a knitting point in the information flow and media.

This book attempts to clarify the route and channel of information transmission for top management's strategic decisions, including interlocking supervisory board members. In this book, through analyzing the network in the extent of "distance 2" including second- and third-party enterprises, not the network that spreads over the linkage of personnel ties in the limitless that many prior studies have considered, it is attempted to grasp not the global centrality measured by the sum distance reaching all other enterprises, but certain enterprises with high centrality in networks of three largest banks. Such analysis can clarify the roles of certain influential companies in information flow and media, as well as the structure of information networks.

Based on analysis of structure of personnel connection between industry and bank built by the largest three banks, this book attempts to grasp changes of personnel ties in relation to the historical conditions in each period. It examines how changes of personnel connection of big banks in each main period were determined by the historical situations of global capitalism and German capitalism in relation to economic and industrial factors without limiting to the factors inherent to the level of enterprises. Analyses to grasp the historical changes of personnel tie in the historical conditions in each period have been not sufficiently developed in prior research.

1.3.2 Primary Points in Question Regarding Function of Interlocking Directorates

The structure of personnel connections formed by interlocking directorates between enterprises serves as an important foundation for demonstrating the function of interfirm relationships. In general, such functions can be seen in the exchange and sharing of information in various industrial departments and many companies where banks are interested in capital financing and investment, as well as the coordination of interests and conflicts between enterprises. As a result, analyzing the functions and roles of personnel connections via interlocking members of large bank supervisory and management boards is an important research topic. This book examines how the function of interfirm relationships, which are commonly seen in relationships between industry and banks, has been demonstrated in exchanging and sharing information, as well as coordinating conflicts and interests between enterprises, including cases in which bank representatives serve as chairman of other enterprises' supervisory boards. According to Edwards and Fischer (1994, p. 220), general coordination, also known as the "consultancy" function, "might best be performed by a relatively small number of banks that had extensive supervisory board representation" among joint-stock companies (Edwards and Fischer 1994, p. 220).

This book discusses two personnel issues related to the functions of interlocking directorates: (1) the election of members who should compose the managing board of an industrial enterprise in which a representative of the bank had a mandate of the supervisory board, and (2) the selection of candidates to the supervisory boards of the industrial enterprise and the concerned bank as proposed at the general meeting. The role and influence of the bank in personnel matters are explored. The selection of management board members is an important function of the supervisory board, and it is closely related to the bank's influence on an industrial enterprise. Given banks' interests, such as the stable collection of financing funds for companies as customers and the increased efficiency of investments in industrial companies, personnel issues such as the election of supervisory board members involved in business policy decisions and the dismissal of members of management boards in charge of execution duties had important significance. It is also important to coordinate various conflicts and interests between banks and industrial firms, as well as between industrial firms, through interlocking discussions rather than market competition. Bank representatives on other companies' supervisory boards can play an important role in this collaboration. In this book, we examine at how they played such a role by gathering, exchanging, and sharing information from their interlocking posts.

The functions and roles of interlocking directorates on personnel issues on other companies' supervisory and management boards, as well as enterprise coordination, including between banks, industrial enterprises, and corporations, are not always fully clarified. This book examines the mechanism of cooperation between enterprises, personnel issues of supervisory board members, and problems of coordination of interests and conflicts between banks and industrial enterprises, as well as between industrial firms, using original materials on the three largest banks and representative enterprises in the major industrial sectors, as well as prior prominent studies.

1.3.3 Primary Points in Question Regarding Structure and Function of Personnel Connection through Bank's Advisory Council System

In Germany, personnel connections in the form of the advisory council system of large banks composed of central and regional advisory councils also played a significant role in interfirm relationships in which interests and various conflicts between enterprises, including between a bank and an industrial enterprise, can be coordinated. It was important for gathering, exchanging, and sharing information about various industrial departments and many companies in which banks were interested in financing and investing capital. As previously stated, the advisory council system was instrumental in supplementing the function of personnel connections via interlocking directorates in top management organs. Therefore, it is critical to clarify the structure and functions of this type of personnel relationship.

Despite the importance of this research on personnel connections through banking advisory council systems, few studies have examined personnel relationships through organizations comprised of central and regional advisory councils, as well as positions in top management organs such as the supervisory board and the board of directors in various companies with advisory council members. The structures of personnel connections between enterprises, as well as between banks and industrial enterprises, and the functions and roles played by personnel relationships through the advisory council system are also unclear (Eglau 1990; Pfeiffer 1987; Gottschalk 1988; Stanzick 1969; Büschgen 1983; Koubek 1971; Schwarz 2003; Aizawa 1988, Aizawa 1994). However, to understand the cooperative mechanisms of interfirm relationships in Germany, it is necessary to conduct a case-by-case analysis of personnel connections between a bank and industrial enterprises and between corporations.

In companies of the personnel structure connected through the advisory council system, the field and scope of information that members of this type of organization can obtain through such an organization are determined by their holding mandates of top management organs. Therefore, this book examines the composition of the central advisory council and each regional advisory council, as well as the conditions under which advisory council members hold top management positions such as supervisory board and board of directors. Such an analysis allowed us to understand the scope of information exchanged and shared between the bank and member enterprises and between member enterprises.

Analyzing the functions and roles of such personnel connections is also an important research area. This book seeks to clarify the functions and roles of such personnel connections by examining the activities of these organizations using original historical materials from large German banks. This study examines at the conditions for holding meetings and their members, the content of each meeting, and personnel issues, such as the election of members of advisory councils, as an important foundation for the organization's operation. The cases of Deutsche Bank, Dresdner Bank, and Commerzbank are examined using a variety of original materials from the three largest banks, including advisory council meeting minutes, letters and documents, and correspondence between bank members, the bank and industrial enterprises, and the bank and advisory council members. This book also attempts to clarify the mechanism of cooperation between a bank and industrial enterprises and between corporations, as well as German corporate behavior that avoids intense price competition and adopts a management style focused on competing with quality (Yamazaki 2013b). This book's analysis has important implications for understanding German capitalism's cooperative mechanism.

The Nazi era is the main period preceding World War II for the object to be examined. In terms of the structure of personnel connections after the war, conditions in the latter half of the 1960s are examined. This is because central advisory councils were typically established to supplement the level of personnel tie influenced by the 1965 Corporations Law. Meanwhile, the analysis of the function and role of such personnel ties is not limited to the 1960s; it covers the period from the 1950s to the 1980s.

1.3.4 Primary Points in Question Regarding German Style of "Finance Capital"

In addition to the three primary research topics mentioned above, understanding the German style of "finance capital" proposed by Lenin as a capital form created by the uniting and knitting of monopolistic capital in industries and the banking sector (Ленин 1962, Chap. 3) and its significance are important research issues. Finance capital refers to forming a management entity that works together to accumulate capital through financing, cross-stockholding, account current business, and personnel connections (Honma 1984, p. 191). Analyzing capital relations (investment and financing) and personnel connections (interlocking directorate) confirms the category of "finance capital," which refers to the uniting and knitting of monopolistic capital in industries and the banking industry. In capital relations, if the bank capital indicated as "asset" on the balance sheet is used for the purchase of industrial enterprise shares and its amount exceeds a certain level, in Germany, the capital invested for this purpose is concerned with "corporate control," which means the ability to enable the composition of the supervisory board of the concerned company at the annual meeting through the exercise of voting rights. In contrast, when bank capital is lent as a source of debt and financing rather than for stock purchases, banks will try to monitor managerial decision-making and business execution of the industrial enterprise in question in terms of fund utilization and remark. Large enterprises that develop business in various economic sectors are united as one body through financing and stockholding, and within a group of large enterprises formed by such fusion, strategy decisions can be coordinated among enterprises. The assignment of directors from a bank to an industrial firm is generally a means of coordinating interests between companies in connected relationships for the common interests of the group as a whole, rather than control over an industrial company (Honma 1984, p. 226).

"Accumulation" of finance capital is understood as acquiring new profits and their reinvestment, which are only possible through knitting industrial and bank monopolies (Honma 1984, p. 232). The common interests of industrial enterprises and their connection to the same bank serve as the foundation for the formation and growth of a group of "finance capital." As a result, the formation of a monopolistic group is based on two axes: (1) the ax of special interest of the industrial sector resulting from economic and technical conditions of production and sale, and (2) the entanglement of financial capitalistic relations. Mutual cross and building of monopolistic group implies both horizontal and vertical coordinates in the monopolistic capital line (Gossweiler 1971, SS. 48–49). The large banks and large industrial enterprises are mutually influenced, and this process can create a consensus among large enterprises about the affairs of an industry (Shonfield 1965, p. 261). Therefore, an important link between banks and industrial enterprises is the establishment of an "industrial system" for the development of enterprises and industries through business management in the form of coordinated and united interests of banks and industries.

Building a capital form is difficult because of the need to create a mechanism that balances the interests of both industry and banks without contradicting or conflicting with either party. Industrial enterprises maximize industrial and commercial profits, while banks maximize interest and dividends. Interest is a cost factor for industrial enterprises, whereas it is a source of profit for banks. As a result, maximizing industrial and commercial profit by exchanging and sharing information between banks and industrial enterprises and promoting control of competition among enterprises through discussion is an important premise for avoiding conflict between industries and banks and maximizing interest and dividends for banks. As a result, an important research topic is how an institution has been built to realize the interests of both industry and banks through a structure of personnel connections and networks via interlocking directorates and information flow and media systems based on such personnel relationships. This book defines an "industrial system" as a German mechanism for developing enterprise, industry, and the economy based on close relationships between industry and banking.

Based on the recognition that the purpose of obtaining information influences the quality of the structure of personnel connections and networks, this book clarifies the structure of personnel ties of three large banks via interlocking directorates and the bank's advisory council system, as well as the functions of such personnel ties. A comprehensive analysis of personnel connections and cooperative mechanisms of interfirm relationships will be attempted, focusing on historical comparison and comparison of the three largest German banks. This study examines the mechanism of cooperative interfirm relationships in Germany and their significance. Thus, the uniqueness and significance of this book stem from its combined analysis of the structure and function of personnel connections between enterprises via interlocking directorates and bank advisory councils.

1.3.5 Primary Points in Question Regarding "Corporate Control" and "Corporate Rule": Issues of Influence of Bank on Industry and Bank's Power

Many previous studies have examined banks' influence and control over important issues such as industrial firm management and business policy through holding the mandate of other firms' supervisory boards and their power in such firms. However, in this regard, it is important to define the term "control" and distinguish between the phenomena of "corporate control" and "corporate rule." In their book on US corporations, A. A. Berle and G. C. Means defined the power to determine the composition of the board of directors as "control." Berle included both "corporate control" regarding the issue of electing members of the management board and "control over business and asset of enterprises," which is concerned with the authority of decision-making of salaried managers in the concept "corporate control" (Berle and Means 1932, pp. 69–70, 220). Regardless of their similarities, both concepts must be clearly distinguished. In this regard, John Scott clearly distinguishes them. He regards the power of determining a member of the board of directors as a top management organ in the USA as "corporate control" and the control over an enterprise's business and assets as "corporate rule" (Scott 1990, pp. 352–353, 371).

In many studies on relationships between industry and banks, the influence of banks on industrial enterprises, the power of banks in German enterprises, and the issues of "corporate control" and "corporate rule" have not been distinguished as concepts, and both are interpreted as "control." This indicates a misunderstanding of the concept of "control." The two phenomena to be distinguished are (1) banks being involved in or exerting decisive influence on management and business policy of the concerned enterprise through the supervisory board mandate of other enterprises, and (2) banks imposing restrictions on decision-making in individual companies through interlocking directorates or personnel networks. Based on an understanding of relations and distinguishing these two concepts, the relationships between industry and banks are analyzed in this book by examining the roles that banks and industrial enterprises play in personnel connections based on networks built by interlocks and the "corporate rule," as well as issues of "corporate control."

1.4 Analytical Framework

1.4.1 Basic Viewpoint of Analysis of Personnel Connection Between Enterprises

The following section attempts to explain an analytical framework [(2)]. This subsection explains the fundamental approach to analyzing personnel connections between industrial enterprises, banks, and corporations. It is important to consider the interlocking directorate in relation to the position of interlocking mandate on the supervisory board, such as chairman and vice-chairman, the number of interlocking posts within the same company, and the distribution of the industrial sector. Through such analysis, it will be possible to understand the strength of the relationship with the enterprise in question, which enterprise plays a central role in personnel connections between companies, and which industrial sector such a core company belongs to. Furthermore, considering indirect interlocking directorates on the supervisory boards of other companies formed among enterprises in the same industry concerning the number of interlocking posts allows us to understand which company with multiple mandates is in the lead and to clarify the industrial sector to which such an enterprise belongs.

When analyzing personnel connections through the bank's advisory council system, understanding the composition of the members of the central advisory council and each regional advisory council, and examining the conditions, each member is mandated by top management organs such as the supervisory board and the board of directors. Such an analysis allowed us to understand the scope of information exchanged and shared between the bank and member enterprises and between member enterprises.

This book will provide a case study of representative companies in the banking sector to clarify the structure of personnel connections. This book also examines the functions and roles of personnel connections through interlocking directorates and advisory councils on the basis of each case, drawing on historical primary materials from the archives of large banks and representative companies in the major producing industries. A comprehensive analysis of personnel connections and cooperative mechanisms of interfirm relationships will be attempted from this analytical perspective.

In Japan, a school of thought analyzes and understands the dynamics of business management on the basis of the mutual relationships between political, industrial, and business economics, which comprise the structure of economics (Maekawa 1970, 1993, 1997; Kanbayashi 1976; Yamazaki 2005). Among these mutual relationships, this school of thought identifies the causes of various problems and the distinct styles and characteristics of business management, particularly in developed countries. It also discusses the social importance of objective changes and the link between the law of change and development. In this book, we go beyond specific corporate-level factors to thoroughly analyze economic and industrial factors of business management and explain the process of corporate activities creating reproduction and accumulation structures in a capitalistic country. Using this analytical approach, this book seeks to understand the relationships between industry and banks based on personnel connections concerning the historical contexts of German capitalism and the issue of industrial concentration.

This book analyzes how relationships between industry and banks have developed over time under historical conditions determined by the characteristics of Germany's social economy. Such a system laid a solid foundation for developing important business management in this country. This book's analysis is extremely useful in clarifying German companies' behavioral modes and competitive strategies. Research focusing on the autonomy of the company as an important element of social economy and mutual interaction between companies and influencing factors of relationships between enterprises as a behavioral entity in the industry and socioeconomic system attempts to add a new perspective to the analysis of business management, industry, and capitalism.

1.4.2 Methodology of Social Network Analysis

Following, the social network analysis methodology is considered (regarding description in this subsection, see Scott 2000, 3 and 4; Hannemann and Riddle 2011; Nakata et al. 1997, pp. 38–41). Two key concepts are required for analyzing the social network of personnel connections between companies. The first is "density," which is used to assess the cohesiveness of a network. The other is "centrality" which determines which company is in the core position among the companies that comprise a network concerned with information flow and media. "Density" describes the characteristics of the network as a whole, whereas "centrality" indicates the importance of each company in the network.

Regarding "density," it is indicated by ratio of number of actual interlocking directorate to that of theoretically possible interlocking directorate. It can be calculated by the following expression. If the number of actual interlocking directorates is L and the total number of enterprises constituting the network is n, then density $= L \div n\,(n-1)/2$. Which enterprise did indicate strong "cohesiveness" of the network and which industry such company belongs to can be grasped through analyzing "density." For instance, let's calculate density of network using Fig. 1.2. Number of actual interlocking directorates is six. The number of theoretically possible interlocking directorates is $7 \times (7\text{–}1)/2 = 21$. Total number of enterprises that constitute the network is seven. Therefore, density $= 6 \div 7\,(7\text{–}1)/2 = 0.286$.

On the other hand, "centrality" is grasped by the indicator called "adjacency" that means number of enterprises in which interlocking directorate is built. It is possible

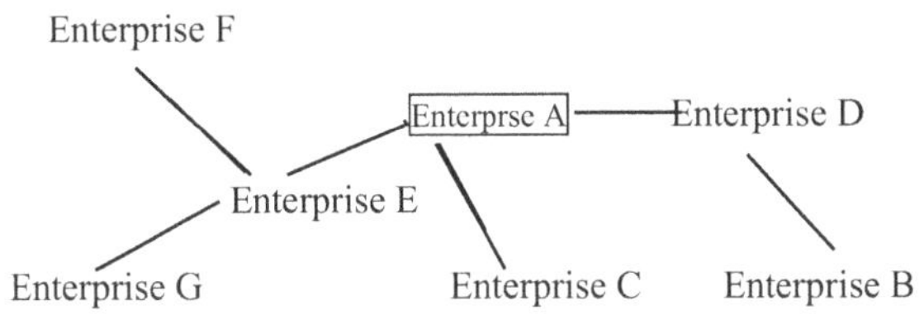

Note: "Enterprise A" enclosed in square is enterprise that is at starting point of this network.

Source: This figure was made by the author.

Fig. 1.2 Density of network and centrality of enterprises concerned in the network

to understand which enterprise is company whose "centrality" is relatively high and to which industry it belongs by analyzing "centrality." Let's measure centrality of each enterprise that constitutes the network using Fig. 1.2. Network indicated in this figure is built including not only second-party enterprises but also third-party enterprises. Whereas adjacency of enterprises A and E is three, respectively, that of D is two. Adjacency of enterprises B, C, F, and G is one, respectively. Therefore, enterprises A and E are regarded as enterprise with relatively high centrality in this network.

The concept of "centrality" is divided into two categories: "global centrality" and "local centrality." Many studies published to date consider personnel networks to be unlimited in scope and comprised of all enterprises. Understanding global centrality as measured by the total distance to all other enterprises is important in such a network. In this book, as networks are analyzed to the extent of "distance 2" including second- and third-party companies, the global centrality that takes connections across the entire network is not considered, but the local centrality is grasped. An enterprise that takes a core position and plays a significant role in the network of the three largest banks and industry to which it belongs is clarified by grasping local centrality.

"Multiplicity" is also important indicator, which means that the number of more than two mandates that build interlocking directorates (Scott 2000, pp. 65–67). Considering "multiplicity" helps to grasp a company that has many mandates on the supervisory board of other enterprise. Methodology of social network analysis is useful for comparing personnel networks among industries and between enterprises (Nakata et al. 1997, pp. 38–41).

Earlier discussions clarified the book's purpose, significance, and analytical framework. Part 1 explains the structures of interlocking directorates of members of large banks who served on supervisory and managing boards of other enterprises before and after World War II, as well as their current positions. Part 2 examines the personnel networks of three large banks formed by interlocking directorates of supervisory board members on the same top management organ of other companies, including second- and third-party companies, using social network analysis. Part 3 examines the role of interlocking directorates on the supervisory board before and after World War II, drawing on original materials from the archives of representative enterprises in the banking and major industries. Part 4 examines the structures and functions of personnel connections between a bank and an industrial enterprise and between corporations via a bank's advisory council system as an important means of supplementing personnel relations formed through interlocking directorates, using original materials analyzed in large bank archives.

(1) In each chapter, the three German large banks analyzed in this book will be referred to as Deutsche Bank, Dresdner Bank, and Commerzbank, even if the company names have changed.

During the period covered in Chap. 2, banks as known as "the Berlin six banks" (Deutsche Bank, Dresdner Bank, Disconto-Gesellschaft, Darmstädter Bank, A. Schaufhausener Banksverein, and Berliner Handels-Gesellschaft) were the most representative. However, the three largest German banks were Deutsche Bank, Dresdner Bank, and Commerzbank, and this large business system in the banking industry lasted until the 2010s, when Dresdner Bank disappeared. As a result, this book considers the cases of these three banks to ensure that the analysis is consistent.

(2) As John Scott pointed out, main models that "have guided inferences about the significance of interlocking directorships" can be seen in the following five: (1) the finance-capital model, (2) the co-ordination and control model, (3) the resource-dependence model, (4) the managerial model, and (5) the class-cohesion model. The finance-capital model emphasizes the existence of finance capital as "units of capital with varying mixes of banking and industrial interests" and "organized groups of companies pursuing a relatively autonomous corporate strategy through the co-ordinated actions of the constituent elements." "Multiple directors would be regarded as the finance capitalists, who may have a home base in a particular company but who also play a role on behalf of the system of finance capital as a whole." The co-ordination and control model is essentially composed of two variants: the bank-control model and the family-control model. According to the former, banks are regarded as "the decision-making centres within the 'empires' of high finance" and "banks are seen as having an independent base of power because of level of their ability to grant or to withhold long- and short-term loans." According to the bank-control model, "banks seek board representation on those companies whose affairs they wish to control." The resource-dependence model is based on "the assumption that large enterprises depend upon one another for access to valued resources and therefore seek to establish links in an attempt to regulate their interdependence." Corporate information obtained by sitting on the board of another company is regarded a valuable resource. However, "according to this model the network of interlocks should have no systematic structure." The managerial model holds that "the top executives of large enterprises have achieved almost total autonomy from control by shareholders and lenders." Because outside directors are "passive and subject to manipulation by the insiders who accutually run the firm," "whatever links may exist between boards are irrelevant to the question of control over corporate strategy." Meanwhile, the class-cohesion model assumes that "directors are recruited from an upper class" and "the patterns of interlocks express and contribute to the cohesion of this class." (scott 1985, pp.6–10) This book is

based on the finance-capital model as an analytical approach due to the significance of forming a management entity that is created by the uniting and knitting industrial and banking capital and works together to accumulate capital through capital and personnel connections.

References

Abelshauser W (2003) Kulturkampf. Der deutsche Weg in die neuen Wirtschaft und die amerikanische Herausforderung. Kulturverlag Kadmos, Berlin

Abshagen HU (2007) Aufsichtsrat und Beirat.Die praktische Arbeit. 2.Aufl., Rudolf Haufe Verlag, München

Adams M (1994) Die Usurpation von Aktionsärsbefugnissen mittels Ringverflechtung in der Deutschland AG. In: Die Aktiengesellschaft 39(4):148–158

Aglietta M (2009) New trends in corporate governance: the prominent role of the long run investor. In: Compet Chang 12(2):203–222

Ahrens R (2013) Bankenmacht im Aufsichtsrat? Der Bankier Jürgen Ponto und die Kontrolle deutscher Groβunternehmen in den 1970er Jahren. In: Ahrens R, Gehlen B, Reckendrees A (Hrsg) Die „Deutschland AG". Historische Annäherung an den bundesdeutschen Kapitalismus. 1. Aufl., Klartext-Verlag, Essen, SS 195–220

Ahrens R (2016) Kreditwirtschaft im "Wirtschaftswunder"—Strukturen und Verflechtungen. In: Hockerts HG, Schulz G (Hersg) Der "Rhenischen Kapitalismus" in der Ära denauer. Ferdinand Schnigh, Paderborn, SS 121–141

Ahrens R (2022) Financing Rhenish capitalism: 'bank power' and the business of crisis management in the 1960s and 1970s. In: Marx C, Leitmeyer M (eds) Rhenish capitalism. new insights from a business history perspective. Routledge, London, New York, pp 119–134

Ahrens R, Bähr J (2013) Jürgen Ponto. Bankier und Bürger. Eine Biografie. C. H. Beck, München

Aizawa K (1994) Oshu Saikyo no Kinyu Teikoku (The Strongest Financial Empire in Europe). Nihon Keizai Shinbunsha, Tokyo

Aizawa K (1988) Nishi Doitsu no kinyu sijyo to kozo (Financial markets in West Germany and their structure). Toyo keizai shinposya, Tokyo

Albach H (1993) Gleitwort. In: Pfannschmidt A, Personelle Verflechtungen über Aufsichtsräte, Mehrfachmandate in deutschen Unternehmen. Gabler, Wiesbaden

Albert M (1991) Capitalisme contre Capitalisme. du Seuil, Paris

Armour J, McCahery JA (2006) After enron. improving corporate law and modernising securities regulation in Europe and the US. Hart Publishing, Oxford

Arndt H (1974) Wirtschaft und Macht.Tatsachen und Theorien. C. H. Beck, München

Berghoff H (2016) Varieties of financialization? evidence from German industry in the 1990s. Business Hist Rev 90(1):81–108

Berle AA, Means GC (1932) The modern corporation and private property. Macmillan Press, New York

Beyer J (2006) Pfadabhängigkeit. Über institutionelle Kontinuität, anfällige Stabiltät und fundamentalen Wandel. Campus, Frankfurt am Main

Beyer J (2013) Die Sreukuturen der Deutschlans AG. Ein Rückblick auf ein Modfell der Unternehmenskontrolle. In: Ahrens R, Gehlen B, Reckendrees A (Hrsg) Die „Deutschland AG". Historische Annäherung an den bundesdeutschen Kapitalismus. Klartext-Verlag, Essen, SS 31–56

Bleicher K, Bortel K-D, Kleinmann R et al (1984) Unternehmungsverfassung und Spitzenorganisation. In: Zeitschrift Fürung+ Organisation 53(1):21–29

Bleicher K, Diethard LK, Paul H (1989) Unternehmungsverfassung und Spitzenorganisation. Führung und überwachung von Aktiengesellschaften im internationalen Vergleich. Gabler, Wiesbaden
Bol A (2021) Corporate Governance. Normen, Legitimation und Praktiken in Deutschen Unternehmen, 1870–1930. De Gruyter, Oldenbourg
Brendel G (2001) Zur Macht der Banken in Deutschland. LIT Verlag, Münster, Eine empirisch-historische Untersuchung
Brullebaut B, Allemand I, Prinz E, Thépot F (2021) Persistence in corporate networks through boards of directors? a longitudinal study of interlocks in France, Germany, and the United Kingdom. RMS 16:1743–1782
Bundesministerium der Finanzen (Hrsg) (1979) Bericht der Studienkommission. Grundsatzfragen der Kreditwirtschaft (Schriftenreihe des Bundesministeriums der Finanzen, Heft 28), Stollfuss, Frankfurt am Main
Burhop C (2006) Banken, Aufsichtsräte und Corporate Governance in Deutschen Reich (1871–1913). In: Bankhistorisches Archiv 32(1):1–25
Büschgen HE (1983) Die Groβbanken. Fritz Knapp Verlag, Frankfurt am Main
Chandler A (1990) Scale and scope: the dynamics of industrial capitalis. Harvard University Press, Berkeley, Massachusetts
Cioffi HW, Höpner M (2006) Das parteipolitische Paradox des Finanzmarkt-kapitalismus. Aktionärsorientierte Reformen in Deutschland, Frankreich, Italien und den USA. In: Politische Vierteljahresschrift 47(3):419–440
Cioffi JW (2010) Public law and private power. corporate governance reforms in the age of finance capitalism. Cornell University Press, Ithaca, New York
Cromme G (2005) Corporate governance in Germany and the German corporate governance code. In: Corporate Govern: An Int Rev 13(3):362–367
Dahlem M (2009) Der Professionalisierung des Bankbetriebs.Studien zur Institutionellen Struktur Deutschen Banken im Kaiserreich 1871–1914. Klartext Verlag, Essen
David T, Weserhuis G (2014) Comparing corporate networks in a long-term perspective. In: David T, Weserhuis G (eds) The power of corporate networks. A comparative and historical perspective. Routledge, New York, pp.1–28
Der Spiegel (1965) Ordner an der Orgel. In: Der Spiegel 19 (45): 49–69
Deutsche Bank AG (1986) Geschäftsbericht für das Jahr 1986. Deutsche Bank AG, Frankfurt am Main
Edwards J, Fischer K (1994) Banks, finance and investment in Germany. Cambridge University Press, Cambridge
Eggenkämper B, Modert G, Pretzlik S (2015) Die Allianz. Geschichte des Unternehmens 1890–2015. Verlag C. H. Beck, München
Eglau HO (1990) Wie Gott in Frankfurt: Die Deutsche Bank und die deutsche Industrie, 3rd edn. Econ Verlag, Düsseldorf
Engenhardt, GF (1995) Die Macht der Banken. Politische Positionen zur Neuregelung der gesetzlichen Grundlagen. Gabler Verlag, Deutsche Universitäts Verlag, Wiesbaden
Fear J, Kobrak CP (2010) Banks on board: German and American corporate governance, 1870–1914. In: Business Hist Rev 84(4):703–736
Feldenkirchen W (1979) Banken und Stahlindustrie im Ruhrgebiet. Zur Entwicklung ihrer Beziehungen 1873–1914. In: Bankhistorisches Archiv 5(2):26–52
Feldenkirchen W (1991) Banking and economic growth: banks and industry in Germany in the nineteenth century and their changing relationship during industrialization. In: Lee WR (ed) German industry and German industrialization. Essay in German economic and business history in the nineteenth and twentieth century. Routledge, London, pp 116–143
Fiedler M (2005) Zur Rolle des Vertrauens in der „Deutschland AG“: Verflechtungen zwischen Franz- und Nichtfinanzunternehmen im 20.Jahrhundert. In: Jahrbuch für Wirtschaftsgeschichte, Teil 1, SS 93–106
Fohlin C (1999) The rise of interlocking directorates in imperial Germany. In: The Econ Hist Rev 52(2):307–333

Fohlin C (2007) Financial capitalism and Germany's rise to industrial power. Cambridge University Press, Cambridge

Furch D (2012) Marktwirtschaften unter dem Druck globalisierter Finanzmärkte, Finanzsysteme und Corporate-Governance-Strukturen in Deutschland und Italien. Springer NV, Wiesbaden

Gall L (2004) Der Bankier Hermann Josef Abs. Eine Biographie, C. H. Beck, München

Gehlen B (2022) Corporate law and corporate control in West Germany after 1945. In: Marx C, Leitmeyer M (eds) Rhenish capitalism. new insights from a business history perspective. Routledge, London, New York, pp 66–80

Gerschenkron A (1962) Economic backwardness in historical perspective. a book of essay. Cambridge, Massachusetts

Goergen M, Manjon MC, Renneboog L (2008) Recent developments in German corporate governance. In: International Rev Law Econ 28(3):175–193

Gossweiler K (1965) Die Vereinigte Stahlwerke und die Groβbanken. Eine Studie über das Verhlätnis von Bank- und Industriekapital in der Weimarer Repulik und unter der Faschistischen Diktatur (1926 bis 1936). In: Jahrbuch für Wirtschaftsgechichte, Teil IV, SS 11–53

Gossweiler K (1971) Die Rolle der Grossbanken im Imperialismus. In: Jahrbuch für Wirtschaftsgeschichte 12(III):35–54

Gottschalk A (1988) Der Stimmrechtseinfluβ der Banken in den Aktionärversammlungen von Groβunternehmen. In: WSI Mitteilungen 41(5):294–304

Goutas L, Lane C (2009) The translation of shareholder value in the German business system: a comparative study of DaimlerChrysler and Volkswagen AG. In: Compet Chang 13(4):327–346

Gutenberg E (1970) Funktionswandel des Aufsichtsrats. In: Zeitschrift für Betriebswirtschaft 40, Ergänzungsheft, SS 1–10

Hagemann H (1931) Das Verhältnis der deutschen Grossbanken zur Industrie. W. Christian, Berlin

Hall PA, Soskice D (eds) (2001) Varieties of capitalism: the institutional foundations of comparative advantage. Oxford University Press, Oxford

Hannemann RA (2011) Riddle M (2011) Concepts and measures for basic network analysis. In: Scott J, Carrington PJ (eds) The Sage handbook of social network analysis. SAGE, London, pp 340–369

Hansen H (1994) Die Zusammensetzung von Aufsichtsräten der DAX-Gesellschaften und die Auswirkungen auf ihre Effizienz. In: Die Aktiengesellschaft 39(11):R.403–404

Heiber MJ (2010) Unternehmens- und Arbeitssstrukturen von Automobilkonzernen im Wandel. Die Beispiele Daimler-Benz, Volkswagen und General Motors, University of Bamberg Press, Bamberg

Heinze T (2001) Transformation der deutschen Unternehmenskontroll-System? Eine empirische Analyse zum Stellenwert der feindlichen Übernahme der Mannesmann-AG für die Unternehmenskontroll-Debatte. Kölner In: Zeitschrift für Soziologie und Sozialpsychologie 53(4):641–674

Heinze T (2002) Die Struktur der Personalverflechtung großer deutscher Aktiengesellschaften zwischen 1989 und 2001. In: Zeitschrift für Soziologie 31(5):391–410

Heinze T (2004) Dynamics in the German system of corporate governance? Empirical findings regarding interlocking directorates. In: Economy and Society 33(2):218–238

Hilferding R (1923) Das Finanzkapital.Eine Studie über die jüngste Entwicklung des Kapitalismus. Verlag der Wiener Volksbuchhandlung, Wien

Honma Y (1984) Gendai Shihonshugi Bunseki no Kiso Riron (An analysis of modern capitalism). Iwanami shoten, Tokyo

Hopt KJ (1979) Zur Funktion des Aufsichtsrats im Verhältnis von Industrie und Bankensystem. In: Horn N, Kocka J (Hrsg) Recht und Entwicklung der Groβunternehmen im 19. und frühen 20. Jahrhundert. Wirtschaft-,sozial- und rechtshistorische Untersuchungen zur Industrialisierung im Deutschland, Frankreich, England und den USA. Vandenhoeck & Ruprecht, Göttingen, SS 227–242

Ifrim S (2007) Erosion der Deutschland AG-Ursachen und konsequenzen Veränderter Personal- und Kapitalverflechtungen aud dem deutschen Kapitalmarkt. Examicus Verlsg, Frankfurt am Main

James H (2003) Die Deutsche Bank im Dritten Reich. C. H. Beck, München

Jeidels O (1905) Das Verhältnis der deutschen Groβbanken zur Industrie mit besonderer Berücksichtigung der Eisenindustrie. Duncker & Humblot, Leipzig
Joly H (1998) Groβunternehemer in Deutschland: Soziologie einer industriellen Elite, 1933–1989. Leipziger Universitätsverlag, Leipzig
Kanbayashi T (1976) Keieikeizaigaku・Kigyo Riron (Businenn economics and theory of enterprise). Tokoro Shoten, Tokyo
Klages P (2006) Zwischen institutioneller Innovation und Reproduktion. Zum Wandel des deutschen Corporate Governance-Systems in den 1990ern. In: Berliner Journal für Soziologie 16(1):37–54
Koubek N (1971) Personelle und institutionelle Verbindung der Bereiche „Produktion" und „Kapital" in der Wirtschaftsgesellschaft der BRD. In: WWI-Mitteilungen 24(8/9):258–274
Krenn K (2012) Alle Macht den Banken? Zur Struktur personaler Netzwerke deutscher Unternehmen am Beginn des 20.Jahrhunderts. Springer, Wiesbaden
Krenn K (2013) Die sozaile Infrastruktur als Wegbereiterin. Aufsichtsratsverflechtung in der Weimarer Republik. In: Ahrens R, Gehlen B, Reckendrees A (Hrsg) Die „Deutschland AG". Historische Annäherung an den bundesdeutschen Kapitalismus. Klartext-Verlag, Essen, SS 85–115
Ленин ВИ (1962) *Империализм, как высшая стадия капитализма: популярный очерк.* In: *Полное собрание сочинений.* Том 27, ос. изд-во полит. лит-ры, Москва, pp 299–426
Maekawa K (1970) Doitsu dokusen kigyo no hatten katei (Development of German monopolistic enterpreises). Mineruva Shobo, Kyoto
Maekawa K (1993) Gendai Kigyo Kenkyu no Kiso (Foundation of study of contemporary enterprise). Moriyama Shoten, Tokyo
Maekawa K (1997) Nichidoku Hikaku Kigyoron eno Michi (Comparative study of Japanese and German enterprise). Moriyama Shoten, Tokyo
Marshall A (1970) Industry and trade. A study of institutional technique and business organization; and of their influences on the conditions of various classes and nations, 4th edn. Augustus M. Kelley, New York
Marx C, Leitmeyer M (2022a) Rhenish capitalism. In: Marx C, Leitmeyer M (eds) Rhenish capitalism. New insights from a business history perspective. Routledge, London, New York
Marx C, Leitmeyer M (2022b) Introduction: Rhenish capitalism and business history. In: Marx C, Leitmeyer M (eds) Rhenish capitalism. New insights from a business history perspective. Routledge, London, New York, pp 1–40
Meyen HG (1992) 120 Jahre Dresdner Bank. Unternehmens-Chronik. Dresdner Bank, Frankfurt am Main
Monopolkommission (1978) Fortschreitende Konzentration bei Groβunternehmen: Hauptgutachte 1976/77 (Haupugutachten der Monopolkommission; 2), 1st edn. Nomos-Verlagsgesellschaft, Baden-Baden
Monopolkommission (2010) Mehr Wettbewerb, wenig Ausnahme (Hauptgutachten, 2008/2009), 1st edn. Nomos Verlagsgesellschaft, Baden-Baden
Monopolkommission (2022) Wettbewerb 2022 (XXIV.Hauptgutachten: Gutachten der Monopolkommission gemäβ §44 Abs.1 Satz 1 GWB), Nomos, Wiesbaden
Nakata N, Hosoi K, Iwanami F (1997) Kigyokan no jinteki nettowaku—Torishimariyaku kenninsei no nichibei hikaku—(Personnel networks between enterprises—Comparison of interlocking directorships in Japan and the United States). Dobunkan, Tokyo
Pfeiffer H (1986) Das Netwerk der Groβbanken. Personelle Verflechtungen mit Konzernen, Staat und ideologischen Apparaten. In: Blätter für deutsche und Internationale Politik 31(2):161–177
Pfeiffer H (1986b) Groβbanken und Finanzgruppen.Ausgewählte Ergebnisse einer Untersuchung der personellen Verflechtungen von Deutscher, Dresdner und Commerzbank. In: WSI Mitteilungen 39(7):473–481
Pfeiffer H (1993) Die Macht der Banken. Die personellen Verflechtungen der Commerzbank, der Deutschen Bank und der Dresdner Bank mit Unternehemen. Campus, Frankfurt am Main
Plumpe W, Nützenadel A, Schenk R (2020) Deutsche Bank. Die globale Hausbank 1870–2020. Propyläen, Berlin

Pönisch S (2007) Die Entwicklung des deutschen Systems der Corporate Governance. Analyse und Entwicklungsdynamiken. Verlag Dr. Müller, Saarbrücken

Prambeck A (2001) Probleme von Mehrfachorganschaften bei Bankenvertretern im Aufsichtsrat bankfremdem der Unternehmen. Grin Verlag, München

Prinz P (2012) Der Einfluss von Mehrfachmandatsträgern auf die Unternehmens-Performance. Neue Erkenntnisse zum Personennetzwerk des Deutschland AG. In: Zeitschrift fur Beteriebswirtschaft 82(9):875–911

Rennert K (2015) Wettbewerber in einer reifen Branche. Die Unternehmensstrategien von Thyssen, Hoesch und Mannesmann 1955–1975, 1st edn. Auflage, Karltext Verlag, Essen

Riesser J (1971) Die deutsche Groβbanken und ihre Konzentration im Zusammenhang mit der Entwicklung der Gesamtwirtschaft in Deutschland. Vierrte verbesserte und vermehrte Auflage, Verlag Detlev Auvermann KG, Glashutten im Taunus

Ringe W-G (2015) Changing law and ownership patterns in Germany: Corporate governance and the erosion of Deutschland AG. In: American Journal of Comparative Law 63(2):493–538

Sato Y (1986) Yakuin kennin to kigyokan kankei no sokutei (Measuring of interlocking directorate and interfirm relationships). In: Keizai ronso (Econoc Review) 137(1):21–41

Sattler F (2009) Ernst Matthiensen (1900–1980). Ein deutscher Bankier im 20. Jahrhundert. Eugen-Gutmann-Gesellschaft, Berlin

Schiffels EW (1981) Der Aufsichtsrat als Instrument der Unternehmenskooperation. Eine empirische Untersuchung zur Zusammensetzung des Aufsichtsrates aller Aktiengesellschaften in 15 Wirtschaftszweigen des Verarbeitenden Gewerbes in der Bundesrepublik Deutschland. R. G. Fischer Verlag, Frankfurt am Main

Schönwitz D, Weber H-J (1981) Indirekte personeelle Verflechtungen zwischen Groβunternehmen über Organe der Geschäftsführungskontrolle. In: Konjunkturpolitik 27(1):12–37

Schönwitz D, Weber H-J (1982) Unternehmenskonzentration,Personelle Verflechtungen und Wettbewerb. Eine Untersuchung auf der Grundlage der hundert gröβten Konzerne der Bundesrepublik Deutschland. Nomos Verlagsgesellschaft, 1.Aufl., Baden-Baden

Schwarz F (2003) Die Deutsche Bank. Riese auf tönerner Füβen. Campus, Frankfurt am Main

Schwein LG, Krosigk von (1958) Die Grosse Zeit des Feuers. Der Weg der deutschen Industrie. 2.Bd, Reiner Wunderlich Verlag, Tübingen

Scott (1985) Theoretical framework and research design. In: Stokman, FN, Ziegler R, Scott J (eds) Networks of corporate power. A comparative analysis of ten countries. Polity Press, Cambridge, pp. 1–19

Scott J (1990) Corporate control and corporate rule: Britain in an international Perspective. In: The Britisch Journal of Sociology 41(3):351–373

Scott J (2000) Social network analysis. A Handbook. 2nd edition, Sage, London

Seibert U (2004) Stand und Perspeltive der Reformbestrebungen zur Verbesserung der Coporate Governance—eine Betrachtung aus dem Blickwinkel des Aufsichtsrats. In: Freidank C-C (Hesg) Reform der Rechnungslegung und Corporate Governance in Deutschland und Japan. Deutscher Universitäts-Verlag, Wiesbaden, SS 191–222

Shonfield A (1965) Modern capitalism. The changing balance of public and private power, Oxford University Press, London, New York

Stanzick K-H (1969) Der ökonomische Konzentrationsproze. In: Schäfer G, Nedelmann C (Hrsg) Der CDU-Staat. Analysen zur Verfassungswriklichkeit der Bundesrepublik, Bd.I, 2. Aufl., Schurkamp, München, SS 48–79

Streeck W (1992) Social institutions and economic performance. Studies of industrial relations in advanced capitalist economies, Sage, London

Streeck W, Höpner M (Hrsg) (2003) Alle Macht dem Markt? Fallstudien zur Abwicklung der Deustchland AG. Campus, Frankfurt am Main, New York

Streeck W (2009) Re-forming capitalism. Institutional change in the German political economy. Oxford University Press

Tilly R (1980) Banken und Industrialisierung in Deutschland. Quantifizieungsversuche. In: F. W. Henning (Hrsg.), Entwicklungen und Aufgaben von Versicherungen und Banken in der Industrilisierung, Berlin, SS 165–193

Tilly R (2005) Trust and mistrust: banks, giant debtors, and enterprise crises in Germany, 1960–2002. In: Jahrbuch für Wirtschaftsgeschichte 1:107–135

Velte P, Weber SC (2011) Outsider-und Insider-Systeme der Corporate Governance. In: Zeitschrift für Planung & Unternehmenssteuerung 21(4):473–482

Vitols S (2003) From banks to markets: the political economy of liberalization of the German and Japanese financial systems. In: Yamamura K, Streeck W (eds) The end of diversity? prospects for German and Japanese capitalism. Cornell University Press, Ithaca, NY, pp 240–260

Volkmann G, Kronenberg B (1994) Bankenmacht und Aufsichtsrat. In: WSI Mitteilungen 47(8):481–487

Wellhöner V (1989) Groβbanken und Groβindustrie im Kaiserreich. Vandenhoeck & Ruprecht, Göttingen

Windolf P (2002) Corporate networks in Europe and the United States. Oxford University Press, New York

Windolf P (2005a) Die neuen Eigentümer. In: Windolf P (ed) Finanzmarkt-Kapitalismus: Analysen zum Wandel von Prodktionsregimen. VS Verlag für Sozialwissenschaften, Wiesbaden, SS 8–19

Windolf P (2005b) Was ist Finanzmarkt-Kapitalismus? In: Windolf P (ed) Finanzmarkt-Kapitalismus: Analysen zum Wandel von Prodktionsregimen. VS Verlag für Sozialwissenschaften, Wiesbaden, SS 20–57

Windolf P (2014) The corporate networks in Germany, 1896–2010. In: David T, Weserhuis F (ed) The power of corporate networks. A comparative and historical perspective. Routledge, New York, pp 66–85

Wixforth H (1995) Banken und Schwereindustrie in der Weimarer Republik. Böhlau, Köln, Weimar, Wien

Wixforth H (2006) Expansion der Dresdner Bank in Europa. R. Oldenbourg Verlag, München

Wixforth H, Ziegler D (1995) Bankenmacht: universal banking and German industry in historical perspective. In: Cassis Y, Feldmann GD, Olsson U (eds) Evolution of financial institutions and markets in twentieth century Europe. Scblar Press, Aldershot, pp 247–272

Yamazaki T (2005) Gendai Keieigaku no Saikoutiku (A study of the reconstruction of business management study). Moriyama Shoten, Tokyo

Yamazaki T (2013a) Gendai no Doitsu kigyo—Sono gurobaru chiikika to keiei tokusitsu—(Comtemporary German enterprises—Their Global-Regionalization and characteristics of business management—). Moriyama shoten, Tokyo

Yamazaki T (2013b) German business management: a Japanese perspective on regional development factors. Springer Tokyo

Yamazaki T (2017) Kigyo keiei no nichidoku hikaku—Sangyo shuchu taisei oyobi "Amerikaka" to "Saikozoka" (Comparative study of business management in Japan and Germany—the system of industrial concentration and the "Americanization" and "re-framing" of business management—). Moriyama shoten, Tokyo

Yamazaki T (2019) Doitu no Kigyokan Kankei—Kigyokan Jinteki Ketugo no Kozo to Kino—(Interfirm relationships in Germany—structure and functions of personnel connections between enterprises—). Moriyama shoten, Tokyo

Ziegler D (1998) Die Aufsichtsrate der deutschen Aktiengesellschaften in den Zwanziger Jahren. Eine empirische Untersuchung zum Probleme der "Bankenmacht". In: Zeitschrift für Unternehmensgeschichte 43(2): 194–215

Ziegler R (1984) Das Netz der Personen- und Kapitalverflechtungen deutscher und österreichischer Wirtschaftsunternehmen. In: Zeitschrift für Soziologie und Sozialpsychologie 36(3):585–618

Ziegler R (1985) Conclusion. In: Stokman FN, Ziegler R, Scott J (eds) Networks of corporate power. A comparative analysis of ten countries. Polity Press, Cambridge, pp 267–287

Ziegler R, Bender D, Biehler H (1985) Industry and Banking in the German Corporate Network. In: Stokman, FN, Ziegler R, Scott J (eds) Networks of corporate power. A comparative analysis of ten countries. Polity Press, Cambridge, pp 91–111

Zugehör R (2003) Die Zukunft des rheinischen Kapitalismus: Unternehmen zwischen Kapitalmarkt und Mitbestimmung. Leske+Budrich, Opladen

Part I
Structure of Interlocking Directorates of Banks

Chapter 2
Interlocking Directorates of Bank's Supervisory Board and Managing Board Members in Other Enterprises in the Period of Establishment of the Monopolistic Capitalism

Abstract In Germany, industry–bank relationships were founded before World War II. They served as a cooperative system between industries and banks. These relationships acted as means of banks' influence on industrial enterprises. The system of industry–bank relationships was established in the early twentieth century as the period of the shift to a monopolistic capitalism. In industry–bank relationships, assignment of directors from banks to industrial enterprises and interlocking directorates on supervisory board of other enterprises were important mechanisms for developing interfirm relationships. This chapter analyzes personnel connections through direct and indirect interlocking directorates of members of top management, such as the supervisory and managing board of large banks on the supervisory board of other enterprises.

Keywords Commerz- und Disconto-Bank · Deutsche Bank · Dresdner Bank · Industry–bank relationship · Direct interlocking directorate · Indirect interlocking directorate · Supervisory board

Part I considers the structure of interlocking directorates of members of large banks belonging to their supervisory or managing boards on the supervisory boards of other enterprises. It discusses not only the direct interlocking directorate of each bank but also the indirect interlocking directorates established among the three large banks and between two of the banks on the supervisory board of another company.

Before World War II, three periods of the shift to a monopolistic capitalism in Germany, that is, in the early twentieth century, the inflation period following World War I, and the mid-1930s during National Socialism are examined. After World War II, three periods, namely in the late 1950s, the late 1960s, and the latter half of the 2010s are considered. In the latter half of the 2010s, cases of Deutsche Bank AG and Commerzbank AG are examined because Dresdner Bank no longer exists.

This chapter examines big banks' personnel connections through direct and indirect interlocking directorates of members of top management, such as the supervisory board and board of directors on the supervisory board of other companies in the early twentieth century when the shift to a monopolistic capitalism had almost completed in

T. Yamazaki, *Relationships Between Industry and Bank in Germany*,
https://doi.org/10.1007/978-981-97-4996-6_2

Germany. The period considered in this chapter is similar to that when Otto Jeildels's classical work on banks' control over industrial enterprises was published in 1905 (Jeidels 1905). However, issues to be clarified in this chapter are total structure of the personnel connection between banks and enterprises in various industrial sectors through direct and indirect interlocking directorates of members of the supervisory board and the managing board of large banks on the supervisory board of other enterprises. For banks, such personnel connections were significant for obtaining, exchanging, and sharing information between banks and a foundation of strong cooperation among banks over each industrial enterprise. Cases of Deutsche Bank, Dresdner Bank, and Commerz- und Disconto-Bank AG (below, Commerzbank) are examined.

This chapter considers the conditions of interlocking directorates in relation to the positioning of interlocking mandates and distribution of industries where personnel connections existed and companies in which interlocking directorates were established through plural mandates. In Germany, although there were several cases where members of the supervisory and managing boards of banks had mandates on the supervisory board of industrial enterprises, members of top management of companies in industrial sectors had posts on the supervisory board of banks. In such cases, it is difficult to understand whether the interlocking directorates in other third-party enterprises are established through assignment of a bank representative or industrial enterprise. Therefore, situations of the three big banks' interlocking directorates in other enterprises are analyzed without considering the direction of interlocking directorates through the dispatch. The analysis in this chapter is based on "*Adressbuch der Direktoren und Aufsichtsrats-Mitglieder der Aktien-Gesellschaften 1908*," Jahrgang 1908 (Finanz-Verlag, Berlin).

In Sect. 2.1, the direct interlocking directorates of members of supervisory board and managing board of each bank on the supervisory board of other companies are analyzed. Next, Sect. 2.2 analyzes the indirect interlocking directorates established through direct interlocking directorates among three banks and between two of the banks.

2.1 Direct Interlocking Directorate of Members of Supervisory Board and Managing Board of Banks on the Supervisory Board of Other Enterprises

2.1.1 Direct Interlocking Directorate of Members of Supervisory Board and Managing Board of Deutsche Bank

First, in examining the situations of the direct interlocking directorate by members of the supervisory board and managing board of Deutsche Bank on the supervisory board of other enterprises (see Table 2.1), there were 188 companies in which such cases were observed and 241 interlocking mandates. Considering the distribution of industrial sectors, Deutsche Bank built direct interlocking directorates in 16 companies and had 18 interlocking mandates in the mining industry, and similarly, nine and 10 in the iron and steel industry; seven and eight in the metal producing and processing industries; 11 each in the chemical industry; five and 11 in the electrical industry; three and four in the automobile industry; 11 and 12 in the machine industry; six and nine in the oil industry; six and seven in the textile, spinning, and woven goods industries; nine and 10 in the distillation industry; one each in the distributing industry; 31 and 47 in the banking industry; 14 and 21 in the insurance industry; eight and 10 in the electric power, gas, and energy industries; 19 and 26 in the transportation industry; and 32 and 36 in other industries, respectively. Among the various industries, except for the banking industry and the insurance sector, for example, in Deutsch Bank, there were several interlocking relations in the mining, iron and steel, chemical, electrical, machine, and transportation industries. Therefore, Deutsche Bank had close and strong relationships with companies in the heavy and chemical industries as the key industrial sectors in Germany.

Considering the situation of interlocking directorates, regarding the position of mandate of supervisory board, in 67 enterprises, interlocking directorates on the supervisory boards of other companies were formed through the mandate of chairman of the supervisory board in several cases, with 69 mandates. Regarding the distribution among industrial sectors, the numbers of enterprises and mandates in which interlocking directorates were formed were two each in the mining industry respectively; similarly, one each in iron and steel; three each in metal producing and processing; four each in chemical; one each in electrical; one each in automobile; four each in machine; four each in oil; two each in textile, spinning, and woven goods; six each in distillation; one each in distributing; 11 each in banking; eight and 10 in insurance; one each in electric power, gas, and energy; seven each in transportation; and 11 each in other industries, respectively. Cases of interlocking directorate in representative companies of each industry were seen in Vereinigte Glanzstofffabriken AG in the chemical industry and Deutsche Petroleum-AG in the oil industry.

In 21 enterprises, interlocking directorates on the supervisory boards of other companies were formed through the mandate of the vice-chairman of the supervisory

Table 2.1 Direct interlocking directorates of the members of the supervisory board and the managing board of Deutsche Bank on the supervisory board of other companies (period of shift to monopolistic capitalism)

Industries	Position							
	Chairman		Vice-chairman		Supervisory board member excluding chairman and vice-chairman		Total[a]	
	Number of companies	Number of posts	Number of companies	Number of posts	Number of companies	Number of posts	Number of companies	Number of posts
Mining	2	2	1	1	15	15	16	18
Iron and steel	1	1	3	3	6	6	9	10
Metal producing and processing	3	3	–	–	5	5	7	8
Chemical	4	4	1	1	6	6	11	11
Electrical	1	1	2	2	4	8	5	11
Automobile	1	1	2	2	1	1	3	4
Machine	4	4	1	1	7	7	11	12
Oil	4	4	–	–	4	5	6	9
Textile, spinning, and woven goods	2	2	1	1	4	4	6	7
Distillation	6	6	2	2	2	2	2	10
Distributing	1	1	–	–	–	–	1	1
Banking	11	11	4	4	22	32	31	47
Insurance	8	10	1	1	6	10	14	21
Electric power, gas, and energy	1	1	1	1	6	8	8	10

(continued)

Table 2.1 (continued)

Industries	Position							
	Chairman		Vice-chairman		Supervisory board member excluding chairman and vice-chairman		Total[a]	
	Number of companies	Number of posts	Number of companies	Number of posts	Number of companies	Number of posts	Number of companies	Number of posts
Transportation	7	7	1	1	14	18	19	26
Other industries	11	11	1	1	22	24	32	36
All industries	67	69	21	21	124	151	188	241

[a] There are cases in which the total number of companies establishing interlocking directorates differed from the total number of companies measured by each position of the supervisory board due to the existence of companies where interlocking directorates through more than two posts were built

Source This table was compiled by the author, based on Arends and Mossner (Hrsg) (1908)

board and the total number of mandates with 21. The numbers of enterprises and mandates in which such interlocking cases were formed were one each in the mining industry; similarly, three each in iron and steel; one each in chemical; two each in electrical; two each in automobile; one each in machine; one each in textile, spinning, and woven goods; two each in distillation; four each in banking; one each in insurance; one each in electric power, gas, and energy; one each in transportation; and one each in other industries, respectively. In these companies, there were major companies in each industry, such as "Allianz" Versicherungs-AG in the insurance industry.

Interlocking directorates built through mandates of the supervisory board except for the chairman and vice-chairman were observed in 124 companies, totaling 151 mandates. Regarding the distribution among industrial sectors, the numbers of enterprises and mandates in which interlocking directorates were formed were 15 each in the mining industry respectively; similarly, six each in iron and steel; five each in metal producing and processing; six each in chemical; four and eight in electrical; one each in automobile; seven each in machine; four and five in oil; four each in textile, spinning, and woven goods; two each in distributing; 22 and 32 in banking; six and 10 in insurance; six and eight in electric power, gas, and energy; 14 and 18 in transportation; and 22 and 24 in other industries, respectively. These companies included leading firms in each industry, such as Gelsenkirchener Bergwerks-AG and Harpener Bergbau AG in mining, Siemens & Halske AG in electrical, and Rheinisch-Westfälisches Electricitätswerk AG in electric power, gas, and energy.

The numbers of enterprises and mandates were 39 and 92, respectively, when considering cases where members of the supervisory board and board of directors of Deutsche Bank had more than two mandates on the supervisory boards of other companies (see Table 2.2). Considering the distribution among industries, the numbers of companies and mandates were as follows: two and four in mining; one and two in iron and steel; one and two in metal producing and processing; two and eight in electrical; one and two in automobile; one and two in machine; two and five in oil; one and two in textile, spinning, and woven goods; one and two in distillation; nine and 25 in banking; seven and 14 in insurance; two and four in electric power, gas, and energy; five and 12 in transportation; and four and eight in other industries, respectively.

Of these 39 companies, in seven enterprises, direct interlocking directorates were built through more than three mandates; the total number of mandates was 48. These enterprises were Siemens & Halske AG and Elektrische Licht- und Kraftanlagen AG in the electrical industry, Deutsche Petroleum-AG in the oil industry, Deutsche Ueberseeische Bank, Deutsche Vereinsnbank, and Sächsische Bank in the banking industry, and Ostafrikanische Eisenbahngesellschaft in the transportation industry. Enterprises in which direct interlocking directorates were formed through seven mandates, five mandates, and four mandates were each one, respectively. Cases in which such interlocking directorates were established through three mandates were three. In the rest 32 companies Deutsche Bank had two mandates on the supervisory board of other companies.

Table 2.2 Cases in which Deutsche Bank built direct interlocking directorates through more than two posts on the supervisory board of other companies (period of shift to monopolistic capitalism)

Industries	Number of posts											
	2		3		4		5		7		Total	
	Number of companies	Number of posts	Number of companies	Number of posts	Number of companies	Number of posts	Number of companies	Number of posts	Number of companies	Number of posts	Number of companies	Number of posts
Mining	2	4	–	–	–	–	–	–	–	–	2	4
Iron and steel	1	2	–	–	–	–	–	–	–	–	1	2
metal producing and processing	1	2	–	–	–	–	–	–	–	–	1	2
Electrical	–	–	1	3	–	–	1	5	–	–	2	8
Automobile	1	2	–	–	–	–	–	–	–	–	1	2
Machine	1	2	–	–	–	–	–	–	–	–	1	2
Oil	1	2	1	3	–	–	–	–	–	–	2	5
Textile, spinning, and woven goods	1	2	–	–	–	–	–	–	–	–	1	2
Distillation	1	2	–	–	–	–	–	–	–	–	1	2
Banking	6	12	2	6	–	–	–	–	1	7	9	25
Insurance	7	14	–	–	–	–	–	–	–	–	7	14
Electric power, gas, and energy	2	4	–	–	–	–	–	–	–	–	2	4
Transportation	4	8	–	–	1	4	–	–	–	–	4	8

(continued)

Table 2.2 (continued)

Industries	Number of posts											
	2		3		4		5		7		Total	
	Number of companies	Number of posts	Number of companies	Number of posts	Number of companies	Number of posts	Number of companies	Number of posts	Number of companies	Number of posts	Number of companies	Number of posts
Other Industries	4	8	–	–	–	–	–	–	–	–	4	8
All industries	32	64	4	12	1	4	1	5	1	7	39	92

Source This table was compiled by the author, based on Arends and Mossner (Hrsg) (1908)

Regarding the kind of mandate for these interlocking directorates, in Deutsche Ueberseeische Bank Deutsche Bank AG built interlocking directorates through seven mandates consisting of one chairman and six posts of the supervisory board except for chairman and vice-chairman. In Elektrische Licht- und Kraftanlag AG interlocking directorates were formed through five mandates consisting of one each of mandate of chairman and vice-chairman and three posts of the supervisory board excluding chairman and vice-chairman. In Ostafrikanische Eisenbahngesellschaft Deutsche Bank built interlocking directorates through four mandates consisting of a post of chairman and three mandates of the supervisory board except for chairman and vice-chairman. Regarding companies with three mandates, whereas in Deutsche Petroleum-AG interlocking directorates were established through a mandate of chairman and two posts of the supervisory board except for chairman and vice-chairman, in Siemens & Halske AG, Deutsche Vereinsbank, and Sächsische Bank, interlocking directorates were built through three mandates of the supervisory board except for chairman and vice-chairman, respectively.

When considering 32 enterprises with two mandates on the supervisory board of other enterprise in relation to distribution of industrial sector, there were two in mining, one in iron and steel, one in metal producing and processing, one in automobile, one in machine, one in oil, one in textile, spinning, and woven goods, one in distillation, six in banking, seven in insurance, two in electric power, gas, and energy, four in transportation, and four in other industries.

In Union, Allgemeine Versicherungs-AG and Transatlantische Güterversicherungs-Gesellschaft in the insurance industry, interlocking directorates were formed through two mandates of chairman, respectively. In Schultheiss' Brauerei AG in the distillation industry and Essener Bankverein in the banking industry, interlocking directorates were built through two mandates consisting of chairman and vice-chairman, respectively. Cases in which interlocking directorates were formed through a mandate of chairman and one post of the supervisory board except for chairman and vice-chairman can be observed in 10 enterprises: Essener Bergwerks-Verein König Wilhelm in the mining industry, Westfälische Kupfer- und Messingwerke AG vorm. Casp. Noell in the metal producing and processing industry, Dinglersche Maschinenfabrik AG in the machine industry, Steaua Romana AG für Petroleumindustrie in the oil industry, Sächsische Kammgarnspinnerei in the textile, spinning, an woven goods industries, Essener Credit-Anstalt and Rheinische Creditbank in the banking industry, Norddeutscher Lloyd in the transportation industry, and Neu-Westend AG für Grundstücksverwertung and Deutsche Treuhandgesellschaft in other industries. There were enterprises in which interlocking directorates were formed through a mandate of vice-chairman and one post of the supervisory board excluding chairman and vice-chairman were seven, namely Essener Steinkohlen-Bergbau AG in the mining industry, Gussstahl-Werk Witten in the iron and steel industry, Rheinische Automobil, Gesellschaft AG in the automobile industry, Hannoversche Bank and Mecklenburgische Hypotheken- und Wechselbank in the banking industry, "Allianz," Versicherungs-AG in the insurance industry, and Gesellschaft für elektrische Hoch- und Untergrundbahnen in the transportation industry. Enterprises where interlocking directorates were established through two mandates of the supervisory board except for chairman and vice-chairman were 11. Such cases were Berg- und Metallbank, AG in the banking industry, Nordstern, Lebensversicherungsgesellschaft and Nordstern, Unfall- und Alters-Versicherungs-AG, Allgemeine Versicherungs-Gesellschaft für See-. Fluss- und Land-Transport, and Sächsische Rückversicherungs-Gesellschaft in the insurance industry, Rheinisch-Westfälisches Electricitätswerk AG and Bergmann-Elektricitäts-Werke AG in the electric power, gas, and energy industries, Leipziger Elektrische Strassenbahn AG and Schantung-Eisenbahn-Gesellschaft in the transportation industry, and AG für Überseeische Bauunternehmungen and A. Goerz & Company, Limited in other industries.

Thus, Deutsche Bank's direct interlocking directorates on the supervisory boards of other enterprises were spread over a wide range of industries and had personnel connections with several competitive companies mutually in the same industrial sector through several mandates of the supervisory board. Such cases can be observed for instance in Gelsenkirchener Bergwerke-AG and Harpener Bergbau AG in the mining industry. Deutsche Bank established close and strong personnel connections with many companies in various industries through direct interlocking directorates of members of the supervisory board and management board, which greatly contributed to securing much information for its own financial business and decision of policies over industrial enterprises.

2.1.2 Direct Interlocking Directorate of Members of Supervisory Board and Managing Board of Dresdner Bank

Next, regarding the conditions of the interlocking directorate by members of the supervisory and management board of Dresdner Bank on the supervisory board of other enterprises (see Table 2.3), there were 224 companies in which such cases were observed and 321 interlocking mandates. The numbers of both enterprises and mandates were much more than those of Deutsche Bank (corresponding numbers 188 and 241, respectively). Considering the distribution of industrial sectors, Dresdner Bank built direct interlocking directorates in 12 companies and 20 interlocking mandates in the mining industry, and similarly, 20 and 27 in iron and steel; five and 10 in metal producing and processing; eight and 11 in chemical; six and 13 in electrical; 25 and 34 in machine; one each in shipbuilding; one each in oil; 13 and 14 in textile, spinning, and woven goods; three and five in distillation; 30 and 55 in banking; 14 and 15 in insurance; 12 each in electric power, gas, and energy; 26 and 39 in transportation; and 48 and 64 in other industries, respectively. Numbers of enterprises in which direct interlocking directorates were built and interlocking mandates were much more compared with those of Deutsche Bank. Among the various industries, except for the banking industry and the insurance industry, for example, there were many interlocking relations in mining, iron and steel, chemical, machine, textile spinning, and woven goods, and electric power, gas, and energy industries. Therefore, Dresdner Bank had close and strong relationships with companies in the key industrial sectors in Germany—the heavy and chemical industries.

Considering the situation of interlocking directorates regarding the mandate of the supervisory board, in 59 enterprises, interlocking directorates on the supervisory boards of other companies were formed through a mandate of the chairman of the supervisory board with 59 mandates. In each enterprise, the number of mandates was one. The numbers of enterprises and mandates were fewer than those of Deutsche Bank (corresponding numbers 67 and 69, respectively). Considering the distribution among industrial sectors, the number of enterprises in which interlocking directorates were formed was two in the mining industry; similarly, seven in iron and steel industry; two in chemical; 10 in machine; one in shipbuilding; two in textile, spinning, and woven goods; eight in banking; two in insurance; and one in electric power, gas, and energy; 10 in transportation, and 14 in other industries, respectively. There were many enterprises and mandates in the banking, machine, and transportation industries. Cases of interlocking directorate in representative companies of each industry were seen in Fried. Krupp AG in the iron and steel industry, AG "Weser" in the shipbuilding industry, and A. Schauhausenische Bankverein in the banking industry.

In 41 enterprises, interlocking directorates were formed through a mandate of the vice-chairman of the supervisory board and the total number of mandates was 42. The numbers of both enterprise and mandate were much more than those of Deutsche Bank (corresponding numbers 21 and 21, respectively). The numbers of enterprises and mandates in which such interlocking cases were formed were two each in the mining industry; similarly, four and five in iron and steel; three each in chemical; one each in electrical; four each in machine; three each in textile, spinning, and woven goods; six each in banking; two each in electric, gas, and energy; four each in transportation; and 12 each in other industries, respectively. In these companies, there were major companies in each industry, such as Phönix, AG für Bergbau und Hüttenbetrieb in the iron and steel industry and Ludw. Loewe & Co, AG in the machine industry.

Interlocking directorates through mandates of the supervisory board except for the chairman and vice-chairman were observed in 165 companies, and the total number of mandates was 220. The numbers of enterprises and mandates were more than those of Deutsche Bank (124 and 151, respectively). Considering the distribution among industrial sectors, the numbers of enterprises and mandates in which Dresdner Bank built interlocking directorates were 10 and 16 in the mining industry respectively; similarly, 13 and 15 in iron and steel; five and 10 in metal producing and processing; four and six in chemical; five and 12 in electrical; 18 and 20 in machine; one each in oil; nine each in textile, spinning, and woven goods; three and five in distributing; 24 and 41 in banking; 13 each in insurance; nine each in electric power, gas, and energy; 18 and 25 in transportation; and 33 and 38 in other industries, respectively. These companies included representative firms in each industry, such as Gelsenkirchener Bergwerks-AG and Harpener Bergbau AG in the mining industry, AEG in the

Table 2.3 Direct interlocking directorates of the members of the supervisory board and the managing board of Dresdner Bank on the supervisory board of other companies (period of shift to monopolistic capitalism)

Industries	Position							
	Chairman		Vice-chairman		Supervisory board member excluding chairman and vice-chairman		Total[a]	
	Number of companies	Number of posts	Number of companies	Number of posts	Number of companies	Number of posts	Number of companies	Number of posts
Mining	2	2	2	2	10	16	12	20
Iron and steel	7	7	4	5	13	15	20	27
Metal producing and processing	–	–	–	–	5	10	5	10
Chemical	2	2	3	3	4	6	8	11
Electrical	–	–	1	1	5	12	6	13
Machine	10	10	4	4	18	20	25	34
Shipbuilding	1	1	–	–	–	–	1	1
Oil	–	–	–	–	1	1	1	1
Textile, spinning, and woven goods	2	2	3	3	9	9	13	14
Distillation	–	–	–	–	3	5	3	5
Banking	8	8	6	6	24	41	30	55
Insurance	2	2	–	–	13	13	14	15
Electric power, gas, and energy	1	1	2	2	9	9	12	12
Transportation	10	10	4	4	18	25	26	39

(continued)

Table 2.3 (continued)

Industries	Position							
	Chairman		Vice-chairman		Supervisory board member excluding chairman and vice-chairman		Total[a]	
	Number of companies	Number of posts	Number of companies	Number of posts	Number of companies	Number of posts	Number of companies	Number of posts
Other industries	14	14	12	12	33	38	48	64
All industries	59	59	41	42	165	220	224	321

[a] There are cases in which the total number of companies establishing interlocking directorates differed from the total number of companies measured by each position of the supervisory board due to the existence of companies where interlocking directorates through more than two posts were built

Source This table was compiled by the author, based on Arends and Mossner (Hrsg) (1908)

electrical industry, A. Schauhausenische Bankverein in the banking industry, and "Allianz" Versicherungs-AG in the insurance industry.

The numbers of enterprises and mandates were 62 and 159, respectively, when considering cases where members of the supervisory board and board of directors of Dresdner Bank had more than two mandates on the supervisory boards of other companies (see Table 2.4). Numbers of both enterprises and mandates were much more than those of Deutsche Bank (39 and 92, respectively). Considering the distribution among industries, the numbers of companies and mandates were as follows: five and 13 in mining; four and 11 in iron and steel; one and six in metal producing and processing; two and five in chemical; four and 11 in electrical; eight and 17 in machine; one and two in textile, spinning, and woven goods; two and four in distillation; 14 and 39 in banking; one and two in insurance; eight and 21 in transportation; and 12 and 28 in the other industries, respectively. In these companies, there were major companies in each industry, such as Gelsenkirchener Bergwerks-AG and Harpener Bergbau AG in the mining industry, Phönix, AG für Bergbau und Hüttenbetrieb in the iron and steel industry, AEG in the electrical industry, and Ludw. Loewe & Co, AG in the machine industry.

Of these 62 companies, 22 enterprises had direct interlocking directorates built through more than three mandates, and the total number of mandates was 79. The numbers of both enterprises and mandates were much more than those of Deutsche Bank (seven and 28, respectively). Enterprises where direct interlocking directorates were formed through seven mandates, six mandates, and four mandates were one, one, and six, respectively. Cases in which such interlocking directorates were established through three mandates were 14. In the remaining 40 companies, Dresdner Bank had two mandates on the supervisory board of other companies.

When considering these interlocking directorates in relation to supervisory board position mandates, in A. Schauhausenische Banksverein Dresdner Bank AG built interlocking directorates through seven mandates consisting of one chairman and six posts of the supervisory board except for chairman and vice-chairman. In Deutsche Waffen- und Munitionsfabriken in the metal producing and processing industries, interlocking directorates were formed through six mandates of the supervisory board except for chairman and vice-chairman. In four company, namely Saar- und Mosel-Bergwerks-Gesellschaft in the mining industry, Rheinisch-Westfälische Boden-Credit-Bank in the banking industry, Grosse Berliner Strassenbahn and Continentale Eisenbahn-Bau und Betriebsgesellschaft in the transportation industry, Dresdner Bank built interlocking directorates through one post of chairman and three mandates of the supervisory board excluding chairman and vice-chairman, respectively. In Deutsch-Atlantische Telegraphengesellschaft in other industries, interlocking directorates were established through mandate of vice-chairman and three posts of the supervisory board except for chairman and vice-chairman. On the other hand, in Felten und Guilleaume-Lahmeyerwerke AG in the electrical industry, there were interlocking directorates through four mandates of the supervisory bard except for chairman and vice-chairman.

Regarding 14 companies with three mandates, in AG Lauchhammer in the iron and steel industry, interlocking directorates were built through a mandate

Table 2.4 Cases in which Dresdner Bank built direct interlocking directorates through more than two posts on the supervisory board of other companies (period of shift to monopolistic capitalism)

Industries	Number of posts											
	2		3		4		6		7		Total	
	Number of companies	Number of posts	Number of companies	Number of posts	Number of companies	Number of posts	Number of companies	Number of posts	Number of companies	Number of posts	Number of companies	Number of posts
Mining	3	6	1	3	1	4	–	–	–	–	5	13
Iron and steel	1	2	3	9	–	–	–	–	–	–	4	11
metal producing and processing	–	–	–	–	–	–	1	6	–	–	1	6
Chemical	1	2	1	3	–	–	–	–	–	–	2	5
Electrical	2	4	1	3	1	4	–	–	–	–	4	11
Machine	7	14	1	3	–	–	–	–	–	–	8	17
Textile, spinning, and woven goods	1	2	–	–	–	–	–	–	–	–	1	2
Distillation	2	4	–	–	–	–	–	–	–	–	2	4
Banking	8	16	4	12	1	4	–	–	1	7	14	39
Insurance	1	2	–	–	–	–	–	–	–	–	1	2
Transportation	5	10	1	3	2	8	–	–	–	–	8	21
Other Industries	9	18	2	6	1	4	–	–	–	–	12	28
All industries	40	80	14	42	6	24	1	6	1	7	62	159

Source This table was compiled by the author, based on Arends and Mossner (Hrsg) (1908)

of chairman and two vice-chairmen. In Deutsche Orientbank AG in the banking industry and Deutsch-Niederländische Telegraphen-Gesellschaft, Osteuropäische Telegraphengesellschaft in other industries, there were interlocking directorates through one post of chairman and two mandates of the supervisory board excluding chairman and vice-chairman, respectively. In six enterprises, namely Phönix, AG für Bergbau und Hüttenbetrieb, and Faconeisen-Walzwerk L. Mannstaedt & Co. in the iron and steel industry, Vereinigte Köln-Rotweiler Pulverfabriken in the chemical industry, Ludw. Loewe & Co, AG in the machine industry, and Rheinische Bank and Schwarzburgische Landesbank in the banking industry, Dresdner Bank had a mandate of vice-chairman and two posts of the supervisory board except for chairman and vice-chairman, respectively. In Gelsenkirchener Bergwerks-AG in the mining industry, Norddeutsche Seekabelwerke in the electrical industry, Schwarzburgische Hypothekenbank in the banking industry, and Braunschweig, Landes-Eisenbahn-Gesellschaft in the transportation industry, interlocking directorates were formed though three posts of the supervisory board except for chairman and vice-chairman, respectively.

Considering 40 enterprises with two mandates on the supervisory board of other enterprise in relation to distribution of industrial sector, there were three in mining industry, one in iron and steel industry, one in chemical industry, two in electrical, seven in machine industry, one in textile, spinning, and woven goods industries, two in distillation industry, eight in banking industry, one in insurance industry, five in transportation industry, and nine in other industries.

In AG für Rheinisch-Westphälische Industrie in the banking industry and AG für Rheinisch-Westfälische Cement-Industrie, Bodengesell-schaft Kurfürstendam, Schmargendorfe Boden-AG, and Vereinigte Bautzner Papierfabriken, interlocking directorates were formed through one each of mandate of chairman and vice-chairman, respectively. Cases in which interlocking directorates were built through a post of chairman and one mandate of the supervisory board except for chairman and vice-chairman can be observed in 12 companies. Such cases were Deutsch-Oestrreeiche Bergwerksgesellschaft in the mining industry, Vereinigte Stahlwerke v. d. Zypen und Wissen. Eisenhütten AG in the iron and steel industry, Berlin-Anhaltische Maschinenbau-AG, Walther & Co., Sächsische Maschinenfabrik vorm. Rich. Hartmann, and AG für Feld- und Kleinbahnen-Bed, v. Orenstein & Koppel in the machine industry, Centralbank für Eisenbahnwerthe in the banking industry, Kölnische Unfall-Versicherungs-AG in the insurance industry, Berlin-Charlottenburge Strassenbahn-Gesellschaft, Westliche Berliner Vorortbahn, and Lausitzer Eisenbahngesellschaft in the transportation industry, and Terraingesellschaft am Central Viehhof AG and Berlinische Boden-Gesellschaft in other industries. In Deutsch-Oesterreiche Bergwerksgesellschaft in the mining industry, Maschinenbau-Anstalt Humboldt and Waggonfabrik AG vorm. P. Herbrand & Co. in the machine industry, Erdmannsdorfe AG für Flachsgarn-Masch. -Spinnerei und Weberei in the textile, spinning, and woven goods industries, Mecklenburgische Bank in the banking industry, Rhein- und Seeschifffahrts-Gesellschaft in the transportation industry, and Dresdner Bau-Gesellschaft and Allgemeine Boden-AG in other industries, there were interlocking directorates through a mandate of vice-chairman and one post of the supervisory board excluding chairman and vice-chairman, respectively. Enterprises where interlocking directorates were established through two mandates of the supervisory board except for chairman and vice-chairman were 15. Such cases were Eschweiler Bergwerks-Verein and Harpener Bergbau AG in the mining industry, Rheinisch-Westfälische Sprengstoff AG in the chemical industry, Land- und Seekabelwerke and AEG in the electrical industry, Kalker Werkzeugmaschinenfabrik Breuer, Schumacher & Cie. in the machine industry, Actien-Bier-Brauerei Reisewitz and Sächsische Malzfabrik in the distillation industry, Deutsche Grundcredit-Bank, Berliner Bodenkredit-Bank, Mittelrheinische Bank, Preussische Pfandbriefbank, and Württembergische Landesbank in the banking industry, Sächsisch-Böhmische Dampfschifffahrts-Gesellschaft in the transportation industry, and Treuhand-Vereinigung AG in other industries.

Thus, Dresdner Bank's direct interlocking directorates on the supervisory boards of other enterprises were spread over a wide range of industries and had personnel connections with several competitive companies mutually in the same industrial sector through several mandates of the supervisory board. Such cases can be observed, for instance, in Bergwerke-AG and Harpener Bergbau AG in the mining industry and Fried. Krupp AG and Phönix, AG für Bergbau und Hüttenbetrieb in the iron and steel industry. Dresdner Bank built close and strong personnel connections with many companies in various industries through direct interlocking directorates of supervisory board and management board members, which enabled this bank to secure much information for its own financial business and decision of policies over industrial enterprises.

2.1.3 Direct Interlocking Directorate of Members of Supervisory Board and Managing Board of Commerzbank

Furthermore, regarding the direct interlocking directorate by members of the supervisory board and managing board of Commerzbank on the supervisory board of other enterprises (see Table 2.5), there were 80 companies in which such cases were observed and 96 interlocking mandates. Both enterprises and mandates were much fewer those of Deutsche Bank (corresponding numbers 188 and 241, respectively) and those of Dresdner Bank (similarly 224 and 321, respectively). Considering the distribution of industrial sectors, Commerzbank built direct interlocking directorates in seven companies and had nine interlocking mandates in the mining industry, respectively, and similarly, four each in iron and steel; three each in metal producing and processing; four and five in chemical; two each in electrical; seven and eight in machine; two each in shipbuilding; two each in oil; two each in textile, spinning, and woven goods; five each in distillation; five and six in banking; one each in insurance; three and five in electric power, gas, and energy; eight and nine in transportation; and 25 and 33 in other industries, respectively. Therefore, Commerzbank had close and strong relationships with companies in the heavy and chemical industries as the key industrial sectors in Germany.

Given the situation of interlocking directorates, concerning the position of mandate of the supervisory board, Commerzbank built interlocking directorates through mandates of the chairman of the supervisory boards of 25 companies. In each company, number of mandates was one. The total number of mandates was 25. Numbers of both enterprises and mandates were much fewer those of Deutsche Bank (67 and 69, respectively) and those of Dresdner Bank (59 and 59, respectively). Considering the distribution of industrial sectors, the numbers of enterprises and mandates in which Commerzbank built interlocking directorates were two each in the mining industry, respectively; similarly, three each in iron and steel; two each in metal producing and processing; one each in chemical; one each in machine; one each in oil; one each in textile, spinning, and woven goods; one each in distillation; two each in banking; four each in transportation; and seven each in other industries, respectively.

In five enterprises, interlocking directorates were formed through mandate of vice-chairman of the supervisory board, totaling five mandates. In each company, the number of mandates was one. The numbers of enterprises and mandates were much fewer those of Deutsche Bank (21 and 21, respectively) and those of Dresdner Bank (41 and 42, respectively). The numbers of enterprises and mandates in which such interlocking cases were formed were one each in chemical; one each in shipbuilding; one each in electric power, gas, and energy; and two each in other industries, respectively.

Interlocking directorates through mandates of the supervisory board's mandates except for chairman and vice-chairman were observed in 56 companies, totaling 66 mandates. The numbers of both enterprises and mandates were much fewer those of Deutsche Bank (124 and 151, respectively) and those of Dresdner Bank (165 and 220, respectively). Considering the distribution among industrial sectors, the numbers of enterprises and mandates in which interlocking directorates were formed were five and seven in the mining industry respectively; similarly, one each in the iron and steel industry; one each in the metal producing and processing industries; two and three in the chemical industry; respectively; two each in the electrical industry; seven each in the machine industry; one each in the shipbuilding; one each in the oil industry; one each in the textile, spinning, and woven goods industries; four each in the distillation industry; four each in the banking industry; one each in the insurance industry; three and four in the electric power, gas, and energy industries; respectively; five each in the transportation industry; and 18 and 24 in other industries, respectively.

The numbers of enterprises and mandates were 12 and 28, respectively, when considering cases where members of the supervisory board and board of directors of Commerzbank had more than two mandates on the supervisory boards of other companies (see Table 2.6). Numbers of both enterprises and mandates were much fewer those of Deutsche Bank (39 and 92, respectively) and those of Dresdner Bank (62 and 159, respectively). Considering the distribution among industries, the numbers of companies and mandates were as follows: one and three in the mining industry; one and two in chemical; one and two in machine; one and two in banking;

Table 2.5 Direct interlocking directorates of the members of the supervisory board and the managing board of Commerzbank Bank on the supervisory board of other companies (period of shift to monopolistic capitalism)

	Position							
Industries	Chairman		Vice-chairman		Supervisory board member excluding chairman and vice-chairman		Total[a]	
	Number of companies	Number of posts	Number of companies	Number of posts	Number of companies	Number of posts	Number of companies	Number of posts
Mining	2	2	–	–	5	7	7	9
Iron and steel	3	3	–	–	1	1	4	4
Metal producing and processing	2	2	–	–	1	1	3	3
Chemical	1	1	1	1	2	3	4	5
Electrical	–	–	–	–	2	2	2	2
Machine	1	1	–	–	7	7	7	8
Shipbuilding	–	–	1	1	1	1	2	2
Oil	1	1	–	–	1	1	2	2
Textile, spinning, and woven goods	1	1	–	–	1	1	2	2
Distillation	1	1	–	–	4	4	5	5
Banking	2	2	–	–	4	4	5	6
Insurance	–	–	–	–	1	1	1	1
Electric power, gas, and energy	–	–	1	1	3	4	3	5
Transportation	4	4	–	–	5	5	8	9

(continued)

Table 2.5 (continued)

Industries	Position							
	Chairman		Vice-chairman		Supervisory board member excluding chairman and vice-chairman		Total[a]	
	Number of companies	Number of posts	Number of companies	Number of posts	Number of companies	Number of posts	Number of companies	Number of posts
Other industries	7	7	5	2	18	24	25	33
All industries	25	25	5	5	56	66	80	96

[a] There are cases in which the total number of companies establishing interlocking directorates differed from the total number of companies measured by each position of the supervisory board due to the existence of companies where interlocking directorates through more than two posts were built

Source This table was compiled by the author, based on Arends and Mossner (Hrsg) (1908)

one and three in electric power, gas, and energy; one and two in transportation; and six and 14 in other industries, respectively.

Of these 12 companies, there were four enterprises in which direct interlocking directorates were built through three mandates. These enterprises were Norddeutsche Braunkohlenwerke AG in the mining industry, Hamburgische Elektricitäts-Werke in the electric power, gas, and energy industries, and Terrain-Gesellschaft am Teltow-Canal Rudow-Johannstahl and Norddeutsche Zucker-Raffinerie AG in other industries. In the remaining eight companies Commerzbank had two mandates on the supervisory board of other companies.

Considering these interlocking directorates with respect to supervisory board position mandates, in Terrain-Gesellschaft am Teltow-Canal Rudow-Johannstahl, interlocking directorates were built through three mandates consisting of a mandate of chairman and two posts of the supervisory board except for chairman and vice-chairman. In Hamburgische Elektricitäts-Werke interlocking directorates were formed through one mandate of vice-chairman and two posts of the supervisory board except for chairman and vice-chairman. Meanwhile, in Norddeutsche Braunkohlenwerke AG and Norddeutsche Zucker-Raffinerie AG, there were interlocking directorates through three mandates of the supervisory board excluding chairman and vice-chairman, respectively.

When considering eight enterprises with two mandates on the supervisory board of other enterprise in relation to distribution of industrial sector, there were one in chemical, one in machine, one in banking, one in transportation, and four in other industries. Considering these interlocking directorates in relation to kind of mandate, cases in which interlocking directorates were built through a mandate of chairman and one post of the supervisory board except for chairman and vice-chairman can be observed in four enterprises. Such case were Maschinenbau-Anstalt und Eisengiesserei vorm.

Table 2.6 Cases in which Commerzbank built direct interlocking directorates through more than two posts on the supervisory board of other companies (period of shift to monopolistic capitalism)

Industries	Number of posts					
	2		3		Total	
	Number of companies	Number of posts	Number of Companies	Number of posts	Number of companies	Number of posts
Mining	–	–	1	3	1	3
Chemical	1	2	–	–	1	2
Machine	1	2	–	–	1	2
Banking	1	2	–	–	1	2
Electric power, gas, and energy	–	–	1	3	1	3
Transportation	1	2	–	–	1	2
Other industries	4	8	2	6	6	14
All industries	8	16	4	12	12	28

Source This table was compiled by the author, based on Arends and Mossner (Hrsg) (1908)

Th. Flöther in the machine industry, Credit- und Sparbank in the banking industry, Hamburg-Amerikamische Packetfahrt-AG in the transportation industry, and Lichtenberger Terrain-AG in other industries, In four companies, namely in Chemische Fabr. Harburg-Stassfurt vorm. Thörl & Heidtmann AG in the chemical industry and Savoy Hotel AG, Admiralsgarten-Bad AG, and Grundstücks-AG in other industries, Commerzbank established interlocking directorates through two mandates of the supervisory board except for chairman and vice-chairman, respectively.

In this way, Commerzbank also established close and strong personnel connections with many companies in various industries through direct interlocking directorates of members of the supervisory board and management board, which greatly contributed to securing much information for its own financial business and decision of policies over industrial enterprises. However, Commerzbank's direct interlocking directorates on the supervisory boards of other enterprises did not spread over a wide range of industries as Deutsch Bank and Dresdner Bank did and conditions of personnel connections through direct interlocking directorate on the supervisory board of other enterprises differed between Commerzbank and Deutsche Bank and between Commerzbank and Dresdner Bank. Therefore, how was such condition afterward, for instance during the Weimar Republic and National Socialism is important problem to be clarified.

In foregoing discussions, conditions of personnel connections that large banks, such as Deutsche Bank, Dresdner Bank, and Commerzbank built through direct interlocking directorates of members of the supervisory board and management board on the supervisory board of other enterprises were considered. How were conditions indirect interlocking directorates on the supervisory board of other firms among these three banks and between two banks of them is also important problem to be clarified. Therefore, these research topics are analyzed in the next section.

2.2 Indirect Interlocking Directorates Between Banks on the Supervisory Board of Other Enterprises

When in looking at indirect interlocking directorate established on supervisory board of other enterprise among Deutsche Bank, Dresdner Bank, and Commerzbank, there was only one case. Such case can be observed in Santa Katharina Eisenbahn-Aktiengesellschaft in the transportation industry. In this enterprise, each bank of three banks had one mandate, respectively. Whereas Deutsche Bank had chairman post, other two banks had each one supervisory board post except for chairman and vice-chairman (Arends and Mossner 1908, pp. 543, 993, 1195). Therefore, this section considers indirect interlocking directorates built between Deutsche Bank and Dresdner Bank, between Deutsche Bank and Commerzbank, and between Dresdner Bank and Commerzbank.

2.2.1 Indirect Interlocking Directorates Between Deutsche Bank and Dresdner Bank on the Supervisory Board of Other Enterprises

Next, in examining the situations related to indirect interlocking directorates between Deutsche Bank and Dresdner Bank on the supervisory board of other enterprises (see Table 2.7), such cases can be observed in 24 companies and the total number of mandates was 64 except cases of indirect interlocking directorates among three big banks. Considering the interlocking directorate in relation to the kind of mandate, the numbers of enterprises and mandates in which indirect interlocking directorates were built through the mandate of chairman were five each, respectively. Similar numerical figures through mandate of vice-chairman and post of the supervisory board except for chairman and vice-chairman were seven each and 23 and 52, respectively. When considering the distribution of industry, numbers of companies and mandates of interlocking directorate were two and seven in mining, two and five in iron and steel, one and two in metal producing and processing, two and five in chemical, one and five in electrical, one and two in machine, two and four in banking, three and nine in insurance, six and 13 in electric power, gas, and energy; three and 10 in transportation, and one and two in other industries, respectively.

Understanding bank that was at the leading position in indirect interlocking relation requires examining cases in which one bank or both Deutsche Bank and Dresdner Bank had more than two mandates on the supervisory board of other company. Such cases were observed in 11 companies with a total of 38 mandates. When considering the distribution of industry, number of companies, and mandates of interlocking directorate, there were, respectively, two and seven in mining; one and three in iron and steel; one and three in chemical; one and five in electrical; three and nine in insurance; one and three in electric power, gas, and energy; and two and eight in the transportation industry.

The number of companies in which Deutsche Bank and Dresdner Bank built indirect interlocking directorate through total of five mandates was two. Similar numerical figures through total four mandates and three mandates were one and eight, respectively. In the remaining 13 enterprises, indirect interlocking directorates were built through total of two mandates, respectively.

Regarding enterprises with total of five mandates in each enterprise, in Grosse Berliner Strassenbahn in the transportation industry, whereas Dresdner Bank had one mandate of chairman and three posts of the supervisory board except for chairman and vice-chairman, Deutsche Bank had one post of the supervisory board except for chairman and vice-chairman. In Felten und Guilleaume-Lahmeyerwerke AG in the electrical industry, whereas Dresdner Bank had four mandates of the supervisory board excluding chairman and vice-chairman, Deutsche Bank had a mandate of the supervisory board excluding chairman and vice-chairman. In Gelsenkirchener Bergwerks-AG in the mining industry, whereas Dresdner Bank had 3 mandates of the supervisory board other than chairman and vice-chairman, Deutsche Bank had a mandate of the supervisory board except for chairman and vice-chairman.

Table 2.7 Indirect interlocking directorates of the members of the supervisory board and the managing board on the supervisory board of other companies between Deutsche Bank and Dresdner Bank[a] (period of shift to monopolistic capitalism)

Industries	Number of posts									
	2		3		4		5		Total	
	Number of companies	Number of posts	Number of companies	Number of posts	Number of companies	Number of posts	Number of companies	Number of posts	Number of companies	Number of posts
Mining	–	–	1	3	1	4	–	–	2	7
Iron and steel	1	2	1	3	–	–	–	–	2	5
Metal producing and processing	1	2	–	–	–	–	–	–	1	2
Chemical	1	2	1	3	–	–	–	–	2	5
Electrical	–	–	–	–	–	–	1	5	1	5
Machine	1	2	–	–	–	–	–	–	1	2
Banking	2	4	–	–	–	–	–	–	2	4
Insurance	–	–	3	9	–	–	–	–	3	9
Electric power, gas, and energy	5	10	1	3	–	–	–	–	6	13
Transportation	1	2	1	3	–	–	1	5	3	10
Other industries	1	2	–	–	–	–	–	–	1	2
All industries	13	26	8	24	1	4	2	10	24	64

[a] The cases of indirect interlocking directorates built among Deutsche Bank, Dresdner Bank, and Commerzbank are excluded

Source This table was compiled by the author, based on Arends and Mossner (Hrsg) (1908)

Of eight enterprises totaling three mandates in each enterprise, in Gussstahl-Werk Witten in the iron and steel industry, whereas Deutsche Bank had a mandate of vice-chairman and one post of the supervisory board except for chairman and vice-chairman, Dresdner Bank held a mandate of chairman. In "Allianz," Versicherungs-AG in the insurance industry, Deutsche Bank had a mandate of vice-chairman and one post of the supervisory board excluding chairman and vice-chairman. Meanwhile, Dresdner Bank held a mandate of the supervisory board except for chairman and vice-chairman. In Harpener Bergbau AG in the mining industry and Rheinisch-Westfälische Sprengstoff AG in the chemical industry, whereas Dresdner Bank had two mandates of the supervisory board except chairman and vice-chairman, Deutsche Bank had one similar post. In four companies, namely Nordstern, Lebensversicherungsgesellschaft, Nordstern, Unfall- und Alters-Versicherungs-AG in the insurance industry, Rheinisch-Westfälisches Electricitätswerk AG in the electric power, gas, and energy industries, and Schantung-Eisenbahn-Gesellschaft in the transportation industry, whereas Deutsche Bank had two mandates of the supervisory board except for chairman and vice-chairman, Dresdner Bank had one similar post.

The other 13 enterprises were cases in which Deutsche Bank AG and Dresdner Bank AG established interlocking directorates through one mandate of the supervisory board, respectively. When considering the distribution of industry, number of companies of interlocking directorate was one in the iron and steel industry, one in the metal producing and processing industries, one in the chemical industry, one in the machine industry, two in the banking industry, five in the electric power, gas, and energy industries, one in the transportation industry, and one in other industries, respectively.

Cases in which each of two banks had one chairman or a vice-chairman can be observed in AG für Anilin-Fabrikation in the chemical industry. In this enterprise, whereas Deutsche Bank had a mandate of chairman, Dresdner Bank had one post of vice-chairman. Cases where each of two banks had a chairman or one post of the supervisory board except for chairman and vice-chairman were seen in two companies: Deutsch-Ueberseeische Elektricitäts-Geselslchaft in the electric power, gas, and energy industries and Maschinenfabrik "Deutschland" in the machine industry. In Deutsch-Ueberseeische Elektricitäts-Geselslchaft, whereas Deutsche Bank had a mandate of chairman, Dresdner Bank had one mandate of the supervisory board excluding chairman and vice-chairman. In Maschinenfabrik "Deutschland," whereas Dresdner Bank had a mandate of chairman, Deutsche Bank AG had one mandate of the supervisory board excluding for chairman and vice-chairman. Cases in which each of two banks had a vice-chairman or one post of the supervisory board other than chairman and vice-chairman were observed in four enterprises: Sächsische Gusstahlfabrik in the iron and steel industry, Sächsische Bodencreditanstalt in the banking industry, and Elektrizitäts-AG vorm. W. Lahmeyer und Co. and Kraftübertragungswerke Rheinfelden in the electric power, gas, and energy industries. In Sächsiche Gusstahlfabrik, Sächsische Bodencreditanstalt, and Kraftübertragungswerke Rheinfelden, whereas Deutsche Bank had a mandate of vice-chairman, Dresdner Bank had one mandate of the supervisory board except for chairman and vice-chairman, respectively. In Elektrizitäts-AG vorm. W. Lahmeyer und Co., whereas

Dresdner Bank had a mandate of vice-chairman, Deutsche Bank had one mandate of the supervisory board excluding chairman and vice-chairman. Cases where each of two banks had one each post of the supervisory board except for chairman and vice-chairman, respectively, can be observed in six enterprises, namely Kupferwerke Deutschland in the metal producing and processing industries, Deutsche-Asiatische Bank in the banking industry, Berliner Elektricitäts-Werke and Deutsche Continental-Gas-Gesellschaft in the electric power, gas, and energy industries, Norddeutsche Lloyd in the transportation industry, and Berliner Makler-Verein in other industries.

2.2.2 Indirect Interlocking Directorates Between Deutsche Bank and Commerzbank on the Supervisory Board of Other Enterprises

Next, in examining the situations related to indirect interlocking directorates between Deutsche Bank and Commerzbank on the supervisory board of other enterprises (see Table 2.8), such cases can be observed in four companies with a total of six mandates except for cases of indirect interlocking directorates among three big banks. The numbers of enterprises and mandates were much fewer than those of indirect interlocking directorate built between Deutsche Bank and Dresdner Bank (24 and 64, respectively). Considering the interlocking directorate in relation to the kind of mandate, the numbers of enterprises and mandates in which indirect interlocking directorates were formed through the mandate of chairman were one each, respectively. Similar numerical figures through mandate of vice-chairman and post of the supervisory board except for chairman and vice-chairman were two each and four and six, respectively. When considering the distribution of industry, numbers of companies and mandates of interlocking directorate were one and three in the mining industry, one and two in the iron and steel industry, one and two in the banking industry, and one and two in other industries, respectively.

Case in which one bank or both Deutsche Bank and Commerzbank had more than two mandates on the supervisory board of other company can be observed in one company, namely Essener Steinkohlen-Bergbau in the mining industry. The total number of mandare was three. In this enterprise, whereas Deutsche Bank had a mandate of vice-chairman and one post of the supervisory board except for chairman and vice-chairman, Commerzbank held one mandate of the supervisory board excluding chairman and vice-chairman.

In the remaining three enterprises, indirect interlocking directorates were built through total of two mandates, respectively. In Oberschlesische Eisenbahn-Bedarfs-AG in the iron and steel industry, Commerzbank had a mandate of chairman and Deutsche Bank had a post of vice-chairman. In Norddeutsche Creditanstal in the banking industry and Hamburg Freihafen, Lagerhaus-Gesellschaft in other industries, Deutsche Bank and Commerzbank held a post of the supervisory board other than chairman and vice-chairman, respectively.

Table 2.8 Indirect interlocking directorates of the members of the supervisory board and the managing board on the supervisory board of other companies between Deutsch Bank and Commerzbank[a] (period of shift to monopolistic capitalism)

Industries	Number of posts					
	2		3		Total	
	Number of companies	Number of posts	Number of companies	Number of posts	Number of companies	Number of posts
Mining	–	–	1	3	1	3
Iron and steel	1	2	–	–	1	2
Banking	1	2	–	–	1	2
Other industries	1	2	–	–	1	2
All industries	3	6	1	3	4	9

[a] The cases of indirect interlocking directorates built among Deutsche Bank, Dresdner Bank, and Commerzbank are excluded
Source This table was compiled by the author, based on Arends and Mossner (Hrsg) (1908)

2.2.3 Indirect Interlocking Directorates Between Dresdner Bank and Commerzbank on the Supervisory Board of Other Enterprises

Furthermore, in examining the situations related to indirect interlocking directorates between Dresdner Bank and Commerzbank on the supervisory board of other enterprises (see Table 2.9), such cases can be observed in four companies and the total number of mandates was nine except for cases of such interlocking directorates among three big banks. The numbers of enterprises and mandates were much fewer than those of indirect interlocking directorate established between Deutsche Bank and Dresdner Bank (24 and 64, respectively) and were same as those of such interlocking directorate built between Deutsche Bank and Commerzbank (four and nine, respectively). Considering interlocking directorate in relation to supervisory board position mandates, the numbers of enterprises and mandates in which indirect interlocking directorates were established through the mandate of chairman were two each, respectively. Similar numerical figures through mandate of vice-chairman and post of the supervisory board except for chairman and vice-chairman were one each and four and six, respectively. When considering the distribution of industry, numbers of companies and mandates of interlocking directorate were one and two in the mining industry, one and two in the chemical industry, one and three in the machine industry, and one and two in the transportation industry, respectively.

Case in which one bank or both Dresdner Bank and Commerzbank had more than two mandates on the supervisory board of other company was one company, namely Waggonfabrik AG vorm. P. Herbrand & Co. in the machine industry. The

Table 2.9 Indirect interlocking directorates of the members of the supervisory board and the managing board on the supervisory board of other companies between Dresdner Bank and Commerzbank[a] (period of shift to monopolistic capitalism)

Industries	Number of posts					
	2		3		Total	
	Number of companies	Number of posts	Number of companies	Number of posts	Number of companies	Number of posts
Mining	1	2	–	–	1	2
Chemical	1	2	–	–	1	2
Machine	–	–	1	3	1	3
Transportation	1	2	–	–	1	2
All industries	3	6	1	3	4	9

[a] The cases of indirect interlocking directorates built among Deutsche Bank, Dresdner Bank, and Commerzbank are excluded

Source This table was compiled by the author, based on Arends and Mossner (Hrsg) (1908)

total number of mandare was three. In this enterprise, whereas Dresdner Bank had a mandate of vice-chairman and one post of the supervisory board except for chairman and vice-chairman, Commerzbank held one mandate of the supervisory board except for chairman and vice-chairman.

In the rest three enterprises, indirect interlocking directorates were established through total of two mandates. In Zechau Kriebitzsche Kohlenwerke "Glückauf" AG in the mining industry and Chemische Fabrik Hönningen vorm. Walther Feld & Co in the chemical industry, whereas Commerzbank had a mandate of chairman, Dresdner Bank had a post of the supervisory board excluding chairman and vice-chairman, respectively. In Schlesische Dampfer-Compagnie in the transportation industry, Dresdner Bank and Commerzbank held a post of the supervisory board other than chairman and vice-chairman, respectively.

Indirect interlocking directorate formed on supervisory board of other enterprise among Deutsche Bank, Dresdner Bank, and Commerzbank or between some two banks of them built important foundation of strong cooperative relationships regarding enterprise in which banks established interlocking directorate between large banks. Numbers of enterprises in which indirect interlocking directorates were formed between Deutsche Bank and Commerzbank or between Dresdner Bank and Commerzbank and total number of interlocking supervisory mandate in each case were fewer than those in cases between Deutsche Bank and Dresdner Bank. Such difference in indirect interlocking directorate was due to the situation that enterprise where direct interlocking directorate of top management members of Commerzbank in other company were built and a total number of interlocking post were fewer in comparison with cases of other two banks.

This chapter discussed the conditions of direct interlocking directorates of members of the supervisory and managing board of three banks on the supervisory board of other enterprises and indirect interlocking directorates among three banks and between two of the banks. Such a system of personnel connections had significant implications for exchanging and sharing information and coordinating interests and conflicts between banks and between a bank and industrial enterprises.

In the period before World War II, relationships between a bank and industrial enterprises were deeply concerned with the characteristics of cooperative capitalism in Germany (Chandler 1990). Generally, studies have shown that during inflation following World War I, banks' influence on industrial enterprises became weaker with changes in capital demand of industrial enterprises, inflation-induced loss of bank assets, and a change in corporate financing (Duschnitzky 1927; Hagemann, 1931, SS. 20–21, 186; Krause 2004, S. 350; Lampe 2004, SS. 370, 372). Analyzing whether there were similar conditions of personnel connections through interlocking directorates of members of large banks on the supervisory board of industrial enterprises is important. It is imperative to deeply analyze the conditions of such personnel relations between a bank and industrial enterprises. Therefore, this issue will be addressed in the following chapter.

References

Arends H, Mossner C (Hrsg) (1908) Adressbuch der Direktoren und Aufsichtsrats-Mitglieder der Aktien-Gesellschaften 1908, Jahrgang 1908. Finanz-Verlag, Berlin

Chandler AD Jr (1990) Scale and scope: the dynamics of industrial capitalism. Harvard University Press, Berkeley, Massachusetts

Duschnitzky S (1927) Das Konzern-Problem unter Berücksichtigung der schwerindustriellen Wirtschaft im Nachkriegs-Deutschland: Eine sozialökonomischen Studie zu den Phänomenen der modernen kapitalistischen Konzentration. Kommissionsverlag der Deutschen Buchhandlung, Kaunas, p 1927

Hagemann W (1931) Das Verhältnis der deutschen Grossbanken zur Industrie. W. Christian, Berlin

Jeidels O (1905) Das Verhältnis der deutschen Groβbanken zur Industrie mit besonderer Berücksichtigung der Eisenindustrie. Duncker & Humblot, Leipzig

Krause D (2004) Die Commerz- und Disconto-Bank 1870–1920/23. Bankgeschichte als Systemgeschichte. Franz Steiner Verlag, Stuttgart,

Lampe W (2004) Der Bankbetrieb in Krieg und Inflation. Deutsche Groβbanken in den Jahren 1914 bis 1923, Franz Steiner Verlag, Stuttgart

Chapter 3
Interlocking Directorates of Bank's Supervisory Board and Managing Board Members in Other Enterprises During the Inflation Period After World War I

Abstract In Germany, industry–bank relationships built through various mechanisms, such as bank credit and securities businesses, shareholdings, and deposited stock systems, and the assignment of directors from banks to corporation boards were established during the shift to monopolistic capitalism in the early twentieth century. During inflation after World War I, studies have clarified that banks' influence on industrial enterprises in capital financing decreased. Moreover, industrial companies developed their businesses independently from banks because of the tremendous changes resulting from inflation. Can such a change be observed in personnel connections built through interlocking directorates of top management members of large banks on the supervisory boards of other enterprises? This chapter clarifies the actual conditions of the direct and indirect interlocking directorates of the three largest banks, namely Deutsche Bank, Dresdner Bank, and Commerzbank.

Keywords Bank control · Commerz- und Privat-Bank · Deutsche Bank · Dresdner Bank · Industry–bank relationship · Direct interlocking directorate · Indirect interlocking directorate · Personnel connection

This chapter analyzes personnel connections between a bank and enterprises in various industrial sectors through direct and indirect interlocking directorates of members of the supervisory and management boards of the three largest banks on the supervisory board of other enterprises during inflation after World War I. According to studies, the control and influence of banks on industrial enterprises tend to weaken because of the movement of industrial enterprises to escape from value in money to tangible assets, the change of fund demand of industrial enterprises, the structural change of corporate financing under strong inflation, and the tremendous loss of bank assets (Duschnitzky 1927; Hagemann 1931, SS. 20–21, 186; Krause 2004, S. 350; Lampe 2004, SS. 370, 372). Such an understanding is true for conditions of providing funds by banks to companies and corporate finance. However, the conditions of such personal relationships should be analyzed in detail regarding the personal connections between a bank and a corporation in diverse industries through direct interlocking directorates of top management of the three largest banks. This chapter considers

T. Yamazaki, *Relationships Between Industry and Bank in Germany*,
https://doi.org/10.1007/978-981-97-4996-6_3

how Deutsche Bank, Dresdner Bank, and Commerz- und Privat-Bank AG (below, Commerzbank) established personnel connections through interlocking directorates of members of the supervisory and management boards on the supervisory boards of other enterprises. Chapter 2 compares the situations during the shift to monopolistic capitalism. These discussions are complemented by studies on the conditions of the Nazi era in Chap. 4.

Therefore, this chapter considers the conditions of direct interlocking directorates of members of the supervisory and management boards of the three largest banks, namely Deutsche Bank, Dresdner Bank, and Commerzbank, on the supervisory boards of other enterprises and indirect interlocking directorates built among these three banks and between two of the banks. The fundamental material used in the analysis of this chapter is "*Adressbuch der Direktoren und Aufsichtsräte 1922*" (Finanzverlag, Berlin).

Section 3.1 examines the direct interlocking directorates of members of each bank's supervisory and management boards on the supervisory boards of other companies. Section 3.2 considers the indirect interlocking directorates built through direct interlocking directorates among three banks and between two banks.

3.1 Direct Interlocking Directorate of Members of Supervisory and Managing Boards of Banks on the Supervisory Board of Other Enterprises

3.1.1 Direct Interlocking Directorate of Members of Supervisory and Managing Boards of Deutsche Bank

First, in examining conditions of the direct interlocking directorate by members of the supervisory and management boards of Deutsche Bank on the supervisory board of other enterprises (see Table 3.1), such cases were observed in 456 companies, with 580 interlocking mandates. The number of enterprises and mandates was approximately 2.5 times that of Deutsche Bank at the beginning of the twentieth century in the shift to monopolistic capitalism (corresponding numbers 188 and 241, respectively) (Chap. 2).

Considering the distribution of industrial sectors, Deutsche Bank built direct interlocking directorates in 35 companies and had 47 interlocking mandates in the mining industry, and similarly, 26 and 35 in the iron and steel industry; 10 and 14 in the metal producing and processing industries; 34 and 40 in the chemical industry; 15 and 19 in the electrical industry; four and five in the automobile industry; 45 and 58 in the machine industry; four each in the precious machine and optical industries; five and six in the shipbuilding industry; six and seven in the oil industry; three each in the food industry; 16 each in the textile, spinning, and woven goods industries; 22 and 23 in the distillation industry; six and seven in the distributing industry; 45 and 79 in the banking industry; 32 and 40 in the insurance industry; 21 and 26 in the electric

Table 3.1 Direct interlocking directorates of the members of the supervisory board and the managing board of Deutsche Bank on the supervisory board of other companies (period of inflation after World War I)

Industries	Position							
	Chairman		Vice-chairman		Supervisory board member excluding chairman and vice-chairman		Total[a]	
	Number of companies	Number of posts	Number of companies	Number of posts	Number of companies	Number of posts	Number of companies	Number of posts
Mining	9	9	7	7	28	31	35	47
Iron and steel	6	6	5	5	20	24	26	35
Metal producing and processing	2	2	2	2	8	10	10	14
Chemical	9	9	3	3	25	28	34	40
Electrical	6	6	1	1	11	12	15	19
Automobile	3	3	–	–	2	2	4	5
Machine	13	13	10	10	26	35	45	58
Precious machine and optical	1	1	–	–	3	3	4	4
Shipbuilding	1	1	–	–	4	5	5	6
Oil	1	1	1	1	5	5	6	7
Food	2	2	–	–	1	1	3	3
Textile, spinning, and woven goods	5	5	2	2	9	9	16	16
Distillation	9	9	2	2	12	12	22	23
Distributing	3	3	1	1	3	3	6	7

(continued)

Table 3.1 (continued)

Industries	Position							
	Chairman		Vice-chairman		Supervisory board member excluding chairman and vice-chairman		Total[a]	
	Number of companies	Number of posts	Number of companies	Number of posts	Number of companies	Number of posts	Number of companies	Number of posts
Banking	17	17	4	4	34	58	45	79
Insurance	4	4	4	4	27	32	32	40
Electric power, gas, and energy	4	4	3	3	17	19	21	26
Transportation	12	13	2	2	28	34	38	49
Other industries	28	28	14	15	52	59	89	102
All industries	135	136	61	62	315	382	456	580

[a] There are cases in which the total number of companies establishing interlocking directorates differed from the total number of companies measured by each position of the supervisory board due to the existence of companies where interlocking directorates through more than two posts were built

Source This table was compiled by the author, based on Arends and Mossner (Hrsg) (1922)

power, gas, and energy industries; 38 and 49 in the transportation industry; and 89 and 102 in other industries, respectively. Among the various industries, except the banking and insurance sectors, for example, in Deutsch Bank, many interlocking relations existed in the mining, iron and steel, chemical, electrical, machine, and transportation industries. Therefore, Deutsche Bank had close and strong relationships with companies in the heavy and chemical industries, the key industrial sectors in Germany.

When considering the situation of interlocking directorates concerning supervisory board position mandates in 135 enterprises, in some cases, interlocking directorates on the supervisory boards of other companies were formed through the mandate of the chairman of the supervisory board, with 136 mandates. The number of enterprises and mandates was approximately two times that of Deutsche Bank at the beginning of the twentieth century (corresponding numbers 67 and 69, respectively). Considering the distribution among industrial sectors, the numbers of enterprises and mandates in which interlocking directorates were formed were nine each in the mining industry; similarly, six each in the iron and steel industry; two each in the metal producing and processing industries; nine each in the chemical industry; six each in the electrical industry; three each in the automobile industry; 13 each in the machine industry; one each in the precious machine and optical industries; one each in the shipbuilding industry; one each in the oil industry; two each in the food industry; five each in the textile, spinning, and woven goods industries; nine each in the distillation industry; three each in the distributing industry; 17 each in the banking industry; four each in the insurance industry; four each in the electric power, gas, and energy industries; 12 and 13 in the transportation industry, respectively; and 28 each in other industries. Cases of interlocking directorates in representative companies of each industry were observed in Mannesmannröhren-Werke in the iron and steel industry, Siemens & Halske AG and Siemens-Schuckertwerke GmbH in the electrical industry, Daimler Motoren-Gesellschaft in the automotive industry, Deutsche Petroleum-AG in the oil industry, and Deutsche Ueberseeische Bank and Deutsche Vereinsbank in the banking industry.

In 61 enterprises, in some cases, interlocking directorates on the supervisory boards of other companies were formed through the mandate of the vice-chairman of the supervisory board, with 62 mandates. The number of enterprises and mandates was three times that of Deutsche Bank at the beginning of the twentieth century (corresponding numbers 21 and 21, respectively). The numbers of enterprises and mandates in which such interlocking cases were formed were seven each in the mining industry; similarly, five each in the iron and steel industry; two each in the metal producing and processing industries; three each in the chemical industry; one each in the electrical industry; 10 each in the machine industry; one each in the oil industry; two each in the textile, spinning, and woven goods industries; two each in the distillation industry; one each in the distributing industry; four each in the banking industry; four each in the insurance industry; three each in the electric power, gas, and energy industries; two each in the transportation industry; and 14 and 15 in other industries, respectively.

Interlocking directorates through supervisory board mandates, except for the chairman and vice-chairman, were observed in 315 companies, and the total number of mandates was 382. The number of enterprises was approximately three times, and the number of mandates was more than two times that of Deutsche Bank at the beginning of the twentieth century (corresponding numbers 124 and 151, respectively). Considering the distribution among industrial sectors, the numbers of enterprises and mandates in which interlocking directorates were formed were 28 and 31 in the mining industry, respectively; similarly, 20 and 24 in the iron and steel industry; eight and 10 in the metal producing and processing industries; 25 and 28 in the chemical industry; 11 and 12 in the electrical industry; two each in the automobile industry; 26 and 35 in the machine industry; three each in the precious machine and optical industries; four and five in the shipbuilding industry; five each in the oil industry; one each in the food industry; nine each in the textile, spinning, and woven goods industries; 12 each in the distillation industry; three each in the distributing industry; 34 and 58 in the banking industry; 27 and 32 in the insurance industry; 17 and 19 in the electric power, gas, and energy industries; 28 and 34 in the transportation industry; and 52 and 59 in other industries, respectively. These companies included leading firms in each industry, such as Gelsenkirchener Bergwerks-AG and Harpener Bergbau AG in the mining industry; Gutehoffnungshütte, Actienverein für Bergbau und Hüttenbetrieb, Rheinische Stahlwerke, and Bochumer Verein für Bergbau und Guβstahlfabrikation in the iron and steel industry; BASF AG in the chemical industry; Siemens & Halske AG, Siemens-Schuckertwerke GmbH, and Brown, Boveri und Co., AG in the electrical industry; Borsig AG and Maschinenfabrik Ausburg-Nürnberg AG (MAN) in the machine industry; Deutsche Werft AG in the shipbuilding industry; Allianz Versicherungs-AG in the insurance industry, and Rheinisch-Westfälisches Electricitätswerk AG in the electric power, gas, and energy industries.

The numbers of enterprises and mandates were 83 and 207, respectively, when considering cases where members of the supervisory board and the board of directors of Deutsche Bank had more than two mandates on the supervisory boards of other companies (see Table 3.2). The number of enterprises and mandates was approximately two times that of Deutsche Bank at the beginning of the twentieth century (corresponding numbers 39 and 92, respectively). Considering the distribution among industries, the number of companies and mandates were as follows: nine and 21 in the mining industry; five and 14 in the iron and steel industry; three and seven in the metal producing and processing industries; six and 12 in the chemical industry; three and seven in the electrical industry; one and two in the automobile industry; nine and 22 in the machine industry; one and two in the shipbuilding industry; one and two in the oil industry; one and two in the distillation industry; one and two in the distributing industry; 15 and 49 in the banking industry; seven and 15 in the insurance industry; four and nine in the electric power, gas, and energy industries; six and 17 in the transportation industry; and 11 and 24 in other industries, respectively.

Of these 83 companies, direct interlocking directorates were built through more than three mandates in 24 enterprises, and the total number of mandates was 89. One, one, and three enterprises formed direct interlocking directorates through seven,

Table 3.2 Cases in which Deutsche Bank built direct interlocking directorates through more than two posts on the supervisory board of other companies (period of inflation after World War I)

Industries	Number of posts													
	2		3		4		5		6		7		Total	
	Number of companies	Number of posts	Number of companies	Number of posts	Number of companies	Number of posts	Number of companies	Number of posts	Number of companies	Number of posts	Number of companies	Number of posts	Number of companies	Number of posts
Mining	6	12	3	9	–	–	–	–	–	–	–	–	9	21
Iron and steel	3	6	1	3	–	–	1	5	–	–	–	–	5	14
metal producing and processing	2	4	1	3	–	–	–	–	–	–	–	–	3	7
Chemical	6	12	–	–	–	–	–	–	–	–	–	–	6	12
Electrical	2	4	1	3	–	–	–	–	–	–	–	–	3	7
Automobile	1	2	–	–	–	–	–	–	–	–	–	–	1	2
Machine	7	14	1	3	–	–	1	5	–	–	–	–	9	22
Shipbuilding	1	2	–	–	–	–	–	–	–	–	–	–	1	2
Oil	1	2	–	–	–	–	–	–	–	–	–	–	1	2
Distillation	1	2	–	–	–	–	–	–	–	–	–	–	1	2
Distributing	1	2	–	–	–	–	–	–	–	–	–	–	1	2
Banking	7	14	3	9	2	8	1	5	1	6	1	7	15	49
Insurance	6	12	1	3	–	–	–	–	–	–	–	–	7	15
Electric power, gas, and energy	3	6	1	3	–	–	–	–	–	–	–	–	4	9
Transportation	3	6	1	3	2	8	–	–	–	–	–	–	6	17

(continued)

Table 3.2 (continued)

Industries	Number of posts													
	2		3		4		5		6		7		Total	
	Number of companies	Number of posts	Number of companies	Number of posts	Number of companies	Number of posts	Number of companies	Number of posts	Number of companies	Number of posts	Number of companies	Number of posts	Number of companies	Number of posts
Other Industries	9	18	2	6	–	–	–	–	–	–	–	–	11	24
All industries	58	118	15	45	4	16	3	15	1	6	1	7	83	207

Source This table was compiled by the author, based on Arends and Mossner (Hrsg) (1922)

six, and five mandates, respectively. Such interlocking directorates were established through four and three mandates in four and 15 cases, respectively. In the remaining 59 companies, Deutsche Bank had two mandates on the supervisory board of other companies.

Considering these interlocking directorates concerning the type of mandate, in Deutsche Ueberseeische Bank in the banking industry, Deutsche Bank built interlocking directorates through seven mandates consisting of one each of chairman and vice-chairman and five posts of the supervisory board except for chairman and vice-chairman. In Deutsche Hypothekenbank (Meiningen) in the banking industry, interlocking directorates were built through six mandates of the supervisory board, except for the chairman and vice-chairman. Regarding enterprises with five mandates, in Mannesmannröhren-Werke in the iron and steel industry, interlocking directorates were built through one each of the chairman and vice-chairman and three posts of the supervisory board excluding the chairman and vice-chairman. Then, in Deutsche Maschinenfabrik AG in the machine industry, interlocking directorates were formed through a mandate of the chairman and four mandates of the supervisory board except for the chairman and vice-chairman. From another aspect, in Württembergische Vereinsbank in the banking industry, Deutsche Bank had five posts on the supervisory board, excluding the chairman and vice-chairman. Concerning companies with four mandates, in Gesellschaft für elektrische Hoch- und Untergrundbahnen in the transportation industry, interlocking directorates were established through two mandates of chairman and two posts of the supervisory board except for the chairman and vice-chairman. In Deutsche Vereinsbank, Hildesheimer Bank in the banking industry, and Mitteleuropäische Schlafwagen- und Speisewagen-AG in the transportation industry, interlocking directorates were formed through a post of the chairman and three mandates of the supervisory board except for the chairman and vice-chairman.

Regarding 15 enterprises with three mandates, in Deutsche Treuhandgesellschaft in other industries, interlocking directorates were built through a mandate of the chairman and two posts of the vice-chairman. In Rheinische AG für Braunkohlenbergbau und Brikettfabrikation in the mining industry, interlocking directorates were built through one each of the chairman and vice-chairman and one post of the supervisory board excluding the chairman and vice-chairman. In six enterprises, Deutsche Bank established an interlocking directorate through a mandate of the chairman and two posts of the supervisory board, except for the chairman and vice-chairman: Bergwerks-AG Consolidation in the mining industry; Hirsch Kupfer und Messingwerke AG in the metal producing and processing industry; Elektrische Licht- und Kraftanlagen AG in the electrical industry; Preußische Hypotheken-Actien-Bank in the banking industry; Kronos Deutsche Lebensversicherungs-AG in the insurance industry; and Rheinisches Elektricitätswerk im Braunkohlenrevier AG in the electric power, gas, and energy industries. In three enterprises, namely Niederlausitzer Kohlenwerke in the mining industry, Kattowitzer AG für Bergbau und Hüttenbetrieb in the iron and steel industry, and Allgemeine Berliner Omnibus-AG in the transportation industry, interlocking directorates were established through one mandate of the vice-chairman and a post of the supervisory board, except for the chairman and vice-chairman. In four companies, interlocking directorates were built through three mandates of the supervisory board, excluding the chairman and vice-chairman, that is, Amme, Giesecke, und Konegen AG in the machine industry, Westdeutsche Bodencreditanstalt and Essener Credit-Anstalt in the banking industry, and Reichsanleihe AG in other industries.

When considering 59 enterprises with two mandates on the supervisory board of other enterprises concerning the distribution of the industrial sector, six were in the mining industry; three in the iron and steel industry; two in the metal producing and processing industries; six in the chemical industry; two in the electrical industry; one in the automobile industry; seven in the machine industry; one in the shipbuilding industry; one in the oil industry; one in the distillation industry; one in the distributing industry; seven in the banking industry; six in the insurance industry; three in the electric power, gas, and energy industries; three in the transportation industry; and nine in other industries.

Considering these interlocking directorates with respect to supervisory board position mandates, in Braunkohlen- und Brikett-Industrie AG in the mining industry, "Kronprinz" AG für Metallindustrie in the metal producing and processing industries, and Bayer Stickstoff-Werke AG in the chemical industry, interlocking directorates were built through two mandates consisting of the chairman and vice-chairman. Cases in which interlocking directorates were formed through the mandate of a chairman and one post of the supervisory board, except for the chairman and vice-chairman, can be observed in 25 enterprises. These enterprises were Braunkohlen- und Brikettwerk Berggeist und Brikettwerk BerggeistAG and Clarenberg AG für Kohlen- und Ton-Industrie in the mining industry; Baroper Walzwerk AG and Rheinisch-Nassauische Bergwerks- und Hütten-AG in the iron and steel industry; Deutsche Südseephosphat AG and J. D. Riedel AG in the chemical industry; Siemens & Halske AG and Siemens-Schuckertwerke GmbH in the electrical industry; Daimler Motoren-Gesellschaft in the automobile industry; Maschinenfabrik Eβlingen and Eisenbahn-Verkehrsmittel AG in the machine industry; Deutsche Petroleum-AG in the oil industry; Hermes AG in the distributing industry; Düsseldorfer Baubank, Bergisch-Märkische Industrie-Gesellschaft, Mecklenburgische Depositen- und Wechselbank, Preussische Boden-Credit-Actien-Bank, and Rheinische Creditbank in the banking industry; Mannheimer Versicherungs-Gesellschaft in the insurance industry; Bergmann-Elektrizitätswerke AG in the electric power, gas, and energy industries; Santa Catharina Eisenbahn-AG in the transportation industry; and Zuckerfabrik Stuttgart, Tempelhofer-Feld-AG für Grundstückverwertung, Universum-Film AG, and Bodengesellschaft am Hochbahnhof Schönhauser Allee AG in other industries. In some enterprises, interlocking directorates that were formed through a mandate of the vice-chairman and one post of the supervisory board excluding the chairman and vice-chairman were six, namely AG Deutsche Kaliwerke and Preuβengrube, AG in the mining industry; Maschinenfabrik Baum AG in the machine industry; Brauereigesellschaft zur Sonne vorm. H. Weltz in the distillation industry, Düssel- dorfer Allgemeine Versicherungs-AG in the insurance industry; and Deutsche Continental-Gas-Gesellschaft in the electric power, gas, and energy industries. The number of interlocking directorates established through two mandates of the supervisory board, except for the chairman and vice-chairman, was 25. The cases were Gelsenkirchener Bergwerks-AG in the mining industry; Deutsch-Luxemburgische Bergwerks- und Hütten-AG in the iron and steel industry; Fritz Neumeyer AG in the metal producing and processing industries; Rütgerwerke AG, Franz Clouth Rheinische Gummiwarenfabrik AG, and Oberschlesische Kokswerke und Chemisch Fabriken AG in the chemische industry; Berlin-Anhaltische Maschinenbau AG, MAN, R. Stock & Co., Spiralbohrer-, Werkzeug- und Maschinenfabrik, and F. Küppersbusch und Söhne AG in the machine industry; Deutsche Werft AG in the shipbuilding industry; Deutsche Orientbank and Rheinisch-Schlesische Versicherungs-Bank, AG in the banking industry; Indemnitas, Versicherungs-AG, "Vaterländische" und "Rhenania" Vereinigte Versicherungs-Gesellschaft AG, Allianz Versicherungs-AG, and Union, Allgemeine Versicherungs-AG in the insurance industry; Rhein-Main-Donau AG in the electric power, gas, and energy industries; Norddeutscher Lloyd and Hamburg-Amerikanische Packetfahrt-AG (Hamburg-Amerika Linie) in the transportation industry; and Wayβ und Freytag, AG, AG für Erwerb und Verwaltung von Industrie- und Hafen-geländen, Philipp Holzmann AG, Stettiner Chamotte-Fabrik vorm. Didier, Hamburger Freihafen, Lagerhaus-Gesellschaft in other industries.

Thus, Deutsche Bank's direct interlocking directorates on the supervisory boards of other enterprises spread over a wide range of industries and had personnel connections with several competitive companies in the same industrial sector through several supervisory board mandates. Such cases can be observed, for instance, in Gelsenkirchener Bergwerks-AG and Harpener Bergbau AG in the mining industry and Mannesmannröhren-Werke, Gutehoffnungshütte, Actienverein für Bergbau und Hüttenbetrieb, Rheinische Stahlwerke, Bochumer Verein für Bergbau und Guβstahlfabrikation, and "Phoenix" AG für Bergbau- und Hüttenbetrieb in the iron and steel industry. Similar cases were also observed in BASF AG and Vereinigte Glanzstofffabriken AG in the chemical industry; Siemens & Halske AG, Siemens-Schuckertwerke GmbH, and Brown, Boveri und Co., AG in the electrical industry; Daimler Motoren-Gesellschaft and Benz & Cie., in the automobile industry; and MAN, Borsig AG, and Linke-Hofmann-Werke AG in the machine industry.

Deutsche Bank established close and strong personnel connections with many companies in various industries through direct interlocking directorates of members of the supervisory and management boards, which significantly contributed to securing much information for its own financial business and policy decisions over industrial enterprises.

3.1.2 Direct Interlocking Directorate of Members of Supervisory Board and Managing Board of Dresdner Bank

Direct interlocking directorates by the supervisory and management board members of Dresdner Bank on the supervisory board of other enterprises (see Table 3.3) were observed in 381 companies and 453 interlocking mandates. The number of enterprises and mandate was much more than that of Dresdner Bank at the beginning of the twentieth century in the shift to monopolistic capitalism (corresponding numbers 224 and 321, respectively) (Chap. 2). However, the number of enterprises in which Dresdner Bank built interlocking directorates and interlocking mandates was fewer than that of Deutsche Bank in the period of inflation after World War I (corresponding numbers 456 and 580, respectively).

Regarding the distribution of industrial sectors, Dresdner Bank developed direct interlocking directorates in 24 companies and 27 interlocking mandates in the mining industry, and similarly, 27 and 35 in the iron and steel industry; 16 and 22 in the metal producing and processing industries; 22 and 25 in the chemical industry; 15 and 20 in the electrical industry; five and six in the automobile industry; 34 and 40 in the machine industry; two each in the precious machine and optical industries; one each in the shipbuilding industry; three and five in the oil industry; four and five in the food industry; 27 and 29 in the textile, spinning, and woven goods industries; three each in the distillation industry; eight each in the distributing industry; 35 and 49 in the banking industry; 22 and 25 in the insurance industry; 21 and 25 in the electric power, gas, and energy industries; 30 and 37 in the transportation industry; and 82 and 89 in other industries, respectively. Among the various industries, except for the banking and insurance industries, for example, many interlocking relationships exist in the mining; iron and steel; chemical; machine; textile, spinning, and woven goods; electric power; gas; energy; and transportation industries. Therefore, Dresdner Bank had close and strong relationships with companies in key industrial sectors in Germany, such as the heavy and chemical industries.

Given the situation of interlocking directorates concerning supervisory board position mandates, Dresdner Bank built interlocking directorates through the mandate of the honorary chairman of the supervisory board in one company. Such a case was Deutsche Orientbank AG in the banking industry.

In 87 enterprises, in some cases, interlocking directorates on the supervisory boards of other companies were formed through the mandate of the chairman of the supervisory board, with 87 mandates. In each company, the number of mandates was one. The number of enterprises and mandates was fewer than that of Deutsche Bank (corresponding numbers 135 and 136, respectively). However, the number of enterprises and mandates was higher than that of Dresdner Bank at the beginning of the twentieth century (corresponding numbers 59 and 59, respectively). Considering the distribution among industrial sectors, the number of enterprises in which Dresdner Bank formed an interlocking directorate was four in the mining industry; similarly, five in the iron and steel industry; three in the metal producing and processing industries; seven in the chemical industry; two in the electrical industry; one in the automobile industry; 11 in the machine industry; one in the shipbuilding industry; two in the food industry; 10 in the textile, spinning, and woven goods industries; one in the distributing industry; nine in the banking industry; two in the insurance industry; one in the electric power, gas, and energy industries; six in the transportation industry; and 22 in other industries. Cases of interlocking directorates in representative companies of each industry were observed in Siemens &

Table 3.3 Direct interlocking directorates of the members of the supervisory board and the managing board of Dresdner Bank on the supervisory board of other companies (period of inflation after World War I)

Industries	Position									
	Honorary Chairman		Chairman		Vice-chairman		Supervisory board member excluding chairman and vice-chairman		Total[a]	
	Number of companies	Number of posts	Number of companies	Number of posts	Number of companies	Number of posts	Number of companies	Number of posts	Number of companies	Number of posts
Mining	–	–	4	4	3	3	18	20	24	27
Iron and steel	–	–	5	5	4	5	21	25	27	35
Metal producing and processing	–	–	3	3	2	2	13	17	16	22
Chemical	–	–	7	7	2	2	16	16	22	25
Electrical	–	–	2	2	2	2	12	16	15	20
Automobile	–	–	1	1	1	1	4	4	5	6
Machine	–	–	11	11	7	7	20	22	34	40
Precious machine and optical	–	–	–	–	–	–	2	2	2	2
Shipbuilding	–	–	1	1	–	–	–	–	1	1
Oil	–	–	–	–	–	–	3	5	3	5
Food	–	–	2	2	1	1	2	2	4	5
Textile and spinning	–	–	10	10	1	1	17	18	27	29

(continued)

Table 3.3 (continued)

Industries	Position									
	Honorary Chairman		Chairman		Vice-chairman		Supervisory board member excluding chairman and vice-chairman		Total[a]	
	Number of companies	Number of posts	Number of companies	Number of posts	Number of companies	Number of posts	Number of companies	Number of posts	Number of companies	Number of posts
Distillation	–	–	–	–	1	1	2	2	3	3
Distributing	–	–	1	1	2	2	5	5	8	8
Banking	1	1	9	9	8	8	29	31	35	49
Insurance	–	–	2	2	3	3	19	20	22	25
Electric power, gas, and energy	–	–	1	1	4	4	18	20	21	25
Transportation	–	–	6	6	5	5	24	26	30	37
Other industries	–	–	22	22	13	13	52	54	82	89
All industries	1	1	87	87	59	60	277	305	381	453

[a] There are cases in which the total number of companies establishing interlocking directorates differed from the total number of companies measured by each position of the supervisory board due to the existence of companies where interlocking directorates through more than two posts were built

Source This table was compiled by the author, based on Arends and Mossner (Hrsg) (1922)

Halske AG and Siemens-Schuckertwerke GmbH in the electrical industry, Daimler Motoren-Gesellschaft in the automotive industry, and Deutsche Petroleum-AG in the oil industry.

In 59 enterprises, in some cases, interlocking directorates were formed through the mandate of the vice-chairman of the supervisory board, and the total number of mandates was 60. The number of enterprises and mandates was higher than that of Dresdner Bank at the beginning of the twentieth century (corresponding numbers 41 and 42, respectively) and was almost the same as that of Deutsche Bank in the inflationary period after World War I (corresponding numbers 61 and 62, respectively). The numbers of enterprises and mandates in which such interlocking cases were formed were three each in the mining industry; similarly, four and five in the iron and steel industry, respectively; two each in the metal producing and processing industries; two each in the chemical industry; two each in the electrical industry; one each in the automobile industry; seven each in the machine industry; one each in the food industry; one each in the textile, spinning, and woven goods industries; one each in the distillation industry; two each in the distributing industry; eight each in the banking industry; three each in the insurance industry; four each in the electric power, gas, and energy industries; five each in the transportation industry; and 13 each in other industries. Each industry has major companies, such as Gelsenkirchener Bergwerks-AG in the mining industry and Allianz Versicherungs-AG in the insurance industry.

Interlocking directorates through supervisory board mandates, except for the chairman and vice-chairman, were observed in 277 companies, and the total number of mandates was 305. The number of enterprises and mandates was much higher than that of Dresdner Bank at the beginning of the twentieth century (corresponding numbers 165 and 220, respectively). However, the number of enterprises and mandates was slightly less than that of Deutsche Bank in the inflationary period after World War I (corresponding numbers 315 and 382, respectively). The numbers of enterprises and mandates in which Dresdner Bank built interlocking directorates were formed were 18 and 20 in the mining industry, respectively; similarly, 21 and 25 in the iron and steel industry; 13 and 17 in the metal producing and processing industries; 16 each in the chemical industry; 12 and 16 in the electrical industry; four each in the automobile industry; 20 and 22 in the machine industry; two each in the precious machine and optical industries; three and five in the oil industry; two each in the food industry; 17 and 18 in the textile, spinning, and woven goods industries; two each in the distillation industry; five each in the distributing industry; 29 and 31 in the banking industry; 19 and 20 in the insurance industry; 18 and 20 in the electric power, gas, and energy industries; 24 and 26 in the transportation industry; and 52 and 54 in other industries, respectively. Each industry has major companies, such as Gelsenkirchener Bergwerks-AG and Harpener Bergbau AG in the mining industry; Rheinische Stahlwerke and Phoenix, AG für Bergwerks- und Hüttenbetrieb in the iron and steel industry; AEG and Siemens & Halske AG in the electrical industry; Bayerische Motoren-Werke AG (BMW) in the automobile industry; Ludwig Loewe & Co. AG and MAN in the machine industry; Deutsche Erdöl-AG in the oil industry; Münchener Rückversicherungs-Gesellschaft in the insurance industry; and Rheinisch-Westfälisches Elektricitätswerk AG in the electric power, gas, and energy industries.

The numbers of enterprises and mandates were 58 and 130, respectively, when considering cases in which the member of the supervisory board and board of directors of Dresdner Bank had more than two mandates on the supervisory boards of other companies (see Table 3.4). The number of enterprises and mandates was less than that of Deutsche Bank (corresponding numbers 83 and 207, respectively). It was slightly less than that of Dresdner Bank at the beginning of the twentieth century (corresponding numbers 62 and 159, respectively). Considering the distribution among industries, the numbers of companies and mandates were as follows: two and five in the mining industry; four and 12 in the iron and steel industry; four and 10 in the metal producing and processing industries; three and six in the chemical industry; three and eight in the electrical industry; one and two in the automobile industry; six and 12 in the machine industry; two and four in the oil industry; one and two in the food industry; two and four in the textile, spinning, and woven goods industries; 11 and 25 in the banking industry; two and five in the insurance industry; four and eight in the electric power, gas, and energy industries; seven and 14 in the transportation industry; and six and 13 in other industries, respectively. Of these enterprises, each industry has representative companies, such as Gelsenkirchener Bergwerks-AG in the mining industry, AEG in the electrical industry, Ludwig Loewe & Co. AG in the machine industry, and Deutsche Erdöl-AG in the oil industry.

Of these 58 companies, direct interlocking directorates were built through more than three mandates in 12 enterprises, and the total number of mandates was 38. The number of enterprises and mandates was much fewer than that of Deutsche Bank (corresponding numbers 24 and 89, respectively). It was almost half of that of Dresdner Bank at the beginning of the twentieth century (corresponding numbers 22 and 79, respectively). Direct interlocking directorates were formed through four mandates in two enterprises. Then, such interlocking directorates were established through three mandates in 10 cases. In the remaining 46 companies, Dresdner Bank had two mandates on the supervisory board of other companies.

Concerning enterprises with four mandates, in AG Lauchhammer in the iron and steel industry, interlocking directorates were built through two mandates of the vice-chairman and two posts of the supervisory board, except for the chairman and vice-chairman. Then, in AEG in the electrical industry, interlocking directorates were formed through four mandates of the supervisory boards except for the chairman and vice-chairman. Regarding companies with three mandates, in Deutsche Südamerikanische Bank in the banking industry and Aachener und Münchener Feuer-Versicherungs-Gesellschaft in the insurance industry, interlocking directorates were built through one each of the mandate of the chairman and vice-chairman and one post of the supervisory board, excluding the chairman and vice-chairman. Interlocking directorates were formed through the chairman's mandate and two supervisory board mandates, except for the chairman and vice-chairman in five companies: Hrzogliche Eisen- und Emaillier-Werke AG and Deutsche Waffen- und Munitions-Fabriken in the metal producing and processing industries; Sächsische Bodencreditanstalt

Table 3.4 Cases in which Dresdner Bank built direct interlocking directorates through more than two posts on the supervisory board of other companies (period of inflation after World War I)

Industries	Number of posts							
	2		3		4		Total	
	Number of companies	Number of posts	Number of companies	Number of posts	Number of companies	Number of posts	Number of companies	Number of posts
Mining	1	2	1	3	–	–	2	5
Iron and steel	1	2	2	6	1	4	4	12
Metal producing and processing	2	4	2	6	–	–	4	10
Chemical	3	6	–	–	–	–	3	6
Electrical	2	4	–	–	1	4	3	8
Automobile	1	2	–	–	–	–	1	2
Machine	6	12	–	–	–	–	6	12
Oil	2	4	–	–	–	–	2	4
Food	1	2	–	–	–	–	1	2
Textile, spinning, and woven goods	2	4	–	–	–	–	2	4
Banking	8	16	3	9	–	–	11	25
Insurance	1	2	1	3	–	–	2	5
Electric power, gas, and energy	4	8	–	–	–	–	4	8
Transportation	7	14	–	–	–	–	7	14
Other industries	5	10	1	3	–	–	6	13
All industries	46	92	10	30	2	8	58	130

Source This table was compiled by the author, based on Arends and Mossner (Hrsg) (1922)

and Deutsche Grundcreditbank in the banking industry; and Berlinische Boden-Gesellschaft in other industries. In Gelsenkirchener Bergwerks-AG in the mining industry and Vereinigte Königs- und Laurahütte AG für Bergbau und Hüttenbetrieb in the iron and steel industry, interlocking directorates were established through one post of the vice-chairman and two mandates of the supervisory board, except for the chairman and vice-chairman. From another aspect, in Deutsch-Luxemburgische Bergwerks- und Hütten-AG in the iron and steel industry, interlocking directorates were built through three posts of the supervisory board, except for the chairman and vice-chairman.

When considering 46 enterprises with two mandates on the supervisory board of other enterprises concerning distribution of the industrial sector, there was one in the mining industry; one in the iron and steel industry; two in the metal producing and processing industries; three in the chemical industry; two in the electrical industry; one in the automobile industry; six in the machine industry; two in the oil industry; one in the food industry; two in the textile, spinning, and woven goods industries; eight in the banking industry; one in the insurance industry; four in the electric power, gas, and energy industries; seven in the transportation industry, and five in other industries.

Considering these interlocking directorates concerning the type of mandate, in Deutsche Orientbank AG in the banking industry, interlocking directorates were built through a mandate of honoring the chairman and one post of the supervisory board, except for the chairman and vice-chairman. In Sarotti-AG in the food industry and Eisenbahn-Bank in the banking industry, interlocking directorates were formed through one each of the directorates of chairman and vice-chairman. Interlocking directorates were established through one post of chairman and a mandate of the supervisory board except for chairman and vice-chairman in 15 enterprises: Berlin-Burger Eisenwerk AG in the iron and steel industry; Gehe und Co., AG in the chemical industry; Vereinigte Isolatorenwerke AG in the electrical industry; Düsseldorfer Eisenbahnbedarf vorm. Carl Weyer & Co, Wanderer-Werke vorm. Winklhofer und Jaenicke, AG, Max Hasse und Comp. AG, and Orenstein und Koppel, AG (Orenstein und Koppel–Arthur Koppel, AG) in the machine industry; Kammgarnwerke AG in the textile, spinning, and woven goods industries; Preuβische Pfandbrief-bank, Dürener Bank, and Berliner Bodencredit-AG in the banking industry; Lausitzer Eisenbahngesellschaft and Rhein- und Seeschifffahrts-Gesellschaft in the transportation industry; and Gemeinnützige Baugesellschaft and Treuhand-Vereinigung AG in other industries. Interlocking directorates were built through a mandate of the vice-chairman and one post of the supervisory board, excluding the chairman and vice-chairman in 13 enterprises. Such cases include Dr. Hugo Remmler AG and AG Lignose in the chemical industry; Nationale Automobil-Gesellshaft in the automobile industry; Landgräflich Hessische concessionierte Landesbank, Mecklenburgische Bank, and Oldenburgische Landesbank in the banking industry; Deutsche Elektricitätswerke Garbe, Lahmeyer & Co. AG, and Elektricitätswerk Südwest in the electric power, gas, and energy industries; Schantung-Eisenbahn-Gesellschaft, AG für Bahn-Bau und -Betrieb, and Mitteleuropäische Schlafwagen- und Speisewagen-AG in the transportation industry; and Tempelhofer Feld-AG für Grundstückverwertung and Schmargendorfer Boden-AG in other industries. Cases in which Dresdner Bank had two supervisory board mandates, except for the chairman and vice-chairman, can be observed in 15 companies. Such enterprises included Vereinigte Kohlen-AG in the mining industry, F. Butzke und Co., AG für Metallindustrie and Westfälische Metallindustrie AG in the metal producing and processing industries; Dr. Cassirer und Co. AG in the electrical industry; AG vorm. Seidel und Naumann and Ludwig Loewe & Co. AG in the machine industry; Deutsche Erdöl-AG and Internationale Petroleum-Union in the oil industry; Vereinigte Strohstoff-Fabriken in the textile, spinning, and woven goods industries; Sächsisch-Türingische Versicherungs-AG in the insurance industry; Schlesische Elektricitäts- und Gas-Gesellschaft and Rheinische Elektrizitäts- und Kleinbahnen-AG in the electric power, gas, and energy industries; Aachener Kleinbahn-Gesellschaft and Santa Catharina Eisenbahn-AG in the transportation industry; and Terrain-AG Park Witzleben in other industries.

Thus, Dresdner Bank's direct interlocking directorates on the supervisory boards of other enterprises were spread over a wide range of industries and had personnel connections with several competitive companies in the same industrial sector through several supervisory board mandates. Such cases can be observed, for example, in Gelsenkirchener Bergwerks-AG and Harpener Bergbau AG in the mining industry; Rheinische Stahlwerke, Bochmer Verein für Bergbau und Gusstahlfabrikation, and Phoenix, AG für Bergwerks- und Hüttenbetrieb in the iron and steel industry; Siemens & Halske AG and AEG in the electrical industry; and MAN and Ludwig Loewe & Co. AG in the machine industry. Dresdner Bank established close and strong personnel connections with many companies in various industries through direct interlocking directorates of members of the supervisory and management boards, which played a significant role in securing much information for its own financial business and in deciding policies over industrial enterprises.

3.1.3 Direct Interlocking Directorate of Members of Supervisory Board and Managing Board of Commerzbank

Furthermore, in examining the conditions of the direct interlocking directorate by members of the supervisory and management boards of Commerzbank on the supervisory board of other enterprises (see Table 3.5), such cases were observed in 368 companies, with 431 interlocking mandates. The number of enterprises and mandates was much greater than that of Commerzbank at the beginning of the twentieth century in the shift to monopolistic capitalism (corresponding numbers 80 and 96, respectively) (Chap. 2). The number of enterprises and mandates was less than that of Deutsche Bank in the inflation period after World War I (corresponding numbers 456 and 580, respectively) and almost the same as those of Dresdner Bank in the same period (corresponding numbers 381 and 453, respectively).

Table 3.5 Direct interlocking directorates of the members of the supervisory board and the managing board of Commerzbank on the supervisory board of other companies (period of inflation after World War I)

Industries	Position							
	Chairman		Vice-chairman		Supervisory board member excluding chairman and vice-chairman		Total[a]	
	Number of companies	Number of posts	Number of companies	Number of posts	Number of companies	Number of posts	Number of companies	Number of posts
Mining	3	3	2	2	17	17	20	22
Iron and steel	3	4	4	4	14	15	19	23
Metal producing and processing	7	7	–	–	5	5	12	12
Chemical	3	3	3	3	13	14	18	20
Electrical	9	9	1	1	11	11	19	21
Automobile	2	2	1	1	4	5	6	8
Machine	13	13	5	5	24	30	37	48
Precious machine and optical	–	–	–	–	1	1	1	1
Shipbuilding	–	–	–	–	4	4	4	4
Oil	–	–	–	–	4	4	4	4
Food	1	1	–	–	1	1	2	2
Textile, spinning, and woven goods	14	14	2	2	26	29	42	45
Distillation	7	7	3	3	18	21	24	31
Distributing	2	2	–	–	5	5	7	7

(continued)

Table 3.5 (continued)

Industries	Position							
	Chairman		Vice-chairman		Supervisory board member excluding chairman and vice-chairman		Total[a]	
	Number of companies	Number of posts	Number of companies	Number of posts	Number of companies	Number of posts	Number of companies	Number of posts
Banking	6	6	1	1	21	29	23	36
Insurance	1	1	4	4	7	7	12	12
Electric power, gas, and energy	2	2	2	2	8	9	10	13
Transportation	2	2	1	1	12	12	13	15
Other industries	30	31	15	15	56	61	95	107
All industries	105	107	44	44	251	280	368	431

[a] There are cases in which the total number of companies establishing interlocking directorates differed from the total number of companies measured by each position of the supervisory board due to the existence of companies where interlocking directorates through more than two posts were built

Source This table was compiled by the author, based on Arends and Mossner (Hrsg) (1922)

Considering the distribution of industrial sectors, Commerzbank built direct interlocking directorates in 20 companies and had 22 interlocking mandates in the mining industry; similarly, 19 and 23 in the iron and steel industry; 12 each in the metal producing and processing industries; 18 and 20 in the chemical industry; 19 and 21 in the electrical industry; six and eight in the automobile industry; 37 and 48 in the machine industry; one each in the precious machine and optical industries; four each in the shipbuilding industry; four each in the oil industry; two each in the food industry; 42 and 45 in the textile, spinning, and woven goods industries; 24 and 31 in the distillation industry; seven each in the distributing industry; 23 and 36 in the banking industry; 12 each in the insurance industry; 10 and 13 in the electric power, gas, and energy industries; 13 and 15 in the transportation industry; and 95 and 107 in other industries, respectively. Commerzbank had close and strong relationships with companies in the heavy and chemical industries and the mining industry, which are key industrial sectors in Germany. Many interlocking directorates existed in industrial sectors, such as the textile, spinning, and woven goods industry; the banking industry; the insurance industry; and the electric power, gas, and energy industries.

Given the situation of interlocking directorates concerning the position of the mandate of the supervisory board, in 105 enterprises, in some cases, interlocking directorates on the supervisory boards of other companies were formed through the mandate of the chairman of the supervisory board with 107 mandates. The number of enterprises and mandates was much greater than those of Commerzbank at the beginning of the twentieth century (corresponding numbers 25 and 25, respectively). The number of enterprises and mandates was fewer than that of Deutsche Bank in the period of inflation after World War I (corresponding numbers 135 and 136, respectively). It was more than that of Dresdner Bank in the same period (corresponding numbers 87 and 87, respectively). Considering the distribution among industrial sectors, the numbers of enterprises and mandates in which Commerzbank formed interlocking directorates were three each in the mining industry; similarly, three and four in the iron and steel industry; seven each in the metal producing and processing industries; three each in the chemical industry; nine each in the electrical industry; two each in the automobile industry; 13 each in the machine industry; one each in the food industry; 14 in the textile, spinning, and woven goods industries; seven each in the distillation industry; two each in the distributing industry; six each in the banking industry; one each in the insurance industry; two each in the electric power, gas, and energy industries; two each in the transportation industry; and 30 and 31 in other industries, respectively.

In 44 enterprises, interlocking directorates were formed through the mandate of the vice-chairman of the supervisory board, and the total number of mandates was 44. In each company, the number of mandates was one. The number of enterprises and mandates was much more than that of Commerzbank at the beginning of the twentieth century (corresponding numbers five and five, respectively) and was fewer than that of Deutsche Bank in the inflationary period after World War I (corresponding numbers 61 and 62, respectively) and those of Dresdner Bank in the same period (corresponding numbers 59 and 60, respectively). The numbers of enterprises and mandates in which such interlocking cases were developed were two each in the mining industry; similarly, four each in the iron and steel industry; three each in the chemical industry; one each in the electric industry; one each in the automobile industry; five each in the machine industry; two each in the textile, spinning, and woven goods industries; three each in the distillation industry; one each in the banking industry; four each in the insurance industry; two each in the electric power, gas, and energy industries; one each in the transportation industry; and 15 each in other industries. Each industry had major companies, such as Gelsenkirchener Bergwerks-AG in the mining industry and Allianz Versicherungs-AG in the insurance industry.

Interlocking directorates through mandates of supervisory boards, except for the chairman and vice-chairman, were observed in 251 companies, and the total number of mandates was 280. The number of enterprises and mandates was more than four times that of Commerzbank at the beginning of the twentieth century (corresponding numbers 56 and 66, respectively). However, the number of enterprises and mandates was fewer than those of Deutsche Bank in the inflationary period after World War I (corresponding numbers 315 and 382, respectively). It was slightly less than that of Dresdner Bank in the same period (corresponding numbers 277 and 305, respectively). The numbers of enterprises and mandates in which Commerzbank built interlocking directorates were formed were 17 each in the mining industry; similarly, 14 and 15 in the iron and steel industry; five each in the metal producing and processing industries; 13 and 14 in the chemical industry; 11 each in the electrical industry; four and five in the automobile industry; 24 and 30 in the machine industry; one each in the precious machine and optical industries; four each in the shipbuilding industry; four each in the oil industry; one each in the food industry; 26 and 29 in the textile, spinning, and woven goods industries; 18 and 21 in the distillation industry; five each in the distributing industry; 21 and 29 in the banking industry; seven each in the insurance industry; eight and nine in the electric power, gas, and energy industries; 12 each in the transportation industry; and 56 and 61 in other industries, respectively. Each industry has major companies, such as Gelsenkirchener Bergwerks-AG in the mining industry; Rheinsiche Stahlwerke in the iron and steel industry; AEG and Siemens-Schuckertwerke GmbH in the electrical industry; Horchwerke AG in the automotive industry; Howaldtswerke in the shipbuilding industry; and Deutsche Petroleum-AG in the oil industry, and Allianz Versicherungs-AG in the insurance industry.

The numbers of enterprises and mandates were 52 and 115, respectively, when considering cases where members of the supervisory board and board of directors of Commerzbank had more than two mandates on the supervisory boards of other companies (Table 3.6). The number of enterprises and mandates was almost four times that of Commerzbank at the beginning of the twentieth century (corresponding numbers 12 and 28, respectively). The number of enterprises and mandates was fewer than that of Deutsche Bank in the inflation period after World War I (corresponding numbers 83 and 207, respectively). It was almost the same as that of Dresdner Bank in the same period (corresponding numbers 58 and 130, respectively). Regarding the distribution among industries, the numbers of companies and mandates were as follows: two and four in the mining industry; four and eight in the iron and steel industry; two and four in the chemical industry; two and four in the electrical industry;

two and four in the automobile industry; 10 and 21 in the machine industry; three and six in the textile, spinning, and woven goods industries; six and 13 in the distillation industry; seven and 20 in the banking industry; two and five in the electric power, gas, and energy industries; two and four in the transportation industry; and 10 and 22 in other industries, respectively.

Of these 52 companies, direct interlocking directorates were built through more than three mandates in nine enterprises, and the total number of mandates was 29. The number of enterprises and mandates was more than that of Commerzbank at the beginning of the twentieth century (corresponding numbers four and 12, respectively) and much less than that of Deutsche Bank in the period of inflation after World War I (corresponding numbers 24 and 89, respectively) and was less than that of Dresdner Bank in the same period (corresponding numbers 12 and 38, respectively). In two enterprises, direct interlocking directorates were formed through four mandates. In seven cases, such interlocking directorates were established through three mandates. In the remaining 43 companies, Commerzbank had two mandates on the supervisory board of other companies.

Regarding enterprises with four mandates, in Chemnitzer Bank-Verein in the banking industry, interlocking directorates were built through a mandate of the chairman and three posts of the supervisory board except for the chairman and vice-chairman. Then, in Löbauer Bank in the banking industry, interlocking directorates were formed through four mandates of the supervisory board excluding the chairman and vice-chairman. Of companies with three mandates, in Waren-Commissionz-Bank in Hamburg, interlocking directorates were built through one each of mandate of the chairman and vice-chairman and one post of the supervisory board except for the chairman and vice-chairman. In Deutsche Schiffsbeleihungs-Bank AG in the banking industry, Commerzbank had one post of the chairman and two mandates of the supervisory board, except for the chairman and vice-chairman. In four enterprises, namely Leipziger Werkzeug-Maschinenfabrik vorm. W. von Pittler, AG (Pittler Werkzeugmaschinenfabrik) in the machine industry; Schultheiss-Patzenhofer Brauerei AG in the distillation industry; Hamburgische Elektrizitätswerke in the electric power, gas, and energy industries; and Industrie-Film-AG in other industries, interlocking directorates were established through one mandate of the vice-chairman and two posts of the supervisory board except for the chairman and vice-chairman, respectively. From another aspect, in one enterprise, interlocking directorates were built through three mandates of the supervisory board except for the chairman and vice-chairman, namely Reichsanleihe AG, in other industries.

When considering 43 enterprises with two mandates on the supervisory board of other enterprises concerning the distribution of the industrial sector, two existed in the mining industry; four in the iron and steel industry; two in the chemical industry; two in the electrical industry; two in the automobile industry; nine in the machine industry; three in the textile, spinning, and woven goods industries; five in the distillation industry; three in the banking industry; one in the electric power, gas, and energy industries; two in the transportation industry; and eight in other industries.

Considering these interlocking directorates concerning supervisory board position mandates, in AG für Montanindustrie in the iron and steel industry and Held &

Table 3.6 Cases in which Commerzbank built direct interlocking directorates through more than two posts on the supervisory board of other companies (period of inflation after World War I)

Industries	Number of posts							
	2		3		4		Total	
	Number of companies	Number of posts	Number of companies	Number of posts	Number of companies	Number of posts	Number of companies	Number of posts
Mining	2	4	–	–	–	–	2	4
Iron and steel	4	8	–	–	–	–	4	8
Chemical	2	4	–	–	–	–	2	4
Electrical	2	4	–	–	–	–	2	4
Automobile	2	4	–	–	–	–	2	4
Machine	9	18	1	3	–	–	10	21
Textile, spinning, and woven goods	3	6	–	–	–	–	3	6
Distributing	5	10	1	3	–	–	6	13
Banking	3	6	2	6	2	8	7	20
Electric power, gas, and energy	1	2	1	3	–	–	2	5
Transportation	2	4	–	–	–	–	2	4
Other industries	8	16	2	6	–	–	10	22
All industries	43	86	7	21	2	8	52	115

Source This table was compiled by the author, based on Arends and Mossner (Hrsg) (1922)

Francke AG in other industries, interlocking directorates were formed through two posts of the chairman. In Terrain Gesellschaft am Teltow-Canal in other industries, interlocking directorates were built through one each of the mandates of the chairman and vice-chairman. Cases of interlocking directorates built through a mandate of a chairman and one post of the supervisory board except for the chairman and vice-chairman can be observed in 18 enterprises. Enterprises were Norddeutsche Braunkohlenwerke AG and Bergbaugesellschaft Teutonia AG in the mining industry; Oberschlesische Eisenbahn-Bedarfs-AG and Milowicer Eisenwerk in the iron and steel industry; Chemische Fabrik Harburg-Staßfurt in the chemical industry; Bayerische Telefonfabrik AG and C. Lorenz AG in the electrical industry; Waggon- und Maschinenbau AG and Th. Flöther Maschinenbau AG in the machine industry; Malzfabriken J. Eisenberg und Etgersleben AG and C. T. Hünlich AG in the distillation industry; Vogtländische Creditanstalt AG in the banking industry; AG für Energiewirtschaft in the electric power, gas, and energy industries; Neue Deutsch-Bömische Elbeschifffahrts AG in the transportation industry; and Lichtenberger Terrain-AG, Aktien-Bauverein "Passage," Rositzer Zucker-Raffinerei, and Baltische Zucker-Raffinerie AG in other industries. Five enterprises had interlocking directorates through a mandate of the vice-chairman and one post of the supervisory board except for the chairman and vice-chairman: Horchwerke AG in the automobile industry; Hille-Werke AG and R. Wolf AG, Bierbrauerei AG vorm. Gebr. Hugger in the distillation industry; and Cohrs und Ammé AG in the transportation industry. In 17 companies, Commerzbank had two supervisory board mandates, excluding the chairman and vice-chairman. Such enterprises were Lothringer Hütten- und Bergwerks-Verein AG in the iron and steel industry; Chemische Fabrik Buckau in the chemical industry; AG für Automobilbau in the automotive industry; Stock, Motorpflug AG, Maschinenfabrik Buckau AG, Wotan-Werke AG, Maschinenbau-Anstalt Humblodt, and Linke-Hofmann-Werke AG, Waggonfabrik in the machine industry; Dresdner Nähmaschinenzwirn-Fabrik, Chemnitzer Aktien-Spinnerei, and Jutespinnerei und Weberei Berlin-Bautzen AG in the textile, spinning, and woven goods industries; C. A. F. Kahlbaum AG and H. A. Winkelhausen-Werke AG in the distillation industry; Thüringische Landesbank AG and Liquidations-Kasse in Hamburg AG in the banking industry; and Norddeutsche Zucker-Raffinerie and AG für Pappenfabrikation in other industries.

Thus, Commerzbank's direct interlocking directorates on the supervisory boards of other enterprises spread over a wide range of industries and had personnel connections with several competitive companies in the same industrial sector through several supervisory board mandates. Such cases can be observed in enterprises such as Siemens-Schuckertwerke GmbH and AEG in the electrical industry; Maschinenbau-Anstalt Humboldt, Maschinenfabrik Buckau AG, and Leipziger Werkzeug-Maschinenfabrik vorm. W. von Pittler, AG (Pittler Werkzeugmaschinenfabrik) in the machine industry; Germanischer Lloyd and Howaldtswerke in the shipbuilding industry; and Deutsche Petroleum-AG and Deutsche Mineralöl-Industrie AG in the oil industry. Commerzbank established close and strong personnel connections with many companies in various industries through direct interlocking directorates of members of the supervisory and management boards, which significantly contributed to securing much information for its own financial business and policy decisions over industrial enterprises.

The number of enterprises and mandates in which direct interlocking directorates were built by members of top management organs of banks, such as the supervisory board and the board of directors on the supervisory board and interlocking mandates of other companies, tended to increase enormously in comparison with those in the period of the shift to monopolistic capitalism. How were conditions regarding indirect interlocking directorates formed among three large banks, namely Deutsche Bank, Dresdner Bank, and Commerzbank, or between two of them? The following section considers the members of the supervisory and management boards of the three biggest banks in the supervisory board of other enterprises.

3.2 Indirect Interlocking Directorates Between Banks on the Supervisory Board of Other Enterprises

Section 3.2 examines how indirect interlocking directorates among three large banks on the supervisory boards of other companies were built through the direct interlocking of members of the supervisory and management board of each bank.

First, Sect. 3.2.1 explores indirect interlocking directorates among the three big banks. Sections 3.2.2 and 3.2.3 examine personnel connections between Deutsche Bank and Dresdner Bank and between Deutsche Bank and Commerzbank, except for those among the three banks. Section 3.2.4 considers the conditions of indirect interlocking directorates built between Dresdner Bank and Commerzbank.

3.2.1 Indirect Interlocking Directorates Among Three Large Banks on the Supervisory Board of Other Enterprises

Section 3.2.1 considers the situations related to indirect interlocking directorates among three large banks on the supervisory boards of other enterprises (see Table 3.7). Such cases can be observed in 16 companies, and the total number of mandates was 70. The number of enterprises and mandates in which three large banks built indirect interlocking directorates was much greater than that at the beginning of the twentieth century, during the shift to monopolistic capitalism (corresponding numbers one and three, respectively) (Chap. 2).

Regarding the interlocking directorate concerning the kind of mandate, number of enterprises, and mandates in which indirect interlocking through the mandate of the chairman was six each. Similarly, the numbers of enterprises and mandates with indirect interlocking directorates through the mandate of the vice-chairman were 10 and 11, respectively. That through the mandate of the supervisory board, except for the chairman and vice-chairman, were 16 and 53, respectively. When considering

Table 3.7 Indirect interlocking directorates of the members of the supervisory board and the managing board on the supervisory board of other companies among Deutsche Bank, Dresdner Bank, and Commerzbank (period of inflation after World War I)

Industries	Number of posts											
	3		4		5		6		7		Total	
	Number of companies	Number of posts	Number of companies	Number of posts	Number of companies	Number of posts	Number of companies	Number of posts	Number of companies	Number of posts	Number of companies	Number of posts
Mining	–	–	–	–	–	–	1	6	–	–	1	6
Iron and steel	3	9	–	–	1	5	2	12	–	–	6	26
Machine	–	–	2	8	–	–	–	–	–	–	2	8
Distillation	1	3	–	–	–	–	–	–	–	–	1	3
Insurance	–	–	2	8	–	–	–	–	–	–	2	8
Transportation	–	–	–	–	1	5	–	–	–	–	1	5
Other Industries	1	3	1	4	–	–	–	–	1	7	3	14
All industries	5	15	5	20	2	10	3	18	1	7	16	70

Source This table was compiled by the author, based on Arends and Mossner (Hrsg) (1922)

the distribution of the industry, number of companies, and mandates of interlocking directorate, there were one and six in the mining industry; six and 26 in the iron and steel industry; two and eight in the machine industry; one and three in the distillation industry; two and eight in the insurance industry; one and five in the transportation industry; and three and 14 in other industries, respectively.

To understand banks in leading positions in indirect interlocking relations, cases in which one bank or some banks of three large banks had more than two mandates on the supervisory board of another company were observed in 11 companies. The total number of mandates was 55. When considering the distribution of industry, number of companies, and mandates of interlocking directorate, there were, respectively, one and six in the mining industry; three and 17 in the iron and steel industry; two and eight in the machine industry; two and eight in the insurance industry; one and five in the transportation industry; and two and 11 in other industries.

The number of companies in which Deutsche Bank, Dresdner Bank, and Commerzbank built indirect interlocking directorates through seven mandates was one. Similarly, the number of companies with numerical figures through six, five, and four mandates was three, two, and five, respectively. In the remaining five enterprises, indirect interlocking directorates were established through three mandates.

Regarding enterprises with a total of seven mandates in each enterprise, in Reichsanleihe AG in other industries, Deutsche Bank and Commerzbank had three mandates of the supervisory board except for the chairman and vice-chairman, whereas Dresdner Bank AG had a mandate of the vice-chairman. Of the enterprises with a total of six mandates, in Gelsenkirchener Bergwerks-AG in the mining industry, Dresdner Bank had three mandates consisting of a mandate of the vice-chairman and two posts of the supervisory board except for the chairman and vice-chairman. Then, Deutsche Bank held two posts on the supervisory board, excluding the chairman and vice-chairman. From another aspect, Commerzbank had one post on the supervisory board, except for the chairman and vice-chairman. In AG Lauchhammer in the iron and steel industry, Dresdner Bank had two mandates of the vice-chairman and two posts of the supervisory board except for the chairman and vice-chairman, whereas Deutsche Bank and Commerzbank had one post of the supervisory board except for the chairman and vice-chairman. In Deutsch-Luxemburgische Bergwerks- und Hütten-AG in the iron and steel industry, Dresdner Bank had three supervisory board mandates, excluding the chairman and vice-chairman, whereas Deutsche Bank had two supervisory board posts, excluding the chairman and vice-chairman. Commerzbank had one post on the supervisory board, except for the chairman and vice-chairman.

Concerning enterprises with a total of five mandates in each enterprise, in Kattowitzer AG für Bergbau und Hüttenbetrieb in the iron and steel industry, Deutsche Bank had three mandates consisting of a post of the vice-chairman and two posts of the supervisory board except for the chairman and vice-chairman. Then, Dresdner Bank and Commerzbank held one mandate of the supervisory board except for the chairman and vice-chairman. In Santa Catharina Eisenbahn-AG, in the transportation industry, Deutsche Bank held the mandate of the chairman and one post on the supervisory board, except for the chairman and vice-chairman, whereas Dresdner

Bank had two posts on the supervisory board, except for chairman and vice-chairman. From another aspect, Commerzbank had one supervisory board mandate, excluding the chairman and vice-chairman.

Of the five companies with four posts in each company, in Eisenbahn-Verkehrsmittel AG in the machine industry, Deutsche Bank had a mandate of the chairman and one post of the supervisory board except for the chairman and vice-chairman. Then, Dresdner Bank held one mandate of the vice-chairman, and Commerzbank had one post of the supervisory board except for the chairman and vice-chairman. In Allianz Versicherungs-AG in the insurance industry, Deutsche Bank held two mandates of the supervisory board, excluding the chairman and vice-chairman. Then, Dresdner Bank held one mandate of vice-chairman, and Commerzbank had one post of the supervisory board, except for the chairman and vice-chairman. In "Vaterländische" und "Rhenania" Vereinigte Versicherungs-Gesellschaft AG in the insurance industry, Deutsche Bank held two mandates of the supervisory board except for the chairman and vice-chairman. Then, Commerzbank had one mandate of vice-chairman, and Dresdner Bank had one post of the supervisory board except for the chairman and vice-chairman. In Universum-Film AG, in other industries, Deutsche Bank had a mandate for the chairman and one mandate for the supervisory board, excluding the chairman and vice-chairman. Then, Dresdner Bank and Commerzbank had one mandate of the supervisory board, excluding the chairman and vice-chairman. In Linke-Hofmann-Werke AG in the machine industry, Commerzbank had two mandates of the supervisory board except for the chairman and vice-chairman. Then, Deutsche Bank and Dresdner Bank had one post on the supervisory board except for the chairman and vice-chairman.

Of the five companies with a total of three mandates in each company, in Bismarckhütte, AG and AG Charlottenhütte in the iron and steel industry, Deutsche Bank had a mandate of chairman, Commerzbank had a post of vice-chairman, and Dresdner Bank had one mandate of the supervisory board except for the chairman and vice-chairman. In Rheinische Baugesellschaft, in other industries, Dresdner Bank had one mandate of the chairman, Commerzbank had a mandate of the vice-chairman, and Deutsche Bank held one post of the supervisory board except for the chairman and vice-chairman. In Rheinische Stahlwerke in the iron and steel industry and Deutsche Bierbrauerei AG in the distillation industry, Deutsche Bank, Dresdner Bank, and Commerzbank held one post on the supervisory board, excluding the chairman and vice-chairman.

3.2.2 Indirect Interlocking Directorates Between Deutsche Bank and Dresdner Bank on the Supervisory Board of Other Enterprises

Next, situations related to indirect interlocking directorates between Deutsche Bank and Dresdner Bank on the supervisory board of other enterprises (see Table 3.8) can be observed in 37 companies. The total number of mandates was 90, except for the cases of indirect interlocking directorates among the three largest banks. The number of enterprises and mandates in which Deutsche Bank and Dresdner Bank built indirect interlocking directorates was much greater than that at the beginning of the twentieth century, which was the period of the shift to monopolistic capitalism (corresponding numbers 24 and 64, respectively).

Considering interlocking directorates concerning supervisory board position mandates, the numbers of enterprises and mandates in which indirect interlocking directorates were built through the mandate of the honor chairman were one each. Similarly, the numbers of enterprises with the mandate of the chairman, vice-chairman, and post of the supervisory board except for the chairman and vice-chairman were 11 each, six each, and 37 and 72, respectively. When considering the distribution of industry, the numbers of companies and mandates of interlocking diredirectorates were four and eight in the mining industry; three and six in the iron and steel industry; two and four in the chemical industry; two and five in the electrical industry; five and 14 in the machine industry; one and two in the food industry; one and three in the distributing industry; five and 12 in the banking industry; five and 10 in the insurance industry; four and nine in the electric power, gas, and energy industries; three and 11 in the transportation industry; and two and six in other industries, respectively.

To understand the bank at the leading position in the indirect interlocking relation, cases in which one bank or both Deutsche Bank and Dresdner Bank had more than two mandates on the supervisory board of another company were observed in 11 companies. The total number of mandates was 38. When considering the distribution of industry, number of companies, and mandates of interlocking directorate, there were, respectively, one and three in the electrical industry; four and 12 in the machine industry; one and three in the distributing industry; one and four in the banking industry; one and three in the electric power, gas, and energy industries; two and nine in the transportation industry; and one and four in other industries.

The number of companies in which Deutsche Bank and Dresdner Bank built indirect interlocking directorates through six mandates was one. Similarly, the number of companies with four and three mandates was two and eight, respectively. In the remaining 26 enterprises, indirect interlocking directorates were built through two mandates.

In Mitteleuropäische Schlafwagen- und Speisewagen-AG in the transportation industry, Deutsche Bank had four mandates consisting of one mandate of the chairman and three posts of the supervisory board except for the chairman and vice-chairman. Then, Dresdner Bank had one post of the vice-chairman and one post of the supervisory board, except for the chairman and vice-chairman. Of the companies with four mandates in each company, Deutsche Orientbank AG in the banking industry, Dresdner Bank had a mandate of the chairman and one post of the supervisory board except for the chairman and vice-chairman. Then, Deutsche Bank had two mandates of the supervisory board, excluding the chairman and vice-chairman. In Tempelhofer-Feld-AG für Grundstückverwertung, in other industries, Deutsche Bank had a mandate for the chairman and one post on the supervisory board except

Table 3.8 Indirect interlocking directorates of the members of the supervisory board and the managing board on the supervisory board of other companies between Deutsche Bank and Dresdner Bank[a] (period of inflation after World War I)

Industries	Number of posts									
	2		3		4		6		Total	
	Number of companies	Number of posts	Number of companies	Number of posts	Number of companies	Number of posts	Number of companies	Number of posts	Number of companies	Number of posts
Mining	4	8	–	–	–	–	–	–	4	8
Iron and steel	3	6	–	–	–	–	–	–	3	6
Chemical	2	4	–	–	–	–	–	–	2	4
Electrical	1	2	1	3	–	–	–	–	2	5
Machine	1	2	4	12	–	–	–	–	5	14
Food	1	2	–	–	–	–	–	–	1	2
Distributing	–	–	1	3	–	–	–	–	1	3
Banking	4	8	–	–	1	4	–	–	5	12
Insurance	5	10	–	–	–	–	–	–	5	10
Electric power, gas, and energy	3	6	1	3	–	–	–	–	4	9
Transportation	1	2	1	3	–	–	1	6	3	11
Other industries	1	2	–	–	1	4	–	–	2	6
All industries	26	52	8	24	2	8	1	6	37	90

[a] The cases of indirect interlocking directorates built among Deutsche Bank, Dresdner Bank, and Commerzbank are excluded
Source This table was compiled by the author, based on Arends and Mossner (Hrsg) (1922)

for the chairman and vice-chairman. Then, Dresdner Bank had a mandate of the vice-chairman and one post of the supervisory board except for the chairman and vice-chairman.

Of the eight enterprises with a total of three mandates in each enterprise, in Siemens & Halske AG in the electrical industry and Hermes AG in the distributing industry, Deutsche Bank had a mandate of the chairman and one post of the supervisory board excluding the chairman and vice-chairman. Then, Dresdner Bank held a mandate of the supervisory board excluding the chairman and vice-chairman. In Deutsche Continental-Gas-Gesellschaft in the electric power, gas, and energy industries, Deutsche Bank had a mandate of the vice-chairman and one post on the supervisory board, except for the chairman and vice-chairman. Then, Dresdner Bank held the mandate of the supervisory board except for the chairman and vice-chairman. In Berlin-Anhaltische Maschinenbau AG in the machine industry, Deutsche Bank had two mandates of the supervisory board except for the chairman and vice-chairman, whereas Dresdner Bank had one mandate of chairman. In Düsseldorfer Eisenbahnbedarf vorm. Carl Weyer & Co. in the machine industry, Dresdner Bank had a mandate of the chairman and one post of the supervisory board except for the chairman and vice-chairman. Then, Deutsche Bank had one mandate of the supervisory board except for the chairman and vice-chairman. In Schantung-Eisenbahn-Gesellschaft in the transportation industry, Dresdner Bank held one post of the vice-chairman and a mandate of the supervisory board, except for the chairman and vice-chairman. Then, Deutsche Bank had one post on the supervisory board, excluding the chairman and vice-chairman. In MAN in the machine industry, Deutsche Bank had two mandates of the supervisory board except for the chairman and vice-chairman, whereas Dresdner Bank held one post of the supervisory board except for the chairman and vice-chairman.

Concerning the remaining 26 firms with a total of two mandates in each firm, the number of interlocking directorate companies was four in the mining industry; three in the iron and steel industry; two in the chemical industry; one in the electrical industry; one in the machine industry; one in the food industry; four in the banking industry; five in the insurance industry; three in the electric power, gas, and energy industries; one in the transportation industry; and one in other industries.

Cases in which each of the two banks had one chairman post or a supervisory board post, except for the chairman and vice-chairman, can be observed in four enterprises. In two enterprises, namely Deutsche Jürgenswerke AG in the food industry and Speicherei und Speditions-AG in other industries, Deutsche Bank had a mandate of the chairman, whereas Dresdner Bank had one post of the supervisory board except for chairman and vice-chairman. In AG für Anilin-Fabrikation in the chemical industry and Hypothekenbank in Hamburg in the banking industry, Dresdner Bank had a mandate of chairman, whereas Deutsche Bank had one post of the supervisory board excluding the chairman and vice-chairman. A case where each of the two banks had a vice-chairman or one post of the supervisory board except for the chairman and vice-chairman was observed in one enterprise: Niedersächsische Versicherungs-AG in the insurance industry. In this enterprise, Deutsche Bank had the mandate of the vice-chairman. Then, Dresdner Bank had one supervisory board mandate, except for the chairman and vice-chairman. The number of companies in which each of the two banks had one post on the supervisory board except for the chairman and vice-chairman was 21. They were Oberschlesische Kokswerke und chemische Fabriken, Eschweiler Bergwerks-Verein, Harpener Bergbau AG, and AG Reichskohlenverband in the mining industry; "Phoenix" AG für Bergbau- und Hüttenbetrieb, Bochmer Verein für Bergbau und Gusstahlfabrikation, and Oberschlesische Eisen-Industrie AG in the iron and steel industry; Dessauer Werke für Zucker- und Chemische Industrie, AG in the chemical industry; Carl Lindström AG in the electrical industry; Mühlenbauanstalt und Maschinenfabrik vorm. Gebr. Steck in the machine industry; Deutsch-Asiatische Bank, Rheinisch-Westfälische Boden-Credit-Bank, and Berliner Makler-Verein in the banking industry; Schlesische Feuerversicherungs-Gesellschaft, Sächsische Rückversicherungs-Gesellschaft, Allgemeine Versicherungs-Geselslchaft für See-, Fluβ- und Landtransport, and Transatlantische Güterversicherungs-Gesellschaft in the insurance industry; Neckarwerke AG, Rheinisch-Westfälisches Elektricitätswerk AG, and Berliner Elektricitätswerke in the electric power, gas, and energy industries; and Hamburg-Amerikanische Packetfahrt-AG (Hamburg-Amerika Linie).

3.2.3 Indirect Interlocking Directorates Between Deutsche Bank and Commerzbank on the Supervisory Board of Other Enterprises

Furthermore, cases related to indirect interlocking directorates between Deutsche Bank and Commerzbank on the supervisory board of other enterprises (see Table 3.9) can be observed in 34 companies. Moreover, the total number of mandates was 91, except for cases of such interlocking directorates among three large banks. The numbers of enterprises and mandates in which Deutsche bank and Commerzbank established indirect interlocking directorates were almost the same as that of indirect interlocking directorates built between Deutsche Bank and Dresdner Bank (corresponding numbers 37 and 90, respectively). These numbers were much more than those at the beginning of the twentieth century (corresponding to numbers four and nine, respectively).

Considering interlocking directorates concerning the type of mandate, the numbers of enterprises and mandates in which indirect interlocking directorates were formed through the mandate of the chairman were 12 each. Similarly, the numbers of enterprises and mandates with the mandate of the vice-chairman and post of the supervisory board except for the chairman and vice-chairman were six each and 34 and 73, respectively. When considering the distribution of industry, the numbers of companies and mandates of interlocking directorates were three and seven in the mining industry; two and six in the iron and steel industry; one and four in the metal producing and processing industries; three and seven in the chemical industry; one

Table 3.9 Indirect interlocking directorates of members of the supervisory board and the managing board on the supervisory board of other companies between Deutsche Bank and Commerzbank[a] (period of inflation after World War I)

Industries	Number of posts									
	2		3		4		7		Total	
	Number of companies	Number of posts	Number of companies	Number of posts	Number of companies	Number of posts	Number of companies	Number of posts	Number of companies	Number of posts
Mining	2	4	1	3	–	–	–	–	3	7
Iron and steel	–	–	2	6	–	–	–	–	2	6
Metal producing and processing	–	–	–	–	1	4	–	–	1	4
Chemical	2	4	1	3	–	–	–	–	3	7
Electrical	–	–	1	3	–	–	–	–	1	3
Machine	1	2	2	6	–	–	–	–	3	8
Shipbuilding	2	4	–	–	–	–	–	–	2	4
Oil	1	2	1	3	–	–	–	–	2	5
Distillation	–	–	1	3	1	4	–	–	2	7
Banking	3	6	1	3	1	4	1	7	6	20
Insurance	1	2	1	3	–	–	–	–	2	5
Electric power, gas, and energy	2	4	–	–	–	–	–	–	2	4
Transportation	1	2	–	–	–	–	–	–	1	2
Other industries	3	6	1	3	–	–	–	–	4	9
All industries	18	36	12	36	3	12	1	7	34	91

[a] The cases of indirect interlocking directorates built among Deutsche Bank, Dresdner Bank, and Commerzbank are excluded

Source This table was compiled by the author, based on Arends and Mossner (Hrsg) (1922)

and three in the electrical industry; three and eight in the machine industry; two and four in the shipbuilding industry; two and five in the oil industry; two and seven in the distillation industry; six and 20 in the banking industry; two and five in the insurance industry; two and four in the electric power, gas, and energy industries; one and two in the transportation industry; and four and nine in other industries, respectively. Cases in which one bank or both Deutsche Bank and Commerzbank had more than two mandates on the supervisory board of another company were observed in 16 companies. The total number of mandates was 55. When considering the distribution of industry, number of companies, and mandates of interlocking directorate, there were, respectively, one and three in the mining industry; two and six in the iron and steel industry; one and four in the metal producing and processing industries; one and three in the chemical industry; one and three in the electrical industry; two and six in the machine industry; one and three in the oil industry; two and seven in the distillation industry; three and 14 in the banking industry; one and three in the insurance industry; and one and three in other industries.

In 16 enterprises, Deutsche Bank and Commerzbank built indirect interlocking directorates through more than three mandates on the supervisory board of other enterprises. The total number of mandates was 55. The number of companies in which indirect interlocking directorates were formed through seven mandates was one. Similarly, the numbers of companies with four and three mandates were three and 12, respectively. In the remaining 18 enterprises, indirect interlocking directorates were built through two mandates.

In Deutsche Hypothekenbank, Meiningen in the banking industry, Deutsche Bank had six mandates of the supervisory board except for the chairman and vice-chairman. Then, Dresdner Bank had one post of the vice-chairman and one post of the supervisory board, except for the chairman and vice-chairman. Of companies with four mandates in each company, in Hirsch Kupfer und Messingwerke AG in the metal producing and processing industries, Deutsche Bank had a mandate of the chairman and two posts of the supervisory board excluding the chairman and vice-chairman. Then, Commerzbank had one mandate of the supervisory board, excluding the chairman and vice-chairman. In Deutsche Schiffsbeleihungs-Bank AG in the banking industry, Commerzbank had a mandate of the chairman and two posts of the supervisory board except for the chairman and vice-chairman, Deutsche Bank had one mandate of the supervisory board except for the chairman and vice-chairman. In Schultheiss-Patzenhofer Brauerei AG in the distillation industry, Commerzbank had a mandate of the vice-chairman and two posts on the supervisory board, except for the chairman and vice-chairman. Then, Deutsche Bank had a mandate of the vice-chairman and one post on the supervisory board, except for the chairman and vice-chairman.

Of the 12 enterprises with three mandates in each enterprise, in R. Wolf AG in the machine industry, Commerzbank had a mandate of a vice-chairman and one post of the supervisory board except for the chairman and vice-chairman. Then, Deutsche Bank held a mandate of chairman. In four companies, namely Baroper Walzwerk AG in the iron and steel industry, Siemens-Schuckertwerke GmbH in the electrical industry, Deutsche Petroleum-AG in the oil industry, and Preussische Boden-Credit-Actien-Bank in the banking industry, Deutsche Bank had a mandate of the chairman and one post of the supervisory board except for the chairman and vice-chairman. Then, Commerzbank held a mandate of the supervisory board except for the chairman and vice-chairman. In Oberschlesische Eisenbahn-Bedarfs-AG in the iron and steel industry, Commerzbank had a mandate of the chairman and one post of the supervisory board except for the chairman and vice-chairman. Then, Deutsche Bank had one mandate of the chairman. In Maschinenfabrik Buckau AG in the machine industry, Deutsche Bank had a mandate of the chairman and one post of the supervisory board excluding the chairman and vice-chairman. Then, Commerzbank had one mandate of the supervisory board, excluding the chairman and vice-chairman. In Preußengrube AG in the mining industry, Deutsch Bank held one post of vice-chairman and a mandate of the supervisory board except for the chairman and vice-chairman. Then, Commerzbank held one post of the supervisory board except for the chairman and vice-chairman. In three firms, namely Rütgerwerke AG in the chemical industry, Union, Allgemeine Versicherungs-AG in the insurance industry, and Hamburger Freihafen-Lagerhaus-Gesellschaft in other industries, Deutsche Bank had two supervisory board mandates except for chairman and vice-chairman. Then, Commerzbank held one supervisory board post except for the chairman and vice-chairman. In C. A. F. Kahlbaum AG in the distillation industry, Commerzbank had two mandates of the supervisory board, excluding the chairman and vice-chairman. Then, Deutsche Bank held one post of the supervisory board, excluding the chairman and vice-chairman.

Regarding the remaining 18 firms with a total of two mandates in each firm, the number of interlocking directorate companies was two in the mining industry; two in the chemical industry; one in the machine industry; two in the shipbuilding industry; one in the oil industry; three in the banking industry; one in the insurance industry; two in the electric power, gas, and energy industries; one in the transportation industry; and three in other industries.

Cases in which each of the two banks had one chairman post or a supervisory board post except for the chairman and vice-chairman can be observed in three enterprises. In two enterprises, namely Schubert und Salzer Maschinenfabrik AG in the machine industry and Deutsche Versicherungsbank AG in the banking industry, Deutsche Bank had the mandate of chairman, and Commerzbank had one post on the supervisory board except for chairman and vice-chairman. In Rheinische Glashütten AG in other industries, Commerzbank had a mandate of the chairman, Deutsche Bank had one post on the supervisory board, excluding the chairman and vice-chairman. The case where each of the two banks had a vice-chairman or one post of the supervisory board excluding the chairman and vice-chairman was observed in three enterprises. In Allianz Lebensversicherungsbank AG in the banking industry and Kraftübertragungswerke Rheinfelden in the electric power, gas, and energy industries, Deutsche Bank had a mandate of vice-chairman, whereas Commerzbank held one mandate of the supervisory board except for chairman and vice-chairman. In Deutsche Lloyd Versicherungs-AG in the insurance industry, Commerzbank had a mandate of the vice-chairman. Then, Deutsche Bank held one mandate of the supervisory board, except for the chairman and vice-chairman. The number of companies in which each of the two banks had one post on the supervisory board except for the chairman and vice-chairman was 12. They were "Königsborn" AG für Bergbau-, Salinen- und Soolbad-Betrieb and Braunkohlen-Industrie AG "Zukunft" in the mining industry; Stassfurter Chemischen Fabrik vorm. Vorster und Grüneberg and Union Fabrik chemischer Produkte in the chemical industry; Deutsche Werke AG and Germanischer Lloyd in the shipbuilding industry; AG für Petroleum-Industrie in the oil industry; Norddeutsche Grund-Credit-Bank in the banking industry; Elektrizitäts-AG vorm. Schuckert und Co. in the electric power, gas, and energy industries; Hamburger Hochbahn-AG in the transportation industry; and "Adler" Deutsche Portland-Zement-Fabrik AG and Tiefbau und Kälte-Industrie AG in other industries.

3.2.4 Indirect Interlocking Directorates Between Dresdner Bank and Commerzbank on the Supervisory Board of Other Enterprises

Next, cases related to indirect interlocking directorates between Dresdner Bank and Commerzbank on the supervisory board of other enterprises (see Table 3.10) can be observed in 23 companies. The total number of mandates was 53, except for cases of such interlocking directorates among three large banks. The number of enterprises and mandates in which Dresdner Bank and Commerzbank formed indirect interlocking directorates was less than that of indirect interlocking directorates built between Deutsche Bank and Dresdner Bank (corresponding numbers 37 and 90, respectively) and those of such interlocking directorates built between Deutsche Bank and Commerzbank (corresponding numbers 34 and 91, respectively). This number was much more than that at the beginning of the twentieth century (corresponding numbers four and nine, respectively).

Considering interlocking directorates concerning the type of mandate, the numbers of enterprises and mandates in which indirect interlocking directorates were established through the mandate of the chairman were four each. Similarly, the numbers of enterprises and mandates with a mandate of the vice-chairman and a post of the supervisory board except for the chairman and vice-chairman were six each and 23 and 43, respectively. When considering the distribution of industry, the numbers of companies and mandates of the interlocking directorate were two and four in the mining industry; three and seven in the iron and steel industry; one and five in the electrical industry; two and five in the machine industry; one and two in the oil industry; one and two in the textile, spinning, and woven goods industries; one and two in the distributing industry; three and seven in the banking industry; two and four in the insurance industry; one and two in the electric power, gas, and energy industries; three and seven in the transportation industry; and three and six in other industries, respectively.

Cases in which one bank or both Dresdner Bank and Commerzbank had more than two mandates on the supervisory board of another company were observed in

Table 3.10 Indirect interlocking directorates of the members of the supervisory board and the managing board on the supervisory board of other companies between Dresdner Bank and Commerzbank[a] (period of inflation after World War I)

Industries	Number of posts							
	2		3		5		Total[a]	
	Number of companies	Number of posts	Number of companies	Number of posts	Number of companies	Number of posts	Number of companies	Number of posts
Mining	2	4	–	–	–	–	2	4
Iron and steel	2	4	1	3	–	–	3	7
Electrical	–	–	–	–	1	5	1	5
Machine	1	2	1	3	–	–	2	5
Oil	1	2	–	–	–	–	1	2
Textile, spinning, and woven goods	1	2	–	–	–	–	1	2
Distributing	1	2	–	–	–	–	1	2
Banking	2	4	1	3	–	–	3	7
Insurance	2	4	–	–	–	–	2	4
Electric power, gas, and energy	1	2	–	–	–	–	1	2
Transportation	2	4	1	3	–	–	3	7
Other industries	3	6	–	–	–	–	3	6
All industries	18	36	4	12	1	5	23	53

[a] The cases of indirect interlocking directorates built among Deutsche Bank, Dresdner Bank, and Commerzbank are excluded

Source This table was compiled by the author, based on Arends and Mossner (Hrsg) (1922)

five companies. The total number of mandates was 17. The number of enterprises and mandates was much fewer than that of indirect interlocking directorates built between Deutsche Bank and Dresdner Bank (corresponding numbers 11 and 38, respectively) and that of such interlocking directorates built between Deutsche Bank and Commerzbank (corresponding numbers 16 and 55, respectively). When considering the distribution of industry, number of companies, and mandates of interlocking directorate, there were one and three in the iron and steel industry; one and five in the electrical industry; one and three in the machine industry; one and three in the banking industry; and one and three in the transportation industry, respectively.

Dresdner Bank and Commerzbank built an indirect interlocking directorate through more than three mandates on the supervisory board of other enterprises in five enterprises. The total number of mandates was 17. The number of companies in which indirect interlocking directorates were formed through five mandates was one. Similarly, the number of companies with three mandates was four. In the remaining 18 enterprises, indirect interlocking directorates were built through two mandates.

In AEG in the electrical industry, Dresdner Bank had four mandates of the supervisory board except for the chairman and vice-chairman, whereas Commerzbank had one post of the vice-chairman and one post of the supervisory board except for the chairman and vice-chairman. Of enterprises with three mandates in each company, in Preußische Pfandbriefbank in the banking industry, Deutsche Bank had a mandate of the chairman and one post of the supervisory board excluding the chairman and vice-chairman. Then, Commerzbank had one mandate of the supervisory board, excluding the chairman and vice-chairman. In Cohrs und Amme AG in the transportation industry, Commerzbank had a mandate of the vice-chairman and one post of the supervisory board except for the chairman and vice-chairman, Dresdner Bank had one mandate of the supervisory board except for the chairman and vice-chairman. Then, in Lothringer Hütten- und Bergwerks-Verein AG in the iron and steel industry and Maschinenbau-Anstalt Humboldt in the machine industry, Commerzbank had two supervisory board mandates, except for the chairman and vice-chairman. Then, Dresdner Bank held one supervisory board post, except for the chairman and vice-chairman.

Regarding the remaining 18 firms with a total of two mandates in each firm, the number of interlocking directorate companies was two in the mining industry; two in the iron and steel industry; one in the machine industry; one in the oil industry; one in the textile, spinning, and woven goods industries; one in the distributing industry; two in the banking industry; two in the insurance industry; one in the electric power, gas, and energy industries; two in the transportation industry; and three in other industries.

Cases in which each of the two banks had one chairman post or a supervisory board post excluding the chairman and vice-chairman can be observed in three enterprises. In Zwickauer Maschinenfabrik in the machine industry, Dresdner Bank had the mandate of chairman, whereas Commerzbank had one post on the supervisory board, except for the chairman and vice-chairman. In two enterprises, namely Bank für Brau-Industrie in the banking industry and Terrain-AG Kleinburg in other industries, Commerzbank had a mandate of the chairman, whereas Dresdner Bank had one post of the supervisory board except for the chairman and vice-chairman. The case where each of the two banks had a vice-chairman or one post of the supervisory board except for the chairman and vice-chairman was five companies. In Anhaltische Kohlenwerke in the mining industry, Dresdner Bank had the mandate of the vice-chairman. Then, Commerzbank held one mandate of the supervisory board, except for the chairman and vice-chairman. In four enterprises, namely Alkaliwerke Ronnenberg in the mining industry; Düsseldorfer Eisen- und Drahtindustrie in the iron and steel industry; Vaterländische und Rhenania Verein. Versicherungsgesellschaft AG in the insurance industry; and Hasserröder Papierfabrik AG in other industries, Commerzbank had a mandate of vice-chairman. Then, Dresdner Bank held one mandate of the supervisory board except for the chairman and vice-chairman. The number of companies in which each of the two banks had one post on the supervisory board except for the chairman and vice-chairman was 10. They were Mansfeld AG für Bergbau und Hüttenbetrieb in the iron and steel industry; Deutsche Mineralölindustrie AG in the oil industry; Persische Teppich-Gesellschaft AG in the textile, spinning, and woven goods industries; Deutsche Eisenhandel-AG in the distributing industry; Berliner Hypothekenbank AG in the banking industry; Beamtenversicherungs-Verein des deutschen Bank- und Bankier-Gewerbes in the insurance industry; Branden-burgische Carbid- und Elektrizitäts-Werke AG in the electric power, gas, and energy industries; Lothringische Eisenbahn-AG and Schlesische Dampfer-Compagnie-Berliner Lloyd, AG in the transportation industry; and Rheinisch-Westfälische "Revision" Treuhand AG in other industries.

An earlier analysis examined how Deutsche Bank, Dresdner Bank, and Commerzbank formed personnel connections with enterprises in various industrial sectors through direct and indirect interlocking directorates of the members of their own supervisory and management boards. The structures of the interlocking directorates of the three large banks were clarified through these discussions. In the inflation period after World War I, earlier studies have shown a weak control and influence of banks over industrial enterprises under changes in the fund demand of industrial enterprises, changes in corporate financing, and the movement of industrial enterprises toward escape from value in money to real assets. However, there were different situations of personnel connection through direct interlocking of members of the three largest banks on the supervisory board of industrial enterprises. The number of enterprises in which interlocking directorates were formed and interlocking mandates significantly increased in this period. Enterprises in which interlocking directorates were formed belonged to various industrial sectors. However, personnel connections were also established through indirect interlocking on the supervisory boards of other firms among members of multiple banks without direct interlocking directorates. Both types of interlocking directorates were significant in exchanging and sharing information and coordinating interests and conflicts among companies.

Regarding the increase in interlocking directorates in the inflation period after World War I, building and maintaining personnel connections with many enterprises in close relationships had great significance for large banks. This case is under the trend of decreasing industrial enterprises' independence from banks where financial transactions do not exist. This case also applies to pursuing cooperation in managing enterprises with which banks had friendly relations (Berliner Handels-Gesellschaft 1956, S. 172). This approach was one of the countermeasures for maintaining business relationships with industrial companies.

How the conditions of interlocking directorates changed during National Socialism after a relatively stable period from 1924 to 1929 and the big crisis period from 1929 to 1933 needs to be clarified. Therefore, the conditions of interlocking directorates of the three large banks during this period are examined in Chap. 4.

References

Arends H, Mossner C (Hrsg) (1922) Adressbuch der Direktoren und Aufsichtsräte 1922. Finanz-Verlag-Gesellschaft, Berlin

Berliner Handels-Gesellschaft B (1956) Die Berliner Handels-Gesellschaft in einem Jahrhundert deutscher Wirtschaft 1856–1956. Berlin Hartmann, Berlin

Duschnitzky S (1927) Das Konzern-Problem unter Berücksichtigung der schwerindustriellen Wirtschaft im Nachkriegs-Deutschland: Eine sozialökonomischen Studie zu den Phänomenen der modernen kapitalistischen Konzentration. Kommissionsverlag der Deutschen Buchhandlung, Kaunas

Hagemann W (1931) Das Verhältnis der deutschen Grossbanken zur Industrie. W. Christian, Berlin

Krause D (2004) Die Commerz- und Disconto-Bank 1870–1920/23. Franz Steiner Verlag, Stuttgart, Bankgeschichte als Systemgeschichte

Lampe W (2004) Der Bankbetrieb in Krieg und Inflation. Deutsche Großbanken in den Jahren 1914 bis 1923, Franz Steiner Verlag, Stuttgart

Chapter 4
Interlocking Directorates of Bank's Supervisory Board and Managing Board Members in Other Enterprises During National Socialism

Abstract Large business systems established on ties between industries and banks were the cornerstone of German capital accumulation and important for the process of German corporate development. Assignment of bank directors to industrial enterprises and interlocking directorates were two of the most important means of sharing information and coordinating the interests of industries and banks. During inflationary after World War I, numbers of companies in which banks built interlocking directorates and interlocking supervisory boards mandate in other enterprises increased than during the shift to a monopolistic capitalism in the early-twentieth century. How did conditions of interlocking directorates of members of top management organs on the supervisory board of other enterprise change during National Socialism? This chapter clarifies the actual conditions of such personnel connections between a bank and enterprises and between banks.

Keywords Commerz- und Privat-Bank · Deutsche Bank und Disconto-Gesellschaft · Dresdner Bank · Industry–bank relationship · Direct interlocking directorate · Indirect interlocking directorate · National socialism · Personnel connection

Chapter 3 analyzed the personnel connections that Deutsche Bank und Disconto-Gesellschaft (below Deutsche Bank), Dresdner Bank, and Commerz- und Privat-Bank AG (below Commerzbank) established through direct and indirect interlocking directorates of the members of the supervisory and managing boards on the supervisory board of other enterprises during inflation after World War I. During this period, the numbers of enterprises in which interlocking directorates were built and interlocking mandate increased than during the shift to a monopolistic capitalism in the early-twentieth century.

In the Nazi era after the relatively stable period from 1924 to 1929 and the big crisis period from 1929 to 1933, there was a strong economic control and influence of the state on economy and enterprises. During National Socialism, a situation of full employment was realized under the economic policy of Nazis state. How were the personnel connections in which the three large banks established through interlocking

T. Yamazaki, *Relationships Between Industry and Bank in Germany*,
https://doi.org/10.1007/978-981-97-4996-6_4

directorates of members of top management organs such as the supervisory board and managing board on the supervisory board of other enterprises? It is crucial to clarify the conditions of direct interlocking directorates of each bank and indirect interlocking directorates built among the three large banks and between two of the banks.

This chapter examines the structures of the personnel connection through direct and indirect interlocking directorates by comparing with the conditions during inflation after World War I. Cases of Deutsche Bank und Disconto-Bank, Dresdner Bank, and Commerz- und Privat-Bank AG are considered. The material used in analysis of this chapter is "*Adressbuch der Direktoren und Aufsichtsräte 1936*" (Bd.I, Nach personen geordnet, Finanzverlag, Berlin).

Section 4.1 considers direct interlocking directorates of members of supervisory board and managing board of each bank on the supervisory board of other companies. Section 4.2 analyzes indirect interlocking directorates built through direct interlocking directorate among three banks and between two banks of them.

4.1 Direct Interlocking Directorate of Members of Supervisory Board and Managing Board of Banks on the Supervisory Board of Other Enterprises

4.1.1 Direct Interlocking Directorate of Members of Supervisory Board and Managing Board of Deutsche Bank

First, in considering the direct interlocking directorate by supervisory board and managing board members of Deutsche Bank on the supervisory board of other enterprises (see Table 4.1), there were 340 companies in which such cases were observed and 415 interlocking mandates. Numbers of both enterprises and mandates were much fewer than those of Deutsche Bank in the period of inflation after World War I (corresponding numbers 456 and 580, respectively) (see Chap. 3).

Regarding the distribution of industrial sectors, Deutsche Bank built direct interlocking directorates in 33 companies and had 44 interlocking mandates in the mining industry, and similarly, 25 and 33 in the iron and steel industry; 14 and 17 in the metal producing and processing industries; 44 and 51 in the chemical industry; 12 and 17 in the electrical industry; four and six in the automobile industry; 34 and 43 in the machine industry, respectively; two each in the precious machine and optical industries; one each in the shipbuilding industry; two each in the oil industry; one each in the food industry; 12 and 13 in the textile, spinning, and woven goods industries, respectively; nine each in the distillation industry; 11 each in the distributing industry; 24 and 35 in the banking industry; 28 and 34 in the insurance industry; 31 and 36 in the electric power, gas, and energy industries; 15 and 16 in the transportation industry;

Table 4.1 Direct interlocking directorates of the members of the supervisory board and the managing board of Deutsche Bank on the supervisory board of other companies (period of National Socialism)

Industries	Position							
	Chairman		Vice-chairman		Supervisory board member excluding chairman and vice-chairman		Total[a]	
	Number of companies	Number of posts	Number of companies	Number of posts	Number of companies	Number of posts	Number of companies	Number of posts
Mining	10	10	7	7	19	27	33	44
Iron and steel	10	10	7	7	12	16	25	33
Metal producing and processing	3	3	1	1	11	13	14	17
Chemical	14	14	7	7	27	30	44	51
Electrical	3	3	2	2	9	12	12	17
Automobile	4	4	2	2	–	–	4	6
Machine	15	15	4	4	20	24	34	43
Precious machine and optical	–	–	–	–	2	2	2	2
Shipbuilding	–	–	–	–	1	1	1	1
Oil	1	1	–	–	1	1	2	2
Food	1	1	–	–	–	–	1	1
Textile, spinning, and woven goods	2	2	2	2	9	9	12	13`
Distillation	3	3	1	1	5	5	9	9
Distributing	2	2	–	–	9	9	11	11
Banking	5	5	6	6	18	24	24	35

(continued)

Table 4.1 (continued)

Industries	Position							
	Chairman		Vice-chairman		Supervisory board member excluding chairman and vice-chairman		Total[a]	
	Number of companies	Number of posts	Number of companies	Number of posts	Number of companies	Number of posts	Number of companies	Number of posts
Insurance	6	6	4	4	21	24	28	34
Electric power, gas, and energy	4	4	4	4	25	28	31	36
Transportation	6	6	2	2	8	8	15	16
Other industries	8	9	2	2	28	33	38	44
All industries	97	98	51	51	225	266	340	415

[a] There are cases in which the total number of companies establishing interlocking directorates differed from the total number of companies measured by each position of the supervisory board due to the existence of companies where interlocking directorates through more than two posts were built

Source This table was compiled by the author, based on Mossner (Hrsg) (1936)

and 38 and 44 in other industries, respectively. Among the various industries, except for the banking industry and the insurance sector, for example, Deutsch Bank had many interlocking relationships in the mining, iron and steel, chemical, machine, and electric power, gas, and energy industries. Therefore, Deutsche Bank had strong and close relationships with companies in the heavy and chemical industries as the key industrial sectors in Germany.

When in examining the situation of interlocking directorates with respect to the position of mandate of supervisory board, in 97 enterprises, there were cases in which interlocking directorates on the supervisory boards of other companies were formed through mandate of chairman of the supervisory board with a total of 98 mandates. Numbers of enterprises and mandates were approximately 70% of those of Deutsche Bank in the period of inflation after World War I (corresponding numbers 135 and 136, respectively). Considering the distribution among industrial sectors, the numbers of enterprises and mandates in which interlocking directorate were formed were 10 each in the mining industry, respectively; similarly, 10 each in the iron and steel industry; three each in the metal producing and processing industries; 14 each in the chemical industry; three each in the electrical industry; four each in the automobile industry; 15 each in the machine industry; one each in the oil industry; one each in the food industry; two each in the textile, spinning, and woven goods industries; three each in the distillation industry; two each in the distributing industry; five each in the banking industry; six each in the insurance industry; four each in the electric power, gas, and energy industries; six each in the transportation industry; and eight and nine in other industries, respectively. Cases of interlocking directorate in representative companies of each industry were observed in Klöckner-Werke AG in the iron and steel industry, Henkel & Cie. AG and Vereinigte Glanzstoff-Fabriken AG in the chemical industry, Siemens & Halske AG and Siemens-Schuckertwerke AG in the electrical industry, Daimler-Benz AG and Bayerische Motoren Werke AG (BMW) in the automobile industry, Demag AG and A. Borsig Maschinenbau AG in the machine industry, Deutsche Ueberseeische Bank in the banking industry, and Deutsche Luft-Hansa AG in thc transportation industry.

In 51 enterprises, there were cases in which interlocking directorates on the supervisory boards of other companies were formed through mandate of vice-chairman of the supervisory board with a total of 51 mandates. In each enterprise, the number of mandates was one. Numbers of both enterprises and mandates were fewer than those of Deutsche Bank in the period of inflation after World War I (corresponding numbers 61 and 62, respectively). The number of enterprises in which such interlocking cases were formed was seven in the mining industry; similarly, seven in the iron and steel industry; one in the metal producing and processing industries; seven in the chemical industry; two in the electrical industry; two in the automobile industry; four in the machine industry; two in the textile, spinning, and woven goods industries; one in the distillation industry; six in the banking industry; four in the insurance industry; four in the electric power, gas, and energy industries; two in the transportation industry; and two in other industries, respectively. There were cases of interlocking directorate in major companies of each industry. Such cases can be observed in Mannesmannröhren-Werke and Klöckner-Werke AG in the iron and steel industry and Daimler-Benz AG and Bayerische Motoren Werke AG in the automobile industry.

Interlocking directorates through mandates of supervisory board except for chairman and vice-chairman were seen in 225 companies and the total number of mandates was 266. The number of enterprises was much fewer than those of Deutsche Bank in the period of inflation after World War I, respectively (corresponding numbers 315 and 382, respectively). Considering the distribution among industrial sectors, the numbers of enterprises and mandates in which interlocking directorates were formed were 19 and 27 in the mining industry, respectively; similarly, 12 and 16 in the iron and steel industry; 11 and 13 in the metal producing and processing industries; 27 and 30 in the chemical industry; nine and 12 in the electrical industry; 20 and 24 in the machine industry, respectively; two each in the precious machine and optical industries; one each in the shipbuilding industry; one each in the oil industry; nine each in the textile, spinning, and woven goods industries; five each in the distillation industry; nine each in the distributing industry; 18 and 24 in the banking industry; 21 and 24 in the insurance industry; 25 and 28 in the electric power, gas, and energy industries, respectively; eight each in the transportation industry; and 28 and 33 in other industries, respectively. These companies included leading firms in each industry, such as Gelsenkirchener Bergwerks-AG and Harpener Bergbau AG in the mining industry, Vereinigte Stahlwerke AG and Mannesmannröhren-Werke in the iron and steel industry, I.G. Farbenindustrie AG in the chemical industry, Siemens & Halske AG, Siemens-Schuckertwerke AG, and AEG in the electrical industry, Demag AG, A. Borsig Maschinenbau AG, and Maschinenfabrik Augsburg-Nürnberg AG (MAN) in the machine industry, Blohm & Voss Kommanditgesellschaft auf Aktien in the shipbuilding industry, Rudolph Karstadt AG in the distributing industry, and Rheinisch-Westfälisches Elektrizitätswerk AG in the electric power, gas, and energy industries.

The numbers of enterprises and mandates were 57 and 132, respectively, when considering cases in which Deutsche Bank's supervisory board and managing board members had more than two mandates on the supervisory boards of other companies (see Table 4.2). Numbers of both enterprises and mandates were even fewer than those of Deutsche Bank in the period of inflation after World War I (corresponding numbers 83 and 207, respectively). Regarding the distribution among industries, the numbers of companies and mandates were as follows: seven and 18 in the mining industry; five and 13 in the iron and steel industry; two and five in the metal producing and processing industries; seven and 14 in the chemical industry; four and nine in the electrical industry; two and four in the automobile industry; six and 15 in the machine industry; one and two in the textile, spinning, and woven goods industries; seven and 18 in the banking industry; five and 11 in the insurance industry; five and 10 in the electric power, gas, and energy industries; one and two in the transportation industry; and five and 11 in other industries, respectively.

Of these 57 companies, direct interlocking directorates were built through more than three mandates in 13 enterprises and the total number of mandates was 44. Numbers of both enterprise and mandate were much fewer than those of Deutsche Bank in the period of inflation after World War I (corresponding numbers 24 and 89,

Table 4.2 Cases in which Deutsche Bank built direct interlocking directorates through more than two posts on the supervisory board of other companies (period of National Socialism)

Industries	Number of posts									
	2		3		4		5		Total	
	Number of companies	Number of posts	Number of companies	Number of posts	Number of companies	Number of posts	Number of companies	Number of posts	Number of companies	Number of posts
Mining	5	10	1	3	–	–	1	5	7	18
Iron and steel	3	6	1	3	1	4	–	–	5	13
Metal producing and processing	1	2	1	3	–	–	–	–	2	5
Chemical	7	14	–	–	–	–	–	–	7	14
Electrical	3	6	1	3	–	–	–	–	4	9
Automobile	2	4	–	–	–	–	–	–	2	4
Machine	4	8	1	3	1	4	–	–	6	15
Textile, spinning, and woven goods	1	2	–	–	–	–	–	–	1	2
Banking	4	8	2	6	1	4	–	–	7	18
Insurance	4	8	1	3	–	–	–	–	5	11
Electric power, gas, and energy	5	10	–	–	–	–	–	–	5	10
Transportation	1	2	–	–	–	–	–	–	1	2
Other industries	4	8	1	3	–	–	–	–	5	11
All industries	44	88	9	27	3	12	1	5	57	132

Source This table was compiled by the author, based on Mossner (Hrsg) (1936)

respectively). Enterprise where direct interlocking directorates were formed through five mandates was one. Enterprises in which direct interlocking directorates were developed through four posts were three. Cases where interlocking directorates were formed through three mandates were nine. In the remaining 44 companies, Deutsche Bank had two mandates on the supervisory board of other companies.

Considering these interlocking directorates with respect to supervisory board position mandates, in Rheinisch-Westfälisches Kohlen-Syndikat in the mining industry, interlocking directorates were established through a mandate of vice-chairman and four posts of the supervisory board except for chairman and vice-chairman. In Deutsche Ueberseeische Bank in the banking industry, Deutsche Bank built interlocking directorates through four mandates consisting of one chairman and three mandates of the supervisory board except for chairman and vice-chairman. Meanwhile, there were two enterprises in which interlocking directorates were formed through four mandates of the supervisory board excluding chairman and vice-chairman. Such cases were observed in Vereinigte Stahlwerke AG in the iron and steel industry and Rheinische Metallwaaren- und Maschinenfabrik in the machine industry.

Regarding enterprises with three mandates, in Siemens & Halske AG in the electrical industry, Demag AG in the machine industry, and Deutsche Centralbodenkredit AG in the banking industry, interlocking directorate were established through a mandate of chairman and two posts of the supervisory board other than chairman and vice-chairman, respectively. Enterprises in which interlocking directorates were formed through a post of vice-chairman and two mandates of the supervisory board except for chairman and vice-chairman were Mannesmannröhren-Werke in the iron and steel industry and Deutsche Hypothekenbank, Meiningen in the banking industry. In four companies, namely, Essener Steinkohlenbergwerke AG in the mining industry, Metallgesellschaft AG in the metal producing and processing industry, Union und Rhein Versicherungs-AG in the insurance industry, and Deutsche Atlantische Telegraphengesellschaft in other industries, Deutsche Bank built interlocking directorates through three mandates of the supervisory board excluding chairman and vice-chairman, respectively.

When considering 44 enterprises with two mandates on the supervisory board of other enterprise in relation to distribution of industrial sector, there were five in mining industry, three in iron and steel industry, one in metal producing and processing industries, seven in chemical industry, three in electrical industry, two in automobile industry, four in machine industry, one in textile, spinning, and woven goods industries, four in banking industry, four in insurance industry, five in electric power, gas, and energy industries, one in transportation industry, and four in other industries.

Examining these interlocking directorates in relation to kind of mandate, in Porzellanfabrik Lorenz Hutschenreuther AG in other industries, there were interlocking directorates through two mandates of chairman. Cases in which interlocking directorates were built through two mandates consisting of chairman and vice-chairman can be observed in nine enterprises: Klöckner-Werke AG in the iron and steel industry, A. Riebeck'sche Montanwerke AG and Siemens-Planiawerke

AG in the chemical industry, Daimler-Benz AG and BMW in the automobile industry, Deutsche-Asiatische Bank in the banking industry, Nordstein Allgemeine Versicherungs-AG and Rückversicherungs-Vereinigung AG in the insurance industry, and Otavi Minen- und Eisenbahn-Gesellschaft in the transportation industry. Cases in which interlocking directorates were formed through a mandate of chairman and one post of the supervisory board except for chairman and vice-chairman can be observed in eight enterprises. These enterprises were Mansfeld AG für Bergbau und Hüttenbetrieb in the iron and steel industry, AG für Bergbau, Blei- und Zinkfabrikation in the metal producing and processing industries, Siemens-Schuckertwerke AG in the electrical industry, A. Borsig Maschinenbau AG, Maschinenbsau-Unternehmungen AG, and Vereinigte Kugellagerfabrikation AG in the machine industry, Berliner Feuer-Versicherungs-Anstalt in the insurance industry, and Bergmann-Elektrizitäts-Werke AG in the electric power, gas, and energy industries. There were nine enterprises in which interlocking directorates were formed through a mandate of vice-chairman and one post of the supervisory board excluding chairman and vice-chairman. They were Kaliwerke Aschersleben AG and Kaliwerk Salzdetfurth AG in the mining industry, Rheinische Stahlwerke in the iron and steel industry, Kokswerke und Chemische Fabriken AG and Dynamit AG vorm. Alfred Nobel & Co in the chemical industry, Berliner Maschinenbau AG vorm. L. Schwartzkopff in the machine industry, Kammgarnspinnerei Stöhr & Co. AG in the textile, spinning, and woven goods industries, Sächsische Bodencredit-Anstalt in the banking industry, and Deutsche Continental Gas-Gesellschaft in the electric power, gas, and energy industries. Cases where interlocking directorates were established through two mandates of the supervisory board other than chairman and vice-chairman were 17. Such cases were Gelsenkirchener Bergwerks-AG, Harpener Bergbau AG, and Rheinische AG. für Braunkohlenbergbau und Brikettfabrikation in the mining industry, Deutsche Gold- und Silber-Scheideanstalt vormals Roessler, I.G. Farbenindustrie AG, and Westfälisch-Anhaltische Sprengstoff AG in the chemical industry, AEG and Gesellschaft für elektrische Unternehmungen-Ludw. Loewe & Co. AG in the electric industry, Allgemeine Deutsche Credit-Anstalt and Rheinisch-Westfälische Boden-Credit-Bank in the banking industry, Magdeburger Feuer-Versicherungs-Gesellschaft in the insurance industry, Elektrowerke AG, Elektrizitäts-Aktiengesellschaft vorm. Schuckert und Co., and Ruhrgas AG in the electric power, gas, and energy industries, and Süddeutsche Zucker AG, Rheinisch-Westfälische Kalkwerke, and Hochtief AG. für Hoch- und Tiefbauten vorm. Gebrüder Helfmann in other industries.

Thus, Deutsche Bank's direct interlocking directorates on the supervisory boards of other enterprises were spread over a wide range of industries and had personnel connections with several competitive companies in the same industrial sector through several mandates of the supervisory board. Such cases can be observed, for instance, in Gelsenkirchener Bergwerks-AG and Harpener Bergbau AG in the mining industry, Vereinigte Stahlwerke AG, Klöckner-Werke AG, and Mannesmannröhren-Werke in the iron and steel industry, I.G. Farbenindustrie AG and Deutsche Gold- und Silber-Scheideanstalt vormals Roessler in the chemical industry, AEG and enterprises under Siemens capital line such as Siemens & Halske AG and Siemens-Schuckertwerke AG in the electrical industry, Daimler-Benz AG and BMW in the automobile industry, Demag AG, A. Borsig Maschinenbau AG, and Maschinenfabrik Augsburg-Nürnberg AG (MAN) in the machine industry.

Deutsche Bank established close and strong personnel connections with many companies in various industries through direct interlocking directorates of members of the supervisory board and management board. Such personnel ties enabled this bank to secure much information for its own financial business and decision of policies over industrial enterprises.

4.1.2 Direct Interlocking Directorate of Members of Supervisory Board and Managing Board of Dresdner Bank

Next, regarding the direct interlocking directorate by Dresdner Bank's supervisory board and managing board members on the supervisory board of other enterprises (see Table 4.3), there were 286 companies in which such cases were observed and 333 interlocking mandates. Numbers of both enterprises and mandates were much fewer than those of Deutsche Bank (corresponding numbers 340 and 415, respectively) and those of Dresdner Bank in the period of inflation after World War I (corresponding numbers 381 and 453, respectively) (see Chap. 3).

Considering the distribution of industrial sectors, Dresdner Bank built direct interlocking directorates in 17 companies and had 20 interlocking mandates in the mining industry, and similarly, 14 and 17 in the iron and steel industry, respectively; three each in the metal producing and processing industries; 17 and 18 in the chemical industry; nine and 12 in the electrical industry; six and nine in the automobile industry; 24 and 26 in the machine industry, respectively; one each in the precious machine and optical industries; one each in the shipbuilding industry; four and five in the oil industry; three each in the food industry; 15 each in the textile, spinning, and woven goods industries; 10 and 11 in the distillation industry; eight each in the distributing industry; 55 and 69 in the banking industry; 18 and 19 in the insurance industry; eight and 11 in the electric power, gas, and energy industries; nine each in the transportation industry; and 64 and 76 in other industries, respectively. Among the various industries, excluding the banking industry and the insurance industry, for example, there were many interlocking relations in the mining, iron and steel, chemical, and machine industries. Therefore, Dresdner Bank had close and strong relationships with companies in the key industrial sectors in Germany—the heavy and chemical industries.

Given the situation of interlocking directorates with respect to supervisory board position mandates, in 62 enterprises, there were cases in which interlocking directorates on the supervisory boards of other companies were formed through mandate of chairman of the supervisory board with a total of 62 mandates. In each company, the number of mandates was one, respectively. Numbers of both enterprises and

Table 4.3 Direct interlocking directorates of the members of the supervisory board and the managing board of Dresdner Bank on the supervisory board of other companies (period of National Socialism)

Industries	Position							
	Chairman		Vice-chairman		Supervisory board member excluding chairman and vice-chairman		Total[a]	
	Number of companies	Number of posts	Number of companies	Number of posts	Number of companies	Number of posts	Number of companies	Number of posts
Mining	4	4	2	2	13	14	17	20
Iron and steel	5	5	1	1	9	11	14	17
Metal producing and processing	–	–	1	1	2	2	3	3
Chemical	3	3	2	2	13	13	17	18
Electrical	–	–	5	5	6	7	9	12
Automobile	2	2	1	1	4	6	6	9
Machine	4	4	8	8	14	14	24	26
Precious machine and optical	–	–	–	–	1	1	1	1
Shipbuilding	–	–	1	1	–	–	1	1
Oil	1	1	–	–	3	4	4	5
Food	–	–	–	–	3	3	3	3
Textile, spinning, and woven goods	4	4	6	6	5	5	15	15
Distillation	1	1	1	1	9	9	10	11
Distributing	3	3	1	1	4	4	8	8

(continued)

Table 4.3 (continued)

Industries	Position							
	Chairman		Vice-chairman		Supervisory board member excluding chairman and vice-chairman		Total[a]	
	Number of companies	Number of posts	Number of companies	Number of posts	Number of companies	Number of posts	Number of companies	Number of posts
Banking	13	13	2	2	43	54	55	69
Insurance	–	–	1	1	17	18	18	19
Electric power, gas, and energy	1	1	2	3	6	7	8	11
Transportation	2	2	–	–	7	7	9	9
Other industries	19	19	8	8	43	49	64	76
All industries	62	62	42	43	202	228	286	333

[a] There are cases in which the total number of companies establishing interlocking directorates differed from the total number of companies measured by each position of the supervisory board due to the existence of companies where interlocking directorates through more than two posts were built

Source This table was compiled by the author, based on Mossner (Hrsg) (1936)

mandates were fewer than those of Deutsche Bank (corresponding numbers 97 and 98, respectively) and were those of Dresdner Bank in the period of inflation after World War I (corresponding numbers 87 and 87, respectively). Considering the distribution among industrial sectors, the number of enterprises in which Dresdner Bank formed interlocking directorate was four in the mining industry; similarly, five in the iron and steel industry; three in the chemical industry; two in the automobile industry; four in the machine industry; one in the oil industry; four in the textile, spinning, and woven goods industries; one in the distillation industry; three in the distributing industry; 13 in the banking industry; one in the electric power, gas, and energy industries; two in the transportation industry; and 19 in other industries, respectively. There were cases of interlocking directorate in representative companies of each industry such as Harpener Bergbau AG in the mining industry.

In 42 enterprises, in some cases, interlocking directorates were formed through mandate of vice-chairman of the supervisory board, and the total number of mandates was 43. The numbers of enterprises and mandates were a little fewer than those of Deutsche Bank (corresponding numbers 51 and 51, respectively) and were fewer than those of Dresdner Bank in the inflationary period after World War I (corresponding numbers 59 and 60, respectively). The numbers of enterprises and mandates in which such interlocking cases were formed were two each in the mining industry; similarly, one each in the iron and steel industry, respectively; one each in the metal producing and processing industries; two each in the chemical industry; five each in the electrical industry; one each in the automobile industry; eight each in the machine industry; one each in the shipbuilding industry; six each in the textile, spinning, and woven goods industries; one each in the distillation industry; one each in the distributing industry; two each in the banking industry; one each in the insurance industry; two and three in the electric power, gas, and energy industries, respectively; and eight each in other industries, respectively. In these companies, there were major companies in each industry, such as AEG in the electrical industry.

Interlocking directorates through mandates of supervisory board other than chairman and vice-chairman were observed in 202 companies and the total number of mandates was 228. The numbers of enterprises and mandates were almost same as those of Deutsche Bank (corresponding numbers 225 and 266, respectively). However, the numbers of enterprises and mandates were fewer than those of Dresdner Bank in the inflationary period after World War I (corresponding numbers 277 and 305, respectively). The numbers of enterprises and mandates in which Dresdner Bank built interlocking directorates were 13 and 14 in the mining industry, respectively; similarly, 9 and 11 in the iron and steel industry, respectively; two each in the metal producing and processing industries; 13 each in the chemical industry; six and seven in the electrical industry; four and six in the automobile industry, respectively; 14 each in the machine industry; one each in the precious machine and optical industries; three and four in the oil industry, respectively; three each in the food industry; five each in the textile, spinning, and woven goods industries; nine each in the distillation industry; four each in the distributing industry; 43 and 54 in the banking industry; 17 and 18 in the insurance industry; six and seven in the electric power, gas, and energy industries, respectively; seven each in the transportation industry; and 43 and

49 in other industries, respectively. In these companies, there were major companies in each industry, such as Harpener Bergbau AG in the mining industry, Vereinigte Stahlwerke AG and Rheinische Stahlwerke AG in the iron and steel industry, AEG and Brown, Boveri & Cie. AG in the electrical industry, Daimler-Benz AG and BMW in the automotive industry, Maschinenfabrik Augsburg-Nürnberg AG (MAN) in the machine industry, Deutsch Erdöl-AG in the oil industry, Allianz und Stuttgarter Verein Versicherungs-AG and Münchener Rückversicherungs-Gesellschaft in the insurance industry, and Rheinisch-Westfälisches Elektrizitätwerk AG in the electric power, gas, and energy industries. It is worth stating that Dresdner Bank built interlocking directorate with Commerzbank (Commerz- und Privat-Bank AG) as one of three largest banks and strong competitor for Dresdner Bank.

The numbers of enterprises and mandates were 41 and 88, respectively, when considering cases where supervisory board and managing board members of Dresdner Bank had more than two mandates on the supervisory boards of other companies (see Table 4.4). Numbers of both enterprises and mandates were fewer than those of Deutsche Bank (corresponding numbers 57 and 132, respectively) and those of Dresdner Bank in the period of inflation after World War I (corresponding numbers 58 and 130, respectively). Considering the distribution among industries, the numbers of companies and mandates were as follows: three and six in the mining industry; two and five in the iron and steel industry; one and two in the chemical industry; two and five in the electrical industry; two and five in the automobile industry; two and four in the machine industry; one and two in the oil industry; one and two in the distillation industry; 13 and 27 in the banking industry; one and two in the insurance industry; three and six in the electric power, gas, and energy industries; and 10 and 22 in other industries, respectively. Of these enterprises, there were representative companies in each industry, such as Harpener Bergbau AG in the mining industry, Vereinigte Sthalwerke AG in the iron and steel industry, AEG in the electrical industry, Adlerwerke vorm. Heinrich Kleyer AG in the automobile industry, Deutsch Erdöl-AG in the oil industry, and Allianz und Stuttgarter Verein Versicherungs-AG in the insurance industry.

Of these 41 companies, there were six enterprises in which direct interlocking directorates were built through more than three mandates and the total number of mandates was 18. Numbers of both enterprises and mandates were approximately half of those of Deutsche Bank (corresponding numbers 13 and 44, respectively) and those of Dresdner Bank in the period of inflation after World War I (corresponding numbers 12 and 38, respectively). In the remaining 35 companies, Dresdner Bank had two mandates on the supervisory board of other companies.

Concerning enterprises with three mandates, in Treuhand-Vereinigung AG in other industries, interlocking directorate was formed through a mandate of chairman and two mandates of the supervisory boards except for chairman and vice-chairman. Enterprises in which there were interlocking directorates through one mandate of vice-chairman and two posts of the supervisory board except for chairman and vice-chairman were two: AEG in the electrical industry and Adlerwerke vorm. Heinrich Kleyer AG in the automotive industry. Meanwhile, cases where interlocking directorates were built through three posts of the supervisory board excluding chairman

Table 4.4 Cases in which Dresdner Bank built direct interlocking directorates through more than two posts on the supervisory board of other companies (period of National Socialism)

Industries	Number of posts					
	2		3		Total	
	Number of companies	Number of posts	Number of companies	Number of posts	Number of companies	Number of posts
Mining	3	6	–	–	3	6
Iron and steel	1	2	1	3	2	5
Chemical	1	2	–	–	1	2
Electrical	1	2	1	3	2	5
Automobile	1	2	1	3	2	5
Machine	2	4	–	–	2	4
Oil	1	2	–	–	1	2
Distillation	1	2	–	–	1	2
Banking	12	24	1	3	13	27
Insurance	1	2	–	–	1	2
Electric power, gas, and energy	3	6	–	–	3	6
Other industries	8	16	2	6	10	22
All industries	35	70	6	18	41	88

Source This table was compiled by the author, based on Mossner (Hrsg) (1936)

and vice-chairman can be observed in three enterprises. They were Vereinigte Stahlwerke AG in the iron and steel industry, Allianz und Stuttgarter Lebensversicherungsbank AG in the insurance industry, and Universum-Film AG in other industries.

When considering 35 enterprises with two mandates on the supervisory board of other enterprise in relation to distribution of industrial sector, there were three in the mining industry; one in the iron and steel industry; one in the chemical industry; one in the electrical industry; one in the automobile industry; two in the machine industry; one in the oil industry; one in the distillation industry; 12 in the banking industry; one in the insurance industry; three in the electric power, gas, and energy industries; eight in the transportation industry; and five in other industries.

Considering these interlocking directorates with respect to supervisory board position mandates, in Hotelbetriebs-AG in other industries, interlocking directorates were built through one each of mandate of chairman and vice-chairman. Enterprises in which interlocking directorates were established through one post of chairman and a mandate of the supervisory board except for chairman and vice-chairman were nine. These enterprises were Harpener Bergbau AG and Grube

Leopold AG in the mining industry, Mitteldeutsche Stahlwerke AG in the iron and steel industry, Wintershall AG in the chemical industry, Engelhardt-Brauerei AG in the distillation industry, Deutsche Bau- und Bodenbank AG and Hermes Kreditversicherungsbank AG in the banking industry, and Berliner Druck- und Zeitungsbetriebe AG and Norddeutsche Eiswerke AG in other industries. In Brandenburgische Elektricitäts-, Gas- und Wasser-Werke AG in the electric power, gas, and energy industries, interlocking directorates were formed through two mandates of vice-chairman. There were seven enterprises where interlocking directorates were built through a mandate of vice-chairman and one post of the supervisory board other than chairman and vice-chairman. Such cases were observed in Gesellschaft für elektrische Unternehmungen-Ludw. Loewe & Co. AG in the electrical industry, Waggon- und Maschinenfabrik vorm. Busch and Rheinmetall-Borsig AG (Rheinische Metallwaaren- und Maschinenfabrik) in the machine industry, Mercurbank in banking industry, Elektricitäts-Lieferungs Gesellschaft in the electric power, gas, and energy industries, and Deutsche Atlantische Telegraphengesellschaft AG and Norddeutsche Portland-Cementfabtik Misburg, AG in other industries. Cases where Dresdner Bank had two mandates of the supervisory board excluding chairman and vice-chairman can be observed in 17 companies. Such enterprises were Rheinische AG für Braunkohlenbergbau und Brikettfabrikation in the mining industry, Daimler-Benz AG in the automobile industry, Deutsch Erdöl-AG in the oil industry, Bank von Danzig, Bank des Berliner Kassenvereins, Commerz- und Privat-Bank AG, Akzeptbank AG, Allgemeine Deutsche Creditanstalt, Norddeutsche Kreditbank AG, Nordstern Lebensversicherungsbank AG, Bank für Brau-Industrie, and Deutsche Hypothekenbank, Meiningen in the banking industry, Allianz und Stuttgarter Verein Versicherungs-AG in the insurance industry, Deutsche Electrizitätswerke zu Aachen Garbe, Lahmeyer & Co., AG in the electric power, gas, and energy industries, and Zucker-Raffinerei Hildesheim GmbH, Zuckerfabrik Klein-Wanzleben vorm. Rabbethge & Giesecke AG, and Gemeinnützige Baugesellschaft für Aachen und Burtscheid AG in other industries.

Thus, Dresdner Bank's direct interlocking directorates on the supervisory boards of other enterprises spread over a wide range of industries and had personnel connections with several competitive companies mutually in the same industrial sector through several mandates of the supervisory board. Such cases can be observed, for example, in Harpener Bergbau AG and Gebrüder Stumm GmbH in the mining industry, Vereinigte Stahlwerke AG and Rheinische Stahlwerke AG in the iron and steel industry, AEG and Brown, Boveri & Cie. AG in the electrical industry, Daimler-Benz AG, Bayerische Motoren Werke AG, and Adlerwerke vorm. Hein- rich Kleyer AG in the automotive industry, Commerz- und Privat-Bank AG as one of the strongest competitors for Dresdner Bank in the banking industry. Dresdner Bank established strong and close personnel relationships with many companies in various industrial sectors through direct interlocking directorates of supervisory board and management board members, which had great significance for securing much information on its own financial business and decision of policies over industrial enterprises.

4.1.3 Direct Interlocking Directorate of Members of Supervisory Board and Managing Board of Commerzbank

Furthermore, in examining the direct interlocking directorate by members Commerzbank's supervisory board and managing board members on the supervisory board of other enterprises (see Table 4.5), there were 240 companies in which such cases were observed and 286 interlocking mandates. Numbers of both enterprises and mandates were much fewer than those of Deutsche Bank (corresponding numbers 340 and 415, respectively) and were fewer than those of Dresdner Bank (similarly 286 and 333, respectively). They were also even fewer than those of Commerzbank in the period of inflation after World War I (corresponding numbers 368 and 431, respectively) (see Chap. 3).

Considering the distribution of industrial sectors, Commerzbank built direct interlocking directorates in 12 companies and had 15 interlocking mandates in the mining industry, and similarly, 13 and 18 in the iron and steel industry; nine and 10 in the metal producing and processing industries; 11 and 14 in the chemical industry, respectively; 12 each in the electrical industry; four and five in the automobile industry; 23 and 24 in the machine industry; three and four in the shipbuilding industry, respectively; two each in the oil industry; two each in the food industry; nine each in the textile, spinning, and woven goods industries; 11 and 15 in the distillation industry, respectively; nine each in the distributing industry; 29 and 37 in the banking industry; 13 and 15 in the insurance industry; six and nine in the electric power, gas, and energy industries; 11 and 13 in the transportation industry; and 61 and 73 in other industries, respectively. Among the various industries, except for the banking industry and the insurance industry, for example, there were many interlocking relationships in the mining, iron and steel, chemical, electrical, machine, distillation, and transportation industries. Therefore, Commerzbank had close and strong relationships with companies in the heavy and chemical industries as the key industrial sectors in Germany and the banking industry.

Given the situation of interlocking directorates concerning the position of mandate of supervisory board, in 53 enterprises, there were cases in which interlocking directorates on the supervisory boards of other companies were formed through mandate of chairman of the supervisory board with a total of 53 mandates. In each company, number of mandates was one. Numbers of both enterprises and mandates were much fewer than those of Deutsche Bank (corresponding numbers 97 and 98, respectively) and were a little fewer than those of Dresdner Bank (similarly 62 and 62, respectively). They were even fewer than those of Commerzbank in the period of inflation after World War I (corresponding numbers 105 and 107, respectively). Regarding the distribution among industrial sectors, the number of enterprises in which Commerzbank formed interlocking directorate was three in the mining industry; similarly, three in the iron and steel industry; one in the metal producing and processing industries; two in the chemical industry; three in the electrical industry; one in the automotive industry; six in the machine industry; four in

Table 4.5 Direct interlocking directorates of the members of the supervisory board and the managing board of Commerzbank on the supervisory board of other companies (period of National Socialism)

Industries	Position							
	Chairman		Vice-chairman		Supervisory board member excluding chairman and vice-chairman		Total[a]	
	Number of companies	Number of posts	Number of companies	Number of posts	Number of companies	Number of posts	Number of companies	Number of posts
Mining	3	3	1	1	8	11	12	15
Iron and steel	3	3	–	–	12	15	13	18
Metal producing and processing	1	1	3	3	6	6	9	10
Chemical	2	2	–	–	10	12	11	14
Electrical	3	3	2	2	7	7	12	12
Automobile	1	1	–	–	3	4	4	5
Machine	6	6	4	4	14	14	23	24
Shipbuilding	–	–	–	–	3	4	3	4
Oil	–	–	–	–	2	2	2	2
Food	–	–	1	1	1	1	2	2
Textile, spinning, and woven goods	4	4	1	1	4	4	9	9
Distillation	2	2	4	4	7	9	11	15
Distributing	3	3	–	–	6	6	9	9
Banking	2	2	1	1	28	34	29	37
Insurance	1	1	–	–	12	14	13	15

(continued)

Table 4.5 (continued)

Industries	Position							
	Chairman		Vice-chairman		Supervisory board member excluding chairman and vice-chairman		Total[a]	
	Number of companies	Number of posts	Number of companies	Number of posts	Number of companies	Number of posts	Number of companies	Number of posts
Electric power, gas, and energy	–	–	1	1	5	8	6	9
Transportation	4	4	1	2	7	7	11	13
Other industries	18	18	7	7	45	48	61	73
All industries	53	53	26	27	180	206	240	286

[a] There are cases in which the total number of companies establishing interlocking directorates differed from the total number of companies measured by each position of the supervisory board due to the existence of companies where interlocking directorates through more than two posts were built

Source This table was compiled by the author, based on Mossner (Hrsg) (1936)

the textile, spinning, and woven goods industries; two in the distillation industry; three in the distributing industry; two in the banking industry; one in the insurance industry; four in the transportation industry; and 18 in other industries, respectively.

In 26 enterprises, interlocking directorates were formed through mandate of vice-chairman of the supervisory board, and the total number of mandates was 27. The numbers of enterprises and mandates were approximately half of those of Deutsche Bank (corresponding numbers 51 and 51, respectively) and were much fewer than those of Dresdner Bank (similarly 42 and 43, respectively). They were also fewer than those of Commerzbank in the inflationary period after the World War I (corresponding numbers 44 and 44, respectively). The numbers of enterprises and mandates in which such interlocking cases were formed were one each in the mining industry; similarly, three each in the metal producing and processing industries; two each in the electrical industry; four each in the machine industry; one each in the food industry; one each in the textile, spinning, and woven goods industries; four each in the distillation industry; one each in the banking industry; one each in the electric power, gas, and energy industries; one and two in the transportation industry, respectively; and seven each in other industries, respectively.

Interlocking directorates through mandates of supervisory board other than chairman and vice-chairman were observed in 180 companies and the total number of mandates was 206. The numbers of enterprises and mandates were fewer than those of Deutsche Bank (corresponding numbers 225 and 266, respectively) and were a little fewer than those of Dresdner Bank (similarly 202 and 228, respectively). However, numbers of enterprises and mandates were much fewer than those of Commerzbank Bank in the inflationary period after the World War I (corresponding numbers 251 and 280, respectively). The numbers of enterprises and mandates in which Commerzbank built interlocking directorates were eight and 11 in the mining industry, respectively; similarly, 12 and 15 in the iron and steel industry, respectively; six each in the metal producing and processing industries; 10 and 12 in the chemical industry; seven each in the electrical industry; three and four in the automobile industry; 14 each in the machine industry; three and four in the shipbuilding industry; two each in the oil industry; one each in the food industry; four each in the textile, spinning, and woven goods industries; seven and nine in the distillation industry; six each in the distributing industry; 28 and 34 in the banking industry; 12 and 14 in the insurance industry; five and eight in the electric power, gas, and energy industries, respectively; seven each in the transportation industry; and 45 and 48 in other industries, respectively. There were many interlocking directorates in industries such as the iron and steel, chemical, machine, banking, and insurance industries. In these companies, there were major companies in each industry, such as Vereinigte Stahlwerke AG and Klöckner-Werke AG in the iron and steel industry, AEG in the electrical industry, Daimler-Benz AG and Auto-Union AG in the automobile industry, Howaldtswerke AG and Deutsche Werft AG in the shipbuilding industry, and Allianz und Stuttgarter Verein Versicherungs-AG and companies of Gerling grouping in the insurance industry. In addition, Commerzbank built interlocking directorate with Dresdner Bank as one of largest banks in Germany and strong competitor for Commerzbank in banking industry, which had great significance for exchanging and sharing information.

The numbers of enterprises and mandates were 39 and 85, respectively, when considering cases where Commerzbank's supervisory board and managing board members had more than two mandates on the supervisory boards of other companies (see Table 4.6). Numbers of both enterprises and mandates were fewer than those of Deutsche Bank (corresponding numbers 57 and 132, respectively) and were almost same as those of Dresdner Bank (similarly 41 and 88, respectively). They were also fewer than those of Commerzbank in the period of inflation after World War I (corresponding numbers 52 and 115, respectively). Considering the distribution among industries, the numbers of companies and mandates were as follows: two and five in the mining industry; five and 10 in the iron and steel industry; one and two in the metal producing and processing industries; three and six in the chemical industry; one and two in the automobile industry; one and two in the machine industry; one and two in the shipbuilding industry; three and seven in the distillation industry; six and 14 in the banking industry; two and four in the insurance industry; two and five in the electric power, gas, and energy industries; two and four in the transportation industry; and 10 and 22 in other industries, respectively.

Of these 39 companies, there were six enterprises in which direct interlocking directorates were built through more than three mandates and the total number of mandates was 19. Numbers of both enterprise and mandate were fewer than those of Deutsche Bank (corresponding numbers 13 and 44, respectively) and were almost same as those of Dresdner Bank (similarly 6 and 18, respectively). They were fewer than those of Commerzbank in the period of inflation after World War I (corresponding numbers nine and 29, respectively). In the rest 33 companies, Commerzbank had two mandates on the supervisory board of other companies.

Regarding enterprises with more than three mandates, in Hansa-Mühle AG (Hanseatische Mühlenwerke AG) in other industries, interlocking directorates were built through one each of mandate of chairman and vice-chairman and two posts of the supervisory board except for chairman and vice-chairman. Of companies with three mandates, in Brauerei Gebr. Dietrich AG in the distillation industry and Deutsche Hypothekenbank, Meiningen and Deutsche Schiffsbeleihungs-Bank in the banking industry, there were interlocking directorates through a post of chairman and two mandates of the supervisory board except for chairman and vice-chairman, respectively. Meanwhile, cases in which interlocking directorates were formed through three posts of the supervisory board excluding chairman and vice-chairman can be observed in two enterprises: Burbach-Kaliwerke AG in the mining industry and Hamburgische Elektricitäts-Werke AG in the electric power, gas, and energy industries.

When considering 33 enterprises with two mandates on the supervisory board of other enterprise in respect to distribution of industrial sector, there were one in mining industry, five in iron and steel industry, one in metal producing and processing industries, three in chemical industry, one in automotive industry, one in machine industry, one in shipbuilding industry, two in distillation industry, four in banking

Table 4.6 Cases in which Commerzbank built direct interlocking directorates through more than two posts on the supervisory board of other companies (period of National Socialism)

Industries	Number of posts							
	2		3		4		Total	
	Number of companies	Number of posts	Number of companies	Number of posts	Number of companies	Number of posts	Number of companies	Number of posts
Mining	1	2	1	3	–	–	2	5
Iron and steel	5	10	–	–	–	–	5	10
Metal producing and processing	1	2	–	–	–	–	1	2
Chemical	3	6	–	–	–	–	3	6
Automobile	1	2	–	–	–	–	1	2
Machine	1	2	–	–	–	–	1	2
Shipbuilding	1	2	–	–	–	–	1	2
Distillation	2	4	1	3	–	–	3	7
Banking	4	8	2	6	–	–	6	14
Insurance	2	4	–	–	–	–	2	4
Electric power, gas, and energy	1	2	1	3	–	–	2	5
Transportation	2	4	–	–	–	–	2	4
Other industries	9	18	–	–	1	4	10	22
All industries	33	66	5	15	1	4	39	85

Source This table was compiled by the author, based on Mossner (Hrsg) (1936)

industry, two in insurance industry, one in electric power, gas, and energy industries, two in transportation industry, and nine in other industries.

Considering these interlocking directorates in relation to supervisory board position mandates, in Neußer Papier- und Pergamentpapierfabrik AG in other industries, interlocking directorates were built through one each of mandate of chairman and vice-chairman. Enterprises in which interlocking directorates were established through one post of chairman and a mandate of the supervisory board except for chairman and vice-chairman were seven. These enterprises were Buderus'sche Eisenwerke and Hüttenwerke C. Wilhelm Kayser & Co. in the iron and steel industry, Chemische Fabrik Buckau in the chemical industry, Neue Deutsch-Böhmische Elbeschifffahrts-AG in the transportation industry, and Portland Cementwerk Saxonia vorm. Heinr. Laas Söhne, Zuckerfabrik Froebeln AG, and Treuhand AG in other industries. In Neue Norddeutsche und Vereinigte Elbeschifffahrt-AG in the transportation industry, interlocking directorates were formed through two mandates of vice-chairman. There were six enterprises where interlocking directorates were built through a mandate of vice-chairman and one post of the supervisory board excluding chairman and vice-chairman. Such cases were Berlin-Karlsruher Industrie-Werke AG in the metal producing and processing industries, Pittler Werkzeugmaschinenfabrik AG in the machine industry, Schultheiss-Patzenhofer Brauerei AG in the distillation industry, and Portland-Zementwerke Dyckerhoff-Wickung AG, Feldmühle, Papier- und Zellstoffwerke AG, and Zuckerfabrik Fraustadt in other industries. Cases where Commerzbank established interlocking directorates through two mandates of the supervisory board except for chairman and vice-chairman were 18 enterprises. They were Braunkohlen-Industrie AG Zukunft in the mining industry, Klöckner-Werke AG, Vereinigte Stahlwerke AG, and Mitteldeutsche Stahlwerke AG in the iron and steel industry, A. Riebeck'sche Montanwerke AG and Consolidierte Alkaliwerke in the chemical industry, Daimler-Benz AG in the automobile industry, Howaldtswerke AG in the shipbuilding industry, Bavaria und St. Pauli-Brauerei in the distillation industry, Waaren-Commissions-Bank, Westdeutsche Bodenkreditanstalt AG, Dresdner Bank, and Deutsche Centralbodenkredit AG in the banking industry, Elbe und Saale Versicherungs-AG and Köln-Düsseldorfer Versicherungs-AG in the insurance industry, Allgemeine Gas- und Elektrizitäts-Gesellschaft in the electric power, gas, and energy industries, and Boswau & Knauer AG and Hotelbetriebs-AG in other industries.

Thus, Commerzbank's direct interlocking directorates on the supervisory boards of other enterprises were spread over a wide range of industries and had personnel connections with several competitive companies mutually in the same industrial sector through several mandates of the supervisory board. Such cases can be observed in for instance in Vereinigte Stahlwerke AG and Klöckner-Werke AG in the iron and steel industry, Daimler-Benz AG, Auto-Union AG, and Brennabor-Werke AG in the automotive industry, Maschinenbau AG, Balcke, Maschinenfabrik Buckau R. Wolf AG, Orenstein & Koppel AG, and Pittler Werkzeugmaschinenfabrik AG in the machine industry, Howaldtswerke AG and Deutsche Werft AG in the shipbuilding industry, Allianz und Stuttgarter Verein Versicherungs-AG and some companies which belonged to the Gerling group such as Gerling-Konzern Allgemeine Versicherungs-AG, Gerling-Konzern Lebensversicherungs-AG, and Gerling-Konzern Rheinische Versicherungsgruppe AG in the insurance industry. In addition, interlocking directorates were built through two mandates on the supervisory board between Commerzbank AG and Dresdner Bank, which built important foundation for collecting, exchanging, and sharing information between these banks. Commerzbank established close and strong personnel connections with many companies in various industries through direct interlocking directorates of members of the supervisory board and management board, which had great significance for securing much information for its own financial business and decision of policies over industrial enterprises.

In the foregoing analysis, we examined how three largest banks, such as Dresdner bank, Dresdner Bank, and Commerzbank, built personnel connection through direct interlocking directorate of members of supervisory board and managing board on the supervisory board of other enterprises. In comparing with conditions in the period of inflation after World War I, numbers of both companies in which each bank formed direct interlocking directorate and interlocking mandates were smaller. There were differences in the absolute number itself of interlocking directorate of all three large banks. How did such conditions reflect in indirect interlocking directorate built among three banks and between two banks of them? Next section considers conditions of indirect interlocking directorate formed on the supervisory boards of other enterprises among three large banks and between two banks of them in comparison with situations in the period of inflation after World War I.

4.2 Indirect Interlocking Directorates Between Banks on the Supervisory Board of Other Enterprises

Section 4.2 examines how indirect interlocking directorates among three large banks on the supervisory board of other companies were built through direct interlocking of members of the supervisory board and the managing board of each bank.

First, Sect. 4.2.1 explores indirect interlocking directorates among three big banks. Sections 4.2.2 and 4.2.3 consider such personnel connections between Deutsche Bank and Dresdner Bank and between Deutsche Bank and Commerzbank except cases of those among three banks, respectively. Section 4.2.4 examines conditions of indirect interlocking directorates built between Dresdner Bank and Commerzbank.

4.2.1 Indirect Interlocking Directorates Among Three Large Banks on the Supervisory Board of Other Enterprises

Section 4.2.1 considers the situations related to indirect interlocking directorate among three large banks on the supervisory board of other enterprises (see Table 4.7). Such cases can be observed in 36 companies and the total number of mandates was 152. The numbers of enterprises and mandates in which three large banks built indirect interlocking directorates were more than two times than those in the period of inflation after World War I(corresponding numbers 16 and 70, respectively) (see Chap. 3).

Considering interlocking directorate in relation to the kind of mandate, numbers of enterprises and mandates in which indirect interlocking directorates were built through the mandate of chairman were 13 and 14, respectively. Similar numerical figures regarding indirect interlocking directorate through the mandate of vice-chairman were 19 and 25, respectively, and those through mandate of the supervisory board except chairman and vice-chairman were 36 and 113, respectively. When considering the distribution of industry, number of companies, and mandates of interlocking directorate, there were, respectively, three and 11 in the mining industry, four and 21 in the iron and steel industry, five and 17 in the chemical industry, two and 11 in the electrical industry, one and six in the automobile industry, three and nine in the machine industry, one and four in the distillation industry, three and nine in the distributing industry, 10 and 47 in the banking industry, one and four in the insurance industry, and three and 13 in other industries.

To understand bank that was at the leading position in indirect interlocking relation, in examining cases in which one bank or some banks of three large banks had more than two mandates on the supervisory board of other company, such cases were observed in 24 companies. The number of total mandates was 116. Numbers of enterprises and mandates in which such indirect interlocking directorates were built were almost two times than those in the period of inflation after World War I (corresponding numbers 11 and 55, respectively). When considering the distribution of industry, number of companies, and mandates of interlocking directorate, there were, respectively, two and eight in the mining industry, three and 18 in the iron and steel industry, two and eight in the chemical industry, two and 11 in the electrical industry, one and six in the automobile industry, one and four in the distillation industry, nine and 44 in the banking industry, one and four in the insurance industry, and three and 13 in other industries.

The number of companies in which Deutsche Bank, Dresdner Bank, and Commerzbank built indirect interlocking directorate through total nine mandates was one. Similar figures through total eight, six, five, and four mandates were one, three, five, and 14, respectively. In the rest 12 enterprises, indirect interlocking directorates were built through total three mandates, respectively.

Regarding enterprise with total nine mandates in each enterprise, in Vereinigte Stahlwerke AG in the iron and steel industry, whereas Deutsche Bank had four mandates of the supervisory board except for chairman and vice-chairman,

Table 4.7 Indirect interlocking directorates of the members of the supervisory board and the managing board on the supervisory board of other companies among Deutsche Bank, Dresdner Bank, and Commerzbank (period of National Socialism)

Industries	Number of posts													
	3		4		5		6		8		9		Total	
	Number of companies	Number of posts	Number of companies	Number of posts	Number of companies	Number of posts	Number of companies	Number of posts	Number of companies	Number of posts	Number of companies	Number of posts	Number of companies	Number of posts
Mining	1	3	2	8	–	–	–	–	–	–	–	–	3	11
Iron and steel	1	3	1	4	1	5	–	–	–	–	1	9	4	21
Chemical	3	9	2	8	–	–	–	–	–	–	–	–	5	17
Electrical	–	–	–	–	1	5	1	6	–	–	–	–	2	11
Automobile	–	–	–	–	–	–	1	6	–	–	–	–	1	6
Machine	3	9	–	–	–	–	–	–	–	–	–	–	3	9
Distillation	–	–	1	4	–	–	–	–	–	–	–	–	1	4
Distributing	3	9	–	–	–	–	–	–	–	–	–	–	3	9
Banking	1	3	5	20	2	10	1	6	1	8	–	–	10	47
Insurance	–	–	1	4	–	–	–	–	–	–	–	–	1	4
Other Industries	–	–	2	8	1	5	–	–	–	–	–	–	3	13
All industries	12	36	14	56	5	25	3	18	1	8	1	9	36	152

Source This table was compiled by the author, based on Mossner (Hrsg) (1936)

Dresdner Bank and Commerzbank had three and two similar mandates, respectively. In Deutsche Hypothekenbank, Meiningen in the banking industry, whereas Commerzbank had a mandate of chairman and two posts of the supervisory board except for chairman and vice-chairman, Deutsche Bank held a mandate of vice-chairman and two post of the supervisory board except for chairman and vice-chairman. Meanwhile, Dresdner Bank had two mandates of the supervisory board excluding chairman and vice-chairman. Of three enterprises with total six mandates in each enterprise, in AEG the electrical industry, whereas Dresdner Bank had three mandates consisting of a mandate of vice-chairman and two posts of the supervisory board except for chairman and vice-chairman, Deutsche Bank held two posts of the supervisory board except for chairman and vice-chairman. Commerzbank had one post of the supervisory board except for chairman and vice-chairman. In Daimler-Benz AG in the automobile industry, whereas Deutsche Bank had one each of mandate of chairman and vice-chairman, Dresdner Bank and Commerzbank held two posts of the supervisory board except for chairman and vice-chairman, respectively. In Deutsche Centralbodenkredit AG in the banking industry, whereas Deutsche Bank had three mandates consisting of a mandate of chairman and two posts of the supervisory board excluding chairman and vice-chairman, Commerzbank held two posts of the supervisory board excluding chairman and vice-chairman. Meanwhile, Dresdner Bank had one post of the supervisory board other than chairman and vice-chairman.

Of five enterprises with total five mandates in each enterprise, in Mitteldeutsche Stahlwerke AG in the iron and steel industry, whereas Dresdner Bank had a mandate of chairman and one post of the supervisory board except for chairman and vice-chairman, Commerzbank had two mandates of the supervisory board except for chairman and vice-chairman. Meanwhile, Deutsche Bank held one post of the supervisory board excluding chairman and vice-chairman. In Gesellschaft für elektrische Unternehmungen-Ludw. Loewe & Co. AG in the electrical industry, whereas Dresdner Bank held a mandate of vice-chairman and one post of the supervisory board except for chairman and vice-chairman, Deutsche Bank had two posts of the supervisory board except for chairman and vice-chairman. Commerzbank had one mandate of the supervisory board except for chairman and vice-chairman. In Universum-Film AG in other industries, whereas Dresdner Bank held three mandates of the supervisory board excluding chairman and vice-chairman, Deutsche Bank had a mandate of chairman and Commerzbank had one mandate of the supervisory board excluding chairman and vice-chairman. In Allianz und Stuttgarter Lebensversicherungsbank AG in the banking industry, whereas Dresdner Bank had three mandates of the supervisory board except for chairman and vice-chairman, Deutsche Bank and Commerzbank had a mandate of the supervisory board except for chairman and vice-chairman, respectively. In Allgemeine Deutsche Credit-Anstalt in the banking industry, whereas Deutsche Bank and Dresdner Bank held two mandates of the supervisory board except for chairman and vice-chairman, respectively, Commerzbank had a mandate of the supervisory board except for chairman and vice-chairman.

Concerning 14 companies with total four posts in each company, in Mansfeld AG für Bergbau und Hüttenbetrieb in the iron and steel industry, whereas

Deutsche Bank had a mandate of chairman and one post of the supervisory board except for chairman and vice-chairman, Dresdner Bank held one mandate of vice-chairman, and Commerzbank had one post of the supervisory board except for chairman and vice-chairman. In Deutsche-Asiatische Bank in the banking industry, whereas Deutsche Bank held one each of mandate of chairman and vice-chairman, Dresdner Bank and Commerzbank held one mandate of vice-chairman, and Commerzbank had one post of the supervisory board excluding chairman and vice-chairman, respectively. In Westdeutsche Bodenkreditanstalt in the banking industry, whereas Commerzbank held two mandates of the supervisory board except for chairman and vice-chairman, Deutsche Bank had one mandate of chairman and Dresdner Bank had one post of the supervisory board other than chairman and vice-chairman. In Kaliwerke Aschersleben AG and Kaliwerk Salzdetfurth AG in the mining industry, whereas Deutsche Bank had two mandates of the supervisory board excluding chairman and vice-chairman, Dresdner Bank had one mandate of vice-chairman and Commerzbank held one post of the supervisory board excluding chairman and vice-chairman, respectively. In Consolidierte Alkaliwerke in the chemical industry, whereas Commerzbank had two mandates of the supervisory board excluding chairman and vice-chairman, Deutsche Bank and Dresdner Bank had one post of vice-chairman, respectively. In Kokswerke und Chemische Fabriken AG in the chemical industry, whereas Deutsche Bank held a mandate of vice-chairman and one post of the supervisory board except for chairman and vice-chairman, Dresdner Bank and Commerzbank had one post of the supervisory board except for chairman and vice-chairman, respectively. In Schultheiss-Patzenhofer Brauerei AG in the distillation industry, whereas Commerzbank held one post of vice-chairman and a mandate of the supervisory board except for chairman and vice-chairman, Deutsche Bank and Dresdner Bank had one post of vice-chairman, respectively. In Portland-Zementwerke Dyckerhoff-Wickung AG in other industries, whereas Commerzbank held one post of vice-chairman and a mandate of the supervisory board except for chairman and vice-chairman, Dresdner Bank had one post of vice-chairman and Deutsche Bank held one post of the supervisory board except for chairman and vice-chairman. In Akzeptbank AG in the banking industry, whereas Dresdner Bank held two mandates of the supervisory board excluding chairman and vice-chairman, Commerzbank held one mandate of vice-chairman and Deutsche Bank had one post of the supervisory board excluding chairman and vice-chairman. In Feldmühle, Papier- und Zellstoffwerke AG in other industries, whereas Commerzbank held one post of vice-chairman and a mandate of the supervisory board except for chairman and vice-chairman, Deutsche Bank and Dresdner Bank had one post of the supervisory board except for chairman and vice-chairman, respectively. In Bank des Berliner Kassenvereins in the banking industry and Allianz und Stuttgarter Verein Versicherungs-AG in the insurance industry, whereas Dresdner Bank had two mandates of the supervisory board except for chairman and vice-chairman, Deutsche Bank and Commerzbank held one mandate of the supervisory board except for chairman and vice-chairman, respectively. In Rheinisch-Westfälische Boden-Credit-Bank in the banking industry, whereas Deutsche Bank held two mandates of the supervisory board excluding chairman and vice-chairman, Dresdner Bank and Commerzbank had one post of the supervisory board excluding chairman and vice-chairman, respectively.

Of 12 firms with total three mandates in each firm, in Orenstein & Koppel AG in the machine industry, whereas Deutsche Bank and Dresdner Bank had a mandate of chairman, respectively, Commerzbank had a post of the supervisory board except for chairman and vice-chairman. In Bergbau AG Lothringen in the mining industry, whereas Deutsche Bank had one mandate of chairman, Commerzbank had a mandate of vice-chairman and Dresdner Bank held one post of the supervisory board except for chairman and vice-chairman. In Einheitspreise AG in the distributing industry, whereas Commerzbank had one mandate of chairman, Dresdner Bank had a mandate of vice-chairman and Deutsche Bank held one post of the supervisory board excluding chairman and vice-chairman. In Eisenwerk-Gesellschaft Maximilianshütte in the iron and steel industry and Gesellschaft für Getreidehandel AG in the distributing industry, whereas Dresdner Bank had one mandate of chairman, Deutsche Bank and Commerzbank held one post of the supervisory board except for chairman and vice-chairman, respectively. In Kali-Chemie AG in the chemical industry, whereas Deutsche Bank had one mandate of chairman, Dresdner Bank and Commerzbank had one post of the supervisory board except for chairman and vice-chairman, respectively. In Eisenbahn-Verkehrsmittel AG in the machine industry, whereas Deutsche Bank had one mandate of vice-chairman, Dresdner Bank and Commerzbank had a mandate of the supervisory board excluding chairman and vice-chairman, respectively. In AG für Waggonbauwerte in the machine industry, whereas Dresdner Bank had one mandate of vice-chairman, Deutsche Bank and Commerzbank held one post of the supervisory board other than chairman and vice-chairman, respectively. In four enterprises, namely, Rütgers Werke AG and Königsberger Zellstoff-Fabriken und Chemische Werke Koholyt AG in the chemical industry, Deutscher Eisenhandel AG in the distributing industry, and Deutsche Hypothekenbank AG in the banking industry, Deutsche Bank, Dresdner Bank, and Commerzbank held one post of the supervisory board excluding chairman and vice-chairman, respectively.

4.2.2 Indirect Interlocking Directorates Between Deutsche Bank and Dresdner Bank on the Supervisory Board of Other Enterprises

Next, in examining the situations related to indirect interlocking directorates between Deutsche Bank and Dresdner Bank on the supervisory board of other enterprises (see Table 4.8), such cases can be observed in 35 companies and the total number of mandates was 93 except cases of indirect interlocking directorates among three big banks. The numbers of enterprises and mandates in which Deutsche Bank and Dresdner Bank built indirect interlocking directorates were almost same as those in the period of inflation after World War I (corresponding numbers 37 and 90, respectively).

Table 4.8 Indirect interlocking directorates of the members of the supervisory board and the managing board on the supervisory board of other companies between Deutsche Bank and Dresdner Bank[a] (period of National Socialism)

Industries	Number of posts											
	2		3		4		5		6		Total	
	Number of companies	Number of posts	Number of companies	Number of posts	Number of companies	Number of posts	Number of companies	Number of posts	Number of companies	Number of posts	Number of companies	Number of posts
Mining	3	6	–	–	3	12	–	–	–	–	6	18
Iron and steel	–	–	1	3	–	–	–	–	–	–	1	3
Metal producing and processing	1	2	–	–	–	–	–	–	–	–	1	2
Chemical	3	6	3	9	–	–	–	–	–	–	6	15
Automobile	–	–	1	3	–	–	–	–	–	–	1	3
Machine	1	2	–	–	–	–	–	–	1	6	2	8
Precious machine and optical	1	2	–	–	–	–	–	–	–	–	1	2
Oil	–	–	1	3	–	–	–	–	–	–	1	3
Banking	4	8	3	9	–	–	–	–	–	–	7	17
Insurance	1	2	–	–	–	–	–	–	–	–	1	2
Electric power, gas, and energy	2	4	–	–	–	–	–	–	–	–	2	4

(continued)

Table 4.8 (continued)

Industries	Number of posts											
	2		3		4		5		6		Total	
	Number of companies	Number of posts	Number of companies	Number of posts	Number of companies	Number of posts	Number of companies	Number of posts	Number of companies	Number of posts	Number of companies	Number of posts
Other Industries	4	8	1	3	–	–	1	5	–	–	6	16
All industries	20	40	10	30	3	12	1	5	1	6	35	93

[a] The cases of indirect interlocking directorates built among Deutsche Bank, Dresdner Bank, and Commerzbank are excluded

Source This table was compiled by the author, based on Mossner (Hrsg) (1936)

Considering interlocking directorate in relation to the kind of mandate, the numbers of enterprises and mandates in which indirect interlocking directorates were formed through the mandate of chairman were nine each, respectively. Similar numerical figures through mandate of vice-chairman and post of the supervisory board except chairman and vice-chairman were 11 each and 33 and 73, respectively. When considering the distribution of industry, the numbers of companies and mandates of interlocking directorate were six and 18 in the mining industry, one and three in the iron and steel industry, one and two in the metal producing and processing industries, six and 15 in the chemical industry, one and three in the automobile industry, two and eight in the machine industry, one and two in the precious machine and optical industries, one and three in the oil industry, seven and 17 in the banking industry, one and two in the insurance industry, two and four in the electric power, gas, and energy industries; and six and 16 in other industries, respectively.

To understand bank at the leading position in indirect interlocking relation, in examining cases in which one bank or both Deutsche Bank and Dresdner Bank had more than two mandates on the supervisory board of other company, such cases were observed in 15 companies. The total number of mandates was 53. When considering the distribution of industry, number of companies, and mandates of interlocking directorate, there were, respectively, three and 12 in mining industry, one and three in iron and steel industry, three and nine in chemical industry, one and three in automobile industry, one and six in machine industry, one and three in oil industry, three and nine in banking industry, two and eight in other industries.

The number of companies in which Deutsche Bank and Dresdner Bank built indirect interlocking directorate through total six mandates was one. Similar figures through total five mandates, four mandates, and three mandates were one, three, and 10, respectively. In the remaining 20 enterprises, indirect interlocking directorates were built through total two mandates, respectively.

In Rheinische Metallwaaren- und Maschinenfabrik (Rheinmetall-Borsig AG) in machine industry, whereas Deutsche Bank had four mandates of the supervisory board except for chairman and vice-chairman, Dresdner Bank had one post of vice-chairman and one post of the supervisory board except for chairman and vice-chairman. In Deutsche Atlantische Telegraphengesellschaft in other industries, whereas Deutsche Bank had three mandates of the supervisory board except for chairman and vice-chairman, Dresdner Bank had a mandate of vice-chairman and one post of the supervisory board except for chairman and vice-chairman.

Of three enterprises with total four mandates in each enterprise, in Harpener Bergbau AG in the mining industry, whereas Dresdner Bank had a mandate of chairman and one post of the supervisory board excluding chairman and vice-chairman, Deutsche Bank held two mandates of the supervisory board excluding chairman and vice-chairman. In Rheinische AG für Braunkohlenbergbau und Brikettfabrikation in the mining industry, Deutsche Bank and Dresdner Bank held two posts of the supervisory board except for chairman and vice-chairman, respectively. In Essener Steinkohlenbergwerke AG in the mining industry, whereas Deutsche Bank had three mandates of the supervisory board except for chairman and vice-chairman,

Dresdner Bank held a mandate of the supervisory board except for chairman and vice-chairman.

Regarding enterprises with total three mandates in each enterprise, in BMW in the automobile industry, whereas Deutsche Bank had one each of mandate of chairman and vice-chairman, Dresdner Bank held a mandate of the supervisory board except for chairman and vice-chairman. In Sächsische Bodencreditanstalt in the baking industry, Deutsche Bank had a mandate of vice-chairman and one post of the supervisory board except for chairman and vice-chairman. Meanwhile, Dresdner Bank held a mandate of chairman. In Wintershall AG in the chemical industry, whereas Dresdner Bank had a mandate of chairman and one post of the supervisory board excluding chairman and vice-chairman, Deutsche Bank had one mandate of chairman. In Rheinische Stahlwerke in the iron and steel industry and Dynamit AG, vormals Alfred Nobel & Co. in the chemical industry, whereas Deutsche Bank had a mandate of vice-chairman and one post of the supervisory board other than chairman and vice-chairman, Dresdner Bank had one mandate of the supervisory board excluding chairman and vice-chairman, respectively. In Bank von Danzig in the banking industry, whereas Dresdner Bank held two posts of the supervisory board except for chairman and vice-chairman, Deutsche Bank had one post of vice-chairman. In Deutsche Gold- und Silber-Scheideanstalt vormals Roessler in the chemical industry and Süddeutsche Zucker AG in other industries, whereas Deutsche Bank had two mandates of the supervisory board except for chairman and vice-chairman, Dresdner Bank held one post of the supervisory board except for chairman and vice-chairman, respectively. In Deutsche Erdöl-AG in the oil industry and Nordstern Lebensversicherungsbank AG in the banking industry, whereas Dresdner Bank had two mandates of the supervisory board except for chairman and vice-chairman, Deutsche Bank had one mandate of the supervisory board except for chairman and vice-chairman.

Concerning the remaining 20 companies with total two mandates in each company, the number of companies of interlocking directorate was three in the mining industry, one in the metal producing and processing industries, three in the chemical industry, one in the machine industry, one in the precious machine and optical industries, four in the banking industry, one in the insurance industry, two in the electric power, gas, and energy industries, and four in other industries, respectively.

Cases wherein each of two banks had one chairman post or a post of vice-chairman can be observed in two enterprises. In two enterprises, namely, Hugo Schneider AG in the metal producing and processing industries and Charlottenburger Wasser- und Industriewerke AG in other industries, whereas Deutsche Bank had a mandate of chairman, Dresdner Bank had one post of vice-chairman, respectively. Cases in which each of two banks had one chairman post or a post of the supervisory board except for chairman and vice-chairman can be observed in three enterprises. In Bayerische Stickstoff-Werke AG in the chemical industry, whereas Deutsche Bank had a mandate of chairman, Dresdner Bank held a post of the supervisory board excluding chairman and vice-chairman. Meanwhile, in Gebrüder Stumm GmbH in the mining industry and Dessauer Werke für Zucker- und Chemische Industrie AG in the chemical industry, whereas Dresdner Bank had a mandate of chairman, Deutsche

Bank had one post of the supervisory board except for chairman and vice-chairman, respectively. Cases where each of two banks had a vice-chairman or one post of the supervisory board except for chairman and vice-chairman were seen in two enterprises: Industriefinanzierungs-AG Ost in the banking industry and Wesermühlen AG in other industries. In these enterprises, whereas Deutsche Bank had a mandate of vice-chairman, Dresdner Bank had one mandate of the supervisory board excluding chairman and vice-chairman, respectively. Companies in which each of two banks had one post of the supervisory board except for chairman and vice-chairman, respectively, were 13. They were Braunkohlen- und Brikettwerke Roddergrube and Essener Bergwerks-Verein König Wilhelm in the mining industry, Joseph Gautsch AG in the chemical industry, Maschinenfabrik Augsburg-Nürnberug AG (MAN) in the machine industry, Zeiss Ikon AG in the precious machine and optical industries, Amsterdamsche Crediet Maatschappij N. V., Reischs-Kredit Gesellschaftb AG, and Karlsruher Lebensversicherungsbank AG in the banking industry, Aachener und Münchener Feuer-Versicherungs-Gesellschaft in the insurance industry, Rheinisch-Westfälisches Elektrizitätwerk AG and Main-Kraftwere AG in electric power, gas, and energy industries, and Stärke-Zuckerfabrik-AG vorm. C.A. Koehlmann and AG für Zellstoff- und Papierfabriktion in other industries.

4.2.3 Indirect Interlocking Directorates Between Deutsche Bank and Commerzbank on the Supervisory Board of Other Enterprises

Furthermore, in examining the situations related to indirect interlocking directorates between Deutsche Bank and Commerzbank on the supervisory board of other enterprises (see Table 4.9), such cases can be observed in 32 companies and the total number of mandates was 76 except cases of indirect interlocking directorates among three big banks. The numbers of enterprises and mandates in which Deutsche Bank and Commerzbank formed indirect interlocking directorate were less than those of indirect interlocking directorate built between Deutsche Bank and Dresdner Bank (corresponding number 35 and 93, respectively) and those in which Deutsche Bank and Commerzbank built indirect interlocking directorate in the period of inflation after World War I (corresponding numbers 34 and 91, respectively).

Considering interlocking directorate concerning the kind of mandate, the numbers of enterprises and mandates in which indirect interlocking directorates were established through the mandate of chairman were 15 each, respectively. Similar numerical figures through mandate of vice-chairman and post of the supervisory board except chairman and vice-chairman were 11 each and 30 and 50, respectively. When considering the distribution of industry, the numbers of companies and mandates of interlocking directorate were five and 11 in the mining industry, three and nine in the iron and steel industry, three and eight in the metal producing and processing industries, four and 11 in the chemical industry, one and two in the electrical industry,

Table 4.9 Indirect interlocking directorates of the members of the supervisory board and the managing board on the supervisory board of other companies between Deutsche Bank and Commerzbank[a] (period of National Socialism)

Industries	Number of posts							
	2		3		4		Total	
	Number of companies	Number of posts	Number of companies	Number of posts	Number of companies	Number of posts	Number of companies	Number of posts
Mining	4	8	1	3	–	–	5	11
Iron and steel	1	2	1	3	1	4	3	9
Metal producing and processing	1	2	2	6	–	–	3	8
Chemical	2	4	1	3	1	4	4	11
Electrical	1	2	–	–	–	–	1	2
Machine	2	4	–	–	–	–	2	4
Distributing	2	4	–	–	–	–	2	4
Insurance	1	2	–	–	–	–	1	2
Electric power, gas, and energy	1	2	1	3	–	–	2	5
Transportation	2	4	–	–	–	–	2	4
Other industries	5	10	2	6	–	–	7	16
All industries	22	44	8	24	2	8	32	76

[a] The cases of indirect interlocking directorates built among Deutsche Bank, Dresdner Bank, and Commerzbank are excluded
Source This table was compiled by the author, based on Mossner (Hrsg) (1936)

two and four in the machine industry, two and four in the distributing industry, one and two in the insurance industry, two and five in the electric power, gas, and energy industries; two and four in the transportation industry, and seven and 16 in other industries, respectively.

There were 10 enterprises in which Deutsche Bank and Commerzbank built indirect interlocking directorate through more than total three mandates on the supervisory board of other enterprise. The total number of mandates was 32. The number of companies in which Deutsche Bank and Commerzbank built such indirect interlocking directorate through total four mandates was two. Similar numerical figure through total three mandates was eight. In the rest 22 enterprises, indirect interlocking directorates were built through total two mandates, respectively.

Regarding enterprises with total four mandates, in Klöckner-Werke AG in the iron and steel industry and A. Riebweck'sche Montanwerke AG in the chemical industry, whereas Deutsche Bank had one each of mandate of chairman and vice-chairman, Commerzbank held two posts of the supervisory board excluding chairman and vice-chairman, respectively.

Of eight companies with total three mandates in each company, in Hüttenwerke C. Wilhelm Kayser & Co. in the iron and steel industry, whereas Commerzbank had a mandate of chairman and one post of the supervisory board except for chairman and vice-chairman, Deutsche Bank held one mandate of vice-chairman. In AG für Bergbau, Blei- und Zinkfabrikation in the metal producing and processing industries, whereas Deutsche Bank had a mandate of chairman and one post of the supervisory board excluding chairman and vice-chairman, Commerzbank had one mandate of the supervisory board excluding chairman and vice-chairman. In Chemische Fabrik Buckau in the chemical industry, Commerzbank had a mandate of chairman and one post of the supervisory board except chairman and vice-chairman. Meanwhile, Deutsche Bank had a mandate of vice-chairman and one post of the supervisory board other than chairman and vice-chairman. In Braunkohlen-Industrie AG Zukunft in the mining industry, whereas Commerzbank had two mandates of the supervisory board except for chairman and vice-chairman, Deutsche Bank had a mandate of chairman. In Berlin-Karlsruher Industrie-Werke AG in the metal producing and processing industries, whereas Commerzbank had a mandate of vice-chairman and one post of the supervisory board except for chairman and vice-chairman, Deutsche Bank had one post of the supervisory board except for chairman and vice-chairman. In Hochtief AG für Hoch- und Tiefbauten vorm. Gebrüder Helfmann and Rheinisch-Westfälische Kalkwerke in other industries, whereas Deutsche Bank had two mandates of the supervisory board except for chairman and vice-chairman, Commerzbank had one mandate of the supervisory board except for chairman and vice-chairman. In Allgemeine Gas- und Elektricitäts-Gesellschaft in the electric power, gas, and energy industries, whereas Commerzbank had two mandates of the supervisory board excluding chairman and vice-chairman, Deutsche Bank held one mandate of the supervisory board excluding chairman and vice-chairman.

Concerning the rest 22 firms with total two mandates in each firm, the number of companies of interlocking directorate was four in the mining industry, one in the iron and steel industry, one in the metal producing and processing industries, two in the chemical industry, one in the electrical industry, two in the machine industry, two in the distributing industry, one in the insurance industry, one in the electric power, gas, and energy industries, two in the transportation industry, and five in other industries, respectively.

Cases in which each of two banks had one chairman post or a post of vice-chairman were two companies: "Eintracht" Braunkohlenwerke und Briketfabriken in the mining industry and Deutsche Eisenbahn-Betriebs-Gesellschaft in the transportation industry. In these two companies, whereas Commerzbank had a mandate of chairman, Deutsche Bank had one post of vice-chairman, respectively. Cases where each of two banks had one chairman post or a post of the supervisory board except for chairman and vice-chairman can be observed in seven enterprises. In six enterprises, namely Gewerkschaft Salzbergwerk Neu-Stassfurt in the mining industry, Isselburger Hütte AG in the iron and steel industry, Humboldt-Deutzmotoren AG in the machine industry, Eckhardt & Co. AG in the distributing industry, Santa. Catharnia Eisenbahn AG in the transportation industry, and Porzellanfabrik Kahla in other industries, whereas Deutsche Bank had a mandate of chairman, Commerzbank had one post of the supervisory board except for chairman and vice-chairman, respectively. Meanwhile, in Ilse Bergbau AG in the mining industry, whereas Commerzbank had a mandate of chairman, Deutsche Bank held one mandate of the supervisory board except for chairman and vice-chairman. Enterprises in which each of two banks had a vice-chairman or one post of the supervisory board except for chairman and vice-chairman was five enterprises. In four enterprises, namely, Mansfeld'sche Kupferschieferbergbau AG in the mining industry, Th. Goldschmidt AG in the chemical industry, Elektrische Licht- und Kraftanlagen AG in the electrical industry, and Beamtenversicherungsverein des Deutschen Bank- und Bankiergewerbes (a.G.) zu Berlin in the insurance industry, whereas Deutsche Bank had a mandate of vice-chairman, Commerzbank held one mandate of the supervisory board excluding chairman and vice-chairman, respectively. In Dürener Metallwerke AG in the metal producing and processing industries, whereas Commerzbank had a mandate of vice-chairman, Deutsche Bank held one mandate of the supervisory board other than chairman and vice-chairman. Companies in which each of two banks had one post of the supervisory board except for chairman and vice-chairman, respectively, were eight. They were Schering-Kahlbaum AG in the chemical industry, Flottmann AG in the machine industry, Rudolf Karstadt AG in the distributing industry, Vereinigte Elektrizitätswerke Westfalen AG in the electric power, gas, and energy industries, and Vereinigte Industrie-Unternehmungen AG, Berliner Victoriamühle AG, Didier-Werke AG, and Buxtehunder Lederfabrik AG in other industries.

4.2.4 *Indirect Interlocking Directorates Between Dresdner Bank and Commerzbank on the Supervisory Board of Other Enterprises*

Next, in examining the situations related to indirect interlocking directorates between Dresdner Bank and Commerzbank on the supervisory board of other enterprises (see Table 4.10), such cases can be observed in 20 companies and the total number of mandates was 44 except cases of such interlocking directorates among three big banks. The numbers of enterprises and mandates were fewer than those of indirect interlocking directorate built between Deutsche Bank and Dresdner Bank (corresponding number 35 and 93, respectively) and those of such interlocking directorate built between Deutsche Bank and Commerzbank (corresponding numbers 32 and 76, respectively). They were a little fewer than those in the period of inflation after World War I (corresponding numbers 23 and 53, respectively).

Considering interlocking directorate in relation to supervisory board position mandates, the numbers of enterprises and mandates in which indirect interlocking directorates were built through the mandate of chairman were seven and eight, respectively. Similar numerical figures through mandate of vice-chairman and post of the supervisory board except for chairman and vice-chairman were six and seven, respectively, and 18 and 29, respectively When considering the distribution of industry, numbers of companies, and mandates of interlocking directorate were one and two in the metal producing and processing industries, one and two in the electrical industry, one and two in the automobile industry, four and nine in the machine industry, six and 13 in the banking industry, two and four in the insurance industry, and five and 12 in other industries, respectively. Of these indirect interlocking directorates, there was a case in which same person who had posts of the supervisory board of both Dresdner Bank and Commerzbank held interlocking mandate on the supervisory board of other enterprise.

There were three cases in which Dresdner Bank and Commerzbank built indirect interlocking directorate through more than total three mandates on the supervisory board of other enterprise. The total number of mandates was 10. The number of companies in which such indirect interlocking directorates were built through total four mandates was one. Similar figure through total three mandates was two. In the rest 17 enterprises, indirect interlocking directorates were built through total two mandates, respectively.

Regarding enterprises with total four mandates in each enterprise, in Hotelbetriebs-AG in other industries, whereas Dresdner Bank had one each of mandate of chairman and vice-chairman, Commerzbank had two posts of the supervisory board except for chairman and vice-chairman. Of two enterprises with three mandates in each enterprise, in Pittler Werkzeugmaschinenfabrik AG in the machine industry, whereas Commerzbank had a mandate of vice-chairman and one post of the supervisory board except for chairman and vice-chairman, Dresdner Bank held one mandate of the supervisory board except for chairman and vice-chairman. In Bank für Brau-Industrie in the banking industry, Dresdner Bank held two mandates

Table 4.10 Indirect interlocking directorates of the members of the supervisory board and the managing board on the supervisory board of other companies between Dresdner Bank and Commerzbank[a] (Period of National Socialism)

Industries	Number of posts							
	2		3		4		Total	
	Number of companies	Number of posts	Number of companies	Number of posts	Number of companies	Number of posts	Number of companies	Number of posts
Metal producing and processing	1	2	–	–	–	–	1	2
Electrical	1	2	–	–	–	–	1	2
Automobile	1	2	–	–	–	–	1	2
Machine	3	6	1	3	–	–	4	9
Banking	5	10	1	3	–	–	6	13
Insurance	2	4	–	–	–	–	2	4
Other industries	4	8	–	–	1	4	5	12
All industries	17	34	2	6	1	4	20	44

[a] The cases of indirect interlocking directorates built among Deutsche Bank, Dresdner Bank, and Commerzbank are excluded
Source This table was compiled by the author, based on Mossner (Hrsg) (1936)

of the supervisory board excluding chairman and vice-chairman, and Commerzbank had one similar mandate.

Concerning the remaining 17 firms with total two mandates in each firm, the number of companies of interlocking directorate was one in the metal producing and processing industries, one in the electrical industry, one in the automobile industry, three in the machine industry, five in the banking industry, two in the insurance industry, and four in other industries, respectively. Of these 17 companies, one company in which same person who had posts of the supervisory board of both Dresdner Bank and Commerzbank held interlocking mandate on the supervisory board of other enterprise was included. Such case was Deutsche Zündwaren-Monopol-Gesellschaft in other industries.

There was one case in which each of two banks had one chairman post or a post of vice-chairman. In Deutsche Gesellschaft für öffentliche Arbeiten AG in other industries, whereas Commerzbank had a mandate of chairman, Dresdner Bank had one post of vice-chairman. Cases where each of two banks had one chairman post or a post of the supervisory board except for chairman and vice-chairman can be observed in four enterprises. In Bank für Landwirtschaft and Hamburgische Baukassen AG in the banking industry, whereas Dresdner Bank had a mandate of chairman, Commerzbank had one post of the supervisory board except for chairman and vice-chairman, respectively. In Busch-Jaeger Lüdenscheider Metallwerke AG in the metal producing and processing industries and Mauser-Werke AG in the machine industry, whereas Commerzbank held a mandate of chairman, Dresdner Bank had one post of the supervisory board excluding chairman and vice-chairman, respectively. Enterprises in which each of two banks had a vice-chairman or one post of the supervisory board except for chairman and vice-chairman were three enterprises. In Linke-Hofmann-Werke AG in the machine industry and Frankona Rück- und Mitversicherungs-AG in the insurance industry, whereas Dresdner Bank had a mandate of vice-chairman, Commerzbank held one mandate of the supervisory board other than chairman and vice-chairman, respectively. In Maschinenfabrik Buckau R. Wolf AG in the machine industry, whereas Commerzbank had a mandate of vice-chairman, Dresdner Bank held one mandate of the supervisory board except for chairman and vice-chairman. Companies in which each of two banks had one post of the supervisory board excluding chairman and vice-chairman, respectively, were eight. They were C. Lorenz AG in the electrical industry, Eduard Winter AG für Kraftfahrzeuge in the automobile industry, Deutsche Schiffskreditbank AG, Frankfurter Hypothekenbank, and Hamburgische Bank von 1923 in the banking industry, Gerling-Konzern Lebensversicherungs-AG in the insurance industry, and Julius Berger Tiefbau AG and Deutsche Revisions- und Treuhand AG in other industries.

Earlier discussions examined how Deutsche Bank, Dresdner Bank, and Commerzbank formed personnel connections through direct and indirect interlocking directorates of members of the supervisory and managing boards on the supervisory board of other companies. The structures of interlocking directorates were examined in this chapter. In comparing with the conditions during inflation after World War I, while the numbers of enterprises where each of the three largest banks established relationships of direct interlocking directorates and interlocking mandates were fewer, different conditions were observed in indirect interlocking directorates. In indirect interlocking among the three banks, the enterprises in which such personnel connections were established and interlocking mandate were more than those during the inflation period after World War I. These numbers were similar in the indirect interlocking between Deutsche Bank and Dresdner Bank to those during the inflation period after World War I. While these numbers were a fewer than those during the inflation period in the indirect interlocking between Deutsche Bank and Commerzbank, these numbers were more in the indirect interlocking between Dresdner Bank and Commerzbank.

Considering the period after the World War II, victorious nations deconcentrated monopolies in banking industry and some industrial sectors, followed by reconcentration of dissolved banks and industrial enterprises. How reconcentrated large banks, such as Deutsche Bank, Dresdner Bank, and Commerzbank, build personnel connections through direct and indirect interlocking directorates of members of top management organs such as the supervisory board and the managing board on the supervisory board of other enterprises? This issue needs further clarification on the structure of interlocking directorate as an important foundation of the system of industrial concentration after the war. Therefore, the next chapter considers the conditions of interlocking directorates of the three large banks in the late 1950s.

Reference

Mossner J (Hrsg) (1936) Adressbuch der Direktoren und Aufsichtsräte 1936. Bd.I, Nach Personen geordnet, Finanz-Verlag, Berlin

Chapter 5
Interlocking Directorates of Bank's Supervisory Board and Managing Board Members in Other Enterprises in the Postwar Period Before the Enactment of the 1965 Corporations Law

Abstract In Germany, a system of interlocking directorates led by large banks was established on the basis of a deposit stock system that allowed a bank to exercise voting rights at a general meeting under the expansion of the secondary stock market and cooperation between banks after World War II. Such a system formed the basis of the banks' influence on corporations and exchanging and sharing information, and coordination of interests and conflicts between a bank and industrial enterprises and among corporations. How did the three largest banks that realized reconcentration after deconcentration under the postwar reforms directed by victorious nations build personnel connections with enterprises in various industrial sectors? This chapter analyzes the interlocking directorates of large banks in the late 1950s. During this period, the interlocking directorates were developed in various industries and companies because there was no limit to the number in which one person might have mandates in the supervisory board by law, such as the 1965 Corporations Law. The conditions of a direct interlocking directorate between a bank and enterprises in diverse industries and the indirect interlocking directorate established between banks on the supervisory board of other enterprises are explained through the distribution of industries where interlocking directorates existed, kinds of interlocking mandates of the supervisory board, and holding of plural posts. In this regard, the cases of Deutsche Bank, Dresdner Bank, and Commerzbank are examined.

Keywords Commerzbank · Deutsche Bank · Direct interlocking directorate · Dresdner Bank · Industry–bank relationship · Indirect interlocking directorate · Personnel connection

Chapters 2–4 examined the situations of direct interlocking directorates of members of supervisory and managing boards of three large banks on the supervisory board of other enterprises and indirect interlocking directorates built among these three banks and between two of the banks before World War II. Through these discussions, the structures of personnel connections that Deutsche Bank, Dresdner Bank, and Commerzbank established through interlocking directorates with the mandates of

T. Yamazaki, *Relationships Between Industry and Bank in Germany*,
https://doi.org/10.1007/978-981-97-4996-6_5

the supervisory board of other companies during the shift to monopolistic capitalism, the period of inflation after World War I, and National Socialism were clarified.

In Chaps. 5–7, the interlocking directorates that top management, such as the supervisory board and board of directors, of three leading banks built on the supervisory board of other enterprises after World War II are analyzed. The conditions of direct and indirect interlocking directorates among three banks and between two of the banks are considered. Three periods, the late 1950s, the late 1960s, and the latter half of the 2010s, are considered for the study. The cases of Deutsche Bank and Commerzbank are examined for the latter half of the 2010s because Dresdner Bank no longer exists.

In Germany, monopolies were dissolved by victorious countries following World War II. Large enterprises in the banking and some industrial sectors were dissolved under the occupation policy. The banking industry was split into 30 small-scale regional banks, with specific bank operations limited to specific state regions (Pohl 1986, pp.102–104; Djelic 1998; Stolper et al. 1964, pp. 227–228; Horstmann 1991, S.302). However, for banks, the abolition and cancelation of allied nation regulations were a great opportunity for reconcentration[*National Archives*, RG59, 862A.14, Reconcentration of German Commercial Banks (10.1.1957), p.1; *National Archives*, RG59, 862A.14, Reconcentration of German Commercial Banks (10.1. 1957), p.1; Djelic 1998, p. 165; Pohl 1986, S.102–105; Wandel 1998, S.40–41; Aizawa 1994, p. 9], which occurred in the latter half of the 1950s[*National Archives*, RG59, 862A.14, Present and Forthcoming Bank Merger in West Germany (3.5.1957)]. A similar movement was observed in the iron and steel industry. Therefore, the 1960s are regarded as the period when industrial concentration system after the war was established. Such conditions were strongly associated with the formation of banks' personnel connections with industrial enterprises through interlocking directorates. In Germany, the 1965 Corporations Law significantly influenced situations of the interlocking directorates on the supervisory board. It regulated the limit of the number in which one person might have mandates on the supervisory board (Pfeiffer 1993, S.158–159; Pfeiffer 1986a, S.477, 1986b, S.164; Stanzick 1969, S.72: Eglau 1990, S.128). Thus, a basic system of interlocking directorates in postwar Germany was established and maintained for a long time. Therefore, the conditions of banks' interlocking directorates on supervisory boards of other enterprises both before and after this law need further research.

Chapters 5 and 6 examine the total direct and indirect interlocking directorates of members of supervisory board and management board of three biggest banks on the supervisory board of other companies in the late 1950s as the time before the 1965 Corporation Law and the late 1960s as that after this law, respectively. Chapter 7 considers the conditions of interlocking directorates of Deutsche Bank and Commerzbank as the two largest banks in the latter half of the 2010s to explain the changes in bank's personnel connections with other enterprises observed since the 1990s.

This chapter considers the situations of interlocking directorates in the late 1950s. "*Adressbuch der Direktoren und Aufsichtsräte 1960*" (Bd.I, Nach personen geordnet, Finanzverlag, Berlin) is the basic material used for analysis.

Section 5.1 considers direct interlocking directorates of members of supervisory board and managing board of each bank on the supervisory board of other companies. Section 5.2 analyzes indirect interlocking directorates built through direct interlocking directorate among three banks and between two banks of them.

5.1 Direct Interlocking Directorate of Members of Supervisory Board and Managing Board of Banks on the Supervisory Board of Other Enterprises

5.1.1 Direct Interlocking Directorate of Members of Supervisory Board and Managing Board of Deutsche Bank

First, in examining the direct interlocking directorate by members of the supervisory board and managing board of Deutsche Bank on the supervisory board of other enterprises (see Table 5.1), there were 306 companies where such cases were observed and 373 interlocking mandates. The numbers of enterprises and mandates were almost identical to those in the mid-1930s during the period of National Socialism (corresponding numbers 340 and 415, respectively) (see Chap. 4). Considering the distribution of industrial sectors, Deutsche Bank built direct interlocking directorates in 24 companies and had 31 interlocking mandates in the mining industry, and similarly, 30 and 38 in the iron and steel industry; nine and 13 in metal producing and processing industries; 34 and 44 in the chemical industry; 17 and 24 in the electrical industry; eight each in the automobile industry; 25 and 31 in the machine industry; one each in precious machine and optical industries; four each in the shipbuilding industry; four and five each in the oil industry; two each in the food industry; 24 and 26 in textile, spinning, and woven goods industries; eight each in the distillation industry; seven each in the distributing industry; 23 and 31 in the banking industry; 24 and 30 in the insurance industry; five and six in electric power, gas, and energy industries; 11 and 12 in the transportation industry; and 46 and 52 in other industries, respectively. Among the various industries, except the banking and insurance sector, for example, in Deutsch Bank, there were several interlocking relations among the mining, iron and steel, chemical, electrical, machine, and textile, spinning, and woven goods industries. Therefore, Deutsche Bank had close, strong relationships with companies in the heavy and chemical industries as Germany's key industrial sectors.

Considering the situation of interlocking directorates, regarding the position of mandate of the supervisory board, Deutsche Bank built an interlocking directorate through a mandate of the honorary chairman of the supervisory board in only one company, namely, Mannesmann AG in the iron and steel industry.

Table 5.1 Direct interlocking directorates of the members of the supervisory board and the managing board of Deutsch Bank on the supervisory board of other companies (period before the 1965 Corporations Law)

	Positions									
Industries	Honorary chairman		Chairman		Vice-chairman		Supervisory board member excluding chairman and vice-chairman		Total[a]	
	Number of companies	Number of posts	Number of companies	Number of posts	Number of companies	Number of posts	Number of companies	Number of posts	Number of companies	Number of posts
Mining	–	–	15	15	–	–	11	16	24	31
Iron and steel	1	1	11	11	11	11	13	15	30	38
Metal producing and processing	–	–	2	2	5	5	4	6	9	13
Chemical	–	–	13	13	5	6	21	25	34	44
Electrical	–	–	9	9	6	6	6	9	17	24
Automobile	–	–	6	6	–	–	2	2	8	8
Machine	–	–	14	14	3	3	13	14	25	31
Precious machine and optical	–	–	–	–	1	1	–	–	1	1
Shipbuilding	–	–	1	1	2	2	1	1	4	4
Oil	–	–	2	2	3	3	–	–	4	5
Food	–	–	–	–	2	2	–	–	2	2

(continued)

Table 5.1 (continued)

	Positions									
Industries	Honorary chairman		Chairman		Vice-chairman		Supervisory board member excluding chairman and vice-chairman		Total[a]	
	Number of companies	Number of posts	Number of companies	Number of posts	Number of companies	Number of posts	Number of companies	Number of posts	Number of companies	Number of posts
Textile, spinning, and woven goods	–	–	10	10	7	7	9	9	24	26
Distillation	–	–	3	3	1	1	4	4	8	8
Distributing	–	–	3	3	1	1	3	3	7	7
Banking	–	–	10	10	10	11	9	10	23	31
Insurance	–	–	7	7	7	7	13	16	24	30
Electric power, gas, and energy	–	–	5	5	–	–	1	1	5	6
Transportation	–	–	3	3	4	4	5	5	11	12
Other industries	–	–	20	20	8	8	22	24	46	52
All industries	1	1	134	134	76	78	137	160	306	373

[a] There are cases in which the total number of companies establishing interlocking directorates differed from the total number of companies measured by each position of the supervisory board due to the existence of companies where interlocking directorates through more than two posts were built

Source This table was compiled by the author, based on JMorr (Hrsg) (1960)

In 134 enterprises, interlocking directorates on the supervisory boards of other companies were formed through the mandate of chairman of the supervisory board in several cases, with 134 mandates. There was one mandate in each enterprise. The numbers of enterprises and mandates were much more than those in the 1930s (corresponding numbers 97 and 98, respectively). Regarding the distribution among industrial sectors, 15 enterprises where interlocking directorates were formed in the mining industry; similarly, 11 in iron and steel; two each in metal producing and processing; 13 in chemical; nine in electrical; six in automobile; 14 in machine; one in shipbuilding; two in oil; 10 in textile, spinning, and woven goods; three in distillation; three in distributing; 10 in banking; seven in insurance; five in electric power, gas, and energy; three in transportation; and 20 in other industries, respectively. Interlocking directorates in representative companies of each industry were seen in Mannesmann AG, Klöckner-Werke AG, Hoesch AG, Hüttenwerk Salzgitter AG, and Dortmund-Hörder Hüttenunion AG in the iron and steel industry, BASF AG, Vereinigte Glanzstoff-Fabriken AG, and Agfa AG in the chemical industry, Siemens & Halske AG, Siemens-Schuckert AG, Siemens-Reininger-Werke AG, and Osram GmbH in the electrical industry, Daimler-Benz AG in the automobile industry, Klöckner-Humboldt-Deutz AG, Borsig AG, and Maschinenfabrik Buckau R. Wolf AG in the machine industry, Kieler Howaldtswerke AG in the shipbuilding industry, Deutsche Erdöl AG in the oil industry, Deutsche Ueberseeische Bank and Berliner Disconto-Bank AG in the banking industry, Allianz Lebensversicherungs-AG and Gerling-Konzern Allgemeine Versicherungs-AG in the insurance industry, and Rheinisch-Westfälisches Elektrizitätswerk AG in the electric power, gas, and energy industries.

In 76 enterprises, interlocking directorates on the supervisory boards of other companies were formed through the mandate of the vice-chairman of the supervisory board with 78 mandates. The numbers of enterprises and mandates were more than those in the mid-1930s (corresponding numbers 51 each, respectively). With regard to the distribution of industrial sectors, there were eleven enterprises and mandates where interlocking directorates were formed in iron and steel; similarly, five each in metal producing and processing; five and six in chemical; six each in electrical; three each in machines; one each in precious machines and optical; two each in shipbuilding; three each in oil; two each in food; seven each in textile, spinning, and woven goods; one each in distillation; one each in distribution; ten and eleven in banking; seven each in insurance; four each in transportation; and eight each in other industries. There were interlocking directorates in the major companies of each industry. For example, the cases were observed in Klöckner-Werke AG, Ilseder Hütte, and Buderus'sche Eisenwerke in iron and steel, BASF AG and Bayer AG in chemical, AEG, Siemens & Halske AG, and Siemens-Electrogeräte AG in electrical, Auto Union GmbH in automobile, DEMAG AG, and Orenstein-Koppel und Lübecker Maschinenbau AG in machine, Zeiss Ikon AG in precious machine and optical, Howaldtswerke Hamburg AG in shipbuilding, Deutsche Shell AG and Mobil Oil AG in Deutschland in oil, Rudolph Karstadt AG in distributing, and Allianz Versicherungs-AG in insurance.

Interlocking directorates through mandates of the supervisory board except for the chairman and vice-chairman were observed in 137 companies, totaling 160 mandates. The numbers of enterprises and posts were much fewer than in the mid-1930s, i.e., 225 and 266, respectively. Regarding the distribution among the industrial sectors, the numbers of enterprises and mandates in which interlocking directorates were formed were 11 and 16 in mining; 13 and 15 in iron and steel; four and six in metal producing and processing; 21 and 25 in chemical; six and nine in electrical; two each in automobile; 13 and 14 in machine; one each in shipbuilding; nine each in textile, spinning, and woven goods; four each in distillation; three each in distributing; nine and 10 in banking; 13 and 16 in insurance; one each in electric power, gas, and energy; five each in transportation; and 22 and 24 in other industries, respectively. These companies included leading firms in each industry, such as Gelsenkirchener Berkwerke AG in mining, August Thyssen-Hütte AG, Mannesmann AG, Hoesch AG, Rheinische Stahlwerke, and Hüttenwerk Salzgitter AG, and Metallgesellschaft AG in metal producing and metal processing, Hoechst AG, Degussa AG, Bunawerke Hüls GmbH, and Vereinigte Glanzstoff-Fabriken AG in chemical, Siemens & Halske AG, Siemens-Schuckert AG, and Brown, Boveri & Cie, AG in electrical, Maschinenbau AG Balcke and Schubert & Salzer Maschinenfabrik AG in machine, Kaufhof AG in distributing, Münchener Rückversicheruns-Gesellschaft, Gerling-Konzern Globale Versicherungs-AG, and Gerling-Konzern Lebensversicherungs-AG in insurance.

The numbers of enterprises and mandates were 49 and 116, respectively, when considering cases in which members of the supervisory board and board of directors of Deutsche Bank had more than two mandates on the supervisory boards of other companies (see Table 5.2). The numbers of enterprises and mandates were slightly lower than in the mid-1930s (57 and 132, respectively). Considering the distribution among industries, the numbers of companies and mandates were as follows: four and 11 in mining; six and 14 in iron and steel; three and seven in metal producing and processing; eight and 18 in chemicals; three and 10 in electrical; five and 11 in machines; one and two in oil; two and four in textile, spinning, and woven goods; six and 14 in banking; four and 10 in insurance; one and two in electric power, gas, and energy; one and two in transportation; and five and 11 in other industries, respectively.

Of these 49 companies, in 14 enterprises, direct interlocking directorates were built through more than three mandates; the total number of mandates was 46. The numbers of enterprises and mandates were almost identical to those in the 1930s (13 and 44, respectively). For one enterprise, direct interlocking directorates were formed through five mandates. In two companies, interlocking directorates were formed through four mandates. In 11 cases, interlocking directorates were formed through three mandates. In the remaining 35 companies, Deutsche Bank had two mandates on the supervisory board of other companies.

With Siemens-Schuckert AG in the electrical industry, interlocking directorates were built through one mandate of chairman and four posts of the supervisory board except for the chairman and vice-chairman. Regarding enterprises with four mandates, while in Mannesmann AG in the iron and steel industry, there were interlocking directorates through one mandate of the honor chairman and chairman and

Table 5.2 Cases in which Deutsche Bank built direct interlocking directorates through more than two posts on the supervisory board of other companies (period before the 1965 Corporations Law)

Industries	Number of posts									
	2		3		4		5		Total	
	Number of companies	Number of posts	Number of companies	Number of posts	Number of companies	Number of posts	Number of companies	Number of posts	Number of companies	Number of posts
Mining	1	2	3	9	–	–	–	–	4	11
Iron and steel	5	10	–	–	1	4	–	–	6	14
Metal producing and processing	2	4	1	3	–	–	–	–	3	7
Chemical	6	12	2	6	–	–	–	–	8	18
Electrical	1	2	1	3	–	–	1	5	3	10
Machine	4	8	1	3	–	–	–	–	5	11
Oil	1	2	–	–	–	–	–	–	1	2
Textile, spinning, and woven goods	2	4	–	–	–	–	–	–	2	4
Banking	4	8	2	6	–	–	–	–	6	14
Insurance	3	6	–	–	1	4	–	–	4	10
Electric power, gas, and energy	1	2	–	–	–	–	–	–	1	2
Transportation	1	2	–	–	–	–	–	–	1	2
Other industries	4	8	1	3	–	–	–	–	5	11
All industries	35	70	11	33	2	8	1	5	49	116

Source This table was compiled by the author, based on Morr (Hrsg) (1960)

two posts of the supervisory board except for the chairman and vice-chairman; in Allianz Versicherungs-AG in the insurance industry, interlocking directorates were formed through one post of vice-chairman and three mandates of the supervisory board except for the chairman and vice-chairman. Meanwhile, in the Deutsche Ueberseeische Bank in the banking industry interlocking directorates were established through a mandate of the chairman and two posts of vice-chairman. Furthermore, one each of the post of chairman and vice-chairman and one mandate of the supervisory board except for the chairman and vice-chairman were seen in Siemens & Halske AG in the electrical industry. Deutsche Bank built interlocking directorates through a mandate of chairman and two posts of the supervisory board except for the chairman and vice-chairman in six companies; namely, Salzdetfurth AG in mining, Vereinigte Glanzstoff-Fabriken AG and Zellstofffabrik Waldhof in chemical, Schubert & Salzer Maschinenfabrik AG in machine, Deutsche Bank, Berlin in banking, and Portland Cementfabrik Hemmoor in other industries. There were three enterprises where interlocking directorate was formed through three posts of the supervisory board except for the chairman and vice-chairman—Gelsenkirchener Bergwerks-AG and Rheinpreußen Aktiengesellschaft für Bergbau und Chemie in the mining industry and Metallgesellschaft AG in the metal producing and metal processing industries.

Considering 35 enterprises with two mandates on the supervisory board of other enterprises in relation to the distribution of the industrial sector, there were one in mining, five in iron and steel, two in metal producing and processing, six in chemicals, one in electrical, four in machines, one in oil, two in textile, spinning, and woven goods, four in banking, three in insurance, one in electric power, gas, and energy, one in transportation, and four in other industries.

Regarding these interlocking directorates with respect to the kind of mandate, there were eight companies where there were interlocking directorates through one each of the mandate of chairman and vice-chairman: Klöckner-Werke AG in iron and steel, Duisburger Kupferhütte in metal producing and metal processing, BASF AG in chemical, Siemens-Reininger-Werke AG in electrical, Deutsche Erdöl AG in oil, J. P. Bemberg AG in textile, spinning, and woven goods, Berliner Disconto-Bank AG in banking, and Eisenbahn-Verkehrmittel AG in transportation. In 15 enterprises, cases where interlocking directorates were built through one post of chairman and a mandate of the supervisory board except chairman and vice-chairman can be observed. They were Gebrüder Stumm GmbH in mining, Hoesch AG and Hüttenwerk Salzgitter AG in iron and steel, Agfa AG in chemical, Klöckner-Humboldt-Deutz AG and Maschinenfabrik Buckau R. Wolf AG in machine, Christian Dierig AG in textile, spinning, and woven goods, Deutsche Centralbodenkredit-AG, Ausfuhrkredit-AG, and Saarländische Kreditbank AG in banking, Allianz Lebensversicherungs-AG and Gerling-Konzern Allgemeine Versicherungs-AG in insurance, Rheinisch-Westfälisches Elektrizitätswerk AG in electric power, gas, and energy, and Portland Cementfabrik Germania AG and Reemtsma Cigarettenfabriken GmbH in other industries. In one case, interlocking directorates were formed through two mandates of the vice-chairman—Bayer AG in chemical. There were six enterprises where interlocking directorates were formed through one mandate of a vice-chairman and one post of the supervisory board except for the chairman and vice-chairman. These enterprises were Ilseder Hütte in iron and steel, J. A. Schmalbach AG in metal producing and metal processing, Rütgerswerke AG in chemical, DEMAG AG and Orenstein-Koppel und Lübecker Maschinenbau AG in machine, and Rheinisch-Westfälische Kalkwerke AG in other industries. In five cases, interlocking directorates were established through two mandates of the supervisory board except the chairman and vice-chairman: Rheinische Stahlwerke in iron and steel, Degussa AG and Bunawerke Hüls GmbH in chemical, Gerling-Konzern Lebensversicherungs-AG in insurance, and Physikalische Studiengesellschaft mbH in other industries.

Deutsche Bank's direct interlocking directorates on the supervisory boards of other enterprises were spread over a wide range of industries and had personnel connections with several competitive companies in the same industrial sector through several mandates of the supervisory board. Such cases can be observed in Gelsenkirchener Bergwerks-AG, Friedrich Thyssen Bergbau AG, Rheinstahl Bergbau AG, and Hoesch Bergwerks-AG in the mining industry, Mannesmann AG, Klöckner-Werke AG, Hoesch AG, Rheinische Stahlwerke, August Thyssen-Hütte AG, Hüttenwerk Salzgitter AG, and Dortmund-Hörder Hüttenunion AG in the iron and steel industry, BASF AG, Bayer AG, Hoechst AG, Degussa AG, and Vereinigte Glanzstoff-Fabriken AG in the chemical industry, AEG, Brown, Boveri & Cie, AG, and large enterprises of the Siemens Group such as Siemens & Halske AG, Siemens-Schuckert AG, and Siemens-Reininger-Werke AG in the electrical industry, Klöckner-Humboldt-Deutz AG, DEMAG AG, Borsig AG, Orenstein-Koppel und Lübecker Maschinenbau AG, and Maschinenfabrik Buckau R. Wolf AG in the machine industry, Kieler Howaldtswerke AG, Howaldtswerke Hamburg AG, and Lübecker Flender-Werke AG in the shipbuilding industry, Deutsche Erdöl AG, Deutsche Shell AG, and Mobil Oil Aktiengesellachaft in Deutschland in the oil industry, and Rudolph Karstadt AG, Kaufhof AG, and Kepa Kaufhaus GmbH in the distributing industry. Similar cases can be observed in Münchener Rückversicheruns-Gesellschaft, representative companies of the Allianz group such as Allianz Versicherungs-AG and Allianz Lebensversicherungs-AG, and large enterprises of the Gerling group such as Gerling-Konzern Allgemeine Versicherungs-AG and Gerling-Konzern Lebensversicherungs-AG in the insurance industry. In banking as well, Deutsche Bank established interlocking directorates with banks in special fields; banks such as Frankfurter Hypothekenbank, Deutsche Hypothekenbank, and Pfälzische Hypothekenbank, alongside leading banks such as Deutsche Ueberseeische Bank, Berliner Disconto-Bank AG, Deutsche Centralbodenkredit-AG, and Ausfuhrkredit-AG.

Thus, Deutsche Bank established close, strong personnel connections with several companies in various industries through direct interlocking directorates of members of the supervisory board and management board, greatly contributing to securing information for its financial business and policy decisions regarding industrial enterprises.

5.1.2 Direct Interlocking Directorate of Members of Supervisory Board and Managing Board of Dresdner Bank

Next, regarding Dresdner Bank on the supervisory board of other enterprises (see Table 5.3), there were 268 companies in which such cases were observed and 326 interlocking mandates. The numbers of both enterprises and mandates were fewer than those of Deutsche Bank (306 and 373, respectively) and were almost identical as those of Dresdner Bank around the mid-1930s during the Nazi era (286 and 333, respectively) (see Chap. 4). Considering the distribution of industrial sectors, Dresdner Bank built direct interlocking directorates in ten companies and 13 interlocking mandates in the mining industry, and similarly, 23 and 27 in iron and steel; 15 and 16 in metal producing and processing; 23 and 29 in chemical; 16 and 19 in electrical; nine and 11 in automobile; 19 and 22 in machine; four and five in shipbuilding; five and six in oil; three each in food; eight and 10 in textile, spinning, and woven goods; 10 and 11 in distillation; five each in distributing; 24 and 34 in banking; 19 and 28 in insurance; 23 and 26 in electric power, gas, and energy; 14 and 15 in transportation; and 38 and 46 in other industries, respectively. Among the various industries, except for the banking and insurance industries, for example, there were many interlocking relations in mining, iron, and steel, chemical, electrical, machine, electric power, gas, and energy, and transportation. Therefore, Dresdner Bank had close and strong relationships with companies in the heavy and chemical industries as the key industrial sectors.

Considering the situation of interlocking directorates regarding the mandate of the supervisory board, the interlocking directorate was built through a mandate of the honorary chairman of the supervisory board in only one company: Preußische Elektrizitäts-AG in electric power, gas, and energy industries.

In 86 enterprises, interlocking directorates on the supervisory boards of other companies were formed through a mandate of the chairman of the supervisory board with 86 mandates. In each enterprise, the number of mandates was one, respectively. Both enterprises and mandates were much fewer than those of Deutsche Bank (134 and 134, respectively) and those of Dresdner Bank around the mid-1930s (62 and 62, respectively). Considering the distribution among industrial sectors, the number of enterprises in which interlocking directorates were formed was two in the mining industry; similarly, four in iron and steel; nine in metal producing and processing; nine in chemical; seven in electrical; two in automobile; six in machine; two in shipbuilding; four in textile, spinning, and woven goods; four in distillation; one in distributing; seven in banking; six in insurance; five in electric power, gas, and energy; three in transportation; and 15 in other industries, respectively. There were many enterprises in the metal producing and metal processing, chemical, and electrical industries. Cases of interlocking directorate in representative companies of each industry were seen in Gelsenkirchener Bergwerks-AG in mining, Deutsche Edelstahlwerke AG in iron and steel, Metallgesellschaft AG in metal producing and metal processing, Hoechst AG, Degussa AG, Chemische Werke Hüls AG, and Kalle

Table 5.3 Direct interlocking directorates of the members of the supervisory board and the managing board of Dresdner Bank on the supervisory board of other companies (period before the 1965 Corporations Law)

Industries	Position									
	Honorary chairman		Chairman		Vice-chairman		Supervisory board member excluding chairman and vice-chairman		Total[a]	
	Number of companies	Number of posts	Number of companies	Number of posts	Number of companies	Number of posts	Number of companies	Number of posts	Number of companies	Number of posts
Mining	–	–	2	2	–	–	9	11	10	13
Iron and steel	–	–	4	4	6	6	14	17	23	27
Metal producing and processing	–	–	9	9	2	2	5	5	15	16
Chemical	–	–	9	9	10	11	8	9	23	29
Electrical	–	–	7	7	3	3	8	9	16	19
Automobile	–	–	2	2	2	3	6	6	9	11
Machine	–	–	6	6	4	4	11	12	19	22
Shipbuilding	–	–	2	2	2	2	1	1	4	5
Oil	–	–	–	–	1	1	4	5	5	6
Food	–	–	–	–	–	–	3	3	3	3
Textile, spinning, and woven goods	–	–	4	4	3	3	3	3	8	10
Distillation	–	–	4	4	4	4	3	3	10	11
Distributing	–	–	1	1	1	1	3	3	5	5

(continued)

Table 5.3 (continued)

Industries	Position									
	Honorary chairman		Chairman		Vice-chairman		Supervisory board member excluding chairman and vice-chairman		Total[a]	
	Number of companies	Number of posts	Number of companies	Number of posts	Number of companies	Number of posts	Number of companies	Number of posts	Number of companies	Number of posts
Banking	–	–	7	7	11	11	15	16	24	34
Insurance	–	–	6	6	9	9	11	13	19	28
Electric power, gas, and energy	1	1	5	5	6	6	13	14	23	26
Transportation	–	–	3	3	4	4	8	8	14	15
Other industries	–	–	15	15	10	11	18	20	38	46
All industries	1	1	86	86	78	81	143	158	268	326

[a] There are cases in which the total number of companies establishing interlocking directorates differed from the total number of companies measured by each position of the supervisory board due to the existence of companies where interlocking directorates through more than two posts were built

Source This table was compiled by the author, based on Morr (Hrsg) (1960)

AG in chemical, AEG and Telefunken GmbH in electrical, MSU Werke AG in automobile, Blohm & Voss AG and Aktiengesellschaft "Weser" in shipbuilding, Disconto und Kredit AG, Frankfurter Hypothekenbank, Bank für Handel und Industrie AG, and Deutsch-Südamerikanische Bank AG in banking, and Allianz Versicherungs-AG in insurance.

In 78 enterprises, interlocking directorates were formed through a mandate of the vice-chairman of the supervisory board and the total number of mandates was 81. The numbers of enterprises and mandates were almost the same as those of Deutsche Bank (76 and 78, respectively) and were even more than those of Dresdner Bank around the middle of the 1930s (42 and 43, respectively). The numbers of enterprises and mandates in which such interlocking cases were formed were six each in the iron and steel industry; similarly, two each in metal producing and metal processing; 10 and 11 in chemical; three each in electrical; two and three in automobile; respectively; four each in machine; two each in shipbuilding; one each in oil; three each in textile, spinning, and woven goods; four each in distillation; one each in distributing; 11 each in banking; nine each in insurance; six each in electric power, gas, and energy; four each in transportation; and 10 and 11 in other industries, respectively. In these companies, there were major companies in each industry, such as Hugo Stinnes GmbH in iron and steel, Metallgesellschaft AG in metal producing and metal processing, Degussa AG, Chemische Werke Hüls AG, and Behlingwerke AG in chemical, Brown, Boveri & Cie, AG and Osram GmbH in electrical, NSU Werke AG in automobile, Orenstein-Koppel und Lübecker Maschinenbau AG and Westfalia Dinnendahl Gröppel AG in machine, Deutsche Werft Agand Lübecker Flender-Werke AG in shipbuilding, Kaufhof AG in distributing, Münchener Rückversicherungs-Gesellschaft, Allianz Lebensversicherungs-AG, and Frankfurter Versicherungs-AG in insurance, and Rheinisch-Westfälisches Elektrizitätswerk AG in electric power, gas, and energy.

Interlocking directorates through mandates of the supervisory board except the chairman and vice-chairman were observed in 143 companies and the total number of mandates was 158. The numbers of enterprises and mandates were almost the same as those of Deutsche Bank (137 and 160, respectively). However, the numbers of enterprises and mandates were fewer than those of Dresdner Bank around the mid-1930s (202 and 228, respectively). The numbers of enterprises and mandates in which Dresdner Bank built interlocking directorates were nine and 11 in the mining industry; similarly, 14 and 17 in iron and steel; five each in metal producing and metal processing; eight and nine in chemical;eight and nine in electrical; six each in automobile; 11 and 12 in machine; one each in shipbuilding; four and five in oil; three each in food; three each in textile, spinning, and woven goods; three each in distillation; three each in distributing; 15 and 16 in banking; 11 and 13 in insurance; 13 and 14 in electric power, gas, and energy; eight each in transportation; and 18 and 20 in other industries, respectively. Among the various industries, excluding banking and insurance, for example, there were many interlocking relations in mining, iron and steel, chemical, electrical, machine, and electric power, gas, and energy industries. There were major companies in each industry, such as Steinkohlenbergwerke Mathias Stinnes AG and Essener Steinkohlenbergwerks-AG in mining industry, August Thyssen-Hütte AG, Mannesmann AG, Rheinische Stahlwerke, and Hüttenwerke Salzgitter AG in iron and steel, BASF AG and Buna-Werke Hüls GmbH in chemical, Siemens & Halske AG, Siemens-Schuckertwerke AG, and Robert Bosch GmbH in electrical, Daimler-Benz AG and Volkswagenwerk AG in automobile, DEMAG AG, Ludwig Loewe & Co. AG, and Pittler Maschinenfabrik AG in machine, Deutsche Erdöl AG and Esso AG in oil, Rudolph Karstadt AG in distributing, and Deutsche Lufthansa AG in transportation.

The numbers of enterprises and mandates were 47 and 105, respectively, when considering cases where members of the supervisory board and board of directors of Dresdner Bank had more than two mandates on the supervisory boards of other companies (see Table 5.4). The numbers of both enterprises and mandates were almost identical as those of Deutsche Bank (49 and 116, respectively) and were slightly more than those of Dresdner Bank around the mid-1930s (41 and 88, respectively). Considering the distribution among industries, the numbers of companies and mandates were as follows: two and five in mining; three and seven in iron and steel; one and two in metal producing and metal processing; five and eleven in chemicals; two and five in electrical; one and three in automobiles; three and six in machines; one and two in shipbuilding; one and two in oil; two and four in textile, spinning, and woven goods; one and two in distillation; seven and 17 in banking; six and 15 in insurance; three and six in electric power, gas, and energy; one and two in transportation; and eight and 16 in other industries, respectively.

Of these 47 companies, 10 enterprises had direct interlocking directorates built through more than three mandates, and the total number of mandates was 31. The numbers of both enterprises and mandates were approximately half of those of Deutsche Bank (14 and 46, respectively) and those of Dresdner Bank around the middle of the 1930s (6 and 18, respectively). In the remaining companies, Dresdner Bank had two mandates on the supervisory board of other companies.

In Allianz Versicherungs-AG in the insurance industry, interlocking directorates were formed through one each of chairman and vice-chairman mandates and two mandates of the supervisory boards except chairman and vice-chairman. Of enterprises with three mandates, there were interlocking directorates through a mandate of chairman and two posts of vice-chairman: Degussa AG in the chemical industry and NSU Werke AG in the automobile industry. Cases where interlocking directorates were established through one each of a chairman and vice-chairman mandate and one post of the supervisory board except chairman and vice-chairman were two enterprises: Bank für Handel und Industrie AG and Deutsch-Südamerikanische Bank AG in the banking industry. There were two companies in which Dresdner Bank formed interlocking directorates through a mandate of chairman and two posts of the supervisory board except chairman and vice-chairman. Such cases were Barbara Erzbergbau AG in the mining industry and Deutsche Edelstahlwerke AG in the iron and steel industry. Meanwhile, cases where interlocking directorates were built through one post of vice-chairman and two mandates of the supervisory board except chairman and vice-chairman can be observed in three enterprises: Brown, Boveri & Cie, AG in electrical, Ausfuhrkredit-AG in banking, and Münchener Rückversicherungs-Gesellschaft in insurance.

Table 5.4 Cases in which Dresdner Bank built direct interlocking directorates through more than two posts on the supervisory board of other companies (period before the 1965 Corporations Law)

Industries	Number of posts							
	2		3		4		Total	
	Number of companies	Number of posts	Number of companies	Number of posts	Number of companies	Number of posts	Number of companies	Number of posts
Mining	1	2	1	3	–	–	2	5
Iron and steel	2	4	1	3	–	–	3	7
Metal producing and processing	1	2	–	–	–	–	1	2
Chemical	4	8	1	3	–	–	5	11
Electrical	1	2	1	3	–	–	2	5
Automobile	–	–	1	3	–	–	1	3
Machine	3	6	–	–	–	–	3	6
Shipbuilding	1	2	–	–	–	–	1	2
Oil	1	2	–	–	–	–	1	2
Textile, spinning, and woven goods	2	4	–	–	–	–	2	4
Distillation	1	2	–	–	–	–	1	2
Banking	4	8	3	9	–	–	7	17
Insurance	4	8	1	3	1	4	6	15
Electric power, gas, and energy	3	6	–	–	–	–	3	6
Transportation	1	2	–	–	–	–	1	2

(continued)

Table 5.4 (continued)

Industries	Number of posts							
	2		3		4		Total	
	Number of companies	Number of posts	Number of companies	Number of posts	Number of companies	Number of posts	Number of companies	Number of posts
Other industries	8	16	–	–	–	–	8	16
All industries	37	74	9	27	1	4	47	105

Source This table was compiled by the author, based on Morr (Hrsg) (1960)

When considering 37 enterprises with two mandates on the supervisory board of other enterprises in relation to the industrial distribution sector, there were one in mining, two in iron and steel, one in metal producing and metal processing, four in chemicals, one in electrical, three in machines, one in shipbuilding, one in oil, two in textile, pinning, and woven goods, one in distillation, four in banking, four in insurance, three in electric power, gas, and energy, one in transportation, and eight in other industries.

Considering these interlocking directorates in relation to the kind of mandate, interlocking directorates were built through one each of a chairman and vice-chairman mandate that can be observed in seven enterprises. They were Metallgesellschaft AG in metal producing and metal processing industry, Chemische Werke Hüls AG and Kalle AG in chemical, Wollgartenfabrik Tittel & Krüger und Sternwoll-Spinnerei AG in textile, spinning, and woven goods, Elbschloss-Brauerei in distillation, Disconto und Kredit AG in banking, and Hochtief Aktiengesellschaft für Hoch- und Tiefbauten vorm and Gebrüder Helfmann in other industries. Enterprises in which interlocking directorates were established through one post of chairman and a mandate of the supervisory board except chairman and vice-chairman were 12. These enterprises were Telefunken GmbH in electrical, Blohm & Voss AG in shipbuilding, Spinnerei und Zwirnerei Ramie AG in textile, spinning, and woven goods, Dresdner Bank, Berlin and Frankfurter Hypothekenbank in banking, Karlsruher Lebensversicherungs-AG and Hermes Kreditversicherungs-AG in insurance, Norddeutscher Lloyd in transportation, and Allgemeine Bauverein Essen AG, BAUBOAG Bau und Boden AG, Grün & Bilfinger AG, and Hotelbetriebs-AG in other industries. Companies where interlocking directorates were formed through two mandates of the vice-chairman were one: Chemie Verwaltungs AG in other industries. There were eight enterprises where interlocking directorates were built through a mandate of vice-chairman and one post of the supervisory board except chairman and vice-chairman. These were Zellstofffabrik Waldhof in chemical, Westfalia Dinnendahl Gröppel AG and L. Schuler AG in machine, Industriekreditbank AG in banking, Allianz Lebensversicherungs-AG and Frankfurter Versicherungs-AG in insurance, and Rheinisch-Westfälisches Elektrizitätswerk AG and Rheinische Energie AG in electric power, gas, and energy. Cases where Dresdner Bank established interlocking directorates through two mandates of the supervisory board except chairman and vice-chairman are observable in nine companies. Such enterprises were Hamborner Bergbau AG in mining, August Thyssen-Hütte AG and Hütten- und Bergwerke Rheinhausen AG in iron and steel, Rütgerswerke AG in chemical, DEMAG AG in machine, Deutsche Erdöl AG in oil, Lech-Elektrizitätswerke AG in electric power, gas, and energy, and Deutsche Investment-Trust Gesellschaft für Wertpapieranlagen mbH and Bonner Portland-Zementwerke AG in other industries.

Thus, Dresdner Bank's direct interlocking directorates on the supervisory boards of other enterprises spread over a wide range of industries and had personnel connections with several competitive companies mutually in the same industrial sector through several mandates of the supervisory board. Such cases can be observed in Gelsenkirchener Bergwerks-AG, Steinkohlenbergwerke Mathias Stinnes AG and Essener Steinkohlenbergwerks-AG in mining, August Thyssen-Hütte AG,

Mannesmann AG, Rheinische Stahlwerke, Hüttenwerk Salzgitter AG, and Hugo Stinnes GmbH in iron and steel, BASF AG, Hoechst AG, Degussa AG, Chemische Werke Hüls AG, and Kalle AG in chemical, Siemens & Halske AG, Siemens-Schuckertwerke AG, AEG, Brown, Boveri & Cie, AG, and Robert Bosch GmbH in electrical, Daimler-Benz AG and Volkswagenwerk AG in automobile, DEMAG AG, Orenstein-Koppel und Lübecker Maschinenbau AG, Ludwig Loewe & Co. AG, and Pittler Maschinenfabrik AG in machine, Blohm & Voss AG, "Aktiengesellschaft Wesser," and Deutsche Werft AG in shipbuilding, Deutsche Erdöl AG, Esso AG, and BP Benzin und Petroleum AG in oil industry, and Kaufhof AG and Rudolph Karstadt AG in distributing. In the financial sectors, there were leading enterprises in each industrial sector such as Allianz Versicherungs-AG, Allianz Lebensversicherungs-AG, and Münchener Rückversicherungs-Gesellschaftin in the insurance industry. Dresdner Bank built strong and close personnel connections with many companies in various industries through direct interlocking directorates, which had a significant meaning for securing information for its own financial business and decisions of policies over industrial enterprises.

5.1.3 Direct Interlocking Directorate of Members of Supervisory Board and Managing Board of Commerzbank

In considering the direct interlocking directorate built by members of the supervisory board and managing board of Commerzbank on the supervisory board of other enterprises (see Table 5.5), there were 196 companies in which such cases were observed and 226 interlocking mandates. Both enterprises and mandates were much fewer than those of Deutsche Bank (corresponding numbers 306 and 373, respectively) and those of Dresdner Bank (similarly 268 and 326, respectively). They were also fewer than those of Commerzbank around the 1930s (240 and 286, respectively) (see Chap. 4). Considering the distribution of industrial sectors, Commerzbank built direct interlocking directorates in 10 companies and 10 interlocking mandates in the mining industry, and similarly, 15 each in iron and steel; one each in metal producing and processing; 12 and 18 in chemicals; 17 and 18 in electrical; one each in automobiles; 16 and 17 in machines; two and three in precious machines and optical; one and two in shipbuilding; five each in oil; three each in food; six each in textile, spinning, and woven goods; 10 and 13 in distillation; eight and nine in distributing; 25 and 31 in banking; 14 and 21 in insurance; four each in electric power, gas, and energy; six each in transportation; and 40 and 43 in other industries, respectively. Among the various industries, excluding the banking and insurance industries, for example, there were many interlocking relations in mining, iron and steel, chemical, electrical, machine, and distillation. Therefore, Commerzbank had close and strong relationships with companies in the heavy and chemical industries as key industrial sectors and the banking industry.

Table 5.5 Direct interlocking directorates of the members of the supervisory board and the managing board of Commerzbank on the supervisory board of other companies (period before the 1965 Corporations Law)

	Position									
Industries	Honorary chairman		Chairman		Vice-chairman		Supervisory board member excluding chairman and vice-chairman		Total[a]	
	Number of companies	Number of posts	Number of companies	Number of posts	Number of companies	Number of posts	Number of companies	Number of posts	Number of companies	Number of posts
Mining	–	–	2	2	2	2	6	6	10	10
Iron and steel	–	–	2	2	2	2	11	11	15	15
Metal producing and processing	–	–	1	1	–	–	–	–	1	1
Chemical	–	–	5	6	1	1	9	11	12	18
Electrical	–	–	7	7	1	1	9	10	17	18
Automobile	–	–	–	–	–	–	1	1	1	1
Machine	–	–	4	4	5	5	8	8	16	17
Precious machine and optical	–	–	2	2	–	–	1	1	2	3
Shipbuilding	–	–	1	1	1	1	–	–	1	2
Oil	–	–	3	3	1	1	1	1	5	5
Food	–	–	1	1	1	1	1	1	3	3

(continued)

Table 5.5 (continued)

	Position									
Industries	Honorary chairman		Chairman		Vice-chairman		Supervisory board member excluding chairman and vice-chairman		Total[a]	
	Number of companies	Number of posts	Number of companies	Number of posts	Number of companies	Number of posts	Number of companies	Number of posts	Number of companies	Number of posts
Textile, spinning, and woven goods	–	–	1	1	2	2	3	3	6	6
Distillation	–	–	4	4	3	3	5	6	10	13
Distributing	1	1	1	1	4	4	3	3	8	9
Banking	–	–	5	5	8	8	17	18	25	31
Insurance	–	–	7	7	5	5	7	9	14	21
Electric power, gas, and energy	–	–	–	–	–	–	4	4	4	4
Transportation	–	–	1	1	–	–	5	5	6	6
Other industries	–	–	13	13	7	7	23	23	40	43
All industries	1	1	60	61	43	43	114	121	196	226

[a] There are cases in which the total number of companies establishing interlocking directorates differed from the total number of companies measured by each position of the supervisory board due to the existence of companies where interlocking directorates through more than two posts were built

Source This table was compiled by the author, based on Morr (Hrsg) (1960)

Examining the situation of interlocking directorates, concerning the position of mandate of the supervisory board, Commerzbank built an interlocking directorate through one mandate of the honorary chairman of the supervisory board in only one company: Handelsunion AG in the distributing industry.

Given the situation of interlocking directorates regarding the position of mandate of the supervisory board, in 60 enterprises, cases in which interlocking directorates on the supervisory boards of other companies were formed through the mandate of chairman of the supervisory board with a total of 61 mandates. The numbers of both enterprises and mandates were less than half of those of Deutsche Bank (134 and 134, respectively) and fewer than those of Dresdner Bank (86 and 86, respectively). However, they were a little more than those of Commerzbank around the mid-1930s (53 and 53, respectively). Considering the distribution of industrial sectors, the numbers of enterprises and mandates in which interlocking directorates were formed were two each in mining; two each in iron and steel; one each in metal producing and processing; five and six in chemicals; seven each in electrical; four each in machines; two each in precious machines and optical; one each in shipbuilding; three each in oil; one each in food; one each in textile, spinning, and woven goods; four each in distillation; one each in distributing; five each in banking; seven each in insurance; one each in transportation; and 13 each in other industries, respectively. In these companies, there were major companies in each industry, such as Buderus'sche Eisenwerke in iron and steel, Bayer AG, Bunawerke Hüls GmbH, and Behringwerke AG in chemical, Lübecker Flender-Werke AG in shipbuilding industry, Rudolph Karstadt AG in distributing, Deutsche Hypothekenbank and Rheinische Hypothekenbank in banking, and Gerling-Konzern Lebensversicherungs-AG, Gerling-Konzern Spezialle Kreditversicherungs-AG, Friedrich Wilhelm Magdeburger Lebensversicherungs-AG, and Bayerische Rückversicherungs-AG in insurance.

In 43 enterprises, interlocking directorates were formed through the mandate of vice-chairman of the supervisory board, totaling 43 mandates. In each company, the number of mandates was one, respectively. The numbers of enterprises and mandates were much fewer than those of Deutsche Bank (76 and 78, respectively) and those of Dresdner Bank (78 and 81, respectively). However, they were more than those of Commerzbank around the 1930s (26 and 27, respectively). The numbers of enterprises and mandates in which such interlocking cases were formed were two each in mining; two each in iron and steel; one each in chemical; one each in electrical; five each in machine; one each in shipbuilding; one each in oil; one each in food; two each in textile, spinning, and woven goods; three each in distillation; four each in distributing; eight each in banking; five each in insurance; and seven each in other industries, respectively. These enterprises included representative enterprises in each industry such as Lübecker Flender-Werke AG in shipbuilding industry, Kaufhof AG and Kaufhalle GmbH in the distributing industry, Gerling-Konzern Spezialle Kreditversicherungs-AG in the insurance industry.

Interlocking directorates through mandates of the supervisory board except the chairman and vice-chairman were observed in 114 companies, totaling 121 mandates. The numbers of enterprises and mandates were fewer than those of Deutsche Bank (137 and 160, respectively) and those of Dresdner Bank (143 and 158, respectively).

They were also much fewer than those of Commerzbank Bank around the mid-1930s (180 and 206, respectively). The numbers of enterprises and mandates in which Commerzbank built interlocking directorates were six each in mining; 11 each in iron and steel; nine and 11 in chemical; nine and 10 in electrical; one each in automobiles; eight each in machine; one each in precious machines and optical; one each in oil; one each in food; three each in textile, spinning, and woven goods; five and six in distillation; three each in distributing; 17 and 18 in banking; seven and nine in insurance; four each in electric power, gas, and energy; five each in transportation; and 23 each in other industries, respectively. There were many enterprises in iron and steel, chemical, electrical, machine, banking, and insurance. There were many interlocking directorates in industries such as iron and steel, chemical, machine, banking, and insurance. In these companies, there were major companies in each industry, such as Gelsenkirchener Bergwerks-AG, Steinkohlenbergwerke Mathias Stinnes AG, and Bergwerksgesellschaft Hibernia AG in mining, Guthoffnungshütte Aktienverein and Ruhrstahl AG in iron and steel, Bayer AG, Hoechst AG, Chemische Werke Hüls AG, and Wintershall AG in chemical, AEG and Brown, Boveri & Cie AG in electrical, Daimler-Benz AG in automobile, Rudolph Karstadt AG in distributing, Gerling-Konzern Allgemeine Versicherungs-AG, Friedrich Wilhelm Lebensversicherungs-AG, and Hermes Kreditversicherungs-AG in insurance, and Rheinisch-Westfälisches Elektrizitätswerk AG in electric power, gas, and energy.

The numbers of enterprises and mandates were 22 and 52, respectively, when considering cases where members of the supervisory board and board of directors of Commerzbank had more than two mandates on the supervisory boards of other companies (see Table 5.6). The numbers of both enterprises and mandates were almost half of those of Deutsche Bank (49 and 116, respectively) and those of Dresdner Bank (47 and 105, respectively). They were also much fewer than those of Commerzbank around the 1930s (39 and 85, respectively). Considering the distribution among industries, the numbers of companies and mandates were as follows: two and eight in the chemical industry; one and two in electrical; one and two in machines; one and two in precious machines and optical; one and two in shipbuilding; two and five in distillation; one and two in distributing; four and 10 in banking; six and 13 in insurance; and three and six in other industries, respectively.

Of these 39 companies, six enterprises in which direct interlocking directorates were built through more than three mandates, totaling 20 mandates. The numbers of both enterprises and mandates were fewer than those of Deutsche Bank (14 and 46, respectively) and those of Dresdner Bank (10 and 31, respectively). However, they were almost exactly as those of Commerzbank in the 1930s (6 and 19, respectively). In the remaining companies, Commerzbank had two mandates on the supervisory board of other companies.

Concerning enterprises with four mandates, for Th. Goldschmidt AG in the chemical industry interlocking directorates were built through two mandates of chairman and one each of vice-chairman and the supervisory board except chairman and vice-chairman, and Bayer AG in the chemical industry interlocking directorates were formed through one post of chairman and three mandates of the supervisory board except chairman and vice-chairman. Of four companies with three

Table 5.6 Cases in which Commerzbank built direct interlocking directorates through more than two posts on the supervisory board of other companies (period before the 1965 Corporations Law)

Industries	Number of posts							
	2		3		4		Total	
	Number of companies	Number of posts	Number of companies	Number of posts	Number of companies	Number of posts	Number of companies	Number of posts
Chemical	–	–	–	–	2	8	2	8
Electrical	1	2	–	–	–	–	1	2
Machine	1	2	–	–	–	–	1	2
Precious machine and optical	1	2	–	–	–	–	1	2
Shipbuilding	1	2	–	–	–	–	1	2
Distillation	1	2	1	3	–	–	2	5
Distributing	1	2	–	–	–	–	1	2
Banking	2	4	2	6	–	–	4	10
Insurance	5	10	1	3	–	–	6	13
Other industries	3	6	–	–	–	–	3	6
All industries	16	32	4	12	2	8	22	52

Source This table was compiled by the author, based on Morr (Hrsg) (1960)

mandates, in Berliner Commerzbank AG in banking, Commerzbank established interlocking directorates through one each of the mandate of chairman and vice-chairman and a post of the supervisory board except chairman and vice-chairman, whereas in Holsten-Brauerei in distillation, there were interlocking directorates through a mandate of chairman and two posts of the supervisory board except chairman and vice-chairman, and in Ausfuhrkredit-AG in banking, interlocking directorates were established through a mandate of vice-chairman and two posts of the supervisory board except chairman and vice-chairman. In Gerling-Konzern Allgemeine Versicherungs-AG in insurance, interlocking directorates were built through three mandates of the supervisory board except chairman and vice-chairman.

When considering 16 enterprises with two mandates on the supervisory board of other enterprises in relation to the distribution of the industrial sector, there were one in electrical, one in machine, one in precious machines and optical, one in shipbuilding, one in distillation, one in distributing, two in banking, five in insurance, three in other industries.

Considering these interlocking directorates in relation to the kind of mandate, cases in which interlocking directorates were built through one each of the mandate of chairman and vice-chairman are observable in six enterprises: Lübecker Flender-Werke AG in shipbuilding, Bavaria- und St. Pauli-Brauerei in distillation, Deutsche Hypothekenbank in banking, and Gerling-Konzern Lebensversicherungs-AG, Gerling-Konzern Spezialle Kreditversicherungs-AG, and Gerling-Konzern Globale Rückversicherungs-AG in insurance. Enterprises in which interlocking directorates were established through one post of chairman and a mandate of the supervisory board except chairman and vice-chairman were six. These enterprises were Krauss-Maffei AG in machine, Ernst Leitz GmbH in precious machine and optical, Rudolph Karstadt AG in distributing, Rheinische Hypothekenbank in banking, Gerling-Konzern Versicherungs-Zentrale AG in insurance, and Beton- und Monierbau AG in other industries. Cases where interlocking directorates were built through a mandate of vice-chairman and one post of the supervisory board except chairman and vice-chairman were seen in three companies: Friedrich Wilhelm Magdeburger Versicherungs-AG in insurance and Allgemeine Deutsche Investment-Gesellschaft mbH and Treuhand AG in other industries. In contrast, in Süddeutsche Telefon-Apparate, Kabel- und Drahtwerke AG in electrical, Commerzbank built interlocking directorates through two mandates of the vice-chairman.

Thus, Commerzbank's direct interlocking directorates on the supervisory boards of other enterprises spread over a wide range of industries and had personnel connections with several competitive companies mutually in the same industrial sector through several mandates of the supervisory board. Such cases are seen in Gelsenkirchener Bergwerks-AG, Steinkohlenbergwerke Mathias Stinnes AG, Eschweiler Bergwerksverein, and Bergwerksgesellschaft Hibernia AG in mining, Guthoffnungshütte Aktienverein, Buderus'sche Eisenwerke, Stahlwerke Röchling-Buderus AG, and Ruhrstahl AG in iron and steel, Bayer AG, Hoechst AG, Chemische Werke Hüls AG, and Wintershall AG in chemical, AEG, Brown, Boveri & Cie AG, Felten & Guilleaume Fernmeldnanlagen GmbH, Kabelwerk Wilhelminenhof AG, and Kabel- und Metallwerke Neumeyer AG in electrical, Krauss-Maffei

AG, L. Schuler AG, Maschinenfabrik, and Maschinenfabrik Grevenbroich AG in machine, Holsten-Brauerei, Bavaria- und St. Pauli-Brauerei, and Wicküler-Küpper-Brauerei AG in distillation, Rudolph Karstadt AG, Kaufhof AG, and Kaufhalle GmbH in distributing, Ausfuhrkredit-AG, Deutsche Hypothekenbank, Rheinische Hypothekenbank, Niederrheinische Bank AG, and Bayerische Hypotheken- und Wechsel-Bank and some enterprises of the Gerling Group such as Gerling-Konzern Allgemeine Versicherungs-AG and Gerling-Konzern Lebensversicherungs-AG, Hermes Kreditversicherungs-AG, and Bayerische Rückversicherungs-AG in insurance. In this way, Commerzbank established close and strong personnel connections with many companies in various industries through direct interlocking directorates of members of the supervisory and management boards, which greatly contributed to securing information for its own financial business and decision of policies over industrial enterprises.

5.2 Indirect Interlocking Directorates Between Banks on the Supervisory Board of Other Enterprises

Three large banks built direct interlocking directorates with many enterprises in the very wide extent of industries. Building upon our previous discussions, the next issue to be explored is how indirect interlocking directorates were formed among these three banks and between some two banks through the direct interlocking directorate of members of the supervisory and managing boards of each bank. Therefore, such research topics will be considered in Sect. 5.2.

First, Sect. 5.1 explores indirect interlocking directorates among the three big banks. Sections 5.2 and 5.3 examine such personnel connections between Deutsche Bank and Dresdner Bank and between Deutsche Bank and Commerzbank. Section 5.4 considers the conditions of indirect interlocking directorates built between Dresdner Bank and Commerzbank.

5.2.1 Indirect Interlocking Directorates Among Three Large Banks on the Supervisory Board of Other Enterprises

This section considers the situations related to indirect interlocking directorates among three large banks on the supervisory board of other enterprises (see Table 5.7). Such cases can be observed in 29 companies, where the total number of mandates was 110. The numbers of enterprises and mandates where the three large banks built indirect interlocking directorates were less than two times those in the mid-1930s during the period of National Socialism (36 and 152, respectively) (see Chap. 4). Considering the interlocking directorate in relation to the kind of mandate, there were 21 and 31 enterprises and mandates which featured indirect interlocking through the mandate of chairman. Similar figures regarding the indirect interlocking directorate through the mandate of vice-chairman were 20 and 28, respectively; those through the mandate of the supervisory board except the chairman and vice-chairman were 27 and 61, respectively. As regards the distribution of industry, number of companies, and mandates of interlocking directorates, there were, respectively, three and 13 in the mining industry, one and three in iron and steel, three and 10 in chemical, two and eight in electrical, one and three in automobile, one and four in shipbuilding, two and six in textile, spinning, and woven goods, two and seven in distributing, seven and 30 in banking, one and four in insurance, two and eight in electric power, gas, and energy, one and three in transportation, and three and 11 in other industries.

To understand the bank at the leading position in an indirect interlocking relation requires examining cases where one or more of the three large banks had more than two mandates on the supervisory board of other companies; such cases were observed in 15 companies with a total of 68 mandates. The numbers of enterprises and mandates in which such indirect interlocking directorates were built were much lower than in the mid-1930s (24 and 116, respectively). When considering the distribution of industry, number of companies, and mandates of interlocking directorates, there were, respectively, two and 10 in mining, one and four in chemical, one and five in electrical, one and four in shipbuilding, one and four in distributing, five and 24 in banking, one and four in insurance, one and five in electric power, gas, and energy, and two and eight in other industries.

In one company, Deutsche Bank, Dresdner Bank, and Commerzbank built indirect interlocking directorates through eight mandates. Similar numerical figures through a total of five and four mandates were four and 10, respectively. In the others, indirect interlocking directorates were built through a total of three mandates each.

Regarding the enterprises with a total of eight mandates, in Ausfuhrkredit-AG in the banking industry, Deutsche Bank had two mandates consisting of one mandate of chairman and a post of the supervisory board except chairman and vice-chairman. Meanwhile, Dresdner Bank and Commerzbank had one mandate of vice-chairman and two posts of the supervisory board except chairman and vice-chairman. For the four enterprises with a total of five mandates in each enterprise, in Gelsenkirchener Bergwerks-AG in the mining industry, Dresdner Bank had one mandate of chairman, Deutsche Bank held three mandates of the supervisory board except chairman and vice-chairman, and Commerzbank had one similar mandate. In Brown, Boveri & Cie, AG in electrical, Dresdner Bank held a mandate of vice-chairman and two posts of the supervisory board except for chairman and vice-chairman, whereas Deutsche Bank and Commerzbank had one post of the supervisory board except for chairman and vice-chairman, respectively. In Rheinisch-Westfälisches Elektrizitätswerke AG in electric power, gas, and energy, Deutsche Bank held a mandate of chairman and one post of the supervisory board except chairman and vice-chairman, and Dresdner Bank had a mandate of vice-chairman and one post of the supervisory board except chairman and vice-chairman. In contrast, Commerzbank held one mandate of the supervisory board except for chairman and vice-chairman. In Salzdetfurth AG in mining, Deutsche Bank had a mandate of chairman and two posts of the supervisory

Table 5.7 Indirect interlocking directorates of the members of the supervisory board and the managing board on the supervisory board of other companies among Deutsche Bank, Dresdner Bank, and Commerzbank (period before the 1965 Corporations Law)

Industries	Number of posts									
	3		4		5		8		Total	
	Number of companies	Number of posts	Number of companies	Number of posts	Number of companies	Number of posts	Number of companies	Number of posts	Number of companies	Number of posts
Mining	1	3	–	–	2	10	–	–	3	13
Iron and steel	1	3	–	–	–	–	–	–	1	3
Chemical	2	6	1	4	–	–	–	–	3	10
Electrical	1	3	–	–	1	5	–	–	2	8
Automobile	1	3	–	–	–	–	–	–	1	3
Shipbuilding	–	–	1	4	–	–	–	–	1	4
Textile, spinning, and woven goods	2	6	–	–	–	–	–	–	2	6
Distributing	1	3	1	4	–	–	–	–	2	7
Banking	2	6	4	16	–	–	1	8	7	30
Insurance	–	–	1	4	–	–	–	–	1	4
Electric power, gas, and energy	1	3	–	–	1	5	–	–	2	8
Transportation	1	3	–	–	–	–	–	–	1	3
Other industries	1	3	2	8	–	–	–	–	3	11
All industries	14	42	10	40	4	20	1	8	29	110

Source This table was compiled by the author, based on Morr (Hrsg) (1960)

board except chairman and vice-chairman, Commerzbank had one mandate of vice-chairman, and Dresdner Bank had a mandate of the supervisory board except for chairman and vice-chairman.

For the ten enterprises totaling four mandates, in Deutsche Hypothekenbank in banking industry, Commerzbank had one mandate each of chairman and vice-chairman, and Deutsche Bank and Dresdner Bank held one post of vice-chairman, respectively. In Lübecker Flender-Werke AG in shipbuilding, Commerzbank had one mandate each of chairman and vice-chairman, Dresdner Bank held one post of vice-chairman, and Deutsche Bank had one post of the supervisory board except chairman and vice-chairman. In Deutsche Centralbodenkredit-AG in banking, Deutsche Bank had a mandate of chairman and one post of the supervisory board except chairman and vice-chairman, Dresdner Bank had a mandate of vice-chairman, and Commerzbank held one post of the supervisory board except chairman and vice-chairman. In Rudolph Karstadt AG in distributing, Commerzbank had one post of chairman and a mandate of the supervisory board except chairman and vice-chairman, Deutsche Bank held a mandate of vice-chairman, and Dresdner Bank had one post of the supervisory board except chairman and vice-chairman. In Rheinisch-Westfälische Kalkwerke AG in other industries, Deutsche Bank held a mandate of vice-chairman and one post of the supervisory board except chairman and vice-chairman, Dresdner Bank had a mandate of chairman, and Commerzbank had one mandate of the supervisory board except chairman and vice-chairman. In Bunawerke Hüls GmbH in chemical, Deutsche Bank had two posts of the supervisory board except chairman and vice-chairman, Commerzbank held a mandate of chairman, and Dresdner Bank had one mandate of the supervisory board except chairman and vice-chairman. In Rheinische Hypothekenbank in banking industry, Commerzbank held a mandate of chairman and one post of the supervisory board except chairman and vice-chairman, whereas Deutsche Bank and Dresdner Bank held a mandate of the supervisory board except chairman and vice-chairman. In Hermes Kreditversicherungs-AG in insurance, Dresdner Bank had a post of chairman and one mandate of the supervisory board except chairman and vice-chairman, and Deutsche Bank and Commerzbank had one mandate of the supervisory board except chairman and vice-chairman, respectively. In Chemie Verwaltungs AG in other industries, Dresdner Bank held two mandates of vice-chairman, and Deutsche Bank and Commerzbank had a mandate of the supervisory board except chairman and vice-chairman. In Industriekreditbank AG in banking, Dresdner Bank had one post of vice-chairman and one mandate of the supervisory board except chairman and vice-chairman, and Deutsche Bank and Commerzbank had a mandate of the supervisory board except chairman and vice-chairman, respectively.

Of 14 companies with a total of three mandates, in Phrix-Werke AG in textile, spinning, and woven goods, Deutsche Bank had a mandate of chairman and Dresdner Bank and Commerzbank had one mandate of vice-chairman. In Buderus'sche Eisenwerke in iron and steel, Commerzbank had one mandate of chairman, Deutsche Bank held a mandate of vice-chairman, and Dresdner Bank had one post of the supervisory board except chairman and vice-chairman. In Deutsche Schiffahrtsbank in banking, where Dresdner Bank had a mandate of chairman, Deutsche Bank had a mandate of vice-chairman, and Commerzbank held one post of the supervisory board except chairman and vice-chairman. In Deutsche Continental-Gas-Gesellschaft in electric power, gas, and energy, Deutsche Bank had one mandate of chairman, Dresdner Bank held a mandate of vice-chairman, and Commerzbank had one post of vice the supervisory board except chairman and vice-chairman. In Knapsack-Griesheim AG in chemical, Dresdner Bank had one mandate of chairman, while Deutsche Bank and Commerzbank had one post of the supervisory board except chairman and vice-chairman, respectively. In contrast, in three companies, namely, Daimler-Benz AG in automobile, Hamburg-Amerikanische Packetfahrt-AG in transportation, and Vereinigte Industrie-Unternehmungen AG in other industries, Deutsche Bank had one mandate of chairman, and Dresdner Bank and Commerzbank had a mandate of the supervisory board except chairman and vice-chairman, respectively. In AEG in electrical, Deutsche Bank and Dresdner Bank had one mandate of vice-chairman, respectively, Commerzbank held a mandate of the supervisory board except chairman and vice-chairman. In Kaufhof AG in distributing, Dresdner Bank and Commerzbank had one mandate of vice-chairman each and Deutsche Bank held a mandate of the supervisory board except chairman and vice-chairman. In Hoechst AG in chemical, where Dresdner Bank held one mandate of vice-chairman, Deutsche Bank and Commerzbank held one post of the supervisory board except chairman and vice-chairman. Finally, in Privatediskont-AG in banking, Deutsche Bank held one mandate of vice-chairman and Dresdner Bank and Commerzbank held one post of the supervisory board except chairman and vice-chairman, respectively.

5.2.2 Indirect Interlocking Directorates Between Deutsche Bank and Dresdner Bank on the Supervisory Board of Other Enterprises

Next, in examining the indirect interlocking directorate between Deutsche Bank and Dresdner Bank (see Table 5.8), cases can be observed in 52 companies and the total number of mandates was 148 except cases of indirect interlocking directorates among the three big banks. The numbers of enterprises and mandates in which Deutsche Bank and Dresdner Bank built indirect interlocking directorates were more than those around the 1930s (35 and 93, respectively). Considering the interlocking directorate in relation to the kind of mandate, the numbers of enterprises and mandates in which indirect interlocking directorate was built through the mandate of honor chairman were one each, respectively. Similar numerical figures through the mandate of chairman, vice-chairman, and post of the supervisory board except chairman and vice-chairman were 31 each, 35 and 41, and 40 and 75, respectively. When considering the distribution of industry, the numbers of companies and mandates of interlocking directorates were two and four in mining, eight and 22 in iron and steel, four and 12 in metal producing and metal processing, 10 and 29 in chemical, four and 15 in electrical, three and nine in machine, one and four in oil, four and nine in banking, 10 and 32 in insurance, three and six in transportation, and three and six in other industries, respectively.

Understanding the bank that was leading in an indirect interlocking relation requires examining cases in which one bank or both Deutsche Bank and Dresdner Bank had more than two mandates on the supervisory board of other companies; such cases were observed in 22 companies with a total of 88 mandates. When considering the distribution of industry, number of companies, and mandates of interlocking directorate, there were, respectively, four and 14 in iron and steel, two and eight in metal producing and metal processing, four and 17 in chemical, three and 13 in electrical, two and seven in machine, one and four in oil, one and three in banking, and five and 22 in insurance.

The number of companies in which Deutsche Bank and Dresdner Bank built an indirect interlocking directorate through a total of eight mandates was one. Similar numerical figures through a total of six, five, four, and three mandates were one, four, six, and 10, respectively. In the remaining 30 enterprises, indirect interlocking directorates were built through two mandates, respectively.

In Allianz ersicherungs-AG in the insurance industry, Dresdner Bank had four mandates consisting of a mandate of chairman, one mandate of vice-chairman, and two mandates of the supervisory board except chairman and vice-chairman, and Deutsche Bank had four mandates consisting of one post of vice-chairman and three posts of the supervisory board except chairman and vice-chairman. In Siemens-Schuckert AG in electrical, Deutsche Bank had five mandates consisting of a mandate of chairman and five mandates of the supervisory board except chairman and vice-chairman, and Dresdner Bank had one post of the supervisory board except chairman and vice-chairman.

Of four enterprises with five mandates in each enterprise, in Mannesmann AG in the iron and steel industry, Deutsche Bank had four mandates consisting of one mandate each of honor chairman and chairman and two mandates of the supervisory board except chairman and vice-chairman, and Dresdner Bank held one post of the supervisory board except chairman and vice-chairman. In Metallgesellschaft AG in metal producing and metal processing, where Dresdner Bank held one mandate each of chairman and vice-chairman, Deutsche Bank had three mandates of the supervisory board except chairman and vice-chairman. In Zellstofffabrik Waldhof in chemical, Deutsch Bank had a mandate of chairman and two mandates of the supervisory board except chairman and vice-chairman, and Dresdner Bank held a mandate of vice-chairman and one post of the supervisory board except chairman and vice-chairman. In Degussa AG in chemical, Dresdner Bank had a mandate of vice-chairman and two mandates of the supervisory board except chairman and vice-chairman, while Deutsche Bank held two posts of the supervisory board except chairman and vice-chairman.

Regarding six companies with four mandates in each company, in Siemens & Halske AG in electrical industry, Deutsche Bank had one each of mandate of chairman and vice-chairman and one post of the supervisory board except chairman and vice-chairman, and Dresdner Bank held a mandate of the supervisory board

Table 5.8 Indirect interlocking directorates of the members of the supervisory board and the managing board on the supervisory board of other companies between Deutsche Bank and Dresdner Bank[a] (period before the 1965 Corporations Law)

Industries	Number of posts													
	2		3		4		5		6		8		Total	
	Number of companies	Number of posts	Number of companies	Number of posts	Number of companies	Number of posts	Number of companies	Number of posts	Number of companies	Number of posts	Number of companies	Number of posts	Number of companies	Number of posts
Mining	2	4	–	–	–	–	–	–	–	–	–	–	2	4
Iron and steel	4	8	3	9	–	–	1	5	–	–	–	–	8	22
Metal producing and processing	2	4	1	3	–	–	1	5	–	–	–	–	4	12
Chemical	6	12	1	3	1	4	2	10	–	–	–	–	10	29
Electrical	1	2	1	3	1	4	–	–	1	6	–	–	4	15
Machine	1	2	1	3	1	4	–	–	–	–	–	–	3	9
Oil	–	–	–	–	1	4	–	–	–	–	–	–	1	4
Banking	3	6	1	3	–	–	–	–	–	–	–	–	4	9
Insurance	5	10	2	6	2	8	–	–	–	–	1	8	10	32
Transportation	3	6	–	–	–	–	–	–	–	–	–	–	3	6
Other industries	3	6	–	–	–	–	–	–	–	–	–	–	3	6
All industries	30	60	10	30	6	24	4	20	1	6	1	8	52	148

[a] The cases of indirect interlocking directorates built among Deutsche Bank, Dresdner Bank, and Commerzbank are excluded

Source This table was compiled by the author, based on Morr (Hrsg) (1960)

except chairman and vice-chairman. In Deutsche Erdöl AG in oil, Deutsche Bank had one mandate each of chairman and vice-chairman, and Dresdner Bank held two posts of the supervisory board except chairman and vice-chairman. In Allianz Lebensversicherungs-AG in insurance, where Deutsche Bank had a mandate of chairman and one post of the supervisory board except chairman and vice-chairman, Dresdner Bank had one mandate of vice-chairman and a mandate of the supervisory board except chairman and vice-chairman. In Rütgerswerke AG in chemical and DEMAG AG in machine, where Deutsche Bank had a mandate of vice-chairman and one post of the supervisory board except chairman and vice-chairman, Dresdner Bank had two mandates of the supervisory board except chairman and vice-chairman, respectively. In Münchener Rückversicheruns-Gesellschaft in insurance, Dresdner Bank held a mandate of vice-chairman and two posts of the supervisory board except chairman and vice-chairman. Notably, Deutsche Bank had one post of vice-chairman.

Of ten enterprises totaling three mandates in each enterprise, in BASF AG in chemical and Duisburger Kupferhütte in metal producing and metal processing, Deutsche Bank had one each of mandate of chairman and vice-chairman, and Dresdner Bank held a mandate of the supervisory board except chairman and vice-chairman, respectively. In Frankfurter Hypothekenbank in banking and Karlsruher Lebensversicherungs-AG in insurance, Dresdner Bank had a mandate of chairman and one post of the supervisory board except chairman and vice-chairman, whereas Deutsche Bank held a mandate of vice-chairman, respectively. In Frankfurter Versicherungs-AG in insurance, Dresdner Bank had a mandate of vice-chairman and one post of the supervisory board except chairman and vice-chairman, while Deutsche Bank had one mandate of chairman. In Hüttenwerk Salzgitter AG in iron and steel, where Deutsche Bank had a mandate of chairman and one post of the supervisory board except chairman and vice-chairman, Dresdner Bank had one mandate of the supervisory board except chairman and vice-chairman. In Telefunken GmbH in electrical, Dresdner Bank held a mandate of chairman and one post of the supervisory board except chairman and vice-chairman. In contrast, Deutsche Bank had one post of vice-chairman. In Orenstein-Koppel und Lübecker Maschinenbau AG in machine, where Deutsche Bank had a mandate of vice-chairman and one mandate of the supervisory board except chairman and vice-chairman, Dresdner Bank held one post of the supervisory board except chairman and vice-chairman. In Rheinische Stahlwerke in insurance, Deutsche Bank had two mandates of the supervisory board except chairman and vice-chairman, and Dresdner Bank had one mandate of the supervisory board except chairman and vice-chairman. In August Thyssen-Hütte AG in iron and steel, Dresdner Bank had two mandates of the supervisory board except chairman and vice-chairman, and Deutsche Bank had one mandate of the supervisory board except chairman and vice-chairman.

Concerning the remaining 30 companies with two mandates in each company, the number of companies of interlocking directorate was two in the mining industry, four in iron and steel, two in metal producing and metal processing, six in chemical, one in electrical, one in machine, three in banking, five in insurance, three in transportation, and three in other industries, respectively.

Cases in which each of the two banks had one chairman post or a post of vice-chairman can be observed in nine enterprises. In seven enterprises, namely, Stahl- und Walzwerke Rasselstein/Andernach AG in iron and steel, Osram GmbH in electrical, Pfälzische Hypothekenbank in banking, Hamburg-Mannheimer Versicherungs-AG and Kraft Versicherungs-AG in insurance, and Elsa Zement- und Kalkwerke AG and Süddeutsche Zucker-AG in other industries, Deutsche Bank had a mandate of chairman, and Dresdner Bank had one post of vice-chairman, respectively. In Eisen- und Hüttenwerke AG in iron and steel and Deutsche Schiffspfandbriefbank AG in banking, where Dresdner Bank had a mandate of chairman, Deutsche Bank had one post of vice-chairman, respectively. Cases in which each of the two banks had one chairman post or a post of the supervisory board except chairman and vice-chairman are observable in six enterprises. In Rheinstahl Bergbau AG in mining and Berlinische Feuer-Versicherungs-Anstalt in insurance, where Deutsche Bank had a mandate of chairman, Dresdner Bank had one post of the supervisory board except chairman and vice-chairman, respectively. In four enterprises, namely, Scheidemandel-Motard-Werke AG and "Sachtleben" AG für Bergbau und Chemische Industrie in chemical, Dinglerwerke AG in machine, and Gesellschaft für Kernenergieverwertung in Schiffbau und Schiffahrt GmbH in other industries, Dresdner Bank had a mandate of chairman, while Deutsche Bank had one post of the supervisory board except chairman and vice-chairman, respectively. Enterprises where two banks had one mandate of vice-chairman were three, namely, Hypothekenbank in Hamburg in banking and Deutsche Kranken-Versicherungs-AG and Hansa Lebensversicherungs-AG in industry. Cases where each of the two banks had a vice-chairman or one post of the supervisory board except chairman and vice-chairman are observable in seven enterprises. In Rheinsthal Eisenwerke Mülheim/Meiderich AG in iron and steel, Stolberger Zink Aktiengesellschaf für Bergbau und Hüttenbetriebe in metal producing and metal processing, Chemische Werke Albert AG in chemical, and Allgemeine Lokalbahn- und Kraftwerke-AG in transportation, Deutsche Bank had a mandate of vice-chairman and Dresdner Bank had one mandate of the supervisory board except chairman and vice-chairman, respectively. In Norddeutsche Affinerie and IG Farbenindustrie in chemical and Fendel-Schiffahrts-AG in transportation, where Dresdner Bank had a mandate of vice-chairman, Deutsche Bank held one post of the supervisory board except chairman and vice-chairman, respectively. Companies in which each bank had one post of the supervisory board except chairman and vice-chairman, respectively, were five. They were Essener Steinkohlenbergwerke AG in mining, Aktiengesellschaft für Berg- und Hüttenbetriebe in iron and steel, Vereinigte Aluminum-Werke in metal producing and metal processing, Phoenix Gummiwerke AG in chemical, and Aktiengesellschaft für Verkehrswesen und Industrie in transportation.

5.2.3 Indirect Interlocking Directorates Between Deutsche Bank and Commerzbank on the Supervisory Board of Other Enterprises

In examining the situations related to indirect interlocking directorates between Deutsche Bank and Commerzbank Bank on the supervisory board of other enterprises (see Table 5.9), such cases can be observed in 22 companies with a total of 63 mandates except for cases of indirect interlocking directorates among the three big banks. The numbers of enterprises and mandates in which Dresdner Bank and Commerzbank formed indirect interlocking directorate were much fewer than those of indirect interlocking directorates built between Deutsche Bank and Dresdner Bank (52 and 148, respectively). They were fewer than cases where Deutsche Bank and Commerzbank built indirect interlocking directorates around the mid-1930s (32 and 76, respectively). Considering the interlocking directorate in relation to the kind of mandate, the numbers of enterprises and mandates in which indirect interlocking directorates were formed through the mandate of chairman were 17 and 18, respectively. Similarly, figures through the mandate of vice-chairman and post of the supervisory board except chairman and vice-chairman were nine and 10, respectively, and 21 and 35, respectively. When considering the distribution of industry, the numbers of companies and mandates of interlocking directorate were one and two in iron and steel, two and 11 in chemical, two and four in electrical, four and 11 in machine, two and four in textile, spinning, and woven goods, one and two in banking, five and 18 in insurance, two and four in transportation, and three and seven in other industries, respectively.

There were ten enterprises in which Deutsche Bank and Commerzbank built indirect interlocking directorates through more than a total of three mandates on the supervisory board of other enterprises. The total number of mandates was 39. The number of companies in which Deutsche Bank and Commerzbank built such indirect interlocking directorates totaling six mandates was one. Other figures through a total five, four, and three mandates were two, two, and five, respectively. In the remaining 12 enterprises, indirect interlocking directorates were built through two mandates, respectively.

Regarding enterprises with six mandates in each enterprise, in Bayer AG in chemical, Commerzbank had four mandates consisting of a mandate of chairman and three posts of the supervisory board except chairman and vice-chairman, and Deutsche Bank had two posts of the supervisory board except chairman and vice-chairman. In Th. Goldschmidt AG in chemical, where Commerzbank held four mandates consisting of two mandates of chairman, one mandate of vice-chairman, and one post of the supervisory board except chairman and vice-chairman, Deutsche Bank had a mandate of the supervisory board except chairman and vice-chairman. In contrast, in Gerling-Konzern Allgemeine Versicherungs-AG in insurance, Deutsche Bank had a mandate of chairman and one post of the supervisory board except

Table 5.9 Indirect interlocking directorates of the members of the supervisory board and the managing board on the supervisory board of other companies between Deutsche Bank and Commerzbank[a] (period before the 1965 Corporations Law)

Industries	Number of posts											
	2		**3**		4		**5**		**6**		Total	
	Number of companies	Number of posts	Number of companies	Number of posts	Number of companies	Number of posts	Number of companies	Number of posts	Number of companies	Number of posts	Number of companies	Number of posts
Iron and steel	1	2	–	–	–	–	–	–	–	–	1	2
Chemical	–	–	–	–	–	–	1	5	1	6	2	11
Electrical	2	4	–	–	–	–	–	–	–	–	2	4
Machine	2	4	1	3	1	4	–	–	–	–	4	11
Textile, spinning, and woven goods	2	4	–	–	–	–	–	–	–	–	2	4
Banking	1	2	–	–	–	–	–	–	–	–	1	2
Insurance	–	–	3	9	1	4	1	5	–	–	5	18
Transportation	2	4	–	–	–	–	–	–	–	–	2	4
Other industries	2	4	1	3	–	–	–	–	–	–	3	7
All industries	12	24	5	15	2	8	2	10	1	6	22	63

[a] The cases of indirect interlocking directorates built among Deutsche Bank, Dresdner Bank, and Commerzbank are excluded
Source This table was compiled by the author, based on Morr (Hrsg) (1960)

chairman and vice-chairman, while Commerzbank held three mandates of the supervisory board except chairman and vice-chairman. In Schubert & Salzer Maschinenfabrik AG in machine, Deutsche Bank had a mandate of chairman and two posts of the supervisory board except chairman and vice-chairman, and Commerzbank held one mandate of vice-chairman. In Gerling-Konzern Lebensversicherungs-AG in insurance, where Commerzbank had one each of mandate of chairman and vice-chairman, Deutsche Bank held two mandates of the supervisory board except chairman and vice-chairman.

Of five companies with three mandates in each company, in Gerling-Konzern Speziale Kreditversicherungs-AG in the insurance industry, Commerzbank had one mandate each of chairman and vice-chairman, and Deutsche Bank held one post of the supervisory board except chairman and vice-chairman. In Krauss-Maffei AG in machine, Commerzbank had one post of chairman and a mandate of the supervisory board except chairman and vice-chairman, while Deutsche Bank had a mandate of vice-chairman. In Reemtsma Cigarettenfabriken GmbH in other industries, where Deutsche Bank had a mandate of chairman and one mandate of the supervisory board except chairman and vice-chairman, Commerzbank held one post of the supervisory board except chairman and vice-chairman. In Gerling-Konzern Versicherungs-Zentrale AG in insurance, Commerzbank held a mandate of chairman and one post of the supervisory board except chairman and vice-chairman, and Deutsche Bank had one mandate of the supervisory board except chairman and vice-chairman. In Friedrich Wilhelm Magdeburger Versicherungs-AG in insurance, Commerzbank had one post of vice-chairman and a mandate of the supervisory board except chairman and vice-chairman, whereas Deutsche Bank held one post of the supervisory board except for chairman and vice-chairman.

Concerning the remaining 12 firms totaling two mandates in each firm, the number of companies of interlocking directorate was one in iron and steel, two in electrical, two in machine, two in textile, spinning, and woven goods, one in banking, two in transportation, and two in other industries, respectively.

Cases in which each of the two banks had one chairman post or a post of vice-chairman were one company (Maschinenfabrik Grevenbroich AG in the machine industry). In this enterprise, Deutsche Bank had a mandate of chairman and Commerzbank had one post of vice-chairman. Cases where each bank had one chairman post or a post of the supervisory board except for chairman and vice-chairman are observable in seven enterprises. In six companies, namely, Hans Still AG in electrical, Henschel-Werke GmbH in machine, Deutsch-Asiatische Bank in banking, Deutsche Eisenbahn-Betriebs-Gesellschaft AG in transportation, and Didier-Werke AG and Porzellanfabrik Kahla in other industries, where Deutsche Bank had a mandate of chairman, Commerzbank had one post of the supervisory board except chairman and vice-chairman, respectively. In Vereinigte Jute-Spinnereien und Webereien AG in textile spinning, and woven goods, where Commerzbank had a mandate of chairman, Deutsche Bank held one mandate of the supervisory board except chairman and vice-chairman. Enterprises in which each bank had a vice-chairman or one post of the supervisory board except chairman and vice-chairman were two enterprises. In Preußische Bergwerks- und Hütten-AG in iron and steel and Gebhard & Co. AG in textile, spinning, and woven goods, where Deutsche Bank had a mandate of vice-chairman, Commerzbank held one mandate of the supervisory board except chairman and vice-chairman, respectively. Companies where each bank had one post of the supervisory board except chairman and vice-chairman, respectively, were two: Osnabrücker Kupfer- und Drahtwerk in electrical and Vorwohle-Emmerthaler Eisenbahn-Gesellschaft in transportation.

5.2.4 *Indirect Interlocking Directorates Between Dresdner Bank and Commerzbank on the Supervisory Board of Other Enterprises*

Next, in examining Dresdner Bank and Commerzbank (see Table 5.10), cases can be observed in 23 companies with a total of 51 mandates except cases of indirect interlocking directorates among the three big banks. The numbers of enterprises and mandates were much fewer than those of indirect interlocking directorates built between Deutsche Bank and Dresdner Bank (52 and 148, respectively) and were fewer than the indirect interlocking directorates built between Deutsche Bank and Commerzbank (22 and 63, respectively). They were a little fewer than the cases in which Dresdner Bank and Commerzbank built indirect interlocking directorates around the mid-1930s (20 and 44, respectively). Considering interlocking directorates in relation to the kind of mandate, the numbers of enterprises and mandates in which indirect interlocking was established through the mandate of honor chairman were one and one, respectively. Similar numerical figures through mandate of chairman and vice-chairman and post of the supervisory board except chairman and vice-chairman were 13 each, 10 and 10, respectively, and 19 and 27, respectively. When considering the distribution of industry, number of companies and mandates of interlocking directorate were one and two in mining, one and two in iron and steel, two and five in chemical, one and two in electrical, two and five in machine, one and two in oil, one and two in food, one and three in textile, spinning, and woven goods, two and four in distributing, three and six in banking, two and four in insurance, one and two in electric power, gas, and energy, and five and 12 in other industries, respectively.

There were five cases in which Dresdner Bank and Commerzbank built indirect interlocking directorates through more than three mandates on the supervisory board of other enterprises. The total mandates were 15. The number of companies in which such indirect interlocking directorates were built through three mandates was five. In the remaining enterprises, indirect interlocking directorates were built through two mandates, respectively.

Regarding enterprises with three mandates in each enterprise, in all cases, where Dresdner Bank had two mandates, Commerzbank had one mandate. In L. Sachuler AG in machine, Dresdner Bank had a mandate of vice-chairman and one post of the supervisory board except chairman and vice-chairman, Commerzbank had a

Table 5.10 Indirect interlocking directorates of the members of the supervisory board and the managing board on the supervisory board of other companies between Dresdner Bank and Commerzbank[a] (period before the 1965 Corporations Law)

Industries	Number of posts					
	2		3		Total	
	Number of companies	Number of posts	Number of companies	Number of posts	Number of companies	Number of posts
Mining	1	2	–	–	1	2
Iron and steel	1	2	–	–	1	2
Chemical	1	2	1	3	2	5
Electrical	1	2	–	–	1	2
Machine	1	2	1	3	2	5
Oil	1	2	–	–	1	2
Food	1	2	–	–	1	2
Textile, spinning, and woven goods	–	–	1	3	1	3
Distributing	2	4	–	–	2	4
Banking	3	6	–	–	3	6
Insurance	2	4	–	–	2	4
Electric power, gas, and energy	1	2	–	–	1	2
Other industries	3	6	2	6	5	12
All industries	18	36	5	15	23	51

[a] The cases of indirect interlocking directorates built among Deutsche Bank, Dresdner Bank, and Commerzbank are excluded
Source This table was compiled by the author, based on Morr (Hrsg) (1960)

mandate of chairman. In Chemische Werke Hüls AG in chemical, Wollgartenfabrik Tittel & Krüger und Sternwoll-Spinnerei AG in textile, spinning, and woven goods, and Hochtief Aktiengesellschaft für Hoch- und Tiefbauten vorm. Gebrüder Helfmann in other industries, Dresdner Bank had one each of mandate of chairman and vice-chairman, and Commerzbank held one mandate of the supervisory board except chairman and vice-chairman, respectively. In Hotelbetriebs-AG in other industries, Dresdner Bank held a mandate of chairman and one post of the supervisory board except chairman and vice-chairman, and Commerzbank had one mandate of vice-chairman.

Concerning the remaining 18 firms with two mandates in each firm, the number of companies of interlocking directorate was one in the mining industry, one in iron and steel, one in chemical, one in electrical, one in machine, one in oil, one in food, two in distributing, three in banking, two in insurance, one in electric power, gas, and energy, and three in other industries, respectively.

Cases in which each of Dresdner Bank and Commerzbank had one honorary chairman post or a post of chairman were one enterprise. In Handelsunion AG in distributing, Commerzbank had a mandate of honor chairman, and Dresdner Bank had one post of chairman. Cases where each bank of two banks had a mandate of chairman or a post of vice-chairman are observable in three enterprises. In Papierfabrik GmbH vorm. Brüder Kämmerer in other industries, Dresdner Bank had a mandate of chairman, and Commerzbank held one mandate of vice-chairman. In Behringwerke AG in chemical and Julius Berger Tiefbau AG in other industries, Commerzbank had one post of chairman, and Dresdner Bank held a mandate of vice-chairman, respectively. Cases in which each bank had one chairman post or a post of the supervisory board except for chairman and vice-chairman can be observed in four enterprises. In Olympia Werke AG in machine and Frankona Rück- und Mitversicherungs AG in insurance, where Dresdner Bank had a mandate of chairman, Commerzbank had one post of the supervisory board except chairman and vice-chairman, respectively. In Gewerkschaft Erdöl-Raffinerie Deurag-Nerag in oil and Mitteldeutsche Hartstein-Industrie AG in other industries, Commerzbank held a mandate of chairman and Dresdner Bank had one post of the supervisory board except chairman and vice-chairman, respectively. Enterprises in which each bank had a vice-chairman or one post of the supervisory board except chairman and vice-chairman were two enterprises. In Eisen- und Stahlhandel AG in distributing and Beamtenversicherungsverein des Deutschen Bank- und Bankiergewerbes (aG) in insurance, where Commerzbank had a mandate of vice-chairman, Dresdner Bank held one mandate of the supervisory board except chairman and vice-chairman, respectively. Companies in which each of the two banks had one post of the supervisory board except chairman and vice-chairman, respectively, were eight. They were Steinkohlenbergwerke Mathias Stinnes AG in mining, Hein, Lehmann & Co AG in iron and steel, Standard Elektrik Lorenz AG in electrical, "Sarotti" AG in food, Westdeutsche Bodenkreditanstalt, Braunschweig-Hannoversche Hypothekenbank, and Rhein-Westfälische Boden-Credit-Bank in banking, and Hamburgischer Elektricitäts-Werke AG in electric power, gas, and energy.

This chapter discussed how the three largest banks established direct interlocking directorates on the supervisory board with other companies in various industrial sectors in the late 1950s when the industrial concentration system of postwar Germany was established through reconcentration of large banks and enterprises dissolved by the occupation policy of the victorious countries. Also explained were the structures of indirect interlocking directorates established among these three banks and between two of them. As there were no regulations to limit the number in which one person might have mandates on the supervisory board that influenced situations of interlocking directorates on supervisory boards, such as the 1965 Corporations Law, interlocking directorates with several enterprises were developed in various industries. Strong relationships were developed with companies in heavy and chemical industries as the key industrial sectors, such as iron and steel, electrical, automobile, machine, and electric power, gas, and energy industries, and the banking and insurance sectors. A bank's interlocking directorate on the supervisory board of other enterprises spread over various industries and three large banks established personnel connections with several competing companies in the same industrial sector through supervisory board mandates.

Such broad establishment of personnel connections through both direct and indirect interlocking directorates was deeply concerned with the two-layer top management system composed of the supervisory board and the board of directors. It was also based on a deposit stock system and relationships with many enterprises in various industries through financing business. Industry–bank relationships based on tie through interlocking directorates built the basis of exchanging and sharing information, coordination of interests and various conflicts between a bank and industrial enterprises and among corporations through discussion rather than market competition, and the banks' influence on corporations. Such a system played a significant role in cooperation.

Thus, personnel connection of big banks with many companies in various industries has formed the foundation of an industry–bank relationship. Individual enterprises as independent behavioral agents developed businesses using the relationships of interaction and interdependence between companies, including competing enterprises. In Germany, at the time, a typical pattern can be observed in such interactive and interdependent relations between enterprises developed through various contacts and exchanges of information based on an interlocking directorate system, which not only differed from those in other countries but also is an important element determining the characteristics of a social economic system called "cooperative capitalism" as well as corporate behavior.

However, the 1965 Corporations Law regulated the number of mandates of the supervisory board that one person could have. Consequently, how did situations regarding the interlocking directorates of members of the supervisory and managing boards of banks change? Was there a trend toward the decrease of interlocking directorates and careful selection of enterprises in which large banks attempted to build interlocking directorate relationships in the period after the law's enactment? Influenced by the regulation of this law, a basic system of interlocking directorates in postwar Germany was established and had been maintained for long.

Extending the discussions in this chapter, the issue of how these large banks established personnel connections through interlocking directorates in the supervisory board of other companies should be examined. Therefore, Chap. 6 further examines these topics.

References

Aizawa K (1994) Oshu saikyo no kinyu teikoku. Doitsu Ginko (The Strongest financial empire in Europe). Nihon keizai shinbunsya, Tokyo

Djelic M-L (1998) Exporting the American model. The postwar transformation of European business. Oxford University Press, Oxford
Eglau HO (1990) Wie Gott in Frankfurt: Die Deutsche Bank und die deutsche Industrie, 3rd edn. Econ Verlag, Düsseldorf
Horstmann T (1991) Die Alliierten und die deutschen Groβbanken. Bankenpolitik nach dem Zweiten Welkrieg in Westdeutschland. Bouvier, Bonn
Morr JM (Hrsg) (1960) Adreßbuch der Direktoren und Aufsichtsräte. Jahrgang 1960, Bd.I, Nach Persönlichkeiten geordnet, Finanzverlag G.m.b.H., Berlin
Pfeiffer (1986a) Groβbanken und Finanzgruppen. Ausgewählte Ergebnisse einer Untersuchung der personellen Verflechtungen von Deutscher, Dresdner und Commerzbank. In: WSI Mitteilungen 39(7):473–481
Pfeiffer (1986b) Das Netwerk der Groβbanken.Personelle Verflechtungen mit Konzernen, Staat und ideologischen Apparaten. In: Blätter für deutsche und internationale Politik 31(2):161–177
Pfeiffer (1993) Die Macht der Banken. Die personellen Verflechtungen der Commerzbank, der Deutschen Bank und der Dresdner Bank mit Unternehemen. Campus, Frankfurt am Main
Pohl M (1986) Entstehung und Entwicklung des Universalbanksystems: Konzentration und Krise als wichtige Faktoren. Fritz Knapp Verlag, Frankfurt am Main
Stanzick K-H (1969) Der ökonomische Konzentrationsproze. In: Schäfer G, Nedelmann C (Hrsg) Der CDU-Staat.Analysen zur Verfassungswirklichkeit der Bundesrepublik, Bd.I, 2. Aufl., Schurkamp, München, SS 48–79
Stolper G, Hauser K, Borchardt K (1964) Deutsche Wirtschaft seit 1870. J. C. B. Mohr, Tübingen
Wandel E (1998) Banken und Versicherungen im 19. und 20. Jahrhundert. R. Oldenbourg, München

Chapter 6
Interlocking Directorates of Bank's Supervisory Board and Managing Board Members in Other Enterprises in the Postwar Period After the Enactment of the 1965 Corporations Law

Abstract In Germany's large banks, the direct and indirect interlocking directorates of members of the supervisory and managing boards on the supervisory board of other enterprises were developed again with the re-concentration of these large banks dissolved after World War II. However, the 1965 Corporations Law that regulates the number of supervisory board members states that one person might have strongly influenced personnel connection through interlocking directorates on the supervisory board. What were the changes after the enactment of this law? The system of personnel connection established during this period continued to be the basic system of interlocking directorates in postwar Germany for long. Extending the discussions in Chap. 5, this chapter compares the conditions of interlocking directorates of three largest banks' top management team on the supervisory board of other enterprises in the late 1960s with the conditions before the enforcement of this law. This analysis shows which enterprise was at a central position in personnel connection between bank and enterprise and its industrial sector.

Keywords Commerzbank · Deutsche Bank · Dresdner Bank · Industry–bank relationship · Direct interlocking directorate · Indirect interlocking directorate · Personnel connection · The 1965 Corporations Law

Chapter 5 considered how Deutsche Bank, Dresdner Bank, and Commerzbank established personnel connections with other enterprises through direct interlocking directorates of their members of supervisory and managing boards and how were indirect interlocking directorates formed among the three banks and between banks in the late 1950s. During this period, there was no influence of the 1965 Corporations Law that regulated the number of supervisory board mandates that a person might have (Pfeiffer 1993, SS. 158–159; Pfeiffer 1986a, S. 477, 1986b, S. 164; Stanzick 1969, S. 72: Eglau 1990, S. 128), which was related to such conditions. However, this law influenced the situations of the interlocking directorates on the supervisory board. What were the changes made by this law under conditions of interlocking directorates of bank's members of the supervisory board and the managing board on the supervisory board of other enterprises? This chapter analyzes the conditions

T. Yamazaki, *Relationships Between Industry and Bank in Germany*,
https://doi.org/10.1007/978-981-97-4996-6_6

of interlocking directorate of members of the top management of the three largest banks on the supervisory board of enterprises in various industrial sectors in the late 1960s following the enactment of the 1965 Corporations Law compared with that in the late 1950s. The basic material used in analysis of this chapter is "*Handbuch der Direktoren und Aufsichtsräte 1970/71*" (Bd.I, Nach personen geordnet, Finanz- und Korrespondenz-Verlag).

Section 6.1 considers direct interlocking directorates of members of supervisory board and managing board of each bank on the supervisory board of other companies. Section 6.2 analyzes indirect interlocking directorates built through direct interlocking directorate among three banks and between two banks of them.

6.1 Direct Interlocking Directorate of Members of Supervisory Board and Managing Board of Banks on the Supervisory Board of Other Enterprises

6.1.1 Direct Interlocking Directorate of Members of Supervisory Board and Managing Board of Deutsche Bank

First, conditions of direct interlocking directorates are examined. Considering the direct interlocking directorate established by supervisory board and managing board members of Deutsche Bank on the supervisory board of other enterprises (see Table 6.1), there were 167 companies in which such cases were observed and 201 interlocking mandates. Numbers of both enterprises and mandates were much fewer than those around the end of the 1950s (corresponding numbers 306 and 373, respectively) (see Chap. 5).

Considering the distribution of industrial sectors, Deutsche Bank built direct interlocking directorates in 15 companies and had 16 interlocking mandates in the mining industry, and similarly, 12 and 15 in the iron and steel industry; six and seven in the metal producing and processing industries; 15 and 21 in the chemical industry; 10 and 15 in the electrical industry; five and five in the automobile industry; 12 and 15 in the machine industry; four and six in the precious machine and optical industries; one each in the shipbuilding industry; two each in the oil industry; two each in the food industry; nine and 11 in the textile, spinning, and woven goods industries; two each in the distillation industry; five and seven in the distributing industry; 15 and 18 in the banking industry; six and 10 in the insurance industry; 10 and 12 in the electric power, gas, and energy industries; six each in the transportation industry; and 30 and 30 in other industries, respectively. Among the various industries, except for the banking industry, for example, Deutsch Bank developed many interlocking relations in the mining, iron and steel, chemical, electrical, and machine industries.

Table 6.1 Direct interlocking directorates of the members of the supervisory board and the managing board of Deutsche Bank on the supervisory board of other companies (period after the 1965 Corporations Law)

Industries	Position									
	Honorary chairman		Chairman		Vice-chairman		Supervisory board member excluding chairman and vice-chairman		Total[a]	
	Number of companies	Number of posts	Number of companies	Number of posts	Number of companies	Number of posts	Number of companies	Number of posts	Number of companies	Number of posts
Mining	1	1	4	4	1	1	9	10	15	16
Iron and steel	–	–	6	6	3	3	6	6	12	15
Metal producing and processing	–	–	3	3	–	–	3	4	6	7
Chemical	1	1	6	6	4	5	9	9	15	21
Electrical	–	–	6	6	4	4	4	5	10	15
Automobile	–	–	4	4	–	–	1	1	5	5
Machine	1	1	6	6	3	3	5	5	12	15
Precious machine and optical industries	–	–	3	3	–	–	3	3	4	6
Shipbuilding	–	–	–	–	–	–	1	1	1	1
Oil	–	–	1	1	–	–	1	1	1	2
Food	–	–	1	1	1	1	–	–	2	2

(continued)

Table 6.1 (continued)

Industries	Position									
	Honorary chairman		Chairman		Vice-chairman		Supervisory board member excluding chairman and vice-chairman		Total[a]	
	Number of companies	Number of posts	Number of companies	Number of posts	Number of companies	Number of posts	Number of companies	Number of posts	Number of companies	Number of posts
Textile, spinning, and woven goods	–	–	5	5	5	5	1	1	9	11
Distillation	–	–	1	1	1	1	–	–	2	2
Distributing	–	–	2	2	2	3	2	2	5	7
Banking	1	1	8	8	7	7	2	2	15	18
Insurance	–	–	1	1	2	2	5	7	6	10
Electric power, gas, and energy	–	–	8	8	2	2	2	2	10	12
Transportation	–	–	3	3	1	1	2	2	6	6
Other industries	2	2	16	16	5	5	7	7	30	30
All industries	6	6	84	84	41	43	63	68	167	201

[a] There are cases in which the total number of companies establishing interlocking directorates differed from the total number of companies measured by each position of the supervisory board due to the existence of companies where interlocking directorates through more than two posts were built

Source This table was compiled by the author, based on Mossner (Hrsg) (1971)

Therefore, it had close and strong relationships with companies in the heavy and chemical industries as the key industrial sectors in Germany.

When considering the situation of interlocking directorates with respect to supervisory board position mandates, Deutsche Bank built interlocking directorates through mandate of the honorary chairman of the supervisory board in six companies, namely, Gebr. Stumm GmbH in the mining industry, Zellstofffabrik Waldhof in the chemical industry, Pitler Maschinenfabrik AG in the machine industry, Deutsche Ueberseeische Bank in the banking industry, and Salamander AG and Süddeutsche Zucker-AG in other industries. All of them were interlocking directorates through mandates with Hermann J. Abs.

In 84 enterprises, there were cases in which interlocking directorates on the supervisory boards of other companies were formed through mandate of chairman of the supervisory board with a total of 84 mandates in the following industries: four in mining industry, six in iron and steel industry, three in metal producing and processing industries, six in chemical industry, six in electrical industry, four in automobile industry, six in machine industry, three in precious machine and optical industries, one in oil industry, one in food industry, five in textile, spinning, and woven goods industries, one in distillation industry, two in distributing industry, eight in banking industry, one in insurance industry, eight in electric power, gas, and energy industries, three in transportation industry, and 16 in other industries. In each company, an interlocking directorate through one mandate was formed. Numbers of both enterprises and mandates were fewer than those around the end of the 1950s (corresponding numbers 134 and 134, respectively). Cases of interlocking directorate in representative companies of each industry were observed in Fried. Krupp GmbH, Klöckner-Werke AG, Mannesmann AG, Rheinische Stahlwerke, Hugo Stinnes AG, and Otto Wolff AG in the iron and steel industry; BASF and Glanzstoff AG in the chemical industry; Siemens AG, Robert Bosch GmbH, and Brown Boveri & Cie. AG in the electrical industry; Daimler-Benz AG in the automobile industry; Klöckner-Humboldt Deutz AG, Pitler Maschinenfabrik AG, and Maschinenfabrik Buckau R. Wolf AG in the machine industry; Allianz Versicherungs-AG in the insurance industry; and Rheinisch-Westfälisches Elektrizitätswerke AG in the electric power industry.

In 41 enterprises, in some cases, interlocking directorates were formed through mandate of vice-chairman of the supervisory board and the total number of mandates was 43. The numbers of enterprises and mandates in which such interlocking cases were formed were one each in the mining industry; similarly, three each in the iron and steel industry; four and five in the chemical industry; four each in the electrical industry; three each in the machine industry; one each in the foods industry; five each in the textile, spinning, and woven goods industries; one each in the distillation industry; two and three in the distributing industry; seven each in the banking industry; two each in the insurance industry; two each in the electric power, gas, and energy industries; one each in the transportation industry; and five each in other industries, respectively. Numbers of both enterprises and mandates were much fewer than those around the end of the 1950s (corresponding numbers 76 and 78, respectively). In these companies, there were major companies in each industry, such as

Hoesch AG in iron and steel industry, BASF AG and Bayer AG in the chemical industry, Siemens AG and AEG in the electrical industry, and Karstadt AG in the distributing industry.

Interlocking directorates through mandates of supervisory board except for chairman and vice-chairman were observed in 63 companies and the total number of mandates was 68. Considering the distribution among industrial sectors, the numbers of enterprises and mandates in which interlocking directorates were formed were nine and 10 in the mining industry, respectively; similarly, six each in the iron and steel industry; three and four in the metal producing and processing industries; nine each in the chemical industry; four and five in the electrical industry; one each in the automobile industry; five each in the machine industry; three each in the precious machine and optical industries; one each in the shipbuilding industry; one each in the oil industry; one each in the textile, spinning, and woven goods industries; two each in the distributing industry; two each in the banking industry; five and seven in the insurance industry; two each in the electric power, gas, and energy industries; two each in the transportation industry; and seven each in other industries, respectively. Numbers of both enterprises and mandates were less than half of those around the end of the 1950s (corresponding numbers 137 and 160, respectively). These companies included leading firms in each industry, such as Gelsenkirchener Bergwerke AG and Harpener Bergbau AG in the mining industry, August Thyssen-Hütte AG and Salzgtter AG in the iron and steel industry, Metallgesellschaft AG in the metal producing and processing industries, Degussa AG in the chemical industry, Volkswagen AG in the automobile industry, DEMAG AG and Orenstein-Koppel und Lübecker Maschinenbau AG in the machine industry, Carl Zeiss in the precious machine and optical industries, Deutsche Shell AG in the oil industry, Kaufhof AG in the distributing industry, and Allianz Lebensversicherungs-AG and Münchener Rückversicherungs-Gesellschaft in the insurance industry.

The numbers of enterprises and mandates were 25 and 59, respectively, when considering cases where Deutsche Bank's supervisory board and managing board members had more than two mandates on the supervisory boards of other companies (see Table 6.2). Numbers of both enterprises and mandates were approximately half of those around the end of the 1950s (corresponding numbers 49 and 116, respectively). Considering the distribution among industries, the numbers of companies and mandates were as follows: one and two in the mining industry; three and six in the iron and steel industry; one and two in the metal producing and processing industries; five and 11 in the chemical industry; three and eight in the electrical industry; two and five in the machine industry; two and four in precious machine and optical industries, one and three in the textile, spinning, and woven goods industries; one and three in the distributing industry; two and five in the banking industry; two and six in the insurance industry; and two and four in the electric power, gas, and energy industries, respectively. In the mining industry and the manufacturing industrial sectors, such cases were observed in representative enterprises in each sector such as Gelsenkirchener Bergwerke AG in the mining industry; Hoesch AG, Hugo Stinnes AG, and Otto Wolff AG in the iron and steel industry; Metallgesellschaft AG in the metal producing and processing industry; BASF AG, Bayer

AG, Glanzstoff AG, Zellstofffabrik Waldhof, and Rütgerswerke und Teerverwertung AG in the chemical industry; Siemens AG, Robert Bosch GmbH, and Brown, Boveri & Cie. AG in the electrical industry; Klöckner-Humboldt Deutz AG and Pittler Maschinenfabrik AG in the machine industry; Zeiss Ikon AG and Voigtländer AG in precious machine and optical industries, and Deutsche Linoleum-Werke AG in the textile, spinning, and woven goods industries. In sectors except for the mining and manufacturing industrial sectors, there were similar cases in Karstadt AG in the distributing industry, Deutsche Uebersseische Bank and Berliner Disconto-Bank AG in the banking industry, Allianz Versicherungs-AG and Albingia Versicherungs-AG in the insurance industry, and Nordwestdeutshe Kraftwerke AG and Preussische Elektrizitätswerke AG in the electric power, gas, and energy industries.

Of these 25 companies, there were seven enterprises in which direct interlocking directorates were built through more than three mandates and the total number of mandates was 23. Numbers of both enterprises and mandates were half of those around the end of the 1950s (corresponding numbers 14 and 46, respectively). Enterprises wherein direct interlocking directorates were formed through four mandates were two. Cases in which there were interlocking directorates through three mandates were five companies. In the rest 18 companies, Deutsche Bank had two mandates on the supervisory board of other companies, respectively.

In two companies, namely, Siemens AG and Allianz Versicherungs-AG, Deutsche Bank had four mandates on the supervisory board of other companies. In five companies, namely, BASF AG, Klöckner-Humboldt Deutz AG, Deutsche Linoleum-Werke AG, Karstadt AG, and Deutsche Ueberseeische Bank, interlocking directorates were built through three mandates on the supervisory board of other companies, respectively.

Considering the interlocking directorates in these enterprises in relation to supervisory board position mandates, in Siemens AG and Allianz-Versicherngs-AG Deutsche Bank built interlocking directorates through four mandates consisting of one chairman, one vice-chairman, and two posts of the supervisory board except for chairman and vice-chairman, respectively. Regarding companies with three mandates, in Deutsche Ueberseeische Bank, there was interlocking directorate through mandates of each one of honor chairman, chairman, and vice-chairman. In BASF AG, interlocking directorate was formed through mandates of one chairman and two vice-chairmans. In Klöckner-Humboldt Deutz AG, and Deutsche Linoleum-Werke AG interlocking directorates were built through mandates of one each of chairman, vice-chairman, and post of the supervisory board excluding chairman and vice-chairman, respectively.

Regarding 18 enterprises with two mandates on the supervisory board of other enterprise with respect to distribution of industrial sector, there were one in mining industry, three in iron and steel industry, one in metal producing and processing industries, four in chemical industry, two in electrical industry, one in machine industry, two in precious machine and optical industries, one in banking industry, one in insurance industry, and two in electric power, gas, and energy industries.

Table 6.2 Cases in which Deutsche Bank built direct interlocking directorates through more than two posts on the supervisory board of other companies (period after the 1965 Corporations Law)

Industries	Number of posts							
	2		3		4		Total	
	Number of companies	Number of posts	Number of companies	Number of posts	Number of companies	Number of posts	Number of companies	Number of posts
Mining	1	2	–	–	–	–	1	2
Iron and steel	3	6	–	–	–	–	3	6
Metal producing and processing	1	2	–	–	–	–	1	2
Chemical	4	8	1	3	–	–	5	11
Electrical	2	4	–	–	1	4	3	8
Machine	1	2	1	3	–	–	2	5
Precious machine and optical industries	2	4	–	–	–	–	2	4
Textile, spinning, and woven goods	–	–	1	3	–	–	1	3
Distributing	–	–	1	3	–	–	1	3
Banking	1	2	1	3	–	–	2	5
Insurance	1	2	–	–	1	4	2	6
Electric power, gas, and energy	2	4	–	–	–	–	2	4
All industries	18	36	5	15	2	8	25	59

Source This table was compiled by the author, based on Mossner (Hrsg) (1971)

In Pitler Maschinenfabrik AG, interlocking directorates were formed through mandates of honor chairman and chairman. In Zellstofffabrik Waldhof, interlocking directorates through mandate of honor chairman and post of the supervisory board except for chairman and vice-chairman were built. In Hugo Stinnes AG and Berliner Disconto-Bank AG, interlocking directorates were established through two mandates consisting of chairman and vice-chairman, respectively. In Otto Wolff AG, Glanzstoff AG, Rütgerswerke und Teerverwertung AG, Robert Bosch GmbH, Brown, Boveri & Cie. AG, and Voigtländer AG, Zeiss Ikon AG, Nordwestdeutshe Kraftwerke AG, Preussische, and Elektrizitätswerke AG, interlocking directorates were formed through a mandate of chairman and one post of the supervisory board excluding chairman and vice-chairman, respectively. In Hoesch AG and Bayer AG, Deutsche Bank formed interlocking directorates through a mandate of vice-chairman and one post of the supervisory board except for chairman and vice-chairman, respectively. In Gelsenkirchener Bergwerke AG, Metallgesellschaft AG, and Albingia Versicherung-AG, interlocking directorates through two mandates except for chairman and vice-chairman existed, respectively.

Thus, Deutsche Bank's direct interlocking directorates on the supervisory boards of other enterprises were spread over a wide range of industries and had personnel connections with several competitive companies mutually in the same industrial sector through several mandates of the supervisory board. In the mining industry, such cases can be observed in Gelsenkirchener Bergwerke AG, Pressag AG, Harpener Bergbau AG, Hibernia AG, Ruhrkohle AG, and Steinkohlenwerke Mathias Stinnes AG. In the iron and steel industry, similar cases are seen in representative companies, such as Fried. Krupp GmbH, Klöckner-Werke AG, Mannesmann AG, Rheinische Stahlwerke, Hugo Stinnes AG, and Otto Wolff AG. In the chemical industry, Deutsche Bank built interlocking directorate in BASF, Bayer AG, and Glanzstoff AG. Whereas Deutsche Bank built interlocking directorate through two mandates of vice-chairman in BASF AG, it was formed through one mandate of vice-chairman in Bayer AG. In the electrical industry, interlocking directorates were established in Siemens AG, Robert Bosch GmbH, and Brown Boveri & Cie. AG through mandate of chairman of the supervisory board, respectively. In the machine industry, Deutsche Bank built interlocking directorate in Klöckner-Humboldt Deutz AG, Pitler Maschinenfabrik AG, Maschinenfabrik Buckau, and R. Wolf AG.

In this way, Deutsche Bank established close and strong personnel connections with many companies in various industries through direct interlocking directorates of members of the supervisory board and management board. Such personnel ties had great meaning for securing much information for its own financial business and decision of policies over industrial enterprises.

6.1.2 Direct Interlocking Directorate of Members of Supervisory Board and Managing Board of Dresdner Bank

Next, in examining the direct interlocking directorate by members of the supervisory board and managing board of Dresdner Bank on the supervisory board of other enterprises (see Table 6.3), there were 151 companies in which such cases were observed and 177 interlocking mandates. Numbers of both enterprises and mandates were a little fewer than those of Deutsche Bank (corresponding numbers 167 and 201, respectively) and were much fewer than those of Dresdner Bank around the end of the 1950s (corresponding numbers 268 and 326 respectively) (see Chap. 5).

Considering the distribution of industrial sectors, Dresdner Bank built direct interlocking directorates in five companies and six interlocking mandates in the mining industry, and similarly, 14 and 15 in the iron and steel industry; five and six in the metal producing and processing industries; 18 and 22 in the chemical industry; six and seven in the electrical industry; four each in the automobile industry; 11 and 11 in the machine industry; one each in the precious machine and optical industries; two each in the shipbuilding industry; three each in the oil industry; one each in the food industry; three each in the textile, spinning, and woven goods industries; two and three in the distillation industry; six each in the distributing industry; 21 and 29 in the banking industry; 11 and 17 in the insurance industry; five and six in the electric power, gas, and energy industries; three and four in the transportation industry; and 30 and 31 in other industries, respectively. Among the various industries, except for the banking industry and the insurance industry, for example, there were many interlocking relations in the mining, iron and steel, chemical, electrical, and machine industries. Therefore, Dresdner Bank built strong relationships with companies in the key industrial sectors in Germany—the heavy and chemical industries.

Given the situation of interlocking directorates with respect to the position of mandate of supervisory board, in 46 enterprises, there were cases in which interlocking directorates on the supervisory boards of other companies were formed through mandate of chairman of the supervisory board with a total of 47 mandates. Numbers of both enterprises and mandates were much fewer than those of Deutsche Bank (corresponding numbers 84 and 84, respectively) and were much fewer than those of Dresdner Bank around the end of the 1950s (corresponding numbers 86 and 86, respectively). Regarding the distribution among industrial sectors, the numbers of enterprises and mandates in which interlocking directorate were formed were two each in the mining industry; similarly, one each in the iron and steel industry; three each in the metal producing and processing industries; 10 each in the chemical industry; three each in the electrical industry; one each in the automobile industry; three each in the machine industry; one each in the textile, spinning, and woven goods industries; one each in the distillation industry; one each in the distributing industry; four each in the banking industry; six and seven in the insurance industry; one each in the transportation industry; and nine each in other industries, respectively. Cases of interlocking directorate in representative companies of each industry were observed

Table 6.3 Direct interlocking directorates of the members of the supervisory board and the managing board of Dresdner Bank on the supervisory board of other companies (period after the 1965 Corporations Law)

Industries	Position							
	Chairman		Vice-chairman		Supervisory board member excluding chairman and vice-chairman		Total[a]	
	Number of companies	Number of posts	Number of companies	Number of posts	Number of companies	Number of posts	Number of companies	Number of posts
Mining	2	2	–	–	4	4	5	6
Iron and steel	1	1	–	–	13	14	14	15
Metal producing and processing	3	3	–	–	3	3	5	6
Chemical	10	10	4	4	8	8	18	22
Electrical	3	3	–	–	3	4	6	7
Automobile	1	1	2	2	1	1	4	4
Machine	3	3	3	3	5	5	11	11
Precious machine and optical industries	–	–	1	1	–	–	1	1
Shipbuilding	–	–	1	1	1	1	2	2
Oil	–	–	–	–	3	3	3	3
Food	–	–	–	–	1	1	1	1
Textile, spinning, and woven goods	1	1	1	1	1	1	3	3
Distillation	1	1	1	1	1	1	2	3
Distributing	1	1	2	2	3	3	6	6

(continued)

Table 6.3 (continued)

Industries	Position							
	Chairman		Vice-chairman		Supervisory board member excluding chairman and vice-chairman		Total[a]	
	Number of companies	Number of posts	Number of companies	Number of posts	Number of companies	Number of posts	Number of companies	Number of posts
Banking	4	4	11	13	11	12	21	29
Insurance	6	7	4	4	4	6	11	17
Electric power, gas, and energy	–	–	1	1	4	5	5	6
Transportation	1	1	1	1	2	2	3	4
Other industries	9	9	9	9	13	13	30	31
All industries	46	47	41	43	81	87	151	177

[a] There are cases in which the total number of companies establishing interlocking directorates differed from the total number of companies measured by each position of the supervisory board due to the existence of companies where interlocking directorates through more than two posts were built

Source This table was compiled by the author, based on Mossner (Hrsg) (1971)

in Gelsenkirchener Bergwerks-AG in the mining industry; Deutsche Edelstahlwerke AG in the iron and steel industry; Metallgesellschaft AG in the metal producing and processing industries; Hoechst AG, Degussa AG, Chemische Werke Hüls AG, Kalle AG, and Ruhrchemie AG in the chemical industry; AEG and Brown Boveri & Cie. AG in the electrical industry; Auto Union GmbH in the automotive industry; DEMAG AG and Kientzle Apparate GmbH in the machine industry; Frankfurter Hypothekenbank AG and Deutsche Hypothekenbank in the banking industry; and Münchener Rückversicherungs-Gesellschaft in the insurance industry.

In 41 enterprises, there were cases where interlocking directorates were formed through mandate of vice-chairman of supervisory board and the total number of mandates was 43. Numbers of both enterprises and mandates were same as those of Deutsche Bank (corresponding numbers 41 and 43, respectively) and were almost half of those of Dresdner Bank around the end of the 1950s (corresponding numbers 78 and 81 respectively). Numbers of enterprises and mandates in which such interlocking cases were formed were four each in the chemical industry; two each in the automobile industry; three each in the machine industry; one each in the precious machine and optical industries; one each in the shipbuilding industry; one each in the textile, spinning, and woven goods industries; one each in the distillation industry; two each in the distributing industry; 11 and 13 in the banking industry; four each in the insurance industry; one each in the electric power, gas, and energy industries; one each in the transportation industry; and nine each in other industries, respectively. In these companies, there were major companies in each industry, such as AUDI NSU AUTO UNION AG in the automobile industry, Kaufhof AG in the distributing industry, Ausfuhrkredit-GMBH and Diskont und Kredit AG in the banking industry, and Allianz Versicherungs-AG, Allianz Lebensversicherngs-AG, and Münchener Rückversicherungs-Gesellschaft in the insurance industry.

Interlocking directorates through mandates of supervisory board excluding chairman and vice-chairman were observed in 81 companies and the total number of mandates was 87. Numbers of both enterprises and mandates were more than those of Deutsche Bank (corresponding numbers 63 and 68, respectively) and were fewer than those of Dresdner Bank around the end of the 1950s (corresponding numbers 143 and 158, respectively). Considering the distribution among industrial sectors, the numbers of enterprises and mandates in which interlocking directorate were formed were four each in the mining industry; similarly, 13 and 14 in the iron and steel industry; three each in the metal producing and processing industries; eight each in the chemical industry; three and four in the electrical industry; one each in the automobile industry; five each in the machine industry; one each in the shipbuilding industry; three each in the oil industry; one each in the food industry; one each in the textile, spinning, and woven goods industries; one each in the distillation industry; three each in the distributing industry; 11 and 12 in the banking industry; four and six in the insurance industry; four and five in the electric power, gas, and energy industries; two each in the transportation industry; and 13 each in other industries, respectively. These companies included leading firms in each industry, such as August Thyssen-Hütte AG, Fried. Krupp GmbH, Fried. Krupp Hüttenwerk AG, Rheinische

Stahlwerke, and Salzgitter AG in the iron and steel industry, Volkswagen AG in the automotive industry, and Karstadt AG in the distributing industry.

The numbers of enterprises and mandates were 21 and 47, respectively, when considering cases where Dresdner Bank's supervisory board and managing board members had more than two mandates on the supervisory boards of other companies (see Table 6.4). Numbers of both enterprises and mandates were a little fewer than those of Deutsche Bank (corresponding numbers 25 and 59, respectively) and were almost half of those of Dresdner Bank around the end of the 1950s (corresponding numbers 47 and 105, respectively). Considering the distribution among industries, the numbers of companies and mandates were as follows: one and two in the mining industry; one and two in the iron and steel industry; one and two in the metal producing and processing industries; four and eight in the chemical industry; one and two in the electrical industry; one and two in the distillation industry; six and 14 in the banking industry; three and nine in the insurance industry; one and two in the electric power, gas, and energy industries; one and two in the transportation industry; and one and two in other industries, respectively. In the mining industry and manufacturing industrial sectors, such cases were observed in representative enterprises in each sector such as Gelsenkirchener Bergwerke AG in the mining industry; Mannesmann AG in the iron and steel industry; Metallgesellschaft AG in the metal producing and processing industry; Hoechst AG, Chemische Werke Hüls AG, Degussa AG, and Kalle AG in the chemical industry; Siemens AG in the electrical industry; and Dortmunder Ritterbrauerei AG in the distillation industry. In sectors except for the mining and manufacturing industrial sectors, there were similar cases in Bank für Handel und Industrie AG, Diskont und Kredit AG, Frankfurter Hypothekenbank AG, Deutsch-Südamerikanische Bank AG, Ausfuhrkredit-GMBH, and Societe Financiere Europeenne in the banking industry, Allianz Versicherungs-AG, Münchener Rückversicherungs-Gesellschaft, and Allianz Lebensversicherngs-AG in the insurance industry, Rheinisch-Westfälisches Elektrizitätswerk AG in the electric power, gas, and energy industries, Norddeutscher Lloyd in the transportation industry, and BAUBOAG AG für Ingenieurbauten des Hoch- und Tiefbaues in other industries..

Of these 21 companies, there were four enterprises in which direct interlocking directorates were built through more than three mandates and the total number of mandates was 13. Numbers of both enterprises and mandates were approximately half of those of Deutsche Bank (corresponding numbers seven and 23, respectively) and were fewer than those of Dresdner Bank in the period at the end of the 1950s (corresponding numbers 10 and 31, respectively). In the remaining 17 companies, Dresdner Bank had two mandates on the supervisory board of other companies, respectively.

In one company, namely, Allianz Versicherungs-AG, Dresdner Bank had four mandates on the supervisory board. In three companies, namely, Bank für Handel und Industrie AG, Diskont und Kredit AG, and Münchener Rückversicherungs-Gesellschaft, there were interlocking directorates through three mandates on the supervisory board, respectively.

Table 6.4 Cases in which Dresdner Bank built direct interlocking directorates through more than two posts on the supervisory board of other companies (period after the 1965 Corporations Law)

Industries	Number of posts							
	2		3		4		Total	
	Number of companies	Number of posts	Number of companies	Number of posts	Number of companies	Number of posts	Number of companies	Number of posts
Mining	1	2	–	–	–	–	1	2
Iron and steel	1	2	–	–	–	–	1	2
Metal producing and processing	1	2	–	–	–	–	1	2
Chemical	4	8	–	–	–	–	4	8
Electrical	1	2	–	–	–	–	1	2
Distillation	1	2	–	–	–	–	1	2
Banking	4	8	2	6	–	–	6	14
Insurance	1	2	1	3	1	4	3	9
Electric power, gas, and energy	1	2	–	–	–	–	1	2
Transportation	1	2	–	–	–	–	1	2
Other industries	1	2	–	–	–	–	1	2
All industries	17	34	3	9	1	4	21	47

Source This table was compiled by the author, based on Mossner (Hrsg) (1971)

Considering the interlocking directorates in these enterprises concerning supervisory board position mandates, in Allianz-Versicherngs-AG, Dresdner Bank built interlocking directorates through four mandates consisting of one vice-chairman and three posts of the supervisory board excluding chairman and vice-chairman, respectively. Regarding companies with three mandates, in Münchener Rückversicherungs-Gesellschaft, there was interlocking directorate through mandates of two chairmans and one post of vice-chairman. In Bank für Handel und Industrie AG, Dresdner Bank formed interlocking directorate through two mandates of vice-chairman and one post of the supervisory board other than chairman and vice-chairman. In Diskont und Kredit AG, interlocking directorate was established through one mandate of vice-chairman and two posts of the supervisory board except for chairman and vice-chairman.

Regarding 17 enterprises with two mandates on the supervisory board of other enterprise in relation to distribution of industrial sector, there were one in mining industry, one in iron and steel industry, one in metal producing and processing industries, four in chemical industry, one in electrical industry, one in distillation industry, four in banking industry, one in insurance industry, one in electric power, gas, and energy industries, one in transportation industry, and one in other industry.

In Deutsch-Südamerikanische Bank AG and Norddeutscher Lloyd, interlocking directorates were formed through two mandates consisting of chariman and vice-chairman, respectively. In Gelsenkirchener Bergwerke AG, Metallgesellschaft AG, Chemische Werke Hüls AG, Degussa AG, Kalle AG, Hoechst AG, Dortmunder Ritterbrauerei AG, Frankfurter Hypothekenbank AG, and BAUBOAG AG für Ingenieurbauten des Hoch- und Tiefbaues, interlocking directorates were built through a mandate of chairman and one post of the supervisory board except for chairman and vice-chairman, respectively. In Ausfuhrkredit-GMBH, there were interlocking directorates through two mandates of vice-chairman. In Societe Financiere Europeenne and Allianz Lebensversicherngs-AG, interlocking directorates were formed through a mandate of vice-chairman and one post of the supervisory board except for chairman and vice-chairman, respectively. In Mannesmann AG, Siemens AG, and Rheinisch-Westfälisches Elektrizitätswerk AG, Dresdner Bank built interlocking directorates through two mandates excluding chairman and vice-chairman existed, respectively.

Thus, Dresdner Bank's direct interlocking directorates on the supervisory boards of other enterprises were spread over a wide range of industries and had personnel connections with several competitive companies mutually in the same industrial sector through several mandates of the supervisory board. In the mining industry, such cases can be observed in Gelsenkirchener Bergwerke AG, Ruhrkohle AG, and Steinkohlenwerke Mathias Stinnes AG. In the iron and steel industry, similar cases are seen in representative companies, such as August Thyssen-Hütte AG, Fried. Krupp Hüttenwerke AG, Mannesmann AG, Rheinische Stahlwerke, Salzgitter AG, Hugo Stinnes AG, and Otto Wolff AG. In the chemical industry, Dresdner Bank built interlocking directorate with enterprises which were competitive condition mutually such as Hoechst AG, Chemische Werke Hüls AG, Degussa AG, and Kalle AG through two mandates. In the electrical industry, interlocking directorates were built in Siemens AG, AEG and Brown Boveri & Cie. AG. In the machine industry,

Dresdner Bank built interlocking directorate in representative enterprises such as DEMAG AG, Kienzle Apparate GmbH, and Pittler Maschinenfabrik AG. Thus, Dresdner Bank established close personnel connections with numerous companies in various industries through direct interlocking directorates of supervisory board and management board members, which had great significance for securing much information regarding its own financial business and decision of policies over industrial enterprises.

6.1.3 Direct Interlocking Directorate of Members of Supervisory Board and Managing Board of Commerzbank

Furthermore, regarding the direct interlocking directorate by members of the supervisory board and managing board of Commerzbank on the supervisory board of other enterprises (see Table 6.5), there were 103 companies in which such cases were observed and 110 interlocking mandates. Numbers of both enterprises and mandates were fewer than those of Deutsche Bank (corresponding numbers 167 and 201, respectively) and those of Dresdner Bank (similarly 151 and 177, respectively). They were approximately half of those of Commerzbank around the end of the 1950s (corresponding numbers 196 and 226, respectively) (see Chap. 5).

Examining the distribution of industrial sectors, Commerzbank built direct interlocking directorates in three companies and three interlocking mandates in the mining industry, and similarly, seven each in the iron and steel industry; three each in the metal producing and processing industries; eight and nine in the chemical industry; five each in the electrical industry; one each in the automobile industry; eight each in the machine industry; two each in the precious machine and optical industries; two each in the shipbuilding industry; two each in the oil industry; one and two in the food industry; six each in the textile, spinning, and woven goods industries; eight each in the distillation industry; three and five in the distributing industry; 12 and 14 in the banking industry; 11 each in the insurance industry; three each in the electric power, gas, and energy industries; three each in the transportation industry; and 15 and 16 in other industries, respectively. Among the various industries, except the banking industry and the insurance industry, for example, there were many interlocking relations in the mining, iron and steel, chemical, electrical, and machine industries. Therefore, Commerzbank had close and strong relationships with companies in the heavy and chemical industries as the key industrial sectors in Germany.

Considering the situation of interlocking directorates with respect to the position of mandate of supervisory board, in 27 enterprises, there were cases in which interlocking directorates on the supervisory boards of other companies were formed through mandate of chairman of the supervisory board with a total of 27 mandates. Numbers of both enterprises and mandates were much fewer than those of Deutsche Bank (corresponding numbers 84 and 84, respectively) and those of Dresdner Bank

Table 6.5 Direct interlocking directorates of the members of the supervisory board and the managing board of Commerzbank on the supervisory board of other companies (period after the 1965 Corporations Law)

Industries	Position									
	Chairman		Vice-Chairman		Supervisory board member excluding chairman and vice-chairman		Deputy supervisory board member		Total[a]	
	Number of companies	Number of posts	Number of companies	Number of posts	Number of companies	Number of posts	Number of companies	Number of posts	Number of companies	Number of posts
Mining	–	–	1	1	2	2	–	–	3	3
Iron and steel	3	3	1	1	2	2	1	1	7	7
Metal producing and processing	–	–	1	1	2	2	–	–	3	3
Chemical	2	2	2	2	5	5	–	–	8	9
Electrical	2	2	–	–	3	3	–	–	5	5
Automobile	–	–	–	–	1	1	–	–	1	1
Machine	–	–	3	3	5	5	–	–	8	8
Precious machine and optical industries	2	2	–	–	–	–	–	–	2	2
Shipbuilding	–	–	1	1	1	1	–	–	2	2
Oil	–	–	1	1	1	1	–	–	2	2
Food	–	–	1	1	1	1	–	–	1	2

(continued)

Table 6.5 (continued)

Industries	Position									
	Chairman		Vice-Chairman		Supervisory board member excluding chairman and vice-chairman		Deputy supervisory board member		Total[a]	
	Number of companies	Number of posts	Number of companies	Number of posts	Number of companies	Number of posts	Number of companies	Number of posts	Number of companies	Number of posts
Textile, spinning, and woven goods	2	2	1	1	3	3	–	–	6	6
Distillation	–	–	2	2	6	6	–	–	8	8
Distributing	2	2	–	–	2	3	–	–	3	5
Banking	4	4	2	2	7	8	–	–	12	14
Insurance	2	2	1	1	8	8	–	–	11	11
Electric power, gas, and energy	–	–	–	–	2	2	1	1	3	3
Transportation	1	1	1	1	1	1	–	–	3	3
Other industries	7	7	1	1	8	8	–	–	15	16
All industries	27	27	19	19	60	62	2	2	103	110

[a] There are cases in which the total number of companies establishing interlocking directorates differed from the total number of companies measured by each position of the supervisory board due to the existence of companies where interlocking directorates through more than two posts were built

Source This table was compiled by the author, based on Mossner (Hrsg) (1971)

(similarly 46 and 47, respectively). They were approximately half of those of Commerzbank around the end of the 1950s (corresponding numbers 60 and 61, respectively). Regarding the distribution among industrial sectors, the numbers of enterprises and mandates in which interlocking directorate were formed were three each in the iron and steel industry; similarly, two each in the chemical industry; two each in the electrical industry; two each in the precious machine and optical industries; two each in the textile, spinning, and woven goods industries; two each in the distributing industry; four each in the banking industry; two each in the insurance industry; one each in the transportation industry; and seven each in other industries, respectively. Cases of interlocking directorate in representative companies of each industry were observed in Rheinische Stahlwerke in the iron and steel industry; Bayer AG in the chemical industry; Karstadt AG and Kaufhof AG in the distributing industry; enterprises of the Gerling group such as Gerling-Konzern Lebensversicherungs-AG and Gerling-Konzern Speziale Kreditversicherungs-AG in the insurance industry, and Standard Lloyd AG in the transportation industry.

In 19 enterprises, there were cases where interlocking directorates were formed through mandate of vice-chairman of supervisory board and the total number of mandates was 19. Numbers of both enterprises and mandates were approximately half of those of Deutsche Bank (corresponding numbers 41 and 43, respectively) and those of Dresdner Bank (similarly 41 and 43, respectively). They were also about half of those of Commerzbank around the end of the 1950s (corresponding numbers 43 and 43 respectively). Numbers of enterprises and mandates in which such interlocking cases were formed were one each in mining industry; one each in iron and steel industry; one each in metal producing and processing industries; two each in chemical industry; three each in machine industry; one each in shipbuilding industry; one each in oil industry; one each in food industry; one each in textile, spinning, and woven goods industries; two each in distillation industry; two each in banking industry; one each in insurance industry; one each in transportation industry; and one each in other industries, respectively. In these companies, there were major companies in each industry, such as Hoechst AG in the chemical industry and J. M. Voith AG in the machine industry.

Interlocking directorates through mandates of supervisory board except for chairman and vice-chairman were observed in 60 companies and the total number of mandates was 62. Numbers of both enterprises and mandates were almost same as those of Deutsche Bank (corresponding numbers 63 and 68, respectively) and were fewer than those of Dresdner Bank (similarly 81 and 87, respectively). They were approximately half of those of Commerzbank around the end of the 1950s (corresponding numbers 114 and 121, respectively). Considering the distribution among industrial sectors, the numbers of enterprises and mandates in which interlocking directorate were formed were two each in the mining industry; similarly, two each in the iron and steel industry; two each in the metal producing and processing industries; five each in the chemical industry; three each in the electrical industry; one each in the automobile industry; five each in the machine industry; one each in the shipbuilding industry; one each the oil industry; one each in the food industry; three each in the textile, spinning, and woven goods industries; six each in the distillation industry; two and three in the distributing industry; seven and eight in the banking industry; eight each in the insurance industry; two each in the electric power, gas, and energy industries; one each in the transportation industry; and eight each in other industries, respectively. These companies included leading firms in each industry, such as Preussag AG in the mining industry, Gutehoffnungshütte Aktienverein in the iron and steel industry, Bayer AG, Chemische Werke Hüls AG, and Schering AG in chemical industry, AEG, Robert Bosch GmbH, and Brown, Boveri & Cie. AG in the electrical industry, Daimler-Benz AG in the automotive industry, DEMAG AG in the machine industry, Blohm & Voss AG in the shipbuilding industry, Karstadt AG in the distillation industry; and Gerling-Konzern Allgemeine Versicherungs-AG in the insurance industry.

In two enterprises, there were cases where interlocking directorates were formed through mandate of deputy mandate of the supervisory board and the total number of mandates was two. Commerzbank built interlocking directorates in Stahlwerk Augustfehn AG in the iron and steel industry and Rheinisch-Westfälisches Elektrizitätswerk in the electric power, gas, and energy industries through one deputy mandate of the supervisory board, respectively.

The numbers of enterprises and mandates were seven and 14, respectively, when considering cases where members of the supervisory board and board of directors of Commerzbank had more than two mandates on the supervisory boards of other companies (see Table 6.6). Numbers of both enterprises and mandates were much fewer than those of Deutsche Bank (corresponding numbers 25 and 59, respectively) and those of Dresdner Bank (similarly 21 and 47, respectively). They were also even fewer than those of Commerzbank around the end of the 1950s (corresponding numbers 22 and 52, respectively). Considering the distribution among industries, the numbers of companies and mandates were as follows: one and two in the chemical industry; one and two in the food industry; one and two in the distributing industry; one and two in the banking industry; and one and two in other industries, respectively.

Table 6.6 Cases in which Commerzbank built direct interlocking directorates through more than two posts on the supervisory board of other companies (period after the 1965 Corporations Law)

Industries	Number of posts			
	2		Total	
	Number of companies	Number of posts	Number of companies	Number of posts
Chemical	1	2	1	2
Food	1	2	1	2
Distributing	2	4	2	4
Banking	2	4	2	4
Other industries	1	2	1	2
All industries	7	14	7	14

Source This table was compiled by the author, based on Mossner (Hrsg) (1971)

When in examining the interlocking directorates in these enterprises concerning kind of mandate, in Berliner Commerzbank in the banking industry, Commerzbank built interlocking directorates through each one mandate of chairman and vice-chairman. In Bayer AG in the chemical industry, Karstadt AG in the distributing industry, and Beton- und Monierbau AG in other industry, there were interlocking directorates through mandates of a mandate of chairman and one post of the supervisory board excluding chairman and vice-chairman, respectively. In Kaiser's Kaffeegeschäft AG in the food industry interlocking directorate was established through a mandate of vice-chairman and one post of the supervisory board except for chairman and vice-chairman. In Handelsunion AG in the distributing industry and Deutsche Hypothekenbank in the banking industry, Commerzbank formed interlocking directorates through two posts of the supervisory board other than chairman and vice-chairman.

Thus, Commerzbank's direct interlocking directorates on the supervisory boards of other enterprises spread over a wide range of industries and had personnel connections with several competitive companies in the same industrial sector through several mandates of the supervisory board. In the iron and steel industry, such cases can be observed in Rheinische Stahlwerke, Gutehoffnungshütte Aktienverein, and Thyssenrohr International GmbH as a subsidiary company of August Thyssen-Hütte AG. Similar cases are observed in representative companies of chemical industry such as Bayer AG, Hoechst AG, Chemische Werke Hüls AG, and Schering AG. In the electrical industry, interlocking directorates were built in AEG, Brown Boveri & Cie. AG, and Robert Bosch GmbH. In the machine industry, Commerzbank built interlocking directorate in representative enterprises such as DEMAG AG, J. M. Voith AG, Klauss-Maffei AG, and Schubert & Salzer Maschinenfabrik AG. In the distributing industry, similar cases were seen in Karstadt AG and Kaufhof AG. Thus, Commerzbank established close and strong personnel connections with many companies in various industries through direct interlocking directorates of members of the supervisory board and management board, which enabled this bank to secure much information for its own financial business and decision of policies over industrial enterprises. However, number of enterprises in which direct interlocking directorates was built and interlocking mandates were considerably fewer than those of Deutsche Bank and Dresdner Bank.

6.2 Indirect Interlocking Directorates Between Banks on the Supervisory Board of Other Enterprises

In Sect. 6.1, how members of supervisory board and board of directors of three large German banks built the direct interlocking directorates on supervisory board of other enterprises was analyzed. Building upon these discussions, the next issue to be explored is how indirect interlocking directorates were formed among these three banks and between some two of them through such direct interlocking directorates. Therefore, in Sect. 6.2, this research topic will be considered.

Section 6.2.1 first explores indirect interlocking directorates among three big banks. Sections 6.2.2 and 6.2.3 examine such personnel connections between Deutsche Bank and Dresdner Bank and between Deutsche Bank and Commerzbank except cases of those among three banks, respectively. Section 6.2.4 considers conditions of indirect interlocking directorates built between Dresdner Bank and Commerzbank.

6.2.1 Indirect Interlocking Directorates Among Three Large Banks on the Supervisory Board of Other Enterprises

Section 6.2.1 considers the situations related to indirect interlocking directorate among three large banks on the supervisory board of other enterprises (see Table 6.7). Such cases can be observed in 12 companies and the total number of mandates was 43. The numbers of enterprises and mandates in which three large banks built indirect interlocking directorates were less than half of than those around the end of the 1950s (corresponding numbers 29 and 110, respectively) (see Chap. 5).

Considering interlocking directorate in relation to the kind of mandate, numbers of enterprises and mandates in which indirect interlocking directorates was established through the mandate of chairman were 12 and 13, respectively. Similar numerical figures regarding indirect interlocking directorate through the mandate of vice-chairman were 8 and 11, respectively, those through mandate of the supervisory board except for chairman and vice-chairman were 11 and 18, respectively, and those through deputy mandate were one each, respectively. When considering the distribution of industry, number of companies, and mandates of interlocking directorate, there were, respectively, one and three in the iron and steel industry, two and seven in the electrical industry, one and three in the machine industry, two and nine in the distributing industry, three and 11 in the banking industry, two and seven in the electric power, gas, and energy industries, and one and three in other industries. Companies included Rheinische Stahlwerke in the iron and steel industry; AEG and Brown, Boveri & Cie. AG in the electrical industry; Demag AG in the machine industry; Karstadt AG and Kaufhof AG. in the distribution industry; Deutsche Hypothekenbank, Ausfuhrkredit GMBH, and Westdeutsche Bodenkreditanstalt in the banking industry; Rheinisch-Westfälisches Elektrizitätswerke AG and Deutsche Continental-Gas Gesellschaft in the electric power, gas, and energy industries; and Chemie Verwaltungs-AG in other industries.

To understand bank that was at the leading position in indirect interlocking relation, in examining cases in which one bank or some banks of three large banks had more than two mandates on the supervisory board of other company, such cases were observed in five companies. These enterprises were Brown, Boveri & Cie. AG in the

Table 6.7 Indirect interlocking directorates of the members of the supervisory board and the managing board on the supervisory board of other companies among Deutsche Bank, Dresdner Bank, and Commerzbank (period after the 1965 Corporations Law)

Industries	Number of posts							
	3		4		6		Total	
	Number of companies	Number of posts	Number of companies	Number of posts	Number of companies	Number of posts	Number of companies	Number of posts
Iron and steel	1	3	–	–	–	–	1	3
Electrical	1	3	1	4	–	–	2	7
Machine	1	3	–	–	–	–	1	3
Distributing	1	3	–	–	1	6	2	9
Banking	1	3	2	8	–	–	3	11
Electric power, gas, and energy	1	3	1	4	–	–	2	7
Other industries	1	3	–	–	–	–	1	3
All industries	7	21	4	16	1	6	12	43

Source This table was compiled by the author, based on Mossner(Hrsg) (1971)

electrical industry, Karstadt AG in the distributing industry, Deutsche Hypothekenbank and Ausfuhrkredit AG in the banking industry, and Rheinisch-Westfälisches Elektrizitätswerke AG in the electric power, gas, and energy industries. In Karstadt AG, whereas Commerzbank had a mandate of chairman and one supervisory board excluding chairman and vice-chairman, Deutsche Bank had two mandates of vice-chairman and one supervisory board excluding chairman and vice-chairman. Dresdner Bank formed interlocking directorates through one supervisory board mandate except for chairman and vice-chairman. There were four companies in which three large banks had four mandates on the supervisory board of another company. In Ausfuhrkredit GMBH, whereas Dresdner Bank had two mandates of vice-chairman, Deutsche Bank had one mandate of chairman. Commerzbank Bank had one supervisory board mandate except for chairman and vice-chairman. In Brown, Boveri & Cie. AG, whereas Deutsche Bank had a mandate of vice-chairman and one supervisory board excluding chairman and vice-chairman, Dresdner Bank had one mandate of chairman. Commerzbank Bank had one supervisory board mandate excluding chairman and vice-chairman. In Deutsche Hypothekenbank, Commerzbank had two mandates of the supervisory board. Dresdner Bank had one mandate of chairman and Deutsche Bank had one mandate of vice-chairman. In Rheinisch-Westfälisches Elektrizitätswerke AG, Dresdner Bank had two supervisory board mandates. Whereas Deutsche Bank had the mandate of chairman, Commerzbank Bank had one deputy.

The other seven enterprises were cases in which each of the three large banks established interlocking directorates through one mandate of the supervisory board, respectively. Cases in which each of these banks had one chairman, one vice-chairman, and one post of the supervisory board except for chairman and vice-chairman, respectively, can be observed in four companies: AEG, Kaufhof AG, Westdeutsche Bodenkreditanstalt, and Deutsche Continental-Gas-Gesellschaft. In Deutsche Continental-Gas-Gesellschaft, while Deutsche Bank had the mandate of chairman, Dresdner Bank had one mandate of vice-chairman. Commerzbank had one post of the supervisory board except for chairman and vice-chairman. In AEG and Westdeutsche Bodenkreditanstalt, whereas Dresdner Bank had the mandate of chairman, Deutsche Bank had one mandate of vice-chairman of the supervisory board, respectively. Commerzbank had one supervisory board mandate excluding chairman and vice-chairman in both the enterprises. In Kaufhof AG, Commerzbank and Dresdner Bank had one mandate each of chairman and vice-chairman, respectively. Deutsche Bank had one supervisory board mandate except for chairman and vice-chairman in both the enterprises. There were three companies in which three big banks had one chairman and two mandates of the supervisory board except chairman and vice-chairman, namely, Rheinische Stahlwerke, Demag AG, and Chemie Verwaltungs-AG. In Rheinische Stahlwerke, whereas Deutsche Bank and Commerzbank had the mandate of chairman, respectively, Dresdner Bank had one post of the supervisory board except for chairman and vice-chairman. In both Demag AG and Chemie Verwaltungs-AG, whereas Dresdner Bank had a mandate of chairman, Deutsche Bank and Commerzbank had one mandate each of the supervisory board other than chairman and vice-chairman, respectively.

6.2.2 *Indirect Interlocking Directorates Between Deutsche Bank and Dresdner Bank on the Supervisory Board of Other Enterprises*

Next, the situations related to indirect interlocking directorates between Deutsche Bank AG and Dresdner Bank AG on the supervisory board of other enterprises are examined (see Table 6.8). Such cases can be observed in 32 companies, with the total number of mandates being 88, except in the cases of such interlocking directorates among the three big banks. Numbers of enterprises and mandates in which three large banks built indirect interlocking directorates were fewer than those at the end of the 1950s (corresponding numbers 52 and 148, respectively).

Considering interlocking directorate with respect to supervisory board position mandates, numbers of enterprises and mandates in which indirect interlocking were built through the mandate of honor chairman were three each, respectively. Similar numerical figures through mandate of chairman, vice-chairman, and post of the supervisory board except for chairman and vice-chairman were 18 and 19, respectively, 15 and 16, respectively, 28 and 50, respectively. When considering the distribution of industry, the numbers of companies and mandates were as follows: three and eight in the mining industry; six and 15 in the iron and steel industry; two and six in the metal producing and processing industries; two and six in the chemical industry; one and six in the electrical industry; one and two in the automobile industry; two and five in the machine industry; one and two in the oil industry; one and two in the food industry; four and nine in the banking industry; three and 15 in the insurance industry; one and two in the transportation industry; and five and 10 in other industries, respectively.

To understand bank that was at the leading position in indirect interlocking relation, in examining cases in which one bank or both Deutsche Bank and Dresdner Bank had more than two mandates on the supervisory board of other company, such cases were observed in 13 companies. These enterprises were Gelsenkirchner Bergwerke AG in the mining industry, Hugo Stinnes AG, Mannesmann AG, and Otto Wolff AG in the iron and steel industry, Metallgesellschaft AG in the metal producing and processing industries, Zellstofffabrik Waldhof and Degussa AG in the chemical industry, Siemens AG in the electrical industry, Pittler Maschinenfabrik AG in the machine industry, Frankfurter Hypothekenbank in the banking industry, Allianz Versicherungs-AG, Allianz Lebensversicherungs-AG, and Münchener Rückversicherungs-Gesellschaft in the insurance industry.

Case in which indirect interlocking directorates between Deutsche Bank and Dresdner Bank were built through eight mandates on the supervisory boards of other enterprises together can be observed in one enterprise. In Allianz Versicherungs-AG, whereas Deutsche Bank had one each of mandate of chairman and vice-chairman and two posts of the supervisory board excluding chairman and vice-chairman, Dresdner Bank had a mandate of vice-chairman and three posts of the supervisory board excluding chairman and vice-chairman. In Siemens AG, whereas Deutsche Bank had one each of mandate of chairman and vice-chairman and two posts of the

Table 6.8 Indirect interlocking directorates of the members of the supervisory board and the managing board on the supervisory board of other companies between Deutsche Bank and Dresdner Bank[a] (period after the 1965 Corporations Law)

Industries	Number of posts											
	2		3		4		6		8		Total	
	Number of companies	Number of posts	Number of companies	Number of posts	Number of companies	Number of posts	Number of companies	Number of posts	Number of companies	Number of posts	Number of companies	Number of posts
Mining	2	4	–	–	1	4	–	–	–	–	3	8
Iron and steel	3	6	3	9	–	–	–	–	–	–	6	15
Metal producing and processing industries	1	2	–	–	1	4	–	–	–	–	2	6
Chemical	–	–	2	6	–	–	–	–	–	–	2	6
Electrical	–	–	–	–	–	–	1	6	–	–	1	6
Automobile	1	2	–	–	–	–	–	–	–	–	1	2
Machine	1	2	1	3	–	–	–	–	–	–	2	5
Oil	1	2	–	–	–	–	–	–	–	–	1	2
Food	1	2	–	–	–	–	–	–	–	–	1	2
Banking	3	6	1	3	–	–	–	–	–	–	4	9
Insurance	–	–	1	3	1	4	–	–	1	8	3	15
Transportation	1	2	–	–	–	–	–	–	–	–	1	2
Other industries	5	10	–	–	–	–	–	–	–	–	5	10
All industries	19	38	8	24	3	12	1	6	1	8	32	88

[a] The cases of indirect interlocking directorates built among Deutsche Bank, Dresdner Bank, and Commerzbank are excluded

Source This table was compiled by the author, based on Mossner (Hrsg) (1971)

supervisory board except for chairman and vice-chairman, Dresdner Bank had two posts of the supervisory board except for chairman and vice-chairman. There were three companies in which Deutsche Bank and Dresdner Bank had four mandates on the supervisory board of another company. In Gelsenkirchener Bergwerks-AG and Metallgesellschaft AG, whereas Dresdner Bank had one each of chairman and vice-chairman, Deutsche Bank had two mandates of the supervisory board except for chairman and vice-chairman, respectively. In Münchener Rückversicherungs-Gesellschaft, whereas Dresdner Bank had two mandates of chairman and a mandate of vice-chairman, Deutsche Bank had one mandate of the supervisory board other than chairman and vice-chairman.

There were eight companies in which Deutsche Bank and Dresdner Bank had three mandates on the supervisory board of another company. These companies were Hugo Stinnes AG, Mannesmann AG, Otto Wolff AG in the iron and steel industry, Zellstofffabrik Waldhof and Degussa AG in the chemical industry, Pittler Maschinenfabrik AG in the machine industry, Frankfurter Hypothekenbank in the banking industry, and Allianz Lebensversicherungs-AG in the insurance industry. In Pittler Maschinenfabrik AG, whereas Deutsche Bank had one each of mandate of honor chairman and chairman, Dresdner Bank had one mandate of the supervisory board except for chairman and vice-chairman. In Zellstofffabrik Waldhof, whereas Deutsche Bank had a mandate of honor chairman and one post of the supervisory board except chairman and vice-chairman, Dresdner Bank had one mandate of the supervisory board excluding chairman and vice-chairman. In Hugo Stinnes AG, whereas Deutsche Bank had one each of mandate of chairman and vice-chairman, Dresdner Bank had one mandate of the supervisory board excluding chairman and vice-chairman. In Frankfurter Hypothekenbank, whereas Dresdner Bank had a mandate of chairman and one post of the supervisory board excluding chairman and vice-chairman, Deutsche Bank had one mandate of vice chairman. In Otto Wolff, whereas Deutsche Bank had a mandate of chairman and one post of the supervisory board excluding chairman and vice-chairman, Dresdner Bank had one mandate of the supervisory board excluding chairman and vice-chairman. In Mannesmann AG, whereas Deutsche Bank had a mandate of chairman, Dresdner Bank had two posts of the supervisory board other than chairman and vice-chairman. In Degussa AG, Dresdner Bank had a mandate of chairman and one post of the supervisory board except for chairman and vice-chairman, whereas Deutsche Bank had one mandate of the supervisory board except for chairman and vice-chairman. In Allianz Lebensversicherungs-AG, whereas Dresdner Bank had a mandate of vice-chairman and one post of the supervisory board excluding chairman and vice-chairman, Deutsche Bank had one mandate of the supervisory board excluding chairman and vice-chairman.

The other 19 enterprises were cases in which Deutsche Bank and Dresdner Bank established interlocking directorates through one mandate of the supervisory board, respectively. When considering the distribution of industry, number of companies of interlocking directorate was two in the mining industry, three in the iron and steel industry, one in the metal producing and processing industries, one in the automobile industry, one in the machine industry, one in the oil industry, one in the food industry, three in the banking industry, one in the transportation industry, and five in other industries, respectively.

Cases in which each of two banks had one honor chairman or a vice-chairman can be observed in Süddeutsche Zucker-AG. In this enterprise, whereas Deutsche Bank had a mandate of honor chairman, Dresdner Bank had one post of vice-chairman. Cases in which each of two banks had one chairman or a vice-chairman can be seen in three companies: Pfälzische Hypothekenbank and Hypothekenbank in Hamburg in banking industry and Hochtief AG für Hoch-und Tiefbauten vorm. Gebr. Helfmann in other industries. In three companies, whereas Deutsche Bank had a mandate of chairman, Dresdner Bank had one post of vice-chairman. Cases where each of two banks had a chairman or one post of the supervisory board except for chairman and vice-chairman were seen in four companies: Fried. Krupp GmbH in the iron and steel industry, Honsel-Werke AG in the metal producing and processing industries, Deutsche Erdöl-AG in the oil industry, and Gebrüder Stollwerk AG in the food industry. In Honsel-Werke AG, whereas Dresdner Bank had a mandate of chairman, Deutsche Bank had one mandate of the supervisory board excluding chairman and vice-chairman. In other three enterprises, whereas Deutsche Bank had a mandate of chairman, Dresdner Bank had one mandate of the supervisory board excluding chairman and vice-chairman, respectively. Cases in which each of two banks had a vice-chairman or one post of the supervisory board except for chairman and vice-chairman were observed in five enterprises: Ruhrkohle AG in the mining industry, Schiffshypothekenbank zu Lübeck-AG in the banking industry, Allgemeine Lokalbahn-und Kraftwerke AG in the transportation industry, and Ada-Ada Schuh AG and AG für Industrie und Verkehrswesen in other industries. In Ada-Ada Schuh AG, whereas Dresdner Bank had a mandate of vice-chairman, Deutsche Bank had one mandate of the supervisory board except for chairman and vice-chairman. In other four companies, whereas Deutsche Bank had a mandate of vice-chairman, Dresdner Bank had one mandate of the supervisory board except for chairman and vice-chairman, respectively. Cases where each of two banks had one post of the supervisory board except for chairman and vice-chairman, respectively, can be observed in six enterprises, namely, Steinkohlenbergwerke Mathias Stinnes AG in the mining industry, August Thyssen-Hüttenwerke AG and Salzgitter AG in the iron and steel industry, Volkswagenwerk AG in the automotive industry, G. M. Pfaff AG in the machine industry, and Dyckerhoff Zementwerke AG in other industries.

6.2.3 *Indirect Interlocking Directorates Between Deutsche Bank and Copmmerzbank on the Supervisory Board of Other Enterprises*

Next, in examining the situations related to indirect interlocking directorates between Deutsche Bank and Commerzbank on the supervisory board of other enterprises (see Table 6.9), such cases can be observed in 14 companies and the total number of mandates was 35 except cases of such interlocking directorates among three big banks. Numbers of enterprises and mandates in which Dresdner Bank and Commerzbank formed indirect interlocking directorates were much fewer than those of indirect interlocking directorate built between Deutsche Bank and Dresdner Bank (corresponding numbers 32 and 88, respectively). They were fewer than those of cases in which Deutsche Bank and Commerzbank built indirect interlocking directorate at the end of the 1950s (corresponding numbers 22 and 63, respectively).

Considering interlocking directorate in relation to the kind of mandate, numbers of enterprises and mandates in which indirect interlocking directorate were built through the mandate of honor chairman were one each, respectively. Similar numerical figures through mandate of chairman, vice-chairman, and post of the supervisory board other than chairman and vice-chairman were 11 and 11, respectively, eight and eight, respectively, 11 and 15, respectively. When considering the distribution of industry, number of companies, and mandates of interlocking directorate, there were, respectively, one and two in the mining industry, one and two in the iron and steel industry, one and two in the metal producing and processing industries, two and six in the chemical industry, one and three in the electrical industry, one and two in the automobile industry, two and four in the machine industry, three and eight in the textile, spinning, and woven goods industries, one and four in the banking industry, and one and two in other industries.

To understand bank that was at the leading position in indirect interlocking relation, in examining cases in which one bank or both Deutsche Bank and Commerzbank Bank had more than two mandates on the supervisory board of other company, such cases were observed in four companies. These enterprises were Bayer AG in the chemical industry, Robert Bosch GmbH in the electrical industry, Deutsche Linoleum-Werke AG in the textile, spinning, and woven goods industries, and Deutsche Ueberseeische Bank in the banking industry. Cases in which indirect interlocking directorates between Deutsche Bank and Commerzbank were built through four mandates on the supervisory boards of other enterprises together can be observed in three enterprises. Case where indirect interlocking directorates between these two banks were built through three mandates on the supervisory boards of other enterprises together can be observed in one company.

In Bayer AG, whereas Commerzbank had a mandate of chairman and one post of the supervisory board except for chairman and vice-chairman, Deutsche Bank had a mandate of vice-chairman and one post of the supervisory board except for chairman and vice-chairman. In Deutsche Linoleum-Werke AG, Deutsche Bank had one each of mandate of chairman and vice-chairman and one post of the supervisory board except for chairman and vice-chairman. Meanwhile, Commerzbank had a mandate of the supervisory board excluding chairman and vice-chairman. In Deutsche Uberseeische Bank, whereas Deutsche Bank had one each of mandate of honor chairman, chairman, and vice-chairman, Commerzbank had one post of the supervisory board excluding chairman and vice-chairman. In Robert Bosch GmbH, whereas Deutsche Bank had a mandate of chairman and one post of the supervisory

Table 6.9 Indirect interlocking directorates of the members of the supervisory and the managing board on the supervisory board of other companies between Deutsche Bank and Commerzbank[a] (Period after the 1965 Corporations Law)

Industries	Number of posts							
	2		3		4		Total	
	Number of companies	Number of posts	Number of companies	Number of posts	Number of companies	Number of posts	Number of companies	Number of posts
Mining	1	2	–	–	–	–	1	2
Iron and steel	1	2	–	–	–	–	1	2
Metal producing and processing	1	2	–	–	–	–	1	2
Chemical	1	2	–	–	1	4	2	6
Electrical	–	–	1	3	–	–	1	3
Automobile	1	2	–	–	–	–	1	2
Machine	2	4	–	–	–	–	2	4
Textile, spinning, and woven goods	2	4	–	–	1	4	3	8
Banking	–	–	–	–	1	4	1	4
Other industries	1	2	–	–	–	–	1	2
All industries	10	20	1	3	3	12	14	35

[a] The cases of indirect interlocking directorates built among Deutsche Bank, Dresdner Bank, and Commerzbank are excluded

Source This table was compiled by the author, based on Mossner (Hrsg) (1971)

board other than chairman and vice-chairman, Commerzbank had one mandate of the supervisory board except for chairman and vice-chairman.

The other 10 enterprises were cases in which Deutsche Bank and Commerzbank established interlocking directorates through one mandate of the supervisory board, respectively. When considering the distribution of industry, number of companies of interlocking directorate was one in the mining industry, one in the iron and steel industry, one in the metal producing and processing industries, one in the chemical industry, one in the automotive industry, two in the machine industry, two in the textile, spinning, and woven goods industries, and one in other industries, respectively. In Schmalbach-Lubeca-Werke AG in the metal producing and processing industries, whereas Deutsche Bank had a mandate of chairman, Commerzbank had one mandate of vice-chairman. In Buderus'sche Eisenwerke in the iron and steel industry and Pongs & Zahn AG in the textile, spinning, and woven goods industries, whereas Commerzbank had a mandate of chairman, Deutsche Bank had a mandate of vice-chairman, respectively. In Daimler-Benz AG in the automobile industry, Schubert & Salzer AG in the machine industry, Girmes-Werke AG in the textile, spinning, and woven goods industries, and Didier-Werke AG in other industries, whereas Deutsche Bank had a mandate of chairman, Commerzbank had one post of the supervisory board excluding chairman and vice-chairman, respectively. In Schering AG in the chemical industry and Krauss-Maffei AG in the machine industry, whereas Deutsche Bank had a mandate of vice-chairman, Commerzbank had one post of the supervisory board except for chairman and vice-chairman, respectively. In Preussag AG in the mining industry, each of Deutsche Bank and Commerzbank had one post of the supervisory board other than chairman and vice-chairman, respectively.

6.2.4 Indirect Interlocking Directorates Between Dresdner Bank and Commerzbank on the Supervisory Board of Other Enterprises

Next, regarding the situations related to indirect interlocking directorates between Dresdner Bank and Commerzbank on the supervisory board of other enterprises (see Table 6.10), such cases can be observed in 13 companies and the total number of mandates was 29 except cases of such interlocking directorates among three big banks. The numbers of enterprises and mandates were much fewer than those of indirect interlocking directorate built between Deutsche Bank and Dresdner Bank (corresponding number 32 and 88, respectively) and were a little fewer than those of such interlocking directorate built between Deutsche Bank and Commerzbank (corresponding numbers 14 and 35, respectively). They were fewer than those of cases in which Dresdner Bank and Commerzbank built indirect interlocking directorate in the period at the end of the 1950s (corresponding numbers 23 and 51, respectively).

Examining interlocking directorate with respect to supervisory board position mandates, the numbers of enterprises and mandates in which indirect interlocking

Table 6.10 Indirect interlocking directorates of the members of the supervisory board and the managing board on the supervisory board of other companies between Dresdner Bank and Commerzbank[a] (period after the 1965 Corporations Law)

Industries	Number of posts					
	2		3		Total	
	Number of companies	Number of posts	Number of companies	Number of posts	Number of companies	Number of posts
Mining	1	2	–	–	1	2
Chemical	1	2	2	6	3	8
Precious machine and optical industries	1	2	–	–	1	2
Shipbuilding	2	4	–	–	2	4
Textile, spinning, and woven goods	1	2	–	–	1	2
Distributing	–	–	1	3	1	3
Banking	1	2	–	–	1	2
Insurance	2	4	–	–	2	4
Electric power, gas, and energy	1	2	–	–	1	2
All industries	10	20	3	9	13	29

[a] The cases of indirect interlocking directorates built among Deutsche Bank, Dresdner Bank, and Commerzbank are excluded
Source This table was compiled by the author, based on Mossner (Hrsg) (1971)

directorates were formed through the mandate of chairman were six each, respectively. Similar figures through mandate of vice-chairman and post of the supervisory board excluding chairman and vice-chairman were six and seven, respectively, and 11 and 16, respectively. When considering the distribution of industry, number of companies, and mandates of interlocking directorate, there were, respectively, one and two in the mining industry, three and eight in the chemical industry, one and two in the precious machine and optical industries, two and four in the shipbuilding industry, one and two in the textile, spinning, and woven goods industries, one and three in the distributing industry, one and two in the banking industry, two and four in the insurance industry, and one and two in the electric power, gas, and energy industries.

To understand bank at the leading position in indirect interlocking relation, in examining cases in which one bank or both Dresdner Bank and Commerzbank Bank had more than two mandates on the supervisory board of other company, such cases were observed in three companies. These enterprises were Hoechst AG and Chemische Werke Hüls AG in the chemical industry and Handelsunion AG in the distributing industry. In all cases, indirect interlocking directorates between Dresdner

Bank and Commerzbank were built through three mandates on the supervisory boards of other enterprises together. In Hoechst AG, whereas Dresdner Bank had a mandate of chairman and one post of the supervisory board except for chairman and vice-chairman, Commerzbank had one post of vice-chairman. In Chemische Werke Hüls AG, Dresdner Bank had a mandate of chairman and one post of the supervisory board except for chairman and vice-chairman. Meanwhile, Commerzbank had one post of the supervisory board excluding chairman and vice-chairman. In Handelsunion AG, whereas Dresdner Bank had a mandate of chairman, Commerzbank had two posts of vice-chairman.

The remaining 10 enterprises were cases in which Dresdner Bank and Commerzbank established interlocking directorates through one mandate of the supervisory board, respectively. When considering the distribution of industry, number of companies of interlocking directorate was one in the mining industry, one in the chemical industry, one in the precious machine and optical industries, two in the shipbuilding industry, one in the textile, spinning, and woven goods industries, one in the banking industry, two in the insurance industry, and one in the electric power, gas, and energy industries, respectively. In Ernst Leitz GmbH in the precious machine and optical industries, whereas Commerzbank had a mandate of chairman, Dresdner Bank had one mandate of vice-chairman. In Ruhrchemie AG in the chemical industry and Hermes Kreditversicherung-AG in the insurance industry, whereas Dresdner Bank had a mandate of chairman, Commerzbank had one mandate of the supervisory board except for chairman and vice-chairman, respectively. In Lübecker Flender-Werke AG in the shipbuilding industry, Dresdner Bank and Commerzbank had one mandate of vice-chairman, respectively. In Beamtenversicherungsverein des Deutschen Bank- und Bankiergewerbes in insurance industry and Deutsche Continental-Gas-Gesellschaft in the electric power, gas, and energy industries, whereas Dresdner Bank had a mandate of vice-chairman, Commerzbank had one mandate of the supervisory board excluding chairman and vice-chairman, respectively. In Salzdetfurth AG in the mining industry, Commerzbank had a mandate of vice-chairman of the supervisory board, whereas Dresdner Bank had one mandate of the supervisory board other than chairman and vice-chairman. In Blohm & Voss AG in the shipbuilding industry, Kammgarnspinnerei Stöhr & Co. AG in the spinning, and woven goods industries, and Braunschweig-Hannoversche Hypothekenbank in the banking industry, each of Dresdner Bank and Commerzbank had one post of the supervisory board except for chairman and vice-chairman, respectively.

Indirect interlocking directorates built among three largest banks or between two banks of them through direct interlocking directorate of members of top management organs of each bank on the supervisory board of other enterprises were an important foundation of the strong connection between banks. Such personnel connections were of significance in exchange and sharing of information concerning various industrial departments and many companies in which banks had interest in the points of financing and investment of capital. They also might be an important means of coordination of interests and conflicts through discussions. Therefore, indirect interlocking between banks on the supervisory board of same firm had big meaning in cooperation between enterprises. This point was an important element determining characteristic of the cooperative capitalism in Germany.

This chapter clarifies the structures of direct interlocking directorate of each bank on the supervisory board of other enterprises and indirect interlocking directorates built among the three largest banks and between two of the banks in the late 1960s as the period after the enactment of the 1965 Corporations Law. There were fewer companies in which the interlocking directorates and mandates were observed compared with those in the late 1950s. Such a system of personnel connection continued to be the basic system of interlocking directorates in postwar Germany for long.

There were remarkable changes in the system after the 1990s. Several studies have highlighted that interfirm relationships in Germany tend to change remarkably. Changes in personnel connections between banks and industries through interlocking directorate are also indicated. Globalization of economy and enterprise, the internationalization of financial market, the subsequent change in company financing conditions, and transformation in banks' behavior such as that seen in the movement from credit bank to investment bank business are related to changes in the industry–bank relationship (Höpner 2001, pp. 17–19; Beyer 2003, SS. 6–7, 9–10; Beck et al 2005, p. 228; Kengelbach and Roos 2006, SS. 12, 21; Streeck 1997, p. 51). The change in the industry–bank relationship observed in decreased dispatches of bank's representatives on the supervisory board of other enterprises and the interlocking directorates of banks' top management has been prominent (Monopolkommission 2008, S. 198; Jürgens et al 2000, p. 70; Höpner 2001, pp. 26, 50).

Therefore, further studies explore how the members of the supervisory and managing boards of large banks built direct interlocking directorates on the supervisory board of other companies and how were the conditions of indirect interlocking directorates developed between big banks. The next chapter examines this important research topic.

References

Beck S, Klobes F, Scherrer C (2005) Conclusion. In: Beck S, Klobes F, Scherrer C (eds) Surviving globalization? perspectives for the German economic model. Springer, Dordrecht, pp 225–235

Beyer J (2003) Deutschland AG a.D. Deutsche Bank, Allianz und das Verflechtungszentrum des deutschen Kapitalismus. In: Streeck W, Höpner M (Hrsg) Alle Macht dem Markt? Fallstudien zur Abwicklung der Deutchland AG. Campus, Berlin, New York, SS 118–146

Eglau HO (1990) Wie Gott in Frankfurt: Die Deutsche Bank und die deutsche Industrie, 3rd edn. Econ Verlag, Düsseldorf

Höpner M (2001) Corporate governance in transition: ten empirical findings on shareholder value and industrial relations in Germany. In: MPIfG (MaxPlanck-Institut für Gesellschaftsforschung) Discussion Paper01/5, 1–61

Jürgens U, Naumann K, Rupp J (2000) Shareholder value in an adverse environment: the German case. In: Economy and Society 29(1):54–79

Kengelbach J, Roos A (2006) Entflechtung der Deutschland AG. Empirische Untersuchung der Reduktion von Kapital- und Personalverflechtungen zwischen deutschen börsennotierten Gesellschaften. Mergers and Acquisitions, 1/2006, 12–21

Monopolkommission (2008) Weniger Staat, mehr Wettbewerb.Gesundheitsmärkte und staatliche Beihilfen in der Wettbewerbsordnung: Hauptgutachten 2006/2007 (Hauptgutachten der Monopolkommission; 17). 1. Aufl., Baden-Baden

Mossner G (Hrsg) (1971) Handbuch der Direktoren und Aufsichtsräte. Jahrgang 1970/71, Bd. I, Nach personen geordnet, Finanz- und Korrespondenz-Verlag, Berlin

Pfeiffer (1986a) Groβbanken und Finanzgruppen. Ausgewählte Ergebnisse einer Untersuchung der personellen Verflechtungen von Deutscher, Dresdner und Commerzbank. In: WSI Mitteilungen 39(7):473–481

Pfeiffer (1986b) Das Netwerk der Groβbanken.Personelle Verflechtungen mit Konzernen, Staat und ideologischen Apparaten. In: Blätter für deutsche und internationale Politik 31(2):161–177

Pfeiffer (1993) Die Macht der Banken. Die personellen Verflechtungen der Commerzbank, der Deutschen Bank und der Dresdner Bank mit Unternehemen. Campus, Frankfurt am Main

Stanzick K-H (1969) Der ökonomische Konzentrationsproze. In: Schäfer G, Nedelmann C (Hrsg) *Der CDU*-Staat.Analysen zur Verfassungswriklichkeit der Bundesrepublik, Bd. I, 2. Aufl., Schurkamp, München, SS 48–79

Streeck W (1997) German capitalism. Does it exist? can it survive? In: Crouch C, Streeck W (eds) Political economy of modern capitalism: mapping convergence and diversity. Sage, London, pp 33–54

Chapter 7
Interlocking Directorates of Bank's Supervisory Board and Managing Board Members in Other Enterprises in the Latter Half of the 2010s

Abstract In Germany, large banks had established direct and indirect interlocking directorates of members of supervisory board and managing board on supervisory board of other enterprises again after World War II. Personnel connection system built through interlocking directorate on the supervisory board in the 1950s was greatly influenced by the 1965 Corporations Law that regulated number of mandates of such top management organ that one person could have. Thus, system of personnel connection between enterprises established in the late 1960s became a basic system of interlocking directorate in post-Germany and had been maintained for a long time. However, in the period after the 1990s, such a system of interfirm relationship, in particular, between bank and industrial enterprise has strongly changed under various factors such as globalization of economy and enterprise, internationalization of financial market and change of conditions of company financing brought about by it, and transformation of behavior of bank such as seen in movement from credit bank toward investment bank business. Therefore, building on discussions in Chap. 6, this chapter analyzes situation of interlocking directorates of two largest bank's top management members on supervisory board of other enterprise in the latter half of the 2010s from the comparative perspective with those in the period of the late 1960s. Through these discussions, changes in industry–bank relationship built through interlocking directorate of members of the supervisory board and the board of directors of Deutsche Bank and Commerzbank are clarified.

Keywords Commerzbank · Deutsche Bank · Industry–bank relationship · Direct interlocking directorate · Indirect interlocking directorate · Personnel connection

Chapter 6 examined conditions of direct interlocking directorates on the supervisory board of other enterprises built by members of top management organs such as the supervisory board and the board of directors of Deutsche Bank, Dresdner Bank, and Commerzbank and indirect interlocking directorates established among these three banks and between two banks of them in the period of the end of the 1960s. In this period, the 1965 Corporations Law that regulated number of supervisory board mandates that one person could hold greatly influenced interlocking directorate on

T. Yamazaki, *Relationships Between Industry and Bank in Germany*,
https://doi.org/10.1007/978-981-97-4996-6_7

the supervisory board. The numbers of companies and mandates in which interlocking directorates were established tended to decrease compared with the period in the late 1950s when there was no influence of this law. Thus, a basic system of interlocking directorate in postwar Germany was built and was maintained for long. Thus, German characteristics of industrial concentration included new developments in an industrial system that shared information and coordinated the interests between industry and banks and among corporations. Such system facilitated cooperation between bank and industrial enterprises and between industrial firms and laid the foundation of corporate behavior that avoids intense price competition and adopts a style of management focused on competing with quality.

It was in the period after the 1990s that such system of interfirm relationship, particularly between bank and industrial enterprise, experienced notable changes. In this period, industry–bank relationships in Germany tend to change remarkably. Factors such as globalization of economy and enterprise, internationalization of financial market and change of conditions of company financing brought about by it, and transformation of behavior of bank such as seen in movement from credit bank toward investment bank business are concerned with changes in industry–bank relationship (Höpner 2001, pp. 17–19; Beyer 2006, SS. 110, 153; Beyer 2001, SS. 6–7, 9–10; Beck et al 2005, p. 228; Kengelbach and Roos, 2006, SS. 12, 21; Streeck 1997, p. 51). Interlocking directorate of top management members of large banks on the supervisory board has tended to decrease tremendously. Strong decrease of both dispatch of representative of bank on supervisory board of other enterprise and interlocking directorate through chairman mandate can be observed. Thus, regarding cooperative system called "Germany Inc." ("Deutschland AG") among enterprises including between bank and industrial enterprise and between capital and labor, it has been pointed out that tremendous change can be observed in industry–bank relationship as a core of interfirm relationship (Streeck and Höpner 2003; Zugehör 2003; Cromme 2005; Adams 1994; Beyer 2003).

Therefore, it is an important research topic to consider and clarify situation of changes of interlocking directorate of large German banks on the supervisory board of other enterprises in the period after the 1990s. This chapter analyzes personnel connection in which representative big banks built through interlocking directorate in the latter half of the 2010s as a recent period. As Dresdner Bank as a company of large three banks in Germany no longer exists at the present and big two banks' system has been established and maintained, in this chapter, conditions how members of the top management organs such as the supervisory board and the managing board of Deutsche Bank and Commerzbank build direct interlocking directorate on the supervisory board of other companies and how indirect interlocking directorate relation are established between these two large banks through direct interlocking. This chapter attempts to clarify changes of industry–bank relationship as a core of the enterprise system called "Deutschland AG" and its characteristics as well as changes of cooperative system that determines feature of German capitalism. The basic materials used in analysis of this chapter are "*Handbuch der Grossunternehmen 2017*" (Bd.1 and Bd.2, Bisnode Deutschland GmbH, Darmstadt).

Section 7.1 examines direct interlocking directorates of members of supervisory board and managing board of Deutsche Bank and Commerzbank on the supervisory board of other companies, respectively. Section 7.2 considers indirect interlocking directorates built through direct interlocking directorate between these two banks.

7.1 Direct Interlocking Directorate of Members of Supervisory Board and Managing Board of Banks

7.1.1 Direct Interlocking Directorate of Members of Supervisory Board and Managing Board of Deutsche Bank

First, in examining the direct interlocking directorate by members of the supervisory board and managing board of Deutsche Bank on the supervisory board of other enterprises (see Table 7.1), there were 17 companies in which such cases were observed and 23 interlocking mandates. Numbers of both enterprise and mandate were decisively fewer than those in the late of the 1960s (corresponding numbers 167 and 201, respectively) (see Chap. 6). Considering the distribution of industrial sectors, Deutsche Bank built direct interlocking directorates in one company and had one interlocking mandate in the iron and steel industry, and similarly, one each in the chemical industry; two each in the automobile industry; one each in the machine industry; one each in the distributing industry; three and nine in the banking industry; two each in the insurance industry; four each in the electric power, gas, and energy industries; and two each in other industries, respectively. Among these industries, the number of enterprises interlocking directorates in the electric power, gas, and energy industries was most. In terms of the number of mandates, there were relatively many interlocking relations in the banking industry as industrial sector to which Deutche Bank belongs. However, conditions greatly change compared with those until the late of the 1980s in which Deutsche Bank had close and strong relationships with companies in the heavy and chemical industries as the key industrial sectors in Germany.

Given the situation of interlocking directorates with respect to the position of mandate of supervisory board, Deutsche Bank built interlocking directorates through mandate of chairman of the supervisory board in three companies, namely, Wuppermann AG in the iron and steel industry, Deutsche Postbank AG in the banking industry, and Allianz Real Estate GmbH in other industries. In each firm, the number of mandates was one. Numbers of both enterprise and mandate were decisively fewer than those in the late of the 1960s (corresponding numbers 84 and 84, respectively).

In five enterprises, there were cases where interlocking directorates were formed through mandate of vice-chairman of the supervisory board and the total number of mandates was five. Numbers of enterprises and mandates in which such interlocking cases were formed were two each in the banking industry; one each in the insurance

Table 7.1 Direct interlocking directorates of the members of the supervisory board and the managing board of Deutsche Bank on the supervisory board of other companies (period in the latter half of the 2010s)

Industries	Position							
	Chairman		Vice-chairman		Supervisory board member excluding chairman and vice-chairman		Total[a]	
	Number of companies	Number of posts	Number of companies	Number of posts	Number of companies	Number of posts	Number of companies	Number of posts
Iron and steel	1	1	–	–	–	–	1	1
Chemical	–	–	–	–	1	1	1	1
Automobile	–	–	–	–	2	2	2	2
Machine	–	–	–	–	1	1	1	1
Distributing	–	–	–	–	1	1	1	1
Banking	1	1	2	2	2	6	3	9
Insurance	–	–	1	1	1	1	2	2
Electric power, gas, and energy	–	–	2	2	2	2	4	4
Other industries	1	1	–	–	1	1	2	2
All industries	3	3	5	5	11	15	17	23

[a] There are cases in which the total number of companies establishing interlocking directorates differed from the total number of companies measured by each position of the supervisory board due to the existence of companies where interlocking directorates through more than two posts were built

Source This table was compiled by the author, based on Handbuch der Grossunternehemen (2017a, b)

industry; and two each in the electric power, gas, and energy industries, respectively. Numbers of both enterprise and mandate were much fewer than those around the end of the 1960s (corresponding numbers 41 and 43, respectively). In these five companies, there are major companies such as RWE AG and Innogy SE in the electric power and energy-related industries.

Interlocking directorates through mandates of supervisory board other than chairman and vice-chairman were observed in 11 companies and the total number of mandates was 15. Considering the distribution among industrial sectors, the numbers of enterprises and mandates in which interlocking directorates were formed were one each in the chemical industry; similarly, two each in the automobile industry; one each in the machine industry, one each in the distributing industry, two and six in the banking industry; one each in the insurance industry; two each in the electric power, gas, and energy industries; and one each in other industries, respectively. Numbers of both enterprises and mandates were much few compared with those around the end of the 1960s (corresponding numbers 63 and 68, respectively). Among these ten companies, there were leading firms in each industry, such as Bayer AG in the chemical industry, Daimler AG and BMW AG in the automobile industry, and Münchener Rückversicherungs-Gesellschaft in the insurance industry.

The numbers of enterprises and mandates were only one and seven, respectively, when considering cases where members of the supervisory board and board of directors of Deutsche Bank had more than two mandates on the supervisory boards of other companies. Numbers of both enterprise and mandate were much fewer than those in the late 1960s (corresponding numbers 25 and 59, respectively). Interlocking directorates through total two mandates can be observed in Postbank AG in the banking industry. In this enterprise, there was interlocking directorate through mandates of each one of chairman and vice-chairman in addition to five posts of the supervisory board other than being chairman and vice-chairman.

7.1.2 Direct Interlocking Directorate of Members of Supervisory Board and Managing Board of Commerzbank

Next, looking at the direct interlocking directorate by members of the supervisory board and managing board of Commerzbank on the supervisory board of other enterprises (see Table 7.2), there were 11 companies in which such cases were observed and 13 interlocking mandates. Numbers of both enterprise and mandate were fewer than those of Deutsche Bank (corresponding numbers 17 and 23, respectively). They were much fewer than those of Commerzbank around the end of the 1960s (corresponding numbers 103 and 110, respectively) (see Chap. 6). Considering the distribution of industrial sectors, Commerzbank built direct interlocking directorates in two companies and three interlocking mandates in the banking industry, and similarly, three and four in the insurance industry, and six each in other industries, respectively.

Unlike the period until the end of the 1980s in which close and strong relationships with companies in the heavy and chemical industries as the key industrial sectors in Germany were established through interlocking directorate, scope of industries where personnel connection relations are built became narrower.

Considering the situation of interlocking directorates with respect to the position of mandate of supervisory board, in four enterprises, there were cases in which interlocking directorates on the supervisory boards of other companies were formed through mandate of chairman of the supervisory board with a total of four mandates. Numbers of both enterprise and mandate were almost same as those of Deutsche Bank (corresponding numbers three each, respectively). They were extremely fewer than those of Commerzbank around the late 1960s (corresponding numbers 27 and 27 respectively). Regarding the distribution among industrial sectors, the numbers of enterprises and mandates in which interlocking directorates were formed were one each in the banking industry, one each in the insurance industry, and two each in other industries.

In two enterprises, there were cases where interlocking directorates were formed through mandate of vice-chairman of the supervisory board and the total number of mandates was two. Numbers of both enterprise and mandate were approximately half of those of Deutsche Bank (corresponding numbers five each, respectively). They were also much fewer than those of Commerzbank around the end of the 1960s (corresponding numbers 19 and 19, respectively).

Interlocking directorates through mandates of supervisory board excluding chairman and vice-chairman were observed in seven companies and the total number

Table 7.2 Direct interlocking directorates of the members of the supervisory board and the managing board of Commerzbank Bank on the supervisory board of other companies (period in the latter half of the 2010s)

Industries	Position							
	Chairman		Vice-chairman		Supervisory board member excluding chairman and vice-chairman		Total[a]	
	Number of companies	Number of posts	Number of companies	Number of posts	Number of companies	Number of posts	Number of companies	Number of posts
Banking	1	1	–	–	2	2	2	3
Insurance	1	1	1	1	2	2	3	4
Other industries	2	2	1	1	3	3	6	6
All industries	4	4	2	2	7	7	11	13

[a] There are cases in which the total number of companies establishing interlocking directorates differed from the total number of companies measured by each position of the supervisory board due to the existence of companies where interlocking directorates through more than two posts were built

Source This table was compiled by the author, based on Handbuch der Grossunternehemen (2017a, b)

of mandates was seven. Numbers of both enterprise and mandate were slightly fewer than those of Deutsche Bank (corresponding numbers 11 and 15, respectively). They were extremely fewer compared with those of Commerzbank around the end of the 1960s (corresponding numbers 60 and 62, respectively).

The numbers of enterprises and mandates were two and four, respectively, when considering cases where members of the supervisory board and board of directors of Commerzbank had more than two mandates on the supervisory boards of other companies. Numbers of both enterprise and mandate were fewer than those of Commerzbank around the end of the 1960s (corresponding numbers seven and 14, respectively). Case in which interlocking directorate was built though more than two supervisory board mandates was observed in Commdirectbank AG in the banking industry and BVV Versicherungsverein des Bakngewerbes AG in the insurance industry. Commdirectbank AG is subsidiary company of Commerzbank. In this enterprise, Commerzbank had one chairman mandate and a post of the supervisory board except for chairman and vice-chairman. In BVV Versicherungsverein des Bakngewerbes AG, interlocking directorates were established through each one mandate of vice-chairman post and a mandate other than being chairman and vice-chairman.

7.2 Indirect Interlocking Directorates Between Deutsche Bank and Commerzbank on the Supervisory Board of Other Enterprises

In Sect. 7.1, how members of supervisory board and board of directors of two large German banks built the direct interlocking directorates on supervisory board of other enterprises are analyzed. Building upon these discussions, the next issue to be explored is how indirect interlocking directorates were formed between these two banks through such direct interlocking directorates. Therefore, in Sect. 7.2, this research topic will be considered.

In examining the situations related to indirect interlocking directorates between Deutsche Bank and Commerzbank on the supervisory board of other enterprises (see Table 7.3), such cases can be observed in only three companies and the total number of mandates was seven. Numbers of enterprises and mandates in which Deutsche Bank and Commerzbank formed indirect interlocking directorates were much fewer than those in the late 1960s (see Chap. 6).

In the banking industry, there was one case where Deutsche Bank and Commerzbank built indirect interlocking directorates. In BVV Versorgungskasse des Bankgewerbes e.V., the total number of mandates was two. In the insurance industry, two cases in which indirect interlockings' directorate was built between these two banks can be observed. Whereas in BVV Versicherungsverein des Bakngewerbes AG, total number of interlocking mandates was three, such number was two in Münchener Rückversicherungs-Gesellschaft.

Table 7.3 Indirect interlocking directorates of the members of the supervisory board and the managing board on the supervisory board of other companies between Deutsche Bank and Commerzbank (period in the latter half of the 2010s)

Industries	Number of posts					
	2		3		Total	
	Number of companies	Number of posts	Number of companies	Number of posts	Number of companies	Number of posts
Banking	1	2	–	–	1	2
Insurance	1	2	1	3	2	5
All industries	2	4	1	3	3	7

Source This table was compiled by the author, based on Handbuch der Grossunternehemen (2017a, b)

To understand bank that was at the leading position in indirect interlocking relation, in examining cases in which one bank or both Deutsche Bank and Commerzbank Bank had more than two mandates on the supervisory board of other company, in BVV Versicherungsverein des Bakngewerbes AG, Commerzbank had a vice-chairman mandate and one post of the supervisory board excluding chairman and vice-chairman„ whereas Deutsche Bank held a mandate of the supervisory board except for chairman and vice-chairman. In both cases of BVV Versorgungskasse des Bankgewerbes e.V. and Münchener Rückversicherungs-Gesellschaft, each of Deutsche Bank and Commerzbank held one post of the supervisory board other than being chairman and vice-chairman.

Essentially, indirect interlocking directorates built between large banks through direct interlocking directorate of members of top management organs of each bank on the supervisory board of other enterprises should be an important foundation of the strong connection between banks. However, in the period in the 2010s, establishment of such personnel connections relation is extremely limited to few enterprises and cannot be an important means of coordination of interests and conflicts through informal discussions and effective measure of cooperative behavior between banks. This greatly differs compared with conditions until the end of the 1980s.

In this way, the period after the 1990s has witnessed notable changes under the globalization of economy and enterprise, internationalization of financial market and the corresponding change in conditions of company financing, and transformation of bank behavior, that is, movement from credit bank toward investment bank business. Several studies showed that industry–bank relationships in Germany changed remarkably. Globalization of economy and enterprises, internationalization of financial market, the resulting changes in the conditions of company financing, and transformation of banks' behavior such as that seen in the movement from a credit bank toward an investment bank business are related to changes in the industry–bank relationship. The interlocking directorates of top management members of large banks on the supervisory board sharply decreased. A strong decrease of both dispatch of bank's representative on the supervisory board of other enterprises and interlocking directorates through chairman mandate can be observed.

Thus, regarding the cooperative system called "Germany Inc." ("Deutschland AG") based on cooperative relationships between industry and bank and between industrial enterprises, a tremendous change can be observed in the industry–bank relationship as a basis of interfirm relationship. Personnel connection relations built through interlocking directorate by largest two banks are extremely limited to few enterprises and cannot be an important means of coordination of interests and conflicts through informal discussions and effective measure of cooperative behavior between banks. Condition in which indirect interlocking directorates built between large banks through direct interlocking directorate of members of top management organs of each bank on the supervisory board of other enterprises had been an important foundation of the strong connection between banks in the period until the beginning of the 1990s has tremendously changed. Personnel connection relations between bank and industrial enterprise through both direct and indirect interlocking directorates as a core element have experienced the process of dissolution since the 1990s, which resulted in tremendous changes in German system of "industry–bank relationships" as well as interfirm relationships including those between industrial enterprises. This greatly differs compared with conditions until the end of the 1980s.

References

Adams M (1994) Die Usurpation von Aktionsärsbefugnissen mittels Ringverflechtung in der Deutschland AG. In: Die Aktiengesellschaft 39(4):148–158

Beck S, Klobes F, Scherrer C (2005) Conclusion. In: Beck S, Klobes F, Scherrer C (eds) Surviving globalization? perspectives for the German economic model. Springer, Dordrecht, pp 225–235

Beyer J (2001) Deutschland AG a.D.: Deutsche Bank, Allianz und das Verflechtungszentrum großer deutscher Unternehmen. In: MPIfG (MaxPlanck-Institut für Gesellschaftsforschung) Working Paper 02/4, 1–26

Beyer J (2003) Deutschland AG a.D. Deutsche Bank, Allianz und das Verflechtungszentrum des deutschen Kapitalismus. In: Streeck W, Höpner M (eds) Alle Macht dem Markt? Fallstudien zur Abwicklung der Deutchland AG. Campus, Frankfurt am Main, pp 118–146

Beyer J (2006) Pfadabhängigkeit. Über institutionelle Kontinuität, anfällige Stabiltät und fundamentalen Wandel. Campus, Frankfurt am Main

Cromme G (2005) Corporate governance in Germany and the German corporate governance code. In: Corporate Govern: An Int Rev 13(3):362–367

Handbuch der Grossunternehmen (2017a) Handbuch der Grossunternehmen 2017. 64.Ausgabe, Bd.1, Bisnode Deutschland GmbH, Darmstadt

Handbuch der Grossunternehmen (2017b) Handbuch der Grossunternehmen 2017. 64.Ausgabe, Bd.2, Bisnode Deutschland GmbH, Darmstadt

Höpner M (2001) Corporate governance in transition: ten empirical findings on shareholder value and industrial relations in Germany. In: MPIfG (MaxPlanck-Institut für Gesellschaftsforschung) Discussion Paper01/5, 1–61

Kengelbach J, Roos A (2006) Entflechtung der Deutschland AG. Empirische Untersuchung der Reduktion von Kapital- und Personalverflechtungen zwischen deutschen börsennotierten Gesellschaften. In: Mergers and Acquisitions, 1/2006, 12–21

Streeck W (1997) German capitalism. does it exist? can it survive? In: Crouch C, Streeck W (eds) Political economy of modern capitalism: mapping convergence and diversity. SAGE, London, pp 33–54

Streeck W, Höpner M (Hrsg) (2003) Alle Macht dem Markt? Fallstudien zur Abwicklung der Deutchland AG. Campus, Frankfurt an Main

Zugehör R (2003) Die Zukunft des rheinischen Kapitalismus: Unternehmen zwischen Kapitalmarkt und Mitbestimmung. Leske+Budrich, Opladen

Part II
Personnel Networks Between Enterprises Through Interlocking Directorates

Chapter 8
Bank's Personnel Networks Through Interlocking Directorates of Members of the Supervisory Board on Such Top Management Organs of Other Enterprises Before World War II: Analysis of the Period of National Socialism

Abstract Members of the supervisory boards of several other enterprises in which supervisory board members of a company have interlocking mandates hold many posts in third-party enterprises. A personnel network is established through interlocking directorates, including second- and third-party enterprises. The possibilities of exchanging information and coordinating interests between industry and banks and among corporations can be enlarged through such a system. Using social network analysis, this chapter examines the personnel networks of three large banks, namely, Deutsche Bank (Deutsche Bank und Disconto-Gesellschaft), Dresdner Bank, and Commerzbank (Commerz- und Privat-Bank AG), through interlocking directorates of members of the supervisory board on the same top management of other companies, including second- and third-party enterprises. This chapter clarifies the characteristics of a network as a whole and the importance of each company in the network by analyzing the key indicators of social network analysis, such as "density" and "centrality." Furthermore, this chapter examines the clique of interlocking supervisory board members who play a significant role in the network.

Keywords Bank · Industrial enterprise · Industry–bank relationship · Interlocking · Personnel network · Social network analysis

As analyzed in Part I, personnel connections have two types, direct and indirect interlocking directorates. A direct interlocking directorate is formed when members of the supervisory and management boards of a company have the mandate of the top management organs of other enterprises, such as the supervisory board and board of directors. When companies A and B that establish direct interlocking directorates in another company C belong to the same industry or industrial sector of company

T. Yamazaki, *Relationships Between Industry and Bank in Germany*,
https://doi.org/10.1007/978-981-97-4996-6_8

C, such a system has significant implications in coordinating interests, conflicts, and cooperation among enterprises. Direct and indirect interlocking directorates are significant in exchanging and sharing information and coordinating interests and conflicts among enterprises.

In other cases, members of the supervisory boards of several other enterprises with interlocking mandates also hold many posts in third-party enterprises. In considering the interlocking directorate between a company and another company as a second-party enterprise as that in the level of "distance 1," that between second- and third-party enterprises in which the former has a mandate of the top management organ can be considered "distance 2." Then, the personnel network through interlocking directorates of the members of the supervisory boards in the extent of "distant 2," including second- and third-party enterprises, is built, which is significant for exchanging information, coordinating interests, and resolving conflicts between industry and banks and among corporations by using such information. Therefore, clarifying the structures of personnel networks of large enterprises in major industrial sectors, including second- and third-party companies, is crucial for understanding the functions of interfirm relationships in Germany. Part II examines personnel networks established in the extent of "distant 2," including second- and third-party enterprises. This part uses social network analysis to clarify the structures of personnel networks of three large banks.

In social network analysis of personnel connection among companies, two key concepts (i.e., "density" and "centrality") are very important. "Density" is an indicator for understanding the cohesiveness of a network. "Centrality" is an indicator for understanding which enterprise is in a core position among companies, comprising the network concerned in the information flow and media. Understanding "density" helps clarify the strength of a company's network in "cohesiveness" . By contrast, "centrality" can be understood by the "adjacency," which indicates the number of enterprises in which interlocking directorate is built. Analyzing "centrality" helps understand which enterprise has high "centrality" and its industry.

"Density" explains the characteristics of the network as a whole, whereas "centrality" indicates the importance of each company in the network. In addition to these two key concepts, "multiplicity" is an important indicator. Multiplicity means more than two mandates that build an interlocking directorate. "Multiplicity" helps understand a company with many mandates on the supervisory board of another enterprise and a clique of interlocking members that takes an essential position in the network. Hence, the social network analysis methodology helps compare personnel networks among industries and enterprises (Hannemann and Riddle 2011; Nakata et al. 1997, pp. 38–41).

Part II is composed of three chapters. This chapter considers conditions in the middle of the 1930s during National Socialism regarding the period before the World War II. Chapter 9 investigated situations around the late 1960s concerning the period after the war. This period is after the 1965 Corporations Law that regulated the number of supervisory board posts one person could hold (Eglau 1990, S. 128; Pfeiffer 1986a, S. 477, 1986b, S. 164, 1993, S. 158–159; Stanzick 1969, S. 72:) and greatly influenced conditions of the interlocking directorates on the supervisory board of other enterprises. Consequently, the basic system of interlocking directorate in postwar Germany was established. Hence, this period will be taken up in Chap. 9. Chapter 10 analyzes networks of two largest banks, namely Deutsche Bank and Commerzbank in the latter half of the 2010s.

This chapter examines the personnel networks of three large banks, namely, Deutsche Bank (Deutsche Bank und Disconto-Gesellschaft), Dresdner Bank, and Commerzbank (Commerz- und Privat-Bank AG), through the interlocking directorate of members of the supervisory board on the same top management organ of other companies, including second- and third-party enterprises. The characteristics of the network of each bank will be clarified through social network analysis. In addition, a clique of interlocking supervisory board members with more than two mandates on such a top management organ of multiple companies, which played significant roles in the network, is considered. Interlocking supervisory board members in banks associated with those in industrial enterprises and combining those in industrial enterprises mutually can be analyzed.

8.1 Deutsche Bank's Personnel Network Through Interlocking Directorate of Members of the Supervisory Board on Such Top Management Organ of Other Enterprises

8.1.1 Personnel Network and Its Characteristics

First, in Sect. 8.1, the conditions of Deutsche Bank's network are analyzed. Considering the centrality of each enterprise constituting the network and the upper 10 enterprises among Deutsche Bank and 254 companies with their interlocking directorates on the supervisory board in terms of the adjacency measured by the number of enterprises in which interlocking directorate is built (Table 8.1), the following numbers emerge. There were two in the banking industry as the financial sector, two in the mining industry, and one each in the iron and steel; chemical; electrical; automobile; electric power, gas, and energy industries; and other industries. Adjacencies of the upper 10 enterprises ranged from 180 to 254. The first, second, and third positions in terms of adjacency were Deutsche Bank (Deutsche Bank und Disconto-Gesellschaft) in the banking industry (adjacency 254), AEG in the electrical industry (similarly 246), and Vereinigte Stahlwerke AG in the iron and steel industry (243). Three enterprises below the fourth position were Deutsche Centralbodenkredit-AG in the banking industry (adjacency 229), Rheinische AG für Braunkohlenbergbau und Brikettfabrikation in the mining industry (similarly 207), and Kokswerke und Chemische Fabriken AG in the chemical industry (199). Four enterprises below the seventh position were as follows: Daimler-Benz AG in the automobile industry (adjacency 191), Rheinisch-Westfäflisches Kohlen-Syndikat in the mining industry (similarly 184), Deutsch-Atlantische Telegraphengesellschaft in other industries (183), and Ruhrgas AG in the electric power, gas, and energy industries (180), respectively.

When examining the centrality of enterprises at the upper 11–20 positions, there were three in the electric power, gas, and energy industries; two each in the mining industry and the banking sector; and one each in the iron and steel; chemical; and electrical industries. The adjacency of enterprises at the upper 11–20 positions ranged from 179 to 150. Harpener Bergbau AG in the mining industry (adjacency 179) and Gesellschaft für elektrische Unternehmungen—Ludwig Loewe & Co. AG in the electrical industry (similarly 175) ranked 11th and 12th positions in terms of the adjacency. Rütgerswerke AG in the chemical industry and Elektrowerke AG (Reichselektrowerke) in the electric power, gas, and energy industries (adjacency 172, respectively) ranked 13th. Then, AG für deutsche Elektrizitätswirt in the electric power, gas, and energy industries (adjacency 170), Deutsch-Asiatische Bank in the banking industry (similarly 160), and Mannesmannröhren-Werke in the iron and steel industry (157) ranked 15th, 16th, and 17th, respectively. Preuβische Elektrizitäts-AG in the electric power, gas, and energy industries (adjacency 152) ranked 18th. Essener Steinkohlenbergwerke AG in the mining industry and Sächsische Bodencreditanstalt in the banking industry (adjacency 150) ranked 19th.

Considering firms within the upper fifth positions measured by adjacency, two firms were in the banking industry as the financial sector and one each in the mining; iron and steel; and electrical industries. Deutsche Bank and Deutsche Centralbodenlredit-AG ranked first and fourth, respectively, and the centralities of some banks were relatively high. However, AEG, Vereinigte Stahlwerke AG, and Rheinische AG für Braunkohlenbergbau and Brikettfabrikation ranked second, third, and fifth, respectively. In addition, notably, considerable adjacency of the upper 10 or 20 enterprises existed. The adjacency of AEG at the second position was 246. A similar numerical figure of Kokswerke und Chemische Fabriken AG at sixth position was 199. Adjacency of Ruhrgas AG at 10th position were 180. Moreover, there were several enterprises in which interlocking directorates were built on the supervisory boards of other enterprises. Although the centralities of some banks were relatively high, many were not always in the upper position in terms of adjacency. Rather, companies with high centrality belonged to industries across some key sectors, such as the iron and steel, chemical, electrical, and automobile industries. Therefore, enterprises in important major industries also assumed core positions in information flow and media of networks, including banks.

Concerning the network's cohesiveness, the density of Deutsche Bank's network was 0.004494. Members on the supervisory board of Deutsche Bank built interlocking directorates in a similar top management organ in 254 companies as second-party enterprises. Then, the number of enterprises comprising the network, including second-party enterprises in which Deutsche Bank had mandates of the supervisory board and third-party enterprises in which second-party enterprises had posts of the supervisory board, was 2702.

Table 8.1 Centrality of member companies in the network of Deutsche Bank[a] (period of National Socialism)

Position	Company	Adjacency[b]	Industries
1	*Deutsche Bank und Disconto-Gesellschaft*[c]	254	Banking
2	Allgemeine Elektricitäts-Gesellschaft	246	Electrical
3	Vereinigte Stahlwerke AG	243	Iron and steel
4	Deutsche Centralbodenkredit-AG	229	Banking
5	Rheinische AG für Braunkohlenbergbau und Brikettfabrikation	207	Mining
6	Kokswerke und Chemische Fabriken AG	199	Chemical
7	Daimler-Benz AG	191	Automobile
8	Rheinisch-Westfälisches Kohlen-Syndikat	184	Mining
9	Deutsch-Atlantische Telegraphengesellschaft	183	Other industries
10	Ruhrgas AG	180	Electric power, gas, and energy
11	Harpener Bergbau-AG	179	Mining
12	Gesellschaft für elektrische Unternehmungen-Ludw.Loewe & Co.AG	175	Electrical
13	Rütgerswerke AG	172	Chemical
13	Elektrowerke AG (Reichselektrowerke)	172	Electric power, gas, and energy
15	AG für deutsche Elektrizitätswirtschaft	170	Electric power, gas, and energy
16	Deutsch-Asiatische Bank	160	Banking
17	Mannesmannröhren-Werke	157	Iron and steel
18	Preuβische Elektrizitäts-AG	152	Electric power, gas, and energy
19	Essener Steinkohlenbergwerke AG	150	Mining
19	Sächsische Bodencreditanstalt	150	Banking
21	Gelsenkirchener Bergwerks-AG	149	Mining
22	AG für Waggonbauwerte (Linke-Hofmann-Busch-Werke AG)	145	Machine
23	Metallgesellschaft AG	144	Metal producing and processing
23	Feldmühle, Papier- und Zellstoffwerke AG	144	Other industries
25	Dynamit AG vormals Alfred Nobel & Co	142	Chemical

(continued)

Table 8.1 (continued)

Position	Company	Adjacency[b]	Industries
25	Allgemeine Deutsche Credit-Anstalt	142	Banking
27	Mansfeld AG für Bergbau und Hüttenbetrieb	139	Iron and steel
28	Deutsche Hypothekenbank, Meiningen	137	Banking
29	Reichs-Kredit-Gesellschaft AG	136	Banking
30	Hochtief, AG für Hoch- und Tiefbauten vorm. Gebr.Helfmann	134	Other industries
31	AG für Bergbau, Blei- und Zinkfabrikation zu Stollberg und in Westfalen	133	Metal producing and processing
31	A.Riebeck'sche Montanwerke AG	133	Chemical
33	DEMAG AG	132	Machine
34	Rheinische Metalwaaren- und Maschinenfabrik (Rheinmetall—Borsig)	130	Machine
35	Rheinisch-Westfälische Boden-Credit-Bank	126	Banking
36	Wintershall AG	122	Chemical
37	Universum-Film AG	120	Other industries
37	Vereinigte Industrie-Unternehmungen AG	120	Other industries
39	Rheinische Stahlwerke	119	Iron and steel
40	Leipziger Bierbrauerei zu Reudnitz Riebeck & Co. AG	116	Distillation

Note [a]Of Deutsche Bank und Disconto-Gesellschaft and 254 enterprises in which it built direct interlocking directorates on their supervisory boards, upper 40 companies measured by adjacency are listed up

[b]"Centrality" is measured by an indicator "adjacency" that indicates number of companies in which interlocking directorate is built

[c]Company in italics is Deutsche Bank und Disconto-Gesellschaft as the starting point of this network

Source This table was compiled by the author, based on Mossner (Hrsg) (1936)

8.1.2 Clique of Interlocking Supervisory Board Members

Next, a clique of interlocking supervisory board members with more than two mandates on such a top management organ of multiple companies, which play significant roles in the network, is considered. Interlocking supervisory board members in banks associated with those in industrial enterprises and combining those in industrial enterprises mutually can be analyzed.

Cases in which multiple members of the supervisory board of Deutsche Bank have a mandate on such an organ of other enterprises can be observed in 31 companies. The total number of mandates was 70. Considering the distribution among industrial sectors, the number of enterprises in which interlocking directorate was formed was three in the mining industry; similarly, two in the iron and steel industry; two in the metal producing and processing industries; four in the chemical industry; three in the electrical industry; four in the machine industry; four in the banking industry; three in the insurance industry; three in the electric power, gas, and energy industries; and three in other industries. Such enterprises were Rheinisch-Westfälisches Kohlen-Syndikat, Essener Steinkohlenbergwerke AG, and Gelsenkirchener Bergwerks-AG in the mining industry; Mannesmannröhren-Werke and Vereinigte Stahlwerke AG in the iron and steel industry; AG für Bergbau, Blei- und Zinkfabrikation zu Stolberg und in Westfalen and Metallgesellschaft AG in the metal producing and processing industries; A. Riebeck'sche Montanwerke AG, Dynamit AG vorm. Alfred Nobel & Co., Deutsche Gold- und Silber-Scheideanstalt vormals Roessler, Westfälisch-Anhaltische Sprengstoff AG, and Siemens-Planiawerke AG für Kohlefabrikate in the chemical industry; Siemens & Halske AG and Siemens-Schuckertwerke AG in the electrical industry; Rheinische Metallwaaren- und Maschinenfabrik (Rheimetall-Borsig), Demag AG, A. Borsig Maschinenbau AG, and Maschinenbau-Unternehmungen AG in the machine industry; Deutsche Hypothekenbank, Meiningen, Sächsische Bodencredit-Anstalt, Deutsche Ueberseeische Bank, and Deutsche Centralbodenkredit AG in the banking industry; Nordstein Allgemeine Versicherungs-AG, Rückversicherungs-Vereinigung AG, and Union und Rhein Versicherungs-AG in the insurance industry; Bergmann-Elektrizitäts-Werke AG, Elektrowerke AG, and Ruhrgas AG in the electric power, gas, and energy industries; and Deutsch Atlantische Telegraphengesellschaft, Rheinisch-Westfälische Kalkwerke, and Hochtief AG für Hoch- und Tiefbauten vorm. Gebrüder Helfmann in other industries.

The number of supervisory board members of Deutsche Bank who held mandate on the supervisory board of the same enterprises was 21. Such members were as follows: O. Schlitter, C. von Siemens, J. Hasslacher, G. von Stauss, F Urwig, R. Stahl, H. Schmitz, W. Huber, P. Klöckner, W. de Weerth, E. Schoen von Wildenegg, A. Koepchen, F. Springorum, H. Bierwes, C. E. von Sachsen-Coburg und Gotha, E. E. Rusell, H. Henkel, H. Münchmeyer, K E. Sibel, H. Eckener, and G. Hardt.

Of 31 companies in which plural members of the supervisory board of Deutsche Bank had mandate, O. Schlitter had mandates on the supervisory board of eight other companies. He was the chairman of Demag AG and Maschinenbau-Unternehmungen AG and the vice-chairman of Mannesmannröhren-Werke, Nordstein Allgemeine Versicherungs-AG, and Rückversicherungs-Vereinigung AG. He had a mandate of the supervisory board except for the chairman and vice-chairman of Siemens & Halske AG, Siemens-Schuckertwerke AG, and Elektrowerke AG. C. von Siemens held mandates on the supervisory board of seven other enterprises. He had mandates of the chairman of Siemens & Halske AG, Siemens-Planiawerke AG für Kohlefabrikate, and Siemens-Schuckertwerke AG and posts of the supervisory board except for the chairman and vice-chairman of Gelsenkirchener Bergwerks-AG,

Mannesmannröhren-Werke, Vereinigte Stahlwerke AG, and Metallgesellschaft AG. J. Hasslacher and E. von Stauss held posts in six other enterprises. J. Hasslacher held the mandate of vice-chairman of A. Riebeck'sche Montanwerke AG and posts of the supervisory board except for the chairman and vice-chairman of Rheinisch-Westfälisches Kohlen-Syndikat, Essener Steinkohlenbergwerke AG, Vereinigte Stahlwerke AG, Union und Rhein Versicherungs-AG, and Rheinisch-Westfälische Kalkwerke. E. von Stauss had a mandate of the chairman of A. Borsig Maschinenbau AG and Bergmann-Elektrizitäts-Werke AG, a mandate of the vice-chairman of Siemens-Planiawerke AG für Kohlefabrikate, and posts of the supervisory board excluding the chairman and vice-chairman of Siemens & Halske AG, Rheinische Metallwaaren- und Maschinenfabrik (Rheimetall-Borsig) and Deutsche Centralbodenkredit AG.

F. Urwig and R. Stahl had mandates on the supervisory board of five other companies. F. Uwig held mandates of the supervisory board except for the chairman and vice-chairman of Essener Steinkohlenbergwerke AG, Sächsische Bodencredit-Anstalt, Union und Rhein Versicherungs-AG, Bergmann-Elektrizitäts-Werke AG, and Deutsch Atlantische Telegraphengesellschaft. R. Stahl had a mandate of the chairman of AG für Bergbau, Blei- und Zinkfabrikation zu Stolberg und in Westfalen and posts of the supervisory board except for the chairman and vice-chairman of Deutsche Gold- und Silber-Scheideanstalt vormals Roessler, Westfälisch-Anhaltische Sprengstoff AG, Demag AG, and Maschinenbau-Unternehmungen AG.

H. Schmitz, W. Huber, and P. Klöckner had mandates of the supervisory board of the other four enterprises. H. Schmitz held a mandate of the chairman of A. Riebeck'sche Montanwerke AG, a post of the vice-chairman of Dynamit AG vorm. Alfred Nobel & Co., and posts of the supervisory board excluding the chairman and vice-chairman of Vereinigte Stahlwerke AG and Metallgesellschaft AG. W. Huber had a mandate of the vice-chairman of Rheinisch-Westfälisches Kohlen-Syndikat and posts of Essener Steinkohlenbergwerke AG, Gelsenkirchener Bergwerks-AG, and Ruhrgas AG. Klöckner held mandates of the supervisory board excluding the chairman and vice-chairman of Rheinisch-Westfälisches Kohlen-Syndikat, Dynamit AG vorm. Alfred Nobel & Co., Rheinische Metallwaaren- und Maschinenfabrik (Rheimetall-Borsig), and A. Borsig Maschinenbau AG.

W. de Weerth, E. Schoen von Wildenegg, and A. Koepchen had mandates of the supervisory board of three other firms. W. De Weerth had mandates of the chairman of Nordstein Allgemeine ersicherungs AG and Rückversicherungs-Vereinigung AG and a post of the supervisory board except for the chairman and vice-chairman of Deutsche Hypothekenbank, Meiningen. E. Schoen von Wildenegg held a mandate of the vice-chairman of Sächsische Bodencredit-Anstalt and posts of the supervisory board except for the chairman and vice-chairman of AG für Bergbau, Blei- und Zinkfabrikation zu Stolberg und in Westfalen and Deutsche Hypothekenbank, Meiningen. A. Koepchen had mandates of the supervisory board except for the chairman and vice-chairman of Elektrowerke AG, Ruhrgas AG, and Hochtief AG für Hoch- und Tiefbauten vorm. Gebrüder Helfmann.

F. Springorum, H. Bierwes, and C. E. von Sachsen-Coburg und Gotha had mandates from the supervisory boards of two other companies. All mandates they held were supervisory board mandates except for the chairman and vice-chairman. F. Springprum held mandates of Rheinisch-Westfälisches Kohlen-Syndikat and Rheinisch-Westfälische Kalkwerke. H. Wierwes had posts of Mannesmannröhren-Werke and Westfälisch-Anhaltische Sprengstoff AG. C. E. von Sachsen-Coburg und Gotha held posts of Rheinische Metallwaaren- und Maschinenfabrik (Rheimetall-Borsig) and Deutsche Centralbodenkredit AG.

E. E. Rusell, H. Henkel, H. Münchmeyer, K E. Sibel, H. Eckener, and G. Hardt had a mandate of the supervisory board of one other enterprise. E. E. Rusell held a mandate of the vice-chairman of Deutsche Hypothekenbank, Meiningen. The other five had one mandate of the supervisory board, excluding the chairman and vice-chairman. H. Henkel had a mandate of Deutsche Gold- und Silber-Scheideanstalt vormals Roessler. H. Münchmeyer held a post of Deutsch Atlantische Telegraphengesellschaft. K. E. Sibel had one mandate of Hochtief AG für Hoch- und Tiefbauten vorm. Gebrüder Helfmann. H. Eckener and G. Hardt held each one mandate of Deutsche Ueberseeische Bank (Mossner 1936, S. 115, 314, 543, 554–555, 586, 657, 766, 796, 1063, 1306, 1309, 1364–1365, 1389–1390, 1408, 1481–1482, 1490, 1510, 1514, 1520, 1622, 1672).

Furthermore, considering the network of meetings built among members of enterprises with more than three mandates (Fig. 8.1), the following conditions can be observed. Cases in which strong interlocking directorates were built between Deutsche Bank and a second-party enterprise were observed in seven enterprises. Such enterprises were Rheinisch-Westäflisches Kohlen-Syndikat and Essener Steinkohlenbergwerke AG in the mining industry; Mannesmannröhren-Werke and Vereinigte Stahlwerke AG in the iron and steel industry; Siemens & Halske AG in the electrical industry; Rheinische Metallwaaren- und Maschinenfabrik (Rheinmetall-Borsig) in the machine industry; and Deutsche Hypothekenbank, Meiningen in the banking industry.

The network of meetings built between Deutsche Bank and these seven enterprises comprised 14 interlocking supervisory board members, namely, J. Hasslacher, C. F. von Siemens, P. Klöckner, O. Schitter, W. Huber, E. G. von Stauss, F. Springorum, F. Urwig, H. Bierwes, H. Schmitz, C. E. von Sachsen-Coburg und Gotha, E. E. Rusell, E. Schoen. von Wildenegg, and W. de Weerth. J. Hasslacher and C. F. von Siemens were interlocking supervisory board members of three enterprises. Then, J. Hasslacher had mandates of Rheinisch-Westfälisches Kohlen-Syndikat, Essener Steinkohlenbergwerke AG, and Vereinigte Stahlwerke AG, and C. F. von Siemens held mandates of Mannesmannröhren-Werke, Vereinigte Stahlwerke AG, and Siemens & Halske AG. P. Klöckner, O. Schlitter, W. Huber, and E. G. von Stauss were interlocking supervisory board members of two companies. P. Klöckner had mandates of Rheinisch-Westfälisches Kohlen-Syndikat and Rheinische Metallwaaren- und Maschinenfabrik (Rheimetall-Borsig). O. Schlitter held mandates of Mannesmannröhren-Werke and Siemens & Halske AG. W. Huber had mandates of Rheinisch-Westfälisches Kohlen-Syndikat and Essener Steinkohlenbergwerke. E. G. von Stauss held mandates of Siemens & Halske AG and Rheinische Metallwaaren-

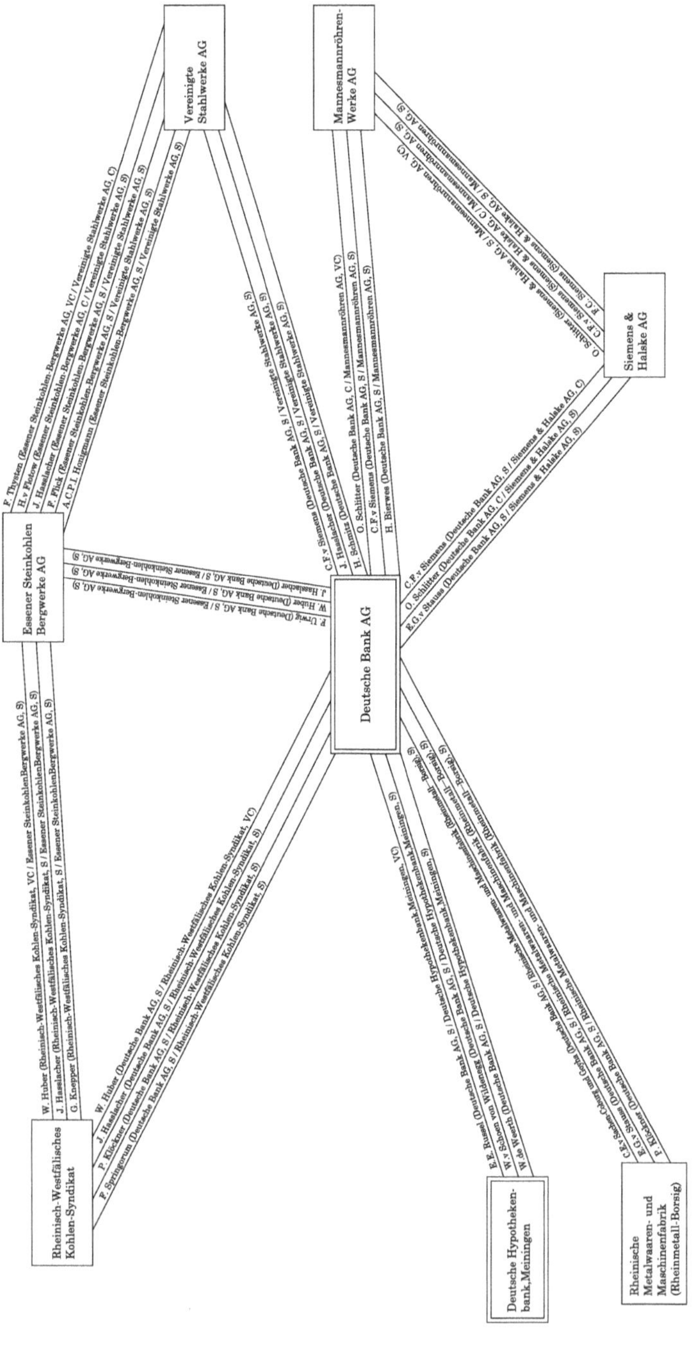

Note : 1) This figure indicates the network composed of companies with more than three interlocking mandates that was connected by the supervisory board members between Deutsche Bank and companies in which this bank had interlocking mandates.
2) Companies enclosed with [double-framed box] were financial institutions.
3) Regarding the positions of mandates on the supervisory board, "C", "VC", and "S" mean chairman, vice-chairman, and mandate other than these two positions, respectively.
Source : This figure was compiled by the author, based on Mossner (Hrsg) (1936).

Fig. 8.1 Network for meeting of Deutsche Bank built among interlocking supervisory board members with more than three mandates in the period of National Socialism (extent of "distance 1")

und Maschinenfabrik (Rheimetall-Borsig). F. Springorum, F. Urwig, H. Bierwes, H. Schmitz, C. E. von Sachsen-Coburg und Gotha, E. E. Rusell, E. Schoen von Wildenegg, and W. de Weerth were interlocking supervisory board members of one enterprise. Then, F. Springorum had the mandate of Rheinisch-Westfälisches Kohlen-Syndikat, and F. Urwig held the mandate of Essener Steinkohlenbergwerke AG. H. Bierwes had post of Mannesmannröhren-Werke. H. Schmitz held post of Vereinigte Stahlwerke AG. C. E. von Sachsen-Coburg und Gotha had mandate of Rheinische Metallwaaren- und Maschinenfabrik (Rheimetall-Borsig). Then, E. E. Rusell, E. Schoen Von Wildenegg, and W. De Weerth held the mandate of Deutsche Hypothekenbank, Meiningen.

In addition, strong relationships of interlocking directorates were built through more than three mandates among seven second-party enterprises. These second-party enterprises also had more than three mandates on the supervisory board of third-party enterprises. The second-party enterprises held more than three mandates on a similar top management organ.

Therefore, conditions of interlocking directorates built through more than three mandates on the supervisory board among seven second-party and third-party enterprises are examined (see Fig. 8.2).

Cases of interlocking directorates formed through more than three mandates between Rheinisch-Westäflisches Kohlen-Syndikat and third-party enterprises were observed in 17 enterprises. They were Concordia Bergbau AG, Essener Steinkohlenbergwerke AG, Gelsenkirchener Bergwerks-AG, Harpener Bergbau AG, and Gesellschaft für Kohlentechnik mbH in the mining industry; Vereinigte Stahlwerke AG in the iron and steel industry; Benzol-Verband GmbH, Dynamit AG vorm. Alfred Nobel & Co., and Ruhrchemie AG in the chemical industry; Ruhrbenzin AG in the oil industry; Deutsche Ammoniakverkaufsvereinigung (GmbH) and Verkaufsvereinigung für Teererzeugnisse GmbH in the distributing industry; Rheinisch-Westfälisches Elektrizitätswerk AG and Ruhrgas AG in the electric power, gas, and energy industries; and Deutsches Kohlen-Depot, GmbH, Wasserwerk für das nördliche westfälische Kohlenrevier, and Westfälische Werkswohnungs-AG in other industries. Among these 17 enterprises, the number of mandates that Rheinisch-Westäflisches Kohlen-Syndikat held was eight in Ruhrgas AG, seven in Ruhrbenzin AG, and six in Ruhrchemie AG. In Gelsenkirchener Bergwerks-AG, Gesellschaft für Kohlentechnik mbH, and Wasserwerk für das nördliche westfälische Kohlenrevier, Rheinisch-Westäflisches Kohlen-Syndikat had four mandates. In the remaining 11 enterprises, interlocking directorates were built through three mandates.

Cases in which Essener Steinkohlenbergwerke AG built interlocking directorates through more than three mandates with third-party enterprises were observed in 15 enterprises. Such companies were Rheinisch-Westäflisches Kohlen-Syndikat, Gelsenkirchener Bergwerks-AG, Harpener Bergbau AG, and Rheinische AG für Braunkohlenbergbau und Brikettfabrikation in the mining industry; August-Thyssen Hütte AG, Bocuhmer Verein für Gußstahlfabrikation AG, Dortmund-Hoerder Hüttenverein AG, Mitteldeutsche Stahlwerke AG, Ruhrstahl AG, and Vereinigte Stahlwerke AG in the iron and steel industry; A. Riebeck'sche Montanwerke AG

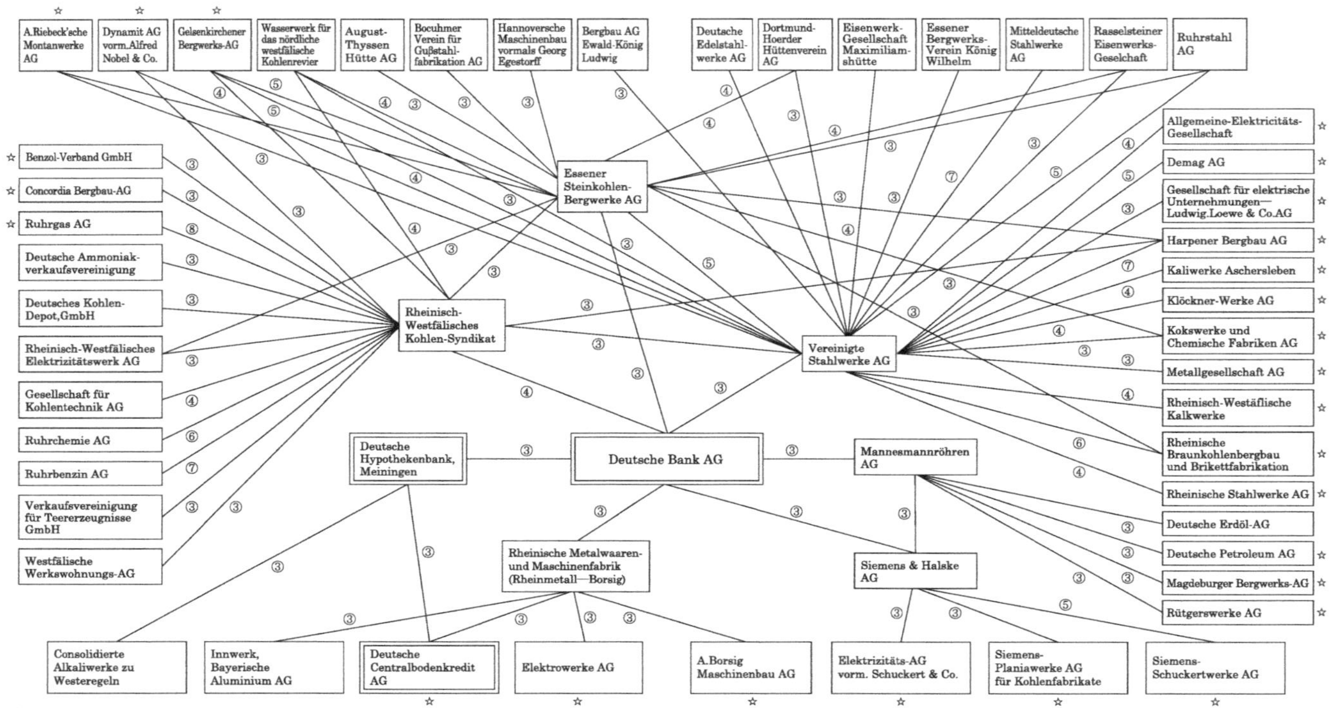

Note : 1) This figure shows the network of companies with more than three interlocking mandates among supervisory board members of the Deutsche Bank; second-party companies in which this bank had interlocking mandates; and third party companies in which these second-party companies had interlocking mandates.
2) Companies enclosed in a ▭ are financial institutions.
3) Companies with mark ☆ were companies in which Deutsche Bank built the interlocking directorates through one or two mandates.
4) The number added to the line connecting a company and other company means the number of the interlocking mandates.
Source : This figure was compiled by the author, based on Mossner (Hrsg) (1936).

Fig. 8.2 Network for meeting of Deutsche Bank built among interlocking supervisory board members with more than three mandates in the period of National Socialims (extent of "distance 2")

and Kokswerke und Chemische Fabriken AG in the chemical industry; Hannoversche Maschinenbau AG vormals Georg Egestorff in the machine industry; Rheinisch-Westfälisches Elektrizitätswerk AG in the electric power, gas, and energy industries; and Wasserwerk für das nördliche westfälische Kohlenrevier in other industries. Among these 15 companies, the number of mandates that Essener Steinkohlenbergwerke AG had was five in Gelsenkirchener Bergwerks-AG and Vereinigte Stahlwerke AG and four in Dortmund-Hoerder Hüttenverein AG, Mitteldeutsche Stahlwerke AG, and Wasserwerk für das nördliche westfälische Kohlenrevier. In the remaining 10 enterprises, interlocking directorates were built through three mandates.

The number of enterprises in which Mannesmannröhren-Werke established interlocking directorates through more than three posts was five, namely, Magdeburger Bergwerks-AG in the mining industry; Rütgerswerke AG in the chemical industry; Siemens & Halske AG in the electrical industry; and Deutsche Erdöl-AG and Deutsche Petroleum AG in the oil industry. In all these five enterprises, interlocking directorates through three mandates were established.

The number of companies where Vereinigte Stahlwerke AG formed interlocking directorates through more than three mandates was 25. They were Bergbau AG Ewald-König Ludwig, Essener Bergwerks-Verein König Wilhelm, Essener Steinkohlenbergwerke AG, Gelsenkirchener Bergwerks-AG, Harpener Bergbau AG, Kaliwerke Aschersleben, Rheinisch-Westäflisches Kohlen-Syndikat, and Rheinische AG für Braunkohlenbergbau und Brikettfabrikation in the mining industry; Deutsche Edelstahlwerke AG, Dortmund-Hoerder Hüttenverein AG, Eisenwerk-Gesellschaft Maxiniliamshütte, Klöckner-Werke AG, Mitteldeutsche Stahlwerke AG, Rasselsteiner Eisenwerks-Gesellschaft AG, Rheinische Stahlwerke, and Ruhrstahl AG in the iron and steel industry; Metallgesellschaft AG in the metal producing and processing industries; A. Riebeck'sche Montanwerke AG, Dynamit AG, vorms. Alfred Nobel & Co., and Kokswerke und Chemische Fabriken AG in the chemical industry; AEG and Gesellschaft für elektrische Unternehmungen—Ludwig. Loewe & Co. AG in the electrical industry; Demag AG in the machine industry; and Rheinisch-Westäflische Kalkwerke and Wasserwerk für das nördliche westfälische Kohlenrevier in other industries. Among these 25 companies, the number of mandates that Vereinigte Stahlwerke AG had was seven in Harpener Bergbau AG and Mitteldeutsche Stahlwerke AG. Similarly, the number of mandates in Rheinische AG für Braunkohlenbergbau und Brikettfabrikation was six. Similar figures in Essener Steinkohlenbergwerke AG, Gelsenkirchener Bergwerks-AG, Ruhrstahl AG, and Demag AG were five, respectively. Vereinigte Stahlwerke AG held four posts in Kaliwerke Aschersleben, Deutsche Edelstahlwerke AG, Eisenwerk-Gesellschaft Maximilianshütte, Klöckner-Werke AG, Rheinische Stahlwerke, Dynamit AG, vorms. Alfred Nobel & Co., AEG, and Rheinisch-Westäflische Kalkwerke. In the remaining 10 enterprises, interlocking directorates were built through three mandates.

Cases where Siemens & Halske AG established interlocking directorates through more than three mandates can be observed in four enterprises: Mannesmannröhren-Werke in the iron and steel industry; Siemens-Planiawerke AG für Kohlefabrikate in the chemical industry; Siemens-Schuckertwerke AG in the electrical industry; and

Elektrizitäts-AG vorm. Schuckert & Co. in the electric power, gas, and energy industries. Among these four enterprises, in Siemens-Schuckertwerke AG, interlocking directorates were formed through five mandates. In the other three companies, Siemens & Halske AG built interlocking directorates through three posts.

The number of enterprises in which Rheinische Metallwaaren- und Maschinenfabrik (Rheinmetall-Borsig) established interlocking directorates through more than three mandates was four, namely, Innwerk, Bayerische Aluminium AG in the metal producing and processing industries; A. Borsig Maschinenbau AG in the machine industry; Deutsche Centralbodenkredit AG in the banking industry; and Elektrowerke AG in the electric power, gas, and energy industries. In all these enterprises, interlocking directorates were built through three posts.

The number of firms where Deutsche Hypothekenbank, Meiningen built interlocking directorates through more than three mandates was two: Consolidierte Alkaliwerke zu Westeregeln in the chemical industry and Deutsche Centralbodenkredit AG in the banking industry. In these firms, interlocking directorates were formed through three mandates.

In this way, in 49 enterprises, strong relationships of interlocking directorates through more than three mandates were established between seven second-party enterprises and third-party enterprises. Deutsche Bank had more than three mandates on the supervisory board of these seven third-party enterprises. Considering the distribution among industrial sectors, the number of enterprises was nine in the mining industry; similarly, ten in the iron and steel industry; two in the metal producing and processing industries; seven in the chemical industry; four in the electrical industry; three in the machine industry; three in the oil industry; two in the distributing industry; one in the banking industry; four in the electric power, gas, and energy industries; and four in other industries.

Such second-party enterprises were as follows: Bergbau AG Ewald-König Ludwig, Essener Bergwerks-Verein König Wilhelm, Magdeburger Bergwerks-AG, Gesellschaft für Kohlentechnik mbH, Concordia Bergbau AG, Gelsenkirchener Bergwerks-AG, Harpener Bergbau AG, Kaliwerke Aschersleben, and Rheinische AG für Braunkohlenbergbau und Brikettfabrikation in the mining industry; August-Thyssen Hütte AG, Bochumer Verein für Guβstahlfabrikation AG, Deutsche Edelstahlwerke AG, Eisenwerk-Gesellschaft Maximilianshütte, Dortmund-Hoerder Hüttenverein AG, Mitteldeutsche Stahlwerke AG, Ruhrstahl AG, Rasselsteiner Eisenwerks-Gesellschaft AG, Klöckner-Werke AG, and Rheinische Stahlwerke in the iron and steel industry; Innwerk, Bayerische Aluminium AG and Metallgesellschaft AG in the metal producing and processing industries; Ruhrchemie AG, Consolidierte Alkaliwerke zu Westeregeln, A. Riebeck'sche Montanwerke AG, Benzol-Verband GmbH, Kokswerke und Chemische Fabriken AG, Rütgerswerke AG, Dynamit AG vorm. Alfred Nobel & Co., and Siemens-Planiawerke AG für Kohlefabrikate in the chemical industry; AEG, Siemens-Schuckertwerke AG, and Gesellschaft für elektrische Unternehmungen—Ludwig. Loewe & Co. AG in the electrical industry; Hannoversche Maschinenbau AG vormals Georg Egestorff, A. Borsig Maschinenbau AG, and Demag AG in the machine industry; Deutsche Erdöl-AG, Ruhrbenzin AG, and Deutsche Petroleum AG in the oil industry; Deutsche

Ammonialverlaufsvereinigung (GmbH) and Verkaufsvereinigung für Teererzeugnisse GmbH in the distributing industry; Deutsche Centralbodenkredit AG in the banking industry; Rheinisch-Westfälisches Elektrizitätswerk AG, Ruhrgas AG, Elektrizitäts-AG vorm. Schuckert & Co., and Elektrowerke AG in the electric power, gas, and energy industries; and Wasserwerk für das nördliche westfälische Kohlenrevier, Westfälische Werkswohnungs-AG, Deutsches Kohlen-Depot, GmbH, and Rheinisch-Westäflische Kalkwerke in other industries.

Of these 49 third-party enterprises, 26 were enterprises in which Deutsche Bank built interlocking directorates through one or two mandates on the supervisory board. They were Magdeburger Bergwerks-AG, Concordia Bergbau AG, Gelsenkirchener Bergwerks-AG, Harpener Bergbau AG, Kaliwerke Aschersleben, and Rheinische AG für Braunkohlenbergbau und Brikettfabrikation in the mining industry; Klöckner-Werke AG and Rheinische Stahlwerke in the iron and steel industry; Metallgesellschaft AG in the metal producing and processing industries; A. Riebeck'sche Montanwerke AG, Benzol-Verband GmbH, Kokswerke und Chemische Fabriken AG, Rütgerswerke AG, Dynamit AG vorm. Alfred Nobel & Co., and Siemens-Planiawerke AG für Kohlefabrikate in the chemical industry; AEG, Siemens-Schuckertwerke AG, and Gesellschaft für elektrische Unternehmungen—Ludwig. Loewe & Co. AG in the electrical industry; A. Borsig Maschinenbau AG and Demag AG in the machine industry; Deutsche Petroleum AG in the oil industry; Deutsche Centralbodenkredit AG in the banking industry; Ruhrgas AG, Elektrizitäts-AG vorm. Schuckert & Co., and Elektrowerke AG in the electric power, gas, and energy industries; and Rheinisch-Westäflische Kalkwerke in other industries. Through interlocking directorates between second- and third-party enterprises, these 26 enterprises constituted the network of meetings built among members of enterprises with more than three mandates.

8.2 Dresdner Bank's Personnel Network Through Interlocking Directorate of Members of the Supervisory Board on Such Top Management Organ of Other Enterprises

8.2.1 Personnel Network and Its Characteristics

Regarding the personnel networks of three large banks, Sect. 8.2 examines the situation of Dresdner Bank's network.

The following numbers emerge when considering the centrality of each enterprise comprising the network and the upper 10 enterprises among Dresdner Bank and 187 companies with their interlocking directorates on the supervisory board in terms of the adjacency measured by the number of enterprises in which interlocking directorate is formed (see Table 8.2). There were two in the banking industry and one in the insurance industry as the financial sectors; two each in the mining and iron and steel industries; and one each in the chemical; electrical; and other industries. Adjacencies of the upper 10 enterprises ranged from 179 to 246. In terms of adjacency, AEG in the electrical industry (adjacency 246), Mitteldeutsche Stahlwerke AG in the iron and steel industry (similarly 244), and Vereinigte Stahlwerke AG in the iron and steel industry (243) ranked first, second, and third, respectively. Deutsche Centralbodenkredit-AG in the banking industry (adjacency 229), Rheinische AG für Braunkohlenbergbau und Brikettfabrikation in the mining industry (similarly 207), and Kokswerke und Chemische Fabriken AG in the chemical industry (199) were below fourth. Then, Allianz und Stuttgarter Verein Versicherungs-AG in the insurance industry (adjacency 197), Dresdner Bank in the banking industry (similarly 187), Deutsch-Atlantische Telegraphengesellschaft in other industries (183), and Harpener Bergbau AG in the mining industry (179) were below seventh.

In examining the centrality of enterprises at the upper 11–20 positions, there were five in the banking industry as the financial sector and one each in the mining; iron and steel; chemical; machine; and electric power, gas, and energy industries. Many enterprises existed in the banking industry. Adjacencies of enterprises at the upper 11–20 positions ranged from 137 to 162. In terms of the adjacency, Commerzbank (Commerz- und Privat-Bank AG) in the banking industry (adjacency 162) and Elektricitäts-Lieferungs-Gesellschaft mbH in the electric power, gas, and energy industries (similarly 153) ranked 11th and 12th, respectively. Then, Essener Steinkoholenbergwerke AG in the mining industry (adjacency 150), Allianz und Stuttgarter Lebensversicherungsbank AG in the banking industry (similarly 146), and AG für Waggonbauwerte AG (Linke-Hofmann-Busch-Werke AG) in the machine industry (145) ranked 13th, 14th, and 15th, respectively. Companies at the 16th position were Dynamit AG vormals Alfred Nobel & Co. in the chemical industry and Allgemeine Deutsche Creditanstalt in the banking industry (adjacency 142, respectively). Eisenwerk-Gesellschaft Maximilianshütte in the iron and steel industry (adjacency 141), Nordstern Lebensversicherungsbank-AG in the banking industry (similarly 138), and Deutsche Hypothekenbank, Meiningen in the banking industry (137) were below 18th.

The number of companies within the upper fifth positions measured by the adjacency was one in the banking industry as the financial sector, two in the iron and steel industry, one each in the mining industry, and one in the electrical industry. Deutsche Centralbodenkredit-AG ranked fourth. Moreover, one bank was within the upper ten enterprises. Dresdner Bank ranked eighth. Although centralities of some banks were relatively high, AEG, Mitteldeutsche Stahlwerke AG, Vereinigte Stahlwerke AG, and Rheinische AG für Braunkohlenbergbau and Brikettfabrikation ranked first, second, third, and fifth, respectively. Furthermore, notably, considerable adjacency of the upper 10 or 20 enterprises existed. The adjacency of AEG at the first position was 246. Similarly, the number of adjacencies of Kokswerke und Chemische Fabriken AG at the sixth position and Harpener Bergbau AG at the 10th position was 199 and 179, respectively. There were several enterprises in which interlocking directorates were built on the supervisory boards of other enterprises. In addition, in the case of Dresdner Bank's network, although some banks indicated relatively high centrality, many were not always in the upper position regarding adjacency. Rather, companies

Table 8.2 Centrality of member companies in the network of Dresdner Bank[a] (period of National Socialism)

Position	Company	Adjacency[b]	Industries
1	Allgemeine Elektricitäts-Gesellschaft	246	Electrical
2	Mitteldeutsche Stahlwerke AG	244	Iron and steel
3	Vereinigte Stahlwerke AG	243	Iron and steel
4	Deutsche Centralbodenkredit-AG	229	Banking
5	Rheinische AG für Braunkohlenbergbau und Brikettfabrikation	207	Mining
6	Kokswerke und Chemische Fabriken AG	199	Chemical
7	Allianz und Stuttgarter Verein Versicherungs AG	197	Insurance
8	*Dresdner Bank*[c]	187	Banking
9	Deutsch-Atlantische Telegraphengesellschaft	183	Other industries
10	Harpener Bergbau-AG	179	Mining
11	Commerz- und Privat-Bank AG	162	Banking
12	Elektricitäts-Lieferungs-Gesellschaft mbH	153	Electric power, gas, and energy
13	Essener Steinkohlenbergwerke AG	150	Mining
14	Allianz und Stuttgarter Lebensvericherungsbank AG	146	Banking
15	AG für Waggonbauwerte (Linke-Hofmann-Busch-Werke AG)	145	Machine
16	Dynamit AG vormals Alfred Nobel & Co	142	Chemical
16	Allgemeine Deutsche Creditanstalt	142	Banking
18	Eisenwerk-Gesellschaft Maximilianshütte	141	Iron and steel
19	Nordstern Lebensversicherungsbank-AG	138	Banking
20	Deutsche Hypothekenbank, Meiningen	137	Banking
21	Reichs-Kredit-Gesellschaft AG	136	Banking
22	Rheinische Metalwaaren- und Maschinenfabrik (Rheinmetall-Borsig)	130	Machine
23	Gesellschaft für Getreidehandel	126	Distributing
23	Gerling-Konzern Lebensversicherungs-AG	126	Insurance
25	Wintershall AG	122	Chemical
26	Universum-Film AG	120	Other industries

(continued)

Table 8.2 (continued)

Position	Company	Adjacency[b]	Industries
27	Deutsche Erdöl AG	119	Oil
28	Bank des Berliner Kassenvereins	109	Banking
29	Bank für Brau-Industrie	108	Banking
30	Niederschlesische Bergbau-AG	107	Mining
30	Kali-Chemie AG	107	Chemical
32	Braunkohlen- und Brikettwerke, Roddergrube AG	99	Mining
32	Norddeutscher Lloyd	99	Transportation
32	Hotelbetriebs-AG (Bistol, Kaiserhof, Bellevue, Balfie, Central-Hotel)	99	Other industries
35	Bayerische Stickstoff-Werke AG	95	Chemical
35	Deutsche Gesellschaft für öffentliche Arbeit AG	95	Other industries
37	Grube Leopold AG	92	Mining
37	Deutsche Bau- und Bodenbank AG	92	Banking
39	Waggon- und Maschinenfabrik AG vorm. Busch	90	Machine
39	Eisenbahn-Verkehrsmittel-AG	90	Machine

Note [a]Of Dresdner Bank AG and 187 enterprises in which it built direct interlocking directorates on their supervisory boards, upper 40 companies measured by adjacency are listed up
b"Centrality" is measured by an indicator "adjacency" that indicates number of companies in which interlocking directorate is built
[c]Company in italics is Dresdner Bank as the starting point of this network
Source This table was compiled by the author, based on Mossner (Hrsg) (1936)

with high centrality belonged to industries across some key sectors, such as iron and steel, chemical, and electrical industries. Therefore, leading companies in important major industries also assumed core positions in information flow and media of networks, including banks.

Regarding network cohesiveness, the density of Dresdner Bank's network was 0.0038978. Members of Dresdner Bank's supervisory board built interlocking directorates in similar top management groups in 187 companies as second-party enterprises. By contrast, the number of enterprises comprising the network, including second-party enterprises in which Dresdner Bank had mandates of the supervisory board and third-party enterprises in which second-party enterprises had supervisory board mandates, was 2331. This number was less than that of companies comprising the network, including second-party companies in which Deutsche Bank held posts of the supervisory board and third-party companies in which second-party companies had mandates of the supervisory board (2, 702).

8.2.2 Clique of Interlocking Supervisory Board Members

Next, a clique of interlocking supervisory board members with more than two mandates on such a top management organ of multiple companies, which plays significant roles in the network, is considered. This section analyzes the interlocking between supervisory board members in banks and those in industrial enterprises.

Cases in which multiple members of the supervisory board of Dresdner Bank have a mandate on such organ of other enterprises were observed in 14 companies. The total number of mandates was 28. The number of enterprises and mandates was much less than that of Deutsche Bank (corresponding numbers 31 and 70, respectively). Considering the distribution among industrial sectors, the number of enterprises in which interlocking directorate was formed was one in the iron and steel industry; similarly, one in the electrical industry; one in the machine industry; five in the banking industry; one in the insurance industry; one in the electric power, gas, and energy industries; and four in other industries. Such enterprises were Vereinigte Stahlwerke AG in the iron and steel industry; AEG in the electrical industry; Waggon- und Maschinenfabrik vorm. Busch in the machine industry; Hermes Kreditversicherungsbank AG, Allianz und Stuttgarter Lebensversicherungsbank AG, Commerz- und Privat-Bank-AG, Allgemeine Deutsche Creditanstalt, and Norddeutsche Kreditbank AG in the banking industry; Allianz und Stuttgarter Verein Versicherungs-AG in the insurance industry; Deutsche Electrizitätswerke zu Aachen Garbe, Lahmeyer & Co., AG in the electric power, gas, and energy industries; and Treuhand-Vereinigung AG, Universum-Film AG, Zucker-Raffinerie Hildesheim GmbH, and Gemeinnützige Baugesellschaft für Aachen und Burtscheid AG in other industries. Notably, interlocking directorates were formed through two posts in Comerz- und Privat-Bank AG as one of the strongest competitors for Dresdner Bank.

The number of supervisory board members of Dresdner Bank who held mandate on the supervisory board of the same enterprises was 15. Such persons were F. Andreae, G. Talbt, W. Kisskalt, F. Flick, B. Claußen, W. Koehler, C. A. Pastor, C. O. Schmelzer, J. Schwandt, K. Lindemann, W. Meinberg, K. Pfeiffer, C. Wenzel, E. Dircks, and F. A. Dufour von Feronce.

Of 14 companies in which multiplesupervisory board members of Dresdner Bank held mandate, F. Andreae and G. Talbot had mandates on the supervisory board of four other companies. F. Andreae had mandate of Waggon- und Maschinenfabrik vorm. Busch and mandates of the supervisory board except for the chairman and vice-chairman of Hermes Kreditversicherungsbank AG, Allianz und Stuttgarter Lebensversicherungsbank AG, and Universum-Film AG. G. Talbot held supervisory board mandates except for the chairman and vice-chairman of Vereinigte Stahlwerke AG, Deutsche Electrizitätswerke zu Aachen Garbe, Lahmeyer & Co., AG, Zucker-Raffinerie Hildesheim GmbH, and Gemeinnützige Baugesellschaft für Aachen und Burtscheid AG.

W. Kisskalt and F. Flick had mandates on the supervisory board of three other enterprises. W. Kisskalt had mandate of the chairman of Hermes Kreditversicherungsbank AG and posts of the supervisory board except for the chairman and vice-chairman of Allianz und Stuttgarter Lebensversicherungsbank AG and Allianz und Stuttgarter Verein Versicherungs-AG. F. Flick held mandate of the vice-chairman of Waggon- und Maschinenfabrik vorm. Busch and posts of the supervisory board except for the chairman and vice-chairman of Vereinigte Stahlwerke AG and AEG.

B. Claußen, W. Koehler, and C. A. Pastor held mandates on the supervisory board of two other companies. All mandates held by these three persons were supervisory board mandates, excluding the chairman and vice-chairman. B. Claußen had mandates of Commerz- und Privat-Bank-AG and Allgemeine Deutsche Creditanstalt. W. Koehler held mandates of Allgemeine Deutsche Creditanstalt and Norddeutsche Kreditbank AG. C. A. Pastr had posts of Deutsche Electrizitätswerke zu Aachen Garbe, Lahmeyer & Co., AG, and Gemeinnützige Baugesellschaft für Aachen und Burtscheid AG.

C. O. Schmelzer, J. Schwandt, K. Lindemann, W. Meinberg, K. Pfeffer, C. Wenzel, E. Dircks, and F. A. Dufour von Feronce had a mandate on the supervisory board of one other enterprise. All posts held by these persons were posts of the supervisory board, excluding the chairman and vice-chairman. O. O. Schmelzer had mandate of Waggon- und Maschinenfabrik vorm. Busch. J. Schwandt held mandate of Commerz- und Privat-Bank-AG. K. Lindemann had post of Norddeutsche Kreditbank AG. W. Mein berg held post of Allianz und Stuttgarter Verein Versicherungs-AG. K. Pfeiffer held mandate of Universum-Film AG. C. Wenzel had mandate of Zucker-Raffinerie Hildesheim GmbH. E. Dircks, and F. A. Dufour von Feronce had the post of Treuhand-Vereinigung AG, respectively (Mossner 1936, S. 23, 232, 280, 304–305, 387, 749, 790, 913–914, 987, 1139, 1158, 1371, 1452, 1569, 1693).

In Dresdner Bank's network, no case in which interlocking directorates were built through more than three mandates of the supervisory board and the network of meetings built among members of enterprises with more than three mandates did not exist. This point differed from the case of Deutsche Bank.

8.3 Commerzbank's Personnel Network Through Interlocking Directorate of Members of the Supervisory Board on Such Top Management Organ of Other Enterprises

8.3.1 Personnel Network and Its Characteristics

Following analysis in Sects. 8.1 and 8.2, conditions of Commerzbank's network are considered in this section.

Considering the centrality of each enterprise constituting the network and the upper 10 enterprises among Commerzbank and 162 companies with interlocking directorates on the supervisory board in terms of the adjacency measured by the number of enterprises where interlocking directorate is developed (see Table 8.3), the following numbers emerge. There were three in the banking industry and one in the insurance industry as the financial sector; two each in the iron and steel and electrical industries; and one each in the chemical and automobile industries. Adjacencies of high 10 enterprises ranged from 162 to 246. In terms of adjacency, AEG in the electrical industry (adjacency 246), Mitteldeutsche Stahlwerke AG in the iron and steel industry (similarly 244), and Vereinigte Stahlwerke AG in the iron and steel (243) ranked first, second, and third, respectively. Then, Deutsche Centralbodenkredit-AG in the banking industry (adjacency 229), Kokswerke und Chemische Fabriken AG in the chemical industry (similarly 199), and Allianz und Stuttgarter Verein Versicherungs-AG in the insurance industry (197) ranked below the fourth position. Daimler-Benz AG in the automobile industry (adjacency 191), Dresdner Bank in the banking industry (similarly 187), Gesellschaft für elektrische Unternehmungen—Ludwig. Loewe & Co. AG in the electrical industry (175), and Commerzbank (Commerz- und Privat-Bank AG) (162) ranked below seventh.

The number of centrality of firms at the upper 11–20 positions was three in the banking industry, one in the insurance industry as the financial sectors, and one each in the iron and steel; metal producing and processing; chemical; electrical; machine industry; and other industries. Adjacencies of enterprises at the upper 11–20 positions ranged from 128 to 160. In terms of the adjacency, Deutsch-Asiatische Bank in the banking industry (adjacency 160), AG für Waggonbauwerte (Linke-Hofmann-Busch AG) in the machine industry (145), and Feldmühle, Papier- und Zellstoffwerke AG in other industries (similarly 144) ranked 11th, 12th, and 13th, respectively. Then, Allgemeine Deutsche Creditanstalt in the banking industry (adjacency 142), Eisenwerk-Gesellschaft Maximilianshütte in the iron and steel industry (similarly 141), and Deutsche Hypothekenbank, Meiningen in the banking industry (137) ranked below the 14th. Gerling-Konzern Allgemeine Versicherungs-AG in the insurance industry (adjacency 134) ranked 17th. Then, AG für Bergbau, Blei- und Zinkfabrikation zu Stollberg und in Westfalen in the metal producing and processing industries and A. Riebeck'sche Montanwerke AG in the chemical industry (adjacency 133) ranked 18th. Furthermore, Elektrische Licht- und Kraftanlagen AG in the electrical industry (adjacency 128) ranked 20th.

When considering companies within the upper fifth positions measured by adjacency, there was one in the banking industry as the financial sector, two in the iron and steel industry, and one each in the chemical and electrical industries. Deutsche Centralbodenkredit-AG ranked fourth. However, one bank was within the upper five enterprises. Dresdner Bank ranked eighth. Commerzbank ranked 10th. AEG, Mitteldeutsche Stahlwerke AG, Vereinigte Stahlwerke AG, and Kokswerke und Chmeische Fabriken AG ranked first, second, third, and fifth, respectively. Furthermore, notably, numerical figures of adjacency of the upper 10 or 20 enterprises were very high. The adjacency of AEG in the first position was 246 and that of Allianz und Stuttgarter Verin Versicherungs-AG in the sixth position was 197. Then, the adjacency of Deutsch-Asiatische Bank was 160 and at the 11th position. There were several enterprises in which interlocking directorates were built on the supervisory board of other enterprises. In addition to the case of Deutsche Bank's network, although some banks indicated relatively high centrality, many were not always in the upper position regarding adjacency. Rather, firms with high centrality belonged

Table 8.3 Centrality of member companies in the network of Commerzbank[a] (period of National Socialism)

Position	Company	Adjacency[b]	Industries
1	Allgemeine Elektricitäts-Gesellschaft	246	Electrical
2	Mitteldeutsche Stahlwerke AG	244	Iron and steel
3	Vereinigte Stahlwerke AG	243	Iron and steel
4	Deutsche Centralbodenkredit-AG	229	Banking
5	Kokswerke und Chemische Fabriken AG	199	Chemical
6	Allianz und Stuttgarter Verein Versicherungs AG	197	Insurance
7	Daimler-Benz AG	191	Automobile
8	Dresdner Bank AG	187	Banking
9	Gesellschaft für elektrische Unternehmungen- Ludw.Loewe & Co.AG	175	Electrical
10	*Commerz- und Privat-Bank AG*[c]	162	Banking
11	Deutsch-Asiatische Bank	160	Banking
12	AG für Waggonbauwerte (Linke-Hofmann-Busch AG)	145	Machine
13	Feldmühle, Papier- und Zellstoffwerke AG	144	Other industries
14	Allgemeine Deutsche Creditanstalt	142	Banking
15	Eisenwerk-Gesellschaft Maximilianshütte	141	Iron and steel
16	Deutsche Hypothekenbank, Meiningen	137	Banking
17	Gerling-Konzern Allgemeine Versicherungs AG	134	Insurance
18	AG für Bergbau, Blei- und Zinkfabrikation zu Stollberg und in Westfalen	133	Metal producing and processing
18	A.Riebeck'sche Montanwerke AG	133	Chemical
20	Elektrische Licht- und Kraftanlagen AG	128	Electrical
21	Gesellschaft für Getreidehandel	126	Distributing
21	Rheinisch-Westfälische Boden-Credit-Bank	126	Banking
21	Gerling-Konzern Lebensversicherungs AG	126	Insurance
24	Vereinigte Industrie-Unternehmungen AG	120	Other industries

(continued)

Table 8.3 (continued)

Position	Company	Adjacency[b]	Industries
25	Deutscher Eisenhandel AG	115	Distributing
26	Kaliwerke Aschersleben	112	Mining
27	Klöckner-Werke AG	110	Iron and steel
28	Westdeutsche Bodenkreditanstalt	108	Banking
29	Kali-Chemie AG	107	Chemical
29	Allgemeine Gas- und Elektricitäts-Gesellschaft	107	Electric power, gas, and energy
29	Braunkohlenindustrie AG Zukunft	107	Mining
32	Maschinenfabrik Buckau R.Wolf AG	105	Machine
33	Schultheiss-Patzenhofer Brauerei-AG	103	Distillation
34	Hotelbetriebs-AG (Bistol, Kaiserhof, Bellevue, Balfie, Central-Hotel)	99	Other industries
35	Buders'sche Eisenwerke	97	Iron and steel
36	Deutsche Gesellschaft für öffentliche Arbeit AG	95	Other industries
37	Concordia Lebens-Versicherungs-Bank AG	93	Banking
38	Schering-Kahlbaum AG	92	Chemical
39	Berlin-Karlsruher Industriewerke AG vormals Deutsche Waffen- und Munitionsfabriken	89	Metal producing and processing
40	Ilse Bergbau-AG	85	Mining
40	Portland-Zementwerke Dyckerhoff-Wicking AG (Mainz-Amneburg)	85	Other industries

Note [a]Of Commerz- und Privat-Bank AG and 162 enterprises in which it built direct interlocking directorates on their supervisory boards, upper about a fourth companies measured by adjacency are listed up

[b]"Centrality" is measured by an indicator "adjacency" that indicates number of companies in which interlocking directorate is built

[c]Company in italics is Commerz- und Privat-Bank AG as the starting point of this network

Source This table was compiled by the author, based on Mossner (Hrsg) (1936)

to industries across some key sectors, such as the iron and steel, chemical, and electrical industries. Therefore, representative enterprises in important major industries also assumed core positions in information flow and media of networks, including banks.

Concerning the network's cohesiveness, the density of Commerzbank's network was 0.003738. Members of Commerzbank's supervisory board developed interlocking directorates in a similar top management organ in 162 companies as second-party enterprises. By contrast, the number of enterprises constituting the network, including second-party enterprises in which Commerzbank had posts of the supervisory board and third-party enterprises where second-party enterprises had posts of the supervisory board, was 2290. This number was less than that of companies comprising the network, including second-party companies in which Deutsche Bank held posts of the supervisory board and third-party companies where second-party companies had mandates of the supervisory board (2702). However, this number was almost the same as that of companies comprising the network, including second-party companies in which Dresdner Bank held mandates of the supervisory board and third-party firms in which second-party companies had posts of the supervisory board (2, 331).

8.3.2 *Clique of Interlocking Supervisory Board Members*

Next, a clique of interlocking supervisory board members with more than two mandates on such a top management organ of multiple companies, which plays significant roles in the network, is considered. This section analyzes the interlocking between supervisory board members in banks and those in industrial enterprises.

Cases in which multiple members of the supervisory board of Commerzbank have a mandate on such an organ of other enterprises were observed in 16 companies. The total number of mandates was 34. Considering the distribution among industrial sectors, the number of enterprises in which interlocking directorates were formed was one in the mining industry; similarly, two in the iron and steel industry; one in the metal producing and processing industries; one in the chemical industry; one in the distillation industry; five in the banking industry; one in the insurance industry; one in the electric power, gas, and energy industries; one in the transportation industry, and two in other industries. Such enterprises were Burbach-Kaliwerke AG in the mining industry, Buderus'sche Eisenwerke and Hüttenwerke C. Wilhelm Kayser & Co. in the iron and steel industry; Berlin-Karlsruher Industrie-Werke in the metal producing and processing industries; Consolidierte Alkaliwerke in the chemical industry; Schultheiss-Patzenhofer Brauerei AG in the distillation industry; Deutsche Hypothekenbank, Meiningen, Deutsche Schiffsbeleihungs-Bank AG, Waaren-Commissions-Bank, Westdeutsche Bodenkreditanstalt AG, and Dresdner Bank in the banking industry; Elbe und Saale Versicherungs-AG in the insurance industry; Hamburgische Elektricitäts-Werke AG in electric power, gas, and energy industries; Neue Deutsch-Böhmische Elbe-Schifffahrts-AG in the transportation industry; and Hansa-Mühle AG (Hanseatische Mühlenwerke AG) and Treuhand AG in other industries.

The number of supervisory board members of Commerzbank who held mandate on the supervisory board of the same enterprises was 15. Such persons were F.

Reinhart, M. Schulze, A. Katzenellenbogen, F. H. Witthoefft, C. L. Nottebohm, P. Rohde, A. Bannwarth, E. Kaempfert, R. Schoepf, E. F. Rechberg, H. von Stein, H. Diederichsen, H. Haney, B. Klaußen, and J. Schwandt.

Of 16 companies in which multiple supervisory board members of Commerzbank held mandate, F. Reinhart had mandates on the supervisory board of six other companies. He had mandates of the chairman of Hüttenwerke C. Wilhelm Kayser & Co. and Deutsche Hypothekenbank, Meiningen, a vice-chairman mandate of Schultheiss Patzenhofer Brauerei AG, and mandates of the supervisory board except for the chairman and vice-chairman of Buderus'sche Eisenwerke, Berlin-Karlsruher Industrie-Werke AG, and Consolidierte Alkaliwerke. M. Schulze and A. Katzenellenbogen had mandates on the supervisory board of four other companies. M. Schulze held mandates of the chairman of Neue Deutsch-Böhmische Elbe-Schifffahrts-AG and Treuhand AG and supervisory board posts except for the chairman and vice-chairman of Burbach-Kaliwerke AG and Hansa-Mühle AG (Hanseatische Mühlenwerke AG). A. Katzenellenbogen held mandates of the chairman of Buderus'sche Eisenwerke and posts of the supervisory board except for the chairman and vice-chairman of Consolidierte Alkaliwerke, Deutsche Hypothekenbank, Meiningen, and Westdeutsche Bodenkreditanstalt AG. F. H. Witthoefft held mandates on the supervisory board of three other firms. He had a mandate of the chairman of Hansa-Mühle AG (Hanseatische Mühlenwerke AG) and supervisory board mandates excluding the chairman and vice-chairman of Waaren-Commissions-Bank and Hamburgische Elektricitäts-Werke AG. Notably, interlocking directorates were built through popular mandates in Dresdner Bank as one of the strongest competitors for Commerzbank.

C. L. Nottebohm, P. Rohde, A. Bannwarth, E. Kaempfert, and R. Schoepf had mandates on the supervisory boards of two other companies. C. L. Nottebohm held the mandate of the chairman of Deutsche Schiffsbeleihungs-Bank AG and the post of the supervisory board except for the chairman and vice-chairman of Hamburgische Elektricitäts-Werke AG. P. Rohde had mandate of the vice-chairman of Berlin-Karlsruher Industrie-Werke AG and supervisory board mandate except for the chairman and vice-chairman of Elbe und Saale Versicherungs-AG. A. Bannwarth had mandates of the supervisory board excluding the chairman and vice-chairman of Hamburgische Elektricitäts-Werke AG and Hansa-Mühle AG (Hanseatische Mühlenwerke AG). E. Kaempfert held similar posts of Neue Deutsch-Böhmische Elbe-Schifffahrts-AG and Treuhand AG. R. Schoepf had mandates similar to Hüttenwerke C. Wilhelm Kayser & Co. and Schultheiss-Patzenhofer Brauerei AG.

E. F. Rechberg, H. von Stein, H. Diederichsen, H. Haney, B. Klaußen, and J. Schwandt had a mandate on the supervisory board of one other enterprise. All mandates held by these six persons were posted on the supervisory board except for the chairman and vice-chairman. E. F. Rechberg had a mandate of Burbach-Kaliwerke AG. H. von Stein held a mandate of Deutsche Schiffsbeleihungs-Bank AG. H. Diederichsen had one post of Waaren-Commissions-Bank. H. Haney held a mandate of Bodenkreditanstalt AG. Then, B. Klaußen and J. Schwandt had one post of Dresdner Bank (Mossner 1936, S. 52, 232, 270, 544–545, 704, 718–719, 1103, 1217, 1231, 1279, 1412, 1439–1440, 1452, 1526, 1736–1737).

Furthermore, considering the network of meetings built among members of enterprises with more than three mandates, the following conditions can be observed in two enterprises. Strong interlocking directorates were established between Commerzbank and Hamburgische Elektricitäts-Werke AG in the electric power, gas, and energy industries and between Commerzbank and Hansa-Mühle AG (Hanseatische Mühlenwerke AG) in other industries. In Hansa-Mühle AG (Hanseatische Mühlenwerke AG), F. H. Witthoefft had a mandate of chairman, whereas A. Bannwarth and M. Schulze held one supervisory board post except for the chairman and vice-chairman. In Hamburgische Elektricitäts-Werke AG, F. H. Witthoefft, C. L. Nottebohm, and A. Bannwarth had one mandate of the supervisory board except for the chairman and vice-chairman. However, these two enterprises were second-party enterprises in which Commerzbank had three mandates on the supervisory boards, and no interlocking directorate was established through three mandates between second-party and third-party enterprises, where second-party enterprises held post the supervisory board. Therefore, the network of meetings built among members of enterprises with more than three mandates did not exist. This point differed from the case of Deutsche Bank.

8.4 Comparison of Personnel Networks of Three Large Banks

Sections 8.1, 8.2 and 8.3 analyzed the personnel networks of three large banks, namely, Deutsche Bank, Dresdner Bank, and Commerzbank, which were built through interlocking directorates of the members of the supervisory board on the same top management organ of other companies, including second- and third-party enterprises. This subsection compares the networks of each bank.

Densities of Deutsche Bank, Dresdner Bank, and Commerzbank indicated the network's cohesiveness: 0.004494, 0.0038978, and 0.003738, respectively. Among these three banks, the cohesiveness of the network of Deutsche Bank was the highest. The cohesiveness of the network of Dresdner Bank was only slightly higher than that of Commerzbank. The total number of enterprises comprising the network, including second- and third-party enterprises in the Deutsche Bank network, was 2702. Similarly, those of Dresdner Bank and Commerzbank networks were 2331 and 2290, respectively. The total numbers of mandates in the networks of Deutsche Bank, Dresdner Bank, and Commerzbank were 16,398, 10,536, and 9891, respectively (these figures were calculated by the author, based on Mossner 1936). The difference in the total number of mandates between Deutsche Bank's network and the other two bank's networks was significant compared to the number of enterprises composing the network. This concerns the difference in the density of the networks between Deutsche Bank and the other two banks. There were no considerable differences in the number of enterprises that constituted a network, including second- and third-party companies and mandate between Dresdner Bank's network and Commerzbank's network, which was concerned with the similarity of densities of these two bank's networks.

Regarding the centrality, in the order of adjacency of three large banks in their own networks, Deutsche Bank, Dresdner Bank, and Commerzbank, in their own networks ranked first, eighth, and tenth, respectively. The number of banks in the upper 10 enterprises was two in the networks of Deutsche Bank and Dresdner Bank, whereas that in the network of Commerzbank was three. The number of banks in the upper five enterprises was two in the networks of Deutsche Bank and each one in the networks of Dresdner Bank and Commerzbank, respectively. The number of banks in the upper 20 enterprises was four, seven, and six in the networks of Deutsche Bank, Dresdner Bank, and Commerzbank, respectively. Then, the number of insurance companies in the upper 10 enterprises was each 1 in the networks of Dresdner Bank and Commerzbank. There was no insurance company in the network of Deutsche Bank. Therefore, in all networks of three large banks, some banks were relatively influential from the centrality perspective. However, the condition in which many banks were in the upper position was not always observed. Rather, industries to which companies with high centrality belonged spread over some key industrial sectors.

When considering industrial enterprise in the upper 10 enterprises in the network of each of the three large banks, the number of enterprises in the mining industry was two in the Deutsche Bank and Dresdner Bank networks. There was no mining company in the network of Commerzbank. Similarly, that in the enterprise in the iron steel industry was one, two, and two in networks of Deutsche Bank, Dresdner Bank, and Commerzbank, respectively. The number of enterprises in the chemical industry in the upper 10 enterprises was one each in networks of three banks. The number of enterprises in the electrical industry in the upper 10 enterprises was two in the network of Commerzbank and one each in the Deutsche Bank and Dresdner Bank networks. Then, similarly, the number of enterprises in the automobile industry was one each in the Deutsche Bank and Commerzbank networks. There was no automobile enterprise in the network of Dresdner Bank. The number of enterprises in the electric power, gas, and energy industries in the upper 10 enterprises was one in the network of Deutsche Bank. However, there was no enterprise in this industrial sector in the networks of the other two banks.

Four companies were in the upper 10 enterprises in all networks of the three largest banks. By adjacency, in networks of Dresdner Bank and Commerzbank, AEG in the electrical industry ranked first. It also ranked second in the network of Deutsche Bank. Then, in networks of Deutsche Bank, Dresdner Bank, and Commerzbank, Vereinigte Stahlwerke AG, in the iron and steel industry, ranked third. In the networks of Deutsche Bank, Dresdner Bank, and Commerzbank, Deutsche Centralbodenkredit-AG in the banking industry ranked fourth. Kokswerke und Chemische Fabriken AG in the chemical industry ranked fifth in the network of Commerzbank and sixth in the networks of Deutsche Bank and Dresdner Bank.

The number of enterprises in the upper 10 in the networks of two banks was five. The number of enterprises in the upper 10 in the networks of Deutsche Bank and Dresdner Bank was two. Rheinische AG für Braunkohlenbergbau und

Brikettfabrikation in the mining industry and Deutsch-Atlantische Telegraphengesellschaft ranked fifth and ninth in the networks of these two banks, respectively. The number of enterprises in the upper 10 in the networks of Deutsche Bank and Commerzbank was only one. Daimler-Benz AG ranked seventh in the networks of these two banks. The number of enterprises in the upper 10 enterprises in the networks of Dresdner Bank and Commerzbank was two. Mitteldeutsche Stahlwerke AG in the iron and steel industry ranked second in the networks of both banks. Allianz und Stuttgarter Verein Versicherungs-AG in the insurance industry ranked sixth in Commerzbank's network and seventh in Dresdner Bank's network. In this way, the same company at the highest position measured by adjacency in networks of three large banks or two banks existed. This is one of the important characteristics of the personnel networks of the three largest banks.

Considering the network of meetings built among members of enterprises with more than three mandates, in the network of Deutsche Bank, there were seven cases in which members of the supervisory board of this bank built interlocking directorates through more than three mandates on the supervisory board of other enterprises. In addition, in many cases, supervisory board members of second-party enterprises in which Deutsche Bank had formed an interlocking directorate had more than three interlocking posts on the supervisory board of third-party enterprises. The number of such enterprises was 49. By contrast, there was no case in which Dresdner Bank built an interlocking directorate through more than three mandates on the supervisory board of other companies. In the network of Commerzbank, there were two cases where supervisory board members of this bank established interlocking directorates through more than three posts on the supervisory board of other enterprises. However, there were no cases in which an interlocking directorate was formed by the supervisor board member of second-party enterprises through three mandates in third-party enterprises. In the networks of Dresdner Bank and Commerzbank, no network of meetings was built among members of enterprises with more than three mandates. Therefore, in Deutsche Bank's network, a close personnel network that connected cliques who played significant roles in information flow and media and the discussion inside the network through more interlocking mandates was established.

In the personnel networks of banks, the centrality of banks was not always high compared with that of industrial enterprises. The centrality of banks was also not necessarily high in their own network. Therefore, banks were not always in a decisive position in the flow and media of information as an essential function of the personnel network. In this meaning, representative large enterprises in the key industrial sector, such as the iron and steel, chemical, electrical, and automobile industries, including large banks, were also at the core position in the function of the network as an information bank.

Extending the analyses in this chapter, the structure of personnel networks of the three largest banks after World War II and their characteristics are explained. The following chapter considers these research topics.

References

Eglau HO (1990) Wie Gott in Frankfurt: Die Deutsche Bank und die deutsche Industrie, 3rd edn. Econ Verlag, Düsseldorf

Hannemann RA, Riddle M (2011) Concepts and measures for basic network analysis. In: Scott J, Carrington PJ (eds) The SAGE handbook of social network analysis. SAGE, London, pp 340–369

Mossner J (Hrsg) (1936) Adressbuch der Direktoren und Aufsichtsräte 1936. Bd.I, Nach Personen geordnet, Finanz-Verlag, Berlin

Nakata N, Hosoi K, Iwanami F (1997) Kigyokan no Jinteki nettowaku—Torishimariyaku kenninsei no nitibei hikaku—(Personnel networks between enterprises—comparison of interlocking directorships in Japan and the United States—). Dobunkan, Tokyo

Pfeiffer H (1986a) Das Netwerk der Groβbanken. Personelle Verflechtungen mit Konzernen, Staat und ideologischen Apparaten. In: Blätter für deutsche und Internationale Politik 31(2):161–177

Pfeiffer H (1986b) Groβbanken und Finanzgruppen. Ausgewählte Ergebnisse einer Untersuchung der personellen Verflechtungen von Deutscher, Dresdner und Commerzbank. In: WSI Mitteilungen 39(7):473–481

Pfeiffer H (1993) Die Macht der Banken. Die personellen Verflechtungen der Commerzbank, der Deutschen Bank und der Dresdner Bank mit Unternehemen. Campus, Frankfurt am Main

Stanzick K-H (1969) Der ökonomische Konzentrationsproze. In: Schäfer G, Nedelmann C (Hrsg) Der CDU-Staat. Analysen zur Verfassungswriklichkeit der Bundesrepublik, Bd.I, 2. Aufl., Schurkamp, München, S. 48–79

Chapter 9
Bank's Personnel Networks Through Interlocking Directorates of Members of the Supervisory Board on Such Top Management Organs of Other Enterprises After World War II: Analysis of Period After the Enactment of the 1965 Corporations Law

Abstract Based on results in Chap. 8, this chapter considers the personnel networks of the three largest banks, including the second- and third-party companies, after World War II using social network analysis. This chapter also compares the network of each bank. Then, this chapter examines the conditions in the late 1960s, the period after the enactment of the 1965 Corporations Law, which regulated the limitation of the number of mandates one person may have on the supervisory board. The late 1960s were chosen because the basic system of interlocking directorates in postwar Germany was established during this time. This chapter analyzes the "cohesiveness" of the network of each bank and enterprise at a core position in the information flow and media of the network and industrial sector to which such an enterprise belonged. Through these discussions, the characteristics of each bank's network are clarified.

Keywords Bank · Industrial enterprise · Industry–bank relationship · Interlocking directorate · Personnel network · Social network analysis · The 1965 Corporations Law

The previous chapter examined the structure of personnel networks of the three largest banks, including second- and third-party enterprises, which were built through interlocking directorates of the members of the supervisory boards during the Social Nationalism period before World War II. Extending the discussions in Chap. 8, this chapter considers the conditions of similar personnel networks of these banks after World War II using social network analysis. This chapter examined the conditions during the late 1960s that were established and maintained as a basic system of interlocking directorates in postwar Germany under the influence of the 1965 Corporations Law. This system regulated the number of mandates that one person may have on

T. Yamazaki, *Relationships Between Industry and Bank in Germany*,
https://doi.org/10.1007/978-981-97-4996-6_9

the supervisory board (Pfeiffer 1986a, S. 477, 1986b, S. 164, 1993, SS. 158–159; Stanzick 1969, S. 72: Eglau 1990, S. 128). Therefore, this chapter analyzes the fundamental structure of a personnel network formed through interlocking directorates between supervisory board members.

As analyzed in Chap. 8, this chapter discusses the personnel network, focusing on two key concepts of social network analysis. Such concepts are "density" as an indicator for grasping the cohesiveness of a network and "centrality" as an indicator of understanding which enterprise is in a core position among companies comprising a concerned network in the information flow and media. In addition, this chapter considers the network paying attention to "multiplicity" as an essential indicator that helps understand which company has many mandates on the supervisory board of other enterprises. Moreover, a clique of interlocking supervisory board members with more than two mandates on such top management organs of multiple companies and play significant roles in the network is considered.

First, Sect. 9.1 considers Deutsche Bank's network built through the interlocking directorate of members of the supervisory board on the same top management organ of other companies, including second- and third-party enterprises. Dresdner Bank's and Commerzbank's networks will be analyzed in Sects. 9.2 and 9.3, respectively.

9.1 Deutsche Bank's Personnel Network Through Interlocking Directorate of Members of the Supervisory Board on Such Top Management Organ of Other Enterprises

9.1.1 Personnel Network and Its Characteristics

First, the conditions of Deutsche Bank's network are analyzed in Sect. 9.1. Regarding the centrality of each enterprise that constituted a network, in looking at the upper 10 enterprises among Deutsche Bank and 65 companies in which this bank developed interlocking directorates on the supervisory board in terms of the adjacency measured by the number of enterprises where interlocking directorate is established (see Table 9.1), the number of such company was two in the banking sector and each one in the insurance, mining, iron and steel, metal and metal processing, chemical, electrical, automobile, and electric power, gas, and energy industries. The adjacency of the upper 10 enterprises ranged from 57 to 80. In terms of the adjacency, Deutsche Ueberseeische Bank in the banking sector (adjacency 80), Rheinisch-Westfälisches Elektrizitätswerke AG in the electric power industry (similar numerical Fig. 77), and Preuβag AG in the mining industry (similar numerical Fig. 74) ranked first, second, and third, respectively. Daimler-Benz AG in the automobile industry (adjacency 66), Deutsche Bank in the banking sector, Degussa AG in the chemical industry (corresponding numbers 65, respectively), and Siemens AG in the electrical industry (corresponding number 63) were below fourth. Then, Allianz Versicherungs-AG in the insurance industry (adjacency 62), Fried. Krupp GmbH in the iron and steel industry, and Metallgesellschaft in the metal producing and processing industries (similar numerical Figs. 57) were below eighth.

The number of companies within the upper fifth positions (six companies owing to the existence of two enterprises in the fifth position) measured by the adjacency was two in the banking sector and each one in the mining, chemical, automobile, and electric power, gas, and energy industries.

In this way, although the centralities of some banks were relatively high, many banks were not always in the upper position in terms of adjacency. Rather, industries to which companies with high centrality belonged spread over some key industrial sectors and the electric power industry. Therefore, enterprises in important major industries also took the core position in information flow and media of networks, including banks. Fried. Krupp GmbH took the ninth position, indicating relatively high network centrality. The reason is that its relationship with banks was important and strong because this enterprise was a parent company of the Krupp Group.

Concerning the network's cohesiveness, the density of Deutsche Bank's network was 0.0077138. The number of companies as second-party enterprises in which members on the supervisory board of Deutsche Bank built an interlocking directorate in a similar top management organ was 65. By contrast, the number of enterprises comprising a network including second- and third-party enterprises was 702.

9.1.2 Clique of Interlocking Supervisory Board Members

Next, a clique of interlocking supervisory board members with more than two mandates on such a top management organ of other companies, which plays a significant role in the network, is considered. Interlocking supervisory board members who connect those in banks with those in industrial enterprises and combine those in industrial enterprises mutually can be grasped through such analysis.

Cases in which plural members of the supervisory board of Deutsche Bank have mandates on such organ of the same other enterprises were observed in 12 companies. These were BASF AG, Zellstofffabrik Waldhof, Glanzstoff AG in the chemical industry, Siemens AG, and Robert Bosch GmbH in the electrical industry; Klöckner-Humboldt Deutz AG and Pittler Maschinenfabrik AG in the machine industry; Deutsche Linoleum-Werke AG in the textile, spinning, and woven goods industries; Allianz Versicherungs-AG, Albingia Versicherungs.-AG in the insurance industry; and Nordwestdeutshe Kraftwerke AG and Preussische Elektrizitätswerke AG in the electric power, gas, and energy industries. The supervisory board members of Deutsche Bank with mandates on the supervisory board of other enterprises were H. J. Abs, H. L. Merkle, G. Henle, C. Wurster, H. P. Kemper, E. von Siemens, H. Küppenbender, H. Helms, and G. Meysenberg.

In these, 12 enterprises, H. J. Abs had mandates on the supervisory board of five other companies. He had posts of the honorary chairman in Zellstofffabrik Waldhof and Pittler Maschinenfabrik AG, the chairman post in Glanzstoff AG, and mandates

Table 9.1 Centrality of member companies in the network of Deutsche Bank[a] (period after the 1965 Corporations Law)

Position	Company	Adjacency[b]	Industries
1	Deutsche Ueberseeische Bank	80	Banking
2	Rheinisch-Westfälisches Elektrizitätswerk AG	77	Electric power, gas, and energy
3	Preussag AG	74	Mining
4	Daimler-Benz AG	66	Automobile
5	*Deutsche Bank AG*[c]	65	Banking
5	Degussa AG 65	65	Chemical
7	Siemens AG	63	Electrical
8	Allianz Versicherungs-AG	62	Insurance
9	Fried. Krupp GmbH	57	Iron and steel
9	Metallgesellschaft AG	57	Metal producing and processing
11	Karstadt AG	56	Distributing
11	Allianz Lebensversicherungs-AG	56	Insurance
13	Süddeutsche Zucker-AG	55	Other industries
14	Rütgerswerke und Teerverwertung AG	51	Chemical
15	VTG (Vereinigte Tanklager und Transportmittel GmbH)	50	Transportation
16	Deutsche Linoleum-Werke AG	46	Textile and spinning and woven goods
17	Gelsenkirchener Bergwerke AG	45	Mining
18	Bayer AG	45	Chemical
19	Otto Wolff AG	44	Iron and steel
20	Deutsche Continental-Gas-Gesellschaft	43	Electric power, gas, and energy
21	Nordwestdeutsche Kraftwerke AG	42	Electric power, gas, and energy
22	Brown, Boveri & Cie AG	42	Electrical
23	Deutsche Lufthansa AG	41	Transportation
24	Hoesch AG	39	Iron and steel
25	Hibernia AG	38	Mining
26	Glanzstoff AG	37	Chemical
27	Preuβische Elektrizitäts AG	36	Electric power, gas, and energy
28	Continental Gummi-Werke AG	35	Chemical
29	Zellstofffabrik Waldhof	35	Chemical
30	Gebr. Stumm GmbH	34	Mining

(continued)

Table 9.1 (continued)

Position	Company	Adjacency[b]	Industries
30	Klöckner-Werke AG	34	Iron and steel
30	Rheinische Braunkohlenwerke AG	34	Mining
33	Hugo Stinnes AG	33	Iron and steel

Note [a] Of Deutsche Bank and 65 enterprises in which it built direct interlocking directorates on their supervisory boards, upper half companies measured by adjacency are listed up
[b] "Centrality" is measured by an indicator "adjacency" that indicates number of companies in which interlocking directorate is built
[c] Company in italics is Deutsche Bank as the starting point of this network
Source This table was compiled by the author, based on Mossner (Hrsg) (1971)

of the vice-chairman in BASF AG and Siemens AG. H. L. Merkle and G Henle held mandates on the supervisory board of four other enterprises. Then, Merkle had posts of the vice-chairman in BASF AG and Deutsche Linoleum-Werke AG and those of the supervisory board except for the chairman and vice-chairman in Zellstofffabrik Waldhof and Glanzstoff AG. G. Henle had mandates of the chairman in Klöckner-Humboldt Deutz AG and Allianz Versicherungs-AG and supervisory board mandates except for the chairman and vice-chairman in Siemens AG and Albingia Versicherungs.-AG. C. Wurster and H. P. Kemper held posts on the supervisory board of three other companies. Wurster had mandates of the chairman in BASF AG and Robert Bosch GmbH and supervisory board post, excluding the chairman and vice-chairman in Allianz Versicherungs-AG. Kemper held posts of the chairman in Nordwestdeutsche Kraftwerke AG and Preussische Elektrizitätswerke AG and supervisory board mandate excluding the chairman and vice-chairman in Deutsche Linoleum-Werke AG. E. von Siemens, H. Küppenbender, and G. Meysenberg had mandates on the supervisory board of two other companies. Then, E. von Siemens held post of the chairman in Siemens and the supervisory board mandate, excluding the chairman and vice-chairman in Klöckner-Humboldt Deutz AG. Küppenbender had the mandate of the chairman in Pittler Maschinenfabrik AG and the supervisory board mandate, excluding the chairman and vice-chairman in Robert Bosch GmbH. Meysenberg had supervisory board mandates except for the chairman and vice-chairman in Nordwestdeutsche Kraftwerke AG and Preussische Elektrizitätswerke AG. Then, Helms had a supervisory board mandate except for the chairman and vice-chairman in Albingia Versicherungs-AG (Mossner 1971, S. 1, 292, 295, 375, 436, 514, 523, 754).

Furthermore, considering the network of meetings built among members of enterprises with more than three mandates (Fig. 9.1), the following conditions can be observed. Strong interlocking directorates were established between Deutsche Bank and BASF AG in the chemical industry; between Deutsche Bank AG and Siemens AG in the electrical industry and between Deutsche Bank AG and Allianz Versicherungs-AG in the insurance industry through three mandates. In addition, strong relationships of interlocking directorates were built through seven posts between Allianz Versicherungs-AG and Siemens AG, which were second-party enterprises in which

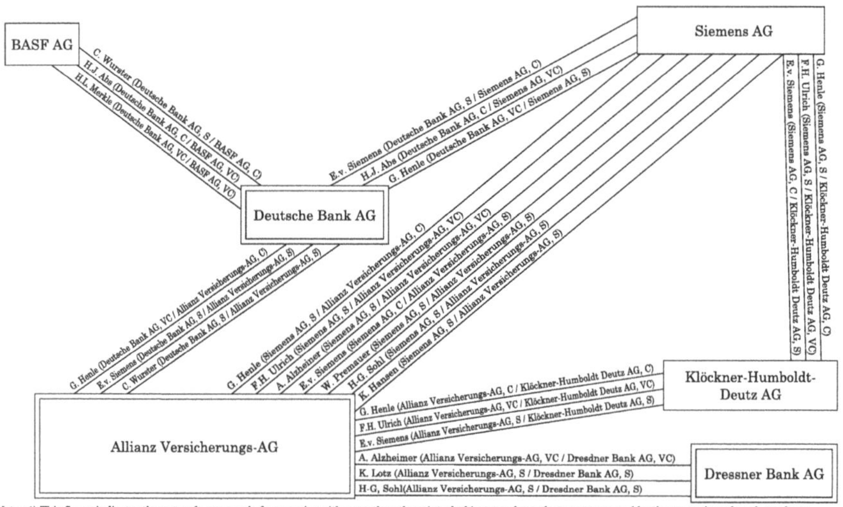

Note : 1) This figure indicates the network composed of companies with more than three interlocking mandates that was connected by the supervisory board members between Deutsche Bank and companies in which this bank had interlocking mandates and between these companies and third-party companies in which these second-party companies had interlocking mandates.

2) Companies enclosed with [double box] were financial institutions.

3) Regarding the positions of mandates on the supervisory board, "C", "VC", and "S" mean chairman, vice-chairman, and mandate other than these two positions, respectively.

Source : This figure was compiled by the author, based on Mossner (Hrsg) (1971).

Fig. 9.1 Network for meeting of interlocking supervisory board members of Deutsche Bank in the end of the 1960s

Deutsche Bank had three mandates on the supervisory boards. Furthermore, interlocking directorates can be observed between Siemens AG and Klöckner-Humboldt Deutz AG; between Allianz Versicherungs-AG and Klöckner-Humboldt Deutz AG; and between Allianz Versicherungs-AG and Dresdner Bank AG, in which these electrical and insurance companies formed interlocking directorates through supervisor board mandates. The network of meetings built among these six enterprises comprised 11 interlocking supervisory board members, namely H. J. Abs, C. Wurster, H. L. Merkle, E. von Siemens, G. Henle, A. Alzheimer, F. H. Ulrich, W. Premauer, H-G. Sohl, K. Hansen, and K. Lotz.

9.2 Dresdner Bank's Personnel Network Through Interlocking Directorate of Members of the Supervisory Board on Such Top Management Organ of Other Enterprises

Regarding the personnel networks of three large banks, the situations of Dresdner Bank's network are examined in Sect. 9.2.

9.2.1 Personnel Network and Its Characteristics

Considering the centrality of each enterprise constituting the network and the upper 10 enterprises among Dresdner Bank and 58 companies with its interlocking directorate on the supervisory board in terms of the adjacency measured by number of enterprises where interlocking directorate is established (see Table 9.2), the following numbers emerge. There were one in the banking sector; three in the insurance sector; two in the electrical industry; and one each in the iron and steel; metal producing and metal processing; chemical; and electric power, gas, and energy industries. The adjacency of the upper 10 enterprises ranged from 56 to 81. In terms of the adjacency, AEG in the electrical industry (adjacency 81), Rheinisch-Westfälisches Elektrizitätswerke AG in the electric power industry (similarly 77), and Degussa AG in the chemical industry (65) ranked first, second, and third, respectively. Then, Siemens AG in the electrical industry (adjacency 63), Allianz Versicherungs-AG in the insurance industry (similarly 62), Münchener Rückversicherungs-Gesellschaft in the insurance industry (61), and Dresdner Bank AG in the banking industry (58) were below fourth. Metallgesellschaft AG in the metal producing and processing industries (adjacency 57), August Thyssen-Hütte AG in the iron and steel industry, and Allianz Lebensversicherungs-AG in the insurance industry (56) were below eighth.

Among companies within the upper 5th positions measured by the adjacency, two were in the electrical industry and one each in the chemical; insurance; and electric power, gas, and energy industries. Thus, although the centralities of some banks were relatively high, many were not always in the upper position in terms of adjacency. Rather, companies with high centrality belonged to industries across some key sectors, including the electric power industry. Therefore, enterprises in important major industries also assumed core positions in information flow and network media, including banks.

Regarding the network's cohesiveness, the density of Dresdner Bank's network was 0.0085992. Dresdner Bank's supervisory board members built interlocking directorates in similar top management groups in 58 companies as second-party enterprises. Then, the number of enterprises comprising the network, including second-party enterprises in which Dresdner Bank AG had mandates of the supervisory board and third-party enterprises where second-party enterprises had posts of the supervisory board was 628.

9.2.2 Clique of Interlocking Supervisory Board Members

Next, a clique of interlocking supervisory board members with more than two mandates on such a top management organ of multiple companies, which plays significant roles in the network, is considered.

Cases in which multiple members of the supervisory board of Dresdner Bank AG have a mandate on such a top management organ of the same enterprises

Table 9.2 Centrality of member of companies in the network of Dresdner Bank[a] (period after the 1965 Corporations Law)

Position	Company	Adjacency[b]	Industries
1	Allgemeine Elektricitäts-Gesellschaft AEG-Telefunken	81	Electrical
2	Rheinisch-Westfälisches Elektrizitätswerk AG	77	Electric power, gas, and energy
3	Degussa AG	65	Chemical
4	Siemens AG	63	Electrical
5	Allianz Versicherungs-AG	62	Insurance
6	Münchener Rückversicherungs-Gesellschaft	61	Insurance
7	*Dresdner Bank AG*[c]	58	Banking
8	Metallgesellschaft AG	57	Metal producing and processing
9	August-Thyssen-Hütte AG	56	Iron and steel
9	Allianz Lebensversicherungs-AG	56	Insueance
11	Mannesmann AG	54	Iron and steel
12	Handelsunion AG	48	Distributing
12	Hermes Kreditversicherungs-AG	48	Insurance
14	Volkswagenwerk AG	46	Automobile
14	AUDI NSU AUTO UNION AG	46	Automobile
16	Gelsenkirchener Bergwerks-AG	45	Mining
16	Chemische Werke Hüls AG	45	Chemical
18	DEMAG AG	44	Machine
19	Brown, Boveri & Cie AG	42	Electrical
19	Frankfurter Hypothekenbank	42	Banking
19	Hamburgische Elektricitäts-Werke AG	42	Electric power, gas, and energy
22	Karlsruher Lebensversicherung A.-G	41	Insurance
23	Chemie-Verwaltungs-AG	37	Other industries
24	Rasselstein AG	36	Iron and steel
24	Hamburg-Amerika Linie (Hamburg-Amerikanische Packet-fahrt-AG)	36	Transportation
26	Ruhrchemie AG	33	Chemical
26	Hoechst AG	33	Chemical
28	Bank für Handel und Industrie	32	Banking

(continued)

Table 9.2 (continued)

Position	Company	Adjacency[b]	Industries
29	Dolomitwerke GmbH	31	Other industries
30	Ruhrkohle AG	30	Mining

Note [a]Of Dresdner Bank and 58 enterprises in which it built direct interlocking directorates on their supervisory boards, upper approximately half companies measured by adjacency are listed up
[b]"Centrality" is measured by an indicator "adjacency" that indicates number of companies in which interlocking directorate is built
[c]Company in italics is Dresdner Bank as the starting point of this network
Source This table was compiled by the author, based on Mossner (Hrsg) (1971)

were observed in eight companies: Mannesmann AG in the iron and steel industry; Metallgesellschaft AG in the metal producing and processing industries; Chemische Werke Hüls AG, Degussa AG, and Hoechst AG in the chemical industry; Siemens AG in the electrical industry; and Münchener Rückversicherungs-Gesellschaft and Allianz Versicherungs-AG in the insurance industry.

In these eight enterprises, supervisory board members of Dresdner Bank with mandates on the supervisory board of other enterprises were as follows: H. C. Boden, K. Winnacker, H. Richter, E. Matthiensen, A. Alzheimer, H-G. Sohl, and K. Lotz. K. Winnacer had mandates on the supervisory board of five other companies. He was the chairman of Münchener Rückversicherungs-Gesellschaft and had supervisory board mandates, excluding the chairman and vice-chairman of Mannesmann AG, Chemische Werke Hüls AG, Degussa AG, and Hoechst AG. H. Richter held mandates on the supervisory board of four other enterprises. He was the chairman of Metallgesellschaft AG, Chemische Werke Hüls AG, Degussa AG, and Hoechst AG. A. Alzheimer had posts on the supervisory board of three other companies. He was the chairman of Münchener Rückversicherungs-Gesellschaft and the vice-chairman of Allianz Versicherungs-AG and had supervisory board mandates except for the chairman and vice-chairman of Siemens AG. E. Matthiensen and H-G. Sohl had mandates on the supervisory board of two other companies. Then, E. Matthiensen was the vice-chairman in Münchener Rückversicherungs-Gesellschaft and held a supervisory board mandate except for the chairman and vice-chairman in Metallgesellschaft AG, H-G. Sohl had supervisory board mandates except for the chairman and vice-chairman in Siemens AG and Allianz Versicherungs-AG. H. C. Boden and K. Lotz had supervisory board mandate except for the chairman and vice-chairman of one other company. H. C. Boden held a post of the supervisory board, excluding the chairman and vice-chairman in Mannesmann AG. Then, K. Lotz had a similar post in Allianz Versicherungs-AG (Mossner 1971, S. 10, 60, 482, 501, 633–634, 761, 873).

Furthermore, considering the network of meetings built among members of enterprises with more than three mandates (Fig. 9.2), the following conditions can be observed. Strong interlocking directorates were established between Dresdner Bank AG and Allianz Versicherungs-AG in the insurance industry and between Dresdner Bank AG and Münchener Rückversierungs-Gesellschaft in the insurance industry through three mandates. In addition, strong relationships of interlocking directorates were built through seven posts between Allianz Versicherungs-AG and Siemens AG, which were third-party enterprises in which Dresdner Bank AG had three mandates on the supervisory boards. Interlocking directorates can be observed between Allianz Versicherungs-AG and Deutsche Bank AG and between Allianz Versicherungs-AG and Klöckner-Humboldt Deutz AG. This insurance company formed interlocking directorates through three supervisor board mandates. The network of meetings built among these six enterprises comprised 11 interlocking supervisory board members, namely A. Alzheimer, E. Matthiensen, K. Winnacker, K. Lotz, H-G. Sohl, E. von Siemens, F. H. Ulrich, G. Henle, W. Premauer, C. Wurster, and K. Hansen.

9.3 Commerzbank's Personnel Network Through Interlocking Directorate of Members of the Supervisory Board on Such Top Management Organ of Other Enterprises

Following the analysis in Sects. 9.1 and 9.2, conditions of Commerzbank's network are considered in this section.

9.3.1 Personnel Network and Its Characteristics

The following numbers emerge when considering the centrality of each enterprise constituting the network, the upper 10 enterprises among Commerzbank AG, and the 54 companies with interlocking directorates on the supervisory board in terms of the adjacency measured by the number of enterprises in which interlocking directorate is established (see Table 9.3). There were two in the banking sector; three in the insurance sector; and two in the distributing industry; and one each in the automobile; textile, spinning, and woven goods; and electric power, gas, and energy industries. The adjacency of more than 10 enterprises ranged from 46 to 80. In terms of the adjacency, Deutsche Ueberseeische Bank in the banking industry (adjacency 80), Rheinisch-Westfälisches Elektrizitätswerke AG in the electric power industry (similarly 77), and Daimler-Benz AG in the automobile industry (66) ranked first, second, and third, respectively. Gerling-Konzern Allgemeine Versicherungs-AG in the insurance industry (adjacency 57), Karstadt AG in the distributing industry (similarly 56), Commerzbank AG in the banking industry (54), and Gerling-Konzern Lebensversicherungs-AG in the insurance industry (53) were below fourth. Handelsunion AG in the distributing industry, Hermes Kreditversicherungs-AG in the insurance industry (adjacency 48, respectively), and Deutsche Linoleum-Werke AG in the textile, spinning, and woven goods industries (corresponding number 46) were below eighth.

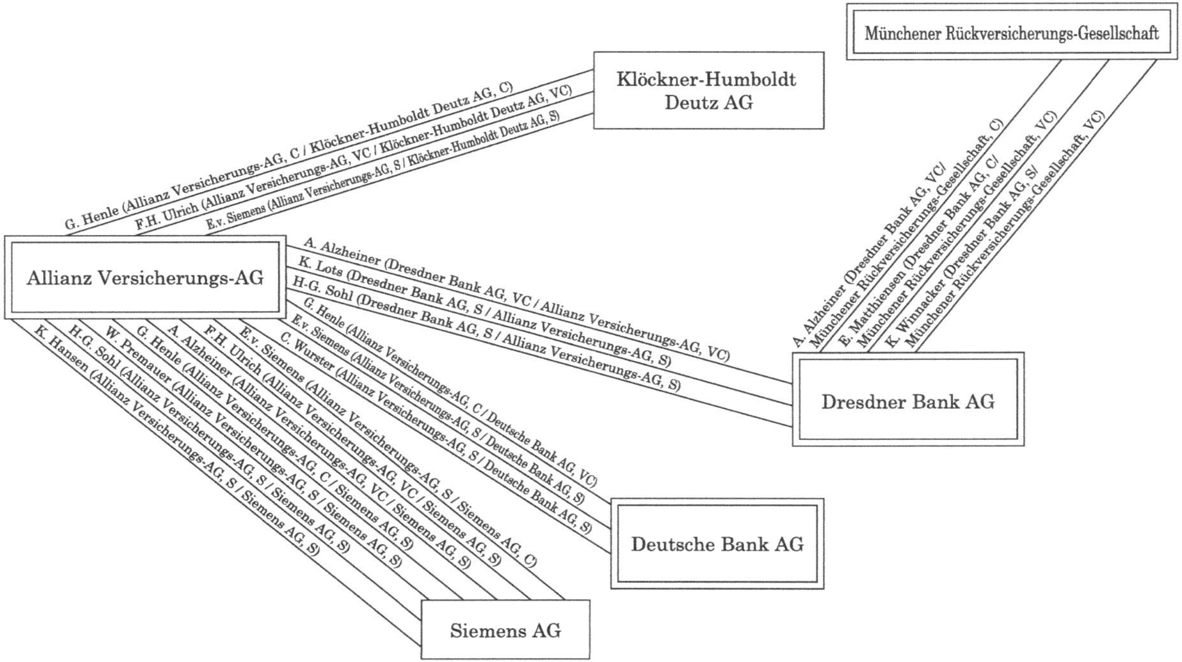

Note : 1) This figure indicates the network composed of companies with more than three interlocking mandates that was connected by the supervisory board members between Dresdner Bank and companies in which this bank had interloking mandates and between these companies and third-party companies in which these second-party companies had interlocking mandates.
2) Companies enclosed with [double-bordered box] were financial institutions.
3) Regarding the positions of mandates on the supervisory board, "C", "VC", and "S" mean chairman, vice-chairman, and mandate other than these two positions, respectively.
Source : This figure was compiled by the author, based on Mossner (Hrsg) (1971).

Fig. 9.2 Network for meeting of interlocking supervisory board members of Dresdner Bank in the end of the 1960s

Table 9.3 Centrality of member companies in the network of Commerzbank[a] (period after the 1965 Corporations Law)

Position	Company	Adjacency[b]	Industries
1	Deutsche Ueberseeische Bank	80	Banking
2	Rheinisch-Westfälisches Elektrizitätswerk AG	77	Electric power, gas, and energy
3	Daimler-Benz AG	66	Automobile
4	Gerling-Konzern Allgemeine Versicherungs-AG	57	Insurance
5	Karstadt AG	56	Distributing
6	*Commerzbank AG*[c]	54	Banking
7	Gerling-Konzern Lebensversicherungs-AG	53	Insurance
8	Handelsunion AG	48	Distributing
8	Hermes Kreditversicherungs-AG	48	Insurance
10	Deutsceh Linoleum-Werke AG	46	Textile and spinning and woven goods
11	Bayer AG	45	Chemical
11	Rheinische Stahlwerke	45	Iron and steel
13	Demag AG	44	Machine
14	Buderus'sche Eisenwerke	43	Iron and steel
14	Deutsche Continental-Gas-Gesellschaft	43	Electric power, gas, and energy
16	Brown, Boveri & Cie AG	42	Electrical
17	Blohm+Voss AG	39	Shipbuilding
18	Beton- und Monierbau AG	35	Other industries
19	Hoechst AG	33	Chemical
19	Ruhrchemie AG	33	Chemical
19	Allgemeine Deutsche Investment-Gesellschaft mbH	33	Other industries
22	Zanräderfabrik Renk AG	27	Machine
22	Süddeutsche Kalkstickstoff-Werke AG	27	Chemical
24	Cassela Farbwerke AG (Cassella Farbwerke Mainkur AG)	26	Chemical
25	Berliner Kidl Brauerei AG	25	Distillation
26	Gutehoffnungshütte Aktienverein	22	Iron and steel
26	Kaiser's Kaffee-Geschäft AG	22	Food
28	Robert Bosch GmbH	21	Electrical

Note [a]Of Commerzbank and 54 enterprises in which it built direct interlocking directorates on their supervisory boards, upper approximately half companies measured by adjacency are listed up
[b]"Centrality" is measured by an indicator "adjacency" that indicates number of companies in which interlocking directorate is built
[c]Company in italics is Commerzbank as the starting point of this network
Source This table was compiled by the author, based on Mossner (Hrsg) (1971)

When considering companies within the upper fifth positions measured by the adjacency, only one such company was in the banking sector and one each in the automotive; distributing; insurance, and electric power, gas, and energy industries. Thus, although the centrality of Deutsche Ueberseeische Bank was high, many banks were not always in the upper position regarding the adjacency. Rather, companies with high centrality belonged to industries across some key sectors and the electric power industry. Therefore, enterprises in important major industries also assumed core positions in information flow and media of networks, including banks.

Concerning the network's cohesiveness, the density of Commerzbank's network was 0.0078716. Members on the supervisory board of Commerzbank AG built an interlocking directorate in a similar top management organ in 54 companies as second-party enterprises. By contrast, the number of enterprises comprising the network, including second-party enterprises, where Commerzbank AG had mandates of the supervisory board and third-party enterprises in which second-party enterprises had supervisory board posts was 606.

9.3.2 Clique of Interlocking Supervisory Board Members

Next, a clique of interlocking supervisory board members with more than two mandates on such a top management organ of multiple companies, which plays significant roles in the network, is considered.

A case in which multiple members of the supervisory board of Commerzbank AG have mandates on such a top management organ of other enterprises was observed only in one company, namely Karstadt AG in the distributing industry. This case significantly differed from the cases of Deutsche Bank and Dresdner Bank. In Karstadt AG, H. Deuss had a mandate of the chairman, and R. Oetker held one post of the supervisory board excluding the chairman and vice-chairman (Mossner 1971, S. 123, 571).

In Commerzbank's network, there was no case in which interlocking directorates were built through more than three mandates of the supervisory board, and the network of meetings built among members of enterprises with more than three mandates did not exist. This point also differed from the cases of Deutsche Bank and Dresdner Bank.

9.4 Comparison of Personnel Networks of Three Large Banks

In Sects. 9.1, 9.2, and 9.3, personnel networks of three large banks, namely Deutsche Bank, Dresdner Bank, and Commerzbank, which were built through the interlocking directorate of members of the supervisory board on the same top management organ of other companies including second-party and third-party enterprises were analyzed. This subsection compares the networks of each bank.

The density of the network of Deutsche Bank, Dresdner Bank, and Commerzbank, which were indicators of grasping the network's cohesiveness, was 0.0077138, 0.0085992, and 0.0078716, respectively. Although the numerical figures of Deutsche Bank's and Commerzbank's networks were almost at the same level, that of Dresdner Bank's network was slightly higher. The number of enterprises comprising networks including second- and third-party companies was 702 in the network of Deutsche Bank, 628 in that of Dresdner Bank, and 606 in that of Commerzbank. Regarding the difference in density of the networks of these two banks, the total number of mandates in Dresdner Bank's network was 1,693, which was more than that in Commerzbank's network (1,443; these figures were calculated by the author, based on Mossner 1971).

Regarding the centrality, Deutsche Ueberseeische Bank ranked first in terms of adjacency in networks of Deutsche Bank and Commerzbank. Regarding the order of adjacency among the three large banks in their own networks, Deutsche Bank, Dresdner Bank, and Commerzbank in their own networks ranked fifth, seventh, and sixth, respectively. The number of banks in the upper 10 enterprises measured by adjacency was two in the networks of Deutsche Bank and Commerzbank. Then, that in the network of Dresdner Bank was only one. Therefore, in all networks of three large banks, although some banks were relatively influential from the centrality perspective, the condition that many banks were in the upper position was not observed. Rather, industries to which companies with high centrality belonged spread over some key industrial sectors and the electric power industry.

Industries to which companies with high centrality belonged spread across some key industrial sectors and the electric power industry. For instance, Rheinisch-Westfälisches Elektrizitätswerke AG in the electric power industry ranked second in all networks of Deutsche Bank AG, Dresdner Bank AG, and Commerzbank AG. Then, Daimler-Benz in the automobile industry ranked third and fourth in the networks of Commerzbank AG and Deutsche Bank AG, respectively. Meanwhile, Siemens AG in the electrical industry ranked fourth and seventh in the networks of Dresdner Bank AG and Deutsche Bank AG, respectively. Degussa AG in the chemical industry ranked third and fifth in the networks of Dresdner Bank AG and Deutsche Bank AG, respectively. Metallgesellschaft AG in the metal producing and processing industries ranked eighth and ninth, respectively.

In the personnel networks of banks, the centralities of banks were not always high compared with those of industrial enterprises. The centrality of banks was also not necessarily high in their own network. Therefore, banks were not always at the decisive position in the flow and media of information as an essential function of personnel networks.

Following the 1990s, the interlocking directorate system and personnel network based on it have undergone significant changes. Therefore, next chapter considers the personnel networks of Deutsche Bank and Commerzbank in the latter half of the 2010s using social network analysis, as Dresdner Bank no longer exists at the present.

References

Eglau HO (1990) Wie Gott in Frankfurt: Die Deutsche Bank und die deutsche Industrie, 3rd edn. Econ Verlag, Düsseldorf

Mossner G (Hrsg) (1971) *Handbuch der Direktoren und Aufsichtsräte.* Jahrgang 1970/71, Bd. I, Nach personen geordnet, Finanz- und Korrespondenz-Verlag, Berlin

Pfeiffer H (1986a) Das Netwerk der Groβbanken. Personelle Verflechtungen mit Konzernen, Staat und ideologischen Apparaten. In: Blätter für deutsche und Internationale Politik 31 (2):161–177

Pfeiffer H (1986b) Groβbanken und Finanzgruppen.Ausgewählte Ergebnisse einer Untersuchung der personellen Verflechtungen von Deutscher, Dresdner und Commerzbank. In: WSI Mitteilungen 39(7):473–481

Pfeiffer H (1993) Die Macht der Banken. Die personellen Verflechtungen der Commerzbank, der Deutschen Bank und der Dresdner Bank mit Unternehemen. Campus, Frankfurt am Main

Stanzick K-H (1969) Der ökonomische Konzentrationsproze. In: Schäfer G, Nedelmann C (Hrsg) Der CDU-Staat. Analysen zur Verfassungswriklichkeit der Bundesrepublik, Bd. I, 2. Aufl., Schurkamp, München, SS 48–79

Chapter 10
Bank's Personnel Networks Through Interlocking Directorates of Members of the Supervisory Board on Such Top Management Organs of Other Enterprises in the Latter Half of the 2010s: Cases of Deutsche Bank and Commerzbank

Abstract Based on the results of the conditions in the late 1960s as the period after the enactment of the 1965 Corporations Law that regulated the limitation of the number in which one person might have mandates on the supervisory board in Chap. 9, this chapter considers the personnel networks of the two largest banks, including the second- and third-party companies, in the latter half of the 2010s using the methods of social network analysis and compares the network of each bank. Following the 1990s, such a system of interfirm relationships, including the relationship between bank and industrial enterprise, has undergone significant change as a result of various factors such as globalization of the economy and enterprise, internationalization of the financial market and the resulting changes in company financing conditions, and transformation of bank behavior, as seen in the shift from credit bank to investment bank business. This chapter analyzes the "cohesiveness" of the networks of each bank that indicates the characteristics of the network as a whole and "centrality" explaining enterprise which plays an important role in the network's information flow and media, as well as the industrial sector to which such an enterprise belonged. These discussions help to clarify the changes to each bank's network.

Keyword Bank · Interlocking directorate · Personnel network · Social network analysis · Supervisory board

Chapter 9 examined the structure of personnel networks of the three largest banks, including second- and third-party enterprises in the late 1960s, which were built through interlocking directorates of supervisory board members. The postwar German basic system of personnel connection was built under the influence of the

T. Yamazaki, *Relationships Between Industry and Bank in Germany*,
https://doi.org/10.1007/978-981-97-4996-6_10

1965 Corporations Law, which regulated the number of mandates that one person could have on the supervisory board and was long maintained until the end of the 1980s. However, since the 1990s, the interlocking directorate system and personnel network based on it have undergone significant changes. Ringe stated in 2015 the erosion of the traditional network between German enterprises that is known as "Germany Inc." (Ringe 2015, p. 494). Paul Windolf also emphasizes that the almost complete dissolution of the network occurred by 2010. (Windolf 2014, pp. 80–81). Beyer insists that the dissolution process of personnel connections resulted from the core of "German Inc." rather than the periphery of the network (Beyer 2006, S. 130).

How have the personnel networks of Germany's two largest banks, Deutsche Bank and Commerzbank, changed? Using social network analysis methodology, this chapter examines the fundamental structure of a personnel network formed by interlocking directorates among supervisory board members. It examines the personnel networks of these two major banks, focusing on key concepts from social network analysis such as "density," "centrality," and "multiplicity."

In addition, this chapter examines a clique of interlocking supervisory board members who hold more than two mandates on such top management organs of multiple other companies and play an important role in the network. Such an analysis can help to understand the interlocking member of the supervisory board that connects banks with industrial enterprises and mutually combines them.

First, Sect. 10.1 considers Deutsche Bank's network, which is built around an interlocking directorate of supervisory board members, to be part of the same top management organ as other companies, including second- and third-party companies. In Sect. 10.2, the Commerzbank network will be examined.

10.1 Deutsche Bank's Personnel Network Through Interlocking Directorate of Members of the Supervisory Board on Such Top Management Organ of Other Enterprises

10.1.1 Personnel Network and Its Characteristics

In Sect. 10.1, the conditions of the Deutsche Bank network are analyzed. In terms of the centrality of each enterprise that comprised the network, when looking at the top ten enterprises among Deutsche Bank and 17 companies in which this bank developed an interlocking directorate on the supervisory board in terms of adjacency measured by the number of companies where an interlocking directorate is established (see Table 10.1), the numbers of such a company in the financial sector were two in the banking and one in the insurance industries. The non-financial sector included four in the electric power, gas, and energy industries, two in the automobile, and one in the chemical industry.

Table 10.1 Centrality of member companies in the network of Deutsche Bank[a] (period in the latter half of the 2010s)

Position	Company	Adjacency[b]	Industries
1	RWE AG	26	Electric power, gas, and energy
2	Stadtwerke Hannau GmbH	25	Electric power, gas, and energy
3	Innogy SE	22	Electric power, gas, and energy
4	Bayer AG	20	Chemical
5	Bayerisch Motoren Werke AG	18	Automobile
6	*Deutsche Bank AG*[c]	17	Banking
7	Daimler AG	16	Automobile
8	E. ON Energie AG	15	Electric power, gas, and energy
9	Münchener Rückversicherungs-Gesellschaft	13	Insurance
10	Deutsche Postbank AG	12	Banking
11	Deutsche Post AG	11	Other industries
11	BVV Versorgungskasse des Bankgewerbes e.V	11	Banking
11	BVV Verischerungsverein des Bankgewerbes a.G	11	Insurance
14	Uniper SE	7	Electric power, gas, and energy
15	BHW Bausparkasse AG	6	Banking
16	Sartorious AG	5	Chemical
17	Allianz Real Estate GmbH	3	Other industries
18	Wuppermann AG	2	Iron and steel

Note [a] Deutsche Bank and 17 enterprises in which it built direct interlocking directorates on their supervisory boards are listed up
[b] "Centrality" is measured by an indicator "adjacency" that indicates number of companies in which interlocking directorate is built
[c] Company in italics is Deutsche Bank as the starting point of this network
Source This table was compiled by the author, based on Handbuch der Grossunternehmen (2017a, b)

The adjacent ten largest companies ranged from 12 to 26. RWE AG (adjacency 26), Stadtwerke Hannau GmbH (similar numerical figure 25), and Innogy SE (similar numerical figure 22) in the electric power, gas, and energy industries ranked first, second, and third in terms of adjacency, respectively. Four companies below the fourth place were Bayer AG in the chemical industry (adjacent 20), BMW AG in the automobile industry (corresponding numbers 18), Deutsche Bank AG in the banking industry (corresponding numbers 17), and Daimler AG in the automobile industry (corresponding numbers 16). Three enterprises below eight position were E. ON Energie AG in the electric power, gas, and energy industries (adjacent 15), Münchener Rückversicherungs-Gesellschaft in the insurance industry (corresponding number 13), and Deutsche Postbank AG in the banking industry (corresponding numbers 12).

When considering companies in the upper fifth position measured by adjacency, there were three in the electric power, gas, and energy industries, and one in the chemical and automobile industries. Unlike the situation at the end of the 1960s, when, in addition to financial sectors such as banking and insurance, major enterprises in key manufacturing industries held core positions measured by adjacency in the network, the scope of industrial sectors included in the personnel network is restricted.

As a result, some companies in the electricity, gas, and energy industries held relatively high positions. Although banks occupied relatively high upper positions in terms of adjacency, the industries to which companies with high centrality belonged were spread across several industrial sectors. Banks do not always play a central role in the network's information flow and media.

In terms of network cohesiveness, the Deutsche Bank network had a density of 0.018481. The number of second-party companies in which Deutsche Bank's supervisory board members established an interlocking directorate in a similar top management organ was 17. In contrast, there were 163 third-party companies with members of the second-party companies' supervisory boards serving in such an organ.

10.1.2 Clique of Interlocking Supervisory Board Members

Next, the clique of interlocking supervisory board members who hold more than two mandates on such top management organs of multiple other companies and play an important role in the network is examined. Seven people served on other companies' supervisory boards with more than two mandates each. Three of the seven people held three mandates. The number of people with two mandates was four.

Paul Achleitner served as chairman of Allianz Real Estate GmbH in other industries and on the supervisory boards of Bayer AG in the chemical industry and Daimler AG in the automobile industry. Frank Bsirske served as vice-chairman of Deutsche Postbank AG in the banking industry and Innogy SE and RWE AG in the electricity, gas, and energy industries. Henning Kagermann served on three supervisory boards, except for the chairman and vice-chairman of Deutsche Post AG, BMW AG in the automobile industry, and Münchener Rückversicherungs-Gesellschaft AG in the insurance industry.

In the banking industry, Timo Heider served as vice-chairman of BHW Bausparkasse AG and had a post on the supervisory board other than chairman and vice-chairman in Deutsche Postbank AG, and Gabriele Platscher served as vice-chairman of BVV Versorgungskasse des Bankgewerbes e.V. She also served on the supervisory board of the BVV Versicherungsverein des Bankgewerbes a.G as vice-chairman. In the insurance industry, Johannes Teyssen served on two supervisory boards, excluding the chairman and vice-chairman of E. Energie AG in the electric power, gas, and energy industries, and Uniper SE in other sectors. Klaus Rüdiger Trützschler held two positions: chairman of Wuppermann AG in the iron and steel industry and supervisory board member (other than chairman and vice-chairman) of Sartorius AG in the chemical industry.

10.2 Commerzbank's Personnel Network Through Interlocking Directorate of Members of the Supervisory Board on Such Top Management Organ of Other Enterprises

10.2.1 Personnel Network and Its Characteristics

Regarding large bank's personnel networks, Sect. 10.2 examines situations in the Commerzbank network.

When considering the centrality of each enterprise that makes up the network, the following numbers emerge from the nine companies comprised of Commerzbank and eight companies with its interlocking directorate on the supervisory board in terms of adjacency as measured by the number of companies where the interlocking directorate is established (see Table10.2). There were two in banking, three in insurance, and four in other industries.

The first companies in terms of adjacency were Münchener Rück-Versicherungs-gesellschaft AG in the insurance industry and Fresenius Manage-SE in other

Table 10.2 Centrality of member companies in the network of Commerzbank[a] (period in the latter half of the 2010s)

Position	Company	Adjacency[b]	Industries
1	Münchener Rückversicherungs-Gesellschaft AG	13	Insurance
1	Fresenius Management SE	13	Other industries
3	BVV Versorgungskasse des Bankgewerbes e. V	11	Banking
3	BVV Versicherungsverein des Bankgewerbes a. G	11	Insurance
3	Deutsche Börse AG	11	Other industries
6	Allianz SE	9	Insurance
6	Fresenius SE & Co. KgaA	9	Other industries
8	*Commerzbank AG*[c]	8	Banking
9	GEA Group AG	5	Other industries

Note [a] Commerzbank and eight enterprises in which it built direct interlocking directorates on their supervisory boards are listed up
[b] "Centrality" is measured by an indicator "adjacency" that indicates number of companies in which interlocking directorate is built
[c] Company in italics is Commerzbank as the starting point of this network
Source This table was compiled by the author, based on Handbuch der Grossunternehmen (2017a, b)

industries (adjacency 13). The third position (adjacent 11) was held by BVV Versorgungskasse des Bankgewerbes. V. in the banking industry; BVV Versicherungsverein des Bankgewerbes a.G. in the insurance sector, and Deutsche Börse AG in other industries. Allianz SE, an insurance company, and Fresenius SE & Co. KgaA in other industries (adjacency 9) were the sixth-ranked companies. Commerzbank AG in the banking industry (adjacent 8) and GEA Group AG in other industries (corresponding number 5) ranked eighth and ninth, respectively.

As a result, even the adjacency of the top-tier companies was not always strong. Some companies in the electric, power, and energy industries held relatively high levels of importance. Among Commerzbank's nine enterprises and the eight enterprises in which this bank established the interlocking directorate on the supervisory board, banks no longer played a central role in the network's information flow and media.

When considering the network's cohesiveness, its density was 0.06779. The members of the Commerzbank supervisory board established an interlocking directorate with similar top management groups in eight companies as second-party companies. Conversely, the network consisted of 54 companies, including second-party companies where Commerzbank AG had supervisory board mandates and third-party companies where second-party companies had supervisory board posts.

10.2.2 Clique of Interlocking Supervisory Board Members

This section examines a clique of interlocking supervisory board members who hold plural mandates on the top management organs of multiple other companies and play an important role in the network. There were no individuals with more than three mandates. Three people served on the supervisory boards of other companies, each with two mandates.

Helmut Perlet was the chairman of Allianz SE in the insurance industry and GEA Group AG in other industries. Klau-Peter Müller served on the supervisory boards of both Fresenius Management SE and Fresenius SE & Co. KgaA in other industries. Hans-Hermann Altenschmidt served on the supervisory boards of BVV Versorgungskasse des Bankgewerbes e.V. in the banking industry, BVV Versicherungsverein des Bankgewerbes a.G. in the insurance industry.

10.3 Comparison of the Bank's Personnel Network at the End of the 1960s and the Latter Half of the 2010s

Following the analysis in Sects. 10.1 and 10.2, this section compares the Deutsche Bank and Commerzbank networks in the latter half of 2010s. It also contrasts the banks' networks at the end of the 1960s and the latter half of 2010s.

In the latter half of the 2010s, the Commerzbank network had a higher density than the Deutsche Bank network. This was because the number of companies making up the Commerzbank network was significantly smaller. In terms of centrality, companies in the electric power, gas, and energy industries tended to be among the most centrally located in the Deutsche Bank network, with only a few in major manufacturing industries such as the chemical and automobile companies. Few companies were highly centralized in the banking and insurance industries. Meanwhile, there was no manufacturing company among the companies in which Commerzbank's supervisory board members established the interlocking directorate.

When comparing networks between supervisory board members in the late 1960s and the latter half of 2010, the number of enterprises in which Deutsche Bank or Commerzbank established interlocking directorates fell from 65 or 54 to 17 or eight, respectively. The numbers of enterprises composing each network, including second- and third-party enterprises in the networks of Deutsche Bank and Commerzbank in the latter half of the 2010s (163 and 54, respectively) dramatically decreased compared to that at the end of the 1960s (702 and 606, respectively) (Chap. 9).

In the latter half of the 2010s, unlike the period at the end of the 1960s, the range of industrial sectors to which these enterprises belonged was limited to a few industries, and enterprise in the heavy and chemical industries, which had been a key industrial sector in German capitalism, became scarce, with many representative enterprises disappearing. The adjacencies of enterprises with high centrality in the Deutsche Bank and Commerzbank network decreased. These indicate a significant change in personnel networks in "distant 2," including second- and third-party enterprises, due to the interlocking directorate and the system's role in exchanging and sharing information between banks and industrial enterprises, as well as between industrial enterprises. As the most representative enterprises in the banking industry, these large banks no longer play significant roles as connecting points in the network's information flow and media. Regarding personnel connections, Germany Inc. has observed a significant transformation due to changes in cooperative interfirm relationships between industry and banks, as well as the decline of large bank roles.

Part 1 examined the conditions of the direct interlocking directorates of top management members of the three large banks on the supervisory boards of other enterprises and indirect interlocking directorates formed among the three banks and two of them before and after World War II. In Part 2, we used social network analysis to examine the personnel networks of the three largest banks, including second- and third-party companies before and after World War II, built through interlocking directorates between the supervisory board members. Personnel connection relations between bank and industrial enterprise through both direct and indirect interlocking directorates, as a core element, have been in the process of dissolution since the 1990s, resulting in tremendous changes in the German system of "industry–bank relationships," as well as interfirm relationships, including those between industrial enterprises. This is a significant departure from prevailing conditions until the late 1980s. Such conditions must have a significant impact on the development of the network established in "distant 2," which includes second and third-party companies via the interlocking directorate, as well as the change of the cooperative system based on the collection and exchange of information and common recognition on a specific business issue between banks and between banks and industrial companies.

Extending these discussions, the functions of members of supervisory and management boards in direct interlocking directorates should be explored further. Therefore, these research topics are addressed in several chapters of Part 3.

References

Beyer J (2006) Pfadabhängigkeit. Über institutionelle Kontinuität, anfällige Stabiltät und fundamentalen Wandel. Campus, Frankfurt am Main

Handbuch der Grossunternehmen (2017a) Handbuch der Grossunternehemen 2017, 64. Ausgabe, Bisnode Deutschland GmbH, Darmstadt, Bd.1

Handbuch der Grossunternehmen (2017b) Handbuch der Grossunternehemen 2017, 64. Ausgabe, Bisnode Deutschland GmbH, Darmstadt, Bd.2

Ringe W-G (2015) Changing law and ownership patterns in Germany: corporate governance and the Erosion of Deutschland AG. In: Am J Comp Law 63(2):493–538

Windolf P (2014) The corporate networks in Germany, 1896–2010. In: David T, Weserhuis F (eds) The power of corporate networks. a comparative and historical perspective. Routledge, New York, pp 66–85

Part III
Functions of Interlocking Directorates Between Enterprises

Chapter 11
Functions of Interlocking Directorate Before World War II: Roles of Direct Interlocking Directorate in Personnel Issues of Top Management Organs and Interlocking Supervisory Board Members from Banks in Management of Industrial Enterprises

Abstract Conditions of interlocking directorate of large banks' top management members such as supervisory board and managing board on supervisory board of other enterprises in various industrial sectors were clarified through examinations in the preceding chapters. Structure of personnel connection formed through interlocking directorate between enterprises is an important foundation of exhibition of function of interfirm relationship. Generally, such functions can be observed in exchanging and sharing information and coordination of interests and conflicts between enterprises. This chapter analyzes functions and roles of personnel connections through interlocking members of supervisory boards and managing boards of large banks and industrial enterprises. Functions of direct interlocking directorate will be considered in relation to personnel issues of top management organs of industrial enterprise and bank and roles of interlocking supervisory board members from banks in management of industrial enterprises.

Keywords Bank influence · Corporate control · Deutsche Bank · Election of director · Industry–bank relationship · Direct interlocking · Personnel connections · Supervisory board

Certain portions of Chaps. 2, 3, 4, 5, 6 and 7 in Part I examined personnel connection structures through direct and indirect interlocking of members of the supervisory board and managing board of large banks on the supervisory board of other companies before and after World War II and recent periods, respectively. Personnel networks are established in the case wherein members of the supervisory boards of several other enterprises as second-party enterprises also hold many posts of third-party enterprises. In second-party enterprises, supervisory board members of a company have interlocking mandates. In Part II, these personnel networks were examined

T. Yamazaki, *Relationships Between Industry and Bank in Germany*,
https://doi.org/10.1007/978-981-97-4996-6_11

using the social network analysis. Interlocking directorates system may have significant meaning in exchanging and sharing information and coordinating interests and conflicts between enterprises.

Personnel connections through the interlocking directorate of top management members on the supervisory board of enterprises in various industrial sectors formed an important foundation for the strong relationships between banks and industrial enterprises and among corporations. Such personnel connections were significant in obtaining, exchanging, and sharing information on various industrial departments and on many companies in which banks had an interest related to financing and investing capital. Therefore, the next issue to be discussed is the function of such typical German personnel connections between enterprises in the periods before and after World War II. In Part III, these research topics are analyzed.

This chapter analyzes personnel connection functions through the direct interlocking of members of the supervisory board and the managing board of a bank in other enterprises before World War II. The research topics considered in this chapter are two issues related to personnel problems. One issue is examining the election of members who should compose the managing board of an industrial enterprise in which a representative of the bank had a mandate of the supervisory board. Selecting members of the managing board is one of the important functions of the supervisory board and is deeply concerned with the bank's influence on an industrial enterprise. The other issue is clarifying the selection of candidates to the supervisory board of the bank as proposed at the general meeting.

In many cases in Germany, numerous members of the supervisory board were from other companies, implying that German companies invited individuals outside the company as members of their supervisory board. Such situations were observed not only at industrial companies but also banks. Appointing members of the board of directors by the supervisory board of an industrial enterprise to which a bank dispatches one of its own as a member of that supervisory board and electing candidates to a bank's supervisory board from outside companies occurred given the importance and significance of obtaining useful information for the bank's business, such as providing financing to companies and making investments in other enterprises. Obtaining such information was important to banks' stable collection of financing funds to enterprises and securing higher efficiency of investments in industrial companies.

Regarding the significance of a bank securing a supervisory board mandate of an industrial enterprise, a Deutsche Bank internal document dated February 3, 1944, on the "acceptance of a supervisory board mandate" pointed out that this bank recognized the value of a supervisory board of enterprises only if it had ideal relationships with this bank and should be representative of business interests regarding scale and importance. Such a prerequisite could be secured only by possessing a company's mandate that made approval from this bank necessary [*Historisches Archiv der Deutschen Bank* (bellow HADB), P00033, Übernahme von Aufsichtsratsmandaten (3.2.1944)]. This agreement was important in various aspects regarding the functions of the supervisory board, namely the stable collection of financing funds to companies as customers and securing higher efficiency of investments in industrial companies. Personnel issues concerning electing and dismissing members of the managing board who had charge of executing duties had an especially important meaning.

In the analysis of this chapter, considering the enterprise for which the bank holds the mandate of chairman of the supervisory board as the most critical post is very important when examining the election of members who should attend the managing board of an industrial enterprise where a bank representative has the mandate of the supervisory board. This chapter uses Daimler-Benz as a representative case. Regarding the election of candidates to the supervisory board of a bank who were to be proposed at the general meeting, Deutsche Bank is explored as a typical case.

This chapter discusses these research topics using various historical materials on Deutsche Bank that were kept in the bank's archives. A significant volume of materials, such as letters, documents, and correspondence among Deutsche Bank members, between this bank and industrial enterprises, between bank representatives on the supervisory board of an industrial company and this bank, and between representatives from Deutsche Bank on the supervisory board of industrial companies and members of industrial companies, are used for the analysis.

First, Sect. 11.1 analyzes the election of members who should belong to the managing board of an industrial enterprise in which a Deutsche Bank representative had the mandate of the supervisory board and influenced this bank. Second, Sect. 11.2 considers the selection of candidates for Deutsche Bank's supervisory board who were to be suggested at the general meeting. Whereas Sect. 11.1 examines the functions and roles of a bank representative at other companies and the influences of the bank on an industrial enterprise, the analysis in Sect. 11.2 attempts to clarify how a bank developed relationships with an industrial company through the internal organization of the bank's supervisory board and the intentions in such a cooperative relation. Furthermore, Sect. 11.3 considers roles of interlocking supervisory board members from banks in management of industrial enterprises.

11.1 Industry–Bank Relationships Regarding Personnel Affairs of Members of the Managing Board in an Industrial Enterprise: Case of Daimler-Benz

Section 11.1 examines a bank's influence over personnel issues, such as the electing members of the managing board of an industrial enterprise in which representatives of a large bank had the mandate of the supervisory board. In this section, the case of Daimler-Benz AG—to which Deutsche Bank dispatched its person as chairman of the supervisory board—is considered. Addressing such personnel affairs was one of the most important functions of the supervisory board. For instance, in a meeting of the supervisory board of this automobile company on November 24, 1933, this entity decided to promote J. Werlin, director of the Munich branch, to a member of the board of directors for a temporary period [HADB, P03248, Auszug aus dem Protokoll über die Aufsichtsratssitzung der Daimler-Benz AG vom 24. November 1933, 3 Uhr nachmittags in Stuttgart-Untertürkheim (24.11.1933), S. 1]. In addition, the election of former director Fritz Nallinger as deputy director was decided in the meeting of the supervisory board on March 23, 1940 [HADB, P03251, Der Brief von der Direktion der Daimler-Benz Aktiengesellschaft an Herr Wörner (24.4.1940), S. 1].

Issues concerning employment contracts, including remuneration and term of office for a managing board member, were also important functions of the supervisory board, along with elections and dismissals. For example, in an internal document dated March 26, 1928, regarding "contract of managing board member of Daimler-Benz AG," the problem of disunited contracts that had existed before the merger of Daimler and Benz in 1926 was addressed. The necessity of securing uniformity in the relationships with all members of the board of directors, including remuneration, was pointed out [HADB, P03248, Daimler-Benz Vorstandsverträge (26.3.1928)].

Under such a condition, E. G. von Stauss, chairman of the supervisory board who was dispatched from Deutsche Bank, indicated some points in his document on April 24, 1928. Because the term of the contract with Lang, W. Kissel, Porsche, and Schippert was ending on December 31, 1928, it was highlighted that contract renewal was necessary. E. G. von Stauss also informed that releasing Kissel from office with a term of twelve months from July 1, 1928, was possible. F. Nallinger could also be dismissed within six months from November 1, 1928, and the contracting term with Niebel was twelve months from January 1, 1929. However, regarding Lohrmann, another agreement did not exist and, thus, the legal term of a dismissal notice based on Article 622 of the civil code to be applied was explained [HADB, P03248, Vorstands—Verträge Daimler-Benz. (24.4.1928)].

At Daimler-Benz, cases in which the chairman of the supervisory board was involved in decisions and approvals of the duties that members of the managing board took charge of on the basis of proposals by the board of directors, as well as personnel affairs, such as elections and dismissals of members of the managing board, contracts, and remunerations, were not few in number. For instance, a letter dated November 6, 1929, from the management to E. G. von Stauss, chairman of the supervisory board, indicated that some proposals regarding personnel affairs were adopted and that approval of these affairs was requested. When observing the important issues, the suggestion was made that von Jurgenfeld should take charge of the management of the Gaggenau factory as successor to Lohrmann, who retired and received an annual remuneration of RM 36,000 and an allowance of RM 14,000. Management also proposed that von Hentig would be in charge of the business in Berlin after December 1, 1929, and receive remuneration of RM 12,000 per year. In addition, the appointment of Keil, senior engineer at the automobile enterprise Horch, for the remuneration of RM 26,000 per year was proposed at the same time [HADB, P03248, Der Brief von Direktion der der Daimler-Benz AG an Herrn Dr. E. G. von Stauss (6.11.1929), SS. 1–5]. A letter from Daimler-Benz to von Jurgenfeld dated June 11, 1929, informed that, of these proposals, the issue concerning Jurgenfeld was approved by E. G. von Stauss, his employment was decided, and the company wanted to arrange him as a member of the managing board who could take charge of the Gaggenau factory as a successor to Lohrman [HADB, P03248, Der Brief vom Gesamtvorstand der Daimler-Benz Aktiengesellschaft an Herrn Direktor von Jungenfeld (6.11.1929), S. 1].

In a letter dated November 3, 1936, from Wilhelm Kissel as chairman of the board of directors to E. G. von Stauss, chairman of the supervisory board, the personnel issue related to inviting Wilhelm Schilken of Maschinenfabrik Esslingen to be director of the new Genshagen factory was noted as being entrusted by von Stauss to the board of directors. Sailer and Müller, as members of the managing board, and Kissel regarded Schilken as very competent. Because Schilken intended to accept this request, Kissel informed E. G. von Stauss that he wanted to enter into an agreement with Schilken on the next possible day [HADB, P03250, Der Brief von Dr. W. Kissel an Herrn Staatsrat Dr. E. G. von Stauβ (11.3.1936), SS. 1–2].

In contrast, in another case, Wilhelm Kissel as chairman of the board of directors left a personnel affair to the judgment of E. G. von Stauss. In this case, the personnel issue regarded Scheneeberger in 1940. Kissel indicated the effect of his entrustment on von Stauss in resolving this issue and wrote a letter to E. Wörner, von Stauss's secretary, to discuss the issue with von Stauss [HADB, P0325, Der Brief von Dr. W. Kissel an Herrn E. Wörner (18.11.1940), S. 1; HADB, P03250, Der Brief vom Vorsitzer des Aufsichtsrates der Daimler-Benz AG (25.11.1940)]. In many other cases, the board of directors asked E. G. von Stauss as chairman of the supervisory board to approve of personnel issues and receive admissions. For instance, a document from the managing board to von Stauss dated March 19, 1932, indicated such a situation. One case of the afore-mentioned personnel affair regarding Keil was representative. In this document, the name Deutsche Bank was written as a notation in the address as well as in the position of chairman of the supervisory board of Daimler-Benz [HADB, P03254, Der Brief von der Direktion der Daimler-Benz Aktiengesellschaft an Herrn Dr. E. G. von Stauβ (19.7.1932)]. This point clearly indicated the position of von Stauss. In addition, F. Nallinger, a member of the managing board, demanded in a document to von Stauss dated August 23, 1928, to be admitted as a member of the supervisory board after retiring his post as a member of the managing board [HADB, P03259, Der Brief von Nallinger an Herrn Direktor Dr. von Stauss (23.8.1928), S. 3]. A Daimler-Benz document dated May 24, 1929, informed the supervisory board to accept his request given the expectation of using Nallinger's experience and knowledge in the Daimler-Benz group and proposed him as a candidate for this entity at the next general meeting [HADB, P03259, Persönlich! (24.5.1929)]. Such a demand and a request regarding the personnel affairs of top management were related to problems that deeply concerned Deutsche Bank, its intention that a dispatched representative be the chairman of the supervisory board of another enterprise, and the general condition in which the chairman of the board of such a top management entity play a significant role.

The importance of the approval by the chairman of the supervisory board can also be observed in cases related to Hans Rummel as the successor of E. G. von Stauss as chairman of such an entity of Daimler-Benz. For example, a letter from Eilhelm Haspel, member of the board of directors, to Rummel dated December 29, 1944, noted that the issue of Kampschulte's appointment as a member of the managing board had Rummel's approval [HADB, P03247, Der Brief von Dr. Ing. Wilhelm Haspel an Herrn Direktor Hans Rummel (29.12.1944)].

Regarding the appointment of H. G. Röhr in 1935 as a member of the board of directors, various exchanges and negotiations between the chairman of the supervisory board of Daimler-Benz from Deutsche Bank and individuals of this automobile enterprise were conducted. A letter from H G. Röhr to E. G. von Stauss as chairman of the supervisory board dated April 8, 1938, indicated that negotiations regarding the appointment of Röhr ensued among Röhr, von Stauss, and members of the managing board of Daimler-Benz [HADB, P03262, Der Brief von H. G. Röhr an Herrn Staatsrat Dr. von Stauss (8.4.1935)]. In this industrial company, the conditions for developing a new type of automobile did not match with the economic and financial situation regarding engineers at this enterprise, the type of program, and production possibilities. The need to manage such a problem was the reason for the examination of Röhr's invitation to be a member of the management board [HADB, P03262, Der Brief von Dr. W. Kissel an Herrn Staatsrat Dr. E. G. von Stauss (5.7.1935)].

Individuals from Deutsche Bank were deeply involved in this personnel affair. A letter dated August 19, 1935, from von Lewinski of Deutsche Bank to Wilhelm Kissel as chairman of the managing board of Daimler-Benz pointed out that the thinking and conception of H G. Röhr regarding design did not naturally harmonize with the technical principals and ideas of this automobile enterprise. Therefore, time was necessary to ensure a fit with this company's product line-up. Given such a condition, von Lewinsky indicated that a short-term contract would be considered for the appointment of Röhr. Discussions between E. G. von Stauss and von Lewinski were planned for the day after the date of the letter. However, Lewinski noted that he did not believe that von Stauss would object to further negotiations that depended on the result of the consultation [HADB, P03262, Der Brief von Dr. von Lewinski an Herr Dr. W. Kissel (19.8.1935), S. 1].

This personnel issue was decided with the final approval of E. G. von Stauss [HADB, P03262, Herrn Röhr (5.9.1935); HADB, P03262, Der Brief von E. G. von Stauβ an Herrn Dr. W. Kissel (12.9.1935)]. In the contract for the appointment of H G. Röhr, certain points were decided. Although Röhr was appointed as a member of the board of directors, he had taken charge of technical issues and his position as deputy director. His duties as director of the design department for mass-produced automobiles and the related development department were entrusted to him, along with the usual duties of a member of the managing board. Annual remuneration of RM 4,400 and a bonus equivalent to 2% of shareholder dividends were paid. That this agreement came into effect on September 1, 1935, was also decided [HADB, P03262, Vertrag zwischen der firma. Daimler-Benz Aktiengesellschaft, Berlin und Herr H. G. Röhr, Kronberg/Tn. Juminstrasse 8 (17.9.1935), S. 1; HADB, P03262, Der Brief von der Daimler-Benz A.G. an Herrn Hans Gustav Röhr, SS. 1–2, HADB, P03262, Dr. von Stauss (12.9.1935)]. A letter from H G. Röhr to E. G. von Stauss dated June 1, 1935, indicated that a plan of appointment was sent to Röhr [HADB, P03262, Der Brief von H. G. Röhr an Herrn Staatsrat Dr. von Stauss (1.6. 1935)]. That this personnel affair was decided through the final approval of von Stauss as chairman of Daimler-Benz's supervisory board and who was from Deutsche Bank indicates the bank's deep involvement and the supervisory board's important function in personnel issues such as electing members of the managing board.

In addition, cases existed in which an individual from Deutsche Bank was involved in exchanges and negotiations concerning personnel affairs at the request of E. G. von Stauss, chairman of the supervisory board, on the basis of this bank's intentions. For instance, a letter from Dr. Jahr of Deutsche Bank to E. G. von Stauss dated February 2, 1933, indicated that friendly negotiations with members of the managing board were performed, as von Stauss expected. Moreover, concerning Reumuth Jr., Dr. Jahr had the opportunity to effectively intervene in the board of directors of Brown Boveri & Cie. AG—an entity in which Jahr was involved [HADB, P03253, Der Brief von Dr, Jahr an Herr von Stauβ (2.2.1933)]. Such a case indicates the deep involvement in personnel issues regarding the managing board of industrial enterprises through exchanges and negotiations using personnel relationships and the interlocking between Deutsche Bank and industrial companies.

In other situations, the chairman of the supervisory board and individuals from Deutsche Bank deeply concerned themselves with personnel issues outside those related to the members of the board of directors. For instance, a letter from von Lewinski of Deutsche Bank to W. Kissel dated January 3, 1930, indicated that the employment of Schreiter Jr., the son of a former member of the managing board of Daimler-Benz, would be supported by E. G. von Stauss as chairman of the supervisory board [HADB, P03248, Der Brief von Dr. von Lewinski an Herr W. Kissel (3.1.1930), HADB, P03248, Der Brief von W. Kissel an Herr Dr. von Lewinski (27.1.1930)]. Regarding this issue, a letter from W. Kissel to von Lewinski dated January 27, 1930, also noted that an effort must be made to properly evaluate a person who was a candidate. Schreiter Jr. first accepted an apprenticeship in the technical and commercial departments at the Berlin branch for one year, and whether he could be employed was to be decided within one year [HADB, P03248, Der Brief von W. Kissel an Herr Dr. von Lewinski (27.1.1930)]. In a letter from von Lewinski to W. Kissel dated January 29, 1930, Lewinski thanked Kissel for employing Schreiter, Jr. and indicated that he intended to inform E. G. von Stauss of the contents of the letter from W. Kissel [HADB, P03248, Der Brief von Dr. von Lewinski an Herr Kissel (29.1.1930)]. The intentions and involvement of Deutsche Bank regarding personnel affairs can be observed in these individuals' exchanges and behavior. The bank's intentions are indicated by the Deutsche Bank's name written on the letters from W. Kissel to von Lewinski, and the chairman of the supervisory board of an industrial enterprise, such as E. G. von Stauss, was very important and strongly influenced important personnel issues without limitation to those concerning members of the managing board. Such cases typically indicate E. G. von Stauss's emphasis on Deutsche Bank's interests at Daimler-Benz and the position of representatives of industrial enterprises as chairmen of the supervisory board.

Requests for E. G. von Stauss as a member of the managing board of Deutsche Bank regarding personnel issues can also be observed in numerous other cases. One representative case—not related to a personnel affair of the board of directors—was noted in a letter to E. G. von Stauss dated April 20, 1930. In the letter, von Stauss was informed about the oldest son of Zahn from the Pongs & Zahn company, who worked as an engineer in the repair shop of Daimler-Benz for five years and who sought greater responsibilities as head of a sales office. Zahn stressed that such a request was the first personal demand made by someone who had a business relationship with Deutsche Bank. The sender of this letter pointed out that the demand was based on the close relationship between Deutsche Bank and Pongs & Zahn and requested that the board of directors reexamine this personnel issue [HADB, P03248, Die Schrift an Herrn Dr. von Stauss (10.4.1930)]. In addition, a letter from E. G. von Stauss dated April 23, 1938, pointed out that he gave consent to employ Ewald, who worked as an engineer at the Junkers company in Genshagen at Daimler-Benz [HADB, P03328, Die Schrift von E. G. von Stauss über die Genehmigung der Personalangelegenheit (23.4.1938)]. Thus, the involvement of E. G. von Stauss as chairman of the supervisory board from Deutsche Bank was not limited to the personnel issues of the board of directors.

Regarding the function of the supervisory board and bank representatives in the personnel affairs and developments in the afore-mentioned cases, E. G. von Stauss as chairman of the supervisory board was concerned with personnel issues not only of the managing board but also in the operational departments. In these departments, personnel issues were essentially not the domain of such top management entities. Cases in which von Stauss' support and approval played a significant role in decisions related to personnel issues and requests, and expectations from him on important personnel affairs, were based on the influential power and interest of Deutsche Bank and his role and intention as chairman of the supervisory board of Daimler-Benz. For instance, a letter dated May 13, 1942, from E. Wörner of Deutsche Bank to Wilhelm Haspel as chairman of the managing board of Daimler-Benz indicated that Wörner examined in detail the personnel affairs regarding the election of a new person proposed by Haspel on the previous day [HADB, P03247, Der Brief von E. Wörner an Herrn Dr. Ing. Wilhelm Haspel (13.5.1943)]. In this way, in many cases, the bank strongly influenced the personnel affairs of the managing board of an industrial enterprise through bank representatives' roles on the supervisory board that provided the interconnections.

11.2 Industry–Bank Relationships Regarding Personnel Affairs of Members of a Bank's Supervisory Board

In the foregoing discussions, personnel issues, such as the election of members who should attend the managing board of an industrial enterprise in which a representative of Deutsche Bank held a mandate of the supervisory board, were considerable. Next, Sect. 11.2 examines the election of candidates to the supervisory board of Deutsche Bank who were suggested at the general meeting. How a bank developed relationships with an industrial company through the internal organization of the supervisory board of the bank and the bank's intentions in such a cooperative relation are clarified. This section analyzes the case of Deutsche Bank.

In numerous cases in Germany, many members of the supervisory board were individuals from other companies. That German banks invited individuals outside the company to be members of their supervisory board indicated the importance and significance of obtaining useful information for its business, such as providing financing for companies and making investments in other enterprises. Obtaining such information on various industries and industrial enterprises was significant to the stable collection of financing funds to enterprises by banks and to secure higher efficiency of investments in industrial companies. Therefore, the election of members of the supervisory board was examined and decided on from various perspectives. Important factors were business relations between bank branches and industrial enterprises as their customers; selecting a successor by an individual from the same company as that of the predecessor to reflect in-firm relations; experience and specialty of the candidate; conditions to the installation as a member of a similar organization and another organization; the enterprise's business situation; and the intention of the candidate and his company. In addition, the 1937 Stock Act was also a factor that influenced the election of a member of a managing board.

The following analysis covers the process of selecting and deciding on candidates to the supervisory board who were proposed at the general meeting. Included are cases in which the person selected was not suggested at the stockholders' meeting. Some of the afore-mentioned key points are considered.

First, the influence of the 1937 Stock Act, which regulated the number of supervisory board members [HADB, P00034, Aktenvermerk. (25.2.1939); HADB, P00034, Ihre Schreiben vom 16.2.1939. (24.2.1939)], could be a factor that affected changing the order of priority—that each company emphasized the concrete selection of a candidate—as the standard for electing a member of the supervisory board. A document by K. E. Sippell dated January 9, 1941, pointed out a restriction of the 1937 Stock Act on the number of members of the supervisory board that had already caused difficulties when constituting such an entity [HADB, P00034, Rheinische Hypothekenbank. (9.1.1941), SS. 1–2]. In 1941, the election of Plassmann, a member from Rheinische Hypothekenbank as a member of the supervisory board of Deutsche Bank, was proposed by Soipio, chairman of this mortgage bank. However, Deutsche Bank indicated that this proposal was not acceptable. Restricting the number of supervisory board members was a concern in terms of Deutsche Bank's recognition [HADB, P00034, Rheinische Hypothekenbank/Deutsche Bank Aufsichtsrat. (30.1.1941); HADB, P00034, Rheinische Hypothekenbank. (9.1.1941), S. 1].

Next, business relationships with an industrial enterprise are considered. Assigning a representative from a bank to the supervisory board of an industrial enterprise is useful as a means of building and maintaining friendly relationships. For example, Siemens requested inviting Emil G von Rösler as a member of the supervisory board of Siemens & Halske and Rummel as that of Siemens-Schuckert in 1942 [HADB, P03500, Aufsichtsratevertretung bei Siemens & Halske und bei den Siemens-Schuckertwerken. (9.4.1942)]. Inviting individuals from other companies to serve as supervisory board member is also important for securing cooperative relationships. For example, a letter dated March 14, 1934, from Dietrich Becker of the Essen branch of Deutsche Bank to Georg Solmssen as a member of the managing board of this bank noted the proposal of Klotzbach of Friedrich Krupp AG as a candidate for the supervisory board. This letter pointed out that no member from Krupp who was a member of this bank's supervisory board represented a significant defect when considering the numerous years and business relationships between this bank and Krupp. Although Dietrich Becker did not discuss this personnel affair on the basis of his trust of the Berlin branch but did so only as an individual, he pointed out that he wanted frequent opportunities to discuss and exchange opinions on issues related to the business. Furthermore, he requested that this affair be discussed at the supervisory board meeting on March 23, 1934 [HADB, P00034, Der Brief von Dietrich Becker an Herrn Dr. Georg Solmssen (14.3.1934), SS. 1–2]. Klöckner was a large enterprise in the iron and steel industry with which Deutsche Bank had developed a strong relationship. An internal document dated December 21, 1942, noted that a representative of this iron and steel industrial enterprise was traditionally a member of the supervisory board of Deutsche Bank [HADB, P00034, Akten-Vermerk (21.12.1942), S. 1].

Other related cases existed. A letter dated March 9, 1939, from Oswald Rösler as a member of the managing board of Deutsche Bank to Wolfgang Dietrich indicated that the personnel issue of appointing Dietrich as a member of the supervisory board of this bank was discussed in person between Mosler and Rösler. In this consultation, that the candidate already belonged to the Schlesischen regional advisory council of this bank and regularly participated in its meetings was emphasized [HADB, P00034, Der Brief von Oswald Rösler an Herrn Arnold Maser (9.3.1938); HADB, P00034, Der Brief von Arnold Maser an Herrn Oswald Rösler (10.3.1938); HADB, P00034, Der Brief an Herrn Maser (14.3.1938)]. A letter from Arnold Maser to Oswald Rösler dated March 10, 1939, pointed out that the relationships between Deutsche Bank and Dietrich would be deepened through Dietrich's acceptance. As this letter indicated, further strengthening the connection with an enterprise with which this bank had established a close business relationship had an important meaning in decisions related to the bank's supervisory board members [HADB, P00034, Der Brief von Arnold Maser an Herrn Oswald Rösler (10.3.1938)].

In addition to the afore-mentioned perspectives, the condition for installing a member of a similar organization of another bank was also an important perspective during the election of a member of the supervisory board [*Bundesarchiv Berlin*, R8119F/34, Der Brief von der Deutschen Bank und Disconto-Gesellschaft an Herr Börger (22. Mai 1933), S.1; *Bundesarchiv Berlin*, R8119F/10913, Die Schrift an Herr Becker (15. März 1934); *Bundesarchiv Berlin*, R8119F/10913, Badisch-Pfälzischer Beirat. (16. Juni 1938), S.1]. For instance, a Deutsche Bank internal document dated October 10, 1938, noted that, although a supervisory board candidate's main bank was this bank and his company maintained the best relationships with this bank in both business and personnel aspects, the candidate was asked to give up such a personnel affair because he was already asked to attend the supervisory board of Commerzbank and was to be proposed at the general meeting. That it was appropriate to postpone this issue concerning the election was pointed out [HADB, P00034, Der Brief von Dr. Alfred Pott an Herr Schlitter (10.10.1938), SS. 1–2]. In contrast, Deutsche Bank had a policy that stated that membership on a committee such as the supervisory board excluded participation in a similar organization of another bank; moreover, proposing in such a top management entity of Deutsche Bank the appointment of an individual who attended the supervisory board of another bank was not acceptable [HADB, P00034, Persönlich (12.10.1938); HADB, P00034, Zuwahl des Herrn R. Freudenberg in den Aufsichtsrat der Deutschen Bank. (12.10.1938)].

One such fundamental policy was as follows. Internal Deutsche Bank documents dated July 8, 1944, May 22, 1933, and April 21, 1933, pointed out that it was necessary to refuse other banks'—such as Dresdner Bank, with which Deutsche Bank was in competition—requests to become members of Deutsche Bank's committees, such as the supervisory board [HADB, P00034, Graf von Ballestern'sche Güterdirektor Gleiwitz O/S (8.7.1944), S. 1; HADB, P00034, Der Brief an Herr M. Börger (22.5.1933), S. 1; HADB, P00034, Der Brief von Kurt von Sydow an Herrn Dr. Georg Solmassen (21.4.1933)]. An internal document dated April 2, 1940, concerning the supervisory board, indicated that Dresdner Bank intended to invite Gasper to a post and that Deutsche Bank regarded the installation of another manager as partner on the institute as unacceptable. This document also pointed out that if Gasper's retirement from a Deutsche Bank committee was not expected, his installation onto a Dresdner Bank post could not be considered for the time being [HADB, P00034, Aufsichtsrat Deutsche Bank. (2.8.1940), SS. 1–2].

A similar case is that of Klöckner Werke AG in the iron and steel industry. An Urbig document dated February 18, 1941, indicated that after the death of Florian Klöckner's brother, the problem arose as to how to invite a representative of this industrial enterprise to the Deutsche Bank supervisory board. Henle, as a member of the managing board of this iron and steel company, was the only object for consideration. Florian Klöckner frequently communicated with an individual from Dresdner Bank and intended to belong to this bank's supervisory board in the case that Henle was elected as a member of Deutsche Bank's supervisory board. However, Deutsche Bank stressed that such an installation was impossible and unsuitable for its traditional relationships, and the appointment of a representative of Klöckner Werke AG should be coordinated in the best manner possible to secure a future mandate of the supervisory board as well [HADB, P00034, Akten-Vermerk (18.2.1941), SS. 1–2]. Regarding this personnel affair, Florian Klöckner was proposed as a candidate for the supervisory board in a general meeting [HADB, P00034, Der Brief an Herrn Dr. Florian Klöckner (25.3.1941); HADB, P00034, Der Brief von Dr. Florian Klöckner an Herrn Kimmich (28.3.1941)] and was approved at this meeting (Deutsche Bank 1941, S.7).

Indeed, if plural banks requested and proposed the installation as a member of the supervisory board, the intentions of the concerned individual and the enterprise to which he belonged were important. However, even in such a case, the bank with deep and strong relationships with this enterprise, the closeness of relations between both companies, the history of interfirm relations, and the relationships between individuals considered candidates and individuals of banks were deeply concerned with whether the industrial enterprise accepted the requests of which banks. For instance, in materials such as a letter dated February 10, 1943, to Karl Jarres, Karl Kimmich as chairman of the supervisory board of Deutsche Bank when Marotzke, chairman of Klöckner Werke AG, was taken up as a candidate for the supervisory board of Deutsche Bank, received the same requests from Commerzbank and Dresdner bank. He declined Commerzbank's proposal because he had a long-term business relationship with Dresdner Bank and refusing Dresdner was difficult. Although Deutsche Bank also asked Marotzke to attend the supervisory board, Florian Klöckner from Klöckner Werke AG already belonged to this top management entity. Another reason why requests from Dresdner Bank were accepted was consideration of an exceptional situation: this Klöckner group would have two mandates of the supervisory board of Deutsche Bank if Marotzke was elected [HADB, P00034, Der Brief von Dr. Karl Jarres an Herr Kimmich (10.2.1943); HADB, P00034, Der Brief von Wilhelm Marotzke an den Vorsitzer des Aufsichtsrats der Deutschen Bank Herr Dr. Kimmich (17.4.1943); HADB, P00034, Der Brief an Herr Wilhelm Marotske (20.4.1943); HADB, P00034, Der Brief von Dr. Jarres an Herr Kimmich (31.5.1943)].

In addition, one case involved a request to select candidates by considering the regional constitution of the members of the supervisory board. For example, in a letter from Heinrich Klöckers of the Mannheim branch to K. E. Sippell, a member of the managing board of Deutsche Bank, Klöckers asked that the election of Richard Freudenberg be prepared for because if A. Hackelsberger—who indicated his intent to retire—retires from the supervisory board, no supervisory board member would be from the southwest region of Germany [HADB, P00034, Der Brief von Heinr. Klöckers an Hernn Dr. jur. K. E. Sippell (16.2.1939)]. This request was taken into consideration. As was clarified in a list of members of the supervisory board in the fiscal year 1939 annual report, Richard Freudenberg was installed as successor to Hackelsberger, who retired in February 1939 (Deutsche Bank 1938, S. 3, 1939, S. 7).

For large banks, such as Deutsche Bank, demands were numerous to include on a supervisory board a specific individual. In such cases, whether a person who already had a bank's supervisory board mandate existed at the concerned company could be important. For instance, in an internal Deutsche Bank memorandum dated October 16, 1936, Werner Carp—an elected member of the supervisory board of Gutehoffnungshütte—indicated a frequent desire to become a member of the bank's supervisory board. However, the author of this memorandum pointed out that, regardless of whether the request would be acceptable or not to Deutsche Bank, it should be examined in detail, and he wanted to withhold refusal of the proposal because of the potential business relationships with this industrial enterprise [HADB, P00034, Akten-Vermerk (16.10.1938)].

The foregoing discussions examined the election of a member of the managing board of an industrial enterprise in which a Deutsche Bank representative had a mandate of the supervisory board, and this bank's influence on the personnel affairs and selection of candidates for its supervisory board were to be suggested at a general meeting before World War II. When selecting members of the managing board in industrial companies, a strong concern was the bank's influence over these enterprises. Personnel affairs regarding the appointment of members of the board of directors by the supervisory board in an industrial enterprise and the election of candidates from outside companies to the bank's supervisory board were important foundations to obtaining valuable information for the bank's business, such as providing financing to companies and making investments in other enterprises. By securing such information, a large bank could realize a stable collection of financing funds to enterprises and secure higher efficiency of investments in industrial companies. In this chapter, the roles of a bank regarding such actions and the function and significance of interlocking of members of a supervisory board and a managing board between banks and industrial enterprises were clarified. Through these discussions, the intention and perspectives of a bank that emphasized developing personnel connections through the interlocking function of a supervisory board were clarified. Such a function in an industry–bank relationship was deeply related to the development and accomplishment of a bank's policy for industrial companies and was an important element and the foundation of cooperative capitalism in Germany.

11.3 Roles of Interlocking Supervisory Board Members in Management

There are cases in which interlocking directors from banks who held seats on the supervisory boards of multiple enterprises that were competitors attempted to coordinate with each other to resolve conflicts and oppositions of interests between those enterprises. However, in such a case, a foundation for collaboration was established. For example, in the German automobile industry, under the growing competitive pressure that arose during the Great Depression that began in 1929, using his interlocking mandates, E. G. von Stauss had supervisory board mandates in both Daimer-Benz AG and BMW and helped the companies to build cooperative relationships involving consignment of production and division of labor for certain products (e.g., engines for aircraft) as a survival strategy for both firms. Stauss proposed a division of labor in which Daimler-Benz would produce water cooling engines and BMW would manufacture air cooling engines. Furthermore, F. J. Popp from BMW held a supervisory board post in Daimler-Benz, and Wilhelm Kissel from Daimler-Benz was on the supervisory board of BMW, and their personal connection helped the companies to achieve a smoother coordination. Stauss also made it possible to provide enterprises in which he held interlocking mandates with large amounts of credit by using his position on the working committee within the supervisory board (James 2003, S. 93, 95).

Furthermore, we can observe cases where industrial enterprises appointed a representative from a bank to their supervisory boards to help them acquiring order from other companies. For example, directors of Siemens-Schuckert asked Oscar Schlitter from Deutsche Bank, who was an interlocking supervisory board member in the company, to intercede with Neukirchner Eisenwerk AG Gebr. Stumm to allow the electric company to obtain orders for two motors for a rolling mill. An internal document of Deutsche Bank's dated April 28, 1927, stressed that because AEG, as

Siemens' biggest rival, had already received a request for a large alternating current generator from this steel company, success in accepting an order had special importance for Siemens-Schuckert [HADB, P03525, Neukirchner Eisenwerk AG Gebr. Stumm, Neukirchen (28.4.1927)]. These cases indicate how interlocking directorates play a role in coordinating activities between enterprises.

Many of the interlocking supervisory board members from banks who served on the boards of industrial enterprises provided expertise and information about the field of finance that was highly significant. For example, as seen in the meeting of the supervisory board of AEG on March 1, 1935, special committees such as the finance committee were founded as important organizations within the supervisory board. At the time, bank credit was considered indispensable by AEG for strengthening its liquidity, and based on a proposal by the chairman of the finance committee, details involving technical points on granting a loan were discussed with members from banks who served on this committee [*Historisches Archiv des Deutschen Technikmuseum*, I0.2060A.02381, Sitzung des Ausschusses des Aufsichtsrates. Berlin, den 1. März 1935, vorm. 10 1/2 Uhr. S. 3].

Such cases exemplify the significance of the roles of interlocking directors from banks and expectations industrial enterprise has for their banking relationships.

Cases in which interlocking supervisory board members from banks played an important role as advisors on the boards of industrial enterprises can be observed in the iron and steel industry. Hermann Fischer, who held a mandate on the supervisory board of Hoesch, considered himself an advisor regarding issues of law (economic law) and finance for the board rather than as an agent representing the interests of Schaaffhausen'scher Bankverein and Discontogesellschaft. Harald Wixforth pointed out that although he was involved in important decision-making for business policy as an advisor, the only banker who played such role in Hoesch during the Weimar period was Hermann Fischer (Wixforth 1995, S. 193, 195, 198, 207). Arthur Salmonsohn from Discontogesellschaft and Carl Fürstenberg from Berliner Handels-Gesellschaft acted as intermediaries, advisors, and information providers to the supervisory boards of Rheinische Stahlwerke (Wixforth 1995, S. 330, 356). Trusting relationships among the board of this iron and steel enterprise and its house banks were built through such personal ties (Wixforth 1995, S. 330). In Mannesmann, Max Steinthal from Deutsche Bank, who was chairman of this industrial enterprise's board, coordinated interests of both companies and sought agreement within the board of directors (Wixforth 1995, S. 303). Differences of opinion or conflicts could be addressed through intensive discussions between Steinthal and Mannesmann's managing board on all issues involving business policy (Wixforth 1995, S. 275, 302). Deutsche Bank played a decisive role as a large stockholder (Wixforth 1995, S. 273). Such involvement of the company's biggest bank was due to the company's special position, as Deutsche Bank had been a large stockholder since its establishment (Wixforth 1995, S. 273, 304). In his book discussing the relationships between banks and ten industrial companies during the Weimar Republic, Wixforth stresses the importance of banks functioning as intermediary and advisor in achieving cooperation with respect to business policies in these companies (Wixforth 1995, SS. 507–508).

Within the concepts of "finance capital" proposed by V. I. Lenin, a form of capital created from combining industrial and banking capital, challenges arise in terms of serving the interests of both industry and banks without creating conflicts between the parties. Industrial enterprises attempt to maximize profits from their commercial operations, while banks seek to maximize interest and dividend income. Interest is an expense for industrial enterprises, but is income for banks. Therefore, exchanging information about and promoting a common understanding of a business issue between banks and industrial enterprises through a system of interlocking directorates is an important foundation for maximizing profits not only for industrial and commercial enterprises but also interest and dividends for banks. Until the end of World War II, financial policies such as building concealed reserves were an important part of "the industrial policy" aspect of finance capital and large German banks played substantial role in such policies. For example, the relationships between AEG and Berliner Handels-Geselslchaft, a large bank in Germany, included extensive financial and personal connections, as were Carl Fürstenberg from Berliner Handels-Gesellschaft and Emili Rathenau from AEG, where the former provided valuable financial advice. A principle of business that Fürstenberg, who held a supervisory board mandate in AEG, regarded as important was strengthening the ability to self-finance by regularly raising capital and building ordinary and secret reserves. This principle was applied to AEG as well and affected the special character of the company's financial policies (Berliner Handels-Gesellschaft 1956, SS. 96–97; Fürstenberg 1961, SS. 299–301). This indicates an understanding of the profitability structure of industrial enterprises on the part of banks and highlights the important role of banking executives who held mandates on the supervisory boards of such companies.

What is called "One Mark Account" ("Eine Mark Konto") is based on excessive depreciation whose origin can be seen in the shift to monopolistic capitalism that was significant in the financial policies of companies that at the time were based on hidden reserve funds. It was adopted for the purpose of realizing a stable dividend policy, and banks played a large role in developing such policies (Rosendorff 1932, SS. 97–98, S. 100; Prion 1931, SS. 20–21, 28; Tsumori 1961a; Tsumori 1961b; Tsumori 1964). Capital participation and personal connections were important measures used to transfer the method of drawing up balance sheets of big banks to subsidiary banks and industrial enterprises (Tsumori 1961b, p.62). For example, in AEG, a "one Mark account" was set up and can be almost consistently observed starting in 1893–1894 up to World War II, except for certain years during a depression (Allgemeine Elektricitäts-Gesellschaft, each financial year; *Handbuch der deutschen Aktiengeselslchaften*, each year; Heß 1958, SS. 29–30; Rosendorff 1932, S. 98).

As seen in the example of Carl Fürstenberg and AEG, a supervisory board member from a bank could play a significant role. In addition to supervising a company's business, inspecting and reporting on issues such as the company's financial statements, and evaluating assets based on company by-laws, the decision-making authority regarding the depreciation method was typically given to the supervisory board (Passow 1923, S. 4). In such a situation, the extent of involvement and roles of interlocking supervisory board members significantly impacted policies such as the "one Mark account" as well.

Building on examinations in this chapter, the next issue to be analyzed is the function that personnel connection built through interlocking directorate system exhibit in interfirm relationships, such as industry–bank relationships and relations among industrial companies after World War II. Therefore, the next chapter will explore this research problem.

References

Allgemeine Elektricitäts-Gesellschaft, *Geschäftsbericht*, each financil year.

Berliner Handels-Gesellschaft (1956) Die Berliner Handels-Gesellschaft in einem Jahrhundert deutscher Wirtschaft 1856–1956. Brüder Hartmann, Berlin.

Deusche Bank (1938) Geschäftsbericht für 1938. Deutsche Bank, Berlin

Deusche Bank (1939) Geschäftsbericht für 1939. Deutsche Bank, Berlin

Deutsche Bank (1941) Geschäftsbericht für 1941. Deutsche Bank, Berlin

Fürstenberg C (1961) Die Lebensgeschichte eines deutschen Bankiers. Reinische Verlags-Anstalt, Wiesbaden

Handbuch der deutschen Aktiengeselslchaften, each year.

Heß P (1958) AEG Energie—Profit—Verbrechen, Wirtschaft: Manuskript Nachlass von Eberhard Koebel-Tusk. Verlag Die Wirtschaft, Berlin

James H (2003) Die Deutsche Bank im Dritten Reich. C. H. Beck, München

Passow R (1923) Die Bilanzen der privaten und öffentlichen Unternehmungen. 3, nue durchgesehne Aufl., Bd.II, B. G. Teubner, Leipzig

Rosendorff R (1932) Was müssen die Aktionäre und Verwaltungen vom neuen Aktienrecht wissen? Spaeth & Lind, Berlin, Wien

Tsumori T (1961a) Doitsu dokusen kakuritsuki ni okeru jiko kinyu to kessan seisaku (1) (Self-financing and policy of balancing of accounts in the period of establishment of monopolies in Germany, 1). In: Keizai ronso (The ecomonic review) 88 (5):51–66

Tsumori T (1961b) Doitsu dokusen keiseiki ni okeru jikokinyu to kessanseisaku (2) (Self-financing and policy of balancing of accounts in the period of establishment of monopolies in Germany, 2). In: Keizai ronso (The economic review) 88(6):58–68

Tsumori T (1964) Doitsu dokusen shihonsyugi to himitsu tsumitatekin seisaku (German monopolistic capitalism and hidden reserves policy). Ritsumeikan keiiegaku (The Ritsumeikan business review) 3(2–3):90–118

Wixforth H (1995) Banken und Schwereindustrie in der Weimarer Republik. Böhlau, Köln, Weimar, Wien

Chapter 12
Functions of Interlocking Directorate After World War II: Roles of Direct Interlocking Directorate in Personnel Issues of Top Management Organs and Coordination Between Enterprises

Abstract Personnel connections through the interlocking directorate of members of top management organs such as supervisory boards and managing boards with other enterprises play important roles in obtaining, exchanging, and sharing information on various industrial departments and numerous companies. This chapter considers functions of interlocking directorate of members of top management organs on supervisory board of other enterprise after World War II in relation to roles of interlocking supervisory board member, bank's intention in cooperative interfirm relationships, and influence of bank on industrial enterprises. Personnel issues of member of supervisory board and problems regarding coordination of interests and conflicts between bank and industrial enterprises and between industrial firms will be examined to clarify mechanism of cooperation between enterprises.

Keyword Bank influence · Industry–bank relationship · Interlocking directorate · Interlocking supervisory board member · Personnel connection · Supervisory board

Chapter 11 considered functions and roles of interlocking directorate and interlocking supervisory board member before World War II. Direct interlocking directorate has played significant roles in collecting, exchanging, and sharing information and coordination of interests and conflicts between bank and industrial enterprise and among corporations. Building on discussions in pervious chapter, the next issue to be analyzed is the function that such personnel connections exhibit in interfirm relationships, such as industry–bank relationships and relations among industrial companies after the war. The personnel connections through the interlocking directorate of members of supervisory boards and managing boards of large banks with other enterprises played important roles in obtaining, exchanging, and sharing information on various industrial departments and numerous companies in which banks had an interest regarding financing and capital investments.

In this chapter, research problems concerning the functions of personnel connections through interlocking members of supervisory boards and managing boards of large banks and industrial enterprises are analyzed. The functions related to the selection of candidates who were to be proposed as members of the supervisory board of an

T. Yamazaki, *Relationships Between Industry and Bank in Germany*,
https://doi.org/10.1007/978-981-97-4996-6_12

industrial enterprise at the general meeting and the bank's influence in such personnel affairs is explored. Given banks' interests, such as the stable collection of financing funds for companies as customers and securing higher efficiency of investments in industrial companies, personnel issues regarding the election of supervisory board members engaged in business policy decisions and dismissal of members belonging to managing boards in charge of executing duties had particularly important meanings. In industrial enterprises as well, securing valuable information from banks and other industrial companies and building cooperative interfirm relationships with banks and other representative enterprises in various industries through interlocking directorate at the supervisory board level are important and significant.

This chapter examines the personnel connections from the end of the 1950s to the end of the 1980s. It discusses the afore-mentioned research topics using various original historical materials of Dresdner Bank AG ("Dresdner Bank") and Commerzbank AG ("Commerzbank") that have resided in the Commerzbank archives; the materials of Deutsche Bank AG ("Deutsche Bank") after World War II are not offered for public inspection. In this chapter, historical materials from industrial enterprises were also used. This chapter also analyzes the functions of interfirm relationships through interlocking directorate using original materials on the representative industrial enterprises of August Thyssen-Hütte in the iron and steel sector, Bayer AG ("Bayer") in the chemical sector, and Siemens AG ("Siemens") and AEG in the electrical sector.

First, Sect. 12.1 considers the selection of candidates as members of the supervisory board of an industrial company who were to be proposed at the general meeting. These discussions attempt to clarify the functions and roles of bank representatives on the supervisory boards of other companies and the bank's influence on industrial enterprises through supervisory board mandates considering a bank's intention in such cooperative interfirm relationships. Section 12.2 examines personnel issues regarding selecting candidates as members of a bank's supervisory board. Section 12.3 explores the coordination between banks and industrial enterprises and among industrial enterprises through interlocking supervisory members.

12.1 Functions of Interfirm Relationships Regarding Personnel Affairs of Supervisory Board Members at Industrial Enterprises

Next, Sect. 12.1 examines the function of interfirm relationships concerning personnel issues of supervisory board members at industrial enterprises. The analysis of such a research problem and the influence of banks are important issues.

12.1.1 Industry–Bank Relationships Regarding Personnel Affairs of Supervisory Board Members and Bank Influence

When considering industry–bank relationships with respect to the personnel affairs of supervisory board members and the influence of banks, at Dresdner Bank, the problem of dispatching someone at this bank to fill the supervisory board mandate of another company was proposed and examined in managing board meetings. Securing and maintaining a supervisory board mandate took precedence over other issues related to such behavior [*Historisches Archiv der Commerzbank*, HAC-500/121, 18232-2000, Bd.1, Auszug aus der Niederschrift über die Gemeinschaftssitzung am 21. Juli 1964 (31.7.1964); *Historisches Archiv der Commerzbank*, HAC-500/121, 18232-2000, Bd.1, Auszug aus der Niederschrift über die Gesamtvorstandssitzung am 25. Februar 1965 in Frankfurt a. M. (7.4.1965); *Historisches Archiv der Commerzbank*, HAC-500/121, 18232-2000, Bd.1, Auszug aus der Niederschrift über die Sitzung des Gesamtvorstandes am 24. Mai 1963. (20.6.1963)]. For example, reported at a board of directors meeting on January 25, 1965, was that Carl Goetz, a member of the Dresdner Bank supervisory board, held the supervisory board mandate of chemical company Degussa AG ("Degussa") that should have been handed over to E. Viehub, a member of the managing board of Dresdner, as successor. Concerning this issue, Henkel AG & Co. KGaA ("Henkel") informed the board through a meeting request (*Historisches Archiv der Commerzbank*, HAC-500/121, 18232-2000, Bd.1, Auszug aus der Niederschrift über die Gesamtvorstandes am 25. Januar 1965 in Hamburg) that an active member of the managing board of Dresdner Bank would take charge of this post in the future. Such a case indicates the close relationship between the bank and an industrial enterprise regarding the dispatch of members of top management.

At a Dresdner Bank board of directors meeting on February 25, 1964, regarding a personnel issue of the AEG supervisory board, E. Viehub reported on the conception of Hans Heine in the AEG-Telefunken business areas through a discussion with Hans C. Boden and Heine. The board took counsel considering conformity with the pattern of the house of Siemens regarding the post of the supervisory board as well. This consultation considered the decrease in the number of supervisory board members resulting from the influence of the 1965 Corporations Law, and only one mandate of the vice-chairman of the supervisory board was planned for AEG-Telefunken (*Historisches Archiv der Commerzbank*, HAC-500/121, 18232-2000, Bd.1., Auszug aus der Niederschrift über die Sitzung des Gesamtvorstandes am 25.2.1964). In addition, internal Dresdner Bank documents dated July 11, 1975 and April 4, 1976, showed that the bank engaged in exchanges and negotiations on who should take over the post of chairman of Hoechst AG's ("Hoechst") supervisory board after Karl Winnacker retired from the position at Hoechst and was installed as vice-chairman of Dresdner Bank's supervisory board in the coming year [*Historisches Archiv der Commerzbank*, HAC-500/121, 18093-2000, AR Dresdner Bank (11.7.1975);

Historisches Archiv der Commerzbank, HAC-500/121, 18093-2000AR Dresdner Bank (4.4.1976)].

An internal Dresdner Bank document dated February 2, 1976, described a personnel affair regarding Jürgen Pont, who took over the mandate of chairman of the supervisory board of Degussa as a successor and that was approved by Konrad Henkel through of exchanges with Henkel [Henkel (6.2.1976), *Historisches Archiv der Commerzbank*, HAC-500/121, 18093-2000]. In a meeting of the board of directors on December 21, 1967, a report on the director who would be dispatched was provided [*Historisches Archiv der Commerzbank*, HAC-500/121, 18232-2000, Bd.1, Auszug aus der Niederschrift über die Gesamtvorstandssitzung am 21. Dezember 1967 in Düsseldorf (16.2.1968)], and personnel issues concerning the supervisory boards of many enterprises were discussed and approved in meetings during other fiscal years as well [*Historisches Archiv der Commerzbank*, HAC-500/121, 18232-2000, Bd.1, Auszug aus der Niederschrift über die Gemeinschaftssitzung am 24. Mai 1963 (5.6.1963); *Historisches Archiv der Commerzbank*, HAC-500/121, 18232-2000, Bd.1, Veränderungen von Aufsichtsraten laut Meldung auf Grund des Rundbriefes Nr. 19 vom 5. März 1962; *Historisches Archiv der Commerzbank*, HAC-500/121, 18232-2000, Bd.1, Veränderungen von Aufsichtsrat-Mandaten. (15.9.1966); *Historisches Archiv der Commerzbank*, HAC-500/121, 18232-2000, Bd.1, Aufsichtsratsmandate (24.5.1960)].

In addition, issues regarding the function of an interlocking member of a supervisory board of an industrial enterprise are examined from the angle of personnel affairs using the case of Bayer as a representative large business. For instance, in a supervisory board meeting in 1968, Franz Heinrich Ulrich as a member of the board of directors of Deutsche Bank was selected as a candidate for vice-chairman of the supervisory board [*Bayer Archiv*, 384-1, Bayer AG, Aufsichtsrats-Sitzungen XII, Niederschrift. Neunundfünfzigste Aufsichtsratssitzung der Farbenfabriken Bayer Aktiengesellschaft in Köln-Deutz, Messehalle 8, am 29. Mai 1968; *Bayer Archiv*, 384-1, Bayer AG, Aufsichtsrats-Sitzungen XII, Stichworte für die 59. AR-Sitzung der FFB am 29. Mai 1968 nach der Hauptversammlung in Köln, Messehalle 8 (28.5.1968); *Bayer Archiv*, 384-1, Bayer AG, Aufsichtsrats-Sitzungen XII, Niederschrift. Achtundfünfzigste Aufsichtsratssitzung der Farbenfabriken Bayer Aktiengesellschaft in Leverkusen am 5. April 1968, S. 5; *Bayer Archiv*, 384-1, Bayer AG, Aufsichtsrats-Sitzungen XII, Stichworte für die 58. AR-Sitzung der Farbenfabriken Bayer AG am 5.4.1968, 9.30 Uhr in Leverkusen (28.3.1968), S. 2; *Bayer Archiv*, 384-1; Bayer AG, AR-Sitzungen XXVI, Stichworte für vorgesehene Tischrede von Herrn Prof. Hansen zur Verabschiedung von Herrn Ulrich aus dem Aufsichtsrat, (7.9.1977)]. His election was proposed and approved at a general meeting (Bayer 1968, S. 6). As is clear from an indication in a meeting on July 3, 1974, his contribution to the committee on capital participation as an advisor regarding financial affairs was expected (*Bayer Archiv*, 384-1, Bayer AG, Aufsichtsrats-Sitzungen XX Niederschrift über die dreiundneunzigste Aufsichtsratssitzung der Bayer Aktiengesellschaft am 3. Juli 1974, 17.05 Uhr, in der Messehalle Köln-Deutz, S. 2). For example, in the supervisory board meeting of Bayer on 19 January, 1972, Ulrich pointed out that in addition to influences of currency change, decisive effects of movement of cost on general business conditions and emphasized in particular, as long as manufacturing of mass-produced goods was concerned, true structural problem could occur for larger sectors of German industries under the constant increase of costs (*Bayer Archiv*, 384-1, Bayer AG, Aufsichtsratssitzungen XVI, Niederschrift über die neunundsiebzigste Aufsichtsratssitzung der Farbenfabriken Bayer Aktiengesellschaft am 19. Januar 1972, 10 Uhr, in Leverkusen, S. 3–4). In the meeting of the supervisory board on October 26, 1972, regarding discussion on entering into insurance business through founding of Bayer's own insurance company, Ulrich stressed fundamental apprehension and grounds of risks of such plan (*Bayer Archiv*, 384-1, Bayer AG, Aufsichtsratssitzungen XVII, Niederschrift über die dreiundachtigste Aufsichtsratssitzung der Bayer Aktiengesellschaft am 26. Oktober 1972, 10.00 Uhr, in Leverkusen, S. 5–6). In a document on a conversation on September 8, 1977 between Herbert Grünewald as a member of the managing board of Bayer and Ulrich concerning Ulrich's retirement from the vice-chairman position of the supervisory board of this chemical company, Ulrich indicated valuable opinions on various business policy problems and his prominent knowledge on the development of the economy as a representative of Deutsche Bank, the largest private bank outside the USA, and as chairman or member of the supervisory board of many enterprises in Germany was stressed. Grünewald pointed out that Ulrich's advice based on his clear insight had significant value (*Bayer Archiv*, 384-1, Bayer AG, AR-Sitzungen XXVI, Die Schrift über die Rede von Prof. Grünewald zum Abschied Ulrich am 8.9.1977). Other internal Bayer documents indicated that Ulrich's special field was foreign businesses concerned with specific interests related to investments in foreign financial and international markets as well as industrial finance (*Bayer Archiv*, 384-1, Bayer AG, AR-Sitzungen XXVI, Vorstellung des neuen AR in Bayer-Berichten Anfang 1975). The use of his special knowledge and experience was an important reason why such an experienced and competent bank representative was invited to hold the significant mandate of vice-chairman of a supervisory board.

In a meeting of the supervisory board on April 29, 1976, one proposal was the election of F. Wilhelm Christians from Deutsche Bank as a member of the supervisory board of Bayer for the remaining term of office after the retirement of Fritz Heinz Ulrich from having the mandate of such a top management entity [*Bayer Archiv*, 384-1, Bayer AG, Aufsichtsratssitzungen XXIII, Stichworte für die 101. Aufsichtsratssitzung der Bayer AG am 29.4.1976, 9.30 Uhr, in Leverkusen. (20.4.1976), S. 3, Deutsche Bank 1976, S. 7, 9]. Christians was inaugurated as vice-chairman of the supervisory board [*Bayer Archiv*, 384-1, Bayer AG, Aufsichtsratssitzungen XXIV, Niederschrift über die einhundertvierte Aufsichtsratssitzung der Bayer Aktiengesellschaft am 15. September 1976, 9.30 Uhr, in Dormagen, S. 6; *Bayer Archiv*, 384-1, Bayer AG, Aufsichtsratssitzungen XXIV, Stichworte für die 104. Aufsichtsratssitzung der Bayer AG am 15.9.1976, 9.30 Uhr, in Dormagen (10.9.1976), S. 2]. In this way, deep relationships between Deutsche Bank and Bayer and the significant role of an interlocking supervisory board member from a bank is observed. In the period of the latter half of the 1970s, when reduction of the rubber sector and closing of department of tires for passenger car were proposed by the managing board of Metzler Rubber, Christians regarded decision-making of Metzler Tire regarding this plan as necessary and appropriate (*Bayer Archiv*, 384-1, Bayer AG, Aufsichtsratssitzungen XVIII, Niederschrift über die einhundertunddreizehnte Aufsichtsratssitzung der Bayer Aktiengesellschaft am 1. September 1978, 9.45 Uhr, in Brunsbüttel, S. 5–6; *Bayer Archiv*, 384-1, Bayer AG, Aufsichtsratssitzungen XXVI, Niederschrift über die einhundertundachte Aufsichtsratssitzung der Bayer Aktiengesellschaft am 9. September 1977, 10 Uhr, in Leverkusen, S. 3) and promoted such restructuring. In the supervisory board meeting of Bayer on January 26, 1979, regarding explanation by F-J. Weitkemper, member of the managing board that conditions of interest and costs, situation of Euro bond market, and economical expectation for this company were important for issuing option bonds of Bayer International Finance, based on his expertise, Christians evaluated that Weitkemper's explanation was right at the timing of the issue of this bond (*Bayer Archiv*, 384-1, Bayer AG, Aufsichtsratssitzungen 30, Niederschrift über die einhundertundfünfzehnte Aufsichtsratssitzung der Bayer Aktiengesellschaft am 26. Januar 1979, 10 Uhr, in Leverkusen, S. 7). His advises contributed understanding of board members regarding financial issues.

Interlocking supervisory board members from banks in industrial enterprises played important roles not only in terms of their instructive knowledge regarding the finance and conditions in many industrial sectors but also in the development of financial policies of enterprise such as building of reserve fund. For instance, in Bayer, at the supervisory board meeting on April 16, 1971, F. H. Ulrich from Deutsche Bank pointed out that though structure of balance sheet was sound, profitability and above all its trend was not satisfying and stressed necessity to form reserve funds. Helmut Brands who was a member of the managing board of Commerzbank and interlocking supervisory board member in Bayer strongly insisted building of reserve funds was indispensable (*Bayer Archiv*, 384-1, Bayer AG, Aufsichtsratssitzungen XV, Niederschrift über die Sechsundsiebzigste Aufsichtsratssitzung der Farbenfabriken Bayer Aktiengesellschaft am 16. April 1971, 9.30 Uhr, in Leverkusen, S. 3).

At Bayer, a committee for personnel affairs was developed as an important committee of the supervisory board. This committee was composed of three members, including the chairman. The chairman of the supervisory board became the chairman of this committee, and two other members of the committee were the vice-chairmen [*Bayer Archiv*, 384-1, Bayer AG, Aufsichtsrats-Sitzungen I, Geschäftsordnung des Aufsichtsrats der Farbenfabriken Bayer Aktiengesellschaft (Juli 1954); *Bayer Archiv*, 384-1, Bayer AG, Aufsichtsrats-Sitzungen I, Niederschrift über die erste (konstituierende) Sitzung des Aufsichtsrates der Firma Farbenfabriken Bayer Aktiengesellschaft; *Bayer Archiv*, 384-1, Bayer AG, Aufsichtsrats-Sitzungen I, Niederschrift. Zwite Aufsichtsratssitzung der FARBENFABRIKEN BAYER AKTIENGESELLSCHAFT in Wuppertal-Elberfeld am 5. Juni 1952, S. 1–2; *Byer Archiv*, 384-1, Bayer AG, Aufsichtsrats-Sitzungen, I, Stichworte für die 7. Aufsichtsratssitzungen der Farbenfabriken Bayer Aktiengesellschaft am Mittwoch, den 23. Sept. 1953 12 Uhr in Leverkusen (21.9.1953); *Bayer Archiv*, 384-1, Bayer AG, Aufsichtsrats-Sitzungen

I, Niederschrift. Zwölfte Aufsichtsratssitzung der Farbenfabriken Bayer Aktiengesellschaft in Leverkusen am 20. Juli 1954; *Bayer Archiv*, 384-1, Bayer AG, Aufsichtsrats-Sitzungen II, Niederschrift. Achtzehnte Aufsichtsratssitzung der Farbenfabriken Bayer Aktiengesellschaft in Leverkusen am 29. Mai 1956; *Bayer Archiv*, 384-1, Bayer AG, Aufsichtsrats-Sitzungen IV, Niederschrift. Dreiβigste Aufsichtsratssitzung der Farbenfabriken Bayer Aktiengesellschaft in Leverkusen am 12. Mai 1960; *Bayer Archiv*, 384-1, Bayer AG, Aufsichtsrats-Sitzungen V, Niederschrift. Fünfunddreiβigste Aufsichtsratssitzung der Farbenfabriken Bayer Aktiengesellschaft in Leverkusen am 16. Mai 1962; *Bayer Archiv*, 384-1, Bayer AG, Aufsichtsrats-Sitzungen IX, Stichworte für die 50. AR-Sitzung der FFB am 18. Mai 1966 nach der Hauptversammlung in Köln, Messehalle 8 (16.5.1966); *Bayer Archiv*, 384-1, Bayer AG, Aufsichtsrats-Sitzungen XII, Niederschrift. Neunundfünfzigste Aufsichtsratssitzung der Farbenfabriken Bayer Aktiengesellschaft in Köln-Deutz, Messehalle 8, am 29. Mai 1968; *Bayer Archiv*, 384-1, Bayer AG, Aufsichtsrats-Sitzungen XIV, Stichworte für die 72. AR-Sitzung der Farbenfabriken Bayer AG am 11. Juni 1970 nach der Hauptversammlung in Köln, Messehalle 8 (10.6.1970)]. In the case that a member of this committee was outside the company, the role that the interlocking supervisory board member played in such an important committee could become significant. Moreover, if a person from the bank was elected as vice-chairman of the supervisory board, the possibility that the bank would become involved in the personnel affairs of top management strengthened through his installation as a member of such an important committee. For instance, the election of Fritz Gröning from Deutsche Bank in 1962 (*Bayer Archiv*, 384-1, Bayer AG, Aufsichtsratssitzungen V, Niederschrift über die Fünfunddreiβigste Aufsichtsratssitzung der Farbenfabriken Bayer Aktiengesellschaft am 16. Mai 1962, S. 1), the re-election of him in 1966 (*Bayer Archiv*, 384-1, Bayer AG, Aufsichtsratssitzungen IX, Niederschrift über die fünfzigste Aufsichtsratssitzung der Farbenfabriken Bayer Aktiengesellschaft in Köln-Deutz, Messehalle 8, am 18. Mai 1966, S. 1), and the above-mentioned election of Franz Heinrich Ulrich from Deutsche Bank to the vice-chairman position on the supervisory board of Bayer in 1968 enabled this large bank to become deeply involved with a personnel committee that played an important role in top management's personnel issues. Ulrich's appointment as vice-chairman of the supervisory board was suggested in a meeting of such a top management entity on June 11, 1970, and he was elected as a member of the personnel committee [*Bayer Archiv*, 384-1, Bayer AG, Aufsichtsrats-Sitzungen XIV, Niederschrift über die Zweiundsiebzigste Aufsichtsratssitzung der Farbenfabriken Bayer Aktiengesellschaft in Köln-Deutz, Messehalle 8, am 11. Juni 1970; *Bayer Archiv*, 384-1, Bayer AG, Aufsichtsrats-Sitzungen XIV, Stichworte für die 72. AR-Sitzung der Farbenfabriken Bayer AG am 11. Juni 1970 nach der Hauptversammlung in Köln, Messehalle 8 (10.6.1970)]. Deutsche Bank's special and strong involvement in top management's personnel affairs was maintained through this re-election. In a meeting of the supervisory board on September 15, 1976, the election of F. Wilhelm Christians from Deutsche Bank as a candidate for vice-chairman of the supervisory board was decided, and he was selected as Ulrich's successor and a member of the personnel committee [*Bayer Archiv*, 384-1, Bayer AG, Aufsichtsratssitzungen XXIV, Niederschrift über die einhundertvierte Aufsichtsratssitzung der Bayer Aktiengesellschaft am 15. September 1976, 9.30 Uhr, in Dormagen, S. 6; *Bayer Archiv*, 384-1, Bayer AG, Aufsichtsratssitzungen XXIV, Stichworte für die 104. Aufsichtsratssitzung der Bayer AG am 15.9.1976, 9.30 Uhr, in Dormagen (10.9.1976), S. 2].

The personnel committee was organized as an inner circle of the AEG supervisory board as well. This committee discussed important personnel affairs, such as the election of top management and proposed candidates [*Historisches Archiv des Deutschen Technikmuseums*, I.2.060 U438, Niederschrift über eine Sitzung der Personalausschusse der AEG und Tfk am 25. Mai 1965 in Frankfurt/M.; *Historisches Archiv des Deutschen Technikmuseums*, I.2.060 U440, Niederschrift über eine Sitzung des Personal-Ausschusses des Aufsichtsrats der ALLGEMEINE ELEKTRICITÄT-GESELLSCHAFT AEG-TELEFUNKEN am 25. April 1969 in Frankfurt/M.; *Historisches Archiv des Deutschen Technikmuseums*, I.2.060 U441, Niederschrift über eine Sitzung des Personalausschusses des Aufsichtsrats der ALLGEMEINE ELEKTRICITÄT-GESELLSCHAFT AEG-TELEFUNKEN am 13. April 1973 in Frankfurt/M (9.5.1973); *Historisches Archiv des Deutschen Technikmuseums*, I.2.060 U443, Niederschrift über eine Sitzung des Aufsichtsrats der ALLGEMEINE ELEKTRICITÄT-GESELLSCHAFT AEG-TELEFUNKEN am 12. Dezember 1974 in Frankfurt/M (13.12.1974); *Historisches Archiv des Deutschen Technikmuseums*, I.2.060 U445, Niederschrift über eine Sitzung des Personalausschusses der ALLGEMEINE ELEKTRICITÄT-GESELLSCHAFT AEG-TELEFUNKEN am 4. Dezember 1975 in München (8.12.1975); *Historisches Archiv des Deutschen Technikmuseums*, I.2.060 U446, Ablauf der Sitzung des Personalausschusses des Aufsichtsrats der ALLGEMEINE ELEKTRICITÄT-GESELLSCHAFT AEG-TELEFUNKEN am 21. April 1976, 8.30 Uhr, Frankfurt (Main); *Historisches Archiv des Deutschen Technikmuseums*, I.2.060 Ü-2, 0257, Niederschrift über die Sitzung des Aufsichtsrats von AEG-TELEFUNKEN am 9.11.1976 in Frankfurt/Main (21.1.1977)]. Interlocking members of the supervisory board from large banks were involved in this important committee organization. For instance, seven such individuals were called to a meeting on February 20, 1962, eight such persons were summoned to a meeting on February 20, 1963, nine such persons were called to meetings on November 28, 1963, and May 25, 1964, and seven such persons including one guest were summoned to a meeting on December 1, 1965. Furthermore, combined meetings of AEG and Telefunken occurred on December 10, 1964, and May 25, 1965, and eleven such persons were called to each of these meetings. Eleven such persons were called to a meeting on March 5, 1966, and eleven persons, one guest, and one recorder were called to a meeting on December 8, 1967. Except for the council meeting on May 25, 1965, at these meetings, interlocking supervisory board members from banks were called. Heinz Osterwind from Deutsche Bank and Erich Vierhub and Hans Boden from Dresdner Bank were the concerned individuals. In particular, Boden was called as a guest at a meeting on December 1, 1965, and attended (*Historisches Archiv des Deutschen Technikmuseums*, I.2.060 U438, Niederschrift über eine Sitzung des Personalausschusses am 20. Februar 1962; *Historisches Archiv des Deutschen Technikmuseums*, I.2.060

U438, Niederschrift über die Sitzung des Personalausschusses am 28.11.1963, 10. Uhr.; *Historisches Archiv des Deutschen Technikmuseums*, I.2.060 U438, Niederschrift über eine Sitzung des Personalausschusses am 25. Mai 1964, 10. Uhr.; *Historisches Archiv des Deutschen Technikmuseums*, I.2.060 U438, Niederschrift über eine Sitzung des Personal-Ausschusses der AEG am 1. Dezember 1965 in Frankfurt/M.; *Historisches Archiv des Deutschen Technikmuseums*, I.2.060 U438, Niederschrift über eine Sitzung der Personal-Ausschusse der AEG und Tfk am 5. Mai 1966 in Frankfurt/M.; *Historisches Archiv des Deutschen Technikmuseums*, I.2.060U439, Niederschrift über eine Sitzung des Personal-Ausschusses des Aufsichtsrats der ALLGEMEINE ELEKTRICITÄT-GESELLSCHAFT AEG-TELEFUNKEN am 8. Dezember 1967 in Rotenburg an der Tauber).

Walter Franke, Hans Heyne, Michery, Heinz Osterwind, and Erich Vierhub were elected as members of the personnel committee at a supervisory board meeting on December 10, 1964, and Heyne was selected as the chairman of this committee. Two individuals from banks were re-elected as committee members (*Historisches Archiv des Deutschen Technikmuseums*, I.2.060 U438, Niederschrift über die Sitzung des Aufsichtsräte der AEG und Tfk am 10. Dezember 1964, 11. Uhr., S. 10; *Historisches Archiv des Deutschen Technikmuseums*, I.2.060 U438, Niederschrift über eine Sitzung des Personalausschusses am 25. Mai 1964, 10. Uhr.). In addition, Hans Boden, Heinz Osterwind, Eduard von Schwarzkoppen, Erich Vierhub, Walter Franke, and Hans Rubke were elected at a supervisory board meeting on June 12, 1968. Three of these bank representatives including Osterwind were elected (*Historisches Archiv des Deutschen Technikmuseums*, I.2.060 U439, Niederschrift über die konstituirende Sitzung des Aufsichtsrats am 12. Juni 1968 in Berlin). At a supervisory board meeting on June 18, 1970, Hans C. Boden retired from the chairman position of this entity before the end of his term of office, and Hans Bühler was selected as his successor and simultaneously elected as chairman of the personnel committee [*Historisches Archiv des Deutschen Technikmuseums*, I.2.060 U440, Niederschrift über die Sitzung des Aufsichtsrats der ALLGEMEINE ELEKTRICITÄT-GESELLSCHAFT AEG-TELEFUNKEN am 18. Juni 1970 in Berlin; *Historisches Archiv des Deutschen Technikmuseums*, I.2.060 U440, Aufsichtsratssitzung vom 18. Juni 1970 Sitzung des Personalausschusses vom 18. Juni 1970(14.5.1970)]. Jürgen Ponto from Dresdner Bank was elected as chairman of the supervisory board, and Hans Rubke and Bernhard Timm were selected as vice-chairmen of this top management entity. At a supervisory board meeting on March 17, 1975, Pont was elected as chairman of the personnel committee, and Timm was selected as a committee member [*Historisches Archiv des Deutschen Technikmuseums*, I.2.060 U444, Niederschrift über eine Sitzung der ALLGEMEINE ELEKTRICITÄT-GESELLSCHAFT AEG-TELEFUNKEN am 17. März 1975 in Frankfurt/M. (25.3.1975)]. In addition, at a personnel committee meeting on December 2, 1976, affairs concerning the appointment of managing board members of AEG as members of the managing board of another company were discussed, as were important personnel affairs of this electric company [*Historisches Archiv des Deutschen Technikmuseums*, I.2.060 Ü-2, 0257, Niederschrift über die Sitzung des Personalausschusses des Aufsichtsrats von AEG-Telefunken am 2. Dezember 1976 in Frankfurt/M. (29.12.1976)]. Therefore, the involvement in this committee of interlocking supervisory board members from a bank made it possible that problems spread through the interlocking mechanism to directors in the other enterprise. Such a situation can also be seen in the afore-mentioned case of Bayer. In this way, the meaningful role and significance of the function of interlocking members of supervisory boards in important committees of these boards, which played an important role in the personnel issues of top management, can be observed at AEG as well.

In this way, Deutsch Bank as the largest bank in Germany had the mandate of vice-chairman of the supervisory board at Bayer and, thus, the continuous post of the personnel committee as well. Such a fact indicates that personnel connections through the interlocking directorate of a bank representative on the supervisory board played a significant role in the industry–bank relationship and was important to realize the interest and intention of the bank. The participation of the interlocking members on a supervisory board of a large bank, such as Deutsche Bank or Dresdner Bank, in such an important committee of the top management entity, particularly in the role of chairman of this committee, indicates the industry–bank relationship regarding the personnel affairs of the supervisory board and the bank's significant role in and influence on this board.

In AEG, as well as the personnel committee, the financial committee established in the supervisory board was important committee organization. In 1955, Erich Vierhub from Dresdner Bank who was a managing board member of Rhein-Main Bank, a preceding bank of Dresdner Bank which revived in 1957 through reconcentration of dissolved banks after World War II under the occupation policy of victorious countries was elected as vice-chairman on the supervisory board and chairman of the financial committee of this industrial company (*Historisches Archiv des Deutschen Technikmuseums*, I.2.060A.0995, Niederschrift über die Sitzung des Aufsichtsrats am Freitag, dem 4. November 1955, S. 1–2; Morr 1955, S. 953). Existence of interlocking supervisory board member from bank had great significance in terms of finance for enterprise that invited such person. For example, in the meeting of the financial committee on February 20, 1962, regarding issue of capital increase, H. Osterwind, interlocking supervisory board member form Deutsche Bank pointed out increase of capital equivalent to 70 million DM was needed under the condition of issuing price less than 200% of face value and equity capital could almost cover fixed assets. Thus, he played important advisory role (*Historisches Archiv des Deutschen Technikmuseums*, I.2.060 Ü-V0438, Niederschrift über eine Sitzung des Finanzausschusses am 20. Februar 1962, 11. Uhr, S. 3).

Furthermore, regarding August Thyssen-Hütte, a letter from Hans-Günther Sohl as chairman of the managing board of this enterprise to Fritz Gröning from Dresdner Bank on January 30, 1968, pointed out that Gröning played a significant role as an advisor during his term of office [*thyssenkrupp Corporate Archives* (bellow *tkA*), A/ 132108, Der Brief von Hans-Günther Sohl an Herr Gröning (30.1.1968)]. A letter dated February 9, 1966 from Hans-Günther Sohl to Alfred Hölling, also from the bank, and another letter in 1967 indicated the standpoint of Thyssen, which emphasized and admired Hölling 's contributions through his cooperation, advice, and maintenance of personnel connections, for many years [*tkA*, A/132108, Der Brief von Hans-Günther Sohl an Herrn Bankdirektor Konsul a. D. Alfred Hölling (9.2.1966); *tkA*, A/132108, Der Brief von Hans-Günther Sohl an Herrn Bankdirektor Konsul a. D. Alfred Hölling]. A new member of Thyssen's supervisory board became necessary with the retirement of Alfred Hölling from this top management entity in 1966. Ernst Matthiensen from Dresdner Bank took over as successor the mandate of Hölling. This personnel affair indicated a deep relationship with the banks, a significant role as an interlocking member of the supervisory board of the bank, and an emphasis on the function of the bank representative on the part of the industrial enterprise [*tkA*, A/12108, Der Brief von Hans-Günther Sohl an Herrn Dr. Kurt Birrenbach (10.2.1966)]. In addition, Robert Pferdmenges, chairman of the supervisory board of Thyssen and from Sal. Oppenheim jr. & Cie, played an important role in securing trustworthy and harmonious cooperation with all individuals concerned—including shareholders and employees—that formed the basis of the company's reconstruction after the war. Pferdmenges also exhibited his expert ability through the establishment of Handelsunion as a subsidiary of August Thyssen-Hütte, which faced strong opposition. Pferdmenges' knowledge and ability were very significant in addressing personnel issues of the top mandate of the supervisory board [*tkA*, A/132108, Der Brief von Hans-Günther Sohl an die Teilhaber des Bankhauses Sal. Oppenheim jr. & Cie (1.10.1962); *tkA*, A/132108, Der Brief von Hans-Günther Sohl an die Teilhaber des Bankhauses Sal. Oppenheim jr. & Cie (2.10.1962); *tkA*, A/132108, Der Brief von Hans-Günther Sohl an Frau Dora Pferdmenges (1.10.1962)].

In addition, an examination of the two insurance enterprises Allianz and Münchener Rückversicherung-Gesellschaft showed that close relationships existed through the supervisory board between large banks and these insurance companies. These relationships were deeply concerned with the functions of the personnel connections through interlocking supervisory board members. At Allianz, the tradition was that individuals from Deutsche Bank and Dresdner Bank were members of such a top management entity. A competitive situation existed between the two banks regarding the personnel affairs of supervisory board members. When Franz H. Ulrich from Deutsche Bank retired from the supervisory board in August 1976, the bank requested the appointment of Wilfred Guth. However, Jürgen Pont from Dresdner Bank succeeded this mandate with the support of a strong request from Allianz. At Münchener Rückversicherung-Gesellschaft at the end of 1974, Jürgen Pont took over the traditional and representative post that Carl Goetz or Ernst Matthiensen from Dresdner Bank held. This personnel issue was also based on the imminent strong demand of Horst Jannott as chairman of the managing board of this insurance company. Pont's work mainly focused on personnel affairs and policies related to the strategic capital participation of corporate insurance groups. In these two insurance companies, he functioned as an advisor rather than a supervisor in discussions concerning personnel issues and capital participation (Ahrens and Bähr 2013, S. 132–134). Such demand and intentions of the insurance firms were based on the important roles of interlocking supervisory board members from banks who are well versed in the problems faced by the industry and had the opportunity to obtain volumes of useful information.

Competition among banks over the assignment of their members to mandates on the supervisory boards, above all chairman post of other enterprises was significant issue for banks concerned. German large banks had acquired recognition and insight regarding business policies of enterprises as provider of credits and as members of the supervisory boards of large corporations. Based on internal information, they could evaluate the expected change in the stock market much better than all other speculators (Der Spiegel 1971a, S. 48). In Rheinisch-Westfälisches Elektrizitätswerk AG, one of the biggest electric power enterprises in German, based on suggestion by Hermann J. Abs from Deutsche Bank, Jürgen Pont from Dresdner Bank who had held interlocking mandate on the supervisory board of this company from the financial year 1972/73 succeeded Abs's chairman mandate on February 24, 1977. However, after it was decided that chairmen mandate on the supervisory board should be taken charge of by representative of private economy according to the agreement with the local self-government body as one of the large shareholders, Wilhelm F. Christians from Deutsche Bank became chairman on October 17, 1977. This means all regarding this personnel issue were decided along the line of intention of Deutsche Bank. In AEG in which rebuilding became one of the most important and indispensable issue to be solved in the 1970s, though J. Ponto made use of chairman post on the supervisory board to re-establish this company, in 1977, this influential mandate was succeeded by Bernhard Timm, former chairman on the board of directors of BASF. The house bank of this chemical company had been Deutsche Bank, and for Dresdner Bank, the election of Timm was not conveniently (Der Spiegel 1977a, S. 60, 1977b, S. 113; Rheiniswch-Westflisches Elektrizittswerk AG 1973, S. 5; Rheinisch-Westflisches Elektrizitätswerk AG 1977, S. 5).

12.1.2 Relationships Between Industrial Enterprises Regarding Personnel Affairs of Members of Supervisory Boards of Industrial Companies

This section analyzes the relationships between industrial enterprises regarding the personnel affairs of members of supervisory boards of industrial firms. Many cases existed in which an industrial enterprise accepted members of the supervisory boards of other companies except for banks. For example, at Bayer, the issue of the appointment of Peter von Siemens, vice-chairman of the supervisory board of Siemens-Schuckerwerket AG in the electrical industry, as a member of Bayer's supervisory board was taken up in 1966. Regarding this personnel issue, that von Siemens consistently used his international experiences for entire industries was evaluated and emphasized [*Bayer Archiv*, 384-1, Bayer AG, Aufsichtsrats-Sitzungen IX, NOTAR MARTIN MEYER in Leverkusen-Wiesdorf, S. 14; *Bayer Archiv*, 384-1, Bayer AG, Aufsichtsrats-Sitzungen IX, *Bayer Archiv*, 384-1, Bayer AG, Aufsichtsrats-Sitzungen IV, Niederschrift. Neunundvierzigste Aufsichtsratssitzung der Farbenfabriken Bayer Aktiengesellschaft in Leverkusen am 31. März 1966, S. 5].

Regarding invitations to and acceptances of interlocking supervisory board members from other enterprises, the influence of the 1965 Corporations Law, which regulated the number of mandates for a supervisory board that one person might have, was also observed in industrial enterprises. For instance, at Bayer, the number of members of the supervisory board on the side of shareholders elected at the general meeting was limited to 10. Under such a condition, Richard Freudenberg, Heinrich Köhler, and Bernhard Plettner from Siemens were asked to approve giving up their re-election as members of the supervisory board, unlike other supervisory board members [*Bayer Archiv*, 384-1, Bayer AG, Aufsichtsrats-Sitzungen IX, Die Schrift über die Hauptversammlung am Mittwoch, den 18. Mai 1966, um 10 Uhr in der Kongreβhalle (Halle 8), Messegelände Köln-Deutz (April 1966); *Bayer Archiv*, 384-1, Bayer AG, Aufsichtsrats-Sitzungen IX, NOTAR MART IN MEYER in Leverkusen-Wiesdorf, S. 1, S. 13–14; *Bayer Archiv*, 384-1, Bayer AG, Aufsichtsrats-Sitzungen IX, HV 18.5.1966/Rundschreiben der Direktionsabteilung betr. Ablauf d. HV (15.4.1966); *Bayer Archiv*, 384-1, Bayer AG, Aufsichtsrats-Sitzungen IV., Niederschrift. Neunundvierzigste Aufsichtsratssitzung der Farbenfabriken Bayer Aktiengesellschaft in Leverkusen am 31. März 1966, S. 4]. The re-election of Plettner was canceled because of the cross-post situation between both companies that emerged due to Kurt Hansen's membership of the supervisory board of Siemens. Peter von Siemens from Siemens was elected as the member of the supervisory board whose candidacy was proposed as succeeding Plettner at the general meeting [*Bayer Archiv*, 384-1, Bayer AG, Aufsichtsrats-Sitzungen IX, Stichworte für die 49. Aufsichtsratssitzung der Farbenfabriken Bayer AG am Donnerstag, den 31. März 1966, 9.30 Uhr in Leverkusen. (28.3.1966), S. 2–3; *Bayer Archiv*, 384-1, Bayer AG, Aufsichtsrats-Sitzungen IX, Niederschrift. Neunundvierzigste Aufsichtsratssitzung der Farbenfabriken Bayer Aktiengesellschaft in Leverkusen am 31. März 1966, S. 4–5; *Siemens Archiv Akten*, 4Lr302-20, Der Brief von Prof. Dr. Kurt Hanaen an Herrn Dr. Ernst von Siemens (12.12.1965)]. Regarding this personnel issue, using Peter von Siemens' special abilities and experience as well as appointing a person from the same enterprise as that of the predecessor was emphasized. In addition, at the supervisory board meeting on January 23, 1974, because the term of office of all supervisory board members expired at the general meeting on July 3, personnel issues regarding the election of candidates to be members of such a top management entity were taken up. Regarding the personnel affairs of Helmut Lorenz-Meyer as a candidate, Peter von Siemens pointed out that his experiences in South America was the reason for his election as a candidate [*Bayer Archiv*, 384-1, Bayer AG, Aufsichtsrats-Sitzungen XIX, Niederschrift über die neunundachtzigste Aufsichtsratssitzung der Bayer Aktiengesellschaft am 23. Januar 1974, 10.30 Uhr, in Leverkusen, S. 8–9; *Bayer Archiv*, 384-1, Bayer AG, Aufsichtsrats-Sitzungen XIX, Stichworte für die 89. Aufsichtsratssitzung der Bayer AG am 23.1.1974, 10.30 Uhr in Leverkusen. (11.1.1974), S. 4].

A similar case can be observed in the relationship between Siemens and Mannesmann. For instance, a letter from Peter von Siemens to Wilhelm Zangen on March

3, 1965, indicated that the broad experience and effective advice of Zangen, who was from Mannesmann and was a member of the supervisory board of Siemens-Schckertwerke from February 28 to March 15, 1965, had significance in his appointment to this post and for reinforcing old relationships between both enterprises. This letter also pointed out the expectation of maintaining friendly relationships between the companies through the appointment of Overbeck as a successor of Zangen—who was from the same iron and steel company—as a member of the supervisory board [*Siemens Archiv Akten*, 4Lr302-20, Der Brief von Dr. Peter von Siemens an Herr Wilhelm Zangen (3.3.1965); *Siemens Archiv Akten*, 4Lr302-20, Ein Dokument über Wilhelm Zangen (28.1.1965); Mannesmann AG 1964, S. 8, 1965, S. 6]. Similar recognition and expectations can also be observed in a letter from Zangen to Peter von Siemens, who was chairman of the supervisory board of Siemens [*Siemens Archiv Akten*, 4Lr302-20, Der Brief von Wilhelm Zangen an Herrn Dr.-Ing. E.h. Ernst von Siemens (5.10.1961)].

Furthermore, at August Thyssen-Hütte, for example, Kurt Lots, chairman of the managing board of Volkswagen, was elected as a member of the supervisory board of Thyssen at the general meeting on April 20, 1970. This iron and steel enterprise emphasized that his appointment for this mandate would contribute to recreating the old connection between the companies that was built through the posts of such top management entities [*tkA*, A/132108, Der Brief von Hans-Günther Sohl an Herrn Dr. Kurt Lotz (18.8.1969)]. According to Thyssen's internal documents dated April 26, 1965, and January 5, 1966, concerning the re-election of Bernhard Plettner from Siemens at the end of his tenure of office, cross posts between both companies that were in contradiction to the 1965 Corporations Law were a problem. However, Thyssen sought the re-election of Plettner from the viewpoint that this problem could be avoided because his term of office ended earlier at Thyssen than at Siemens [*tkA*, A/132108, Aufsichtsratsmandat des Herrn Plettner (26.8.1965); *tkA*, A/132108, Der Brief von Hans-Günther Sohl an Herrn Dr. Kurt Birrenbach (5.1.1966)]. This point indicates the importance of interlocking directorate through mandates of supervisory boards to maintain and strengthen the relationships between the enterprises.

The significance of maintaining and reinforcing friendly relationships between companies can also be seen in the cases of Thyssen and Bayer. For example, a letter from Hans-Günther Sohl to Kurt Hansen from Bayer dated January 8, 1962 and an internal Thyssen document dated October 2, 1961 pointed out that the supervisory board and the board of directors of this iron and steel enterprise placed decisive value on maintaining friendly and continuous relationships with Bayer and stressed the role of interlocking members of the supervisory board with respect to personnel connections [*tkA*, A/132107, Der Brief von Hans-Günther Sohl an Herrn Dr. Kurt Hansen (8.1.1962); *tkA*, A/132107, Aufsichtsrat ATH (2.10.1961)].

In a meeting of the supervisory board of Bayer on September 6, 1974, appointing Peter von Siemens from Siemens as a member of the personnel committee was proposed and approved on to help manage personnel problems. Consequentially, decisions regarding important personnel issues, such as for top management, were made by Kurt Hansen as chairman of this committee, Fritz Heinz Ulrich from Deutsche Bank, and Peter von Siemens from Siemens-Schuckertwerke AG

[*Bayer Archiv*, 384-1, Bayer AG, Aufsichtsrats-Sitzungen XX, Niederschrift über die vierundneunzigste Aufsichtsratssitzung der Bayer Aktiengesellschaft am 6. September 1974, 9.30 Uhr, in Wuppertal-Elberfeld, S. 5].

In addition, the election of Peter von Siemens as vice-chairman of the supervisory board of Bayer and the installation of F. Wilhelm Christians from Deutsche Bank as members of the personnel committee were decided on in a supervisory board meeting on September 15, 1976. The mandate of Peter von Siemens was for re-election, and Siemens continued its involvement in important functions of the personnel committee [*Bayer Archiv*, 384-1, Bayer AG, Aufsichtsratssitzungen XXIV, Niederschrift über die einhundertvierte Aufsichtsratssitzung der Bayer Aktiengesellschaft am 15. September 1976, 9.30 Uhr, in Dormagen, S. 6; *Bayer Archiv*, 384-1, Bayer AG, Aufsichtsratssitzungen XXIV; *Bayer Archiv*, 384-1, Bayer AG, Aufsichtsratssitzungen XXIX, Stichworte für die 104. Aufsichtsratssitzung der Bayer AG am 15.9.1976, 9.30 Uhr, in Dormagen (10.9.1976), S. 2, Aufsichtsrat (8.4.1976).]. Thus, not only interlocking supervisory board members from the bank but also from industrial enterprises played a significant role in addressing important topics such as personnel issues of top management. At Bayer, personnel connections through the interlocking members of the supervisory board between Bayer and German largest bank and between Bayer and one of the most representative large enterprises in the electrical industry as a key industry exhibited functions through their participation on the personnel committee.

Between industrial enterprises as well, there were numerous cases in which continuous personnel connections through the interlocking function of the supervisory board were developed from deep interfirm relationships, business relationships, or the specialties of the concerned individuals. Cases in which members of Bayer's managing board had mandates of the supervisory boards of other companies are evaluated. In a meeting of the supervisory board on April 2, 1956, the installation of Otto Bayer as a member of the supervisory board of Cassella Farbwerke Mainkur AG, that of Riedel de Haen at a similar statue as that of Borgwardt, and that of Koziol as a similar member of Beton und Monierbau AG were approved. O. Bayer was a successor of Haberland as a member of Bayer's managing board [*Bayer Archiv*, 384-1, Bayer AG, Aufsichtsrats-Sitzungen II, Niederschrift. Siebzehnte Aufsichtsratssitzung der Farbenfabriken Bayer Aktiengesellschaft in Leverkusen am 27. April 1956, S. 4; *Bayer Archiv*, 384-1, Bayer AG, Aufsichtsrats-Sitzungen II, Stichworte für die 17. Aufsichtsratssitzung der Farbenfabriken Bayer AG am Freitag, den 27. April. 1956 10 Uhr in Leverkusen (25.4.1956)].

In a meeting on July 7, 1971, the installation of Kurt Hansen on the supervisory board of Veba AG and that of Dieter Schaub as a member of the supervisory board of Bayer-Wohnungen GmbH and Gemeinnützige Wohnungs-Gesellschaft mbH were accepted and admitted. F. Schilcher retired from posts on the supervisory board of Bayer-Wohnungen GmbH, and Gemeinnützige Wohnungs-Gesellschaft mbH and Schaup took over these posts [*Bayer Archiv*, 384-1, Bayer AG, Aufsichtsrats-Sitzungen XV, Stichworte für die 77. Aufsichtsratssitzung der Farbenfabriken Bayer AG am 7.7.1971, 9.30 Uhr, im Uerdingen. (29.6.1971), S. 4; *Bayer Archiv*, 384-1, Bayer AG, Aufsichtsrats-Sitzungen XV, Niederschrift über die Siebenundsiebzigste

Aufsichtsratssitzung der Farbenfabriken Bayer Aktiengesellschaft am 7. Juli 1971, 9.30 Uhr, in Uerdingen, S. 5]. In a meeting on April 18, 1973, the mandates to take the office of Metzler AG by W. Meyerheim, of Agfa-Gevaert AG by Herbert Grünewald, and of Agfa AG and Chemie-Verwaltungs-AG by Schaub were recognized. Grünewald succeeded the post of H. Gierlichs, and Schaup's post on Chemie-Verwaltungs-AG was a mandate that F. Schilcher held until then [*Bayer Archiv*, 384-1, Bayer AG, Aufsichtsrats-Sitzungen XVIII, Stichworte für die 86. Aufsichtsratssitzung der Bayer AG am 18. April 1973, 9.30 Uhr, im Leverkusen. (10.4.1973), S. 4; *Bayer Archiv*, 384-1, Bayer AG, Aufsichtsrats-Sitzungen XVIII]. In a meeting on April 24, 1974, the installations of supervisory board mandates in other enterprises by members of Bayer's managing board were approved. Of these, mandates at Wolff Walsrode that were taken over by Fritz and W. Meyerheim were the posts of Kaus and H. Gierlichs, who were both members of Bayer's managing board. The post of chairman of the supervisory board should have been taken charge of by Meyerheim [*Bayer Archiv*, 384-1, Bayer AG, Aufsichtsrats-Sitzungen XIX, Stichworte für die 91. Aufsichtsratssitzung der Bayer AG am 24. April 1974, 9.30 Uhr, im Leverkusen. (11.4.1974), S. 6; *Bayer Archiv*, 384-1, Bayer AG, Aufsichtsrats-Sitzungen XIX, Niederschrift über die einundneunzigste Aufsichtsratssitzung der Bayer Aktiengesellschaft am 24. April 1974, 9.30 Uhr, in Leverkusen, S. 8]. In a meeting on September 6, 1974, acceptance of the mandate of Chemische Werke Hüls AG by W. Meyerheim was admitted, and this personnel issue was a successive post that W. Holzrichter had until that point [*Bayer Archiv*, 384-1, Bayer AG, Aufsichtsrats-Sitzungen XX, Niederschrift über die vierundneunzigste Aufsichtsratssitzung der Bayer Aktiengesellschaft am 6. September 1974, 9.30 Uhr, in Wuppertal-Elberfeld, S. 4; *Bayer Archiv*, 384-1, Bayer AG, Aufsichtsrats-Sitzungen XX, Stichworte für die 94. Aufsichtsratssitzung der Bayer AG am 6.9.1974, 9.30 Uhr, in Wuppertal-Elberfeld. (14.8.1974), S. 2]. In a meeting on September 9, 1977, taking over the supervisory board mandates at Allianz, Deutsche Entwicklungsgesellschaft, and Metallgesellschaft by H. Grünewald and the acceptance of a mandate at Continental Gummi-Werke AG by Weitkemper were approved. Of these, the post at Allianz that was taken over by Grünewald was a mandate that K. Hansen held, and the post at Continental Gummi-Werke AG that was accepted by Weitkemper was a mandate that W. Meyerheim held until that point. The minutes of this meeting noted that these two mandates were dispatched by Bayer and were to be maintained on the basis of such a tradition [*Bayer Archiv*, 384-1, Bayer AG, AR-Sitzungen XXVI, Stichworte für die 108. Aufsichtsratssitzung der Bayer AG am 9.9.1977, 10.00 Uhr, im Leverkusen (6.9.1977), S. 3; *Bayer Archiv*, 384-1, Bayer AG, AR-Sitzungen XXVII, Niederschrift über die einundhundertachte Aufsichtsratssitzung der Bayer Aktiengesellschaft am 9. September 1977, 10 Uhr, in Leverkusen, S. 7]. In a meeting on September 1, 1978, the installation of Dittmar for the Linde AG mandate was admitted. Regarding interlocking directorate through this post, Holzricher—as a member of Bayer's board of directors—asked Linde AG to provide a continuous supervisory board post given the long relationship between this company and Bayer [*Bayer Archiv*, 384-1, Bayer AG, AR-Sitzungen XXVIII, Stichworte für die 113. Aufsichtsratssitzung der Bayer AG am 1.9.1978, 9.45 Uhr, in Brunsbüttel (23.8.1978), S. 4; *Bayer Archiv*, 384-1, Bayer AG, AR-Sitzungen XXVIII, Niederschrift über die einhundertunddreizehnte Aufsichtsratssitzung der Bayer Aktiengesellschaft am 1. September 1978, 9.45 Uhr, in Brunsbüttel, S. 2, 8; *Bayer Archiv*, 384-1, Bayer AG, AR-Sitzungen XXVIII, Die Schrift vom Vorsitzende des Aufsichtsrats an die Mitglieder des Aufsichtsrates der BAYER AG (10.8.1978), S. 2].

When observing the installation of a member of Bayer's managing board as a member of the supervisory board of other enterprises, as well as cases in which interlocking directorate relationships were reinforced by securing and maintaining existing posts on supervisory boards by successors, many cases existed in which personnel connections were created through a new post to establish a new relationship with and to deepen existing relationships between companies. For instance, in a meeting of the Bayer supervisory board on September 9, 1977, the acceptance of supervisory board mandates of Deutsche Bank and Metallgesellschaft AG by Herbert Grünewald were approved. These two mandates were provided for Bayer with a view to building new relationships with this chemical company and to deepening interfirm relationships [*Bayer Archiv*, 384-1, Bayer AG, AR-Sitzungen XXVI, Stichworte für die 108. Aufsichtsratssitzung der Bayer AG am 9.9.1977, 10.00 Uhr, im Leverkusen (6.9.1977), S. 4: *Bayer Archiv*, 384-1, Bayer AG, AR-Sitzungen XXVII]. Furthermore, in a meeting on April 24, 1974, the installation of Fritz and Josef Strenger through supervisory board mandates of Metzeler Kautschuk AG, Metzeler Schaum GmbH, and Correcta-Werke GmbH was recognized as well as some of the afore-mentioned posts. In these three enterprises, each mandate of chairman of the supervisory board was considered to be taken over by either of these two members [*Bayer Archiv*, 384-1, Bayer AG, Aufsichtsrats-Sitzungen XIX, Stichworte für die 91. Aufsichtsratssitzung der Bayer AG am 24. April 1974, 9.30 Uhr, im Leverkusen. (11.4.1974), S. 5; *Bayer Archiv*, 384-1, Bayer AG, Aufsichtsrats-Sitzungen XIX, Niederschrift über die einundneunzigste Aufsichtsratssitzung der Bayer Aktiengesellschaft am 24. April 1974, 9.30 Uhr, in Leverkusen, S. 8]. These cases indicate the establishment of strong personnel connections with important enterprises through interlocking directorates on supervisory boards and the expectation of enterprises that accepted supervisory board members from other companies for the role and function that interlocking supervisory board members would play through important mandates such as chairman of the supervisory board.

In interlocking relationships among industrial enterprises through mandates of the supervisory board, the function of complementing between companies in different industries also had significance. For instance, in a meeting of the Bayer supervisory board on September 1, 1978, the installation of Weitkemper to the supervisory board post of Horten AG in the distribution industry was admitted in addition to the afore-mentioned acceptance of a supervisory board post at Linde AG by Dittmar. The personnel issue regarding Weitkemper was based on the request of Horten AG, and this company intended to complement members of the supervisory board from the industrial sector, including the producing industry [*Bayer Archiv*, 384-1, Bayer AG, AR-Sitzungen XXVIII, Stichworte für die 113. Aufsichtsratssitzung der Bayer AG am 1.9.1978, 9.45 Uhr, in Brunsbüttel (23.8.1978), S. 4; *Bayer Archiv*, 384-1,

Bayer AG, AR-Sitzungen XXVIII, Niederschrift über die einhundertunddreizehnte Aufsichtsratssitzung der Bayer Aktiengesellschaft am 1. September 1978, 9.45 Uhr, in Brunsbüttel, S. 2, 8; *Bayer Archiv*, 384-1, Bayer AG, AR-Sitzungen XXVIII, Schriftliche Stimmabgabe zur Aufsichtsratssitzung der Bayer AG am 1.9.1978 in Brunsbüttel, S. 2, *Bayer Archiv*, 384-1, Bayer AG, AR-Sitzungen XXVIII, Die Schrift vom Vorsitzende des Aufsichtsrats an die Mitglieder des Aufsichtsrates der BAYER AG (10.8.1978), S. 2]. This case indicates the significant nature of meaningful personnel connections through enterprises as well.

In terms of roles of interlocking supervisory board members from industrial enterprises, Heinz P. Kemper from VEBA who held interlocking supervisory board mandate in Bayer played important role in this chemical company. In the meeting of Bayer's supervisory board on January 19, 1972, he referred to case of wage-intensive business in the department of VEVA in which possibility to maintain production was excluded as a result of the rise of wage (*Bayer Archiv*, 384-1, Bayer AG, Aufsichtsrats-Sitzungen XVI, Niederschrift über die neunundsiebzigste Aufsichtsratssitzung der Farbenfabriken Bayer Aktiengesellschaft am 19. Januar 1972, 10 Uhr, in Leverkusen, S. 4) and took up issues with which many enterprises faced at the time. In this way, in the interlocking directorates between industrial enterprises as well, making the most use of experiment and expertise of person concerned in company to which he belonged had great significance.

Personnel connections in the form of indirect interlocking directorate through mandates of supervisory boards of other interlocking mandates of supervisory boards and of establishing personnel connections among industrial companies functioned as a means of personal discussion and contact regarding various problems without being limited to issues of the concerned enterprise. For instance, an internal August Thyssen-Hütte document dated November 26, 1962, indicated that the route between Hans-Günther Sohl from Thyssen and Franz Heinrich Ulrich from Deutsche Bank could be secured through an opportunity to meet at the company in which both individuals had supervisory board mandates—Demag in the machine industry. They discussed personnel affairs concerning the supervisory board member of Thyssen on the basis of this bank's demand [*tkA*, A/132108, Vermerk (26.11.1962)].

12.2 Function of Interfirm Relationships Regarding Personnel Affairs of Members of Banks' Supervisory Boards

Regarding mandates of banks' supervisory boards, negotiations and exchanges with industrial companies were important. For instance, in a Dresdner Bank internal document dated April 7, 1957, Rheinstahl AG and its group proposed Wiedenhof, a member of the managing board of this industrial enterprise, as a successor of von Waldthausen, who was from this group and was a supervisory board member of Dresdner Bank. This personnel affair was suggested on the basis of the demand of

Rheinstahl, and Dresdner Bank agreed with the proposal [*Historisches Archiv der Commerzbank*, HAC-500/192, 1379–2002, Aufsichtsrat Dresdner Bank (8.4.1957)]. In a meeting on April 22, 1968, on the post of the Dresdner Bank supervisory board, this bank indicated the request to install an individual from Volkswagen for the remaining period of duty as a successor to Heinrich Nordhoff, who was from same automobile enterprise and died halfway through his term of office. Two individuals, Lotz and Lust, who were vice-chairman of the managing board and chairman of the supervisory board, respectively, of this automobile enterprise were taken up as candidates for members of Dresdner Bank's supervisory board; the first discussion with Lust occurring during the decision process [*Historisches Archiv der Commerzbank*, HAC-500/211, 109333, Präsidialsitzung (22.4.1968), S. 4].

In many cases, a person who belonged to the same company outside the bank was invited and installed as a member of the bank's supervisory board. For instance, in a meeting of Dresdner Bank's supervisory board on March 22, 1961, Hellmut Ley, chairman of the managing board of Metallgesellschaft AG, and Hermann Heusch, chairman of the supervisory board of Aachener und Münchener Feuerversicherungs-Gesellschaft, were elected as candidates and were proposed at the general meeting. Ley was elected as a successor of the mandate held by Alfred Petersen, who was chairman of the supervisory board of the same metal company (*Historisches Archiv der Commerzbank*, 5014-2002. Ms, Niederschrift über die Sitzung des Aufsichtsrats der Dresdner Bank Aktiengesellschaft am 22. März 1961 im Hause der Hauptverwaltung Düsseldorf; Dresdner Bank AG 1959, S. 9, 1960, S. 12–13). Similar cases can be observed in a meeting of the supervisory board on March 31, 1965. The decision was made at the general meeting to propose Walther Kniep of the Meizena group, Felix Prentzel, chairman of the managing board of Degussa, and Hans Rinn of Hof Hellerholz as members of the supervisory board of Dresdner Bank. Of these three individuals, Kniep was to succeed the post of Werner Rosenbruch, who was chairman of the supervisory board of Deutsche Meizena Werke GmbH, an enterprise of the same capital line as the Meizena group. Plentzel was a successor of the mandate of Hermann Schlosser, who was chairman of the supervisory board of Degussa (*Historisches Archiv der Commerzbank*, 5041-2002. Ms, Niederschrift über die Sitzung des Aufsichtsrats der Dresdner Bank Aktiengesellschaft am 31. März 1965 in den Räumen der Hauptverwaltung Frankfurt a.M.; Dresdner Bank AG 1964, S. 8–9, 1965, S. 11).

In addition, regarding the installation of someone from an industrial enterprise as a member of the supervisory board of a large bank, cases existed in which the concerned company declined the mandate of such a top management entity of another bank that had a competitive relationship with a specific large bank. For instance, Ellscheid from August Thyssen-Hütte AG indicated in a letter dated December 2, 1974, from Robert Ellscheid to Jürgen Pont that he declined the request to install himself as a member of the supervisory board of Commerzbank, given his special relationship with Dresdner Bank approximately twenty years earlier [*Historisches Archiv der Commerzbank*, HAC-500/121, 7909-2002, Bd.1, Der Brief von Robert Ellscheid an Herr Jürgen Pont (12.12.1974)]. In an internal document dated April 4, 1976, that described the exchange and negotiation between Jürgen Pont and Hermann Richter over personnel issues at Dresdner Bank, such as electing members of the supervisory board and the installation of Karl Winnacker from Hoechst as vice-chairman of the Dresdner Bank supervisory board, Pont indicated the opinion that Hans-Günther Sohl of August Thyssen-Hütte was to be regarded as the appropriate person. Although Richter pointed out that the discussion was insufficient and no conditions existed to be judged, that this bank would not invite Karl Winnacker—who had belonged to the directorial meeting from the beginning—was stressed as possibly being regarded as rude [*Historisches Archiv der Commerzbank*, HAC-500/121, 18093-2000, AR Dresdner Bank (4.4.1976)]. The importance of significant personnel issues regarding members of supervisory boards of large banks to relationships with industrial enterprises can be understood from these cases.

Regarding personnel affairs of top management of large banks, cases existed that concerned dispatches from outside the bank, and an individual candidate's relationships with his mandate at another bank became important. For example, a letter from Hans-Günther Sohl to Robert Pferdmenges dated March 16, 1961, pointed out that Hans Deuβ of Commerzbank had demanded that a person from Phoenix be appointed as a member of the supervisory board and considered Mommsen or Vellguth as a candidate. However, because Mommsen belonged to the Deutsche Bank advisory council and Vellguth was a member of a similar organization at Dresdner Bank, Commerzbank faced the necessity to coordinate with both banks [*tkA*, A/132107, Der Brief von Hans-Günther Sohl an Herrn Dr. Robert Pferdmengens (16.3.1961), S. 2].

Also observed were personnel issues that differed from those of supervisory board members of banks. Regarding the personnel affairs of an administrative board, in internal Dresdner Bank documents on the discussion related to the election of Ewaldsen between Jürgen Pont from this bank and von Schwartzkoppen on March 17, 1976, and March 22, 1976, Schwartzkoppen indicated an allergic reaction to the election plan. This reaction was because Ewaldsen belonged to a similar committee at Deutsche Bank, and the other bank was a competitor of Dresdner Bank. Jürgensen, as the sender of this letter, indicated that he requested of Pont an understanding. In the former document, that same situation could also be observed in the case in which the concerned person was a member of the supervisory board of Deutsche Bank [*Historisches Archiv der Commerzbank*, HAC-500/121, 18093-2000, Ewaldsen (17.3.1976); *Historisches Archiv der Commerzbank*, HAC-500/121, 18093-2000, Telefonnozit gesprochen mit Herren Dr. von Schwarzkoppen am 12.3.76], and the relationship of the candidate regarding a personnel affair with the other bank was important to his election as a member of the supervisory board.

12.3 Coordination Function Through Interlocking Supervisory Board Members

This section considers the coordination function of personnel connections through an interlocking supervisory board member between enterprises. In the case in which the person from a bank had the mandate as an interlocking supervisory board member, that person was observed to have played a significant role in many cases in coordinating between the bank and the industrial company and among industrial companies. For instance, in a meeting of the managing board of Dresdner Bank on January 25, 1965, a report was provided on the discussion with someone from Esso AG in the oil industry. Minutes of this meeting pointed out that the existence of a representative from this bank's supervisory board was important when considering favorable business relationships and the efforts of neighboring banks [*Historisches Archiv der Commerzbank*, HAC-500/121, 18232-2000, Bd.1, Auszug aus der Niederschrift über die Sitzung des Gesamtvorstands am 25. Januar 1965 in Hamburg (17.2.1965)].

Hermann Josef Abs, chairman of the supervisory board of Deutsche Bank for a long time and who held numerous chairman posts and mandates of the supervisory boards of many representative enterprises in various industries, played a significant role in the coordination function between companies, including that between banks and industrial enterprises. At the end of the 1960s, a conflict between two enterprises occurred in the rubber products industry. When Firestone's demand to achieve the majority of the stockholdings threatened to hinder a planned increase in the capital of Phoenix Gummiwerke AG, Abs attempted to solve this conflict. Through such an action, he distinguished clearly between involvement as the representative of a large shareholder of these two companies and the interests of Deutsche Bank (Gall 2004, S. 346). As the supervisory board chairman in Phoenix Gummiwerke AG, Abs also pursued confederation with Bayer that sought surer purchaser of artificial rubber in tire business and cooperated with Kurt Hansen who was chairman of the managing board of Bayer (Der Spiegel 1973b, S. 63). An article published in the journal "*Spiegel*" on November 2, 1965, pointed out Abs not only decided whether new wide strip mill was built or high dividend was paid but also performed strict monitoring of management in industrial enterprises (Der Spiegel 1965, S. 60). According to this article, of 2000 h per year Abs spent in business of Deutsche Bank excluding time for trip, 750 h were used in enterprises in which he held supervisory board posts (Der Spiegel 1965, S. 58).

Alfred Herrhausen, a member of the managing board of Deutsche Bank, also played great roles in the interlocking directorates. As chairman of the supervisory board of Continental Gummi-Werke AG, he introduced Carl Huhn from Volkswagen group who had realized mass sale of "the Beetle" as popular car in the USA and had experience of international business to managers of Continental and attempted to improve the terrible profitability with Huhn (Der Spiegel 1973b, S. 63–64). When support from the outside became necessary for Stollwerck AG as chocolate manufacturer in the 1970s, as interlocking supervisory board member of this enterprise, Herrhausen also opened negotiation regarding cooperation with manufactures of foods and confectionery in Germany and foreign countries and started discussion on purchase of other companies (Der Spiegel 1971b, S. 105). Herrhausen also played a leading role in the development of diversification strategy during the 1980s in Daimler-Benz AG as chairman of the supervisory board in this automobile company. He was the architect of the new strategy. In 1987, Herrhausen implemented a change of Werner Breitschwerdt who was a chairman of the managing board of Daimler-Benz and opposed a dramatic move leading to change of this company into a conglomerate despite of remaining his term of office. He appointed Edzard Reuter whom he considered a person with well-equipped for strategic thinking as a successor of Breitschwerdt. Herrhausen also created organizational structure composed with five divisions and four functional departments and added three new members who approved of the diversification strategy in addition to the old eight-member board (Aizawa 1994, Chapters 3 and 4; Der Spiegel 1987a, S. 100, 1987b, S. 70–71, 1988a, S. 116, 1988b, S. 110, 112; 1988c, S.39-43; Ingersoll and Brady 1987, p. 19; Wirtschaftswoche 1987, S. 88–89). Thus, through influence on the decision of fundamental policy of which implementation was taken charge of the managing board, Herrhausen vigorously involved in management of enterprises where he held interlocking supervisory board mandates.

In addition, when observing another case, Carl Würster, chairman of the managing board of BASF, one of the largest chemical companies, sought the advice of Abs for not only finance problems but also operationally important decisions. Würster regarded Abs, who was an interlocking supervisory board member, as an intermediator between the problems and the policies of this industrial company. In the personnel connections through the interlocking function of the supervisory board, as chairman of the BASF supervisory board, Abs could secure his strong position through the influence of the bank he came from and a combination of traditional relationships and actual connections (Gall 2004, S. 350).

As the largest bank, Deutsche Bank was connected with the most profitable enterprises in Germany in the aspects of personnel, intellectual, and financial relations in the 1980s (Der Spiegel 1985, S. 47). The number of mandates of supervisory boards through the interlocking function was forced to decline under the influence of the 1965 Corporations Law. For instance, Hermann Josf Abs and Deutsche Bank decided that interlocking posts should continue. However, even in such a situation, six companies—Siemens & Halske, Daimler-Benz, BASF, Vereingte Glanzstoff-Fabrik, Rheinish-Westfälisches Elektrizitätswerk AG, and Dortmund-Hörder Hüttenunion—were regarded as enterprises in which this bank absolutely maintained these mandates (Gall 2004, S. 338–339, 342–344). When considering such conditions and the important roles and functions of interlocking supervisory board members from large banks, that not the number but the quality of a supervisory board post was important and that such mandates of bank representatives spread over almost all areas of economic life were decisively significant. This significance was attributable to the possibility of bank representatives to obtain volumes of available information regarding conditions and development trends in various economic sectors through interlocking mandates on the supervisory board (Gall 2004, S. 349).

Ernst Matthienssen who was member of top management organs of Dresdner Bank also had many mandates of supervisory boards of other enterprises and was typical for the "Rhenish capitalism" that exhibited the function of cooperative coordination between companies. A study by F. Sattler pointed out that Matthienssen as an interlocking supervisory board member played an important role in intermediating and coordinating difficult conflicts when such serious problems occurred. His role can be clearly observed in the case of Metallgesellschaft AG (Sattler 2009, S. 241, 334). Matthienssen played a significant role in improving the atmosphere and providing advice related to investment decisions by this industrial enterprise and as an interlocking supervisory board member (Ahrens and Bähr 2013, S. 142). Matthiensen was gradually accepted as advisor for decision of investment by the managing board of this company in the 1960s (Ahrens 2016, S. 136). He made efforts to provide advice and to coordinate through close contact with Hellmuth Ley as chairman of the board of directors. Matthienssen used his international connections with banks and bankers in North America and Canada to force Ley to pay attention to the latest development trend in the coal mines in this district. Matthienssen participated in intensive discussions through such involvement, which resulted in this metal company adopting a fundamentally new business policy that far exceeded his concrete views. As an interlocking supervisory board member from Dresdner Bank, Hertmann Richter also played an important role in coordinating the conflict over the dividend policy between Metallgesellschaft and large shareholders that occurred after his participation on the supervisory board in 1956 (Sattler 2009, S. 244–246). Furthermore, Jürgen Ponto, who was member of top management organ of Dresdner Bank, exhibited the function of moderating conflict and mutual blame in discussions between Ernstberger and Schieren and by coordinating their interests to secure common advantages through the role as a moderator in consultation when rumors persisted that Allianz in the insurance industry made efforts to secure control of Bayern-Hypo (Ahrens and Bähr 2013, S. 133).

The coordination functions of a bank representative who was an interlocking supervisory board member at other enterprises were usually more influential than those of an individual from an industrial enterprise. In addition to such functions, the roles of an interlocking supervisory board member and, particularly as a member of a bank—coordinating through activities such as advising and making suggestions within the company through such a member in its top management entity—were also very significant. Such cases can be observed in, for instance, the behavior of Jürgen Ponto from Dresdner Bank.

Therefore, when examining the roles and functions of interlocking supervisory members from banks, a representative case is observed in the relationship between Mannesmann and Demag. When Mannesmann planned to merge with Demag through capital participation in early 1970s with a view to diversifying the processing department, in particular, machine department (Der Spiegel 1973a), Jürgen Pont as interlocking supervisory board member of Demag attempted to solve the latent conflict of loyalty to the company that he had mandated by supporting the company's independence without injuring his bank's interest. He considered his duty as the interlocking supervisory board member of this machine company to be avoiding the image that the manager of this enterprise was limiting his behavior related to or evading the crisis facing the company. His role was to ward off conflicts and coordinate the final economic development goals of the company through his interlocking mandate and contacts with important individuals and by giving them useful advice through personnel connections (Ahrens and Bähr 2013, S. 138–141).

In **Krupp** as another case, the main function of Jürgen Pont as an interlocking supervisory board member was not the election of a manager or the design of a new structure for a diverse industrial corporate group but steady activities as a "moderate supervisor" who enjoyed high personnel confidence. In the latter half of the 1960s, Krupp had structural weaknesses, developed an intensive growth strategy, and refused to eliminate unprofitable departments. The structural weaknesses became thoroughly apparent with the weakening of the "economic miracle" and the first actual depression of 1966–1967 in West Germany. In 1970, Hermann Josef Abs from Deutsche Bank still played a central role as chairman of the supervisory board in the restructuring negotiations. However, subsequently, Jürgen Pont became deeply involved in the reconstruction of this company. Krupp was managed without paying attention to profitability, and its organization was insufficient (Ahrens 2013, S. 212; 2022, p. 125; Ahrens and Bähr 2013, S. 149–155, 158–161; Der Spiegel 1976d, S. 94).

Structural weakness of the Krupp group became more prominent in the mid-1970s, and almost all departments were in the red (Der Spiegel 1976c, S. 30, 32). Moreover, the integration of production capacity composed of subsidiary companies and centralized managed business units belonging to this group was attempted under such conditions. However, these endeavors were unsuccessful (Der Spiegel 1976d, S. 94). Thus, this group suffered from a great loss, insufficient liquidity, and capital shortages. Jürgen Pont, from Dresdner Bank, made the bank the main provider of funds to Krupp in his capacity as an interlocking supervisory board member (Der Spiegel 1976e, S. 51). Under such conditions, after overcoming the actual weak profitability and subsidiary company sales, urgently needed was a thorough reinforcement of the base of owned capital, which became a decisive problem. Although Günther Vogelsang and Pont engaged in extensive exchanges of opinions, Vogelsang faced the necessity of downsizing the corporate group and selling unprofitable subsidiary companies. Although Ponto already played an important role in intermediating relationships between Beitz and Krupp family members, such as Bohlen and Halbach, before installing Pont as a supervisory board member, after his participating in this top management entity, he sought answers to the financial condition with tenacious energy that reflected the structural problems in the metallurgical and processing departments. He declared unconditional support by Dresdner Bank for Krupp's financial difficulties. Thus, Ponto provided expert knowledge of financial issues and pursued the bank's interest in reinforcing the financial base of a large and representative customer to which this bank gave credit. Ponto was a supervisor who was well informed about this company. His activities on the supervisory board secured this bank's profits from diverse and extensive financing businesses. Ralf Ahrens characterized Pont's function as a member of the supervisory board at Krupp as "supervisor as moderator." He pointed out that Ponto considered business affairs from the perspective of not only the bank category but also the entire industry, which had the characteristics of the entire economy and social policy (Ahrens 2013, S. 212; Ahrens and Bähr 2013, S. 153–155, 158–161).

In the case of **Bilfinger & Berger AG ("Bilfinger & Berger")** in the construction industry as well, the significant roles of Jürgen Pont can be observed. In 1966, Dresdner Bank obtained more than 25% of shares of Julius Berger AG and Grün & Bilfinger (Der Spiegel 1966, S. 33). Ponto, who succeeded a mandate of Ernst Matthiessen from Dresdner Bank and in this year became vice-chairman of the supervisory board at this construction enterprise pursued the thorough use of the enlarged influence of this bank for the needed restructuring of this constructing company. He grappled with the concentration policy that included medium construction enterprises by bank earnestly and requested strict reorganization to enable the effective control of business results. However, such attempts failed. The apparent occurrence of a crisis related to profits enabled Pont to become highly involved. When this construction enterprise was faced with a crisis, Pont first began efforts to solve the merger problem in a field in which he had the strongest influence as chairman of the supervisory board. Such a case was observed in the personnel policy given the condition that the constitution of the board of directors was no longer appropriate for managing this company. Whereas no obstacle occurred to implementing a merger because Dresdner Bank had a dominant position in Bauboag, the fusion with Grün & Bilfinger that was planned from the beginning collided with the opinion of the managing board of this enterprise. Ponto played a role as an important driving force of concentration by controlling the reports of the managing board and by initiating an enthusiastic personnel policy. He mainly grappled with issues of management and successors on the board of directors, even after the combination. In addition, a new crisis of profitability enabled the company's second merger in which Dresdner Bank took capital participation. Jürgen Pont could never agree with an intermediate solution and performed a complete merger by enthusiastically pointing out the cost problem. Ponto achieved his goal by establishing Bilfinger & Berger Construction in 1975 (Ahrens 2013, S. 205; Ahrens and Bähr 2013, 162–165). In this way, Pont played a significant role in executing the merger and ensuring a smooth and successful reconstruction (Ahrens 2013, S. 216). This case indicates that a serious management crisis enabled the bank to be involved in the structure of another company through improved monitoring and in conflict with the intentions of the board of directors (Ahrens 2013, S. 205).

However, even in cases in which a reputable person such as Jürgen Ponto was involved, such coordination functions of an interlocking supervisory member from a bank did not always bring good results. In some cases, such activities were regarded as failures. The case of **Metallgesellachaft AG** shows that this company pursued an expansion without sufficiently considering the profitability issue and an effective management structure. Such a growth strategy was supported by banks (Ahrens 2013, S. 209). In the corporate group of Metallgesellschaft, a considerable portion of the investment was secured by debt, in fact, short-term debt in the 1960s, which was an important factor that resulted in structural problems. Vereinigte Deutsche Metallwerke AG and all other departments had the most significant problems. Such a condition was concerned with the problems of organization and investment failure.

In addition, technological inferiority was prominent despite investments made in the 1960s (Ahrens 2013, S. 209–210; Ahrens and Bähr 2013, S. 142, 144–145, 149).

Under such a condition, this corporate group was faced with a structural crisis. Although in 1966, Dresdner Bank already obtained more than 25% of stocks of Metallgesellschaft AG (Der Spiegel 1966, S. 33), this bank purchased shares of this metal company from Henkel, a representative chemical company, for approximately 100 million Mark in 1974 (Ahrens and Bähr 2013, S. 143; Der Spiegel, 1975a, S. 30). Dresdner Bank continued to be the largest shareholder of Metallgesellschaft until the 1980s, when large amounts of share were sold. Ralf Ahrens pointed out the activities of Jürgen Ponto as a member of the supervisory board that were characterized by a close trusting relationship with Karl Gustaf Ratjen. Ratjen, who was from this industrial enterprise, was evaluated as unsuccessful from the perspective of "industrial policy" when he disregarded negotiations with Deutsche Bank on a personnel issue of the chairman of the supervisory board. For Dresdner Bank, important issues included not profiting from direct interest and commissions but securing long-term relationships as a house bank; the bank's social position in the German economy; and—not to mention—avoiding the negative image of an enterprise for which a bank sent its representative as a member of the supervisory board. This case was not unique to Metallgesellschaft AG but a typical case in Germany. The afore-mentioned case of Krupp indicates a similar situation (Ahrens 2013, S. 209–210; Ahrens and Bähr 2013, S. 149).

AEG, which went bankrupt in the former half of the 1980s, also represented a case in which the activities of the interlocking supervisory board member from the bank failed to reconstruct the business despite the pursuit of the functions of management, advice, and coordination. Reconstruction of AEG had to be pursued without the state's assistance (Der Spiegel 1979, S. 74; 1982, S. 66). Jürgen Ponto from Dresdner Bank as the house bank of AEG participated on the supervisory board of this electrical company in 1972 and became chairman of this top management entity on March 17, 1975. The period when he held office as chairman of the supervisory board was the term during which rebuilding the company was pursued (Ahrens 2013, S. 206–207; Ahrens and Bähr 2013, S. 165–166, 168–169; Der Spiegel 1975b, S. 38, 1975c, S. 66, 1977a, S. 60, 1979, S. 84).

The management crisis of this enterprise was the result of an undisciplined expansion, including acquisitions performed under two chairmen of the managing board: Hans Bühler, whose period in office was from 1966 to 1970, and Hans Groebe, whose term in office was from 1970 to 1976 (Ahren 2013, S. 206; Ahrens and Bähr 2013, S. 166; Der Spiegel 1975b, S. 38; Hautsch 1979, S. 71–73, 77, 123; Ipsen and Pfitzinger 2003, S. 63, 66, 70; Strunk 2000, S. 79–82, 86–88, 103). This expansion policy's essential goal was to achieve scale lager than that of Siemens as an important competitor of AEG (Ipsen and Pfitzinger 2003, S. 68). In the latter half of the 1960s, financial conditions of AEG still did not grow seriously, and a definite financial liquidity was maintained (*Historisches Archiv des Deutschen Technikmuseums*, I.2.060 Ü-V0438, Niederschrift über eine Sitzung des Aufsichtsrates am 28. 11.1963, 10.30 Uhr, S. 4–5; *Historisches Archiv des Deutschen Technikmuseums*, I.2.060 Ü-V0438, Pressenotiz. am 25. Mai 1964, S. 2; *Historisches Archiv des Deutschen Technikmuseums*, I.2.060 Ü-V0438, Niederschrift über die Sitzung der Aufsichtsräte der AEG und der Telefunken AG am 10. Dezember 1964, 11 Uhr, S. 6; *Historisches Archiv des Deutschen Technikmuseums*, I.2.060 Ü-V0438, Niederschrift über eine Sitzung des Aufsichtsrats der AEG und Tfk am 25. Mai 1965 in Frankfurt/M., S. 4, S. 10). However, despite the strong expansion policy, the AEG corporate group was in the first position technologically in only a few production departments, and more than 80% of sales were distributed to departments with slow growth (Ahrens and Bähr 2013, S. 166; Hautsch 1979, S. 147–148). In addition, AEG had to secure more than 80% of needed funds from external funds (Ipsen and Pfitzinger 2003, S. 69–70, 76; Strunk 2000, S. 82, 91) and the owned capital base became very weak from acquisitions (Ahrens 2013, S. 207; Ahrens and Bähr 2013, S. 166; Hautsch 1979, S. 74, 123; Ipsen and Pfitzinger 2003, S. 79; Strunk 2000, S. 87–91, 104). This gave rise to the too rapidly increasing expenditures for interest under the conditions of high level of interest in the 1970s (Ipsen and Pfitzinger 2003, S. 76, 79).

A consortium for AEG led by Dresdner Bank provided this electrical enterprise with enormous credit for acquisitions and fund demand meted out by an increase in capital was only a small part. However, when Ponto attended the supervisory board of AEG in 1972, both he and the industrial section of this bank failed to recognize how large the problems were that this electrical company faced. Subsequently, the first measure of Pont as chairman of the supervisory board was to reshuffle the board of directors and appoint two managers outside the company (Ahrens 2013, S. 207; Ahrens and Bähr 2013, S. 170; Der Spiegel 1975b, S. 38, 40; 1976e, S. 51 Ipsen and Pfitzinger 2003, S. 64, 71, 75; Strunk 2000, S. 105–106).

As stressed in a meeting of the financial committee of the supervisory board of AEG on January 19, 1974, in which Jürgen Ponto was the chairman, slash of financial debt had to be prior [*Historisches Archiv des Deutschen Technikmuseums*, I.2.060 Ü-V0442, Niederschrift über eine Sitzung des Finanzausschusses des Aufsichtsrats der Allgemeine Elektricitäts-Gesellschaft AEG-TELEFUNKEN am 19. Januar 1974 in Kronberg (21.1.1974), S. 1]. In a similar meeting on November 14, 1974, Pont recommended the supervisory board to decide that the financial committee must recognize the investment over 5 million DM [*Historisches Archiv des Deutschen Technikmuseums*, I.2.060 Ü-V0442, Niederschrift über eine Sitzung des Aufsichtsrats der Allgemeine Elektricitäts-Gesellschaft AEG-TELEFUNKEN am 4. November 1974 in Frankfurt/M (6.11.1974), S. 1], thus attempting at the control of financial conditions through stricter appraisal of investment. In the supervisory board meeting on December 12, 1974, he also explained materials for proof submitted by the financial committee did not yet clarify conditions of movement of risks brought about from the business related to power plant thoroughly and pointed out the necessity to accurately grasp risk of the power plant business as a business field with the largest and most serious problems with tenacious energy [*Historisches Archiv des Deutschen Technikmuseums*, I.2.060 Ü-V0443, Niederschrift über eine Sitzung des Aufsichtsrats der Allgemeine Elektricitäts-Gesellschaft AEG-TELEFUNKEN am 12. Dezember 1974 in Frankfurt/M (19.12.1974), S. 2; *Historisches Archiv des Deutschen Technikmuseums*, I.2.060 A.Ü-V0443, Niederschrift über eine Sitzung des Aufsichtsrats der ALLGEMEINE ELEKTRICITÄTS-GESELLSCHAFT AEG-TELEFUNKEN am 12. Dezenber 1974 in Frankfurt/M, S. 2]. Thus, Pont played significant roles as interlocking supervisory board member from main bank in financial affairs. His role became larger through taking charge of chairman post of the financial committee [*Historisches Archiv des Deutschen Technikmuseums*, I.2.060 Ü-V0442, Niederschrift über eine Sitzung des Finanzausschusses des Aufsichtsrats der ALLGEMEINE ELLKTRICITÄTS-GESELLSCHAFT AEG-TELEFUNKEN am 19. Januar 1974 in Kronberg (21.1.1974)].

A more urgent necessity than such personnel affairs of the managing board was clearing a substantial amount of debt, and approximately DM 600 million in short-term obligations had to be transformed to long-term debt. Ponto made efforts to perform coordination activities that enabled the maintenance of a line of credit to AEG without limitations to trustworthy discussions with bank representatives as other creditors through his negotiating ability and good reputation in the financial sector (Ahrens 2013, S. 207; Ahrens and Bähr 2013, S. 171; Der Spiegel 1975b, S. 41). He also decided to execute an increase in capital. However, because of this increase in capital of approximately DM 300 million, which was decided at a general meeting on April 19, 1975, issuing new stock at a market price of 140% of its face value was achieved at Dresdner Bank's expense. Such a transaction was executed at considerable risk to the concerned banks, particularly Dresdner Bank [*Historisches Archiv des Deutschen Technikmuseums*, I.2.060 Ü-V0445, Vorlage für die Sitzung des Aufsichtsrats am 19. Juni 1975 (18.6.1975), S. 1–2; *Historisches Archiv des Deutschen Technikmuseums*, I.2.060 Ü-V0445, Tagesordnungspunkt 7 der Sitzunz des Aufsichtsrats am 19. Juni 1975 (13.6.1975), S. 1–2; *Historisches Archiv des Deutschen Technikmuseums*, I.2.060 Ü-V0445, Niederschrift über eine Sitzung des Finanzausschusses des Aufsichtsrats der Allgemeine Elektricitäts-Gesellschaft AEG-TELEFUNKEN am 19. Juni 1975 in Frankfurt/M (30.6.1975), S. 3; *Historisches Archiv des Deutschen Technikmuseums*, I.2.060 Ü-V0445, Ablauf der Sitzung des Finanzausschusses des Aufsichtsrats der Allgemeine Elektricitäts-Gesellschaft AEG-TELEFUNKEN am 19. Juni 1975, 14.00 Uhr, Frankfurt; Ahrens 2013, S. 207; Ahrens and Bähr 2013, S. 171–172; Hautsch 1979, S. 125; Strunk 2000, S. 105]. Pont proposed that banks involved in financing to AEG, in particular, those that held post of the financial committee of the supervisory board should admit interest rate at the best level for this electrical company as much as possible and ought to prepare to abandon requiring higher interest rate against possible risk [*Historisches Archiv des Deutschen Technikmuseums*, I. 2.060 Ü-V0445, Niederschrift über eine Sitzung des Finanzausschusses des Aufsichtsrats der Allgemeine Elektricitäts-Gesellschaft AEG-TELEFUN-KEN am 18. August 1975 in Berlin (1.9.1975), S. 3]. Such behaviors indicate how he efforted to rebuild AEG as interlocking supervisory board member from bank.

Despite these measures to strengthen financial conditions, the ratio of own capital to the sum of balance sheet of AEG in the end of 1975 was only 15% [*Historisches Archiv des Deutschen Technikmuseums*, I.2060 Ü-V 0445, Niederschrift über eine Sitzung des Finanzausschusses des Aufsichtsrats der Allgemeine Elektricitäts-Gesellschaft AEG-TELEFUN-KEN am 4. Dezember 1975 in München,

S. 3], indicating that it did not contribute to improving capital structure and stabilizing finance as goal [*Historisches Archiv des Deutschen Technikmuseums*, I.2.060 Ü-V0445, Vorlage für die Sitzung des Aufsichtsrats am 19. Juni 1975 (18.6.1975), S. 2; *Historisches Archiv des Deutschen Technikmuseums*, I.2060 Ü-V0445, Tagesordnungspunkt 7 der Sitzunz des Aufsichtsrats am 19. Juni 1975 (13.6.1975), S. 1, *Historisches Archiv des Deutschen Technikmuseums*, I.2.060 Ü-V0445, Niederschrift über eine Sitzung des Finanzausschusses des Aufsichtsrats der Allgemeine Elektricitäts-Gesellschaft AEG-TELEFUNKEN am 19. Juni 1975 in Frankfurt/M (30.6.1975), S. 3]. Under such difficult conditions, selling shares at a loss and maintaining the core competence of the corporate electrical group were indispensable to reconstructing AEG. Consequently, sale of many stocks of subsidiary companies and enterprises that AEG held shares were performed [*Historisches Archiv des Deutschen Technikmuseums*, I.2060 Ü-2 4218, GeschäftspolitischeMaβnahmen AEG-Telefunken-Konzern 1975 bis 1978 (7.5.1979), S. 1, S. 3; *Historisches Ar chiv des Deutschen Technikmuseums*, I.2060 Ü-2 4218, Strukturemaβnahmen AEG-TELEFUNKEN Konzern 1975–1982 hier: Ergebnisauswirkungen bis 1982 (9.10.1979), S. 2, S. 4; *Historisches Archiv des Deutschen Technikmuseums*, I.2.060 Ü-V0432, Sitzung des VorstandsAEG-TELEFUNKEN am 13. November 1975 in Frankfurt (Main) (24. November 1975), S. 11; Ahrens 2013, S. 207; Ahrens and Bähr 2013, S. 172–176; Der Spiegel 1979, S. 87, 90; Hautsch 1979, S. 75–76; Ipsen and Pfitzinger 2003, S. 71, Strunk 2000, S. 98–99, 103, 106]. Although development with large risk of AEG was structural problem, it was essentially promoted by business of atomic power plant [Ahrens 2013, S. 206; Strunk 2000, S. 94, 104, *Historisches Archiv des Deutschen Technikmuseums*, I.2.060 Ü-V0446, *Historisches Archiv des Deutschen Technikmuseums*, I.2.060 Ü-V0425, a. o. Sitzung des Vorstands AEG-TELEFUNKEN am 6. Februar 1973 in Frankfurt (Main) (5.3.1973), S. 4; *Historisches Archiv des Deutschen Technikmuseums*,I.2.060 Ü-V0428, Haftung und Risiko aufgrund der Errichtung von Kernkraftwerken durch KWU (5. Juni 1974), S. 1; *Historisches Archiv des Deutschen Technikmuseums*, I.2.060 Ü-V0430, Sitzung des Vorstands AEG-TELEFUNKEN am 12.Juni 1975 in Frankfurt (Main) (14.Juli 1975), S. 7, S. 15; *Historisches Archiv des Deutschen Technikmuseums*, I.2.060 Ü-2-FA0192; Niederschrift über eine Sitzung des Aufsichtsrats der Allgemeine Elektricitäts-Gesellschaft AEG-TELEFUNKEN am 21. April 1976 in Frankfurt (14.5.1976), S. 4, S. 6; *Historisches Archiv des Deutschen Technikmuseums*, I.2.060 Ü-2-FA0192, Niederschrift über die Sitzung des Präsidiums des Aufsichtsrats von AEG-TELEFUNKEN am 6. September 1977 in Frankfurt (29.9.1977), S. 8, S. 10; *Historisches Archiv des Deutschen Technikmuseums*, I0.2.060 Ü-2-FA0192, Niederschrift über die Sitzung des Finanzausschusses des Aufsichtsrats von AEG-TELEFUNKEN am 5. Dezember 1977 in Frankfurt/Main (18. Mai 1978), S. 6]. This is because special burden brought about by atomic power plant business was an important factor of own capital's decline rate from 26 to 14% from December 31, 1973, to December 31, 1975 [*Historisches Archiv des Deutschen Technikmuseums*, I.2.060 Ü-V0430, Eil-Beschluβvorlage für die Sitzung des Vorstands am 17.6.1975 über die Kapitalerhhung (13. Juni 1975), S. 2]. For the board of directors and the supervisory board reducing risks of business in Kraftwerk Union and avoiding of shifting larger burden brought about by rationalization measures on employee became important task (*Historisches Archiv des Deutschen Technikmuseums*, I.2.060 Ü-V0442, Niederschrift über eine Sitzung des Aufsichtsrats der ALLGEMEINE ELLKTRICITÄTS-GESELLSCHAFT AEG-TELEFUNKEN am 6. Dezember 1973 in Frankfurt/M, S. 2). However, AEG could no longer solve problem of loss from power plant business to be expected without assistance by third parties and crisis of continuance of this company (*Historisches Archiv des Deutschen Technikmuseums*, I.2.060 Ü-V0444, Niederschrift über eine Sitzung des Aufsichtsrats der ALLGEMEINE ELLKTRICITÄTS-GESELLSCHAFT AEG-TELEFUNKEN am 23. April 1975 in Frankfurt/M, S. 8).

However, the federal government refused its aid to AEG. Under such difficult conditions, AEG sold its all shares of Kraftwerk Union to Siemens that was partner of this common subsidiary enterprise and was in competitive relation in electrical industry in November 1976 [Ahrens 2013, S. 206–207; Ipsen and Pfitzinger 2003, S. 86–87; Strunk 2000, S. 94, 96–97, 109; *Historisches Archiv des Deutschen Technikmuseums*, I.2.060 V0441, Niederschrift über eine a. o. Sitzung des Aufsichtsrats der Allgemeine Elektricitäts-Gesellschaft AEG-TELEFUNKEN am 14. September 1972 in Frankfurt, S. 3; *Historisches Archiv des Deutschen Technikmuseums*, I.2.060 V0441, Antrag von AEG TELEFUNKEN in der Sitzung der Gesellschafterdelegation der KWU am 18.12.1973 (21.12.1973), S. 1; *Historisches Archiv des Deutschen Technikmuseums*, I.2.060 Ü-V044, Niederschrift über eine Sitzung des Aufsichtsrats der ALLGEMEINE ELLKTRICITÄTS-GESELLSCHAFT AEG-TELEFUNKEN am 23. April 1975 in Frankfurt/M, S. 9; *Historisches Archiv des Deutschen Technikmuseums*, I.2.060 Ü-V0445, Niederschrift über eine Sitzung des Finanzausschusses des Aufsichtsrats der ALLGEMEINE ELLKTRICITÄTS-GESELLSCHAFT AEG-TELEFUNKEN am 9. Juni 1975 in Frank-furt/M, S. 4-7; *Historisches Archiv des Deutschen Technikmuseums*, I.2.060 Ü-2-FA0192, Niederschrift über die Sitzung des Präsidiums des Aufsichtsrats von AEG-TELEFUNKEN am 2. Dezember 1976 in Frankfurt/Main, S. 2; *Historisches Archiv des Deutschen Technikmuseums*, I.2.060 Ü-2 -FA0192, Niederschrift über die Sitzung des Aufsichtsrats von AEG-TELEFUNKEN am 9.11.1976 in Frankfurt/Main (21. Januar 1977), S. 4, 1]. However, it not only lost its power plant business by this selling transaction but also lost the advantage held by the universal corporate electric group. Ponto played roles that far exceeded the usual duties of the chairman of a supervisory board by selling Kraftwerke Union. Despite his great efforts, this sale was contrary to the condition that this type of corporate group could continue only if it secured an energy connection from production to distribution to the final customer (Ahrens 2013, S. 207; Ahrens and Bähr 2013, S. 175–176; Der Spiegel 1975b, S. 40, 1975c; S. 66; Strunk 2000, S. 96,). At the supervisory board meeting on November 9, 1976, Ponto emphasized that complete withdrawal from Kraftwerke Union could imply giving up an important business opportunity (*Historisches Archiv des Deutschen Technikmuseums*, I.2.060 A.Ü-V0192, Niederschrift über die Sitzung des Finanzausschusses des Aufsichtsrats von AEG-TELEFUNKEN am 9. November

1976 in Frankfurt/Main, S. 2). Nevertheless, his attempts to rebuild AEG led to decision-making that greatly influenced the important foundation of this company.

The failure to rebuild AEG caused Dresdner Bank—which had given this electrical enterprise significant credit and had an increase in capital—an enormous loss when its stock price plummeted. Such a significant loss became the factor that changed the connection between the financial sector and large industries: a loosening of the interfirm relationships called "Germany Inc." ("Deutschland AG") after the 1980s (Ahrens 2013, S. 206–207, 216; Ahrens and Bähr 2013, S. 179–181). Jürgen Ponto failed in his attempt to reconstruct AEG using the interlocking supervisory board mandate (Der Spiegel 1979, S. 84). However, this case of AEG indicates not the bank's withdraw from "Deutschland AG" but its "voice strategy" (Ahrens 2013, S. 209). After Jürgen Ponto's death, no one could resist Walther Cipa as chairman of the managing board in AEG's supervisory board (Der Spiegel 1979, S. 87), indicating change in the bank's role of interlocking supervisory board member in corporate governance.

The case in which merger could be smoothly promoted and realized through coordination between members of the board and interlocking supervisory board member from bank can be observed. For instance, **Karstadt AG** attempted to merge Neckerman group in 1976, whereas Walter Deuss from Commerzbank, a managing board member of Karstadt AG, presented conditions of acquisition and made Neckamann Versand KGaA accept them. Such conditions were recognized by Wilhelm Christians who was chairman of Deutsche Bank's supervisory board and held interlocking chairman mandate on similar top management organ of Karstadt and large shareholders beforehand. Coordination and coordination was conducted between Deuss and Christians before all members of the supervisory board decided this issue (Der Spiegel 1976a; S. 94, 96, 1976b, S. 111–113; Gerhardt 1982, S. 169, 172; Wirtschaftswoche 1976, S. 28–29; Handbuch der deutschen Aktiengesellschaften 1977, S. 1615). Members of the managing boards of three largest banks had posts of the controlling bodies (supervisory boards) of Karstadt and bankers played decisive roles when the first preceding conversation regarding issues of merger (Der Spiegel 1976b, S. 112–113).

Regarding the bank's role and intention through an interlocking supervisory board member in industry–bank relationships, a representative of a large bank in the "Deutschland AG" system tended to engage in continually balancing competition and cooperation, above all, securing long-term and expanding housbank relationships (Ahrens 2013, S. 211). For instance, Dresdner Bank and its chairman of the board were not interested in directly controlling other enterprises but in securing long-term house bank relationships. Securing a mandate of the supervisory board that was oriented toward not short-term expectations of dividends or profits from the stock price but toward, first, credit relationships and classical business through services that the bank provided (Ahrens 2013, S. 216).

In contrast, the installation of an individual from an industrial enterprise as a member of the supervisory board of a bank being significant to the advisory role of a bank can be confirmed in some cases. For instance, at a meeting of the administrative board (Verwaltungsrat) of Dresdner Bank on April 22, 1968, one indication concerned two individuals who retired from their positions as members of the supervisory board of this bank because of death. One was Heinrich Nordhoff, who was chairman of the managing board of Volkswagen AG and a member of the supervisory board of Dresdner Bank from September 25, 1952. The other was Hellmuth Greinert of Rheinish-Westfälisches Elektrizitätswerk AG. During this meeting, their advisory roles at this bank and contributions to developing friendly relationships between the bank and the company were stressed [*Historisches Archiv der Commerzbank*, HAC-500/211, 109332, Die Schrift über die Verwaltungsratssitzung (22.4.1968)].

In many cases, an administrative board was established with the view of maintaining and complementing the advisory function for the board of directors under the 1965 Corporations Law, which limited the number of mandates of a supervisory board that one person could have. Persons who were not be able to be elected as members of the supervisory board could belong to the administrative board [*Historisches Archiv der Commerzbank*, HAC-500/337, 447/50, Der Brief von Ernst Matthiensen über den Verwaltungsrat (4.4.1966), S. 1, 4; *Historisches Archiv der Commerzbank*, HAC-500/121, 18232-2000, Bd.1, Auszug aus der Niederschrift über die Gesamtvorstandssitzung am 1. Juli 1965 in Frankfurt a. M. (21.7.1965); Sattler 2009, S. 288]. In case of Dresdner Bank, many old and new members of the supervisory board belonged to this new committee (Meyen 1992, S. 331). Cases in which a person from outside the company joined such an organization were not rare [*Historisches Archiv der Commerzbank*, HAC-500/211, 109332, Die Schrift über die Verwaltungsratssitzung (22.4.1968); *Historisches Archiv der Commerzbank*, HAC-500/337, 447/50, Verwaltungsrat der Dresdner Bank AG. Stand: 26. Mai 1966 (Konstituierung); *Historisches Archiv der Commerzbank*, HAC-500/337, 447/50, Verwaltungsrat der Dresdner Bank AG (Stand: Januar 1978)]. Personnel connections through this entity also supplemented the function of personnel connections through the interlocking function of the supervisory board.

In Germany, the advisory council system of banks played a significant role in collecting, exchanging, and sharing information and cooperation among enterprises. A central advisory council created for banks' head offices and regional advisory councils established in major districts were important means of personnel connection between bank and industrial enterprises and among corporations. Advisory council system played significant roles in supplementing function of personnel connections through interlocking directorate in top management organs. Therefore, next issues to be considered are structures and functions of personnel connections built through such systems. Part 4 will analyze these research topics.

References

Ahrens R (2013) Bankenmacht im Aufsichtsrat? Der Bankier Jürgen Ponto und die Kntrolle deutscher Groβunternehmen in den 1970er Jahren. In: Ahrens R, Gehlen B, Reckendrees A (Hrsg) Die „Deutschland AG". Historische Annährung an den bundesdeutschen Kapitalismus. 1.Aufl., Klartext-Verlag, Essen, S. 195–220

Ahrens R (2016) Kreditwirtschaft im 》Wirtschaftswunder《—Strukturen und Verflechtungen. In: Hockerts HG, Schulz G (Hrsg) *Der* 》Rheinischen Kapitalismus《 in der Ära denauer. Ferdinand Schnigh, Paderborn, S. 121–141
Ahrens R (2022) Financing Rheinish capitalism:'bank power'and the business of crisis management in the 1960s and 1970s. In: Marx C, Leitmeyer M (eds) Rheinish capitalism. new insights from a business history perspective. Routledge, London, New York, pp 119–134
Ahrens R, Bähr J (2013) Jürgen Ponto. Bankier und Bürger. Eine Biografie. C. H. Beck, München
Aizawa K (1994) Oshu Saikyo no Kinyu Teikoku (The strongest financial empire in Europe). Nihon Keizai Shinbunsha, Tokyo
Bayer AG (1968) Geschäftsbericht 1968. Bayer AG, Leverkusen
Der Spiegel (1965) Ordner an der Orgel. In: Der Spiegel 19(45):49–67
Der Spiegel (1966) Richtum im Dunkeln. In: Der Spiegel 20(16):32–34
Der Spiegel (1971a) Die Omnipotenten. In: Der Spiegel 25(4):38–55
Der Spiegel (1971b) Verschüttete Milch. In: Der Spiegel 25(42):102–105
Der Spiegel (1973a) Nicht ewig selbständig. In: Der Spiegel 27(5):60–61
Der Spiegel (1973b) Rote Tinte. In: Der Spiegel 27(9):63–64
Der Spiegel (1975a) Die Lampen brennen. In: Der Spiegel 29(12):30
Der Spiegel (1975b) Krach Im groβen Haus. In: Der Spiegel 29(4):38–41
Der Spiegel (1975c) Verheerende Bilanz. In: Der Spiegel 29(26):65–67
Der Spiegel (1976a) Eine einzige Tragödie. In: Der Spiegel 30(50):94–96
Der Spiegel (1976b) Genug Luschen. In: Der Spiegel 30(48):111–113
Der Spiegel (1976c) Perser-Geld bei Krupp ≫Einiges ändert sich≪. In: Der Spiegel 30(44):30–33
Der Spiegel (1976d) Quelle versiegt. In: Der Spiegel 30(42):92–96
Der Spiegel (1976e) Stellt was dar. In: Der Spiegel 30(32):50–51
Der Spiegel (1977a) Ponts Erben. In: Der Spiegel 31(44):59–60
Der Spiegel (1977b) Ponts Erben in der Industrie. In: Der Spiegel 31(37):113
Der Spiegel (1979) AEG: Weltfirma am Abgrund. In: Der Spiegel 33(47):74–90
Der Spiegel (1982) 》Das Geschäft bricht weg《. In: Der Spiegel 36(27):65–69
Der Spiegel (1985) Das Riesen-Monopoly der Deutschen Bank. In: Der Spiegel 39(7):40–68
Der Spiegel (1987a) Denkt weiter. In: Der Spiegel 41(18):98–101
Der Spiegel (1987b) Schwere Fehler. In: Der Spiegel 41(29): 69–71
Der Spiegel (1988a) Daimler/MBB: Die Niederlage des Grafen. In: Der Spiegel 42(46):116–118
Der Spiegel (1988b) Daimler-Benz: Übernimmt sich der Reise? In: Der Spiegel 42(16):108–113
Der Spiegel (1988c) ≫Ich hoffe, die Rüstungsindustrie schrumpft≪. In: Der Spiegel 42(31):34–43
Deutsche Bank AG (1976) Geschäftsbericht 1976. Deutsche Bank AG, Frankfurt am Main
Dresdner Bank AG (1959) Bericht über das Geschäftsjahr 1959. Dresdner Bank AG, Frankfurt am Main
Dresdner Bank AG (1960) Bericht über das Geschäftsjahr 1960. Dresdner Bank AG, Frankfurt am Main
Dresdner Bank AG (1964) Bericht über das Geschäftsjahr 1964. Dresdner Bank AG, Frankfurt am Main
Dresdner Bank AG (1965) Bericht über das Geschäftsjahr 1965. Dresdner Bank AG, Frankfurt am Main
Gall L (2004) Der Bankier Hermann Josef Abs. Eine Biographie. C. H. Beck, München
Gerhardt M (1982) Industriebezihungen der westdeutschen Banken. Sendler, Frankfurt am Main
Handbuch der deutschen Aktiengesellschaften (1977) KARSTADT Aktiengesellschaft. In: Handbuch der deutschen Aktiengesellschaften 1976/77, S. 1615–1621
Hautsch G (1979) Das Imperium AEG-Telefunken. Verlag Marxistische Blätter, Frankfurt am Main
Ingersoll R, Brady R (1987) The Banker behind the Shakeup at Daimler-Benz. Deutsche Bank's Alfred Herrhausen is pushing the company his way. In: Bus Week 3007:19–20
Ipsen D, Pfitzinger J (2003) Krise in der Deutschland AG: Der Fall AEG. In: Streeck W, Höpner M (Hrsg) Alle Macht dem Markt? Fallstudien zur Abwicklung der Deutschland AG. Campus Verlag, Frankfurt am Main, New York, S. 60–92
Mannesmann AG (1964) Bericht über das Geschäftsjahr 1964. Mannesmann AG, Düsseldorf
Mannesmann AG (1965) Bericht über das Geschäftsjahr 1965. Mannesmann AG, Düsseldorf

Meyen G (1992) 120 Jahre Dresdner Bank. Dresdner Bank, Frankfurt am Main
Morr JM v (Hrsg.) (1955) Adreβbuch der Direktorenund Aufsichtsräte. Bd.II, nach gesellschaften geordnet, Jahrgang 1955. Finanz-Verlag, Berlin
Rheiniswch-Westflisches Elektrizittswerk AG (1973) Bericht über das 75. Geschäftsjahr 1972/73. Rheiniswch-Westflisches Elektrizittswerk AG, Essen
Rheinisch-Westflisches Elektrizitätswerk AG (1977) Bericht über das 79. Geschäftsjahr 1976/77. Rheiniswch-Westflisches Elektrizittswerk AG, Essen
Sattler F (2009) Ernst Matthiensen (1900–1980). Ein deutscher Bankier im 20. Jahrhundert. Eugen Gutmann-Gesellschaft, Berlin
Strunk P (2000) Die AEG. Aufstieg und Niedergang einer Industrieliegende. 2. Aufl., Nicolaische Verlagsbuchhandlung, Berlin
Wirtschaftswoche (1976) Neckermann/Karstadt. Aktionäre werden Geld verlieren. In: Wirtschaftswoche 30(28):28–29
Wirtschaftswoche (1987) Der Herr im Haus. In: Wirtschaftswoche 41(30):88–92

Part IV
Structures and Functions of Personnel Connection Among Enterprises Through Advisory Council System of Bank

Chapter 13
Personnel Connection Among Enterprises Through Advisory Council System of Bank Before World War II

Abstract In Germany, the bank advisory council system is important for collecting, exchanging, and sharing information, as well as fostering cooperation among enterprises. While central advisory councils were formed for bank headquarters following World War II, regional advisory councils were established in the major districts before the war. Such an organization was an important means of connecting personnel between banks, industrial enterprises, and corporations. The advisory council system played significant roles in supplementing personnel connections through interlocking directorates in top management. This chapter describes the conditions of personnel connections established by regional advisory councils between banks and industrial enterprises and between enterprises in various industrial sectors before World War II. The field and scope of information that advisory council members can obtain from such an organization are determined by their holding condition of mandate on top management, such as the supervisory and managing boards of enterprises. Therefore, this chapter examines the holding conditions under which advisory council members hold top management positions and the composition of each regional advisory council. Personnel connections established through Deutsche Bank's regional advisory council systems (Deutsche Bank and Disconto-Bank) are examined as an important case study.

Keywords Advisory council · Bank · Board of directors · Industry–bank relationship · Personnel connection · Regional advisory council · Supervisory board

Parts I and III analyze the structures and functions of personnel connections established via the interlocking directorate. Part II examined the structure of personnel networks established by members of the supervisory boards of several other enterprises as second-party enterprises, in which supervisory board members of a company have interlocking mandates and hold many posts of third-party enterprises, using social network analysis. Both direct and indirect interlocking directorates play important roles in information exchange and sharing, as well as coordinating interests and conflicts among enterprises. Personnel networks formed by interlocking directorates

T. Yamazaki, *Relationships Between Industry and Bank in Germany*,
https://doi.org/10.1007/978-981-97-4996-6_13

of members of supervisory boards, including second- and third-party enterprises, are critical for the flow of information between industry, banks, and corporations.

However, the advisory council system in Germany was important in establishing personnel connections between banks, enterprises in various industrial sectors, and corporations. Prior to World War II, some large banks had regional advisory councils. They were constructed in various areas important to bank businesses and played an important role in the exchange and sharing of information between banks and industrial enterprises and among industrial enterprises. Regional advisory councils comprised management representatives from various corporate sectors who served large banking customers and their regional organizational units. One reason for regional advisory boards was to strengthen relationships among various corporations across business sectors and regions regarding business policy (Büschgen 1983, S. 242–243; Koubek 1971, S. 261). For example, the regional advisory councils for Deutsche Bank and Disconto-Bank (below Deutsche Bank) that were established in major districts were a critical way to develop relationships with significant enterprises in the competent area with whom the bank had a business relationship (Eglau 1990, S. 250–251). These organizations served as a hub for information exchange between banks and industrial enterprises, and among corporations themselves. The advisory council system effectively fostered close and cooperative relationships between banks and industrial enterprises.

A central advisory council was established as the foundation of a special committee that managed information exchange between enterprises and between banks and industrial enterprises for bank headquarters. The Dresdner Bank central advisory council, which served as a liaison between banks and industrial corporations, was established in 1957 (Meyen 1992, S. 331) despite the 1965 Corporations Law, which limited the number of supervisory board mandates a single person could hold. Other large German banks, such as Deutsche Bank and Commerzbank, established central advisory councils in response to the limitation imposed by this law on the number of supervisory board mandates that one person could hold to maintain a level of personnel connection between banks and industrial enterprises (Eglau 1990, S. 128; Pfeiffer 1986a, S. 477, 1986b, S. 164, 1993, S. 156–157, Stanzick 1969, S. 72). Major corporations assigned members to a central advisory board, through which industry leaders regularly reported on the conditions of their markets (Eglau 1990, S. 192–193, 244). The central advisory council was important in supplementing the function of personnel connections via direct and indirect interlocking in top management organs.

Bank advisory council systems also played an important role in information exchange and sharing, allowing for the coordination of interests and conflicts between corporations, banks, and enterprises. Members of the advisory council who hold mandates on top management organs such as supervisory boards and boards of directors of many enterprises in various industries could obtain a wide range of information. Central and regional advisory councils played an important role in bank-industrial cooperation.

As a result, the four chapters of Part IV examine the structures and functions of personnel connections between a bank and an industrial enterprise, as well as between industrial enterprises, as mediated by the three large banks' advisory council systems. This chapter analyzes the conditions of personnel connections through the regional advisory council before World War II, specifically in the mid-1930s during National Socialism. Chapter 14 discusses the functions of such personnel connections prior to the war. Chapter 15 examines the post–World War II conditions of personnel connection through the advisory council system, which consisted of central and regional advisory councils in the late 1960s, when the 1965 Corporations Law limited the number of supervisory board positions that one person could hold. Chapter 16 clarifies the functions of personnel connection via such systems by examining the activities of both central and regional advisory councils following World War II.

This chapter clarifies the conditions of personnel connections made through regional advisory councils prior to World War II. The cases of Deutsche Bank's regional advisory councils are considered. This chapter examines the mid-1930s because that is when most original historical materials were available for analysis. Chapter 14 focuses on the functions of personnel connection through regional advisory councils using documents from the 1930s and 1940s.

Section 13.1 discusses the composition of Deutsche Bank's regional advisory councils. Section 13.2 analyzes the conditions under which members of the regional advisory council hold mandates on top management organs such as the supervisory and management boards.

13.1 Members of the Deutsche Bank's Regional Advisory Council

Around the mid-1930s, Deutsche Bank had 20 regional advisory councils. The organizations have 325 members. The Rhein–Westfalen regional advisory council comprised three suborganizations. (1) Cologne, (2) Essen–Düsseldorf, and (3) Wuppertal. Therefore, if these organizations represented one advisory council in the Rhein–Westfalen region, the total number of regional advisory councils was 18.

The Essen-Düsseldorf organization of the Rhein–Westfalen regional advisory council had one chairman and two vice-chairmen out of 39 members. The Cologne organization had 33 members and, a chairman, and a vice-chairman. The Wuppertal organization, which consisted of 32 members, had one chairman. The Baden-Pfalz regional advisory council consisted of 31 members and had one chairman and one vice-chairman.

The Berlin–Brandenburg regional advisory council consisted of 26 members, with one chairman and two vice-chairmen. The Württemberg regional advisory council, which consisted of 24 members, had one chairman and one vice-chairman. The Schlesien and Bayern regional advisory councils had a total of 18 members. They had one chairman and one vice-chairman, each. The Hamburg–Holstein regional advisory council consisted of 15 members, with one chairperson and one vice-chairman. The Frankfurt-Hessen regional advisory council, which consisted of 13 members, had one chairman. The Magdeburg regional advisory council consisted of 12 members, with one chairman and one vice-chairman. The Sachsen regional advisory council consisted of ten members, with one chairman and one vice-chairman.

The regional advisory councils for Braunschweig, Hannover, and Thüringen each had eight members. They had one chairman. Meanwhile, the Königsberg and Bremer regional advisory councils were made up of seven people. They had a chairman. The Hildesheim regional advisory council, which consisted of six members, had a chairman. The Saarbrücken regional advisory council had six members. However, there was no chairman or vice-chairman. The Stettin regional advisory council, which consisted of four members, had a single chairman.

Considering the enterprises from which a person becomes a member of a representative regional advisory council in relation to the industry to which each enterprise belonged, there were members of multiple enterprises in industries such as iron and steel; chemical; banking; and textile, spinning, and woven goods, as well as companies in electrical, automobile, and oil. Although enterprises from various industries were represented on the Sachsen regional advisory council, the majority of enterprises were from the textile, spinning, and woven goods industries. The Magdeburg regional advisory council comprised companies from various industries, including machine, chemical, distillation, distribution, metal production and processing, electric power, gas and energy, and insurance. Members of the Hannover regional advisory council came from various industries, including metal production and processing, food, and distillation, as well as a number of chemical enterprises. The Bayern regional advisory council included representatives from industries such as iron and steel, metal production and processing, automobile, machine, textile, spinning, and woven goods, distillation, and transportation. The majority of these companies were in the machine, textile, spinning, and goods industries. In the Württenberg regional advisory council, even though there were enterprises in industries such as metal production and processing, automobile, machine, textile, spinning and woven goods, and distillation, there were members of multiple companies in the machine, metal producing and processing, and textile, spinning and woven goods industries.

When considering regional advisory councils in the Rhein–Westfalen district, where Germany's key industries are aggregated, the Cologne organization included members from a variety of firms in industries such as mining, iron and steel, machine, textile, spinning, and woven goods, and insurance. In the Essen–Düsseldorf organization, although there were many members from enterprises in industries such as mining, iron and steel, and machine, there were also members of several companies in the chemical and oil industries. In the Wuppertal organization, there were many members of companies in industries such as iron and steel, metal producing and processing, chemical, and textile, spinning, and woven goods (Deutsche Bank and Disconto-Bank 1935, S. 7–15).

13.2 Holding of Mandates by Members of the Regional Advisory Council on Top Management Organs

These discussions show that the Deutsche Bank regional advisory council was made up of enterprises from a variety of industries. This was important for exchanging and sharing information among banks and member companies. However, the field and scope of information to be exchanged and shared between enterprises can be expanded by having members of each advisory council serve on top management organs such as the supervisory and managing boards of the enterprise.

As a result, this subsection explores the circumstances under which the members of the regional advisory council held the mandates of these top management organs. Although Deutsche Bank had several regional advisory councils, the Württemberg regional advisory council and the Rhein–Westfalen regional advisory councils, which were made up of three suborganizations, were among the most important in the region where Germany's key industries were concentrated. The Rhein–Westfalen regional advisory council's three suborganizations are examined: (1) Cologne, (2) Essen–Düsseldorf, and (3) Wuppertal.

13.2.1 Case of the Württemberg Regional Advisory Council

First, when considering the mandates that members of the Württemberg regional advisory council held on the supervisory board (see Table 13.1), the number of companies totaled 71, with a total of 79 mandates. In terms of industrial sector distribution, the numbers of enterprises and mandates were two each in the iron and steel industries; three each in the metal producing and processing industries; one each in the chemical industry; one each in the automobile industry; five each in the machine industry; two each in the precious machine and optical industries; 20 and 23 in the textile, spinning, and woven goods industries, respectively; four each in the distillation industry; four and five in the banking industry; two each in the insurance industry; three each in the electric power, gas, and energy industries; one in each the transportation industry; and 23 and 27 in other industries, respectively. Although the number of enterprises and mandates in the machine industry was relatively large, the supervisory board of enterprises in the textile, spinning, and woven goods industries held a sizable mandate.

When considering a situation in which members of the Württemberg regional advisory council had a mandate for the position of chairman of the supervisory board, holding the chairman post was observed in 28 companies. Each member of this advisory council had one mandate, bringing the total to 28. There were two such enterprises in the metal producing and processing industries; one in the chemical industry; three in the machine industry; one in the precious machine and optical industries; seven in the textile, spinning, and woven goods industries; two in the distillation industry; and 12 in other industries.

Table 13.1 Supervisory board positions held by members of Deutsche Bank's Württemberg regional council (period of National Socialism)

Industries	Position							
	Chairman		Vice-Chairman		Supervisory board member excluding chairman and vice-chairman		Total[a]	
	Number of companies	Number of posts	Number of companies	Number of posts	Number of companies	Number of posts	Number of companies	Number of posts
Iron and steel	—	—	1	1	1	1	2	2
Metal producing and processing	2	2	—	—	1	1	3	3
Chemical	1	1	—	—	—	—	1	1
Automobile	—	—	—	—	1	1	1	1
Machine	3	3	1	1	1	1	5	5
Precious machine and optical	1	1	—	—	1	1	2	2
Textile, spinning, and woven goods	7	7	5	5	10	11	20	23
Distillation	2	2	2	2	—	—	4	4
Banking	—	—	1	1	4	4	4	5
Insurance	—	—	—	—	2	2	2	2
Electric power, gas, and energy	—	—	—	—	3	3	3	3
Transportation	—	—	—	—	1	1	1	1

(continued)

Table 13.1 (continued)

Industries	Position							
	Chairman		Vice-Chairman		Supervisory board member excluding chairman and vice-chairman		Total[a]	
	Number of companies	Number of posts	Number of companies	Number of posts	Number of companies	Number of posts	Number of companies	Number of posts
Other industries	12	12	6	6	9	9	23	27
All industries	28	28	16	16	34	35	71	79

[a] There are cases in which the total number of companies in which mandate was held differed from the total number of companies measured by each position of the supervisory board due to the existence of companies where more than two posts were held

Source This table was compiled by the author, based on Mossner (Hrsg) (1936) and Deutsche Bank und Disconto-Gesellschaft (1935)

Cases of holding of vice-chairman post can be observed in 16 enterprises. Each member of this advisory council had one mandate, for a total of 16. There was one such enterprise in the iron and steel industry, one in the machine industry, five in the textile, spinning, and woven goods industries, two in the distillation industry, one in the banking industry, and six in other industries.

Except for the chairman and vice-chairman, each member of this advisory council in 34 enterprises held a supervisory board mandate. The total number of mandates was 35. The numbers of companies and mandates were one each in the iron and steel industry, metal producing and processing industries, automobile industry, machine industry, and precious machine and optical industries; 10 and 11 in the textile, spinning, and woven goods industries; respectively; four each in the banking industry; two each in the insurance industry, three each in the electric power, gas, and energy industries; one each in the transportation industry; and nine each in other industries, respectively.

There were representative enterprises in each industry among the 71 enterprises for which Württemberg regional advisory council members held supervisory board mandates. Such cases can be observed in enterprises like Daimler-Benz AG in the automobile industry and Allianz and Stuttgarter Verein Versicherungs-AG in the insurance industry. Local enterprises in the Württemberg region included Draht und Eisenwerk Erlau AG, Württembergische Leinenindustrie, Württembergische Baumwoll-Spinnerei und Weberei, Württembergische Hypothekenbank, Württembergische Notenbank in banking, Württembergische Mittelatandskasse AG, and Württembergische Industrietreuhand AG.

Members of the Württemberg regional advisory council held more than two mandates on the supervisory board of the same enterprise in five companies, totaling 13. These companies included Kammrarnspinnerei Bietingheim in the textile, spinning, and woven goods industries, Württembergische Hypothekenbank in banking, and Schwäbische Treuhand AG, Bleicherei, Färberei und Appreturanstalt AG, as well as Matth. Hohner AG in other industries. In Kammrarnspinnerei Bietingheim, members of this advisory council held four mandates: one for chairman and vice-chairman and two supervisory board positions other than chairman and vice-chairman. In Schwäbische Treuhand AG members of this advisory council held three mandates: one chairman, one vice-chairman, and one supervisory board member other than the chairman or vice-chairman. In the other three companies, Württemberg regional advisory council members held two mandates each. In Bleicherei, Färberei und Appreturanstalt AG and Matth Hohner AG members of this advisory council held one chairman and one vice-chairman mandate each. In contrast, in Württembergische Hypothekenbank members of this advisory council held a vice-chairman mandate and one supervisory board position other than chairman and vice-chairman.

The holding of mandates by members of the Württemberg regional advisory council on the enterprise's management board is then considered. Such cases can be found in four companies. In each company members of this advisory council held one mandate. Thus, the total number of mandates was four. These companies included Daimler-Benz AG in the automotive industry and E. Breuninger AG and Württembergische Cattunmanufactur were textile, spinning, and woven goods manufacturers, while Süddeutsche Zucker AG operated in other industries. The number of companies and mandates was very small when compared to the number of supervisory board mandates. However, in Daimler-Benz AG, each member of this regional advisory council had a mandate from the supervisory board or managing board (Deutsche Bank and Disconto-Bank 1935, S. 11; Mossner 1936).

13.2.2 Case of the Rhein–Westfalen Regional Advisory Council

This subsection examines the status of members of the Rhein–Westfalen regional advisory council's mandates on top management bodies such as the supervisory board and managing board. In this district, three suborganizations of the regional advisory council are examined: (1) Köln, (2) Essen–Düsseldorf, and (3) Wuppertal.

13.2.2.1 Case of Cologne Organization

First, taking into account the mandates held by members of the Rhein–Westfalen regional advisory council's Cologne organization on the supervisory board (see Table 13.2), the total number of companies was 119, with 158 mandates. These numbers were significantly higher than those of the Württemberg regional advisory council. When considering the distribution of industrial sectors, the numbers of companies and mandates were 11 each in the mining industry; 11 and 12 in the iron and steel industry; three and four in the metal producing and processing industries; six each in the chemical industry; two each in the electrical industry; one each in the automobile industry; 10 and 12 in the machine industry; respectively, one each in the oil industry; one each in the textile, spinning, and woven goods industries; eight and 16 in the banking industry; 21 and 43 in the insurance industry; respectively; four each in the electric power, gas, and energy industries; four and five in the transportation industry; respectively, and 36 and 40 in other industries, respectively. There were many firms and mandates in industries such as mining, iron and steel, machine, banking, insurance.

When considering a situation in which the members of the Rhein–Westfalen regional advisory council's Cologne organization had a mandate regarding the supervisory board position, in three companies members of this organization held the honorary chairmanship mandate. The cases involved two mining companies and one iron and steel company. In each company, the number of mandates was active. 32 enterprises observe the chairman's mandate. The total number of mandates was 34. When considering the distribution of industrial sectors, the numbers of companies and mandates were three each in mining; similarly, one each in the iron and steel industry; one each in the chemical industry; one each in the textile, spinning, and

Table 13.2 Supervisory board positions held by members of the Cologne organization of Deutsche Bank's Rhein-Westfalen regional council (period of National Socialism)

Industries	Position									
	Honorary chairman		Chairman		Vice-chairman		Supervisory board member excluding chairman and vice-chairman		Total[a]	
	Number of companies	Number of posts	Number of companies	Number of posts	Number of companies	Number of posts	Number of companies	Number of posts	Number of companies	Number of posts
Mining	2	2	3	3	–	–	6	6	11	11
Iron and steel	1	1	1	1	–	–	10	10	11	12
Metal producing and processing	–	–	–	–	–	–	3	4	3	4
Chemical	–	–	1	1	–	–	5	5	6	6
Electrical	–	–	–	–	–	–	2	2	2	2
Automobile	–	–	–	–	–	–	1	1	1	1
Machine	–	–	–	–	2	2	9	10	10	12
Oil	–	–	–	–	1	1	–	–	1	1
Textile, spinning, and woven goods	–	–	1	1	–	–	–	–	1	1
Banking	–	–	5	6	2	2	5	8	8	16
Insurance	–	–	11	12	3	3	15	28	21	43
Electric power, gas, and energy	–	–	1	1	1	1	2	2	4	4

(continued)

Table 13.2 (continued)

Industries	Position									
	Honorary chairman		Chairman		Vice-chairman		Supervisory board member excluding chairman and vice-chairman		Total[a]	
	Number of companies	Number of posts	Number of companies	Number of posts	Number of companies	Number of posts	Number of companies	Number of posts	Number of companies	Number of posts
Transportation	–	–	1	1	–	–	3	4	4	5
Other industries	–	–	8	8	11	11	19	21	36	40
All industries	3	3	32	34	20	20	80	101	119	158

[a] There are cases in which the total number of companies in which mandate was held differed from the total number of companies measured by each position of the supervisory board due to the existence of companies where more than two posts were held

Source This table was compiled by the author, based on Mossner (Hrsg) (1936) and Deutsche Bank und Disconto-Gesellschaft (1935)

woven goods industries; five and six in the banking industry; 11 and 12 in the insurance industry; one each in the electric power, gas, and energy industries; one each in the transportation industry; and eight in other industries.

The holding of vice-chairman mandate was observed in 20 enterprises. In each company, members of this organization had one mandate, for a total of twenty. There were two such enterprises in the machine industry; one in the oil industry; two in the banking industry; three in the insurance industry; one in the electric power, gas, and energy industries; and 11 in other industries.

Except for the chairman and vice-chairman, cases of holding supervisory board positions can be found in 80 enterprises, with a total of 101 mandates. The number of enterprises and mandates was extremely large. There were six such enterprises and mandates in the mining industry and 10 in the iron and steel industry; three and four in the metal producing and processing industries, respectively; five in the chemical industry; two in the electrical industry; one in the automobile industry; nine and 10 in the machine industry; five and eight in the banking industry; and 15 and 28 in the insurance industry; two each in the electricity, gas, and energy industries; three and four in the transportation industry; and 19 and 21 in other industries, respectively.

Of 119 enterprises where the members of the Cologne organization of the Rhein–Westfalen regional advisory council had mandate of the supervisory board, there were representative large companies in each industry, such as Gelsenkirchener Bergwerk AG and Harpener Bergbau AG in the mining industry, Vereinigte Stahlwerke AG, August Thyssen-Hütte AG, and Mannesmannröhren-Werke in the iron and steel industry, Bayerische Motoren-Werke AG in the automobile industry, and Gerling-Konzern Allgemeine Versicherungs-AG in the insurance industry. In Gerling-Konzern Allgemeine Versicherungs-AG, five mandates of the supervisory board excluding chairman and vice-chairman were held by members of the Cologne organization of the Rhein–Westfalen regional advisory council.

Members of this organization held multiple supervisory board mandates in 25 enterprises. The total number of mandates was 64 (see Table 12.3). The numbers of such enterprises and mandates were one and two in the iron and steel industry, one and two in the metal producing and processing industries, two and four in the machine industry, five and 13 in the banking industry, 12 and 34 in the insurance industry, one and two in the transportation industry, and three and seven in other industries, respectively. One of these 25 companies had five mandates held by Rhein–Westfalen regional advisory council members from Cologne. Two cases involved the execution of four mandates. There were seven cases in which three positions were held. Two mandates were issued to the remaining 15 companies (Table 13.3).

Five supervisory board mandates were held at Gerling-Konzern Allgemeine Versicherungs-AG, an insurance company, except for the chairman and vice-chairman. Four mandates were fulfilled at Nordstern Lebensversicherungsbank AG in the banking industry and Kölnische Glas-Versicherungs-AG in the insurance industry, consisting of a chairman mandate and three supervisory board positions (excluding chairman and vice-chairman). In seven enterprises, three mandates were held: Rheinisch-Westfälische Boden-Credit-Bank in the banking industry and Rückversicherungs-AG, Colonia, and Kölnische Hagel-Versicherungs-Gesellschaft

Table 13.3 Cases in which the members of the Cologne organization of Deutsche Bank's Rhein-Westfalen regional advisory council held more than two posts on the supervisory board (period of National Socialism)

Industries	Number of posts									
	2		3		4		5		Total	
	Number of companies	Number of posts	Number of companies	Number of posts	Number of companies	Number of posts	Number of companies	Number of posts	Number of companies	Number of posts
Iron and steel	1	2	–	–	–	–	–	–	1	2
Metal producing and processing	1	2	–	–	–	–	–	–	1	2
Machine	2	4	–	–	–	–	–	–	2	4
Banking	3	6	1	3	1	4	–	–	5	13
Insurance	5	10	5	15	1	4	1	5	12	34
Transportation	1	2	–	–	–	–	–	–	1	2
Other industries	2	4	1	3	–	–	–	–	3	7
All industries	15	30	7	21	2	8	1	5	25	64

Source This table was compiled by the author, based on Mossner (Hrsg) (1936) and Deutsche Bank und Disconto-Gesellschaft (1935)

in the insurance industry, with one mandate for chairman and vice-chairman and one supervisory board post excluding chairman and vice-chairman, respectively. Three mandates were held by the insurance companies Schlesische Feuerversicherungs-Gesellschaft, Kronprinz Versicherungs-AG, and Rheinische Feuerversicherungs-AG, as well as Kölner Tattersall AG in other industries.

Considering the rest 15 companies in which two posts were held by members of the Cologne organization of the Rhein–Westfalen regional advisory council in respect to the distribution of industrial sectors, the remaining 15 companies included one in the iron and steel industry, one in the metal producing and processing industries, two in the machine industry, three in the banking industry, five in the insurance industry, one in the transportation industry, and two in other industries. Members of the Rhein–Westfalen regional advisory council's Cologne organization held two chairmanship mandates in Concordia Lebens-Versicherungs-Bank AG, a bank, and Kölnische Rückversicherungs-Gesellschaft, an insurance company. In Rheinisch-Westfälische "Revision" Treuhand AG and Glas- and Spiegel-Manufaktur AG, members of this advisory council held mandates of the chairmanship and the vice-chairmanship. In the iron and steel industry, in Hoesch-KölnNeuessen AG für Bergbau und Hüttenbetrieb members of this advisory council held an honorary chairmanship and one supervisory board position other than chairman and vice-chairman. In each company of Westdeutsche Bodenkreditanstalt in the banking industry and Colonia Kölnische Feuer- und Kölnische Unfall-Versicherungs-AG, Hamburger Allgemeine Versicherungs-AG, and Nordstern Allgemeine Versicherungs-AG in the insurance industry, a chairman's mandate and one supervisory board position other than chairman and vice-chairman were held. In the machine industry, in Humboldt-Deutzmotoren AG members of this advisory council had a vice-chairman position and one supervisory board mandate that did not include the chairman and vice-chairman. Enterprises in which two supervisory board mandates, except for the chairman and vice-chairman, were held can be observed in AG für Bergbau, Blei- und Zinkfabrikation zu Stollberg und in Westfalen in the metal producing and processing industries, Walther & Cie., AG in the machine industry, Schlesisch-Kölnische Lebens-Versicherungsbank AG in the banking industry, Aachener und Münchener Feuer-Versicherungs-Gesellschaft in the insurance industry, and Eisern-Siegener Eisenba.

Members of the Rhein–Westfalen regional advisory council's Cologne organization hold mandates on the enterprise's management board. Such cases can be observed in eight companies. The total number of mandates was nine. The number of enterprises and mandates was extremely small. The mining industry and the metal producing and processing industries had two such enterprises and mandates, respectively. In the iron and steel industry and the chemical industry, one mandate was held, respectively. In the machine industry, each member of the Cologne organization of the Rhein–Westfalen regional advisory council had three mandates in two companies.

Members of the Cologne organization of the Rhein–Westfalen regional advisory council served on one enterprise's supervisory and managing boards. In the machine industry, one such case was Vereinigte Westdeutsche Waggonfabriken AG. In this company, a chairman mandate of the managing board and post of the managing board except for chairman and vice-chairman, as well as a chairman mandate of the supervisory board, were held by three members of such regional advisory council (Deutsche Bank and Disconto-Bank 1935, S. 12–13; Mossner 1936).

13.2.2.2 Case of Essen-Düsseldorf Organization

Next, when considering the mandates that members of the Essen-Düsseldorf organization of the Rhein–Westfalen regional advisory council had on the supervisory board (see Table 13.4), in such cases the number of companies was 168 and the total number of mandates was 204. These numbers were very many compared to those of the Württemberg regional advisory council and more than those of the Cologne organization of the Rhein–Westfalen regional advisory council. Taking into account the distribution of industrial sectors, the numbers of companies and mandates, respectively, were 23 and 27 in the mining industry; 26 and 31 in the iron and steel industry; 15 and 18 in the chemical industry; 17 and 28 in the machine industry; and 9 and 10 in the insurance industry. Many firms and mandates existed in mining, iron and steel, chemical, and machine industries.

When considering a situation in which the members of the Essen-Düsseldorf organization of the Rhein–Westfalen regional advisory council had a mandate in relation to the position of the supervisory board, the case of holding of the chairman post was 34 companies. In each company, the number of mandates was one, respectively, and the total number of mandates was 34. When considering the distribution of industrial sectors, the number of companies was three in mining; four in the iron and steel and chemical industries; one in the electrical, machine, oil, and insurance industries; one in the textile, spinning, and woven goods industries; four in the distributing industry; two in the banking and transportation industries; and 10 in other industries.

Holding of mandate of vice-chairman was observed in 19 enterprises. In each company, the number of mandates was one, respectively, and the total number of mandates was 19. The number of such enterprises was five in the mining industry; three in the iron and steel industry; two in the chemical industry; three in the machine industry; two in the oil industry; two in the insurance industry; and two in other industries.

Cases in which supervisory board posts except for chairman and vice-chairman were held can be seen in 126 enterprises, and the total number of mandates was 151. The numbers of both the enterprise and the mandate were very many. The numbers of such enterprises and mandates respectively were 16 and 19 in the mining industry; 21 and 24 in the iron and steel industry; one each in the metal producing and processing industries; 10 and 12 in the chemical industry; five and seven in the electrical industry; one each in the automobile industry; 16 and 24 in the machine industry; one and two in the shipbuilding industry; three each in the oil industry; three each in the textile, spinning and woven goods industries; four each in the distillation industry; two each in the distribution industry; four each in the banking industry; six and seven in the insurance industry; three and seven in the electric power, gas and energy industries; five and six in the transportation industry; and 25 each in other industries.

Table 13.4 Supervisory board positions held by members of the Essen-Düsseldorf organization of Deutsche Bank's Rhein-Westfalen regional advisory council

Industries	Position							
	Chairman		Vice-chairman		Supervisory board member excluding chairman and vice-chairman		Total[a]	
	Number of companies	Number of posts	Number of companies	Number of posts	Number of companies	Number of posts	Number of companies	Number of posts
Mining	3	3	5	5	16	19	23	27
Iron and steel	4	4	3	3	21	24	26	31
Metal producing and processing	–	–	–	–	1	1	1	1
Chemical	4	4	2	2	10	12	15	18
Electrical	1	1	–	–	5	7	6	8
Automobile	–	–	–	–	1	1	1	1
Machine	1	1	3	3	16	24	17	28
Shipbuilding	–	–	–	–	1	2	1	2
Oil	1	1	2	2	3	3	5	6
Textile, spinning, and woven goods	1	1	–	–	3	3	4	4
Distillation	–	–	–	–	4	4	4	4
Distributing	4	4	–	–	2	2	6	6
Banking	2	2	–	–	4	4	5	6
Insurance	1	1	2	2	6	7	9	10

(continued)

Table 13.4 (continued)

Industries	Position							
	Chairman		Vice-chairman		Supervisory board member excluding chairman and vice-chairman		Total[a]	
	Number of companies	Number of posts	Number of companies	Number of posts	Number of companies	Number of posts	Number of companies	Number of posts
Electric power, gas, and energy	–	–	–	–	3	7	3	7
Transportation	2	2	–	–	5	6	6	8
Other industries	10	10	2	2	25	25	36	37
All industries	34	34	19	19	126	151	168	204

[a] There are cases in which the total number of companies in which mandate was held differed from the total number of companies measured by each position of the supervisory board due to the existence of companies where more than two posts were held

Source This table was compiled by the author, based on Mossner (Hrsg) (1936) and Deutsche Bank und Disconto-Gesellschaft (1935)

Of 168 enterprises where the members of the Essen-Düsseldorf organization of the Rhein–Westfalen regional advisory council had a supervisory board mandate, there were representative large companies in each industry, such as Gelsenkirchener Bergwerk AG and Harpener Bergbau AG in the mining industry, Vereinigte Stahlwerke AG, Rheinsiche Stahlwerke, Mannesmannröhren-Werke AG and Klöckner-Werke AG in the iron and steel industry, Brown, Boveri & Cie. AG in the electrical industry, Daimler-Benz AG in the automobile industry, Demag AG and Maschinenfabrik Augsburg-Nürnberg AG (MAN) in the machine industry, Deutsche Werft AG in the shipbuilding industry, Deutsche Erdöl AG in the oil industry and Ruhrgas AG in the electric power, gas, and energy industries. In Gerling-Konzern Allgemeine Versicherungs-AG, five mandates of the supervisory board, except for chairman and vice-chairman, were held by members of the Essen-Düsseldorf organization of the Rhein–Westfalen regional advisory council.

Taking into account the cases in which members of this organization had plural mandates on the supervisory board (see Table 13.5), such cases can be observed in 22 enterprises. The total number of mandates was 58. The numbers of such enterprises and mandates respectively were one and five in the mining industry; three and eight in the iron and steel industry; three and six in the chemical industry; one and three in the electrical industry; seven and 18 in the machine industry; one and two in the shipbuilding industry; one and two in the oil industry; one and two in the banking industry; one and two in the insurance industry; one and five in the electric power, gas and energy industries; one and three in the transportation industry; and one and two in other industries. Of these 22 companies, the case in which five mandates were held by members of the Essen-Düsseldorf organization of the Rhein–Westfalen regional advisory council was two. The cases in which four mandates were held were one. The cases in which three posts were held were six. In the remaining 13 companies, two mandates were held.

In Rheinisch–Westfälisches Kohlen–Syndikat in the mining industry, five mandates consisting of a mandate of vice-chairman and four posts of the supervisory board excluding chairman and vice-chairman were held by the Essen-Düsseldorf organization of the Rhein–Westfalen regional advisory council, in Ruhrgas AG in the electric power, gas and energy industries five mandates of the supervisory board except for chairman and vice-chairman were held. In Rheinsiche Stahlwerke in the iron and steel industry, four mandates consisting of a mandate of chairman and three posts of the supervisory board except for chairman and vice-chairman were held. Regarding enterprises in which three mandates were held, whereas in Oldenburg-Portugiesische Dampfschiffs-Rhederei in the transportation industry, a mandate of chairman and two posts of the supervisory board except for chairman and vice-chairman were held, in Maschinenbauunternehmungen AG in the machine industry, a mandate of vice-chairman and two posts of the supervisory board except for chairman and vice-chairman were held. In contrast, in Kabelwerk Rheydt AG in the electrical industry and Westfalen Dinnendahl Gröppel AG, Demag AG, and Schieß-Defries AG in the machine industry, three supervisory board excluding chairman and vice-chairman, respectively, were held.

Table 13.5 Cases in which the members of the Essen-Düsseldorf organization of Deutsche Bank's Rhein-Westfalen regional advisory council held more than two posts on the supervisory board (period of National Socialism)

Industries	Number of posts									
	2		3		4		5		Total	
	Number of companies	Number of posts	Number of companies	Number of posts	Number of companies	Number of posts	Number of companies	Number of posts	Number of companies	Number of posts
Mining	–	–	–	–	–	–	1	5	1	5
Iron and steel	2	4	–	–	1	4	–	–	3	8
Chemical	3	6	–	–	–	–	–	–	3	6
Electrical	–	–	1	3	–	–	–	–	1	3
Machine	3	6	4	12	–	–	–	–	7	18
Shipbuilding	1	2	–	–	–	–	–	–	1	2
Oil	1	2	–	–	–	–	–	–	1	2
Banking	1	2	–	–	–	–	–	–	1	2
Insurance	1	2	–	–	–	–	–	–	1	2
Electric power, gas, and energy	–	–	–	–	–	–	1	5	1	5
Transportation	–	–	1	3	–	–	–	–	1	3
Other industries	1	2	–	–	–	–	–	–	1	2
All industries	13	26	6	18	1	4	2	10	22	58

Source This table was compiled by the author, based on Mossner (Hrsg) (1936) and Deutsche Bank und Disconto-Gesellschaft (1935)

Taking into account the other 13 companies in which two posts were held by members of the Essen-Düsseldorf organization of the Rhein–Westfalen regional advisory council with respect to the distribution of industrial sectors, the number of companies was two in the iron and steel industry; three in the chemical industry; three in the machine industry; one in the shipbuilding industry; one in the oil industry; one in the banking industry; one in the insurance industry; and one in other industries. In Gesellschaft für Teerverwertung in the chemical industry, one each of the mandates of chairman and vice-chairman was held. In Düsseldorfer Eisenbahnbedarf vormals Carl Weyer & Co. in the machine industry and Deutsche Schiffskreditbank AG in the banking industry, a mandate of chairman and one post of the supervisory board except for chairman and vice-chairman were held, respectively. In Vereinigte Stahlwerke AG in the iron and steel industry, Presswerk AG in the machine industry, Deutsche Erdöl AG in the oil industry, and Deutsche Schachtbau AG in other industries, one post of vice-chairman and a mandate of the supervisory board excluding chairman and vice-chairman were held, respectively. In Mannesmannröhren-Werke AG in the iron and steel industry, Rheinisch-Westfälische Sprengstoff AG and Riebeck'sche Montan-werke AG in the chemical industry, Vereinigte Kesselwerke AG in the machine industry, Deutsche Werft AG in the shipbuilding industry, Nordstein Allgemeine Versicherungs-AG in the insurance industry, two posts of the supervisory board excluding chairman and vice-chairman, respectively.

Furthermore, the holding of mandates by members of the Essen-Düsseldorf organization of the Rhein–Westfalen regional advisory council on the management board of the enterprise is considered. Such cases can be observed in 20 enterprises. The total number of mandates was 23. The numbers of both enterprises and mandates were extremely few compared to the case of holding the supervisory board mandate. The numbers of such enterprises and mandates respectively were three and four in the mining industry; five each in the iron and steel industry; one each in the metal producing and processing industries; one each in the electrical industry; and one each in the machine industry; two each in the oil industry; two each in the textile, spinning, and woven goods industries; one and two in the banking industry; two and three in the electric power, gas, and energy industries; and two each in other industries. The holding of the chairman's mandate of the managing board was observed in five enterprises: three in the iron and steel industry; one in the banking industry and one in other industries. In each company, the number of mandates was one, respectively, and the total number of mandates was five. Cases in which the mandate of the managing board except for chairman and vice-chairman was held can be observed in 16 enterprises. The total number of mandates was 18. The numbers of such enterprises and mandates respectively were three and four in the mining industry; two each in the iron and steel industry; one each in the metal producing and processing industries; one each in the electrical industry; and one each in the machine industry; two each in the oil industry; two each in the textile, spinning, and woven goods industries; one each in the banking industry; two and three in the electric power, gas, and energy industries; and one each in other industries. There were three cases in which two mandates of the managing board were held by members of the Essen-Düsseldorf organization of the Rhein–Westfalen regional advisory council. Such cases were

for each company in the mining, banking, electric power, gas, and energy industries. Whereas in company in the banking industry, a mandate of chairman and one post of the managing board except for chairman and vice-chairman were held, in other two companies, two mandates of the managing board except for chairman and vice-chairman were held, respectively.

Cases in which mandates of the supervisory board and managing board were held by members of the Essen–Düsseldorf organization of the Rhein–Westfalen regional advisory council can be observed in six enterprises: Mannesmann-Röhrenwerke AG, Klöckner-Werke AG, and Stahlwerks-Verband AG in the iron and steel industry, Kabelwerk Duisburg in the electrical industry, Deutsche Erdöl AG, and Deutsche Petroleum AG in the oil industry. In Mannesmann-Röhrenwerke AG, three members held two mandates on the supervisory board except for chairman and vice-chairman, and one post of chairman of the management board. In Deutsche Erdöl AG, three members held a mandate of vice-chairman and one post of the supervisory board except for chairman and vice-chairman, and a mandate of the managing board except for chairman and vice-chairman. In Stahlwerks-Verband AG, two members each occupied a supervisory board mandate excluding the chairman and vice-chairman and chairmen of the managing board. In Kabelwerk Duisburg, a mandate of chairman of the supervisory board and one post of the managing board excluding chairman and vice-chairman were held by two members. In Deutsche Petroleum AG, a mandate of vice-chairman of the supervisory board and one post of the managing board excluding chairman and vice-chairman were held. In Klöckner-Werke AG, a mandate of the supervisory board except for chairman and vice-chairman and one post of the managing board except for chairman and vice-chairman were held by two members (Deutsche Bank und Disconto-Bank 1935, S. 13–14; Mossner 1936).

13.2.2.3 Case of Wuppertal Organization

Finally, when considering the mandates that members of the Wuppertal organization of the Rhein–Westfalen regional advisory council held on the supervisory board (see Table 13.6), the number of companies totaled 51, and the total number of mandates was 57. These numbers were significantly lower than those of the Rhein–Westfalen regional advisory council's Cologne, Essen-Düsseldorf organizations, and the Württemberg regional advisory council.

Examining the conditions regarding the holding of supervisory board mandates in relation to the distribution of industrial sectors, the numbers of companies and mandates respectively were three each in the metal producing and processing industries; similarly, five each in the chemical industry; three each in the machine industry; one each in the food industry; 17 and 19 in the textile, spinning, and woven goods industries; respectively; two each in the banking industry; three and five in the insurance industry; and 17 and 19 in other industries. Although there were many firms and mandates in the textile, spinning, and woven goods industries, the situation differed from that of the Cologne organization, the Essen-Düsseldorf organization of the

Table 13.6 Supervisory board positions held by members of the Wuppertal organization of Deutsche Bank's Rhein-Westfalen regional council (period of National Socialism)

Industries	Position							
	Chairman		Vice-Chairman		Supervisory board member excluding chairman and vice-chairman		Total[a]	
	Number of companies	Number of posts	Number of companies	Number of posts	Number of companies	Number of posts	Number of companies	Number of posts
Metal producing and processing	3	3	–	–	–	–	3	3
Chemical	2	2	–	–	3	3	5	5
Machine	1	1	2	2	–	–	3	3
Food	1	1	–	–	–	–	1	1
Textile, spinning, and woven goods	7	7	2	2	10	10	17	19
Banking	1	1	–	–	1	1	2	2
Insurance	–	–	1	1	3	4	3	5
Other industries	7	7	1	1	10	11	17	19
All industries	22	22	6	6	27	29	51	57

Note [a] There are cases in which the total number of companies in which mandate was held are different from the total number of companies measured by each position of the supervisory board due to the existence of companies where more than two posts were held
Source This table was compiled by the author, based on Mossner (Hrsg) (1936) and Deutsche Bank und Disconto-Gesellschaft (1935)

Rhein–Westfalen regional advisory council, and the Württemberg regional advisory council in terms of industrial sector types.

When Wuppertal organization members of the Rhein–Westfalen regional advisory council had a mandate for the supervisory board position, 22 companies held the chairmanship. Each member of this advisory council had one mandate, bringing the total to 22. Taking into account the distribution of the industrial sectors, there were three companies in the metal production and processing industries, two in the chemical industry, one in the machine industry, one in the food industry, seven in the textile, spinning, and woven goods industries, one in the banking industry, and seven in other industries.

Holding of mandate of vice-chairman was observed in six enterprises. In each company, each member of this advisory council had one mandate, bringing the total to six. There were two such enterprises in the machine industry, two in the textile, spinning, and woven goods industries, one in the insurance industry, and one in other industries.

Except for the chairman and vice-chairman, the supervisory board posts were held in 27 companies, for 29 mandates. The chemical industry had three such enterprises and mandates and the textile, spinning, and woven goods industries had 10 each. The banking industry had one each, the insurance industry had three and four, and the others had ten and eleven, respectively.

Of the 51 enterprises where members of the Rhein–Westfalen regional advisory council's Wuppertal organization held a supervisory board mandate, six of them had multiple supervisory board mandates. Westdeutsche Textil AG and Gebrüder Simon Textil AG were in the textile, spinning, and woven goods industries, while Rheinische Assekuranz AG and Gerling-Konzern Lebensversiche-rung AG were in insurance, and Fiedes Treuhand AG and Ausrüstungsanstalt Wiesental AG were in other industries. The total number of mandates was 12. Although the numbers of enterprises and mandates were small compared to the Rhein–Westfalen regional advisory council's Cologne and Essen-Düsseldorf organizations, they were nearly identical to the Württemberg regional advisory council's numerical figures.

Two members of the Rhein–Westfalen regional advisory council's Wuppertal organization held the chairman and vice-chairman positions at Westdeutsche Textil AG. Except for the chairman and vice-chairman, two members held the mandates of chairman and one supervisory board position at Gebrüder Simon Textil AG and Fiedes Treuhand AG. In Rheinische Assekuranz AG, two members held one vice-chairman position and a supervisory board mandate that excluded the chairman and vice-chairman. In contrast, in each of Gerling-Konzern Lebensversicherung AG and Ausrüstungsanstalt Wiesenthal AG, two members of this advisory council hold two supervisory board positions, excluding the chairman and vice-chairman.

Members of the Wuppertal organization of the Rhein–Westfalen regional advisory council hold mandates on the enterprise's management board. Nine enterprises exhibit such cases. The total number of mandates was nine. The enterprise and mandate numbers were extremely small compared to holding a supervisory board mandate. The number of such enterprises was one in the iron and steel industry, two in the metal producing and processing industries, three in the chemical industry, one in the food industry, one in the textile, spinning, and woven goods industries, and one in others. Except for the chairman and vice-chairman, each of the nine companies had a managing board with one mandate.

In two cases, members of the Rhein–Westfalen regional advisory council's Wuppertal organization served on both the supervisory and managing boards. These cases included J. P. Bemberg AG in the textile, spinning, and woven goods industries and Schlieper & Baum AG in other industries. In other industries, in Schlieper & Baum AG, two members hold the mandate of chairman of the supervisory board and post of the managing board, except for chairman and vice-chairman. In P Bemberg AG, two members held one each of the supervisory and managing board mandates (Deutsche Bank and Disconto-Bank 1935, S. 14–15; Mossner 1936).

The previous discussions show how personnel connections between a bank and industrial enterprises and between enterprises in various industrial sectors were established using the bank's regional advisory council system. This was necessary for exchanging and sharing information between a bank and its members' companies. However, the field and scope of information that can be exchanged and shared between enterprises can be expanded by members of each advisory council holding top management positions, such as the company's supervisory and management boards. Having a supervisory board mandate is common in a variety of industrial sectors. These personnel connections help to exchange and share information, coordinate interests, and resolve conflicts between corporations.

This chapter described the conditions in the mid-1930s for personnel connections between banks, enterprises, and corporations via the bank's regional advisory council system before WWII. The functions and roles of these personnel connections are important factors to consider. Chapter 14 clarifies these research topics by examining the activities of advisory councils.

References

Büschgen HE (1983) Die Groβbanken. Fritz Knapp Verlag, Frankfurt am Main

Deutsche Bank und Disconto-Gesellschaft (1935) Geschäftsbericht für 1935. Deutsche Bank und Disconto-Gesellschaft, Frankfurt am Main

Eglau HO (1990) Wie Gott in Frankfurt: Die Deutsche Bank und die deutsche Industrie, 3rd edn. Econ Verlag, Düsseldorf

Koubek N (1971) Personelle und institutionelle Verbindung der Bereiche "Produktion" und "Kapital" in der Wirtschaftsgesellschaft der BRD. In: WWI-Mitteilungen 24(8/9):258–274

Meyen HG (1992) *120 Jahre Dresdner Bank. Unternehmens-Chronik*. Dresdner Bank, Frankfurt am Main

Mossner J (Hrsg) (1936) Adressbuch der Direktoren und Aufsichtsräte 1936. Bd.I, Nach Personen geordnet, Finanz-Verlag, Berlin

Pfeiffer (1986a) Groβbanken und Finanzgruppen. Ausgewählte Ergebnisse einer Untersuchung der personellen Verflechtungen von Deutscher, Dresdner und Commerzbank. In: WSI Mitteilungen 39(7):473–481

Pfeiffer (1986b) Das Netwerk der Groβbanken.Personelle Verflechtungen mit Konzernen, Staat und ideologischen Apparaten. In: Blätter für deutsche und internationale Politik 31(2):161–177

Pfeiffer (1993) Die Macht der Banken. Die personellen Verflechtungen der Commerzbank, der Deutschen Bank und der Dresdner Bank mit Unternehemen. Campus, Frankfurt am Main

Stanzick K-H (1969) Der ökonomische Konzentrationsproze. In: Schäfer G, Nedelmann C (Hrsg) Der CDU-Staat.Analysen zur Verfassungswriklich- keit der Bundesrepublik, Bd.I, 2. Aufl., Schurkamp, München, S.48-79

Chapter 14
Activities of Banks' Advisory Councils and Roles of Personnel Connections Based on Such Organizations Before World War II

Abstract Based on examinations of conditions of personnel connection between enterprises through regional advisory council system before World War II in the previous chapter, this chapter considers functions and roles of personnel connection through such organization before the war on the basis of original historical materials of large German bank. It examines the conditions for holding meetings and their members, the contents of each meeting, and personnel issues, such as elections of members of regional advisory councils as an important foundation of the functioning of such an organization. Significance and role of advisory council systems and personnel connections through such an organization will be clarified on the basis of these discussions.

Keywords Advisory council · Deutsche Bank · Industry–bank relationship · Interfirm relationships · Personnel connection · Regional advisory council

In Chap. 13, personnel connection structures through bank's advisory councils during the period before World War II were analyzed. Personnel connections through advisory council systems as well as through interlocking directorates played significant roles in the exchange and sharing of information between banks and industrial enterprises and among industrial enterprises. These organizations functioned as a focal point of information exchange between corporations and banks as well as among corporations. They played a significant role as an important means of supplementing the personnel connections through direct and indirect interlocking in top management entities, such as the supervisory board and the board of directors.

This chapter considers personnel connection functions through this type of organization before World War II. Regarding the advisory council system of a bank, only regional advisory councils were created for each region. Therefore, the role played by personnel connections through a bank's regional advisory council is discussed, and the functions of such personnel connections are clarified.

In this chapter, the functions and roles of advisory councils and the personnel connections through them are considered for Deutsche Bank as one of the most representative cases. The analysis in this chapter is done on the basis of various

T. Yamazaki, *Relationships Between Industry and Bank in Germany*,
https://doi.org/10.1007/978-981-97-4996-6_14

original historical materials on Deutsche Bank that were possessed in its archives (Historisches Archiv der Deutschen Bank). A large volume of materials, such as minutes of advisory council meetings, letters, and documents, and correspondence records between members of Deutsche Bank, between this bank and industrial enterprises, and between this bank and members of advisory councils, are used. This chapter examines situations from the latter half of the 1920s to end of the World War II for reasons concerning the existence and possibility of public inspections of original historical materials possessed in the Deutsche Bank archives.

Section 14.1 examines the conditions for holding meetings and the members of each meeting. Section 14.2 considers the contents of each meeting. Section 14.3 analyzes personnel issues, such as elections of members of regional advisory councils as an important foundation of the functioning of such an organization. Building on these discussions, Sect. 14.4 clarifies the significance and role of advisory council systems and personnel connections through such an organization.

14.1 Conditions for Holding Meetings and Meeting Participants of Regional Advisory Councils

Conditions for holding regional advisory council meetings of Deutsche Bank and the participants in each meeting are examined in Sect. 14.1. As was considered in Chap. 13, the Rhein–Westfalen regional advisory council consisted of three suborganizations: (1) Cologne, (2) Essen–Düsseldorf (in the fiscal year 1934, Essen), and (3) Wuppertal (Deutsche Bank 1937, S. 30–33, 1938, S. 29–31, 1939, S. 30–33, 1940, S. 30–33; Deutsche Bank und Disconto-Gesellschaft 1934, S. 12–14, 1935, S. 12–15, 1936, S. 26–29). Here, an analysis is developed mainly regarding the organization of the Cologne advisory council, which had meeting minutes. Two other organizations of this regional advisory council and advisory councils in other regions were considered as important cases.

Observations of meetings held from 1934 to 1942, which were confirmed through minutes in the Deutsche Bank archives, indicated the following. Meetings of the Cologne organization in the Rhein–Westfalen regional advisory council occurred on July 26, 1934, January 9, 1935, June 17, 1935, November 27, 1935, May 5, 1936, November 11, 1936, April 20, 1937, October 28, 1937, March 31, 1938, November 2, 1938, April 30, 1940, May 7, 1941, and April 15, 1942. Using these documents as confirmation, numerous cases exist for organizations that held meetings twice a year.

Regarding the participants of each meeting, 57 individuals were invited to a meeting on July 26, 1934. At this meeting, 47 attended, including individuals from Deutsche Bank, and 10 were absent. Similar numerical figures were 50 attendees and eight absentees, or a total of 58, for a meeting held on January 9, 1935. The numbers of attendees and absentees were 42 and eight on June 17, 1935, meeting, 49 and five on November 27, 1935, meeting, 42 and 14 on May 5, 1936, meeting,

54 and 10 on November 11, 1936, meeting, 52 and nine on April 20, 1937, meeting, 49 and 11 on October 28, 1937, meeting, 51 and 16 on March 31, 1938, meeting, 49 and 15 on November 2, 1938, meeting, 43 and 19 on April 30, 1940, meeting, 46 and 18 on May 7, 1941, meeting, and 46 and 17 on April 15, 1942, meeting. Therefore, the number of invited individuals was 50 on June 17, 1935, 54 on November 27, 1935, 56 on May 5, 1936, 64 on November 11, 1936, 61 on April 20, 1937, 60 on October 28, 1937, 67 on March 31, 1938, 64 on November 2, 1938, 62 on April 30, 1940, 64 on May 7, 1941, and 63 on April 15, 1942 [*Historisches Archiv der Deutschen Bank* (bellow HADB), P00041, Sitzung des Rheinisch-Westfälischen Beirates, Sitz Köln im Gebäude der Deutschen Bank und Disconto-Gesellschaft Filiale Köln am Donnerstag, dem 26. Juli 1934; HADB, P00041, Sitzung des Rheinisch-Westfälischen Beirates, Sitz Köln im Gebäude der Deutschen Bank und Disconto-Gesellschaft Filiale Köln am Mittwoch, dem 9. Januar 1935; Sitz Köln im Gebäude der Deutschen Bank und Disconto-Gesellschaft Filiale Köln am Montag, den 17. Juni 1935; HADB, P00041, Sitzung des Rheinisch-Westfälischen Beirates, Sitz Köln im Gebäude der Deutschen Bank und Disconto-Gesellschaft Filiale Köln am Mittwoch, dem 27. November 1935; HADB, P00041, Sitzung des Rheinisch-Westfälischen Beirates, Sitz Köln im Gebäude der Deutschen Bank und Disconto-Gesellschaft Filiale Köln am Dienstag, dem 5. Mai 1936; HADB, P00041, Sitzung des Rheinisch-Westfälischen Beirates, Sitz Köln im Gebäude der Deutschen Bank und Disconto-Gesellschaft Filiale Köln am Mittwoch, dem 11. November 1936; HADB, P00041, Sitzung des Rheinisch-Westfälischen Beirats, Sitz Köln im Gebäude der Deutschen Bank und Disconto-Gesellschaft Filiale Köln am Dienstag, den 20. April 1937; HADB, P00041, Sitzung des Rheinisch-Westfälischen Beirats, Sitz Köln im Gebäude der DEUTSCHEN BANK FILIALEN KÖLN am Donnerstag, dem 28. Oktober 1937; HADB, P00041, Sitzung des Rheinisch-West-fälischen Beirats, Sitz Köln im Gebäude der DEUTSCHEN BANK FILIALEN KÖLN am Donnerstag, dem 31. März 1938; HADB, P00041, Sitzung des Rheinisch-Westfälischen Beirats, Sitz Köln im Gebäude der DEUTSCHEN BANK FILIALEN KÖLN am Mittwoch, den 2. November 1938; HADB, P00041, Sitzung des Rheinisch-Westfälischen Beirats, Sitz Köln im Gebäude der DEUTSCHEN BANK FILIALEN KÖLN am Dienstag, dem 30. April 1940; HADB, P00041, Sitzung des Rheinisch-Westfälischen Beirats, Sitz Köln im Gebäude der DEUTSCHE NBANK FILIALEN KÖLN am Mittwoch, dem 7. Mai 1941; HADB, P00041, Sitzung des Rheinisch-Westfälischen Beirats, HADB, P00036, Sitz Köln im Gebäude der Deutschen Bank Filialen Köln am Mittwoch, dem 15. April 1942].

The number of members of the Cologne organization in the Rhein–Westfalen regional advisory council as noted in annual reports was 30 in fiscal year 1934, 33 in fiscal year 1935, 32 in fiscal year 1936, 33 in fiscal year 1937, 33 in fiscal year 1938, 34 in fiscal year 1939, and 34 in fiscal year 1940 (Deutsche Bank 1937, S. 30–31, 1938, S. 29, 1939, S. 30–31, 1940, S. 30–31; Deutsche Bank und Disconto-Gesellschaft 1934, S. 12–13, 1935, S. 12–13, 1936, S. 26–27). Therefore, the number of invited individuals except for members of this regional advisory council was 17 in the fewest cases (a meeting on June 17, 1935) and 34 in the highest cases (March 31, 1938).

In addition, conditions for holding meetings of the Cologne organization in the Rhein–Westfalen regional advisory council before 1934 and other organizations in this advisory council are examined. According to the annual report before fiscal year 1932, such a regional organization was not called a "regional advisory council" (Bezirksbeirat) but a "regional committee" (Ortausschuss or Landesausschuss) (Deutsche Bank 1900, 1927, S. 9–15, 1928, S. 9–14; Deutsche Bank und Disconto-Gesellschaft 1932, S. 33–40). The situations of meetings including these organizations were observed. For instance, a letter from Deutsche Bank to K. Kimmich pointed out that committees in the Rhein–Westfalen region were newly divided into three: Elberfeld, Essen, and Cologne. Moreover, the Essen organization succeeded the Osnabrück– Münster committee [HADB, P00042, Der Brief von der Deutschen Bank und Disconto-Gesellschaft an Herrn Dr. Karl Kimmich (10.4.1930)]. In Elberfeld, one of the Rhein–Westfalen regional committees, a meeting occurred on May 1, 1930 [HADB, P00042, Die Schrift über die Einladung für Herrn Dr. Carl Kimmich zur Sitzung des Rheinisch-Westfälischer Ausschuβes, Elberfeld der Deutschen Bank und Disconto-Gesellschaft (8.4.1930)]. Another meeting of the Rhein–Westfalen regional committee occurred in Essen on May 2, 1930 [HADB, P00042, Die Schrift über die Einladung für Herrn Bankdirektor Dr. Karl Kimmich zur Sitzung des Rheinisch-Westfälischer Ausschuβes, Essen der Deutschen Bank und Disconto-Gesellschaft (11.4.1930)]. In the Essen organization of this regional committee, another meeting was also held on October 7, 1930 [HADB, P00042, Die Schrift über die Einladung für Herrn Dr. Karl Kimmich zur Sitzung des Rheinisch-Westfälischer Ausschusses, Essen der Deutschen Bank und Disconto-Gesellschaft (26.9.1930)] and a similar meeting of the Elberfeld organization occurred on October 8, 1930 [HADB, P00042, Die Schrift über die Einladung für Herrn Dr. Karl Kimmich zur Sitzung des Rheinisch-Westfälischer Ausschuβes, Elberfeld der Deutschen Bank und Disconto-Gesellschaft (24.9.1930)]. In Elberfeld of the Rhein–Westfalen regional committee, other meetings also occurred on April 30, 1931 [HADB, P00042, Die Schrift über die Einladung für Herrn Dr. Karl Kimmich zur Sitzung des Rheinisch-Westfälischer Ausschuβes, Erberfeld der Deutschen Bank und Disconto-Gesellschaft (23.3.1910)] and November 31, 1931 [HADB, P00042, Die Schrift über die Einladung für Herrn Dr. Karl Kimmich zur Sitzung des Rheinisch-Westfälischer Ausschuβes, Erberfeld der Deutschen Bank und Disconto-Gesellschaft (30.9.1931)]. In addition, a meeting of the Cologne organization of the Rhein–Westfalen regional committee occurred on December 20, 1932 [HADB, P00042, Die Schrift über die Einladung für Herrn Dr. Karl Kimmich zur Sitzung des Rheinisch-Westfälischer Ausschuβes, Köln der Deutschen Bank und Disconto-Gesellschaft (12.11.1932)].

Furthermore, meetings of the Rhein–Westfalen regional advisory council except for the Cologne organization after its name change from "regional committee" to "regional advisory council" were analyzed. For example, a meeting of the Essen organization occurred on November 4, 1938 [HADB, P00037, Die Schrift über die Einladung für Herrn Dr. Karl Kimmich zur Sitzung des Rheinisch-Westfälischer Ausschuβes, Essen der Deutschen Bank (13.10.1938)]. Meetings in Essen–Düsseldorf occurred on April 5, 1938 [HADB, P00037, Die Schrift über die Einladung für Herrn Dr. Karl Kimmich zur Sitzung des Rheinisch-Westfälischer Ausschuβes,

Essen-Düsseldorf der Deutschen Bank (14.3.1939); HADB, P00042, Der Brief vom Rheinisch-Westfälischer Beirat der Deutschen Bank an Herrn Hermann J. Abs (11.3.1939); HADB, P00042, Der Brief an die Direktion der Deutschen Bank Filiale Köln über die Sitzung des Rheinisch-Westfälischer Beirates am 5. April 1939 (14.3.1939)] and November 6, 1938. The latter was held with the Cologne organization in the Rhein–Westfalen regional advisory council [HADB, P00036, Der Brief über die Einladung für Herrn Direktor Hermann J. Abs zur Sitzung des Rheinisch-Westfälischer Beirates Essen-Düsseldorf gemeinsam mit dem Beirat Köln am 6.11.1940, vormittags 10 Uhr im Geschäftshause der Bank zu im Industrieklub Düsseldorf, Elberfelderstr.5 (21.10.1940); HADB, P00036, Der Brief vom Sekretariat Hermann J. Abs an die Deutschen Bank Filiale Essen (4.11.1940)]. Meetings were also held on April 29, 1940 [HADB, P00037, Die Schrift über die Einladung für Herrn Dr. Karl Kimmich zur Sitzung des Rheinisch-Westfälischer Ausschußes, Essen-Düsseldorf der Deutschen Bank (10.4.1940)] and December 9, 1941. The latter was a unified meeting with the Cologne organization of the Rhein–Westfalen regional advisory council [HADB, P00037, Die Schrift über die Einladung für Herrn Dr. Karl Kimmich zur Sitzung des Rheinisch-Westfälischer Ausschußes, Essen-Düsseldorf der Deutschen Bank (17.11.1941); HADB, P00036, Der Brief über die Einladung für Herrn Hermann J. Abs zur Gemeinschafts-Sitzung der Beiräte Essen-Düsseldorf und Köln am Dienstag, dem 9. Dezember 1941 vormittags 10 1/2 in den Räumen des Industri-Club Düsseldorf, Elberfelderstr.5 (21.11.1941)].

Advisory council meetings of other regions were considered. In the Frankfurt–Hessen regional advisory council, for instance, meetings were held on April 29, 1938 [HADB, P00036, Der Brief von der Deutschen Bank Filiale Frankfurt (Main) an Herr Hermann J. Abs (8.14.1938); HADB, P00036, Der Brief von Deutschen Bank Filiale Frankfurt (Main) über die Sitzung des Frankfurt-Hessischen Beirates am 29. April 1938 (11.4.1938); HADB, P00036, Der Brief über die Einladung für Herrn Hermann J. Abs zu einer Sitzung des Frankfurt-Hessischen Beirates am 29. April 1938, vormittags 11 Uhr, im Bankgebäude der Deutschen Bank Filiale Frankfurt (Main), Frankfurt a.M., Roßmarkt 18. (11.4.1938)], September 19, 1938 [HADB, P00036, Der Brief über die Einladung für Herrn Hermann J. Abs zu einer Sitzung des Frankfurt-Hessischen Beirates am Montag, den 19. September 1938 (8.9.1938)], June 22, 1939 [HADB, P00036, Der Brief über die Einladung für Herrn Hermann J. Abs zu einer Sitzung des Frankfurt-Hessischen Beirates am Donnerstag, den 22. Juni 1939, vorm. 11 Uhr, im Bankgebäude der Deutschen Bank Filiale Frankfurt (Main), Frankkfurt a.M., Roßmarkt 18. (3.6.1939); HADB, P00036, Der Brief an Herrn Hermann J. Abs (17.6.1939)], June 14, 1940 [HADB, P00036, Der Brief über die Einladung für Herrn Hermann J. Abs zu einer Sitzung des Frankfurt-Hessischen Beirates am Freitag, den 14. Juni 1940 (15.5.1940); HADB, P00036, Der Brief an Herrn Dr. R. Frowein (10.6.1940); HADB, P00036, Der Brief von der Deutschen Bank Filiale Frankfurt (Main) an Herrn Hermann J. Abs (12.6.1940); HADB, P00036, Der Brief von der Deutschen Bank Filiale Frankfurt (Main) an Herrn Hermann J. Abs (21.6.1940); HADB, P00036, Niederschrift über den Verlauf der neunten Sitzung des FRANKFURT-HESSISCHEN BEIRATS der DEUTSCHEN BANK am 14. Juni 1940, vormittags 11. Uhr, im Sitzungssaal der Deutschen Bank Filiale Frankfurt

(Main), Rossmarkt 18, S. 1; HADB, P00036, Der Brief von Hermann J. Abs an die Direktion der Deutschen Bank Filiale Frankfurt (Main) (27.6.1940)], June 5, 1941 [HADB, P00036, Frankfurt-Hessischer Beirats. (12.5.1941); HADB, P00036, Der Brief von Dr. Robert Frowein an Herrn Hermann J. Abs (17.5.1941); HADB, P00036, Der Brief von Hermann J. Abs an Herrn Dr. Robert Frowein (20.5.1941); HADB, P00036, Der Brief über die Einladung für Herrn Hermann J. Abs zu einer Sitzung des Frankfurt-Hessischen Beirates am Donnerstag, den 5. Juni 1941, vorm. 11 Uhr, im Bankgebäude der Deutschen Bank Filiale Frankfurt (Main), Frankkfurt a.M., Roβmarkt 18. (15.5.1941); HADB, P00036, Der Brief von der Deutschen Bank Filiale Frankfurt (Main) an Herrn Hermann J. Abs (14.6.1941); HADB, P00036, Niederschrift über den Verlauf der zehnten Sitzung des FRANKFURT-HESSISCHEN BEIRATS der DEUTSCHEN BANK am 5. Juni 1941, vormittags 11. Uhr, im Sitzungssaal der Deutschen Bank Filiale Frankfurt (Main)., S. 1; HADB, P00036, Der Brief über die Sitzung des Frankfurt-Hessischen Beirates am 5. Juni 1941 (20.6.1941)], and May 26, 1942 [HADB, P00036, Der Brief über die Einladung für Herrn Hermann J. Abs zu einer Sitzung des Frankfurt-Hessischen Beirates am Dienstag, den 26. Mai 1942, vorm. 11 Uhr, im Bankgebäude der Deutschen Bank Filiale Frankfurt (Main), Frankfurt a.M., Roβmarkt 18. (5.5.1942); HADB, P00036, Frankfurt-Hessischer Beirat. (4.6.1942); HADB, P00036, Niederschrift über den Verlauf der elften Sitzung des FRANKFURT-HESSISCHEN BEIRATS der DEUTSCHEN BANK am 26. Mai 1942, vormittags 11. Uhr, im Sitzungssaal der Deutschen Bank Filiale Frankfurt (Main)., S. 1; HADB, P00036, Der Brief von Hermann J. Abs an die Deutschen Bank Filiale Frankfurt (Main) am 26. Mai 1942 (6.6.1942)]. Every meeting planned to begin at 11:00 a.m. [HADB, P00036, Der Brief von der Deutschen Bank Filiale Frankfurt (Main) an Herr Hermann J. Abs (8.4.1938); HADB, P00036, Der Brief über die Einladung für Herrn Hermann J. Abs zu einer Sitzung des Frankfurt-Hessischen Beirates am 29. April 1938, vormittags 11 Uhr, im Bankgebäude der Deutschen Bank Filiale Frankfurt (Main), Frankfurt a.M., Roβmarkt 18. (11.4.1938); HADB, P00036, Der Brief über die Einladung für Herrn Hermann J. Abs zu einer Sitzung des Frankfurt-Hessischen Beirates am Montag, den 19. September 1938(8.9.1938); HADB, P00036, Der Brief über die Einladung für Herrn Hermann J. Abs zu einer Sitzung des Frankfurt-Hessischen Beirates am Donnerstag, den 22. Juni 1939, vorm. 11 Uhr, im Bankgebäude der Deutschen Bank Filiale Frankfurt (Main), Frankkfurt a.M., Roβmarkt 18. (3.6.1939); HADB, P00036, Der Brief von der Deutschen Bank Filiale Frankfurt (Main) an Herrn Hermann J. Abs (12.6.1940); HADB, P00036, Niederschrift über den Verlauf der neunten Sitzung des FRANKFURT-HESSISCHEN BEIRATS der DEUTSCHEN BANK am 14. Juni 1940, vormittags 11. Uhr, im Sitzungssaal der Deutschen Bank Filiale Frankfurt (Main), Rossmarkt 18, S. 1; HADB, P00036, Frankfurt-Hessischer Beirat. (12.5.1941); HADB, P00036, Der Brief über die Einladung für Herrn Hermann J. Abs zu einer Sitzung des Frankfurt-Hessischen Beirates am Donnerstag, den 5. Juni 1941, vorm. 11 Uhr, im Bankgebäude der Deutschen Bank Filiale Frankfurt (Main), Frankfurt a.M., Roβmarkt 18. (15.5.1941); HADB, P00036, Niederschrift über den Verlauf der zehnten Sitzung des FRANKFURT-HESSISCHEN BEIRATS der DEUTSCHEN BANK am 5. Juni 1941, vormittags 11. Uhr, im Sitzungssaal der Deutschen Bank Filiale Frankfurt (Main)., S. 1; HADB, P00036, Der Brief über die Einladung für Herrn Hermann J. Abs zu einer Sitzung des Frankfurt-Hessischen Beirates am Dienstag, den 26. Mai 1942, vorm. 11 Uhr, im Bankgebäude der Deutschen Bank Filiale Frankfurt (Main), Frankkfurt a.M., Roßmarkt 18. (5.5.1942); HADB, P00036, Niederschrift über den Verlauf der elften Sitzung des FRANKFURT-HESSISCHEN BEIRATS der DEUTSCHEN BANK am 26. Mai 1942, vormittags 11. Uhr, im Sitzungssaal der Deutschen Bank Filiale Frankfurt (Main)., S. 1]. Meetings from 1939 to the 1940s usually occurred once a year. A document dated December 4, 1940, from K. E. Sippell as a member of the managing board of Deutsche Bank to H. J. Abs pointed out that no meeting of this regional advisory council was held during this period and holding a single meeting in 1940 was agreed on between F. Frowein as a director of the Frankfurt branch of Deutsche Bank and G. von Schnitzler as chairman of this regional advisory council [HADB, P00036, Frankfurt-hessischer Beirat. (4.12.1940)].

Meetings of the Frankfurt–Hessen regional advisory council for which the number in attendance could be confirmed were explored. The numbers of attendees and absentees at the meeting on June 14, 1940 (confirmation on May 15, 1940) were 21 and nine, respectively. Of the 21 attendees, 13 were members of this regional advisory council. The number of people invited was 30, of which 20 were members of this regional advisory council, four were guests, four were concerned with the Frankfurt branch, and one each was from the Mainz and Cassel branches [HADB, P00036, Niederschrift über den Verlauf der neunten Sitzung des FRANKFURT-HESSISCHEN BEIRATS der DEUTSCHEN BANK am 14. Juni 1940, vormittags 11. Uhr, im Sitzungssaal der Deutschen Bank Filiale Frankfurt (Main), Rossmarkt 18, S. 1–2]. At the meeting on June 5, 1941, 23 attended and six were absent, figures that were confirmed on May 15, 1941, for a total number of invited of 29. Of the 23 attendees, 16 were from the regional advisory council. Of the 29 invited, 21 were members of this regional advisory council, three were guests, three were persons concerned with the Frankfurt branch, and one each was from the Mainz and Cassel branches [HADB, P00036, Niederschrift über den Verlauf der zehnten Sitzung des FRANKFURT-HESSISCHEN BEIRATS der DEUTSCHEN Bank am 5. Juni 1941, vormittags 11. Uhr, im Sitzungssaal der Deutschen Bank Filiale Frankfurt (Main)., S. 1–2]. At a meeting on May 26, 1942, 25 attended and five were absent, figures confirmed on May 5, 1942, for a total number of invited of 30. Of the 25 attendees, 16 were from this regional advisory council. Of the 30 invited, 20 were members of this regional advisory council, four were guests, three were persons concerned with the Frankfurt branch, two were from the Mainz branch, and one was from the Cassel branch [HADB, P00036, Niederschrift über den Verlauf der elften Sitzung des FRANKFURT-HESSISCHEN BEIRATS der DEUTSCHEN BANK am 26. Mai 1942, vormittags 11. Uhr, im Sitzungssaal der DeutschenBank Filiale Frankfurt (Main)., S. 1–2].

Meetings of the Hannover–Braunschweig–Hildesheim regional advisory council were evaluated. For example, at a meeting held on May 9, 1939, 27 attended and 12 were absent, for a total of 39 invited. Of the 27 attendees, three were from Berlin, seven were members of this regional advisory council who were from Hannover, two were from the Hannover branch, eight were members of this regional advisory council who were from Braunschweig, one was from the Braunschweig branch, five were members of this regional advisory council who were from Hildesheim, and one was from the Hildesheim branch (HADB, P00039, Protokoll über die Sitzung der Beiräte der Bezirke Hannover, Braunschweig und Hildesheim am 9. Mai 1939 in den Räumen der Deutschen Bank Filiale Hannover in Hannover., S. 1–2). At a meeting held on May 14, 1941, 28 attended and 13 were absent, for a total number of invited of 41. Of the 28 attendees, three were from Berlin, six were members of this regional advisory council who were from Hannover, two were from the Hannover branch, six were from this regional advisory council who were from Braunschweig, one was from the Braunschweig branch, nine were members of this regional advisory council who were from Hildesheim, and one was from the Hildesheim branch (HADB, P00039, Protokoll über die Sitzung der Beiräte der Bezirke Braunschweig, Hildesheim und Hannover am 14. Mai 1941 in den Räumen der Deutschen Bank Filiale Hannover in Hannover., S. 1–2). At a meeting on December 4, 1942, 33 attended and four were absent, for a total number of invited of 37. Of the 33 attendees, three were from Berlin, nine were members of this regional advisory council who were from Hannover, two were from the Hannover branch, eight were members of this regional advisory council who were from Braunschweig, two were from the Braunschweig branch, eight were members of this regional advisory council who were from Hildesheim, and one was from the Hildesheim branch (HADB, P00039, Protokoll über die Sitzung der Beiräte der Bezirke Braunschweig, Hildesheim und Hannover am 4. Dezember 1942 in den Räumen der Deutschen Bank Filiale Hannover in Hannover).

Meetings of the Hamburg–Holstein regional advisory council were also evaluated. At a meeting on May 21, 1935, 22 attended and seven were absent, for a total number of invited of 29 ([HADB, P00040, Niederschrift über die 2. Sitzung des Bezirksbeirats Hamburg-Holstein, am 21. Mai 1935, 12 Uhr, S. 1). At a meeting on November 7, 1935, 28 attended and three were absent, for a total number of invited of 31 (HADB, P00040, Niederschrift über die 3. Sitzung des Bezirksbeirats Hamburg-Holstein, am 7. November 1935, 11 Uhr, S. 1–2). According to internal documents of Deutsche Bank dated August 23, 1941, and April 17, 1942, meetings of the Württemberg regional advisory council were to be held twice a year in the spring and the autumn [HADB, P00035, Der Brief an Herr Kessler, (23.8.1941); HADB, P00035, Der Brief an Herr Doktor Hans Malzacher (17.4.1942), S. 1; HADB, P00034, Der Brief von Rummel an Herrn Generaldirektorn Herald Hamberg (6.3.1936)].

14.2 Contents of Regional Advisory Council Meetings: Cases of the Cologne Organization of the Rhein–Westfalen Regional Advisory Council

Conditions for holding meetings of regional advisory councils and participants in such meetings were evaluated. Section 14.2 discusses the contents of regional advisory council meetings. The meeting minutes of the Cologne organization of the Rhein–Westfalen regional advisory council can be used for analysis and are explored in this section. In addition, the meeting minutes of other regional advisory councils are analyzed.

Meeting on July 26, 1934: A meeting of the Cologne organization of the Rhein–Westfalen regional advisory council was held on July 26, 1934. The meeting began at 10:45 a.m. with a greeting by Gottlieb von Langen as chairman of the organization of this advisory council. After the introduction of new members of the advisory council, lectures were heard.

M. Jörgens explained that the purpose of the advisory council was to develop relationships between banks and the economic world. Deutsche Bank expressed thanks for such a function because actual cooperation became possible only through the institution of problems and reviews. He also pointed out the main problems that hindered the founding of regional banks: because of the significant demand for funds in Rheinland, attempts to establish such a bank would fail given a lack of funds. Banks with branches had a significant advantage in being able to rely on the capital of the central office. This lecturer stated the economic conditions in Cologne and confirmed that the business was characterized by the maintenance of domestic market liveliness on the one hand and a decline in the profitability of extending foreign businesses on the other hand.

Next, Karl Kimmich, a member of the managing board of Deutsche Bank since 1933, lectured on foreign trade conditions. He pointed out the lack of foreign currency given a significant decline in Reichsbank's compensation funds as the central bank in Germany. He also took up the foreign exchange problem and clarified that various foreign exchange settlement agreements with individual countries were important when considering the currency issue. F. Proenen lectured on the problem of the production of commutation materials and themes as related to Jörgens' report. Max Clouth also lectured on the same problem, particularly in the field of rubber production.

K. Kimmich referred to individual problems that were taken up in these lectures. He pointed out that 80% of all credits were already provided by the core branches of leading banks that developed business on a national scale and that the remaining 20%—with which regional banks were concerned—needed to receive approval of the credit committee. G. Solmssen indicated the importance of an economic boycott by foreign countries, in particular, the USA. E. Tgahrt referred to the situation in the Saal region from economic and political perspectives and pointed out that, regarding fundamental transformations through the new custom system in relation to France, the possibility of the appearance of difficulties with returns of this district to Germany was significant for the economic structure at that time.

After these lectures, discussions were held among attendances. The chairman of the regional advisory council thanked the lecturers, and the meeting that began at 10:45 a.m. ended at 3:45 p.m., or five hours later (HADB, P00041, Sitzung des Rheinisch-Westfälischen Beirates, HADB, P00041, Sitz Köln im Gebäude der Deutschen Bank und Disconto-Gesellschaft Filiale Köln am Donnerstag, dem 26. Juli 1934.; HADB, P00041, Sitzung des Rheinisch-Westfälischen Beirats, Sitz Köln im Gebäude der Deutschen Bank Filialen Köln am Mittwoch, dem 15. April 1942).

Meeting on January 9, 1935: Next, the meeting on January 9, 1935, began at 10:40 a.m. and some lectures were heard. M. Jörgens, the first lecturer, reported on the bank's business conditions subsequent to the previous meeting and pointed out issues in the fields of law, organization, and general bank policy that had attracted interest in this period. According to him, demand for credit declined because of an upstream trend in market liveliness, an expansion in employment, and a decrease in the stock in the industry, which resulted in a decrease in debtors and an increase in lenders.

Next, J. B. Rath explained the stock market and the damage to Cologne from the loss of a stock exchange given the integration of the three stock exchanges of the Rheinland region into the Düsseldorf stock exchange. He also reported the stock market conditions in the previous year and a prospective for the new year.

K. Kimmich also reported on the stock market situation. He pointed out that economic conditions were very difficult because of the many laws and regulations that were recently granted. The prospect that a barter transaction would be limited by various foreign currency settlement agreements with individual nations was indicated. He explained that because emergent necessities of foreign countries to export to Germany were very large, whether Germany would be resigned with difficulties in commodity trade would become important.

In addition, P. Klöckner pointed out that the main role of managers in recent years was to reduce unemployment. He also indicated the expectation to produce using domestic materials, relatively favorable prospects in coal and iron, very firm price movements, and low wages in part. Brecht reported on manufacturing methods, such as gasoline synthesis, the Reuna method of IG Farben, and the Fischer–Trop method. G. Solmassen reported his impressions of a trip to the USA. Finally, F. von Schorlemer-Lieser reported on wine production.

Attendees discussed these afore-mentioned themes after these lectures. The chairman of the regional advisory council thanked the lecturers and the meeting that started at 10:40 a.m. ended at 1:40 p.m., after three hours (HADB, P00041, Sitzung des Rheinisch-Westfälischen Beirates, Sitz Köln im Gebäude der Deutschen Bank und Disconto-Gesellschaft Filiale Köln am Mittwoch, dem 9. Januar 1935).

Meeting on June 17, 1935: The contents of the meeting that occurred on June 17, 1935, are considered. This meeting also began at 10:40 a.m., similar to the meeting on January 9 of the same year. After a greeting by the chairman of the regional advisory council, new members were introduced, the duty confidentiality regarding contents of reports and discussions was explained, and lectures were given.

M. Jörgens reported that profits did not increase as did sales despite a rapidly advancing economy. He also reported that, although the securities business had improved, the foreign exchange business had almost perfectly decreased, and the conditions of the consortium and security issues businesses were the same. The general situation in Cologne varied. Whereas railroad transportation increased, water transportation decreased significantly and the consumption of gas, waterworks, and electric power slightly increased. The number of unemployed in Cologne was much higher than that in other neighboring cities, and the number of bankruptcies and reconciliation procedures was higher than the previous year. Regarding industry conditions, although the situations in the machine producing industry, the electrical industry, and the automobile industry were good, the metal processing industry was troubled by a lack of material.

K. Kimmich then reported that conditions in the banking industry were not as good, interest and commissions declined again, the general situation was characterized by a state economic boom, unemployment decreased, and liquidity improved. However, conditions were not sound for the economy to achieve good results without public order. He pointed out that a decrease in Germany's exports in recent years was due to the decline in export to western European countries.

He also pointed out that the foreign exchange settlement agreement was very narrow-minded, world trade was seriously damaged, and devaluation did not reduce unemployment in the concerned nations despite the considerable increase in exports.

In addition, O. Brügelmann reported problems in the textile industry, particularly related to sales, the provision of materials, and organization. W. Hesse of Rheinische Nadelfabriken referred to industry conditions that his company faced. In succession, L. von Boch explained the situation in the ceramic industry.

After these reports and lectures, Kimmich referred again to the competitive situation among countries. He pointed out that Japan had become an important threat to Germany and all European countries. Building on these lectures, discussions ensured among the attendees, and the meeting that started at 10:40 a.m. ended at 1:10 p.m., two and a half hours later (HADB, P00041, Sitzung des Rheinisch-Westfälischen Beirates, Sitz Köln im Gebäude der Deutschen Bank und Disconto-Gesellschaft Filiale Köln am Montag, den 17. Juni 1935).

Meeting on November 27, 1935: The meeting on November 27, 1935, also began at 10:40 a.m. and included lectures. G. von Langen, as chairman of this regional advisory council, informed the attendees that all lecture and discussion contents were secret because a free and open conference was possible only when the contents of the meeting were treated as top secret.

The first lecturer was M. Jörgens. He reported that the iron processing and metal processing industries were in generally favorable conditions. For instance, the material industry, such as brown coal, also indicated a slight improvement. In contrast, the situation in the quarrying industry was as not satisfactory as before given a lack of large road construction orders in Holland. The consumer goods industry, particularly the textile industry, faced various difficulties because the largest part of textile processing and sale was taken over by Judah, as well as a relatively large scale of

stock and decline in purchasing power. He also reported that, although the securities business was in good condition until July 1935, such a situation had calmed down after undertaking treasury bonds, the result of such acceptance was considerably satisfactory, and Deutsche Bank founded a commodity trade department for intermediation of barter transactions with a view to promoting exports and imports.

After the lectures by Jörgens, H. Taake reported on the situation in Siegerland. He pointed out that economic conditions considerably worsened, reported on situations in the labor market using numerical figures, and indicated an outline of the condition and trends in individual industrial sectors.

In addition, K. Kimmich reported on general conditions in the banking sector and industries as a whole and explained that, although Deutsche Bank was the largest creditor, the volume of credit did not increase despite the expansion of production; moreover, new credit often had a long-term characteristic. That industries were not able to continue without state order given insufficient increases in exports and promoting exports through all means as indispensable was pointed out. He also reported on national finance and foreign trade and, finally, recognized that a sharp, critical viewpoint was necessary regarding economic problems.

Furthermore, Freiher von Schorlemer informed a short, general survey on the wine market. F. Monheim reported on the situation in the chocolate industry. In addition, A. Schütte indicated that difficulties in the export business increased.

Various fields were reported on and discussions ensued on the basis of these reports. The meeting started at 10:40 a.m. and ended at 1:10 p.m., after two and a half hours (HADB, P00041, Sitzung des Rheinisch-Westfälischen Beirates, Sitz Köln im Gebäude der Deutschen Bank und Disconto-Gesellschaft Filiale Köln am Mittwoch, dem 27. November 1935).

Meeting on May 5, 1936: The meeting on May 5, 1936, also started at 10:40 a.m. After a greeting by the chairman of the advisory council, some lectures were given. J. E. Rath reported on the business condition of the Cologne branch of Deutsche Bank and indicated that, although commerce and industry were still in a domestic boom situation, Cologne was considerably late relative to the economic region of middle Germany. Whereas the iron processing and metal processing industries were in good condition and production increased strongly in the individual sectors, the textile industry faced the problem of a lack of material. He also indicated that wholesale in Cologne was in a relatively satisfactory condition and, in part, a 20% increase in sales volume was realized, unemployment was under fifty thousand, and the number of bankruptcies also further decreased. The business situation in the Cologne branch was more favorable than that in the year before, as observed through an increase in sales volume of approximately 6% relative to that in the previous year. He explained that, although the number of accounts increased from 31,000 to 31,730, problems caused by foreign exchange and material issues became prominent and—regarding the stock price—securities businesses indicated a clear increasing trend.

Next, Eduard Martin reported on economic conditions in the Saar region and indicated that this district faced difficulties given the sudden movement of the custom boundary. Sales and purchasing changed fundamentally with the return of this region to Germany. Martin also clarified that, although the number of employees indicated considerable improvement and unemployment decreased from 50,000 at the end of February 1935 to 28,000 at the end of March 1935, enterprise profitability was quite low because of insufficient coordination in price formation that resulted from cost increases, such as increases in wages, social insurance costs, subsidies for exports, unemployment insurance, and taxation. Moreover, branches in the Saar region experienced considerable expansion when French banks closed; for example, losses created in foreign exchange businesses were also pointed out.

In addition, K. Kimmich reported Deutsche Bank's business situation and explained the business with Vereinigte Stahlwerke AG. He also indicated that when efforts to reduce armaments began again, the interest in a steady financial economy could be maintained. Moreover, maintaining the condition that short-term public state bonds could be coordinated only by banks and insurance companies and a return to a free fund market was necessary. Although a state economic boom was maintained and the order of the state was indispensable at that time, the connection with the world market was unconditionally necessary because such order had to stop at a certain point. Nevertheless, foreign trade remained moderate. He also explained the problem of control of materials under a considerable increase in materials prices in the world market. The currency problem of not devaluing the currency in the home country under the devaluation of the Pound was pointed out.

Karl Grosse gave a short report on the iron industry in Germany from a comparative perspective. He explained the rapid development of this industry after the Franco–Prussian War in 1870–1871 and pointed out that, although further decreases in exports had to be considered, the Soviet Union and Japan would shortly become competitors.

The final lecturer was Friedrich Proenen. He pointed out that, although the textile industry—which had production of RM five billion—was in the very important position of a producing industrial sector, it depended exclusively on foreign raw materials. He emphasized Kimmich's explanation that exports were unconditionally necessary to secure the raw materials needed for the internal economy in Germany and pointed out that the textile industry had to fight serious difficulties in the foreign market.

Thus, lectures by some persons on various fields were given, and discussions among the attendees ensued. The meeting started at 10:40 a.m. and ended at 1:20 p.m. (HADB, P00041, Sitzung des Rheinisch-Westfälischen Beirates, Sitz Köln im Gebäude der Deutschen Bank und Disconto-Gesellschaft Filiale Köln am Dienstag, dem 5. Mai 1936).

Meeting on November 11, 1936: The meeting on November 11, 1936, also started at 10:40 a.m. After a greeting by the chairman of the advisory council, some lectures were given.

J. B. Rath reported on the business of Deutsche Bank in the Cologne region and pointed out that, although a small amount credit was mainly maintained, new bank credit was becoming a central field, and short-term bridge financing based on the consent of existing mortgages was important. He also provided a detailed report on the securities business, which had developed satisfactorily in recent years, and pointed out that a narrowing of the financial markets had to be considered.

In succession with this lecture, K. Kimmich reported general conditions of Deutsche Bank's business. He indicated that business conditions in the former half of the year were satisfactory and better results could be expected in the latter half. He explained numerical figures on the balance sheet relative to those in the previous report and the privatization of Vereingte Stahlweke AG. Issues of stock prices and state debts were considered, and problems related to the consolidation of public bonds were reported. He also reported on the labor market and explained that such a market was becoming active through public funds and that unemployment of special workers decreased significantly. Regarding the problem of providing raw materials, movements to expand armaments on a worldwide scale brought a considerable increase in metal prices, and Deutsche Bank had already provided funds for five sets of oil production equipment. He also referred to the Second Four-Year Plan and pointed out that, as observed when the price of synthetic rubber was six times that of natural rubber, execution of this plan was possible only through significant sacrifice.

Emil Engels lectured on the textile industry and pointed out that this industry was not in a very desirable condition, that raw material problems were the main cause of the anxiety, and the ability to pay declined. Furthermore, Christian Oertel reported on the position of joint stock companies in the insurance sector in the Nazi state. He indicated that the competition among joint stock companies in this sector and between private mutual insurance companies and public insurance was an important problem.

After these lectures, discussions among attendees ensued. Karl Kimmich informed on the intention of Gottlieb von Langen as chairman of the regional advisory council to retire his post and thanked him for his long years of contributions to this organization. The meeting concluded after these exchanges (HADB, P00041, Sitzung des Rheinisch-Westfälischen Beirates, Sitz Köln im Gebäude der Deutschen Bank und Disconto-Gesellschaft Filiale Köln am Mittwoch, dem 11. November 1936).

Meeting on April 20, 1937: Next, the contents of the meeting on April 20, 1937, were considered. This meeting started at 10:30 a.m., ten minutes earlier than previous meetings. The chairman of the regional advisory council opened the meeting with a greeting and pointed out that this meeting was taking place during an important phase of Deutsche Bank's privatization. After such an explanation, lectures were given.

As the first lecturer, J. B. Rath pointed out some important issues. Adjustment and integration in the Cologne region progressed to an extent. International price increases and the development of important export industries in this region could be expected under a stringent and serious lack of commodities in the world market. Further, strong public activities and initiating large-scale construction by the army would become possible through interim financing from the bank. J. B. Rath also stated that the investment business in fixed-interest securities played a primary role, and such a business in this district had achieved favorable results throughout Deutsche Bank.

Next, Karl Kimmich pointed out that Deutsche Bank increased its dividend from 4 to 5%. He also explained the balance sheet and emphasized an increase in reserve funds to RM 28 million through the creation of RM 2.8 million in reserve funds.

This amount equaled 25% of the capital stock and was much larger than that of neighboring banks. Kimmich stressed that the securities, foreign exchange, money exchange, and interest coupon businesses created profits that were not accumulated within the bank but were used to strengthening internal bank operations as well as profits from capital participation, the consortium, and special businesses. Doing so was indispensable for ensuring that this bank's stock was a first-class investment security with as high a price as before World War I. Kimmich briefly referred to the problem of the complete privatization of Deutsche Bank and reported on the bank's business conditions. That the stock market was not as important as it used to be and did not reflect economic conditions as it did during previous periods was pointed out. He also explained that, regarding the Second Four-Year Plan, the results to be achieved in this plan depended on the extent to which short-term debt could be consolidated and demand deposits would be created, and Deutsche Bank actively provided credits for investments in the framework of this plan. In addition, Kimmich reported on the production of Buna rubber as synthetic rubber, difficult conditions in the market for iron and metal, and situations regarding the provision of ora.

Erich Tgahrt provided a detailed report and explanation of the conditions in the iron and steel industry using numerical production figures for each country. He clarified that a significant difference resulted from newly beginning the production of iron and steel in several nations, and the extraordinary increase in production in other countries was clarified. Subsequent to this lecture, Arnold Langen reported on automobile production.

In discussions after these lectures, Emil Engels described the textile industry and G. Solmassen described the oil industry. After the afore-mentioned lectures and discussions, the meeting came to an end (HADB, P00041, Sitzung des Rheinisch-Westfälischen Beirats, Sitz Köln im Gebäude der Deutschen Bank und Disconto-Gesellschaft Filiale Köln am Dienstag, den 20. April 1937).

Meeting on October 28, 1937: The meeting on October 28, 1937, began at 10:40 a.m. In his greeting, the chairman of the advisory council remarked on the difficulty of correctly evaluating and understanding whether rapid progress of the bank business at that time was continuous or temporary. He asked that some problems be clarified in the discussion after the lectures. Lectures were then given.

First, J. R. Rath informed about the general survey on trends in the Rheinland economic region. He did not take up individual sectors and economic fields but paid attention to sectors in which increases in employment appeared as well as the entire economic field. Rath pointed out that exports were lately hindered by a decline in the international commodity market and that investments within the country were also obstructed in recent years by the tax system. He also noted that such changes were especially decisive in the western region where recovery of the superiority of the domestic economy was an important issue. On the one hand, that unemployment in the Cologne region strongly decreased was informed. Regarding the business of Deutsche Bank, he explained issues, such as debtors, stock of bills, creditors, sales volume of fellow trader deposits, number of employees, profits, and the stock trading business. He stressed that, above all, the stock trading business progressed rapidly in 1937 and continuous improvements in stock prices appeared.

In a succession of lectures by Rath, Karl Kimmich lectured on the overall conditions at Deutsche Bank. The business situation was favorable in the former half of 1937 and profits equivalent to the previous year were achieved, which was mainly the result of the influence from the security issuing and the security trading businesses. Whereas the sales amounts of duties for individuals and businesses for bankers increased to approximately 7.5 billion Reichsmark (RM) and the number of accounts also increased to more than 800,000, the burden of the foreign exchange and the foreign exchange settlement businesses was significant. In addition, he reported on the balance sheet and indicated that it increased further relative to the previous year and amounts of the bills increased from 835 million Reichsmark (RM) to more than 1 billion Reichsmark (RM). State debts amounted to RM 41 billion and in no other country was the ratio of short-term debt to total debt the same as that for Germany. Furthermore, he referred to foreign trade and explained that, whereas finished goods imports slightly decreased, food and raw materials imports increased significantly and exports increased favorably. He stressed that, although the trade surplus was sufficient to expense imports of necessary raw materials and foods until then, forecasting future situations was difficult. He also reported that the demand of iron was inflexible and the state's growing demand had to be absolutely satisfied, which created a situation in which demand except for that of the state was forced to be limited to 30% of the normal level. For instance, 40% of steel production was consumed for armaments and the Second Four Year Plan, and this ratio was only 20% in the UK. That difficulties in securing of raw materials became a factor in determining the ineffective piling up of semi-finished goods in the enterprise was pointed out.

Next, Franz Waechter reported on conditions in the Saar region. In addition, Waldemar Croon referred to the situation in the textile industry and pointed out that, although three million individuals worked in this industry, the problem of provisioning raw materials became serious and no other industry had a ratio of self-sufficiency as high as that for this industry.

In discussions that followed these lectures, F. Proenen supplemented lectures on the textile industry by Croon and pointed out improvements in the finishing of cloth that enabled longer stock as an explanation for the relatively good operating conditions and supplies in the market. In addition, G. Gasper referred to issues of economic association. E. Engels and W. Croon also provided short explanations. Furthermore, K. Kimmich pointed out that the rayon staple that won high praise at the time was refused by industries, and this phenomenon was the fault. Finally, Bürgers as chairman of the regional advisory council ended the meeting and thanked the lecturers, thus ending the meeting (HADB, P00041, Sitzung des Rheinisch-Westfälischen Beirats, Sitz Köln im Gebäude der DEUTSCHEN BANK FILIALEN KÖLN am Donnerstag, dem 28. Oktober 1937).

Meeting on March 31, 1938: The meeting on March 31, 1938, started at 10:40 a.m. After the chairman of the advisory council said a few words at the opening of the meeting, including a greeting and introducing new members to this regional advisory council and guests, some lectures were ensured.

J. R. Rath explained the business situation of the Cologne branch of Deutsche Bank and this region and pointed out that the district's economic condition was generally favorable. Although certain sectors were not yet fully operational, special reasons existed, and the influence of the price stop regulation was one of them. Although prices in the international market tended to decline and the exporting became increasingly difficult, the wholesale situation improved and the situation in the Cologne region was satisfactory. Rath reported that the increase in profits in this region was the result of large-scale bill businesses, such as the Mefo bill, and increases in the commission of ordinary duties. Sales increased by approximately 18%, and commission income also increased depending on the sales increase. The number of accounts was 33,850 and deposit accounts increased considerably. Regarding the securities business, Rath explained that the securities market changed only slightly for several months and further development depended significantly on the funds market.

Next, Karl Kimmich lectured on conditions in the banking industry and the economy in general. He emphasized that the profits of special businesses, the securities business, foreign exchange trading, and the interest coupon business did not contribute to retaining profits but could be used beforehand to reinforce Deutsche Bank's internal operations. After such a report on the bank's business, production problems related to Buna rubber were also discussed, and the prospect of production delays because of a new manufacturing method was indicated. Kimmich explained that the necessity to organize the business to enable it to continue without public order was an important management issue. A report on exports was also provided that indicated that 80% of exports were finished goods. Although this figure was favorable, some problems existed. Kimmich pointed out four difficult situations: (1) too high prices in Germany; (2) long delivery term, (3) too significant difficulties resulting from the control of competent authorities, and (4) insufficient provision of long-term credit relative to other countries.

In addition, Herman J. Abs lectured on a situation in Austria. He indicated that the main export items of this country were iron products, wood, and paper. Abs also pointed out a significant difference in wages, extraordinarily low house rents, and the evils of the monopoly of tobacco as a problem to be solved.

Furthermore, L. von Boch-Galhau lectured on the ceramics industry. He pointed out difficulties in transformations to home products, expectations of glass orders, the high weight of exports to European regions—for all exports that indicated 70%, an increase by 20% of exports from 1936 to 1937—and different conditions in the new year from the conditions of this time.

Next, through the framework of the Second Four-Year Plan, Brecht lectured on the important problem with which the brown coal industry in the Rheinland–Westfalen region was faced. He pointed out that, although the increase in consumption was larger than that of production—in particular, diesel oil consumption by the army increased significantly—diesel oil production cost almost the same as gasoline and, thus, was nearly unprofitable. Brecht also informed both factories that the fuel for and production of Buna rubber were for large-scale consumers of electric power, consumption in Germany was significant, and the decision to rationalize consumption in a short period was to be made.

After these lectures, H. J. Abs reported again on Austria's debt. Discussions among attendances ensued. The meeting started at 10:40 a.m. and finished at 1:20 p.m., two hours and fifty minutes later (HADB, P00041, Sitzung des Rheinisch-Westfälischen Beirats, Sitz Köln im Gebäude der DEUTSCHEN BANK FILIALEN KÖLN am Donnerstag, dem 31. März 1938).

Meeting on November 2, 1938: The contents of the meeting on November 2, 1938, were also examined. This meeting began at 10:45 a.m. The chairman of the advisory council greeted attendees at the opening of this meeting and made statements on some points, such introducing new members of this organization and mourning members who died after the previous meeting. Subsequently, certain individuals lectured on various topics.

As the first lecturer, J. R. Rath reported on the economic conditions in the Rheinland region and pointed out the prospect that, as long as the state was at the head in the domestic market, the economy would be in full operation. However, the transportation system was insufficient, and the Reichs Bahn as the national railroad organization had reduced its program for several years. Rath also reported on Deutsche Bank's business situation and indicated that stock trading was temporarily yet almost completely hindered and the public and corporate bonds business was also in a difficult situation. The result of accepting state borrowing was exactly favorable, and RM 75 million was absorbed by an intermediate of this bank in 1938.

The next lecturer was Karl Kimmich, who reported on general economic conditions and Deutsche Bank's business situation. The bank's profits were satisfactory, and bills decreased from RM 1007.2 million in August 1938 to RM 898 million in September 1938—less than RM 1 billion for the first time. The ratio of commodity bills to all bills was 50% and indicated a favorable figure. Kimmich also pointed out that credit demands were very different among individual industries. Also was indicated that stock trading decreased and the stock price decline extended to the bond market. Kimmich referred to national finances and deficits of several billion RM in 1938. He indicated the prospect that 50% of the national income would be absorbed by state finances and the burden of the national debt's interest, totaling more than RM 51 billion, would become RM 2.2 billion at 4.5% interest per year. Kimmich also reported on conditions in individual industries and pointed out that, whereas the electric industry progressed rapidly, the cost of gasoline production in Germany was very high—at 3.5 to 3.6 times that of foreign commodities—given expensive equipment, and talking about profitability under such a situation was not possible. Kimmich finally referred to improvements in economic conditions through expansions of relations in wide areas from the North Sea to Africa.

Hermann J. Abs explained the significance and results of the annexation of counties in the Sdeden district. He pointed out the problem of a custom union creating difficulties, one of them being whether or not such a union was possible without a currency unit—a custom union was not considered without a currency unit. Furthermore, Abs explained the situation in the textile and the brown coal industries.

In a succession of these lectures, Friedrich Siemssen made an interesting explanation of the limestone industry. Sales in this industry in Germany were RM 1400 million for a year, and the number of factories increased from 890 in Germany before the amalgamation of Austria and the Sdeden region to approximately 1000 given such an annexation. Siemssen also pointed out that the main consumers of limestone were the chemical and iron and steel industries.

Furthermore, Richard Meyer reported on the electric power industry. Karl Kimmich cleared his own standpoint for Meyer's explanation and referred to his lecture again to supplement it. Kimmich stressed the productive activities that Deutsche Bank had developed.

In the discussions that followed these lectures, L. von Boch-Galhau briefly explained the ceramic industry. In addition, W. Croon also referred to the rayon staple, which indicated a qualitative and desirable development. After such lectures and discussions, the meeting that started at 10:45 a.m. ended at 2:00 p.m., lasting three hours and fifteen minutes (HADB, P00041, Sitzung des Rheinisch-Westfälischen Beirats, Sitz Köln im Gebäude der DEUTSCHEN BANK FILIALEN KÖLN am Mittwoch, den 2. November 1938).

Meeting on April 30, 1940: The meeting on April 30, 1940, started at 10:40 a.m. The chairman of the advisory council greeted everyone and explained some points. He lamented over the members who died after the previous meeting and introduced new members. After such a greeting and explanation, lectures ensued.

E. Hoppe reported briefly on the economic regions of Aachen, Siegen, and Saarbrücken. He indicated the prospect that sales would increase by approximately 7% relative to the previous year. Moreover, although loans at the Cologne branch of Deutsche Bank decreased by approximately 15% relative to the prior year, loans at the Siegen and Aachen branches increased, and changes in four afore-mentioned regions as a whole would not happen.

Next, Karl Kimmich lectured on the business condition of Deutsche Bank and the general economic situation. He pointed out that the balance sheet amount increased from RM 3.7 billion at the end of 1938 to approximately RM 4.2 billion at the end of 1939 and to approximately RM 4.6 billion at the time of the meeting. Therefore, an increase of 25% was recorded. The commission and interest that this bank earned were larger by approximately RM 15 million than in the former year. The commission and interest that this bank could earn in 1939 was larger by more than approximately RM 15 million relative to the former year. The bank's consortium business was very active, and Deutsche Bank was positively in the first place regarding the execution of and involvement in this business. Kimmich also pointed out that, although larger credit increased because of the war, smaller credit decreased. Kimmich stressed that one of the most important side effects of wartime finance in this period was the lack of a fair tax system and that dividend payments were influenced by a further reduction in corporate income taxes. Moreover, relations between Europe and the USA fundamentally changed after 1914. Such a change in international relations was observed when the USA as a debtor country became the largest creditor nation in the world after World War I.

In addition, W. Croon reported that, although the textile industry as a typical consumer goods industry was not at the center of public interest before the beginning of the war, the war created new conditions. Croon also indicated that the scale of the business operation depended on the raw materials that this industry could use and the degree of urgency that was graded among the military economy, exports, and private demand. The system of purchasing and supplying clothing tickets provided a guarantee of fairness and saved the distribution of all textile products for private demand. That Germany was third in the world as an export nation of cloth and semi-finished products and its large-scale textile industry was the largest production unit of economic organization in this country was emphasized.

After these lectures, discussions ensued among the attendees. The meeting that began at 10:40 a.m. finished at 1:00 p.m., after two hours and twenty minutes (HADB, P00041, Sitzung des Rheinisch-Westfälischen Beirats, Sitz Köln im Gebäude der DEUTSCHEN BANK FILIALEN KÖLN am Dienstag, dem 30. April 1940).

Meeting on May 7, 1941: The meeting on May 7, 1941, started at 3:40 p.m. After the chairman of the advisory council said a few words at the opening of the meeting, including a greeting, introducing new members of this regional advisory council, and mourning for members who died after the former meeting, some lectures were performed.

J. R. Rath reported on the conditions of the economic region and the business of the branch in Cologne. He indicated that, although liquidity of funds in the economy increased in 1940, the number of bondholders increased by more than 53% relative to that of 1939 and bank deposits increased by approximately 45%, finding opportunities to invest funds within the Cologne region was not possible. The favorable results of the duties were essentially from the profits of the securities and issuing businesses, and the issuing business was very active. The ratio of that of the Cologne branch was very high, and bond trading was in good condition. This branch was in the head position, as was the Manheim and Berlin branches of Deutsche Bank. However, the exchange business experienced a considerable quantitative decrease, and the scale of the commercial bill was in a condition observed before World War I. Rath also explained that the business in the Saar district was interesting and worth referring to, and the state provided a credit guarantee of RM 100 million to support the recovery from the difficulties brought about by the evacuation of more than half the population in this region and the closing or contemporary removal of significantly more than half the companies.

Next, Hermann J. Abs lectured and pointed out the treasury bill of the nation and the states, and that treasury bonds without interest increased from RM 1148 million to RM 2079 million, equivalent to an increase in other credits from RM 2896 million to RM 3830 million. Securities that Deutsch Bank owned increased by more than two times, its treasury bond increased from RM 163 million to RM 573 million, and the total increase in short-term treasury bills, treasury bonds, and securities was approximately RM 1350 million. Capital participation increased from RM 50 million to RM 70 million. Regarding income by item, interest increased by approximately RM 7 million and commissions decreased by RM 7 million. Deutsche Bank was extensively involved in the issuing business, and approximately two-thirds of the securities issuing business was performed as a principle or common underwriter. He also referred to the Dividend Freeze Law and pointed out that the prohibition on issuing had hindered capital adjustments in previous years.

H. Jackowski lectured on the problems of NAZI's Big Space Economy. Karl Haus reported on the foreign business of German insurance companies. He explained that a very important foreign business existed before the outbreak of World War II and most insurance enterprises had their own foreign agencies. The prospect was indicated that even though this business was not as large as that in the UK, it could play an important role. He pointed out that, although the business was in a very difficult condition from the unfortunate results of the World War, a good outlook appeared through the new, large German framework.

Finally, the chairman of the regional advisory council asked the attendees to treat explanations at this meeting as top secret. The meeting that began at 3:40 p.m., late relative to the previous meeting, ended at 5:50 p.m., two hours and ten minutes later (HADB, P00041, Sitzung des Rheinisch-Westfälischen Beirats, Sitz Köln im Gebäude der DEUTSCHEN BANK FILIALEN KÖLN am Mittwoch, dem 7. Mai 1941).

Meeting on April 15, 1942: The contents of the meeting on April 15, 1942, were finally considered. This meeting began at 12:05 p.m. The chairman of the advisory council greeted attendees at the opening of this meeting and said a few words on some points, including the introduction of new members and mourning a member who died after the previous meeting. Then, other individuals lectured.

J. B. Rath, as the first lecturer, reported on the business of the Cologne branch of Deutsche Bank and pointed out that the most noteworthy characteristic was the continuing strong increase in the credit side of the balance sheet at the end of 1941, the result of a significant increase in the deposit account of approximately 2.4 times that of 1938. In addition, Rath indicated that sales of the business to customers except for the bank increased and that the number of accounts rose. Additionally, Rath informed that profits were again in a favorable condition this year and resulted from a satisfactory issuing business. In particular, bond markets became the focus, and sales could be expected to achieve their highest level.

After this lecture, Hermann J. Abs reported on the balance sheets of financial institutions, including savings banks. He pointed out that Deutsche Bank's balance sheet indicated RM 6573 million, Dresdner Bank indicated RM 4900 million, Commerzbank indicated RM 2900 million, and the increasing rates of these three large banks were 23.7%, 19%, and 28%, respectively. Most of the bill amount was composed of the endorsed bill and the Meho bill, and RM 845 million was the Deutsche Bank amount. Other Reichsmark bills were only RM 193 million. Abs also referred to rationalization problems, such as concentration and integration of businesses and factories.

Eugen Gottlieb von Langen lectured on the sugar industry in Germany. Although discussions among attendees ensued after these lectures, attendees did not expressly state their opinions. The chairman of the regional advisory council thanked the lecturers, and the meeting ended. After the meeting, a dinner party was held, and short speeches were given (HADB, P00041, Sitzung des Rheinisch-Westfälischen Beirats, Sitz Köln im Gebäude der Deutschen Bank Filialen Köln am Mittwoch, dem 15. April 1942).

In meetings of regional advisory council, in many cases, dinner was provided after the regional advisory council meeting [HADB, P00042, Die Schrift über die Einladung für Herrn Bankdirektor Dr. Karl Kimmich zur Sitzung des Rheinisch-Westfälischer Ausschuβes, Essen der Deutschen Bank und Disconto-Gesellschaft (11.4.1930); HADB, P00037, Die Schrift über die Einladung für Herrn Dr. Karl Kimmich zur Sitzung des Rheinisch-Westfälischer Ausschuβes, Essen der Deutschen Bank (13.10.1938); HADB, P00037, Die Schrift über die Einladung für Herrn Dr. Karl Kimmich zur Sitzung des Rheinisch-Westfälischer Ausschuβes, Essen-Düsseldorf der Deutschen Bank (14.3.1939); HADB, P00037, Die Schrift über die Einladung für Herrn Dr. Karl Kimmich zur Sitzung des Rheinisch-Westfälischer Ausschuβes, Essen-Düsseldorf der Deutschen Bank (10.4.1940); HADB, P00037, Die Schrift über die Einladung für Herrn Dr. Karl Kimmich zur Sitzung des Rheinisch-Westfälischer Ausschuβes, Essen-Düsseldorf der Deutschen Bank (17.11.1941); HADB, P00038, Die Schrift über die Einladung für Herrn Dr. Eduard Mosler zur Sitzung des Schlesischen Bezirksbeirats der Deutschen Bank und Disconto-Gesellschaft (2.12.1935); HADB, P00038, Die Schrift über die Einladung für Herr Dr. Mosler zur Sitzung des Königsberger Beirats der Deutschen Bank und Disconto-Gesellschaft (6.4.1936)]. For instance, the Frankfurt–Hessen regional advisory council usually provided a meal at 1:30 p.m., after the end of a meeting [HADB, P00036, Der Brief von der Deutschen Bank Filiale Frankfurt (Main) an Herr Hermann J. Abs (8.4.1938)] Such meals indicated the significance of the regional advisory council in developing and maintaining close relationships with enterprises that had deep cooperative relations with Deutsche Bank.

14.3 Personnel Issues of Regional Advisory Councils

Sections 14.1 and 14.2 analyzed the conditions for holding meetings of regional advisory councils and the participants in and contents of such meetings. This section examines the personnel affairs of regional advisory councils that had significant meaning for exhibiting the functions of such an organization.

Although many cases existed in which the election of members of the regional advisory council was decided by the approval of the supervisory board [HADB, P00035, Der Brief an Herr Kessler (23.4.1941); HADB, P00035, Der Brief von Richard Gdynia an Herr Johannes Kiel (27.5.1941); HADB, P00035, Der Brief an Herr Doktor Hans Malzacher (17.4.1942), S. 2; HADB, P00034, Der Brief von der Deutschen Bank an Herr Baron (19.3.1941)], such an issue was considered and decided from various perspectives. Business relations between branches of banks and industrial enterprises as their customers, replacement of a successor by someone from same company that reflected such in-firm relations, the experience and specialty of a candidate, the conditions for installation as a member of a similar organization and other organizations, the business situation of an enterprise, and the intention of a candidate and the company to which he belongs were important points.

For a business relationship with the concerned region's branch, a general phenomenon is the case in which members of an enterprise with such deep relations were elected to the regional advisory council. For instance, a letter dated February 13, 1938, from Deutsche Bank to W. Borner as a member of the managing board of the chemical company Schering and an internal document of this company dated July 8, 1938, pointed out that the importance of the long-term friendly relationships between this enterprise and Deutsche Bank was the main reason a person from this industrial enterprise was invited to be a member of the Berlin–Brandenburg regional advisory council [HADB, P00034, Der Brief an Herrn Dr. Wilhelm Borner (13.7.1938), Schering AG (8.7.1938)]. A document on March 18, 1941, concerning the election of E. Feldl from J. D. Riedel–de Haen as a member of the Berlin–Brandenburg regional advisory council also indicated that the reasons for electing this member were the existence of long-term and close relationships of mutual trust between Deutsche Bank and this industrial company, the possibility of reinforcing such relationships through participation by individuals concerned with this regional advisory council, and the use of his advice and experience [HADB, P00034, Der Brief an Herrn Eugen Feldl (18.3.1941)]. Similar phenomena are also observed in many other cases. The election of Baron as a member of the Berlin–Brandenburg regional advisory council of Deutsche Bank was one such case [HADB, P00034, Der Brief von der Deutschen Bank an Herr Baron (19.3.1941), Carl Freherr von Schröder an Herr Baron (19.3.1941)].

However, other cases existed. For example, although business relations existed, banks refrained from electing someone from a company as a member of the regional advisory council because the competitive relation with other enterprises in the same industry as that of the concerned company took precedence. A typical case is that of AEG, one of the largest companies in the electrical industry. According to a document to E. G. von Stauss dated April 19, 1938, Deutsche Bank did not dispatch its representative to AEG because the bank recognized the value of deepening and reinforcing relationships with Siemens to as great a degree as possible. Under such a condition, Deutsche Bank had not invited an individual from AEG to the Berlin regional advisory council, and the election of a member of this enterprise could not be considered [HADB, P00034, Der Brief an Herrn Dr. von Stauss (19.4.1938)]. In addition, effort was made to avoid electing someone from a company of which business conditions were not healthy. For instance, a letter dated April 20, 1942, from Walter Pohle of Bömische Union -Bank to Johannes Kiehl as a member of the managing board of Deutsche Bank pointed out that Kiehl did not welcome the election of Müller to the Oberschlesien regional advisory council because the business prospects of his company could not be determined [HADB, P00035, Der Brief von Walter Pohle an Herrn Johannes Kiehl (20.4.1942)].

Additionally, in many cases, a branch of Deutsche Bank proposed and recommended a candidate from its perspective of the election to maintain and develop business relationships between branches and important enterprises of this bank. For example, a letter from Heinrich Klöckers of the Mannheim branch of Deutsche Bank to K. E. Sippell dated March 11, 1939, indicated that Klöckers proposed Kurt Barlet, a member of the Baden–Pfalz mortgage bank, as a member of the Baden–Pfalz regional advisory council to emphasize the relations between this bank and him and his demands [HADB, P00034, Badisch-Pfälzischer Beirat (11.3.1939)]. In addition, documents from the Manheim branch dated August 2, 1938, and February 17, 1938, clarified that the election of Ohlodwig Kammerscheid of Deutsche Steinzeugwarenfabrik für Kanalisation und Chemische Industrie was suggested by the Manheim branch of Deutsche Bank because it was considered a desirable development for the Baden–Pfalz regional advisory council to elect Kammersched from the perspective of reputation of duty, candidate personality, and his importance in economic life. This branch requested the approval of this personnel affair [HADB, P00034, Badisch-Pfälzischer Beirat. (2.8.1938); HADB, P00034, Badisch-Pfälzischer Beirat (17.12.1938)].

Similar phenomena can be observed for the Munich branch. In a Munich branch document on the Bayern regional advisory council dated January 13, 1941, several individuals were proposed and recommended by this branch as candidates for the council [HADB, P00034, Bayerischer Beirat. (13.1.1941)]. In addition, in a document dated February 12, 1941, to Hans Rummel, a member of the managing board of Deutsche Bank, the election of some individuals was suggested by the Nürnberg branch because of the depth of the business relations with the concerned companies. For example, Hans Wellhausen of MAN in the machine industry was recommended given the special relation with Rummel, a closer relation with Deutsche Bank than any other bank, and in particular his strengthening of this bank's position against the efforts of Commerzbank toward MAN. Karl Diehl of Metall-, Guss-und Presswerke Heinrich Diehl GmbH was proposed as a candidate for this advisory council because of the significant possibilities for fundamental expansion and the establishment of valuable business relationships with this company through participation on the council. Dresdner Bank had main business relationships with this industrial enterprise until that point. Indeed, Deutsche Bank could succeed in securing small business accounts and maintaining Diehl's large account. However, such results were insufficient for establishing a relationship with this company, and Dhiel's recommendation was considered an important countermeasure. Raabe of Eisenwerke-Gesellschaft Maximilianshütte was recommended given the significant importance of this enterprise for the Nürnberg branch of Deutsche Bank and the criticality of developing personnel relationships with leading individuals at this company [HADB, P00034, Der Brief von Deutschen Bank Filiale Nürnberg an Herr Hans Rummel (12.2.1941); HADB, P00034, Der Brief an die Direktion der Deutschen Bank Filiale Nürnberg (13.2.1941)]. A similar proposal by the Nürnberg branch is also observed in other cases. For instance, a letter from Adolf von Grafenstein to Hans Rummel dated March 8, 1941, noted that, if Terberger was elected as managing director of Eisenwerke-Gesellschaft Maximilianshütte and a successor of Raabe, this branch wanted to recommend Terberger as a candidate for the Bayern regional advisory council because of the deposit results for safekeeping securities and the very favorable personnel relationships with Deutsche Bank [HADB, P00034, Der Brief von Adolf von Grafenstein an Herrn Direktor Hans Rummel (8.3.1941), S. 2].

The same proposal was made by other branches of Deutsche Bank. For example, in a document of the Braunschweig branch dated September 10, 1935, expansion of the Braunschweig regional advisory council was taken over in a recent meeting of this organization. As a result, three individuals were proposed as candidates for election and approval by Osward Rösler, a member of the managing board of Deutsche Bank was required [HADB, P00034, Beirat (10.9.1935)]. A similar proposal was made by the Cassel branch. A document of this branch dated April 14, 1933, pointed out that the proposal for the election of two new members of the Frankfurt–Hessen regional advisory council was performed by examining the expansion of this advisory council [HADB, P00034, Der Brief von der Deutschen Bank und Disconto-Gesellschaft Filiale Kassel an Herr Kaiser (14.4.1933)]. In addition, a document of the Frankfurt branch dated April 18, 1936, indicated that five candidates were suggested for election to the Frankfurt–Hessen regional advisory council [HADB, P00034, Hessischer Beirat. (18.4.1936)]. Furthermore, a similar proposal can also be observed by the Siegen branch. A letter from Rudolf Plaas of this branch to Gustav Schlieper dated September 19, 1935, indicated that the election of von Bodenhausen-Degener as a member of this region's advisory council be investigated because of his relationships with groups of politicians, the importance of establishing such relations for Deutsche Bank, the friendly relationships of this bank with his father, and his importance as an influential customer [HADB, P00034, Der Brief von Rudolf Plaas an Herrn Gustav Schlieper (19.9.1935)].

In the case that a branch in the district of each regional advisory council proposed the election of a member of such an organization, the candidate was decided for the bank through discussions with members of the managing board and the supervisory board of Deutsche Bank and between the two boards. As noted in an internal Deutsche Bank document dated September 21, 1936, regarding the Frankfurt–Hessen regional advisory council, such a case is observed in the discussion between K. E. Sippell as a member of the managing board of this bank and F. Werner as a director of the Frankfurt branch on the expansion of this advisory council and the election of members to this organization. This discussion pointed out that a candidate to be elected as a member of the Cologne regional advisory council or the Frankfurt–Hessen regional advisory council was to be determined through counsel with Karl Kimmich as a member of the managing board of Deutsche Bank [HADB, P00034, Frankfurt-Hessischer Beirat. (21.9.1936)].

Members of the supervisory board and the managing board of Deutsche Bank also recommended individuals who could be considered as candidates of regional advisory councils; these boards also negotiated with individuals with whom this bank had close relationships. Such a case can be observed in the recommendation of Paul Beyer, a member of the managing board of Süddeutsche Zucker-AG, as a member of the South regional advisory council [HADB, P00034, Der Brief von K. E. Sippell an Herr Dr. Beyer (17.2.1940); HADB, P00034, Süddeutsche Zucker A.G.

(Auszug aus dem Aktenvermerk des Herr Dr. Sippell vom 27. März 1940); HADB, P00034, Badisch-Pfälzischer Beirat (15.1.1940)]. Hans Rummel, as a member of the managing board of Deutsche Bank, was strongly involved in the proposal for Harald Hamberg, member of the managing board of Vereinigte Kugellagerfabrik AG, as a member of the Bayern regional advisory council to the supervisory board of this bank in 1936 [HADB, P00034, Der Brief von Rummel an Herrn Generaldirektorn Herald Hamberg (6.3.1936); HADB, P00034, Der Brief von Harald Hamberg an Herrn Bankdirektor Rummel (1.3.1936)].

In addition, in other cases, the election of proposed individuals and those recommended by a branch of Deutsche Bank did not proceed smoothly and were given up because of personnel affairs. For instance, a document from Karl Butsch of the Freiburg branch to K. E. Sippell concerning the Baden–Pfalz regional advisory council dated March 10, 1942, pointed out that this branch had to withdraw its demand to invite a prominent person as a member of the advisory council in the Oberschlesen region because of the difficulty in adjusting the demands of this branch to actual conditions, including new general policies. In such a situation, Karl Butsch welcomed the same exceptional treatment regarding personnel issues of his regional advisory council members, as in the Elsas region that has a newly founded regional advisory council [HADB, P00034, Badisch-Pfälzischer Beirat. (10.3.1942)].

An examination from the perspective of replacing a member of a regional advisory council by a person from the same company as that of the predecessor to maintain and reinforce business relationships with a bank's branch in the concerned district indicated that, generally, many cases existed that considered this point [HADB, P00034, Badisch-Pfälzischer Beirat. (20.2.1937)]. Both cases exist in which the bank had such a demand and the industrial enterprise also had such a desire. For example, concerning supplement personnel affairs of the Berlin–Brandenburg regional advisory council, in 1938, Deutsche Bank selected five individuals as candidates for this regional advisory council and discussed who was to be elected as a member of this committee organization considering the importance of traditional relationships with this enterprise [HADB, P00034, Schering AG (8.7.1938)].

However, cases were also observed in which personnel issues related to replacement by individuals from the same company were not agreed to. Above all, when regional advisory councils were reorganized, such a situation tended to be created. For instance, an internal document concerning the Baden–Pfalz regional advisory council on January 19, 1937, indicated that, regarding the personnel affair of the successor of Franz Bueschler as a member of the managing board of Pfälzische Mühlwerke, the necessity of considering and examining whether the election of a managing board member of the same company who was in active service was purposive under a planned reorganization of this regional advisory council was pointed out [HADB, P00034, Badisch-Pfälzischer Beirat. (19.1.1937)].

Furthermore, when observing from the perspective of an emphasis on the experience and specialty of a candidate of a regional advisory council, such characteristics were very important elements in the election of the candidate. For example, a letter from Deutsche Bank to Adolf Samwer on March 17, 1937, indicated that this bank most recognized the value of his experience and knowledge of the insurance system when inviting him to be a member of the Baden–Pfalz regional committee [HADB, P00034, Der Brief an Herrn Genelaldirektor Adolf Samwer (17.3.1937), S. 1].

However, cases existed in which such an election proposal emphasizing the experience and specialty of the candidate was returned to the branch of Deutsche Bank that suggested it. A document from the Frankfurt branch to K. E. Sippell dated August 19, 1937, pointed out that, although this branch proposed Bauer, who was a member of Spinnerei-und Weberei Offenburg and a large shareholder of this company as a member of the Baden–Pfalz regional advisory council in the previous year, this suggestion was returned to the branch. This branch proposed again and explained that the concerned individual was a most important and active manager of a company in the textile industry of the Baden–Pfalz region, that relations with this enterprise were very old, and this branch sometimes provided significant funds for this industrial enterprise. A decision on the election was expected at the next meeting of the supervisory board [HADB, P00034, Badisch-Pfälzischer Beirat. (19.8.1937)]. This personnel issue was taken over at a meeting of the supervisory board and approved [HADB, P00034, Badisch-Pfälzischer Beirat. (24.8.1937)]. On the one hand, regarding an important issue such as the election of a member of a regional advisory council, cases existed in which discussions, exchanges of opinions with the chairman of the concerned regional advisory council, and his approval were important. For instance, a document of the Munich branch dated March 5, 1942, indicated such an exchange between a branch and the chairman of the regional advisory council [HADB, P00034, Deustche Bank Filiale München (5.3.1942)].

In addition to the afore-mentioned perspectives, the conditions for installing a member of a similar or other organization of another bank was also an important perspective in the election of a member of the regional advisory council. For example, a document from T. Riesterer of the Stuttgart branch dated March 28, 1938, indicated that, concerning Cramer of Cramer and Breuer, developing a close personnel relationship between Deutsche Bank and Cramer was not possible because Dresdner Bank attempted several times to extend business relationships with this industrial company, and Cramer belonged to the Cologne regional advisory council of Dresdner Bank [HADB, P00034, Der Brief von Dr. T. Riesterer über die Beiräte (28.7.1938)]. An internal document of Deutsche Bank dated March 14, 1939, also pointed out that Kurt Barlet, considered by Deutsche Bank as a candidate for the Baden–Pfalz regional advisory council, was asked by Dresdner Bank whether he was prepared to participate in the advisory council last month and accepted such an invitation; therefore, the request of Deutsche Bank was too late [HADB, P00034, Badisch-Pfälzischer Beirat (14.3.1939)].

Similar situations can also be observed in other cases. For instance, in a Deutsche Bank memorandum dated September 8, 1938, although Deutsche Bank asked Kampfmeyerto to participate in the Berlin–Brandenburg regional advisory council, he was not able to accept this request because his installation as a member of the Berlin regional committee of Dresdner Bank had already been decided [HADB, P00034, Auszug aus einer Aktennotiz des Herrn Wintermantel von 8.9.38.]. A letter regarding the Baden–Pfalz regional advisory council from K. E. Sippell to Heinrich Klöckers of the Mannheim branch dated February 24, 1942, pointed out that a relation existed between Dresdner Bank and Seegmüller, and Deutsche Bank was unable to object to Dresdner Bank's behavior given the perspective of an agreement on competition [HADB, P00034, Badisch-Pfälzischer Beirat (24.2.1942)]. An internal document of Deutsche Bank dated February 22, 1939, also indicated similar situations regarding Metallgesellschaft AG in the metal industry. Although Deutsche Bank intended to invite someone on the Frankfurt–Hessen regional advisory council, such a demand was not realized given his installation as a member of the supervisory board of Dresdner Bank. Maintaining relations with this leading metal company through this person became impossible. Therefore, Deutsche Bank decided to elect another person from this company [HADB, P00034, Aktenvermerk (22.2.1939)]. A Deutsche Bank memorandum on January 30, 1941, also indicated the case of an individual who received an invitation to be a member of the regional advisory council from Dresdner Bank and Deutsche Bank [HADB, P00034, Akten-Notiz (30.1.1941)].

However, on the one hand, phenomena also existed in which competition regarding the election of a member to a regional advisory council arose among large banks because of the importance of strengthening business relationships. A document from Heinrich Klöckers as a director of the Manheim branch of Deutsche Bank pointed out that, although Dresdner Bank attempted to expand the scope of the regional advisory council, Deutsche Bank hindered this effort through an agreement [HADB, P00034, Badisch-Pfälzischer Beirat (19.2.1942)]. In addition, a letter from K. E. Sippell to Karl Butzsch of Freiburg branch noted that participation in the regional advisory council of Deutsch Bank was exclusive for this bank and that belonging to the supervisory board or advisory council of another bank was not accepted [HADB, P00034, Der Brief von K. E. Sippell an Herrn Direktor Dr. Karl Butsch (24.10.1941)]. This point was an element that influenced the personnel affairs of a member of the regional advisory council as an important foundation of developing relationships with many enterprises in various industries. An internal document regarding the Württemberg regional advisory council on June 22, 1939, pointed out that Deutsche Bank had intentionally invited members of the managing board of various cellulose enterprises into its regional advisory council. Although doing so created the problem of whether a member of Schwäbische Zellstoff AG was appropriate for the Württemberg regional advisory council, Deutsche Bank paid attention to Carl Schmid as chairman of the supervisory board of both this company and Süddeutsche Zellwolle AG [HADB, P00035, Württembergischer Beirat. (22.6.1939)].

In addition, opposition among banks in competitive relationships strongly influenced the personnel issues of members of the regional advisory council in cases in which multiple banks took note of the same company. A document from the Freiburg branch of Deutsche Bank dated October 21, 1940, pointed out that concerning the personnel affairs of inviting a member of the regional advisory council from Elsässische Machinen-Bau AG, some candidates were proposed, and not taking a very long time was appropriate because other banks also considered similar personnel issues [HADB, P00035, Elsass/Zukünftige Beiratsmitglieder. (21.10.1940)]. Coping with the movements of other banks can be observed in another case. A letter from Richard Gdynia to Johannes Kiehl indicated that, although Deutsche Bank examined the invitation and election of Ludwig as a member of the regional advisory council, Dresdner

Bank had already asked him whether he intended to accept requests to attend similar organizations of this bank [HADB, P00035, Der Brief von Richard Gdynia an Herr Johannes Kiel (22.4.1942)]. In a letter dated November 5, 1938, from Max Richter to Hermann Joseph Abs as a member of the managing board of Deutsche Bank, Richter asked to examine whether the invitation of a specific person to the regional advisory council was possible or not because the concerned person still had not accepted the Dresdner Bank request to participate in a regional committee [HADB, P00035, Der Brief von Max Richter an Herr Hermann J. Abs (5.11.1938)].

Other cases existed in which Deutsche Bank faced the problem of the movement of an individual from its own regional advisory council to a similar organization of another large bank. An internal document of Deutsche Bank dated March 6, 1942, indicated the consultation with Carl Goetz of Dresdner Bank regarding the issue of the movement of Sperl from the Cologne organization of the Rhein–Westfalen regional advisory council of Deutsche Bank to a regional committee of Dresdner Bank. This document also pointed out that, although Deutsche Bank did not want to give up the election of Sperl, this bank had to compromise because of his close relationship with Dresdner Bank [HADB, P00036, Aktenvermerk. (6.3.1942)].

Many cases existed concerning the election, dismissal, and replacement of a member of a regional advisory council, and decisions were made through exchanges and examinations from the afore-mentioned various perspectives. For instance, an internal document of Deutsche Bank dated February 23, 1938, regarding the personnel affair of a member of the Baden–Pfalz regional advisory council indicated that K. E. Sippell of Deutsche Bank took counsel with Jahr on the replacement of Buechler, who was not active with other individuals, the displacement of Weber with Schcht, the dismissal of Hecht, and the new election of Heuer, Eggerss, and Fürstenberg. As a result of such a consultation, Sippell indicated the prospect that Jahr would soon discuss these issues with individuals concerned with the Mannheim branch and would decide [HADB, P00034, Badisch-Pfälzischer Beirat. (23.2.1938)].

14.4 Significance of Regional Advisory Councils

Building on the foregoing discussions, this section clarifies the significance of the regional advisory council. Such organizations had the purpose of developing close and friendly relationships between a large bank and a company in each region and among industrial enterprises, and favorable relationships with representative individuals. They contributed significantly to establishing such interfirm relations [HADB, P00034, Badisch-Pfälzischer Beirat. (29.7.1938)]. For example, a letter from E. Eggerss as a member of the managing board of a spinning company to K. E. Sippell as a member of the managing board of Deutsche Bank dated June 12, 1940, pointed out that the friendly relationships and the many years of cooperation with Sippell and numerous individuals of this bank led to the invitation of Eggerss onto the Baden–Pfalz regional advisory council by the chairman of the supervisory board of this bank. This invitation indicated the significance of the advisory council in further reinforcing relationships between banks and industrial enterprises [HADB, P00034, Der Brief von E. Eggerss an Herrn Dr. Karl Ernst Sippell (12.6.1940)]. A letter from Sippell dated September 14, 1940, also pointed out that belonging to a regional advisory council promoted friendly relationships, close business connections, and personnel contacts, and Eggerss contributed to providing an exchange of information through an interesting lecture on the industry in the Austria district of which the contents were abundant [HADB, P00034, Der Brief von Dr. K. E. Sippell an Herrn Direktor Gerhard Eggerss (14.6.1940)].

In a Deutsche Bank document dated April 17, 1942, the purpose of the advisory councils established in each region was to create special relationships between bank management and important leading managers of enterprises in each economic sector for mutual interest. As observed in the Oberschlesien regional advisory council, famous representative individuals belonging to regional advisory councils of Deutsche Bank and issues in the region concerning general economic problems were discussed through mutual exchange of opinions at meetings that usually took place two times a year [HADB, P00035, Der Brief an Herr Dr. Hans Malzacher (17.4.1942), S. 1]. Valuable advice and sharing of information were possible through such personnel interchanges.

In addition, most individuals who had a mandate of a regional advisory council of Deutsche Bank were elected as members of such an organization given their positions in their home companies [HADB, P00034, Der Brief von J. Fabian an Herrn Direktor Dr. Weigert (29.3.1935), S. 1].

Although most individuals who were elected as members of a regional advisory council of a large bank had important posts in representative companies in each district, understanding that participation in such a Deutsche Bank organization was an honor was indicated by the concerned individuals [HADB, P00034, Der Brief von Geheimrat Fellinger an Herr Direktor Wintermantel (27.11.1939); HADB, P00034, Auszug aus einer Aktennotiz des Herrn Wintermantel von 8.9.39.]. Considering this point, the regional advisory council was an important and effective foundation of personnel connections between banks and industrial enterprises.

Furthermore, the regional advisory council was significant for large banks not only in developing and strengthening business relationships with representative companies in each region and exchanging and sharing information through personnel connections of such an organization with banks and industrial enterprises but also as an important countermeasure for tidying over situations in which the concerned bank was inferior to other banks regarding business relationships with industrial companies as customers and could not establish sufficient business relations with them. As analyzed in this chapter, even if large banks—above all Deutsche Bank as the leading bank with the most power in Germany—such as Dresdner Bank and Commerzbank as strong rival banks had early on established close business and personnel relationships with enterprises, developing and maintaining relationships with industrial enterprises by inviting members of industrial companies to regional advisory councils and interchange and cooperation with these companies could create for concerned banks the possibility of overcoming such a situation.

In addition, remunerations were paid to members of regional advisory councils of Deutsche Bank. These remunerations indicated the importance and significance of such an organization for this bank and the important role of its members. Regarding the regional committee for which the name was not yet changed to "regional advisory council," a document to Karl Kimmich dated April 30, 1930, and other documents regarding rewards for members of the Rhein–Westfalen regional committee dated April 15, 1930, and December 31, 1931, indicated that RM 3000 should be paid per year [HADB, P00042, Der Brief von der Deutschen Bank und Disconto-Gesellschaft an Herrn Dr. Karl Kimmich (10.4.1930); HADB, P00042, Vergütung an den Rheinisch-Westfälischen Ausschuβ Sitz Köln für das Jahr 1931 (31.12.1931); HADB, P00042, Vergütung an den Rheinisch-Westfälischen Ausschuβ Sitz Köln für Die Monate November und Dezember 1929 (15.4.1930)]. A document from Deutsche Bank to Karl Kimmich dated June 30, 1933, informed that remuneration for members of the Cologne organization of the Rhein–Westfalen regional committee was RM 750 in the former half of the year [HADB, P00042, Vergütung an den Rheinisch-Westfälischen Ausschuβ Sitz Köln, für das 1. Halbjahr 1933 (30.6.1933)]. An internal document of Deutsche Bank dated December 6, 1941, also pointed out that members of regional advisory councils were given the right to receive rewards according to the articles of association, work regulations, and decisions of the supervisory board; therefore, this bank had a duty to pay remuneration, and RM 1000 RM was to be paid per year [HADB, P00042, Verzicht auf Beiratsvergütung (6.12.1941)]. Such treatment for members of the regional advisory council, including remuneration and consideration of various special relationships with members of this organization and their home companies, reflected the fact that such bank committees were important to developing and maintaining relationships with representative industrial enterprises in each region and establishing and reinforcing personnel connections.

As was clear in the foregoing analysis, developing and strengthening personnel connections based on relationships through the credit and securities businesses means the development of interdependence and the interplay of relationships among independent enterprises. The personnel connections through banks' regional advisory councils played a significant role in supplementing personnel connections and interfirm relationships between banks and industrial enterprises through interlocking directorates in the supervisory board of other companies and invitations of individuals from companies outside a bank's supervisory boards. Personnel connections through advisory councils could extend relationships between banks and industrial enterprises at a broader scope than through connections of the supervisory board. Such personnel connections could also secure closer linkages with representative companies in specific regions where the bank had business relations. Such entities established by large banks played significant roles as important elements of cooperative capitalism in Germany.

In foregoing examination, functions and roles of personnel connection through regional advisory council before World War II were clarified. After World War II, central advisory council system was created for banks' head offices in addition to regional advisory council founded before the war. It was established as response to influence of the 1965 Corporations Law that regulated number of supervisory board post one person could have for the purpose of maintaining level of personnel connection between bank and industrial enterprises. On the other hand, regional advisory council system was also expanded after the war. Therefore, next issues to be considered are conditions of personnel connection built through central and regional advisory councils of three large banks between enterprises in the period after World War II. In next chapter, this research topic will be analyzed.

References

Deutsche Bank (1900) Einunddreissigster Geschäfts-Bericht des Vorstandes der Deutschen Bank für die Zeit vom 1.Januar bis 31.Dezember 1900. Deutsche Bank, Berlin

Deutsche Bank (1913) Vierundvierzigster Geschäfts-Bericht des Vorstandes der Deutschen Bank für die Zeit vom 1.Januar bis 31.Dezember 1913. Deutsche Bank, Berlin

Deutsche Bank (1927) 58. Geschäftsbericht des Vorstandes der Deutschen Bank für das Jahr 1927. Deutsche Bank, Berlin

Deutsce Bank (1928) Jahresbericht über des 59.Geschäftsjahr 1928. Deutsche Bank, Berlin

Deutsche Bank (1937) Geschäftsbeiricht für 1937. Deutsche Bank, Berlin

Deutsche Bank (1938) Geschäftsbericht für 1938. Deutsche Bank, Berlin

Deutsche Bank (1939) Geschäftsbericht für 1939. Deutsche Bank, Berlin

Deutsche Bank (1940) Geschäftsbericht für 1940. Deutsche Bank, Berlin

Deutsche Bank und Disconto-Gesellschaft (1932) Geschäftsbericht 1932. Deutsche Bank und Disconto-Gesellschaft, Berlin

Deutsche Bank und Disconto-Gesellschaft (1934) Geschäftsbericht 1934. Deutsche Bank und Disconto-Gesellschaft, Berlin

Deutsche Bank und Disconto-Gesellschaft (1935) Geschäftsbericht 1935. Deutsche Bank und Disconto-Gesellschaft, Berlin

Deutsche Bank und Disconto-Gesellschaft (1936) Geschäftsbericht 1936. Deutsche Bank und Disconto-Gesellschaft, Berlin

Chapter 15
Personnel Connection Among Enterprises Through Advisory Council System of Bank After World War II

Abstract For a long time in Germany, the bank advisory council system played an important role in collecting, exchanging, and sharing information, as well as facilitating enterprise cooperation. After World War II, a central advisory council was established for bank head offices, whereas regional advisory councils were established in major districts before the war. These councils served as important means of connecting personnel between banks, industrial enterprises, and corporations. The advisory council system supplemented personnel connections through establishing interlocking directorates in top management bodies. This chapter explains how three large banks' central and regional advisory councils established personnel connections between enterprises after World War II. The analysis considers the membership of such special committees and their mandates in top management organs such as the enterprise's supervisory and management boards. The cases of Deutsche Bank, Dresdner Bank, and Commerzbank are examined.

Keywords Advisory council · Bank · Board of directors · Central advisory council · Industry–bank relationship · Personnel connection · Regional advisory council · Supervisory board

Chapter 13 examined the personnel connections between banks and industrial enterprises and between corporations after World War II through the bank's advisory council system, which included both central and regional councils. Chapter 14 discusses the functions and roles of these personnel connections. This chapter and Chap. 16 analyze the structure and function of personnel connections after World War II.

The advisory council system, which consisted of central and regional advisory councils, played an important role in information exchange and sharing, as well as creating opportunities to coordinate interests and conflicts between banks and industrial enterprises and among enterprises. If members of the advisory council have mandates on top management organs such as supervisory boards and boards of directors of many enterprises in various industries, the opportunity to obtain variable information about many industries will be expanded.

T. Yamazaki, *Relationships Between Industry and Bank in Germany*,
https://doi.org/10.1007/978-981-97-4996-6_15

As a result, this chapter examines the conditions of personnel connections through the advisory council system. Central advisory councils, as a core of the advisory council system of banks, were usually established as a response to the influence of regulation by the 1965 Corporations Law regarding the number of supervisory board posts that one person could hold in order to maintain the level of personnel connection between bank and other enterprises in various important industries. Therefore, this chapter considers the period around the late 1960s.

Section 15.1 examines the conditions of personnel connections between banks and industrial enterprises, as well as between corporations via the central advisory council of the three major banks, Deutsche Bank, Dresdner Bank, and Commerzbank. Section 15.2 examines the structures of personnel connections via the regional advisory councils of these banks.

15.1 Personnel Connection Between Enterprises Through the Central Advisory Council

15.1.1 Personnel Connection Between Companies Through the Central Advisory Council of Deutsche Bank

15.1.1.1 Members of the Central Advisory Council

This section discusses personnel connections between companies via the central advisory council. The central advisory council described in Deutsche Bank's annual reports for fiscal years 1967, 1968, and 1969 consisted of 16, 16, and 14 members. According to the 1969 annual report, all members were from other companies other than Deutsche Bank. Kurt Hansen, chairman of Bayer AG's board of directors in the chemical industry, presided over this committee. Alfred Haase, an insurance executive with Allianz Versicherungs-AG, served as vice-chairman. The other members of the central advisory council were Salzdetfurth AG in the mining industry; Mannesmann AG, Otto Wolff AG, and Hoesch AG in the iron and steel industry; Metallgesellschaft AG in the metal production and processing industries; Norddeutsche Affinerie in the chemical industry; Siemens AG and AEG in the electrical industry; Daimler-Benz AG in the automobile industry; Demag AG in the machine industry; Deutsche Erdöl AG in the oil industry; and Karstadt AG in the distributing industry. People from multiple companies in the same industry sometimes served on the central advisory council. Examples include Mannesmann AG, Hoesch AG, and Otto Wolff AG in the iron and steel industry, as well as Siemens AG and AEG in the electrical industry.

Let us consider the members of the central advisory council who had the mandate of top management organs such as the supervisory board and the managing board in their own enterprises concerning the position. Cases where the chairman of the board of directors was a committee member can be observed in the following eight enterprises. Salzdetfurth AG, Mannesmann AG, Otto Wolff AG, Norddeutsche Affinerie, Bayer AG, Siemens AG, Demag AG, and Allianz Versicherungs-AG. Companies in which the vice-chairman of the board of directors was a member of the central advisory council were Metallgesellschaft AG, AEG, and Deutsche Erdöl AG. In some cases, every managing board member, except the chairman and vice-chairman, served on the committee in Dailmer-Benz AG. Enterprises in which chairman of the supervisory board was a member of this committee was Hoesch AG and case where vice-chairman of a similar top management organ was a member of this advisory organization was Karstadt AG (Deutsche Bank AG 1967, S. 10, 1968, S. 10, 1969, S. 16).

Deutsche Bank built an interlocking directorate through mandates of the supervisory board in 13 enterprises, except Salzdetfurth AG, whose members belonged to the central advisory council (see Chap. 6). As a result, close personnel connections were established between Deutsche Bank and these enterprises via the interlocking directorate and the central advisory council.

15.1.1.2 Holding of Mandates by Members of the Central Advisory Council on Top Management Organs

Holding of Mandates by Members of the Central Advisory Council on the Supervisory Board of Enterprise

Further, this subsection examines how members of the central advisory council held mandates on top management organs such as supervisory boards and boards of directors of enterprises in various industries. In that case, the concerned bank and advisory council member companies can obtain a wide range of information about those industries and companies.

Considering the mandates that members of the central advisory council held on the supervisory board (see Table 15.1), the number of companies totaled 81, and the total number of mandates was 83. Looking at the distribution of industrial sectors, the numbers of companies and mandates, respectively, were two each in the mining industry; 11 each in the iron and steel industry; four each in the metal producing and processing industries; seven each in the chemical industry; four each in the electrical industry; six each in the automobile industry; nine each in the machine industry; one each in the textile, spinning, and woven goods industries; four each in the distributing industry; one each in the banking industry; 17 and 18 in the insurance industry; three and four in the electric power, gas, and energy industries; four each in the transportation industry; and eight each in other industries.

When considering a situation in which members of the central advisory council had a mandate for the supervisory board position, 26 companies held the chairmanship. The total number of mandates was 26. There were four such enterprises in the iron and steel industry, one in the metal producing and processing industries, one in the chemical industry, one in the electrical industry, four in the automobile industry,

Table 15.1 Supervisory board positions held by members of Deutsche Bank's central advisory council (period at the late of the 1960s)

Industries	Position							
	Chairman		Vice-chairman		Supervisory board member excluding chairman and vice-chairman		Tota[a]	
	Number of companies	Number of posts	Number of companies	Number of posts	Number of companies	Number of posts	Number of companies	Number of posts
Mining	–	–	1	1	1	1	2	2
Iron and steel	4	4	4	4	3	3	11	11
Metal producing and processing	1	1	1	1	2	2	4	4
Chemical	1	1	2	2	4	4	7	7
Electrical	1	1	–	–	3	3	4	4
Automobile	4	4	–	–	2	2	6	6
Machine	5	5	–	–	4	4	9	9
Textile, spinning, and woven goods	–	–	–	–	1	1	1	1
Distributing	1	1	1	1	2	2	4	4
Banking	–	–	–	–	1	1	1	1
Insurance	8	8	4	4	6	6	17	18
Electric power, gas, and energy	1	1	1	1	2	2	3	4
Transportation	–	–	1	1	3	3	4	4

(continued)

Table 15.1 (continued)

Industries	Position							
	Chairman		Vice-chairman		Supervisory board member excluding chairman and vice-chairman		Tota[a]	
	Number of companies	Number of posts	Number of companies	Number of posts	Number of companies	Number of posts	Number of companies	Number of posts
Other industries	–	–	3	3	5	5	8	8
All industries	26	26	18	18	39	39	81	83

[a] There are cases in which the total number of companies in which mandate was held differed from the total number of companies measured by each position of the supervisory board due to the existence of companies where more than two posts were held

Source This table was compiled by the author, based on Mossner (Hrsg) (1971) and Deutsche Bank AG (1967, 1968, 1969)

five in the machine industry, one in the distributing industry, eight in the insurance industry, and one in the electric power, gas, and energy industries. Each member of this advisory council had one mandate, respectively. The holding of the chairman position can be observed in representative enterprises in each industrial sector, such as Hoesch AG, Ilseder Hütte and Rasselstein in the iron and steel industry, Agfa-Gevaert AG in the chemical industry, Orenstein-Koppel AG and Maschinenfabrik Esslingen AG in the machine industry, Allianz Lebensversicherungs-AG, Frankfurter Versicherungs-AG, and some companies of the Gerling group (Gerling-Konzern Allgemeine Versicherung AG, Gerling-Konzern Friedlich Wilhelm Lebensversicherung AG, and Gerling-Konzern Versicherungs-Zentrale AG) in the insurance industry.

Examining the situation in which members of the central advisory council held the position of vice-chairman, such cases were found in 18 companies. Each member of this advisory council had one mandate, respectively. Thus, the total number of mandates was 18. There were one such enterprise in the mining industry, four in the iron and steel industry, one in the metal producing and processing industries, two in the chemical industry, one in the distribution industry, four in the insurance industry, one in the electric power, gas, and energy industries, one in transportation, and three in other industries. These companies included major companies from each industry, such as Chemische Werke Hüls AG in the chemical industry, Erdölchemie GmbH in the oil industry, and Münchener Rückversicherungs-Gesellschaft in the insurance industry.

Except for the chairman and vice-chairman positions, in 39 companies members of this advisory council had supervisory board mandates. Taking into account the distribution among industrial sectors, the number of companies in which the advisory council members had a post was one in the mining industry, three in the iron and steel industry, two in the metal producing and processing industries, four in the chemical industry, three in the electrical industry, two in the automobile industry, four in the machine industry, one in the textile, spinning, and woven goods industries, and two in the distributing industry; one in the banking industry; six in the insurance industry; two in the electric power, gas, and energy industries; three in the transportation industry; and five in other industries, respectively. Each member of this advisory council had one mandate. Among these companies were companies in each industry, such as Otto Wolff AG and Stahlwerke Bochum AG in the iron and steel industry, Glanzstoff AG in the chemical industry, Siemens AG in the electrical industry, and Hanomag-Henschel Fahrzeugwerke GmbH in the automotive industry.

Holding of Mandates by Members of the Central Advisory Council on Managing Board of Enterprise

Next, the mandates of members of the central advisory council on the company's managing board are considered. Such cases can be observed in 12 enterprises. Each member of this advisory council had one mandate. As a result, the total number of mandates was 12, with one in mining, iron and steel, chemical, automobile, machine, oil, insurance, and other industries and two in metal producing and processing and electrical industries.

Considering the holding situation in which members of the central advisory council held the post of managing board in relation to their position, those holding the chairman position can be observed in eight companies, with a total of eight mandates. These enterprises were involved in mining, iron and steel, metal production and processing, chemical, electrical, mechanical, insurance, and other industries. There were three companies and three mandates, and each member of the central advisory council had a vice-chairman on the managing board. There was one each in the metal production and processing, electrical, and petroleum industries. Mandates were only observed in the automobile enterprise except for the chairman and vice-chairman of the managing board.

In cases where members of the central advisory council held positions on the managing board, there were representatives from large enterprises in each industrial sector. Such cases can be observed in Metallgesellschaft AG in the metal producing and processing industries, Bayer AG in the chemical industry, Siemens AG and AEG in the electrical industry, Daimler-Benz AG in the automotive industry, Demag AG in the machine industry, Deutsche Erdöl AG in the oil industry, and Allianz Versicherungs-AG in the insurance industry (Mossner 1971).

15.1.2 Personnel Connection Between Enterprises Through Central Advisory Council of Dresdner Bank

15.1.2.1 Members of Central Advisory Council

Dresdner Bank's central advisory council was described in its annual reports for fiscal years 1967, 1968, and 1969 as having 16, 17, and 17 members. According to the 1969 annual report, none of the members were from Dresdner Bank. The two individuals were members of the supervisory boards of their companies. These enterprises included August Thyssen-Hütte AG in the iron and steel industry and Martin Brinkmann AG in the food industry. The companies to which they belonged had nine members on their management boards. Such cases can be observed in Fried. Krupp GmbH and Klöckner-Werke AG in the iron and steel industry, Phrix-Werke AG in the chemical industry, Brown, Boveri & Cie. AG in the electrical industry, Westfalen Separator AG in the machine industry, Allianz Lebensversicherungs-AG in the insurance industry, Ruhrgas AG and Elektrizitäts-Actien-Geseschaft vorm. Lahmeyer AG in the electric power, gas, and energy industries, and Deutsche Bundesbahn in the transportation industry (Dresdner Bank AG 1967, 1968, 1969).

Dresdner Bank established an interlocking directorate through mandates of the supervisory board in five enterprises, namely August Thyssen-Hütte AG; Fried. Krupp GmbH; Phrix-Werke AG; Brown, Boveri, & Cie. AG; and Allianz Lebensversicherungs-AG, whose members belonged to the central advisory council (see Chap. 6). As a result, close personnel connections were established between Dresdner Bank and these companies via the interlocking directorate and central advisory council. However, the number of such enterprises was lower than that of Deutsche Bank (13 enterprises).

15.1.2.2 Holding of Mandates by Members of the Central Advisory Council on Top Management Organs

Holding of Mandates by Members of the Central Advisory Council on the Supervisory Board of Enterprise

Considering the mandates that members of the central advisory council held on the supervisory board (see Table 15.2), the number of companies in such cases totaled 63, with a total of 64 mandates. When examining the distribution of industrial sectors, the numbers of companies and mandates, respectively, were four each in the mining industry; five and six in the iron and steel industry; four each in the metal producing and processing industries; six each in the chemical industry; two each in the electrical industry; one each in the automobile industry; four each in the machine industry; two each in the textile, spinning, and woven goods industries; one each in the distillation industry; two each in the distributing industry; four each in the banking industry; seven each in the insurance industry; eight each in the electric power, gas, and energy industries; one each in the transportation industry; and 12 each in other industries.

When considering a situation in which members of the central advisory council had a mandate concerning the position of the supervisory board, 25 companies held the chairmanship. The total number of mandates was 25. There were three such enterprises in the mining industry, two in the iron and steel industry, three in the metal producing and processing industries, two in the chemical industry, two in the electrical industry, one in the automobile industry, two in the machine industry, one in the textile, spinning, and woven goods industries, one in the banking industry, two in the insurance industry, and six in other industries. Each member of this advisory council had one mandate, respectively. Chairmanship is observed by enterprises from each industrial sector, such as Klöckner-Bergbau AG and Friedrich Thyssen Bergbau AG in mining, August Thyssen-Hütte AG in iron and steel, and Rheinmetall GmbH in metal production and processing.

Four companies reported cases in which members of the central advisory council held the position of vice-chairman. Each member of this advisory council had one mandate, respectively. Thus, the total number of mandates was four. One of these enterprises was in the chemical industry, one was in the machine industry, and two were in the electric power, gas, and energy sectors.

Except for the chairman and vice-chairman positions, 35 companies held supervisory board mandates. Taking into account the distribution of industrial sectors, the number of companies in which the advisory council members had a post was one in the mining industry, four in the iron and steel industry, one in the metal producing and processing industries, three in the chemical industry, one in the machine industry, one

Table 15.2 Supervisory board positions held by members of Dresdner Bank's central advisory council (period at the late of the 1960s)

Industries	Position							
	Chairman		Vice-chairman		Supervisory board member excluding chairman and vice-chairman		Total*	
	Number of companies	Number of posts	Number of companies	Number of posts	Number of companies	Number of posts	Number of companies	Number of posts
Mining	3	3	–	–	1	1	4	4
Iron and steel	2	2	–	–	4	4	5	6
Metal producing and processing	3	3	–	–	1	1	4	4
Chemical	2	2	1	1	3	3	6	6
Electrical	2	2	–	–	–	–	2	2
Automobile	1	1	–	–	–	–	1	1
Machine	2	2	1	1	1	1	4	4
Textile, spinning, and woven goods	1	1	–	–	1	1	2	2
Distillation	–	–	–	–	1	1	1	1
Distributing	–	–	–	–	2	2	2	2
Banking	1	1	–	–	3	3	4	4
Insurance	2	2	–	–	5	5	7	7
Electric power, gas, and energy	–	–	2	2	6	6	8	8
Transportation	–	–	–	–	1	1	1	1

(continued)

Table 15.2 (continued)

Industries	Position							
	Chairman		Vice-chairman		Supervisory board member excluding chairman and vice-chairman		Total*	
	Number of companies	Number of posts	Number of companies	Number of posts	Number of companies	Number of posts	Number of companies	Number of posts
Other industries	6	6	–	–	6	6	12	12
All industries	25	25	4	4	35	35	81	83

[a] There are cases in which the total number of companies in which mandate was held differed from the total number of companies measured by each position of the supervisory board due to the existence of companies where more than two posts were held

Source This table was compiled by the author, based on Mossner (Hrsg) (1971) and Deutsche Bank AG (1967, 1968, 1969)

in the textile, spinning, and woven goods industries, one in the distillation industry, two in the distribution industry; three in the banking industry; five in the insurance industry; six in the electric power, gas, and energy industries; one in the transportation industry; and six in other industries. Each member of this advisory council had one mandate, respectively. Leading companies in various industries included Preuβag AG in mining, August Thyssen-Hütte AG and Deutsche Edelstahlwerke AG in iron and steel, Kaufhof AG in distribution, and Münchener Rückversicherungs-Gesellschaft and Frankfurter Versicherungs-AG in insurance.

Members of Deutsche Bank and Dresdner Bank's central advisory councils served on the supervisory boards of three companies: Frankfurter Versicherungs-AG and Münchener Rückversicherungs-Gesellschaft in the insurance industry, and Vereinigte Deutsche Metallwerke AG in the metal production and processing industries. In Frankfurter Versicherungs-AG, while Alfred Haase, vice-chairman of the central advisory council of Deutsche Bank, held the position of chairman of the supervisory board, Joachim Zahn, a member of the central advisory council of Deutsche Bank, and Hans Fonk, a member of the central advisory council of Dresdner Bank, held supervisory positions other than chairman and vice-chairman, respectively. In Münchener Rückversicherungs-Gesellachaft, Alfred Haase, vice-chairman of Deutsche Bank's central advisory council, served as vice-chairman of the supervisory board, and Heinz Maria Oeftering, a member of Dresdner Bank's central advisory council, served as supervisory board member, except for chairman and vice-chairman. In Vereinigte Deutsche Metallwerke AG, Casimir Prinz Wittgenstein, a member of Deutsch Bank's central advisory council, was vice-chairman. In contrast, Gerd Müller, a member of Dresdner Bank's central advisory council, held the position of supervisory board member, excluding the chairman and vice-chairman.

Holding of Mandates by Members of the Central Advisory Council on Managing Board of Enterprise

Next, the mandates of members of the central advisory council on the company's managing board are considered. Such incidents can be observed in 13 companies. Each member of this advisory council had one mandate. As a result, the total number of mandates was 13, with four in the electric power, gas, and energy industries, three in the iron and steel industry, two in the insurance industry, and one each in the chemical, electrical, machine, and transportation sectors.

When considering the holding situation in which members of the central advisory council held the post of managing board concerning their position, cases of chairmanship can be observed in five companies, with a total of five mandates. These cases occurred in the iron, steel, chemical, electrical, insurance, and transportation industries. There was only one enterprise in the iron and steel industry, and members of the central advisory council were assigned a vice-chairman of the managing board. Except for the chairman and vice-chairman of the managing board, seven enterprises held mandates, for a total of seven. Four were in the electric power, gas, and energy industries, with one each in iron and steel, machine, and insurance.

In cases where members of the central advisory council served on the managing board, there were representatives from major companies in each industrial sector. Such examples can be observed in Kölckner-Werke AG and Fried. Krupp GmbH in the iron and steel industry, Brown, Boveri & Cie. AG in the electrical industry, Allianz Versicherungs-AG and Allianz Lebensversicherungs-AG in the insurance industry, Ruhrgas AG in the electric power, gas, and energy industries, and Deutsche Bundesbahn in the transport industry. Many of them were enterprises from which members of the central advisory council were.

Members of Deutsche Bank and Dresdner Bank's central advisory councils served on the managing board of the same enterprise, Allianz Versicherungs-AG, in the insurance industry. In this company, Alfred Haase, who was vice-chairman of the central advisory council of Deutsche Bank, had the mandate of chairman of the managing board, and Gerd Müller, who was a member of the central advisory council of Dresdner Bank, held the post of managing director except for chairman and vice-chairman (Mossner 1971).

15.1.3 Personnel Connection Between Enterprises Through Central Advisory Council of Commerzbank

15.1.3.1 Members of Central Advisory Council

Commerzbank's central advisory council was described in its annual reports for fiscal years 1967, 1968, and 1969 as having 13, 14, and 14 members, respectively. According to the 1969 annual report, all members were from companies other than Commerzbank. Friedrich Krämer, chairman of Preuβag AG's managing board in the mining industry, led the committee. There were three members of the companies' supervisory boards. Eschweiler Bergwerks-Verein was a mining enterprise, and Kepa Kaufhaus GmbH and Kaufhof AG were in the distributing industry. Persons who were members of the managing board of companies to which they belonged were eight. Examples include Preuβag AG in mining, Hugo Stinnes AG and Buderus'sche Eisenwerke in iron and steel, Chemische Werke Hüls AG in chemical, Helmut Horten AG in distribution, and Ruhrgas AG, Rheinisch-Westfälisches Elektrizitätswerk AG, and VEBA AG in electric power, gas, and energy industries. However, the same person served on the management boards of Hugo Stinnes AG and VEBA AG. As a result, ten members of the central advisory council served on the supervisory or management boards of 11 different enterprises.

Commerzbank's central advisory council includes five member enterprises: Preuβag AG in mining, Buderus'sche Eisenwerke in iron and steel, Chemische Werke Hüls AG in chemical, Kaufhof AG in distribution, and Rheinisch-Westfälisches Elektrizitätswerk AG in electric power, gas, and energy. These enterprises formed an interlocking directorate with their supervisory boards (see Chap. 6). As a result, close personnel connections were established between Commerzbank and these companies via the interlocking directorate and the central advisory council. The number of such enterprises was the same as that of Dresdner Bank, but it was smaller than that of Deutsche Bank (13 enterprises).

In one case, enterprises sent representatives to the central advisory councils of Dresdner Bank and Commerzbank. Ruhrgas AG, which operates in the electric power, gas, and energy industries, appointed Peter-Josef Deckers to the central advisory council of Dresdner Bank and Herrt Schelberger to the central advisory council of Commerzbank (Commerzbank AG 1967, S. 68, 1968, S. 75, 1969, S. 85).

15.1.3.2 Holding of Mandates by Members of the Central Advisory Council on Top Management Organs

Holding of Mandates by Members of the Central Advisory Council on the Supervisory Board of Enterprise

When considering the mandates that members of the central advisory council had on the supervisory board (see Table 15.3), the number of companies totaled 65, with a total of 66 mandates. Looking at the distribution of industrial sectors, the numbers of companies and mandates were three each in the mining industry, and similarly, six each in the iron and steel industry; three each in the metal producing and processing industries; four each in the chemical industry; one each in the electrical industry; five and six in the machine industry; one each in the shipbuilding industry, one each in the oil industry, and eight each in the distributing industry; two each in the banking industry; four each in the insurance industry; 20 each in the electric power, gas, and energy industries; two each in the transportation industry; and five each in other industries.

Examining a situation in which the members of the central advisory council had a mandate regarding the position of the supervisory board, it was discovered that 15 companies held the chairmanship. The total number of mandates was fifteen. There was one in the mining industry, one in metal production and processing, one in chemical, one in electrical, five in distribution, one in banking, four in electric power, gas, and energy, and one in other industries. Each member of this advisory council had one mandate, respectively.

In 14 companies, members of the central advisory council were observed the role of vice-chairman. Each member of this advisory council had one mandate, respectively. Thus, the total number of mandates was 14. There were three such enterprises in the iron and steel industry, one in the metal producing and processing industries, one in the chemical industry, two in the machine industry, three in the distribution industry, one in the electric power, gas, and energy industries, one in the transportation industry, and two in other industries.

There were 37 mandates for supervisory companies, excluding the chairman and vice-chairman. Taking into account the distribution among the industrial sectors, the number of companies in which the advisory council members had a post was two in

Table 15.3 Supervisory board positions held by members of Commerzbank's central advisory council (period at the late of the 1960s)

Industries	Position							
	Chairman		Vice-chairman		Supervisory board member excluding chairman and vice-chairman		Total[a]	
	Number of companies	Number of posts	Number of companies	Number of posts	Number of companies	Number of posts	Number of companies	Number of posts
Mining	1	1	–	–	2	2	3	3
Iron and steel	–	–	3	3	3	3	6	6
Metal producing and processing	1	1	1	1	1	1	3	3
Chemical	1	1	1	1	2	2	4	4
Electrical	1	1	–	–	–	–	1	1
Machine	–	–	2	2	4	4	5	6
Shipbuilding	–	–	–	–	1	1	1	1
Oil	–	–	–	–	1	1	1	1
Distributing	5	5	3	3	–	–	8	8
Banking	1	1	–	–	1	1	2	2
Insurance	–	–	–	–	4	4	4	4
Electric power, gas, and energy	4	4	1	1	15	15	20	20
Transportation	–	–	1	1	1	1	2	2

(continued)

Table 15.3 (continued)

Industries	Position							
	Chairman		Vice-chairman		Supervisory board member excluding chairman and vice-chairman		Total[a]	
	Number of companies	Number of posts	Number of companies	Number of posts	Number of companies	Number of posts	Number of companies	Number of posts
Other industries	1	1	2	2	2	2	5	5
All industries	15	15	14	14	37	37	65	66

[a] There are cases in which the total number of companies in which mandate was held differed from the total number of companies measured by each position of the supervisory board due to the existence of companies where more than two posts were held

Source This table was compiled by the author, based on Mossner (Hrsg) (1971) and Deutsche Bank AG (1967, 1968, 1969)

the mining industry, three in the iron and steel industry, one in the metal producing and processing industries, two in the chemical industry, four in the machine industry, one in the shipbuilding industry, one in the oil industry, one in the banking industry, four in the insurance industry, 15 in the electric power, gas, and energy industries, one in the transportation industry, and two in other industries. Each member of this advisory council had one mandate, respectively.

In five cases, members of Dresdner Bank and Commerzbank's central advisory councils served on the supervisory boards of the same enterprise: Kaufhof AG in the distribution industry and Mittelrheinische Erdgastransport GmbH, Gas Union GmbH, Nordrheinische Erdgastransport GmbH, and Rheinische Energie AG in the electric power, gas, and energy industries. Werner Schulz, a member of Commerzbank's central advisory council, held the position of vice-chairman of the supervisory board at Kaufhof AG, while Robert Ellscheid, a member of Dresdner Bank's central advisory council, held the position of supervisory board member except for chairman and vice-chairman. In Mittelrheinische Erdgastransport GmbH, while Herbert Schelberger, a member of Commerzbank's central advisory council, held the position of chairman of the supervisory board, Peter-Josef Deckers, a member of Dresdner Bank's central advisory council, held the position of supervisory board member, excluding the chairman and vice-chairman. In Gas Union GmbH, whereas Herbert Schelberger, a member of Commerzbank's central advisory council, held the position of vice-chairman, Peter-Josef Deckers, a member of Dresdner Bank's central advisory council, held the position of supervisory board member other than chairman and vice-chairman. Except for the chairman and vice-chairman, the supervisory mandates of Nordrheinische Erdgastransport GmbH and Rheinische Energie AG were held by Peter-Josef Deckers, a member of Dresdner Bank's central advisory council, and Herbert Schelberger, a member of Commerzbank's central advisory council. There was no instance of members of Deutsche Bank and Commerzbank's central advisory councils having supervisory board mandates for the same enterprise.

Holding of Mandates by Members of the Central Advisory Council on Managing Board of Enterprise

Next, the mandates of members of the central advisory council on the company's managing board are considered. Such cases can be addressed in 11 enterprises. Each member of this advisory council had one mandate. As a result, the total number of mandates was 11, with three in the distribution industry and the electric power, gas, and energy industries, two in the mining and iron and steel industries, two in the insurance industry, and one in the chemical industry.

When considering the holding situation in which members of the central advisory council held the post of managing board concerning their position, cases of chairmanship can be observed in three companies, with a total of three mandates. Each member of this advisory council had one mandate. Examples include Preußag AG in mining, Chemische Werke Hüls AG in chemical, and Ruhrgas AG in electric power, gas, and energy industries.

Except for the chairman and vice-chairman of the management board, members of the central advisory council held mandates in eight enterprises, for a total of eight mandates. In each company, each member of this advisory council held one mandate, respectively. There were three in the distribution industry, two in the iron and steel and electric power, gas, and energy industries, and one in mining and other industries. These enterprises were Steinkohlenbergwerke Mathias Stinnes AG in the mining industry, Hugo Stinnes AG and Buderus'sche Eisenwerke in the iron and steel industry, Karstadt AG, Handelsunion AG, and Helmut Horten AG in the distribution industry, and Rheinisch-Westfälisches Elektrizitätswerk AG and VEBA AG in the electric power, gas, and energy sectors.

One case in which members of Dresdner Bank and Commerzbank's central advisory councils served on the management board of the same company was Rhurgas AG, which operated in the electric power, gas, and energy sectors. Herbert Schelberger, a member of Commerzbank's central advisory council, held the mandate of chairman of the enterprise board, and Peter-Josef Deckers, a member of Dresdner Bank's central advisory council, held the mandate excluding the chairman and vice-chairman. There was no case in which members of the central advisory councils of Deutsche Bank and Commerzbank had mandates from the management board of the same enterprise (Mossner 1971).

15.2 Personnel Connection Between Enterprises Through Regional Advisory Council

Section 15.1 examines personnel connections between companies through three large banks' central advisory councils. Section 15.2 addresses the conditions of personnel connection through the regional advisory council.

15.2.1 Personnel Connection Between Enterprises Through Regional Advisory Council of Deutsche Bank

15.2.1.1 Members of Regional Advisory Council

In the annual report for fiscal year 1967, Deutsche Bank described 15 regional advisory councils. There were a total of 453 members in these organizations. The Baden-Pfalz, Bayern, Braunschweig, Bremen, Düsseldorf/Krefeld, Essen/Dortmund/Duisburg, and Hamburg/Schleswig-Holstein regional advisory councils each had 35, 39, 18, 13, 35, 45, and 36 members. Similarly, the regional advisory councils of Hannover, Hessen, Köln/Aachen/Siegen, Oberbaden, Osnabrück,

Rhein/Mosel, Württemberg, and Wuppertal/Bielefeld/Münster had 20, 35, 42, 25, 11, 21, 28, and 50 members. All 15 regional advisory council members were from enterprises other than Deutsche Bank. Five of the 15 regional advisory councils had a chairman: Essen/Dortmund/Duisburg, Hessen, Oberbaden, Rhein/Mosel, and Wuppertal/Bielefeld/Münster. The remaining ten regional advisory councils had one chairman and one vice-chairman each.

Considering the enterprises from which a person becomes a member of the regional advisory council in terms of the industry to which each enterprise belonged, members of the Baden-Pfalz regional advisory council came from industries such as chemical, machine, textile, spinning and woven goods, insurance, electric power, gas, and energy, and transportation. The chemical and machine industries account for the vast majority of these companies. There were representative large companies in each industry, such as BASF in the chemical sector. Although there were several enterprises in the Bayern regional advisory council in industries such as metal production and processing, chemical, electrical, automobile, machine, textile, spinning, and woven goods, banking, and insurance, the majority of the enterprises were in the chemical, electrical, and machine industries. There were major companies in each industry, including Siemens AG in the electrical industry and BMW in the automobile industry. Several mining, iron and steel, automobile, machine, and distillation companies were represented on the Braunschweig regional advisory council. The machine industry had a relatively high number of companies. Each industrial sector had a representative company, such as Salzgitter AG in the iron and steel and Volkswagen AG in the automobile industry.

The Bremen regional advisory council included firms from the iron and steel, machine, distillation, and banking industries. Among these companies were large companies in their respective industries, such as Klöckner-Werke AG in the iron and steel industry. In Düsseldorf/Krefeld regional advisory council, although there were members from enterprises in industries, such as iron and steel; metal producing and processing; chemical; machine; textile, spinning, and woven goods; distillation; and distribution, majority of the members were from enterprises in the iron and steel industry and the machine industry. In Essen/Dortmund/Duisburg regional advisory council, there were members from enterprises in industries such as mining, iron and steel, chemical, machine, distillation, gas, and energy industries. Several members came from the mining and iron and steel industries. Members of chemical companies were also present. These conditions reflected regional industrial aggregation. This advisory council's companies included leading companies such as August Thyssen-Hütte AG, Hoesch AG, Klöckner-Werke AG, and Mannesmann AG in the iron and steel industry, Harpener AG in the mining industry, and DEMAG AG in the machine industry. Hoesch AG held two positions on this regional advisory council.

The Hamburg/Schleswig-Holstein-Pfalz regional advisory council included enterprises from mining, machine, shipbuilding, oil, insurance, energy, gas, and energy, and transportation industries. The majority of these companies were in the machinery, shipbuilding, and oil industries. Large companies represented each industry, including Preußag AG in mining, Howaldtwerke-Deutsche Werft AG and Deutsche Werft AG in shipbuilding, and Mobil Oil AG in Germany in the oil industry.

Howaldtwerke-Deutsche Werft AG and Mobil Oil AG in Deutschland each sent two representatives to this regional advisory council. Although there were several enterprises in the Hannover regional advisory council in industries such as iron and steel, chemical, and distillation, the chemical industry accounted for the majority of the companies. The Hessen Regional Advisors included enterprises from metal production and processing, chemical, electrical, automobile, machine, textile, spinning, woven goods, banking, and transportation industries. The majority of these companies were in the metal production and processing, chemical, electrical, and machine industries. Large companies represented each industry, such as Adam Opel AG in the automotive industry. Several companies from the mining, iron and steel, metal production and processing, chemical, automobile, machine, food, textile, spinning, and woven goods, distillation, distribution, banking, insurance, and electric power, gas, and energy industries were represented on the Köln/Aachen/Siegen regional advisory council. The machine industry had a large number of companies. There were representatives from each industrial sector, including Ford-Werke AG in the automobile industry, Klöckner-Humboldt Deutz AG in the machine industry, and Kaufhof AG in distribution industry. The Oberbaden regional advisory council included enterprises from the following industries: metal production and processing; chemical; machine; food; textile, spinning, and woven goods; and energy; gas, and energy. The majority of these companies were in the machine and textile, spinning, and woven goods industries. Although there were several enterprises in industries such as iron and steel, metal production and processing, chemical, machine, and distillation, the majority of the enterprises were in the machine and distillation industries.

The Württemberg regional advisory council included firms in the metal producing and processing, electrical, automobile, machine, precious machine and optical, textile, spinning and woven goods, and insurance industries. Most of these companies were involved in metal production and processing, as well as machine manufacturing, reflecting the district's industrial accumulation. There were also numerous textile, spinning, and woven goods enterprises. Although there were several enterprises in industries such as iron and steel, metal producing and processing, chemical, machine, and textile, spinning and woven goods in the Wuppertal/Bielefeld/Münster regional advisory council, the majority of the enterprises belonged to the metal producing and processing, chemical, machine, and textile, spinning, and woven goods industries (Deutsche Bank AG 1967, S. 69–85).

15.2.1.2 Holding of Mandates by Members of the Regional Advisory Council on Top Management Organs

These discussions show that the Deutsche Bank regional advisory council was made up of enterprises from various industries. This was critical for exchanging and sharing information among banks and member companies. However, by holding positions on top management organs such as the supervisory and managing boards of new entrants, members of each advisory council can broaden the field and scope of information that can be exchanged and shared between enterprises.

As a result, this subsection explores the circumstances under which the members of the regional advisory council held the mandates of these top management organs. Although Deutsche Bank had several regional advisory councils, the Württemberg regional advisory council and Essen/Dortmund/Duisburg regional advisory council are among the most important advisory councils in the region where the key industries in Germany are aggregated.

Case of the Württemberg Regional Advisory Council

First, when considering the mandates that members of the Württemberg regional advisory council held on the supervisory board (see Table 15.4), there were 34 companies and 34 mandates. Looking at the distribution of industrial sectors, the numbers of companies and mandates were one each in the metal producing and processing industries, and similarly, one each in the electrical industry; three each in the automobile industry; four each in the machine industry; two each in the precious machine and optical industries; four each in the textile, spinning, and woven goods industries; one each in the distillation industry; one each in the distribution industry; three each in the banking industry; seven each in the insurance industry; and seven each in other industries. Each member of this advisory council had one mandate, respectively.

When investigating a situation in which members of the Württemberg regional advisory council had a mandate in relation to the position of the supervisory board, it was observed that seven companies held the chairmanship. Each member of this advisory council had one mandate, bringing the total to seven. There was one such enterprise in the automobile industry, two in the textile, spinning, and woven goods industry, one in the insurance industry, and three in other industries.

In seven enterprises, members of this advisory council had vice-chairman positions. Each member of this advisory council had one mandate, bringing the total to seven. There were two such enterprises in the machine industry, two in the precious machine and optical industries, one in the textile, spinning, and woven goods industries, one in the insurance industry, and one in other industries.

In all 20 enterprises, members of this advisory council held the supervisory board mandate except for the chairman and vice-chairman. Each member of this advisory council had one mandate, for a total of 20. There was one in metal manufacturing and processing, one in electrical, two in automobile, two in machine, one in textile, spinning, and woven goods, one in distillation, one in distribution, three in banking, five in insurance, and three in other industries.

The holding of mandates by members of the Württemberg regional advisory council on the enterprise's management board is then considered. Such incidents can be observed in 13 companies. Each member of this advisory council had one mandate, respectively. Thus, the total number of mandates was 13. There were two such enterprises in the metal producing and processing industries, one in the electrical industry, two in the automobile industry, two in the machine industry, two in the textile, spinning, and woven goods industries, one in the insurance industry, and three in other industries.

Table 15.4 Supervisory board positions held by members of Deutsche Bank's Württemberg regional advisory council (period at the late of the 1960s)

Industries	Position							
	Chairman		Vice-chairman		Supervisory board member excluding chairman and vice-chairman		Total	
	Number of companies	Number of posts	Number of companies	Number of posts	Number of companies	Number of posts	Number of companies	Number of posts
Metal producing and processing	–	–	–	–	1	1	1	1
Electrical	–	–	–	–	1	1	1	1
Automobile	1	1	–	–	2	2	3	3
Machine	–	–	2	2	2	2	4	4
Precious machine and optical	–	–	2	2	–	–	2	2
Textile, spinning, and woven goods	2	2	1	1	1	1	4	4
Distillation	–	–	–	–	1	1	1	1
Distributing	–	–	–	–	1	1	1	1
Banking	–	–	–	–	3	3	3	3
Insurance	1	1	1	1	5	5	7	7
Other industries	3	3	1	1	3	3	7	7
All industries	7	7	7	7	20	20	34	34

Source This table was compiled by the author, based on Mossner (Hrsg) (1971) and Deutsche Bank AG (1967, 1968, 1969)

Considering the holding situation in which members of the Württemberg regional advisory council held the post of managing board in relation to their position, those holding chairman positions can be observed in seven companies, with a total of seven mandates. These enterprises included two in the metal production and processing industries, two in the automobile industry, two in the textile, spinning, and woven goods industries, and one in the insurance sector. There were six enterprises and six mandates in which Württemberg regional advisory council members held positions on the managing board, excluding the chairman and vice-chairman. There was one in the electrical industry, two in the machine industry, and three in other fields.

In one enterprise, Württemberg regional advisory council members held mandates for both top management organs, such as the supervisory and managing boards. These regional advisory council members held a supervisory board mandate and one managing board position at Maschinenfabrik Weingarten AG, a machine industry company (Mossner 1971).

Members of this regional advisory council who held supervisory and managing board mandates were typically from the metal producing and processing industries and the machine industry in general, including the automobile industry. This reflected the state of industrial accumulation in this district.

Case of Essen/Dortmund/Duisburg Regional Advisory Council

Next, when considering the mandates that members of the Essen/Dortmund/Duisburg regional advisory council held on the supervisory board (see Table 15.5), the number of companies was 122, and the total number of mandates was 130. The enterprise and mandate had large numbers. When considering the distribution of industrial sectors, the numbers of companies and mandates were six each in the mining industry and similarly 18 and 22 in the iron and steel industry; respectively, six each in the metal producing and processing industries; 10 each in the chemical industry; two each in the electrical industry; one each in the automobile industry; 15 each in the machine industry; four each in the oil industry; and four each in the distillation industry; six each in the distributing industry; six each in the banking industry; six and seven in the insurance industry, respectively; four and six in the electric power, gas, and energy industries, respectively; four each in the transportation industry; and 30 and 31 in other industries, respectively.

In 43 companies, the chairman position was observed by a member of the Essen/Dortmund/Duisburg regional advisory council who had a mandate for the supervisory board position. Each member of this advisory council had one mandate, bringing the total to 43. The number of such enterprises was seven in the iron and steel industry, three in the metal producing and processing industry, two in the chemical industry, one in the electrical industry, one in the automobile industry, seven in the machine industry, three in the oil industry, one in the distillation industry, three in the distribution industry, two in the insurance industry, one in the electric power, gas, and energy industries, and one in the transportation industry, and 11 in other industries.

Table 15.5 Supervisory board positions held by members of Deutsche Bank's Essen/Dormund/Duisburg regional advisory council (period at the late of the 1960s)

Industries	Position							
	Chairman		Vice-chairman		Supervisory board member excluding chairman and vice-chairman		Total[a]	
	Number of companies	Number of posts	Number of companies	Number of posts	Number of companies	Number of posts	Number of companies	Number of posts
Mining	–	–	1	1	5	5	6	6
Iron and steel	7	7	4	4	11	11	18	22
Metal producing and processing	3	3	1	1	2	2	6	6
Chemical	2	2	4	4	4	4	10	10
Electrical	1	1	–	–	1	1	2	2
Automobile	1	1	–	–	–	–	1	1
Machine	7	7	3	3	5	5	15	15
Oil	3	3	–	–	1	1	4	4
Distillation	1	1	1	1	2	2	4	4
Distributing	3	3	1	1	2	2	6	6
Banking	–	–	1	1	5	5	6	6
Insurance	2	2	1	1	4	4	6	7
Electric power, gas, and energy	1	1	1	1	2	4	4	6
Transportation	1	1	–	–	3	3	4	4

(continued)

Table 15.5 (continued)

Industries	Position							
	Chairman		Vice-chairman		Supervisory board member excluding chairman and vice-chairman		Total[a]	
	Number of companies	Number of posts	Number of companies	Number of posts	Number of companies	Number of posts	Number of companies	Number of posts
Other industries	11	11	4	4	16	16	30	31
All industries	43	43	22	22	63	65	122	130

[a] There are cases in which the total number of companies in which mandate was held differed from the total number of companies measured by each position of the supervisory board due to the existence of companies where more than two posts were held

Source This table was compiled by the author, based on Mossner (Hrsg) (1971) and Deutsche Bank AG (1967, 1968, 1969)

In 22 enterprises, vice-chairman mandates of supervisory board were held. Each member of this advisory council had one mandate, bringing the total to 22. The number of such enterprises was one in the mining industry, four in the iron and steel industry, one in the metal producing and processing industries, four in the chemical industry, three in the machine industry, one in the distillation industry, one in the distribution industry, one in the banking industry, one in the insurance industry, one in the electric power, gas, and energy industries, and four in others.

In all 63 enterprises members of this advisory council held the supervisory board mandate except for the chairman and vice-chairman. The number of mandates was 65. There were five such enterprises and mandates in the mining industry, 11 in the iron and steel industry, two in the metal production and processing industry, four in the chemical industry, one in the electrical industry, five in the machine industry, one in the oil industry, two in the distillation industry, two in the distributing industry, five in the banking industry, four in the insurance industry; two and four in the electric power, gas, and energy industries, respectively; three each in the transportation industry; and 16 each in other industries.

The Essen/Dortmund/Duisburg regional advisory council members occasionally held multiple mandates for the same enterprise. Such cases can be observed in seven enterprises, with 15 mandates. The iron and steel industry had three enterprises and seven mandates, the insurance industry had one and two, the electric power, gas, and energy industries had two and four, and the others had one and two. Three members of this regional advisory council held three mandates at Dortmund-Hörder Hüttenunion AG in the iron and steel industry: chairman, vice-chairman, and supervisory mandate (excluding chairman and vice-chairman). In the insurance industry, Feuerschaden-verband V.a.G. had two members, a chairman and a vice-chairman. In Westfälische Union AG für Eisen- und Drahtindustrie and Hüttewerke Siegerland AG in the iron and steel industry, and Rheinisch-Westfälische Kalkwerke AG in other industries, two members held the chairmanship and one supervisory board position excluding the chairman and vice-chairman, respectively. Two members held two supervisory board mandates in Ruhrgas AG and Steinkohlen-Elektrizität AG, except for chairman and vice-chairman, which operate in the electric power, gas, and energy industries.

There were numerous representative enterprises in each industry among the 122 enterprises where members of the Essen/Dortmund/Duisburg regional advisory council held the supervisory board mandate. Examples include Gelsenkirchener Bergwerks-AG and Bergwerksgesellschaft Hibernia AG in the mining industry, August Thyssen-Hütte AG, Gutehoffnunghütte Aktienverein, Rheinische Stahlwerke, Klöckner-Werke AG, and Dortmund-Hrder Hüttenunion AG in the iron and steel industry, and Deutsche Erdöl AG in the oil industry.

Next, the holding of mandates by Essen/Dortmund/Duisburg regional advisory council members on the enterprise's managing board is discussed. Such instances can be found in 25 companies. The total number of mandates was 27. There were six such enterprises and mandates in the mining industry, seven and nine in the iron and steel industries, one in the chemical industry, three in the machine industry, one in the food industry, one in the distillation industry, one in the distribution industry, one in the electric power, gas, and energy industries, and four in other industries.

Considering the holding situation in which members of the Essen/Dortmund/Duisburg regional advisory council held the position of managing board, those holding the chairman post can be observed in 15 companies, with a total of 15 mandates. Each member of this advisory council had one mandate. These companies included four in mining, four in iron and steel, two in machine, one in electric power, gas, and energy, and four in other industries. The vice-chairman's mandate was only observed by one iron and steel company. There were 11 enterprises and 11 mandates, with Essen/Dortmund/Duisburg regional advisory council members serving on the managing board except for the chairman and vice-chairman. Each member of this advisory council had one mandate. There were two such enterprises in the mining industry, five in the iron and steel industry, one in the chemical industry, one in the machine industry, one in the food industry, and one in the distillation industry.

The Essen/Dortmund/Duisburg regional advisory council members occasionally held multiple mandates for the same enterprise. Examples in the iron and steel industry include Hoesch AG and Hüttenwerk Oberhausen AG. In Hoesch AG, two members had a chairman mandate on the managing board and one mandate other than chairman and vice-chairman. In the Hüttenwerk Oberhausen AG, two posts of a vice-chairman and a post except for the chairman and vice-chairman of the managing board were held.

There were numerous representative enterprises in each industry among the 25 enterprises in which Essen/Dortmund/Duisburg regional advisory council members held managing board mandates. Such examples can be observed in enterprises such as Harpener Bergbau AG and Ruhrkohle AG in the mining industry, August Thyssen-Hütte AG, Hoesch AG, Klöckner-Werke AG, and Deutsche Edelstahlwerke AG in the iron and steel industry, Chemische Werke Hüls AG in the chemical industry, and DEMAG AG and Orenstein & Koppel AG in the machine industry.

In some cases, Württemberg regional advisory council members held mandates for both top management organs, such as the supervisory and managing boards. Members of this regional advisory held a supervisory board mandate and one managing board post at Thyssen-Hütte AG and Klöckner-Werke AG in the iron and steel industry, and Wasserwerk für das nördliche westfälische Kohlenrevier AG in other industries, respectively (Mossner 1971).

As a result, members of the Essen/Dortmund/Duisburg regional advisory council tended to hold many supervisory and managing board mandates. This figure was particularly high in the mining and heavy industries, including iron and steel, metal production and processing, and the machine industry. The regional advisory council members held top management organ mandates in many companies, particularly in the iron and steel industry. This reflected the state of industrial accumulation in this district.

15.2.2 Personnel Connection Between Enterprises Through Regional Advisory Council of Dresdner Bank

15.2.2.1 Members of Regional Advisory Council

Dresdner Bank's regional advisory council was described in its annual report for fiscal year 1967 as ten such organizations. There were a total of 296 members in these organizations. The regional advisory councils in Baden-Württemberg, Bayern, Bremen-Oanabrück, Hamburg/Schleswig-Holstein, Hannover-Braunschweig, and Hessen had 47, 29, 18, 30, 17, and 35 members, respectively. Similarly, the regional advisory councils for Rheinland, Rheinland-Pfalz, Saar, and Westfalen each had 58, 20, 9, and 33 members. All regional advisory council members were from enterprises other than Dresdner Bank. Each of these ten regional advisory councils had one chairman.

Taking into account the enterprises from which a person becomes a member of the regional advisory council in relation to the industry to which each enterprise belongs, members of the Baden-Württemberg regional advisory council came from industries such as metal production and processing, chemical, electrical, automobile, machine, textile, spinning, and woven goods, banking, and electric power, gas, and energy. Most companies in these industries were in the electrical, automobile, machine, textile, spinning and woven goods, and electric power, gas, and energy sectors. Brown, Boveri & Cie AG was a large company in the electrical industry, while Daimler-Benz AG was in the automobile industry. Although there were several enterprises in industries such as iron and steel; chemical; electrical; automobile; machine; precious machine and optical; textile, spinning, and woven goods; distillation; banking; insurance; and electric power, gas, and energy, the majority of the enterprises were in the electrical and machine industries. There were major companies in each industry, such as Siemens AG in electrical engineering and BMW in automobile manufacturing. Several companies from the iron and steel, machine, textile, spinning and weaving, and food industries were represented on the Bremen-Oanabrück regional advisory council. There were companies from each industrial sector, such as Klöckner-Werke AG in the iron and steel industry.

The Hamburg/Schleswig-Holstein regional advisory council included firms from the metal production and processing, chemical, electrical, shipbuilding, oil, insurance, and electric power, gas, and energy sectors. The majority of these companies were in the metal production and processing, chemical, oil, and shipbuilding industries. Large companies were involved in the affected industries, including Howaldtswerke-Deutsche Werft AG and Blohm & Voss AG in shipbuilding and Deutsche Erdöl AG, Esso AG, and BP Benzin und Petroleum AG in oil. The Hannover-Braunschweig regional advisory council members represented companies in industries such as mining, iron and steel, chemical, machine, oil, textile, spinning and woven goods, and electric power, gas, and energy. These companies included major companies in each industry, such as Salzgitter AG in the iron and steel sector. Members of the Hessen Regional Advisors represented companies in the iron and steel, metal producing and processing, chemical, machine, precious machine and optical, distribution, banking, and electric power, gas, and energy industries. Leading companies represented on this advisory council included Metallgesellschaft AG in the metal producing and processing industries and Adam Opel AG in the automotive industry.

The Rheinland regional advisory council included firms from the mining, iron and steel, metal production and processing, chemical, electrical, automobile, machine, distillation, distribution, banking, insurance, and electric power, gas, and energy sectors. The majority of these companies were in the iron and steel, metal production and processing, machine, distribution, and insurance industries. Large companies were in the major industry, such as Volkswagen AG in the automobile industry and Kaufhof AG in the distribution industry. The Rheinland-Pfalz regional advisory council included enterprises from industries such as iron and steel, machine, distillation, and banking. The Saar regional advisory council members represented companies in mining, iron and steel, distillation, and electric power, gas, and energy industries. Although the regional council of Westfalen had several enterprises in industries such as iron and steel, metal production and processing, chemical, textile, spinning and woven goods, distillation, and electric power, gas, and energy, the majority of the enterprises were in the iron and steel and metal production and processing industries. There were some prominent companies, such as Fried. Krupp Hüttenwerke AG operated in the iron and steel industry (Dresdner Bank AG 1967).

15.2.2.2 Holding of Mandates by Members of the Regional Advisory Council on Top Management Organs

These discussions show that the Dresdner Bank regional advisory council was made up of companies from various industries. This subsection explores the circumstances under which members of the regional advisory council were granted the authority of these top management organs. Although Dresdner Bank had several regional advisory councils, the Baden-Württemberg regional advisory council, the Rheinland regional advisory council, and the Westfalen regional advisory council were among the most important in Germany's key industry cluster.

Case of Baden-Württemberg Regional Advisory Council

First, when considering the mandates that members of the Baden-Württemberg regional advisory council held on the supervisory board (see Table 15.6), the total number of companies and mandates was 47. Regarding the distribution of industrial sectors, the numbers of companies and mandates were one each in the iron and steel industry, and similarly, one each in the metal producing and processing industries, three each in the chemical industry, 13 each in the electrical industry, three each in the automobile industry, one each in the machine industry, one each in the precious machine and optical industries, and one each in the textile, spinning, and woven goods industries; five each in the banking industry; two each in the insurance industry; seven each in the electric power, gas, and energy industries, and nine each in other industries. Each member of this advisory council had one mandate, respectively. There were no instances in which these regional advisory council members held dual mandates.

When considering a situation in which members of the Baden-Württemberg regional advisory council had a mandate for the supervisory board position, holding the honorary chairman post was one company in other industries, and the number of mandates was one. In eleven enterprises, the holding of the chairmanship can be observed. Each member of this advisory council had one mandate, for a total of eleven. There were two such enterprises in the electrical industry, one in the automobile industry, one in the banking industry, one in the insurance industry, four in the electric power, gas, and energy industries, and two in other industries.

Vice-chairman positions have been observed in nine enterprises. Each member of this advisory council had one mandate, bringing the total to nine. There was one such enterprise in the metal production and processing industries, one in the chemical industry, six in the electrical industry, and one in the automobile industry.

Except for the chairman and vice-chairman, 26 enterprises held a supervisory board mandate. Each member of this advisory council had one mandate, bringing the total to 26. The number of such enterprises was one in the iron and steel industry, two in the chemical industry, five in the electrical industry, one in the automobile industry, one in the machine industry, one in the precious machine and optical industries, one in the textile, spinning, and woven goods industries, four in the banking industry, one in the insurance industry, three in the electric power, gas, and energy industries, and six in others. There were prominent companies in each industry, such as Fried. Krupp GmbH producing iron and steel, while Bayer AG manufacturing chemicals.

The next consideration is whether Baden-Württemberg regional advisory council members hold mandates on an enterprise's management board. Such cases can be observed in 17 enterprises. Each member of this advisory council had one mandate, respectively. Thus, the total number of mandates was 17. There were three such enterprises in the chemical industry, one in the electrical industry, four in the automobile industry, one in the textile, spinning, and woven goods industry, one in the banking industry, three in the electric power, gas, and energy industries, and four in other industries.

Considering the holding situation in which members of the Baden-Württemberg regional advisory council held the post of managing board in relation to their position, those holding the chairman position can be observed in four companies, with a total of four mandates. There was one such enterprise in the automobile industry, one in the textile, spinning, and woven goods industries, and two in other industries. There were major companies in each industry, such as Audi NSU AUTO UNION AG in the automobile industry. In one case, the Baden-Württemberg regional advisory council members held the position of vice-chairman. This enterprise was called Brown, Boveri & Cie. AG in the electric industry. Except for the chairman and vice-chairman, the Baden-Württemberg regional advisory council members served on the managing boards of ten enterprises. Each member of this advisory council had one mandate,

Table 15.6 Supervisory board positions held by members of Dresdner Bank's Baden-Württemberg regional advisory council (period at the late of the 1960s)

Industries	Position									
	Honorary chairman		Chairman		Vice-chairman		Supervisory board member excluding chairman and vice-chairman		Total	
	Number of companies	Number of posts	Number of companies	Number of posts	Number of companies	Number of posts	Number of companies	Number of posts	Number of companies	Number of posts
Iron and steel	–	–	–	–	–	–	1	1	1	1
Metal producing and processing	–	–	–	–	1	1	–	–	1	1
Chemical	–	–	–	–	1	1	2	2	3	3
Electrical	–	–	2	2	6	6	5	5	13	13
Automobile	–	–	1	1	1	1	1	1	3	3
Machine	–	–	–	–	–	–	1	1	1	1
Precious machine and optical	–	–	–	–	–	–	1	1	1	1
Textile, spinning, and woven goods	–	–	–	–	–	–	1	1	1	1
Banking	–	–	1	1	–	–	4	4	5	5
Insurance	–	–	1	1	–	–	1	1	2	2

(continued)

Table 15.6 (continued)

Industries	Position									
	Honorary chairman		Chairman		Vice-chairman		Supervisory board member excluding chairman and vice-chairman		Total	
	Number of companies	Number of posts	Number of companies	Number of posts	Number of companies	Number of posts	Number of companies	Number of posts	Number of companies	Number of posts
Electric power, gas, and energy	–	–	4	4	–	–	3	3	7	7
Other industries	1	1	2	2	–	–	6	6	9	9
All industries	1	1	11	11	9	9	26	26	47	47

Source This table was compiled by the author, based on Mossner (Hrsg) (1971) and Dresdner Bank AG (1967, 1968, 1969)

respectively. Thus, the total number of mandates was ten. There were three such enterprises in the chemical industry, three in the automobile industry, one in the banking industry, one in the electric power, gas, and energy industries, and two in other industries. There were companies from each industrial sector, including Daimler-Benz AG and Deutsche Fiat AG in the automobile industry. The Baden-Württemberg regional advisory council members held a deputy management board mandate in two enterprises. These companies were in the electric power, gas, and energy industries. Each member of this advisory council had one mandate, respectively. Thus, the total number of mandates was two (Mossner 1971).

The conditions of the supervisory and managing board mandates by members of the Baden-Württemberg regional advisory council were fairly common in the automobile industry. This reflected the state of industrial accumulation in this district.

Case of Rheinland Regional Advisory Council

Next, this subsection considers the mandates that members of the Rheinland regional advisory council had on the supervisory board (see Table 15.7). In such cases, the number of companies totaled 59, and the total number of mandates was 61. When considering the distribution of industrial sectors, the numbers of companies and mandates were three each in the mining industry, and similarly, seven each in the iron and steel industry, one each in the metal producing and processing industries, six each in the chemical industry, two each in the electrical industry; one each in the automobile industry, six each in the machine industry; one each in the oil industry; one each in the distillation industry; two each in the distributing industry, six and eight in the banking industry; respectively, 12 each in the insurance industry; one each in the electric power, gas, and energy industries, two each in the transportation industry, and eight each in other industries. There were many firms and mandates in industries such as banking, insurance, iron and steel, chemicals, and machinery.

When examining a situation in which members of the Rheinland regional advisory council had a mandate in relation to the supervisory board's position, holding the honorary chairman post was one company in the chemical industry, with only one mandate. Fourteen enterprises observe the chairman's mandate. Each member of this advisory council had one mandate, for a total of fourteen. There were two such enterprises in the mining industry, one in the iron and steel industry, one in the metal producing and processing industry, two in the chemical industry, two in the machine industry, one in the oil industry, one in the banking industry, three in the insurance industry, and one in other industries.

Holding of mandate of vice-chairman was observed in nine enterprises. Each member of this advisory council had one mandate, bringing the total to nine. There were two such enterprises in the iron and steel industry, two in banking, three in insurance, and two in other sectors.

Besides the chairman and vice-chairman, 36 enterprises have cases of holding supervisory board positions, for 37 mandates. The numbers of such enterprises and mandates, respectively, were one each in the mining industry; four each in the iron

Table 15.7 Supervisory board positions held by members of Dresdner Bank's Rheinland regional advisory council (period at the late of the 1960s)

Industries	Position									
	Honorary chairman		Chairman		Vice-chairman		Supervisory board member excluding chairman and vice-chairman		Total[a]	
	Number of companies	Number of posts	Number of companies	Number of posts	Number of companies	Number of posts	Number of companies	Number of posts	Number of companies	Number of posts
Mining	–	–	2	2	–	–	1	1	3	3
Iron and steel	–	–	1	1	2	2	4	4	7	7
Metal producing and processing	–	–	1	1	–	–	–	–	1	1
Chemical	1	1	2	2	–	–	3	3	6	6
Electrical	–	–	–	–	–	–	2	2	2	2
Automobile	–	–	–	–	–	–	1	1	1	1
Machine	–	–	2	2	–	–	4	4	6	6
Oil	–	–	1	1	–	–	–	–	1	1
Distillation	–	–	–	–	–	–	1	1	1	1
Distributing	–	–	–	–	–	–	2	2	2	2
Banking	–	–	1	1	2	2	4	5	6	8
Insurance	–	–	3	3	3	3	6	6	12	12
Electric power, gas, and energy	–	–	–	–	–	–	1	1	1	1
Transportation	–	–	–	–	–	–	2	2	2	2

(continued)

Table 15.7 (continued)

Industries	Position									
	Honorary chairman		Chairman		Vice-chairman		Supervisory board member excluding chairman and vice-chairman		Total[a]	
	Number of companies	Number of posts	Number of companies	Number of posts	Number of companies	Number of posts	Number of companies	Number of posts	Number of companies	Number of posts
Other industries	–	–	1	1	2	2	5	5	8	8
All industries	1	1	14	14	9	9	36	37	59	61

[a] There are cases in which the total number of enterprises in which mandate was held differed from the sum of the numbers of company measured by each position of the supervisory board due to the existence of companies where more than two posts were held

Source This table was complied by the author, based on Mossner (Hrsg) (1971), and Dresdner Bank AG (1967, 1968, 1969)

and steel industry; three each in the chemical industry; two each in the electrical industry; one each in the automobile industry; four each in the machine industry; one each in the distillation industry; two each in the distributing industry; four and five in the banking industry; six each in the insurance industry; one each in the electric power, gas, and energy industries; two each in the transportation industry; and five each in other industries. Large companies were represented in each industry, including Preuβag AG in mining, Salzgitter AG in iron and steel, and VEBA AG in electrical, gas, and energy. In the automobile industry, there were some representative foreign capital companies, such as Deutsche Fiat AG.

Two enterprises demonstrate the situation in which Rheinland regional advisory council members held multiple supervisory board mandates. In Deutsche Industriebank, members of this regional advisory council held the position of vice-chairman and one supervisory board mandate, excluding the chairman and vice-chairman. In Deutsche Unionbank in the banking industry, members of this advisory board held two supervisory board posts, excluding the chairman and vice-chairman.

Next, members of the Rheinland regional advisory council's mandates on the enterprise's managing board are considered. Such instances can be observed in 35 companies. Each member of this advisory council had one mandate, respectively. Thus, the total number of mandates was 35. There were four such enterprises in the mining industry, four in the iron and steel industry, two in the metal producing and processing industries, five in the chemical industry, one in the electrical industry, one in the automobile industry, one in the machine industry, one in the distribution industry, two in the banking industry, ten in the insurance industry, two in the electric power, gas, and energy industries, and two in other industries. There were numerous companies in the insurance industry.

Considering the holding situation in which members of the Rheinland regional advisory council held the post of managing board in relation to their position, those holding the chairman position can be observed in 14 companies. Each member of this advisory council had one mandate, respectively. Thus, the total number of mandates was 14. These enterprises included one in the mining industry, one in the iron and steel industry, two in metal production and processing, nine in insurance, and one in other industries. Except for the chairman and vice-chairman, the Rheinland regional advisory council members served on the management boards of 20 companies. Each member of this advisory council had one mandate, respectively. Thus, the total number of mandates was 20. There were three such enterprises in the mining industry, three in the iron and steel industry, five in the chemical industry, one in the electrical industry, one in the automobile industry, one in the machine industry, one in the distribution industry, two in the banking industry, one in the insurance industry, one in the electric power, gas, and energy industries, and one in other industries. There were companies representing each industrial sector, such as Volkswagen AG in the automobile industry and Kaufhof AG in the distribution industry. In one enterprise, the Rheinland regional advisory council members served as the managing board's deputies. This enterprise was Rheinisch-Westfälisches Elektrizitätswerk AG in the electric power, gas, and energy industries and one of the most representative enterprises in this industrial sector (Mossner 1971).

Members of the Rheinland regional advisory council held supervisory and managing board mandates in a number of industries, including mining, iron and steel, insurance, and chemicals. This reflected the state of industrial accumulation in this district.

Case of the Westfalen Regional Advisory Council

Furthermore, when considering the mandates that members of the Westfalen regional advisory council held on the supervisory board (see Table 15.8), the total number of companies and mandates was 28. Looking at the distribution of industrial sectors, there were three companies and mandates in the mining sector, one in the iron and steel industry, three in the chemical industry, nine in the machine industry, two in the distillation industry, one in the banking industry, two in the electric power, gas, and energy industries, and seven in the other industries. There were numerous enterprises and mandates in the machine industry.

When considering a situation in which members of the Westfalen regional advisory council had a mandate regarding the supervisory board position, four companies held the chairmanship. Each member of this advisory council had one mandate, bringing the total to four. There were two such companies in the machine industry, one in the distillation industry, and one in the electric power, gas, and energy industries.

The vice-chairman's mandate is observed in six enterprises. Each member of this advisory council had one mandate, bringing the total to six. There was one such enterprise in the mining industry, two in the machine industry, one in the distillation industry, one in the electric power, gas, and energy industries, and one in other industries.

Except for the chairman and vice-chairman, there are cases of holding supervisory board positions in 18 enterprises. Each member of this advisory council had one mandate, bringing the total to 18. The mining industry had two such enterprises and mandates. The iron and steel industry had one, the chemical industry had three, the machine industry had five, the banking industry had one, and the other industries had six.

Next, the holding of mandates by Westfalen regional advisory council members on the company's management board is considered. Such cases can be observed in ten enterprises. Each member of this advisory council had one mandate, respectively. Thus, the total number of mandates was ten. There were two such enterprises in the iron and steel industry, one in the metal producing and processing industries, one in the chemical industry, one in the machine industry, one in the food industry, two in the distribution industry, and two in the electric power, gas, and energy industries.

When considering the holding situation in which members of the Westfalen regional advisory council held the post of managing board in relation to their position, the case of holding the chairman post was one company in the machine industry, with one mandate. There were two enterprises where Westfalen regional advisory council members served as vice-chairmen. These enterprises were Fried. Krupp GmbH in the iron and steel industry and a company in the food industry. Except for the chairman

Table 15.8 Supervisory board positions held by members of Dresdner Bank's Westfalen regional advisory council (period at the late of the 1960s)

Industries	Position							
	Chairman		Vice-chairman		Supervisory board member excluding chairman and vice-chairman		Total	
	Number of companies	Number of posts	Number of companies	Number of posts	Number of companies	Number of posts	Number of companies	Number of posts
Mining	–	–	1	1	2	2	3	3
Iron and steel	–	–	–	–	1	1	1	1
Chemical	–	–	–	–	3	3	3	3
Machine	2	2	2	2	5	5	9	9
Distillation	1	1	1	1	–	–	2	2
Banking	–	–	–	–	1	1	1	1
Electric power, gas, and energy	1	1	1	1	–	–	2	2
Other industries	–	–	1	1	6	6	7	7
All industries	4	4	6	6	18	18	28	28

Source This table was compiled by the author, based on Mossner (Hrsg) (1971) and Dresdner Bank AG (1967, 1968, 1969)

and vice-chairman, the regional advisory council members served on the managing boards of seven companies. Each member of this advisory council had one mandate, respectively. Thus, the total number of mandates was seven. The number of such enterprises was one in the iron and steel industry; one in the metal producing and processing industries; one in the chemical industry; two in the distribution industry; and two in the electric power, gas, and energy industries (Mossner 1971).

As a result, the conditions of the supervisory and managing board mandates by members of the Westfalen regional advisory council were relatively common in industrial sectors such as mining, iron and steel, and machine manufacturing. This was related to the region's industrial accumulation.

15.2.3 Personnel Connection Between Enterprises Through Regional Advisory Council of Commerzbank Bank

15.2.3.1 Members of Regional Advisory Council

In the annual report for fiscal year 1967, Commerzbank Bank described ten regional advisory councils. These organizations had a total membership of 243. The regional advisory councils in Baden-Württemberg, Bayern, Bremen, Hamburg, and Hessen had 24, 19, 7, 17, and 26 members, respectively. Similarly, the regional advisory councils for Niedersachsen, Nordrhein–Westfalen, Rheinland-Pfalz, Saar, and Schleswig-Holstein each had 36, 93, 10, two, and nine members. The Nordrhein–Westfalen regional advisory council had a large number of members. It was almost identical to the sum of the numbers of the Rheinland regional advisory council (58) and the Westfalen regional advisory council (33).

Taking into account the enterprises from which a person becomes a member of the regional advisory council in relation to the industry to which each enterprise belongs, the Baden-Württemberg regional advisory council had members from industries such as iron and steel, chemical, electrical, automobile, machine, banking, insurance, and electric power, gas, and energy. The majority of these companies were in the automobile, machine, and electrical industries, reflecting the district's industrial accumulation. Large companies represented each industry, such as Daimler-Benz AG and Porsche KG in the automobile industry and Brown, Boveri & Cie. AG in the electrical industry. Although there were several enterprises in industries such as iron and steel, chemical, electrical, machine, and insurance, the majority of the companies were in the electrical industry. There were major companies in each industry, such as Siemens AG in the electrical sector. Although several companies from the chemical, oil, distillation, electric power, gas and energy, and transportation industries were represented on the Hamburg regional advisory council, there were a large number of oil companies. There were companies from each industrial sector, including Deutsche Shell AG and Esso AG in the oil industry.

The Hessen regional advisory council included companies from the mining, iron and steel, chemical, electrical, machine, precious machine, optical, oil, and distillation industries. Most of these companies were in the iron, steel, chemical, and machine industries. Although there were members of companies in industries such as mining, iron and steel, chemical, machine, oil, textile, spinning, and woven goods, insurance, and transportation, the majority of companies were in the iron and steel, mining, and machine industries. These companies included major companies in each industry, such as Klöckner-Werke AG in the iron and steel industry. Although there were members of companies in industries such as mining, iron and steel, metal production and processing, chemical, machine, food, textile, spinning and woven goods, distillation, distribution, banking, insurance, and electric power, gas, and energy industries, the majority of the companies belonged to the chemical, machine, and textile, spinning and woven goods industries, as well as the mining industry and iron and steel industry. Leading companies on this advisory council included Harpener Bergbau AG in mining, Klöckner-Werke AG and Dortmunder-Hörder Hüttenunion AG in iron and steel, Bayer AG and Agfa AG in chemical, and Kaufhof AG in distribution industry. Although there were firms in industries such as machine, distillation, and electric power, gas, and energy, most of the companies in the Rheinland-Pfalz regional advisory council were chemical. The Saar regional advisory council included enterprises from industries such as mining and distillation. The Schleswig-Holstein regional advisory council included firms from the chemical, shipbuilding, textile, spinning and woven goods, and food industries (Commerzbank AG 1967, S. 69–77).

15.2.3.2 Holding of Mandates by Members of the Regional Advisory Council on Top Management Organs

These discussions show that the Commerzbank regional advisory council comprised enterprises from various industries. This subsection explores the circumstances under which members of the regional advisory council were granted the authority of these top management organs. Although Commerzbank had several regional advisory councils, the Baden-Württemberg regional advisory council and the Nordrhein–Westfalen regional advisory council were two of the most important advisory councils in the region where Germany's key industries are concentrated.

Case of Baden-Württemberg Regional Advisory Council

First, when considering the mandates that members of the Baden-Württemberg regional advisory council held on the supervisory board (see Table 15.9), in such cases the number of companies totaled to 34 and the total number of companies and mandates was 34. Considering the distribution of industrial sectors, the numbers of companies and mandates were one each in the mining industry and, similarly, one each in the iron and steel industry; four each in the metal production and processing industries; one each in the chemical industry; four each in the electrical industry; two each in the automobile industry; four each in the machine industry; one each in the textile, spinning, and woven goods industries; one each in the distributing industry; four each in the banking industry; one each in the electric power, gas, and energy industries, and ten each in other industries. In each company, the number of mandates was one.

When considering a situation in which members of the Baden-Württemberg regional advisory council held a supervisory board position, in 11 enterprises members of this advisory council had the chairman mandate. Each member of this advisory council had one mandate, for a total of eleven. There were three such enterprises in the metal manufacturing and processing industries, two in the electrical industry, three in the machine industry, two in the banking industry, and one in other industries.

The holding of the vice-chairman mandate was observed in eight enterprises. Each member of this advisory council had one mandate, bringing the total to eight. There were two such enterprises in the electrical industry, one in the textile, spinning, and woven goods industry, one in the electric power, gas, and energy industry, and four in other industries.

In 15 enterprises, supervisory board positions other than chairman and vice-chairman were held. Each member of this advisory council had one mandate, for a total of fifteen. The mining industry had one such enterprise and mandate, as did the iron and steel industry, the metal producing and processing industries, the chemical industry, the machine industry, and the distribution industry. The automobile industry and the banking industry had two enterprises and mandates, respectively, and other industries had five enterprises and mandates.

Furthermore, members of the Baden-Württemberg regional advisory council's mandates on an enterprise's management board are considered. Such instances can be observed in 15 companies. Each member of this advisory council had one mandate, respectively. Thus, the total number of mandates was 15. There was one such enterprise in the metal production and processing industries, one in the chemical industry, three in the electrical industry, three in the automobile industry, two in the machine industry, one in the banking industry, one in the electric power, gas, and energy industries, and three in other industries.

Considering the holding situation in which members of the Baden-Württemberg regional advisory council held the position of managing board, those holding the chairman post can be observed in five companies, with a total of five mandates. There was one such enterprise in the chemical industry, one in the electrical industry, one in the machine industry, one in the banking industry, and one in other industries. In one case, the Baden-Württemberg regional advisory council members held the position of vice-chairman. Such a case was an electrical enterprise. Except for the chairman and vice-chairman, members of the Baden-Württemberg regional advisory council served on the management boards of nine enterprises. Each member of this advisory council had one mandate, respectively. Thus, the total number of mandates was nine. There was one such enterprise in the metal production and processing industries, one in the electrical industry, three in the automobile industry, one in the

Table 15.9 Supervisory board positions held by members of Commerzbank's Baden-Württemberg regional advisory council (period at the late of the 1960s)

Industries	Position							
	Chairman		Vice-chairman		Supervisory board member excluding chairman and vice-chairman		Total	
	Number of companies	Number of posts	Number of companies	Number of posts	Number of companies	Number of posts	Number of companies	Number of posts
Mining	–	–	–	–	1	1	1	1
Iron and steel	–	–	–	–	1	1	1	1
Metal producing and processing	3	3	–	–	1	1	4	4
Chemical	–	–	–	–	1	1	1	1
Electrical	2	2	2	2	–	–	4	4
Automobile	–	–	–	–	2	2	2	2
Machine	3	3	–	–	1	1	4	4
Textile, spinning, and woven goods	–	–	1	1	–	–	1	1
Distributing	–	–	–	–	1	1	1	1
Banking	2	2	–	–	2	2	4	4
Electric power, gas, and energy	–	–	1	1	–	–	1	1
Other industries	1	1	4	4	5	5	10	10
All industries	11	11	8	8	15	15	34	34

Source This table was compiled by the author, based on Mossner (Hrsg) (1971) and Commerzbank AG (1967, 1968, 1969)

machine industry, one in the electric power, gas, and energy industries, and two in other industries. There were representative companies in each industrial sector, such as Brown, Boveri & Cie AG in the electrical industry and Daimler-Benz AG in the automobile industry (Mossner 1971).

Case of the Nordrhein–Westfalen Regional Advisory Council

Next, considering the mandates that members of the Nordrhein–Westfalen regional advisory council held on the supervisory board (see Table 15.10), the total number of companies and mandates was 56. Looking at the distribution of industrial sectors, the numbers of companies and mandates were three each in the mining industry, and similarly, seven each in the iron and steel industry, one each in the metal producing and processing industries, nine each in the chemical industry, two each in the electrical industry, three each in the machine industry, two each in the textile, spinning, and woven goods industries, five each in the distillation industry, and two each in the distributing industry; two each in the banking industry; three each in the insurance industry; one each in the transportation industry, and 16 each in other industries. Each member of this advisory council had one mandate, respectively. There were numerous companies in both the iron and steel and chemical industries.

When considering a situation in which members of the Nordrhein–Westfalen regional advisory council had a mandate regarding the position of the supervisory board, the case of holding the chairman mandate can be observed in 12 enterprises. Each member of this advisory council had one mandate, for a total of twelve. The number of such enterprises was one in the metal producing and processing industries, two in the chemical industry, one in the electrical industry, one in the machine industry, one in the textile, spinning, and woven goods industries, one in the distillation industry, one in the insurance industry, and four in other industries.

Holding the vice-chairman's mandate was observed in 11 enterprises. Each member of this advisory council had one mandate, for a total of eleven. There was one such enterprise in the mining industry, three in the chemical industry, one in the electrical industry, one in the textile, spinning, and woven goods industry, two in the distillation industry, one in the distribution industry, and two in other industries.

A supervisory board position, excluding the chairman and vice-chairman, can be found in 33 enterprises. Each member of this advisory council had one mandate, bringing the total to 33. The mining industry had two such enterprises and mandates, as did the iron and steel industry, which had seven; the chemical industry had four; the machine industry had two; the distillation industry had two; the distribution industry had one; the banking industry had two; the insurance industry had two; the transportation industry had one; and the other industries had ten.

In contrast, the presence of members of the Nordrhein–Westfalen regional advisory council on an enterprise's managing board is considered. Such cases can be observed in 27 enterprises. Each member of this advisory council had one mandate, respectively. Thus, the total number of mandates was 27. There was one such enterprise in the mining industry, two in the iron and steel industry, one in the metal

Table 15.10 Supervisory board positions held by members of Commerzbank's Nordrhein–Westfalen regional advisory council (period at the late of the 1960s)

Industries	Position							
	Chairman		Vice-chairman		Supervisory board member excluding chairman and vice-chairman		Total	
	Number of companies	Number of posts	Number of companies	Number of posts	Number of companies	Number of posts	Number of companies	Number of posts
Mining	–	–	1	1	2	2	3	3
Iron and steel	–	–	–	–	7	7	7	7
Metal producing and processing	1	1	–	–	–	–	1	1
Chemical	2	2	3	3	4	4	9	9
Electrical	1	1	1	1	–	–	2	2
Machine	1	1	–	–	2	2	3	3
Textile, spinning, and woven goods	1	1	1	1	–	–	2	2
Distillation	1	1	2	2	2	2	5	5
Distributing	–	–	1	1	1	1	2	2
Banking	–	–	–	–	2	2	2	2
Insurance	1	1	–	–	2	2	3	3
Transportation	–	–	–	–	1	1	1	1
Other industries	4	4	2	2	10	10	16	16
All industries	12	12	11	11	33	33	56	56

Source This table was compiled by the author, based on Mossner (Hrsg) (1971) and Commerzbank AG (1967, 1968, 1969)

producing and processing industries, six in the chemical industry, one in the textile, spinning, and woven goods industry, two in the distillation industry, one in the distribution industry, one in the banking industry, four in the insurance industry, two in the electric power, gas, and energy industries, and six in other industries.

Considering the holding situation in which members of the Nordrhein–Westfalen regional advisory council held the post of managing board in relation to their position, those holding chairman positions can be observed in eight companies, with a total of eight mandates. These enterprises included three in the chemical industry, one in textile, spinning, and woven goods, one in distillation, two in electric power, gas, and energy, and one in other industries. Except for the chairman and vice-chairman, Nordrhein–Westfalen regional advisory council members served on the management boards of 19 enterprises. Each member of this advisory council had one mandate, respectively. Thus, the total number of mandates was 19. There was one such enterprise in the mining industry, two in the iron and steel industry, one in the metal producing and processing industries, three in the chemical industry, one in the distillation industry, one in the distribution industry, one in the banking industry, four in the insurance industry, and five in other industries. There were representative companies in each industrial sector, such as Dortmund-Hörder Hüttenunion AG and Otto Wolff AG in the iron and steel industry, Hoechst AG, Ruhrchemie AG, Agfa AG, and Knapsack AG in the chemical industry, and Kaufhof AG in the distributing industry (Mossner 1971).

As a result, members of the Nordrhein–Westfalen regional advisory council held a significant number of supervisory and managing board mandates in industrial sectors such as the iron and steel and chemical industries. The fact that members of this regional advisory council held numerous mandates on top management bodies of enterprises in the iron and steel industry reflected industrial accumulation in this region.

15.2.4 Holding of Mandates of Top Management Organs in Same Enterprise by Members of Regional Advisory Councils of Three Large Banks

This section examines situations in which members of regional advisory councils of three large banks or two of them in the same region held top management positions, such as supervisory and management boards.

Members of the Baden-Württemberg regional advisory councils of Dresdner Bank and Commerzbank had observed supervisory board mandates in the same enterprise, as seen in Bausparkasse Gemeinschaft der Freunde Wüstenrot gemeinnützige GmbH in the banking industry and Hausbau Wüstenrot gemeinnützige GmbH in other industries. Although each member of the advisory councils of Dresdner Bank and Commerzbank held a chairman's mandate of Bausparkasse Gemeinschaft der Freunde Wüstenrot gemeinnützige GmbH, such members were the same. In

Hausbau Wüstenrot gemeinnützige GmbH, while the member of Dresdner Bank's regional advisory council served as chairman, the member of Commerzbank's such a committee held one position on the supervisory board, aside from the chairman and vice-chairman.

Salamander AG in other industries was an example of an enterprise where members of the Württemberg regional advisory council of Deutsch Bank and the Baden-Württemberg regional advisory councils of Dresdner Bank and Commerzbank held managing board mandates. Except for the chairman and vice-chairman, each member of the three banks' regional advisory councils was appointed by the managing board. In the automobile industry, members of the Württemberg regional advisory council of Deutsch Bank and the Baden-Württemberg regional advisory councils of Dresdner Bank held managing board mandates for the same enterprise. In Deutsche Fiat AG, a member of Deutsche Bank's regional advisory council held the position of chairman, whereas a member of Dresdner Bank's committee organization held the mandate of the managing board, excluding the chairman and vice-chairman. In one case, members of the Württemberg regional advisory council of Deutsch Bank and the Baden-Württemberg regional advisory council of Commerzbank held positions in the same enterprise. In the electrical industry, one such case was Standard Elektrik Lorenz AG. In this enterprise, a member of Commerzbank's regional advisory council held the position of chairman, and a member of a similar organization of Deutsche Bank held the position of managing director, with the exception of chairman and vice-chairman. In three cases, members of the Baden-Württemberg regional advisory councils of Dresdner Bank and Commerzbank held management board positions at the same enterprise. Such cases can be observed in Brown, Boveri & Cie. AG in the electrical industry, Daimler-Benz AG in the automobile industry, and Groβkraftwerk Mannheim AG in the electric power, gas, and energy sectors. In Brown, Boveri, and Cie. AG, whereas a member of Dresdner Bank's regional advisory council held the position of vice-chairman, a member of Commerzbank's similar organization held only one management board position other than chairman and vice-chairman. In Daimler-Benz AG and Groβkraftwerk Mannheim, regional advisory council members held management board mandates, except for the chairman and vice-chairman.

Regional advisory councils in the Rhein–Westfalen district included Dresdner Bank's Rheinland and Westfalen regional advisory councils, as well as Commerzbank's Nordrhein–Westfalen regional advisory council. In contrast, Deutsche Bank had regional advisory councils such as the Essen/Dortmund/Duisburg, Düsseldorf/Krefeld, Köln/Aachen/Siegen, and Wuppertal/Bielefeld/Münster regional advisory council in the Rhein–Westfalen district. Members of Deutsche Bank's Essen/Dordmund/Duisburg regional advisory council, Dresdner Bank's Rheinland and Westfalen regional advisory council, and Commerzbank's Nordrhein–Westfalen regional advisory council all had mandates from the same enterprise.

In three cases, members of the regional advisory councils of three large banks held supervisory board mandates for the same enterprise. Such cases included

Neunkircher Eisenwerk AG. Gebrüder Stumm in the iron and steel industry, Nitrochemie GmbH in the chemical industry, and Rheinisch-Westfälische Kalkwerke AG in other industries. In Rheinisch-Westfälische Kalkwerke AG, whereas two members of Deutsche Bank's regional advisory council held the positions of chairman and supervisory board mandate excluding chairman and vice-chairman, a member of Commerzbank AG's committee organization held the position of vice-chairman. In contrast, a Dresdner Bank's Rheinland regional advisory council member held one position on the supervisory board, aside from chairman and vice-chairman. In Nitrochemie GmbH, a Commerzbank regional advisory council member held the position of vice-chairman and members of similar organizations from the other two banks held positions on the supervisory board other than chairman and vice-chairman. In Neunkircher Eisenwerk AG vorm. Gebrüder Stumm, each member of the regional advisory councils of three large banks held a supervisory board mandate, respectively. The Dresdner Bank regional advisory council member also served on the Rheinland regional advisory council.

In seven cases, members of Deutsche Bank AG's Essen/Dortmund/Duisburg regional advisory council and Dresdner Bank AG's Rheinland and Westfalen regional advisory council had the same company's supervisory board mandate. Such cases can be observed in Hilgers AG and Hein, Lehmann & CO in the iron and steel, Deutsche Unionbank GmbH is in banking, Seerederei Frigga AG is in transportation, and Westdeutsche Wohnhäuser AG, Rheinische Wohnstätten AG, and Dolomitwerke GmbH are in other sectors. Two members of the same bank's regional advisory council held company mandates in two of these seven enterprises. In Westdeutsche Wohnhäuser AG, while a member of the Rheinland regional advisory council of Dresdner Bank had a mandate as chairman, each member of the Westfalen regional advisory council of this bank and the Essen/Dortmund/Duisburg regional advisory council of Deutsche Bank had one post of the supervisory board, except for the chairman and vice-chairman. In Deutsche Unionbank GmbH, two members of Dresdner Bank's Rheinland regional advisory council and one member of Deutsche Bank's Essen/Dortmund/Duisburg regional advisory council each held one supervisory board position, with the exception of chairman and vice-chairman. In the remaining five companies, each member of the regional advisory councils of two banks had a single mandate. In Hilgers AG, a member of the regional advisory council of Deutsche Bank held the position of chairman, while a member of the Rheinland regional advisory council of Dresdner Bank held the position of vice-chairman. In Hein, Lehmann & CO AG, a member of Dresdner Bank's Rheinland regional advisory council held one position of chairman, while a member of Deutsche Bank's regional advisory council held a supervisory board mandate except for the chairman and vice-chairman. In Rheinische Wohnstätten AG, while a member of Deutsche Bank's regional advisory council held the position of vice-chairman, a member of Dresdner Bank's Rheinland regional advisory council held one supervisory board position other than chairman and vice-chairman. In Seerederei Frigga AG and Dolomitwerke GmbHs, each member of regional advisory councils of two largest banks had one supervisory board mandate, except for the chairman and vice-chairman.

In two cases, members of Deutsche Bank AG and Commerzbank's regional advisory councils held supervisory board mandates for the same enterprise. Examples include Schwerter Profileisenwalzwerke AG in the iron and steel industry and Dortmunder Union-Brauerei AG in the distillation industry. While a member of Deutsche Bank's regional advisory council held the position of chairman, a member of Commerzbank's similar organization held the position of supervisory board member, except for chairman and vice-chairman.

There was only one case where members of Dresdner Bank and Commerzbank's regional advisory councils held supervisory board mandates for the same company. Eisenwerk Weserhütte AG, an iron and steel company, is one such example. While each member of Dresdner Bank's Rheinland regional advisory council held the company of vice-chairman, members of this bank's Westfalen regional advisory council and Commerzbank's Nordrhein–Westfalen regional advisory council held supervisory board positions other than chairman and vice-chairman.

Let us consider the conditions under which members of Deutsche Bank's Essen/Dordmund/Duisburg regional advisory council, Dresdner Bank's Rheinland and Westfalen regional advisory council, and Commerzbank's Nordrhein–Westfalen regional advisory council held managing board mandates for the same enterprise. Each member of Deutsche Bank and Dresdner Bank's regional advisory councils had a mandate from the managing board of the same enterprise, which was Deutsche Edelstahlwerke AG in the iron and steel industry. Each member of Deutsche Bank's Essen/Dordmund/Duisburg regional advisory council and Dresdner Bank's Rheinland regional advisory council served as chairman in this enterprise. There was only one enterprise in which each member of Deutsche Bank and Commerzbank's regional advisory councils had a mandate from the same company. This case involved Vereinigte Elektrizitätswerke Westfalen AG, which operated in the electric power, gas, and energy industries. In this enterprise, each member of the committee organization of two banks held one position as chairman of the management board. There were six enterprises in which each member of Dresdner Bank's and Commerzbank's regional advisory councils served on the same company's management board. Otto Wolff AG was an iron and steel company; Ruhrchemie AG was a chemical company; Kaufhof AG was a distribution company; and Victoria Lebens-Versicherung AG, Victoria Feuer-Versicherung AG, and Victoria Rückversicherung AG were insurance enterprises. In Victoria Lebens-Versicherung AG, Victoria Feuer-Versicherung AG, and Victoria Rückversicherung AG, a member of Dresdner Bank's Rheinland regional advisory council held the position of chairman. In contrast, a member of Commerzbank's Nordrhein–Westfalen regional advisory council held one managing board position other than chairman and vice-chairman. In Ruhrchemie AG, while a member of Commerzbank AG's regional advisory council held the position of chairman, a member of Dresdner Bank's Rheinland regional advisory council held the position of managing director, except for chairman and vice-chairman. Meanwhile, in Otto Wolff AG and Kaufhof AG, each member of Dresdner Bank's Rheinland regional advisory council and Commerzbank's Nordrhein–Westfalen regional advisory council held one managing board position, with the exception of chairman and vice-chairman.

In this chapter on the connection of personnel through the bank's advisory council system composed of central and regional advisory councils between banks and industrial enterprises and between corporations after World War II, actual conditions were explained in the late 1960s. The functions and roles of these personnel connections require further consideration. Chapter 16 examines this research topic by analyzing advisory council activities.

References

Commerzbank AG (1967) Geschäftsbericht 1967. Commerzbank AG, Frankfurt am Main
Commerzbank AG (1968) Geschäftsbericht 1968. Commerzbank AG, Frankfurt am Main
Commerzbank AG (1969) Geschäftsbericht 1969. Commerzbank AG, Frankfurt am Main
Deutsche Bank AG (1967) Geschäftsbericht 1967. Deutsche Bank AG, Frankfurt am Main
Deutsche Bank AG (1968) Geschäftsbericht 1968. Deutsche Bank AG, Frankfurt am Main
Deutsche Bank AG (1969) Geschäftsbericht 1969. Deutsche Bank AG, Frankfurt am Main
Dresdner Bank AG (1967) Geschäftsbericht 1967. Dresdner Bank AG, Frankfurt am Main
Dresdner Bank AG (1968) Geschäftsbericht 1968. Dresdner Bank AG, Frankfurt am Main
Dresdner Bank AG (1969) Geschäftsbericht 1969. Dresdner Bank AG, Frankfurt am Main
Mossner G (Hrsg) (1971) Handbuch der Direktoren und Aufsichtsräte. Jahrgang 1970/71, Bd.I, Nach personen geordnet, Finanz- und Korrespondenz-Verlag, Berlin

Chapter 16
Activities of Banks' Advisory Councils and Roles of Personnel Connections Based on Such Organizations After World War II

Abstract Whereas regional advisory councils already existed in some large banks before World War II, central advisory council was created for banks' head offices after World War II. Advisory council system composed of bank's central and regional advisory councils played meaningful roles in supplementing the function of personnel connections through interlocking directorates on top management organs. They had big significance for collecting, exchanging, and sharing of information between banks and industrial enterprises and among industrial enterprises. Building upon discussions regarding conditions of personnel connection between enterprises through advisory council system in previous chapter, this chapter attempts to clarify functions and roles of such personnel connection through analyzing activities of these organizations on the basis of original historical materials of large German banks. Analysis in this chapter has significant meaning for grasping cooperative mechanism of German capitalism.

Keywords Advisory council · Central advisory council · Commerzbank · Dresdner Bank · Industry–bank relationship · Personnel connection · Regional advisory council

In Chap. 15, conditions of personnel connection built through central and regional advisory councils of three large banks between bank and industrial enterprise and among corporations after World War II were considered. Central advisory councils as the core of a special committee for the exchange and sharing of information among enterprises played an important role in supplementing the function of personnel connections through direct and indirect interlocking in top management entities. Regional advisory councils also played a significant role in the exchange and sharing of information between banks and industrial enterprises and among industrial enterprises. Building on discussions in previous chapter, this chapter analyzes the functions and roles of personnel connections through banks' advisory councils in interfirm relationships.

In this chapter, such research topics are clarified through analyzing activities of banks' advisory councils from the 1950s to the 1980s without period of the latter half

T. Yamazaki, *Relationships Between Industry and Bank in Germany*,
https://doi.org/10.1007/978-981-97-4996-6_16

of the 1960s, unlike the examination in Chap. 15. This chapter attempts to clarify the functions and roles of personnel connections in interfirm relationships after world War II. In this chapter, such research topics are clarified mainly using various original historical materials of Dresdner Bank and Commerzbank, including documents in the Commerzbank archives (Historisches Archiv Commerzbank). Because post-World War II documents in the Deutsche Bank archive (Historisches Archiv der Deutschen Bank) were not offered for public inspection, cases of advisor councils of Dresdner Bank and Commerzbank are examined. Many original materials, such as minutes of advisory council meetings, letters and documents, and correspondence between members of banks, between the bank and industrial enterprises, and between the bank and members of the advisory council, are used.

Section 16.1 examines the fundamental functions, roles, and characteristics of banks' advisory councils. Section 16.2 analyzes the functions of the personnel connections through central advisory councils of Dresdner Bank. Section 16.3 considers the functions of personnel connections through regional advisory councils of Dresdner Bank and Commerzbank. Through these discussions this chapter clarifies the significance of these advisory council systems and the personnel connections through such organizations.

16.1 Fundamental Function and Characteristics of Banks' Advisory Councils

The advisory council, created for banks' head offices and each region, functioned as a focal point in the information exchange between corporations and banks as well as among corporations. Major corporations assigned members to a central advisory council, through which industry leaders regularly reported to each other on their markets' conditions.

As members of the central advisory council performed their council roles, they received advice and guidance on various business issues (Eglau 1990, SS. 192–193, 244). Many major industrial enterprises sent their person to a central advisory council. Most members of the supervisory board as representatives of shareholders tended to want to become members of the central advisory council because the status as a member of this type of committee was usually regarded as "decorative." An important standard was that a supervisory board member from the labor side did not exist on the central advisory council (*Historisches Archiv der Commerzbank*, HAC-500/337, 447/52, Zentralbeirat der Dresdner Bank AG; Eglau 1990, SS. 243–244). The mission of this organization was to provide advice to management regarding fundamental problems of important business policies (Aizawa 1994, p. 95).

Region-specific advisory councils existed at Deutsche Bank and Dresdner Bank. Regional advisory councils included management representatives from various corporate sectors that served large banking customers and their regional organizational units. One reason for the existence of regional advisory councils was that they strengthened relationships among various corporations across business sectors and in each region regarding business policy matters (Büschgen 1983, SS. 242–243; Koubek 1971, S. 261). For instance, the regional advisory councils for Deutsche Bank that were established in major districts was an important way to develop relationships with significant enterprises in the competent area with which the bank had a business relation (Eglau 1990, SS. 250–251). That the regional advisory council functioned as a committee for coordination can be observed (Pfeiffer 1986, S. 165). Whereas the central advisory council was comprised of members dispatched from large representative companies in Germany, representatives from companies that were customers and with which the bank had small transactions were members of the regional advisory council (Aizawa 1994, p. 96). Individuals appointed by the top three banks to the supervisory or an advisory council were considered "friendly" (Gottschalk 1988, S. 301). For example, it was important for Deutsche Bank's advisory council to create strong ties with its customers through its business and to propose new operations through those ties (Schwarz 2003, S. 32).

In addition, several hundred business associations shared ties with banks through the top three banks' supervisory board, central advisory council, or regional advisory council members (Pfeiffer 1987, SS. 29–31). In one case, contact among companies in the iron and steel industry started before the execution of new investment behavior through an association with the iron and steel industry, and this organization conveyed each company's information concerning the investment plan. Producing enterprises of the iron and steel industry found the merits of commonality of investments in a series of cooperation agreements (Stanzick 1969, S. 61). Given these personal organizational ties, close relationships between banks and industries created information conduits and were not only based on direct relationships between the two groups but also were complemented by intermediary relationships of economic associations, such as business and industrial associations and industry–bank relationships (Koubek 1971, SS. 262–266).

Next, Sect. 16.2 examines the functions of the personnel connection through the central advisory council. The case of Dresdner Bank is explored.

16.2 Activities of Central Advisory Council: Case of Dresdner Bank

16.2.1 Work Regulation of Central Advisory Council

First, in reviewing the statute of Dresdner Bank's central advisory council, an internal document dated March 19, 1964, pointed out that no statute existed concerning this organization [*Historisches Archiv der Commerzbank*, HAC-500/337, 447/51, Turnus unserer Zentralbeirats- und Beiratsmandate (19.3.1964)].

Under such a condition, limitations to the term of office of advisory council members were proposed. The supervisory board took charge over decisions related to statute [*Historisches Archiv der Commerzbank*, HAC-500/337, 447/51, Auszug aus der Niederschrift über die Gemeinschaftssitzung am 25. Februar 1964, *Historisches Archiv der Commerzbank*, HAC-500/337, 447/51, Turnus unserer Zentralbeirats- und Beiratsmandate (19.3.1964)], and these regulations of the central advisory council were created. Clause 1 determined that the objectives of this organization were to provide advice to the bank's management, develop close relationships with groups throughout the economic world, and create friendly support groups for the bank that contributed to strengthening business relationships. The central advisory council did not have a duty, obligation, or authority such as those held by a supervisory board of a joint-stock company. In clause 2, the appointment and dismissal of members of this organization were handled by the chairman of the supervisory board on the basis of suggestions by the board of directors. Clause 3 determined that members of the central advisory council had a duty to keep the secrets of Dresdner Bank [*Historisches Archiv der Commerzbank*, HAC-500/196, 120025, Geschäftsordnung für den Zentralbeirat der Dresdner Bank Aktiengesellschaft]. Although no definite prescription regarding the statute of Dresdner Bank's central advisory council existed, the minutes of the managing board meetings dated January 14, 1971, specified that central advisory council members could not participate in committee organizations of other banks (e.g., advisory councils) [*Historisches Archiv der Commerzbank*, HAC-500/121, 18227-2000, Auszug aus der Niederschrift über die Gesamtvorstandssitzung am 14. Januar 1971 in Frankfurt a. M. (27.4.1971)].

16.2.2 Holding Conditions of Meeting of Central Advisory Council

Next, when considering the conditions for holding a meeting of the central advisory council, although some meetings were held in other cities, such as Düsseldorf and Hamburg, most meetings took place in Frankfurt am Main. For instance, meetings of the central advisory councils were held on July 1, 1957, November 29, 1957, March 26, 1958, January 15, 1959, April 7, 1959, July 15, 1959, November 3, 1959, March 24, 1960, November 9, 1960, March 22, 1961, November 24, 1961, April 11, 1962, and November 20, 1962 [*Historisches Archiv der Commerzbank* , HAC-500/196, 120025, Sitzungstermine; *Historisches Archiv der Commerzbank*, HAC-500/211, 107841, Der Brief vom Vorsitzer des Aufsichhtsrats der Dresdner Bank AG an die Herren Mitglieder des Zentralbeirats der Dresdner Bank AG (20.12.1958); *Historisches Archiv der Commerzbank*, HAC-500/211, 107,841, Zentral-Beirat des Dresdner Bank AG. am 9. November 1960 in Frankfurt a. M.; *Historisches Archiv der Commerzbank*, HAC-500/211, 107841, Der Brief vom Vorsitzer des Aufsichtsrats der Dresdner Bank AG an die Herren Mitglieder des Zentralbeirats der Dresdner Bank AG (28.1.1961); *Historisches Archiv der Commerzbank*, HAC-500/196, 120036, Ablauf der Sitzungen 6. April und folgende Tage]. Such cases were seen in meetings on April 9, 1963, November 19, 1963,

April 9, 1964, November 25, 1966, April 5, 1967, November 28, 1967, April 23, 1968, and November 26, 1969 as well [*Historisches Archiv der Commerzbank*, HAC-500/196,120027, Zentralbeirat. Sitzungstermine; *Historisches Archiv der Commerzbank*, HAC-500/257, 108273, Die Schrift über die Banksitzungen am 24. Und 25.November 1966; *Historisches Archiv der Commerzbank*, HAC-500/221, 109333, Niederschrift über die Sitzung des Zentralbeirats der Dresdner Bank Aktiengesellschaft am 5. April 1967 in den Räumen der Hauptverwaltung Frankfurt a.M. (5.4.1967); *Historisches Archiv der Commerzbank*, HAC-500/221, 109333, Niederschrift über die Sitzung des Zentralbeirats der Dresdner Bank Aktiengesellschaft am 28.November 1967 in Räumen der Hauptverwaltung Frankfurt a. M.; *Historisches Archiv der Commerzbank*, HAC-500/221, 10933, Der Brief von Hermann Röchling an Herr Ernst Matthiensen (4.4.1968); *Historisches Archiv der Commerzbank*, HAC-500/121, 7079–2002, Bd.1, Sitzung des Zentralbeirats des Dresdner Bank AG, am 26. November 1969, 11 Uhr in Frankfurt a. M.]. In the 1970s, meetings of this organization took place on April 8, 1970, November 25, 1970, and December 1, 1971. In the latter half of the 1970s, for example, meetings were held on May 4, 1975, November 30, 1976, March 24, 1977, November 30, 1977, and April 6, 1978 [*Historisches Archiv der Commerzbank*, HAC-500/121, 7079–2002, Bd.1, Sitzung des Zentralbeirats des Dresdner Bank AG am 8. April 1970, 11 Uhr in Frankfurt a. M.; *Historisches Archiv der Commerzbank*, HAC-500/337, 447/51, Der Brief von Hans Fonk an Herrn Jürgen Ponto (19.4.1971); *Historisches Archiv der Commerzbank*, HAC-500/121, 7909–2002, Bd.1, Tagesordnung der Sitzung des Zentralbeirats der Dresdner Bank AG am 1. Dezember 1971, 11 Uhr, in Frankfurt a. M.; *Historisches Archiv der Commerzbank*, HAC-500/337, 447/50, Auszug aus der Niederschrift über die Sitzung des Zentralbeirats am 14. April 1975 in Frankfurt a. M. (6.8.1975); *Historisches Archiv der Commerzbank*, HAC-500/337, 447/50, Auszug aus der Niederschrift über die Sitzung des Zentralbeirates am 6. April 1976 um 10.30 Uhr in Frankfurt a. M. (4.5.1976); *Historisches Archiv der Commerzbank*, HAC-500/121, 8106–2002, Der Brief vom Sitzung des Aufsichtsrates der Dresdner Bank AG an die Herren Mitglieder des Zentralbeirats der Dresdner Bank AG (15.10.1976); *Historisches Archiv der Commerzbank*, HAC-500/121, 8106–2002, Der Brief von der Dresdner Bank AG an Herr Dr. Adolff (11.7.1977)].

16.2.3 Situations Regarding Participants at Central Advisory Council Meetings

This subsection examines representative cases of participants in central advisory council meetings. The number of members of the council on the date on which this organization was created, September 24, 1957, was 16 [*Historisches Archiv der Commerzbank*, HAC-500/337, 447/52, Zentralbeirat der Dresdner Bank AG.]. At the meeting on July 1, 1957, the numbers in attendance and absent were 17 and six, respectively [*Historisches Archiv der Commerzbank*, HAC-500/196,

120038, Sitzung des Zentral-Beirats der Dresdner Bank AG am 1. Juli 1957 mit Abendessen]. Similar numerical figures were 17 and seven at the meeting on January 15, 1959 [*Historisches Archiv der Commerzbank*, HAC-500/196, 120038, Zentralbeirat—Sitzung am 15.1.1959, 17 Uhr, Frankfurt a. M.] and 20 and five at the meeting on April 7, 1959, respectively [*Historisches Archiv der Commerzbank*, HAC-500/196, 120038, Zentralbeirat—Sitzung am 7. April 1959, 17 Uhr, in Frankfurt a. M.]. Twenty individuals participated in the meeting on November 3, 1959 [*Historisches Archiv der Commerzbank*, HAC-500/196,120038, Sitzung des Zentralbeirats der Dresdner Bank AG. am 3.November 1959 in Hamburg].

At the meeting on March 24, 1960, the number in attendance and absent was 21 and six, respectively [*Historisches Archiv der Commerzbank*, HAC-500/196, 120039, Sitzung des Zentralbeirats der Dresdner Bank AG.am 24. März 1960 in Hamburg]. Although the number of members that constituted the central advisory council was 27 on July 20, 1960 [*Historisches Archiv der Commerzbank*, HAC-500/211, 107841, Zentralbeirat der Dresdner Bank AG. (Stand 20.7.1960)], the number in attendance and absent was 22 and seven, respectively, including Dresdner Bank individuals, at the meeting on November 9, 1960 [*Historisches Archiv der Commerzbank*, HAC-500/211, 107841, Zentralbeirat der Dresdner Bank AG. am 9. November 1960 in Frankfurt a.M.]. At the meeting on March 22, 1961, of the 29 invited, 26 attended [*Historisches Archiv der Commerzbank*, HAC-500/196, 120039, Zentralbeirat der Dresdner Bank AG. am 22. März 1961 in Düsseldorf]. At the meeting on November 24, 1961, the number in attendance and absent was 19 and eight, respectively, with the number from Dresdner Bank in attendance and absent was 15 and two, respectively [*Historisches Archiv der Commerzbank*, HAC-500/196, 120039, Sitzung des Zentralbeirats der Dresdner Bank AG am 24. November 1961 in Hamburg]. Twenty-four individuals participated in the meeting on November 20, 1962 [*Historisches Archiv der Commerzbank*, HAC-500/196, 120039, Sitzung des Zentralbeirats der Dresdner Bank AG. am 20. November 1962 in Düsseldorf]. Although the number of members of the central advisory council was 29 on November 6, 1963 [*Historisches Archiv der Commerzbank*, HAC-500/196, 120025, Zentralbeirat der Dresdner Bank AG. (Stand 6.11.1963)], 34 individuals attended the meeting on November 19, 1963. Of these 34, 20 were members of the central advisory council, three were members of the supervisory board of Dresdner Bank, and 11 were members of the managing board of this bank [*Historisches Archiv der Commerzbank*, HAC-500/196, 120025, Niederschrift über die Sitzung des Zentralbeirats der Dresdner Bank Aktiengesellschaft am 19. November 1963 in den Räumen der Hauptverwaltung Frankfurt a.M. (19.11.1963), S. 1].

At the meeting on April 9, 1964, the number in attendance and absent was 25 and four, respectively [*Historisches Archiv der Commerzbank*, HAC-500/196, Sitzung des Zentralbeirats der Dresdner Bank AG. am 9. April 1964, 11 Uhr, in Frankfurt a. M.]. Of the attendees at the central advisory council meeting on November 25, 1966, one person was chairman of the supervisory board of Dresdner Bank, and seven were on the managing board of this bank [*Historisches Archiv der Commerzbank*, HAC-500/257, 108273, Die Schrift über die Banksitzungen am 24. und 25.November 1966]. At a meeting on Mai 4, 1967, one person was chairman of the supervisory board of Dresdner Bank, six were members of the managing board of this bank, 13 were members of the central advisory council, and one person managed the accounts register, for a total of 21 attendees [*Historisches Archiv der Commerzbank*, HAC-500/221, 109333, Niederschrift über die Sitzung des Zentralbeirats der Dresdner Bank Aktiengesellschaft am 5. April 1967 in den Räumen der Hauptverwaltung Frankfurt a. M. (5.4.1967), SS. 1–2]. At the meeting on November 28, 1967, one chairman of the supervisory board, one vice-chairman of the supervisory board, and eight members of the managing board of Dresdner Bank, and ten members of the central advisory council were in attendance, and the total number of attendances was 20 [Niederschrift über die Sitzung des Zentralbeirats der Dresdner Bank Aktiengesellschaft am 28. November 1967 in den Räumen der Hauptverwaltung Frankfurt a.M., *Historisches Archiv der Commerzbank*, HAC-500/221, 109333]. At the meeting on April 23, 1968, two members including the chairman of the supervisory board of Dresdner Bank participated, as well as 12 members of the central advisory council [*Historisches Archiv der Commerzbank*, HAC-500/211, 109333, Sitzung des Zentralbeirates der Dresdner Bank AG. am 23. April 1968, 17 Uhr in Frankfurt a. M.]. In meetings on November 26, 1969, and April 8, 1970, the number in attendance and absent was 14 and three, respectively [*Historisches Archiv der Commerzbank*, HAC-500/121, 7079–2002, Bd.1, Sitzung des Zentralbeirats des Dresdner Bank AG am 26. November 1969, 11 Uhr in Frankfurt a. M.; *Historisches Archiv der Commerzbank*, HAC-500/121, 7079–2002, Bd.1, Sitzung des Zentralbeirats des Dresdner Bank AG am 8. April 1970, 11 Uhr in Frankfurt a.M.]. Similar numerical figures were 17 and five, respectively, in the meeting on March 24, 1977 [*Historisches Archiv der Commerzbank*, HAC-500/337,449/6, Sitzung Zentralbeirat—24. März 1977, 10.30 Uhr].

16.2.4 Contents of Meeting of Central Advisory Council

This subsection considers the contents of meetings of the central advisory council. For instance, at the meeting on November 25, 1966, after a report on the conditions of the business of Dresdner Bank during the period until that point in the year was given by the directors, other issues were taken up [*Historisches Archiv der Commerzbank*, HAC-500/257, 108273, Benütiges Material für Banksitzungen im November (19 66), S. 2; *Historisches Archiv der Commerzbank*, HAC-500/257, 108273, Tagesordnung der Sitzung des Zentralbeirats der Dresdner Bank Aktiengesellschaft am 25. November 1966, 11 Uhr, in Frankfurt a.M.]. Many similar cases were observed in other meetings. Such cases can be seen in, for example, meetings held on March 26, 1958, December 8, 1958, January 15, 1959, April 7, 1959, November 3, 1959, March 24, 1960, November 9, 1960, March 22, 1961, November 24, 1961, April 11, 1962, November 20, 1962, November 19, 1963, April 9, 1964, April 23, 1968, December 1, 1971, and March 24, 1977. Reports on this bank's business during the previous fiscal year and the period up to that point in the current fiscal year were given by the bank's directors, and discussions regarding other issues were undertaken [*Historisches Archiv der Commerzbank*, HAC500/196, 120036, Der Brief vom Vorsitzer des Aufsichtsrats der Dresdner Bank AG an die Herren Mitglieder des Zentralbeirates der Dresdner Bank AG (20.12.1958); *Historisches Archiv der Commerzbank*, HAC500/196, 120038, Der Brief vom Vorsitzer des Aufsichtsrats der Dresdner Bank AG an die Herren Mitglieder des Zentralbeirates der Dresdner Bank AG (20.1.1959); *Historisches Archiv der Commerzbank*, HAC500/196, 120038, Tagesordnung der Sitzung des Zentralbeirats der Dresdner Bank AG. am 7. April 1959, 17 Uhr in Frankfurt a. M.; *Historisches Archiv der Commerzbank*, HAC500/196, 120038, Tagesordnung für der Sitzung des Zentralbeirats der Dresdner Bank AG. am Dienstag, dem 3. November 1959, 17 Uhr im Hause der Dresdner Bank AG. Hamburg, Jungfernstieg 22 (5. Stock); *Historisches Archiv der Commerzbank*, HAC500/196, 120038, Der Brief von der Dresdner Bank AG an die Herren Mitglieder des Zentralbeirates der Dresdner Bank AG (20.1.1960); *Historisches Archiv der Commerzbank*, HAC500/196, 120039, Tagesordnung der Sitzung des Zentralbeirats der Dresdner Bank Aktiengesellschaft am 9. November 1960 10,30 Uhr in Frankfurt a.M.; *Historisches Archiv der Commerzbank*, HAC500/196, 120039, Der Brief vom Voestandes der Dresdner Bank AG an die Herren Mitglieder des Zentralbeirates der Dresdner Bank AG (12.9.1960); *Historisches Archiv der Commerzbank*, HAC500/196, 120039, Der Brief vom Vorsitzer des Aufsichtsrats der Dresdner Bank AG an die Herren Mitglieder des Zentralbeirates der Dresdner Bank AG. (28.1.1961); *Historisches Archiv der Commerzbank*, HAC500/196, 120039, Der Brief vom Vorsitzer des Aufsichtsrats der Dresdner Bank AG an die Herren Mitglieder des Zentralbeirats der Dresdner Bank AG. (29.9.1961); *Historisches Archiv der Commerzbank*, HAC 500/196, 120039, Der Brief vom Vorsitzer des Aufsichtsrats der Dresdner Bank AG an die Herren Mitglieder des Zentralbeirates der Dresdner Bank AG. (22.2.1962); *Historisches Archiv der Commerzbank*, HAC 500/196, 120039, Tagesordnung für die Sitzung des Zentralbeirats der Dresdner Bank AG. am 20. November 1962, 11,30 Uhr, in Düsseldorf; *Historisches Archiv der Commerzbank*, HAC-500/196, 120025, Tagesordnung der Sitzung des Zentralbeirats der Dresdner Bank Aktiengesellschaft am 19. November 1963, 11 Uhr, in Frankfurt a.M.; *Historisches Archiv der Commerzbank*, HAC-500/196, 12044, Der Brief vom Vorsitzer des Aufsichtsrats der Dresdner Bank AG an die Herren Mitglieder des Zentralbeirats der Dresdner Bank AG (3.3.1964); *Historisches Archiv der Commerzbank*, HAC-500/211, 109333, Tagesordnung der Sitzung der Zentralbeirates der Dresdner Bank Aktiengesellschaft am 23. April 1968, 17.00 Uhr in Frankfurt a.M.; *Historisches Archiv der Commerzbank*, HAC-500/121, 7909–2002, Bd.1, Tagesordnung der Sitzung des Zentralbeirats der Dresdner Bank AG am 1. Dezember 1971, 11 Uhr, in Frankfurt a. M.; *Historisches Archiv der Commerzbank*, HAC-500/121, 8106–2002, Tagesordnung der Sitzung des Zentralbeirats der Dresdner Bank Aktiengesellschaft am 24. März 1977, 10.30 Uhr in Königstein/Ts].

However, in many cases, large varieties of contents were taken up. For example, in the meeting on November 19, 1963, not only the business conditions of Dresdner Bank were reported by members of the board of directors but also explanations for the competition between savings banks and other banks by Rheinhold, a report on the general conditions of economic trends in West Germany, and a report on the capital market situation by Henzel. Based on these reports, animated discussions regarding immeasurable reductions in the loan interest rate for the following year occurred among the attendances. In addition, active exchanges of opinions on the introduction of electronic equipment among those present were also developed using the basis of suggestions by members of the central advisory council. Oeftering reported on the introduction of such equipment at the federal bank. Cases also existed in which detailed reports were given, and discussions ensued, even though lectures on specific themes were not prepared [*Historisches Archiv der Commerzbank*, HAC-500/196, 120025, Niederschrift über die Sitzung des Zentralbeirats der Dresdner Bank Aktiengesellschaft am 19. November 1963 in den Räumen der Hauptverwaltung Frankfurt a. M. (19.11.1963), SS. 2–3].

Concrete observations of the contents of each meeting were as follows. For instance, in a meeting on November 29, 1957, Dresdner Bank's business conditions were reported, and Richter lectured on international financial institutions [*Historisches Archiv der Commerzbank*, HAC-500/196, 120038, Auszug aus der Niederschrift über die Gemeinschaftssitzung am 24. Oktober 1957 (18.1.1957)]. In a meeting on November 25, 1966, the bank's financial business was explained by comparing financial information as of October 31, 1966, with that of December 31, 1965, and October 31, 1965. In addition, capital market trends, market prices, and old yield rates of various fixed interest commodities, and noteworthy asset management points for the end of 1966 were reported by Henzel [*Historisches Archiv der Commerzbank*, HAC-500/257, 108273, Zentralratssitzung (25. November 1966, 11 Uhr)]. In a meeting on April 5, 1967, Dresdner Bank's personnel issues and the foundation of the capital market committee of the board of directors, which engaged in decision making or measurements of the affairs of the "stock market and portfolio management," and the consortium business were reported. In addition, Dresdner Bank's settlement of accounts in 1966 and business conditions for the period to that point in 1967 were reported by the managing board. These reports by Schäfer and Henzel lectured on the general situation of the capital market and the stock market and the condition of the security and consortium businesses of this bank. In the following discussions, European market trends and issues regarding the activation of enterprises' investments were argued. In succession, Glück reported on trends in the bank's foreign business. The meeting that started at 5 p.m. ended at 7 p.m. [*Historisches Archiv der Commerzbank*, HAC-500/211, 109333, Niederschrift über die Sitzung des Zentralbeirats der Dresdner Bank Aktiengesellschaft am 5. April 1967 in den Räumen der Hauptverwaltung Frankfurt a.M.(5.4.1967); *Historisches Archiv der Commerzbank*, HAC-500/211, 109333, Sprechzettel für die Zentralbeirats-Sitzung (5.4.1976), S. 5].

After Schäfer reported the business conditions of the period until November 28, 1967, the board of directors reported Dresdner Bank's general profitability situation in a meeting. Henzel explained the capital market condition in Germany and internationally, the security and consortium businesses of this bank, trends of investment trusts throughout the country, and activities in the field of asset management and directions toward its further expansion. Furthermore, Glück reported on a decline in the market price of the Pound and foreign business activities in this bank. In subsequent discussions, the influence of overcoming the limitations of profitability by participants' obligation to social insurance was argued. This meeting began at 5 p.m. and finished at 7:10 p.m. [*Historisches Archiv der Commerzbank*, HAC-500/211, 109333, Niederschrift über die Sitzung des Zentralbeirats der Dresdner Bank Aktiengesellschaft am 28. November 1967 in den Räumen der Hauptverwaltung Frankfurt a. M.]. At Dresdner Bank, the concerned issues were proposed and discussed in the case of personnel changes in the members of the central advisory council [*Historisches Archiv der Commerzbank*, HAC-500/211, 109333, Niederschrift über die Sitzung des Zentralbeirats der Dresdner Bank Aktiengesellschaft am 28. November 1967 in den Räumen der Hauptverwaltung Frankfurt a. M.]. In some cases, decisions on issues suggested by members of this organization were approved by the credit committee [*Historisches Archiv der Commerzbank*, HAC-500/121, 18232-2000, Bd.1, Auszug aus der Niederschrift über die Gesamtvorstandssitzung am 25. Februar 1965 in Frankfurt a. M. (7.4.1965)].

Meetings of the central advisory council were deeply concerned with reports of the supervisory board, and many commonalities existed in the contents of both committees. For instance, a letter from C. Goetz to E. Röchling in 1961 pointed out that reports done in the central advisory council quietly corresponded to those in the supervisory board [*Historisches Archiv der Commerzbank*, HAC-500/121, 18232-2000, Bd.1, Auszug aus der Niederschrift über die Gemeinschaftssitzung am 25. Februar 1965 in Frankfurt a.M. (16.3.1965); *Historisches Archiv der Commerzbank*, HAC-500/121, 18232-2000, Bd.1, Auszug aus der Niederschrift über die Gemeinschaftssitzung am 20. März 1964 (7.4.1964)].

In many cases, a meal was held after the meeting of the central advisory council [*Historisches Archiv der Commerzbank*, HAC-500/211, 107841, Der Brief von Carl Goetz an Herr Dr. Röchling]. Seating arrangements were carefully analyzed and decided [*Historisches Archiv der Commerzbank*, HAC-500/196, 120038, Sitzung des Zentral-Beirats der Dresdner Bank AG am 1. Juli 1957 mit Abendessen; *Historisches Archiv der Commerzbank*, HAC-500/196, 120038, Der Brief vom Vorsizter des Aufsichtsrats der Dresdner Bank Aktiengeselslchaft über dis Sitzung des Zentralbeirats am 1. Juli 1957 (23.5.1957); *Historisches Archiv der Commerzbank*, HAC-500/196, 120038, Der Brief von der Dresdner Bank AG. an Herr Dr. Pastor (31.1.1958); *Historisches Archiv der Commerzbank*, HAC-500/196, 120038, Der Brief vom Vorsitzer des Aufsichtsrats der Dresdner Bank AG an Herren Mitglieder des Zentralbeirates der Dresdner Bank AG (29.9.1958); *Historisches Archiv der Commerzbank*, HAC-500/196, 120038, Der Brief vom Vorsitzer des Aufsichtsrats der Dresdner Bank AG an die Herren Mitglieder des Zentralbeirats der Dresdner Bank AG (20.12.1958); *Historisches Archiv der Commerzbank*, HAC-500/196, 120038, Der Brief vom Vorsitzer des Aufsichtsrats der Dresdner Bank AG an die Herren Mitglieder des Zentralbeirates der Dresdner Bank AG (20.1.1959); *Historisches Archiv der Commerzbank*, HAC-500/196, 120038, Der Brief von der Dresdner Bank AG an die Herren Mitglieder des Zentralbeirats der Dresdner Bank AG (14.9.1959); *Historisches Archiv der Commerzbank*, HAC500/196, 120039, Der Brief von der Dresdner Bank AG an die Herren Mitglieder des Zentralbeirats der

Dresdner Bank AG (20.1.1960); *Historisches Archiv der Commerzbank*, HAC-500/196, 120039, Der Brief vom Vorstandes der Dresdner Bank AG an die Herren Mitglieder des Zentralbeirats der Dresdner Bank AG (12.9.1960); *Historisches Archiv der Commerzbank*, HAC-500/196, 120039, Der Brief vom Vorsitzer des Aufsichtsrats der Dresdner Bank AG an die Herren Mitglieder des Zentralbeirats der Dresdner Bank AG. (28.1.1961); *Historisches Archiv der Commerzbank*, HAC-500/196, 120039, Der Brief vom Vorsitzer des Aufsichtsrats der Dresdner Bank AG an die Herren Mitglieder des Zentralbeirats der Dresdner Bank AG. (29.9.1961); *Historisches Archiv der Commerzbank*, HAC-500/196, 120039, Der Brief vom Vorsitzer des Aufsichtsrats der Dresdner Bank AG an die Herren Mitglieder des Zentralbeirates der Dresdner Bank AG. (22.2.1962); *Historisches Archiv der Commerzbank*, HAC-500/196, 120039, Der Brief vom Vorsitzer des Aufsichtsrats der Dresdner Bank AG an die Herren Mitglieder des Zentralbeirats der Dresdner Bank Aktiengesellschaft (4.10.1962); *Historisches Archiv der Commerzbank*, HAC-500/196, 12044, Der Brief vom Vorsitzer des Aufsichtsrats der Dresdner Bank AG an die Herren Mitglieder des Zentralbeirats der Dresdner Bank AG (3.3.1963); *Historisches Archiv der Commerzbank,* HAC-500/196, 120025, Der Brief von Dresdner Bank AG an die Herren Mitglieder des Zentralbeirats der Dresdner Bank AG (17.10.1963); *Historisches Archiv der Commerzbank*, HAC-500/121, 7909–2002, Bd.1, Brief vom Vorsitzer des Aufsichtsrats der Dresdner Bank AG an die Herren Mitglieder des Zentralbeirats der Dresdner Bank AG (26.10.1971); *Historisches Archiv der Commerzbank*, HAC-500/337, 449/6, Banksitzung 22.-24. März 1977]. Seating arrangements were carefully analyzed and decided [*Historisches Archiv der Commerzbank*, HAC-500/196, 120039, 9. November 1960 Mittagessen Zentralbeirat. Tischordnung Kasino 10. Stock, *Historisches Archiv der Commerzbank*, HAC-500/257, 108273, Tischordnung. Sitzung des Zentralbeirats der Dresdner Bank Aktiengesellschaft (25.11.1966), *Historisches Archiv der Commerzbank*, HAC-500/257,108273, Zentralbeirat 25.11.66, Sitzordnung, 1. Stock, *Historisches Archiv der Commerzbank*, HAC-500/211, 107841, Sitzordnung. Sitzung Zentralbeirat 15.1.1959]. Such an effort indicates the significance of the central advisory council in developing and maintaining further close relationships with enterprises that had deep cooperative relations with Dresdner Bank and clear positions in such relationships.

16.2.5 Significance of Central Advisory Council

Building on the foregoing discussions, this subsection considers the significance of the central advisory council. The company prospectus for the 1966 capital increase pointed out that the supervisory board was able to establish advisory councils to develop further close relationships and to secure contacts with groups in the economic world on the basis of suggestions by the board of directors; a central advisory council and ten regional advisory councils existed at that time [*Historisches*

Archiv der Commerzbank, HAC-500/121,18232-2000, Bd.1, Prospekt für die Zulassung zum Börsenhandel der DM 70000000,—neuen, auf den Inhaber lautenden Aktien aus der Kapitalerhöhung 1966 mit Gewinnberechtigung vom 1.Januar 1966 an Stück 45000 zu je DM1000,—Nr.1000001–1045000 Stück 500000 zu je DM 50,—Nr.2000001–2500000, S. 6]. Reinforcing the amicable and special relationship and contact between Dresdner Bank and the concerned enterprise became possible by appointing and installing an individual from the industrial company as a member of the central advisory council [*Historisches Archiv der Commerzbank*, HAC-500/337, 447/51, Der Brief von Franz Paul Heckschen an Herr Matthiensen (10.2.1971)]. For example, a letter dated August 6, 1971, from F. Gieske as acting director of Rheinisch-Westfälisches Elektrizitätswerk AG to E. Matthiensen as chairman of the supervisory board of Dresdner Bank indicated the intention to foster the existing good relationship between the bank and the electric power enterprise to which Gieske belonged through installation as a member of the central advisory council [*Historisches Archiv der Commerzbank*, HAC-500/337, 447/51, Der Brief von Dr. Friedhelm Giesken an Herrn Ernst Matthiensen (6.8.1971)]. Many indications also existed that belonging to such a committee organization of leading persons in the economic world who had prominent experience enabled the provision of very useful advice and information for Dresdner Bank and this organization [*Historisches Archiv der Commerzbank*, HAC-500/221, 109333, Sprechzettel für die Zentralbeirats-Sitzung (5.4.1976), S. 1; *Historisches Archiv der Commerzbank*, HAC-500/221, 107841, Der Brief von Hermann Röchling an Herrn Carl Goetz (29.7.1961); *Historisches Archiv der Commerzbank*, HAC-500/337, 447/52, Der Brief von Dresdner Bank AG an Herr Dirocks (5.4.1966), *Historisches Archiv der Commerzbank*, HAC-500/337,447/52, Der Brief von Ernst Matthiensen an Herr Carl Julius Brabant (5.4.1966); *Historisches Archiv der Commerzbank*, HAC-500/337, 447/52, Der Brief von Ernst Matthiensen an Herr Dr. E. h. Heinz Gehm (5.4.1966)]. Similar indications can also be observed in the testimonies of individuals who belonged to this type of organization. For instance, J. Weste of Friedrich Krupp, a large enterprise in the iron and steel industry, pointed out that Dresdner Bank's central advisory council was a place for gathering and exchanging abundant information and having frank discussions on fund market and capital market issues [*Historisches Archiv der Commerzbank*, HAC-500/337, 447/52, Der Brief von Dr. Jürgen Weste an Herr Dr. Hermann Richter (30.9.1974)].

In internal historical materials possessed in the archives of large banks, many indications existed that installing a person as a member of the central advisory council enabled close personnel contacts between Dresdner Bank management and other large enterprises, as well as expanding the range of vision of the advisory council members [*Historisches Archiv der Commerzbank*, HAC-500/337, 447/51, Der Brief von Hermann Röchling an Herrn Ernst Matthiensen (4.4.1968); *Historisches Archiv der Commerzbank*, HAC-500/337, 447/52, Der Brief von Dresdner Bank AG an den Vorstand der Brown, Boveri & Cie AktiengesellSchaft (20.7.1964)]. Such functions of the central advisory council played important roles. For example, a letter from Ernst Matthiensen to W. Habig of Westfalia Separator AG, who proposed in 1971 retirement as a member of this organization because of aging pointed out that maintaining the most truthful and friendly relationships and useful close contacts for several decades after Habig's retirement was important [*Historisches Archiv der Commerzbank*, HAC-500/337, 447/51, Der Brief von Ernst Matthiensen an Herr Werner Habig (25.2.1971)]. Such a role of the central advisory council in creating and reinforcing close, friendly, and faithful interfirm relationships and their importance can also be observed in other many documents collected from bank archives [*Historisches Archiv der Commerzbank*, HAC-500/337, 447/52, Der Brief von Dresdner Bank Aktiengesellschaft an Herr Ernst Hagemeier (27.12.1966); *Historisches Archiv der Commerzbank*, HAC-500/337, 447/52, Die Schrift von dem Aufsichtsrat und Vorstand der Dresdner Bank Aktiengesellschaft am 20. Juli 1964; *Historisches Archiv der Commerzbank*, HAC-500/337, 447/52, Der Brief von der Dresner Bank AG an Herrn Dr. Jürgen Weste (14.10.1974)].

In addition, cases in which the transmission of the intention to retire from an installation to the central advisory council was done through contacts or exchange of opinions between individuals at Dresdner Bank and other enterprises were not rare [*Historisches Archiv der Commerzbank*, HAC-500/337, 447/51, Der Brief von Ernst Matthiensen an Herr Werner Habig (25.2.1971)]. For instance, W. Habig proposed a candidate to succeed him after he retired from the central advisory council, and Dresdner Bank informed him that his suggestion would be welcomed [*Historisches Archiv der Commerzbank*, HAC-500/337, 447/51, Der Brief von Dresdner Bank AG. an Herrn Direktor Dr.jur.Franz Paul Heckschen (18.2.1971); *Historisches Archiv der Commerzbank*, HAC-500/337, 447/51, Der Brief von Dresdner Bank AG an Herr Matthiensen (18.12.1971); *Historisches Archiv der Commerzbank*, HAC-500/337, 447/51, Der Brief von Franz Paul Heckschen an Herr Ernst Matthiensen (10.2.1971)]. Such exchanges and negotiations between banks and industrial enterprises, proposals from industrial companies, and the involvement and role of a specific person indicate the deepness of the relationships between banks and enterprises that sent members of the central advisory council and their significant role in strengthening the bank's close relations with leading companies in various industries.

In many cases, close and careful coordination of opinions concerning the election and installation of members of the central advisory council between bank and company concerned or another company occurred because of the importance of this organization. These actions were prominent when a person to be considered as a candidate was a member of the advisory council or another organization of other banks. For instance, in an issue regarding the installation of G. v. d. Goltz of Klöckner Werke AG as a member of Dresdner Bank's central advisory council in 1971, Quandt and Ulrich, who were members of the supervisory board of Deutsche Bank, were involved in exchanging and coordinating and their efforts contributed significantly to obtaining an understanding of Goltz, and such close coordination and negotiations were substantial [*Historisches Archiv der Commerzbank*, HAC-500/121, 7909-2002, Bd.1, Die Schrift von Jürgen Ponto über Graf. v. d. Goltz (4.5.1971); *Historisches Archiv der Commerzbank*, HAC-500/121, 7909-2002, Bd.1, Der Brief von Jürgen Ponto über Graf. v. d. Goltz (19.3.1971)].

Being installed to the central advisory council of a bank had significance for a member of an industrial enterprise and the economic world, which can be observed in cases in which a member of regional advisory council of bank moved to a central advisory council. For example, F. Gieske, who belonged to the Rhein-Westfalen regional advisory council of Dresdner Bank after 1968 moved to the central advisory council in 1971 [*Historisches Archiv der Commerzbank*, HAC-500/337, 447/51, Der Brief von Ernst Matthiensen an Herrn Dr. jur. Friedheim Gieske (1.7.1971); *Historisches Archiv der Commerzbank*, HAC-500/337, 447/51, Die Schrift von der Dresdner Bank AG an Herrn Ernst Matthiensen (5.3.1971)]. H-M. Höcherl, a managing board member of Lahmeyer AG, moved from the Hessen regional advisory council to which he belonged after July 1, 1971 to the central advisory council on July 1, 1975 [*Historisches Archiv der Commerzbank*, HAC-500/121, 7909-2002, Bd.1, Der Brief von der Dresdner Bank AG an Herr Dr. Hans-Michael Höcherl (5.6.1975)]. Similar situations can be observed when D. Spethmann of August Thyssen-Hütte AG moved in 1971 to the central advisory council from the Rheinland Regional advisory council [*Historisches Archiv der Commerzbank*, HAC-500/121, 7909-2002, Bd.1, Der Brief von Ernst Matthiensen an Herr Dr. Dieter Spethmann (21.5.1971)]. Moreover, through a decision made in 1974, P. Henle of Klöckner Werke AG moved from the Rheinland regional advisory council to the central advisory council [*Historisches Archiv der Commerzbank*, HAC-500/121, 7909-2002, Bd.1, Der Brief von Christian-Peter Henle an Herrn Hermann Richter (4.12.1974)].

In such conditions, cases also existed in which an industrial enterprise recommended and proposed candidates for mandates of the concerned regional advisory council as successor to person who moved from regional to central advisory council [*Historisches Archiv der Commerzbank*, HAC-500/337, 447/51, Der Brief von Hans Fonk an Herrn Jürgen Ponto (19.4.1971)]. This finding indicates the significance of a bank's advisory council to an industrial company that dispatched its member. A prominent state can be observed in the following case. Concerning a personnel affair of the advisory council, although Dresdner Bank hoped to invite Götte to the central advisory council as a successor of Müller, Allianz decided not to send someone with experience in the field of asset investments and finance (Götte, Sonnenholzner, and Reuter) to the bank's committee. This bank made efforts to manage such a situation and negotiations [*Historisches Archiv der Commerzbank*, HAC-500/121, 7909-2002, Bd.1, Allianz—hier: Mandatsfrage (16.5.1975), *Historisches Archiv der Commerzbank*, HAC-500/121, 7909-2002, Bd.1, Zentralbeirat—Dr. Götte (11.5.1975), *Historisches Archiv der Commerzbank*, HAC-500/121, 7909-2002, Bd.1, Allianz—Herr Götte (11.11.1973), *Historisches Archiv der Commerzbank*, HAC-500/121, 7909-2002, Bd.1, Allianz (8.3.1971)]. This case indicates the importance of personnel issues at a bank's central advisory council.

In some cases, the members of Dresdner Bank's supervisory board hoped to move to a central advisory council. Such a case was observed in, for example, the case of Dr. Gehm in February 1964 [*Historisches Archiv der Commerzbank*, HAC-500/121, 18232-2000, Bd.1, Auszug aus der Niederschrift über die Gemeinschaftssitzung am 25. Februar 1964 (12.3.1964)]. This case also signifies the strong meaning of being a member of a central advisory council for someone in the economic world and the importance of this organization to relationships between banks and industrial enterprises and among industrial enterprises, which represents the background of such significance for carriers of businesspersons.

For Dresdner Bank, that personnel issues of the central advisory council had the same importance as that of the supervisory board was not rare. For instance, according to a Dresdner Bank internal document dated April 8, 1957, the Rheinische Stahlwerke group proposed Wiedenhof, a member of the managing board of Rheinische Stahlwerke AG, as a successor of von Waldthausen, a member of the supervisory board of this bank, and this bank acknowledged the proposal. Under this approval, that Wiedenhof would become a member of the central advisory council in one year according to circumstances was also considered a possible provisional solution [*Historisches Archiv der Commerzbank*, HAC-500/192, 1379-2002, Aufsichtsrat Dresdner Bank (8.4.1957)]. Furthermore, in another internal document of this bank dated March 19, 1957, personnel issues of the central advisory council, with a foundation that was planned at the time of the reconcentration of dissolved banks, were taken up and discussed [*Historisches Archiv der Commerzbank*, HAC-500/192, 1379-2002, Wiedervereinigung (19.3.1957)]. The importance of the central advisory council for a bank is indicated through this point.

At Dresdner Bank, cases in which members of the central advisory council were asked to participate in the general meeting were also not rare. For instance, nine members attended the general meeting of stockholders on April 29, 1960 [*Historisches Archiv der Commerzbank*, HAC-500/196, 120039, Hauptversammlung Dresdner Bank AG. 29.4.1960 in Frankfurt a.M.]. In addition, documents that asked to join such a meeting dated April 29, 1964, were sent on April 9, 1964 [*Historisches Archiv der Commerzbank*, HAC-500/196, 120044, Der Brief von der Dresdner Bank AG. an die Herren Mitglieder des Zentralbeirats der Dresdner Bank Aktiengesellschaft (9.4.1964)]. Of the 23 members, eight were absent, and 15 participated in this general meeting [*Historisches Archiv der Commerzbank*, HAC-500/196, 120044, Hauptversammlung der Dresdner Bank AG. Am 30. April 1964 in Hamburg]. Attendance of the members of the central advisory council at such a meeting can be observed in subsequent periods. In a document dated October 15, 1976, information on the general meeting held on May 5, 1976, was conveyed [*Historisches Archiv der Commerzbank*, HAC-500/121, 8106-2002, Der Brief vom Vorsitzende des Aufsichtsrates der Dresdner Bank AG an die Herren Mitglieder des Zentralbeirats der Dresdner Bank AG (15.10.1976)]. The importance of this organization as a means of reinforcing close and cooperative relationships between banks and industrial enterprises can be observed through this point.

Remuneration was paid to members of the central advisory council as meritorious consideration. In a meeting of the managing board of Dresdner Bank on November 18, 1963, the issue of rewards for members of the central advisory council and the regional advisory council was taken up as a subject and discussed [*Historisches Archiv der Commerzbank*, HAC-500/196, 120043, Tagesordnung für die Sitzung des Gesamtvorstandes am 18. November 1963, 9 Uhr, in Frankfurt a. M.]. For example, 22,200 Deutsche Mark (DM), including a value-added tax of 2,200 Deutsche Mark (DM), was paid in 1977 to each member as remuneration [*Historisches Archiv der Commerzbank*, HAC-500/ 337, 447/50, Der Brief von der Dresdner Bank AG an die

Herren Mitglieder des Zentralbeirates der Dresdner Bank AG (30.12.1978)]. The significance of the central advisory council and the great role of members of such an organization can be seen in this point.

16.3 Activities of Regional Advisory Council

16.3.1 Activities of Regional Advisory Council of Dresdner Bank

16.3.1.1 Conditions for Holding Regional Advisory Council Meetings

Section 16.3 considers the functions of personnel connections through regional advisory councils. The cases of Dresdner Bank and Commerzbank are explored, and this section analyzes Dresdner Bank's situation. Holding conditions of meetings of regional advisory councils were observed.

For instance, in Rhein–Main Bank as a successor bank of dissolved Dresdner Bank, the meeting of the Baden–Württemberg regional committee occurred on September 16, 1955, in Baden-Baden [*Historisches Archiv der Commerzbank*, HAC-500/211, 108114, Sitzung Lande-Ausschuβ Baden-Württemberg am 16.9.1955 in Baden-Baden]. A meeting of the same regional committee also took place on April 25, 1957, at Frankfurt am Main [*Historisches Archiv der Commerzbank*, HAC-500/211, 108114, Der Brief vom Sitzer des Landesausschusses für Baden-Württemberg der Rhein-Main Bank AG an die Herren Mitglieder des Landesausschusses für Baden-Württemberg der Rhein-Main Bank AG. (22.3.1957)].

During the period before the reconcentration of Dresdner Bank in 1957, some regional committee meetings took place. For example, in 1957, such cases are observed in a united meeting on March 23, a meeting of the Bayern regional committee on September 14, a meeting of the Baden–Württemberg regional committee on September 21, a meeting of the Hessen regional committee on October 26, and a meeting of the Rheinland–Pfalz regional committee on November 2. In 1957, a united meeting was held on April 25, a meeting of the Rheinland–Pfalz regional committee on September 13, a meeting of the Baden–Württemberg regional committee on September 26, a meeting of the Hessen regional committee on October 30, and a meeting of the Bayern regional committee on November 15 [*Historisches Archiv der Commerzbank*, HAC-500/196, 120021, Landes-Ausschuβ-Sitzung].

Changing the name of "regional committee" (Landesausschuss) to "advisory council" (Beirat) was decided on at the meeting on March 28, 1958 [*Historisches Archiv der Commerzbank*, HAC-500/196, 120020, Sitzung des Landesausschusses am 28. März 1958 (31.3.1958); *Historisches Archiv der Commerzbank*, HAC-500/196, 120020, Der Brief von der Dresdner Bank AG an Herrn Dr.Walter Bauer (28.3.1958); *Historisches Archiv der Commerzbank*, HAC-500/196, 120020, Sitzung des Landesaus-Schusses am 28. März 1958 (10.4.1958)]. For instance, meetings of the Baden–Württemberg regional advisory council occurred on October 24, 1958, in Badenweiler [*Historisches Archiv der Commerzbank*, HAC-500/196, 120021, Der Brief von Hinckel an die Herren Mitglieder des Beirats Baden-Württemberg der Dresdner Bank AG], on October 2, 1959, in Mannheim [*Historisches Archiv der Commerzbank*, HAC-500/211, 108114, Anwesenheitsliste. Sitzung Beirat Baden-Württemberg am 2. Oktober 1959 in Mannheim], and on September 30, 1960, in Konstanz [*Historisches Archiv der Commerzbank*, HAC-500/211, 108114, Der Brief vom Vorsitzer des Beirats Baden-Württemberg der Dresdner Bank AG an die Herren Mitglieder des Beirats Baden-Württemberg der Dresdner Bank AG. (5.9.1960)]. During the 1970s, for example, a meeting occurred on October 22, 1971, in Baden-Baden [*Historisches Archiv der Commerzbank*, HAC-500/121, 7909-2002, Bd.2, Der Brief von der Dresdner Bank AG an Herrn Kurt Losten (30.7.1971)].

Regarding the Bayern regional advisory council, for instance, meetings occurred on October 31, 1958, in Rotenburg at the Tauber [*Historisches Archiv der Commerzbank*, HA500/211, 120021, Der Brief von Gassner an die Herren Mitglieder des Beirats Bayern der Dresdner Bank AG (26.9.1958)], on October 30, 1959, in Nürnberg [*Historisches Archiv der Commerzbank*, HAC-500/211, 107847, Der Brief vom Vorsizter des Beirats Bayern der Dresdner Bank AG. an die Herren Mitglieder des Beirats Bayern der Dresdner Bank AG. (7.9.1959)], on October 7, 1960, in Parmisch–Partenkirchen [*Historisches Archiv der Commerzbank*, HAC-500/211, 107847, Teilnehmerliste.Sitzung Beirat Bayern am 7. Oktober 1960 im Riessersee-Hotel, Garmisch-Partemkirchen], and on October 18, 1963, in Rottach–Egern [*Historisches Archiv der Commerzbank*, HAC-500/196, 12005, Der Brief vom Vorsitzer des Beirat Bayern der Dresdner Bank AG an Herren Mitglieder der Beirats Byern der Dresdner Bank AG. (2.9.1963)]. Regarding the Hessen regional advisory council, for example, meetings were held on November 7, 1958, in Bad–Dürkheim [*Historisches Archiv der Commerzbank*, HAC-500/196, 120021, Anwesenheitsliste.Sitzung Beirat Rheinland-Pfalz am 7. November 58 in Bad Dürkheim], and on September 19, 1958, in Kronberg [*Historisches Archiv der Commerzbank*, HAC-500/196, 120020, Der Brief von dem Vorsitzer des Beirat Hessen der Dresdner Bank AG. an die Herren Mitglieder des Beirat Hessen der Dresdner Bank AG. (26.8.1958)].

Furthermore, united meetings of some regional advisory councils also took place. A united meeting of the Baden–Württemberg regional advisory council, the Bayern regional advisory council, the Hessen regional advisory council, the Rheinland–Pfalz regional advisory council, and the Saar regional advisory council occurred on March 28, 1958, in Frankfurt am Main [*Historisches Archiv der Commerzbank*, HAC-500/196, 120020, Der Brief von der Dresner Bank AG. an Herr Josef Schäfer (13.3.1958)]. Representative cases can be observed in, for instance, the unified meeting of the Baden–Württemberg regional advisory council, the Bayern regional advisory council, the Hessen regional advisory council, the Rheinland–Pfalz regional advisory council, and the Saar regional advisory council on April 10, 1960, in Frankfurt am Main [*Historisches Archiv der Commerzbank*, HAC-500/196, 12005, Der Brief vom Vorsitzer des Beirat Rheinland-Pfalz der Dresner Bank AG. an die Herren Mitglieder des Beirat Rheinland-Pfalz der Dresner Bank AG. (4.3.1963);

Historisches Archiv der Commerzbank, HAC-500/196, 12005, Der Brief von der Dresdner Bank AG. an Herrn Dr. Hermann Richter (4.3.1963)]. A similar meeting of the Hessen regional advisory council, Rheinland–Pfalz regional advisory council, and Saar regional advisory council was held on December 3, 1971 [*Historisches Archiv der Commerzbank*, HAC-500/121, 7909-2002, Bd.2, Der Brief vom Vorsitzer des Beirats Saar der Dresdner Bank AG. an die Herren Mitglieder des Beirats Saar der Dresdner Bank AG. (26.10.1971)], a combined meeting of the Baden–Württemberg regional advisory council, the Bayern regional advisory council, the Hessen regional advisory council, and the Southwest regional advisory council was held on December 2, 1975, in Munich [*Historisches Archiv der Commerzbank*, HAC-500/121, 7909-2002, Bd.2, Der Brief vom Vorsitzer des Beirats Bayern der Dresdner Bank AG an die Herren Mitglieder des Beirats Bayern der Dresdner Bank AG (17.10.1975)].

In addition, similar unified meetings of the Baden–Württemberg regional advisory council, the Bayern regional advisory council, the Hessen regional advisory council, and the Southwest regional advisory council were held on December 3, 1976, and March 28, 1978. Whereas the former occurred in Wiesbaden, the latter occurred in Frankfurt am Main [*Historisches Archiv der Commerzbank*, HAC-500/121, 8106-2002, Der Brief von der Dresdner bank Aktiengesellschaft an die Herren Mitglieder der Beiräte Baden-Württemberg, Bayern, Hessen und Südwest der Dresdner Bank AG (27.7.1976); *Historisches Archiv der Commerzbank*, HAC-500/121, 8106-2002, Der Brief von der Dresdner bank AG an die Herren Mitglieder der Beiräte Baden-Württemberg, Bayern, Hessen und Südwest der Dresdner Bank AG (14.2.1977)].

16.3.1.2 Situations Regarding Participants of Meetings of Regional Advisory Councils

This subsection examines situations regarding the participants of meetings of the regional advisory council in representative cases. At a representative meeting of the Baden–Württemberg regional committee on October 2, 1959, the attendees were 29 members of this organization, 12 members of Dresdner Bank top management, 15 individuals from the bank's branches, and one guest. The total number in attendance was 57. The 23 absentees included 14 members of the regional advisory council, five directors of Dresdner Bank, three branch individuals, and one guest, for a total of 80 invited individuals [*Historisches Archiv der Commerzbank*, HAC-500/211, 108114, Anwesenheitsliste. Sitzung Beirat Baden-Württemberg am 2. Oktober 1959 in Mannheim]. The number of attendees at a meeting of the Baden–Württemberg regional advisory council on September 30, 1960, was 68. Of these 68 individuals, 29 were members of this organization, 17 were members of Dresdner Bank's top management, 19 were at branches of this bank, and three were guests. Of 19 absentees, 14 were members of the regional advisory council, two were directors of Dresdner Bank, two were from the bank's branches, and one was a guest, for a total of 87 invited individuals [*Historisches Archiv der Commerzbank*, HAC-500/211, 108114, Teilnehmerliste. Sitzung Beirat Baden-Württemberg am 30. September 1960 in Konstanz].

For instance, an examination of the Bayern regional advisory council indicated that 19 members of this organization, 15 members of Dresdner Bank's top management, 14 bank branch personnel, and two guests participated in a meeting on October 10, 1960, for a total attendance of 50. Six members of this advisory council were absent [*Historisches Archiv der Commerzbank*, HAC-500/211, 107847, Teilnehmerliste.Sitzung Beirat Bayern am 7. Oktober 1960 im Riessersee-Hotel, Garmisch-Partemkirchen]. At a meeting on October 18, 1963, 27 members of the regional advisory council, ten members of Dresdner Bank top management, 11 bank branch personnel, and three guests attended, for a total attendance of 51. Two members of this advisory council and three individuals from Dresdner Bank's top management were absent [*Historisches Archiv der Commerzbank*, HAC-500/196, 12005, Teilnehmerliste.Sitzung Beirat Bayern am 18. Oktober 1963 in Rottbach. Egern]. Regarding the Rheinland–Pfalz regional advisory council, 15 members of the regional advisory council, 12 individuals from Dresdner Bank's top management, and seven individuals from the bank's branches attended a meeting on November 7, 1958, for a total attendance of 34. Three members of this advisory council and one member of Dresdner Bank's top management were absent [*Historisches Archiv der Commerzbank*, HAC-500/196, 120021, Anwesenheitsliste. Sitzung Beirat Rheinland-Pfalz am 7. November 58 in Bad Dürkheim].

In addition, when observing the unified meeting of regional advisory councils, the number of attendees was high given their characteristics. For instance, 28 members of the Baden–Württemberg regional advisory council, 14 members of the Bayern regional advisory council, 28 members of the Hessen regional advisory council, 11 members of the Rheinland–Pfalz regional advisory council, 23 persons of Dresdner Bank's top management, 25 individuals from the bank's branches, and three guests attended the unified meeting on March 28, 1958, for a total attendance of 132 [*Historisches Archiv der Commerzbank*, HAC-500/196, 120020, Teilnehmerliste. Sitzung der Landes-Ausschusse für Baden-Württemberg, Bayern, Hessen, Rheinland-Pfalz am 28. März 1958 in Frankfurt a. M.].

16.3.1.3 Contents of Regional Advisory Council Meetings

Next, the contents of meetings of regional advisory councils are considered in this subsection. For instance, in a meeting of the Baden–Württemberg regional advisory council on October 24, 1958, a member of Dresdner Bank's managing board reported on the bank's business conditions, and R. Ansbach from Dresdner Bank lectured on the international financial market. After these lectures, other issues were taken up [*Historisches Archiv der Commerzbank*, HAC-500/196, 120021, Der Brief von Hinckel an die Herren Mitglieder des Beirats Baden-Württemberg der Dresdner Bank AG]. At a meeting on October 2, 1959, after a member of this bank's managing board reported on its business conditions, V. Erlich as a member of this regional advisory council lectured on the "Latest problems of energy economy." Other affairs were then taken up and discussed [*Historisches Archiv der Commerzbank*, HAC-500/211, 108114, Der Brief vom Vorsizter des Beirats Baden-Württemberg der Dresdner Bank

AG. an die Herren Mitglieder des Beirats Baden-Württemberg der Dresdner Bank AG. (7.9.1960)].

At a meeting on September 30, 1960, a member of Dresdner Bank's managing board reported on the bank's business conditions and then lectured on specific themes. Other issues were then discussed [*Historisches Archiv der Commerzbank*, HAC-500/211, 108114, Der Brief vom Vorsitzer des Beirats Baden-Württemberg der Dresdner Bank AG. an die Herren Mitglieder des Beirats Baden-Württemberg der Dresdner Bank AG. (5.9.1960)].

Meetings of the Bayern regional advisory council were almost the same. For instance, at a meeting on October 31, 1958, member of the managing board of Dresdner Bank reported on the bank's business conditions and W. Huck, a member of this regional advisory council, lectured on the theme "structural charge in the newspaper industry in Germany," after which other issues were discussed [*Historisches Archiv der Commerzbank*, HAC-500/211, 107847, Der Brief vom Vorsitzer des Beirats Bayern der Dresdner Bank AG. an die Herren Mitglieder des Beirats Bayern der Dresdner Bank AG. (26.9.1958)]. At a meeting on October 30, 1959, in addition to a report by a member of Dresdner Bank's managing board on the bank's business situations, K. Lindner lectured on the latest problems in the electrical industry [*Historisches Archiv der Commerzbank*, HAC-500/211, 107847, Der Brief vom Vorsitzer des Beirats Bayern der Dresdner Bank AG. an die Herren Mitglieder des Beirats Bayern der Dresdner Bank AG. (7.9.1959)]. At a meeting on October 18, 1963, a member of Dresdner Bank's managing board reported on the bank's business conditions and T. Schmeller, a member of the Bayern regional advisory council, gave a lecture on an atomic power plant in Germany that provided electric power. After that, other affairs were argued [*Historisches Archiv der Commerzbank*, HAC-500/196, 12005, Der Brief vom Vorsitzer des Beirat Bayern der Dresdner Bank AG. an Herren Mitglieder der Beirats Bayern der Dresdner Bank AG. (2.9.1963), *Historisches Archiv der Commerzbank*, HAC-500/196, 12005, Tagesordnung. Beirat Bayern der Dresdner Bank Aktiengesellschaft. Sitzung am 18. Oktober 1963 in Rottbach-Egern].

Meetings of other regional advisory councils were explored. At a meeting of the Rheinland–Pfalz regional advisory council on November 7, 1958, Dresdner Bank's business conditions were reported, and C. F. von Salmuth lectured on aluminum. Other issues were also taken up [*Historisches Archiv der Commerzbank*, HAC-500/196, 120021, Tagesordnung der Sitzung Beirat Rheinland-Pfalz am 7. November 1958, *Historisches Archiv der Commerzbank*, HAC-500/196, 120021, Anwesenheitsliste. Sitzung Beirat Rheinland-Pfalz am 7. November 58 in Bad Dürkheim]. At a meeting of the Hessen regional advisory council on September 19, 1958, a member of the managing board of Dresdner Bank reported on the bank's business conditions, and R. Ansbach lectured on international financial institutions. After these lectures, other affairs were discussed [*Historisches Archiv der Commerzbank*, HAC-500/196, 120020, Der Brief von dem Vorsitzer des Beirat Hessen der Dresdner Bank AG. an die Herren Mitglieder des Beirat Hessen der Dresdner Bank AG. (26.8.1958)].

In addition, unified meetings of some regional advisory councils were observed. At a meeting on April 10, 1963, member, a of Dresdner Bank's managing board reported on the bank's business in 1962, and M. G von Belling gave a lecture titled "Economic and political situations in Southeast Asia." Other issues were also taken up [*Historisches Archiv der Commerzbank*, HAC-500/196, 12005, Der Brief von der Dresdner, Bank AG. über die Gesamtsitzung der Beiräte am 10. April 1963]. At a combined meeting of the Hessen regional advisory council, the Rheinland–Pfalz regional advisory council, and the Saar regional advisory council on December 3, 1971, a member of Dresdner Bank's managing board reported on the bank's business. After his report, D. Oedkoven lectured on "Economic activities of state: Behavioral scientific and interpretation of economic phenomena," and discussions on other issues ensued [*Historisches Archiv der Commerzbank*, HAC-500/121, 7909-2002, Bd.2, Der Brief vom Vorsitzer des Beirats Saar der Dresdner Bank AG. an die Herren Mitglieder des Beirats Saar der Dresdner Bank AG. (26.10.1971)]. In addition, at a unified meeting of the Baden–Württemberg regional advisory council, the Bayern regional advisory council, the Hessen regional advisory council, and the Southwest regional advisory council, a member of Dresden Bank's managing board reported on the bank's business conditions, and H. Hammerschmidt gave a lecture titled "entrepreneur and media." After these lectures, other issues were discussed [*Historisches Archiv der Commerzbank*, HAC-500/121, 7909-2002, Bd.2, Der Brief von Vorsitzende des Beirats Bayern der Dresdner Bank AG an die Herren Mitglieder des Beirats Bayern der Dresdner Bank AG (17.10.1975)].

In some cases, critical and constructive utterances and proposals were made by members of regional advisory councils. One such case was at a meeting of the Hessen regional advisory council on March 1, 1970. At this meeting, O. Braun pointed out that some materials were to be distributed beforehand and the form, such as the working committee as the form of the regional advisory council, was desired over the mere organizational form that, until then, was comprised of members from companies [*Historische Archiv der Commerzbank*, HAC-500/121, 8106-2002, Beirat Hessen (1.3.1976)]. This case indicated that regional advisory councils were not only places for friendly relationships between banks and industrial enterprises and among industrial companies but also places of active discussions, including critical examinations.

In meetings of the regional advisory council of Dresdner Bank, seating arrangements were carefully examined and decided [*Historische Archiv der Commerzbank*, HAC-500/211, 108114, Sitzordnung Konstanz 30.9.1960]. In many cases, dinners were held after these meetings [*Historische Archiv der Commerzbank*, HAC-500/196, 120021, Veranstaltung der Dresdner Bank am 7. November 1958 in Kurhaus Bad Dürkheim (6.10.1958); *Historisches Archiv der Commerzbank*, HAC-500/196, 120020, Der Brief von der Dresner Bank. an Herr Josef Schäfer (13.3.1958); *Historisches Archiv der Commerzbank*, HAC-500/196, 12005, Der Brief vom Vorsitzer des Beirat Rheinland-Pfalz der Dresner Bank AG. an die Herren Mitglieder des Beirats Rheinland-Pfalz der Dresner Bank AG. (4.3.1963); *Historisches Archiv der Commerzbank*, HAC-500/196, 12005, Der Brief von der Dresdner Bank AG. an den Vorstand der Dresdner Bank AG. (4.3.1963); *Historisches Archiv der*

Commerzbank, HAC-500/196, 12005, Der Brief vom Vorsitzer des Beirats Bayern der Dresdner Bank AG. an die Herren Mitglieder der Beirats Bayern der Dresdner Bank AG. (2.9.1963)]. These dinners indicated the significance of the regional advisory councils in building and maintaining further close and strong relationships with leading companies in each region that had deep cooperative relations with Dresdner Bank. Seating arrangements reflected the differences in the depth of such relations among industrial enterprises and the clear positions of each company for this bank.

16.3.2 Activities of Regional Advisory Council of Commerzbank

16.3.2.1 Conditions for Holding Regional Advisory Council Meetings

In the previous subsection, the functions of the regional advisory council of Dresdner Bank were discussed. This subsection considers the case of Commerzbank. Conditions under which meetings of regional advisory councils were held are considered.

The conditions under which meetings of Commerzbank were held from 1969 to the end of the 1980s were examined. During this period, 24 meetings were held. Meetings of regional advisory councils occurred on April 10, 1969, October 13, 1969, April 6, November 11, 1970, April 5, 1971, November 11, 1971, March 2, 1971, November 3, 1972, March 26, 1973, November 12, 1973, March 25, 1974, November 5, 1974, February 25, 1975, November 5, 1975, March 30, 1976, November 2, 1977, March 30 1977, October 27, 1977, March 31, 1978, October 30, 1978, March 22, 1979, October 31, 1979, March 20, 1980, and October 31, 1980. Of these, the meeting on 31.10.1969 occurred at Baden-Baden, the meeting on 1.11.1971 occurred in Hamburg, and the meeting on 12.11.1973 occurred in Munich. Excluding these cases, most meetings occurred in Frankfurt am Main [*Historisches Archiv der Commerzbank*, HAC-400/1822, Landesbeiratssitzungen].

For Commerzbank's regional advisory councils, unified meetings of some of these councils occurred, as did meetings of each regional advisory council. For example, at representative meetings in the 1960s, a combined meeting of the Baden–Württemberg regional advisory council, the Bayern regional advisory council, the Hessen regional advisory council, the Rheinland–Pfalz regional advisory council, and the Saar regional advisory council was held in Frankfurt am Main on April 8, 1968 [*Historisches Archiv der Commerzbank*, HAC-400/1814, Der Vorstand der Commerzbank Aktiengesellschaft gibt sich die Ehre zu einer Sitzung der Landesbeiräte Baden-Württemberg, Bayern, Hessen, Rheinland-Pfalz und Saar am Montag, dem 8. April, 16.30 Uhr, im Bankgebäude in Frankfurt a.M., Grasse Gallusstrasse 17–19, ergebenst einladen]. Regarding meetings in the 1970s, a unified meeting was held in Hamburg on November 11, 1971 [*Historisches Archiv der Commerzbank*, HAC-400/1817, Gesamtbeiratssitzung am 11.11.1971 in Hamburg (25.8.1971),

Historisches Archiv der Commerzbank, HAC-400/1817, Gesamtbeiratssitzung am 11. November 1971 in Hamburg hier: Tagungsfolge], and a similar meeting was held in Frankfurt on March 31, 1978 [*Historisches Archiv der Commerzbank*, HAC-400/1821, Der Vorstand gibt sich die Ehre, zu einer Sitzung der Landesbeiräte Baden-Württemberg, Bayern, Hessen, Rheinland-Pfalz-Saar am Freitag, dem 31. März 1978, 17.00 Uhr, im Bankgebäude in Frankfurt am Main, Neue Mainzer Strasse 32–36, 24. Stock, einzuladen, *Historisches Archiv der Commerzbank*, HAC-400/1821, Landesbeitartssitzung am 31. März 1978 17.00 Uhr Frankfurt, *Historisches Archiv der Commerzbank*, HAC-400/1821, Landesbeiratssitzung 31.3.1978]. In the 1980s, a unified meeting of the Baden–Württemberg regional advisory council, the Bayern regional advisory council, the Hessen regional advisory council, and the Rheinland–Pfalz–Saar regional advisory council occurred on October 31, 1980 [*Historisches Archiv der Commerzbank*, HAC-400/1822, Teilnehmer an der Sitzung des Landesbeiräte Baden-Württemberg, Bayern, Hessen, Rheinland-Pfalz-Saar in Frankfurt (Main) am 31. Oktober 1980].

Furthermore, at a joint meeting of the regional and central advisory council, members of the supervisory board and the board of directors were observed. Such a case occurred at the meeting on June 16, 1978, in which 328 individuals participated; attendance was high as a characteristic of the form of the meeting [*Historisches Archiv der Commerzbank*, HAC-400/1821, Teilnehmer an dem gesellschaftlichen Treffen der Landesbeiräte mit dem Aufsichtsrat, dem Verwaltungsbeirat und dem Vorstand an Board des MS "Alte Liebe" (16. Juni 1978)].

16.3.2.2 Participants in Regional Advisory Council Meetings

Next, participants of regional advisory council meetings are examined through representative cases. An internal Commerzbank document dated February 28, 1958, indicated that the number of members of the South regional advisory council, the North regional advisory council, and the Nordrhein–Westfalia regional advisory council who attended was 73, 68, and 58, respectively, for a total attendance of 199. Of the 73 individuals from the South regional advisory council, 34, 28, and 11 were from Hessen and Rheinpfalz, Baden–Württemberg, and Bayern, respectively. Of the 68 individuals in the North regional advisory council, 20, 35, nine, and four were from Hamburg, Niderachsen, Schleswig–Holstein, and Bremen, respectively. Previous situations had 14, 31, 12, 7, and 22 members from the North regional advisory council, the West regional advisory council, the South-West regional advisory council, the Middle regional advisory council, and the East regional advisory council, respectively [*Historisches Archiv der Commerzbank*, HAC-400/624, Landesbeiräte der Commerzbank AG. (28.2.1959)].

At one representative unified meeting in Frankfurt am Main on April 9, 1968, number of invited persons was 139. Of these, five were members of the Commerzbank managing board, six were members of the Commerzbank supervisory board, 82 were members of the regional advisory councils, 36 were bank's branch managers, and 10 were other members of this bank. Of these 139 individuals, 105 persons attended this meeting. Four were members of the Commerzbank managing board, three were members of Commerzbank's supervisory board, 55 were members of regional advisory councils, 33 were bank's branch managers, and ten were other members of this bank [*Historisches Archiv der Commerzbank*, HAC-400/1814, Landesbeirats-Tagung am 9. April 1968, 16.30 Uhr, in Frankfurt a. M.]. In preparation for this meeting, issues concerning the invited Commerzbank branch directors and individuals were carefully examined. In such an investigation, the emphasis was on ensuring the attendance of individuals from branches in which members of the regional advisory council and the supervisory board were customers [*Historisches Archiv der Commerzbank*, HAC-400/1814, Landesbeirat-Tagung am 9. April 1968 in Frankfurt a.M.— Teilnahme der Filialleiter und Herren aus dem Haus]. This point was strongly related to the circumstance that regional advisory councils founded in main districts were significant to the business of the branch in the concerned region. According to internal documents of the secretariat office of the managing board and Commerzbank dated September 8 and 9, 1971, the branch director was not usually invited to a unified meeting of regional advisory councils. However, this situation occurred only in Frankfurt and Hamburg [*Historisches Archiv der Commerzbank*, HAC-400/1817, Landesbeiratssitzung am 11.November 1971 in Hamburg (10.9.1971), *Historisches Archiv der Commerzbank*, HAC-400/1817, Landesbeiratssitzung am 11. November 1971 in Hamburg (8.9.1971)].

Situations in the 1970s were observed. At a unified meeting in Hamburg on November 11, 1971, attendees were from French and Italian enterprises as well as German companies, and such personnel relationships contributed to realizing the framework of a friendly cooperation agreement [*Historisches Archiv der Commerzbank*, HAC-400/1817, Begrüβung durch Herrn Dr. Deuβ (11.11.1971)]. An internal document of the secretariat office of the managing board regarding answers from invited persons indicated that, of the 357 individuals who were invited to this meeting, 289 attended, 66 were absent, and two did not decide whether to participate at the time of the writing of the document or not [*Historisches Archiv der Commerzbank*, HAC-400/1817, Gesamtlandesbeiratssitzung am 11. November 1971 in Hamburg (2.11.1971)]. In a combined meeting of the Baden–Württemberg regional advisory council, the Bayern regional advisory council, the Hessen regional advisory council, the Rheinland–Pfalz council, and the Saar regional advisory council, 79 individuals attended [*Historisches Archiv der Commerzbank*, HAC-400/1820, Teilnehmer an Sitzung der Landesbeiräte Baden-Württemberg, Bayern, Hessen, Rheinland-Pfalz und Saar in Frankfurt (Main) am 26. März 1973].

An internal Commerzbank document on November 5, 1974, pointed out that a group of regional advisory councils was expanded somewhat after the latest meeting in March 1974 (*Historisches Archiv der Commerzbank*, HAC-400/1819, Sitzung der Landesbeiräte Baden-Württemberg, Bayern, Hessen und Rheinland-Pfalz-Saar am 5. November 1974 in Frankfurt am Main). At the unified meeting on November 5, 1975, 325 individuals were invited. Of these 325 individuals, 105 were members of the South regional advisory council, 119 were members of the West regional advisory council, 80 were members of the North regional advisory council, 13 were chairmen of the supervisory board and managing board members of Commerzbank, and one was the managing board member of Commerzbank Berlin. The number in attendance was 226 [*Historisches Archiv der Commerzbank*, HAC-400/1820, Organisatorische Ablauf der landesbeiratssitzung am Mittwoch, dem 5. November 1975 in Frankfurt am Main, S. 1, *Historisches Archiv der Commerzbank*, HAC-400/1820, Gesamtlandesbeiratstagung am 5. November 1975 in Frankfurt (29.8.1975)]. In the combined meeting of the Baden–Württemberg regional advisory council, the Bayern regional advisory council, the Hessen regional advisory council, and the Rheinland–Pfalz–Saar regional advisory council on March 30, 1976, 82 attended and 12 were absent [*Historisches Archiv der Commerzbank*, HAC-400/1820, Teilnehmer an der Sitzung der Landesbeiräte Baden-Württemberg, Bayern, Hessen, Rheinland-Pfalz-Saar in Frankfurt (Main) am 30. März 1976]. In a similar unified meeting on March 30, 1997, 78 attended and 15 were absent [*Historisches Archiv der Commerzbank*, HAC-400/1820, Teilnehmer an der Sitzung der Landesbeiräte Baden-Württemberg, Bayern, Hessen, Rheinland-Pfalz-Saar in Frankfurt (Main) am 30. März 1977]. In a meeting in Frankfurt am Main on March 31, 1978, 114 individuals were invited and 67 attended (*Historisches Archiv der Commerzbank*, HAC-400/1821, Landesbeiratssitzung 31. März 1978 17.00 Uhr Frankfurt). At a similar meeting on October 30, 1978, 88 individuals attended and nine were absent [*Historisches Archiv der Commerzbank*, HAC-400/1822, Teilnehmer an der Sitzung der Landesbeiräte Baden-Württemberg, Bayern, Hessen, Rheinland-Pfalz-Saar in Frankfurt (Main) am 30. Oktober 1978]. At a unified meeting on March 22, 1979, 84 attended and ten were absent [*Historisches Archiv der Commerzbank*, HAC-400/1822, Teilnehmer an der Sitzung der Landesbeiräte Baden-Württemberg, Bayern, Hessen, Rheinland-Pfalz-Saar in Frankfurt (Main) am 22. März 1979]. At a meeting on October 31, 1979, similar numerical figures were 85 and 19, respectively [*Historisches Archiv der Commerzbank*, HAC-400/1822, Teilehmer an der Sitzung der Landesbeiräte Baden-Württemberg, Bayern, Hessen, Rheinland-Pfalz-Saar in Frankfurt (Main) am 31. Oktober 1979]. Regarding the conditions in the 1980s, for example, at a similar unified meeting on March 30, 1980, 81 attended and ten were absent [*Historisches Archiv der Commerzbank*, HAC-400/1822, Teilnehmer an der Sitzung der Landesbeiräte Baden-Württemberg, Bayern, Hessen, Rheinland-Pfalz-Saar in Frankfurt (Main) am 20. März 1980]. At a unified meeting on October 31, 1980, 85 attended and 12 were absent, figures that were almost the same as those of the meeting on October 31, 1980 [*Historisches Archiv der Commerzbank*, HAC-400/1822, Teilnehmer an der Sitzung der Landesbeiräte Baden-Württemberg, Bayern, Hessen, Rheinland-Pfalz-Saar in Frankfurt (Main) am 31. Oktober 1980].

16.3.2.3 Contents of Meeting of Regional Advisory Council

In this subsection, the contents of the regional advisory councils meeting are examined. Although a variety of content was taken up at meetings of the regional advisory council of Hansa-Bank and Bankverin Westdeutschland, as a successor bank of the dissolved Commerzbank after the war, issues related to the credit business, the bill business, and credit approvals tended to be the focus of the discussions (*Historisches Archiv der Commerzbank*, HAC-303/3, Niederschrift über die 1. Beiratssitzung der HANSA-BANK am Freitag, dem 9. Juli 1948, um 15 Uhr in den Räumen der Bank; *Historisches Archiv der Commerzbank*, HAC-303/3, Niederschrift über die 16. Beiratssitzung der Hansa-Bank am Mittwoch, den 17. Mai 1950 vorm. 10,30; *Historisches Archiv der Commerzbank*, HAC-303/3, Niederschrift über die 28. Beiratssitzung der Hansa-Bank am Donnerstag, dem 14. Februar 1952 vorm. 10, 30; *Historisches Archiv der Commerzbank*, HAC-S3/A183, Niederschrift über die 23. Beiratssitzung des BANKENVEREIN WESTDEUTSCHLAND am Montag, den 3. September 1951, nachm. 3 Uhr, im Bankgebäude in Düsseldorf; *Historisches Archiv der Commerzbank*, HAC-S3/A183, Niederschrift über die 25. Beiratssitzung des BANKENVEREIN WESTDEUTSCHLAND am Mittowoch, den 16. Januar 1952, nachm. 3 Uhr, im Bankgebäude in Düsseldorf). The contents of the meetings indicate the insufficiency of this type of committee in developing close relationships between banks and industrial enterprises in each important region, as observed during the period after the reconcentration of dissolved banks in 1957. Moreover, after 1957, when Commerzbank was completely reconcentrated, the regional advisory council's function and role in relationships between banks and industrial enterprises and among industrial enterprises were exhibited in earnest.

Therefore, analyzing the contents of meetings of the regional advisory council at Commerzbank indicates themes of the meetings. At a unified meeting of the Baden–Württemberg regional advisory council, the Bayern regional advisory council, the Hessen regional advisory council, the Rheinland–Pfalz regional advisory council, and the Saar regional advisory council on April 8, 1968, a report by the managing board of Commerzbank on the business conditions and settlement of this bank's accounts for fiscal year 1967 and a general discussion of these topics formed the main themes. A dinner party was held after the meeting (*Historisches Archiv der Commerzbank*, HAC-400/1814, Der Vorstand der Commerzbank Aktiengesellschaft gibt sich die Ehre zu einer Sitzung der Landesbeiräte Baden-Württemberg, Bayern, Hessen, Rheinland-Pfalz und Saar am Montag, dem 8. April, 16.30 Uhr, im Bankgebäude in Frankfurt a.M., Grasse Gallusstrasse 17–19, ergebenst einladen). In addition, according to an internal Commerzbank document dated August 25, 1971, at the Hanburg department of unified meetings, although prominent guests from outside the bank lectured at the autumn meeting, only a lecture by a member of the board of directors occurred in the spring meeting up to that point [*Historisches Archiv der Commerzbank*, HAC-400/1817, Gesamtbeiratssitzung am 11.11.1971 in Hamburg (25.8.1971)]. In a combined meeting of the regional advisory council, the supervisory board, the central advisory council, and the consultative board on November 11, 1971, after a greeting by the chairman of the supervisory board of Commerzbank and an introduction of newly elected members of the regional advisory council, Lichtenberg reported on the bank's business conditions. The meeting began at 17:00 and, after serving an aperitif at 19:00, a dinner party started at 19:30. Subsequently, a relaxed meeting was held (*Historisches Archiv der Commerzbank*, HAC-400/1817, Gemeinsame Sitzung der Landesbeiräte mit dem Aufsichtsrat und dem Verwaltungsbeirat am 11. November 1971 im Atlantic Hotel, Hamburg). At such a unified meeting, gifts were distributed for being in attendance. A small silver cup valued at approximately 40 Deutsche Mark (DM) was presented to attendees of the three most recent meetings (*Historisches Archiv der Commerzbank*, HAC-400/1817, Gesamtlandesbeiratssitzung am 11. November 1971 im Hamburg). At a meeting on November 11, 1971, an analysis and evaluation of world conditions were explained in the lecture [*Historisches Archiv der Commerzbank*, HAC-400/1817, Der Brief von Dr. Thilo Pohlert an die Herren des Vorstandes der Commerzbank Aktiengesellschaft (12.11.1971)]. At numerous meetings of the regional advisory council, a member of the managing board of Commerzbank lectured on the latest economic situation and reported on the most recent business conditions and settlement of accounts of this bank [*Historisches Archiv der Commerzbank*, HAC-400/1819, Der Vorstand gibt sich die Ehre, zu einer Sitzung der Landesbeiräte Baden-Württemberg, Bayern, Hessen, Rheinland-Pfalz-Saar am Dienstag, dem 25. März 1975, 17.00 Uhr, im Bankgebäude in Frankfurt (Main), Neue Mainzer Strasse 32–36, Hochhaus 24.Stock, einzuladen (30.1.1975); *Historisches Archiv der Commerzbank*, HAC-400/1820, Der Vorstand gibt sich die Ehre, zu einer Sitzung der Landesbeiräte Baden-Württemberg, Bayern, Hessen, Rheinland-Pfalz-Saar am Mittwoch, dem 30. März 1977, 17.00 Uhr, im Bankgebäude in Frankfurt (Main), Neue Mainzer Strasse 32–36, 24.Stock einzuladen (Februar 1977); *Historisches Archiv der Commerzbank*, HAC-400/1822, Der Vorstand gibt sich die Ehre, zu einer Sitzung der Landesbeiräte Baden-Württemberg, Bayern, Hessen, Rheinland-Pfalz-Saar am Freitag, dem 31. Oktober 1980, 17.30 Uhr, im Bankgebäude in Frankfurt (Main), Neue Mainzer Strasse 32–36, 24.Stock einzuladen (September 1980)].

Other cases were examined. At a meeting in Frankfurt am Main on November 5, 1975, after an inspection of a new training center and a lecture on its duty and purpose, the meeting's key lecture was given [*Historisches Archiv der Commerzbank*, HAC-400/1820, Landesbeiratssitzung am 5. November 1975 in Frankfrt (19.9.1975), *Historisches Archiv der Commerzbank*, HAC-400/1820, Gesamtlandesbeiratstagung am 5. November 1975 in Frankfurt (29.8.1975)]. At a meeting of the South regional advisory council on March 30, 1976, although the central issue was a report on the settlement of accounts of Commerzbank, problems related to economic conditions and financial market trends were discussed after a report was made on these themes [*Historisches Archiv der Commerzbank*, HAC-400/1820, Begrüβung Landesbeirat Süd (30.3.1976), S. 3, 5]. In preparation for the unified meeting in Hamburg on June 16, 1978, the secretariat office of the board of directors suggested that the election of candidates in attendance, the selection of gifts for attendees, and the holding of a meal and reservation of the location were the issues to be decided on, using as a model the unified meeting on March 21, 1978 (*Historisches Archiv der Commerzbank*, HAC-400/1821, Gesamtlandesbeiratssitzung mit Damen am 16. Juni 1978 in Hamburug). The planning for this meeting started early. The participation of 376 individuals, including 302 regional advisory council members, 13 managing board members, and 26 supervisory board members of Commerzbank was planned for November 2, 1977. The total number of attendances was estimated at 750, including members' wives. Thus, the very large scale of combined meeting was planned (*Historisches*

Archiv der Commerzbank, HAC-400/1821, Gesamtbeiratssitzung Juni 1978). Cases in which members of the managing board of Commerzbank lectured and reported on the bank's business condition and issues related to their specialized areas were numerous. In preparation of the meeting on March 20, 1980, the list of individuals on the managing board who should take charge of reports or lectures was examined, and a list of lecturers from previous meetings was distributed (*Historisches Archiv der Commerzbank*, HAC-400/1822, Landesbeirats-Sitzung am 20. März 1980).

At many meetings of the regional advisory council of Commerzbank, a meal was also provided. In such cases, seating arrangements were carefully examined and decided (*Historisches Archiv der Commerzbank*, HAC-400/1814, Sitzordnung anläßlich der Landesbeirats-Tagung am 8. April 1968 um 16.30 Uhr). Hotel reservations for attendees were made by Commerzbank, which defrayed the cost of meals as well as accommodations [*Historisches Archiv der Commerzbank*, HAC-400/1814, Die Schrift vom Hotel Frankfurter Hof an Herrn Direktor von Mengden (24.4.1968), *Historisches Archiv der Commerzbank*, HAC-400/1814, Die Schrift vom Hotel Frankfurt Hof an Commerzbank AG Vorstands-Sekretariat (29.4.1968)].

For instance, at a meeting in Hamburg on November 11, 1971, costs were expended by item, such as the printing cost of the materials, hospitality including accommodations and meals, gifts, travel expenses, and other costs (*Historisches Archiv der Commerzbank*, HAC-400/1817, Kosten Landesbeiratssitzung 11).

16.3.3 Significance of Regional Advisory Council

In the previous subsection, the holding conditions, situations regarding meeting participants, and the contents of regional advisory council meetings for Dresdner Bank and Commerzbank were analyzed. Building on the foregoing discussions, this subsection explores the significance of the regional advisory council.

That belonging to a regional advisory council of a large bank was very useful for the exchange and sharing of information, opinions, and experiences among individuals who were acting vivaciously in the business world. The promotion of such important relationships was pointed out by members of the Dresdner Bank regional advisory council and attendances of meetings of this organization. Furthermore, in many cases, the expectation was that subsequent interchanges through friendly and close relationships were indicated by both banks and industrial enterprises [*Historisches Archiv der Commerzbank*, HAC-500/211, 107847, Der Brief von Carl Goetz an Herrn Alfons Hentzel (18.7.1960); *Historisches Archiv der Commerzbank*, HAC-500/211, 107847, Der Brief von Carl Goetz an Herrn Direktor Hans Böhmer (11.7. 1961); *Historisches Archiv der Commerzbank*, HAC-500/121, 8106- 2002, Der Brief von der Dresdner Bank AG an Herrn Dr. Schwarz (10.12.1976); *Historisches Archiv der Commerzbank*, HAC-500/121, 18227-2000, Der Brief von der Dresdner Bank AG. an Herrn Dr. Giuseppe Benellit (28.9.1970); *Historisches Archiv der Commerzbank*, HAC-500/121, 1227-2000, Der Brief von der Dresdner Bank AG. an Herrn Dr.-Ing. Hermann Roser (19.3.1971); *Historisches Archiv der Commerzbank*, HAC-500/

121, 7909-2002, Bd.2, Der Brief von der Dresdner Bank AG an Herrn Hermann Pfaff (7.11.1972); *Historisches Archiv der Commerzbank*, HAC-500/121,7909-2002, Bd.2, Der Brief von der Dresdner Bank an Herrn Senator E. h. Dipl.-Ing.Ludwig Büchner (9.12.1974); *Historisches Archiv der Commerzbank*, HAC-500/121, 7909-2002, Bd.2, Der Brief von der Dresdner Bank AG an Herrn Ministerdirektor a. D. Dr. Elmar Michel (8.10.1975)].

Similar situations can also be observed in the regional advisory council of Commerzbank. Many individuals concerned with regional advisory councils pointed out that free and open contacts with noticeable leading persons in the German economic world became possible through the bank's council, and opportunities to personally discuss every general issue with attendances were created [*Historisches Archiv der Commerzbank*, HAC-400/1821, Der Brief von August Bilstein an den Vorstand der Commerzbank A.G. zu Hd. Herrn G. Knappertsbusch (26.6.1978), *Historisches Archiv der Commerzbank*, HAC-400/1821, Der Brief von Hermann Kronseder an der Vorstandd/Commerzbank AG (4.7.1978)]. In addition, attendees of regional advisory councils of this bank indicated that they were given the opportunity to actively take counsel, which contributed to developing new personnel contacts and deepening existing personnel relationships [*Historisches Archiv der Commerzbank*, HAC-400/1821, Der Brief von Freidrich Siegert an Herr Lichtenberg (20.6.1978)]. In other cases, participants of unified meetings of some regional advisory councils pointed out that membership in a Commerzbank regional advisory council was attractive because of not only the friendly business relationships created but also the experience of the concerned individuals [*Historisches Archiv der Commerzbank*, HAC-400/1821, Der Brief von Herm. W. Thywissen an den vorstand d/Commerzbank AG (20.6.1978)]. In the unified meeting of the Baden–Württemberg regional advisory council, the Bayern regional advisory council, the Hessen regional advisory council, and the Rheinland–Pfalz–Saar regional advisory council on March 25, 1974, members of Commerzbank specified that the favorable and active cooperation of members of regional advisory councils with this bank through such an organization had significant meaning (*Historisches Archiv der Commerzbank*, HAC-400/1819, Sitzung der Landesbeiräte Baden-Württemberg, Bayern, Hessen, Rheinland-Pfalz-Saar am 25. März 1974 in Frankfurt am Main). Regarding the significance for this bank, a letter dated December 19, 1979, from Commerzbank to E. Denges, a member of the Bayern regional advisory council for eleven years, pointed out that his advice based on expert knowledge promoted the bank's development [*Historisches Archiv der Commerzbank*, HAC-400/1822, Der Brief von der Commerzbank Aktiengesellschaft an Herrn Dr. Dönges (19.12.1979)].

In addition, cases existed in which the invitation of a member from an enterprise with which a large bank had not built a close relationship given the company's relations with other banks became an important way to establish personnel and cooperative relationships based on it. In an internal Dresdner Bank document dated November 12, 1973, no member was from BASF, as one of the largest chemical enterprises on this bank's advisory council, despite the importance of this industrial company in business relations. Such a situation resulted from the participation of BASF individuals on Deutsche Bank's central advisory and regional advisory councils. Bernhard

Timm was a member of the central advisory council and Rolf Magener was a member of the Baden–Pfalz regional advisory council of this bank. At Dresdner Bank, issues related to requests for participation of a BASF individual in the Southeast regional advisory council that would be newly founded were examined [*Historisches Archiv der Commerzbank*, HAC-500121, 7909-2002, Bd.2, Landesbeirat Südwest—Beabsichtigte Zuwahl von Professor Host Pommer, Mitglied des Vorstands der BASF AG. Ludwigshafen (12.11.1973)]. In this way, the appeal of Dresdner Bank to BASF is essential proof that building a close and cooperative relationship between banks and industrial enterprises was emphasized by the large bank.

Regarding the personnel affairs of members and chairmen of regional advisory councils, in numerous cases, minute proposals and discussions were performed, and exchanges and coordination occurred between candidates or their enterprises and banks and between banks and important individuals who could influence such personnel issues [*Historisches Archiv der Commerzbank*, HAC-500/121, 8106-2002, Der Brief von Jürgen Ponto an Herr Zahn (1.6.1977); *Historisches Archiv der Commerzbank*, HAC-500/121, 8106-2002, Beirat Bayern (12.5.1977); *Historisches Archiv der Commerzbank*, HAC-500/121, 8106-2002, Beirat Baden-Württemberg (11.2.1977); *Historisches Archiv der Commerzbank*, HAC-500/121, 8106-2002, Beirat Baden-Württemberg (9.2.1977)]. A careful examination of such personnel affairs revealed the deep concern with the fact that regional advisory councils played important roles in building, maintaining, and reinforcing close and friendly relationships between banks and industrial enterprises and among industrial companies.

Remuneration was paid to members of regional advisory councils as meritorious consideration. In such an organization of Dresdner Bank, 4,000 Deutsche Mark (DM) was paid in 1962 for each member as remuneration. 2,000 Deutsche Mark (DM) was paid to members who had posted only in a half period of one year. Remuneration for the chairman of the regional advisory council was two times that of each member for a year [*Historisches Archiv der Commerzbank*, HAC-500/196, 12005, Beirat (31.12.1962); *Historisches Archiv der Commerzbank*, HAC-500/196, 12005, Der Brief von Dresdner Bank AG. an die Herren Mitglieder des Beirates Baden-Württemberg der Dresdner Bank AG. (31.12.1962)]. This point indicates the significance of the regional advisory council and the important role of members of such an organization.

In the foregoing examinations, the functions of personnel connections through a bank's advisory council system between banks and industrial enterprises and among companies that sent members to such an organization were clarified. Information, opinions, and experiences on general economic issues were exchanged and shared, and conditions in individual fields and advice on important fundamental problems in business policy were developed through these organizations. Such committee entities exhibited the functions of strengthening business relationships of banks with industrial enterprises as customers and coordination between banks and industrial companies and among industrial firms through personnel contacts and connections. In Germany, in many cases, members of advisory councils had mandates of the top management entities of enterprises in various industries, such as the supervisory board. Such personnel connections were an important foundation for displaying the functions of interfirm relationships. As analyzed in the foregoing chapters, extensive systems of exchanging and sharing information and coordinating interests and conflicts between companies through personnel connections between banks and industrial enterprises and among industrial companies were established. Under such relations, personnel connections through advisory council systems of banks supplemented personnel connections through the interlocking of members of the supervisory board and the managing board in top management entities of other companies. Personnel connections functioned as an important element that constituted cooperative capitalism in Germany.

References

Aizawa K (1994) Oshu saikyo no kinyu teikoku. Doitsu ginko (The strongest financial empire in Europe). Nihon Keizai shinbunsha, Tokyo

Büschgen HE (1983) Die Groβbanken. Fritz Knapp Verlag, Frankfurt am Main

Eglau HO (1990) Wie Gott in Frankfurt: Die Deutsche Bank und die deutsche Industrie, 3rd edn. Econ Verlag, Düsseldorf

Gottschalk A (1988) Der Stimmrechtseinfluβ der Banken in den Aktionärver-sammlungen von Groβunternehmen. In: WSI Mitteilungen 41(5):294–304

Koubek N (1971) Personelle und institutionelle Verbindung der Bereiche "Produktion" und "Kapital" in der Wirtschaftsgesellschaft der BRD. In: WWI-Mitteilungen 24(8/9):258–274

Pfeiffer H (1987) Das Imperium der Deutsche Bank. Campus, Frankfurt am Main

Pfeiffer H (1986) Das Netwerk der Groβbanken.Personelle Verflechtungen mit Konzernen, Staat und ideologischen Apparaten. In: Blätter für deutsche und Internationale Politik 31(2):161–177

Schwarz F (2003) Die Deutsche Bank. Reise auf tönerner Füβen. Campus, Frankfurt am Main

Stanzick K-H (1969) Der ökonomische Konzentrationsprozeβ. In: Schäfer G, Nedelmann C (Hrsg) Der CDU-Staat. Analysen zur Verfassungswriklichkeit der Bundesrepublik, Bd. I, 2. Aufl., Schurkamp, München, SS 48–79

Chapter 17
Conclusion: Historical Changes in Personnel Connections and Industry–Bank Relationships in Germany

Abstract This chapter expands on the previous chapters' discussions and clarifies the implications of the analyses presented in this book. The characteristics and significance of changes in personnel connections between industry and banks will be examined in light of the historical conditions in each period analyzed in previous chapters. The special characteristics of interfirm relationships based on personnel relationships in Germany are examined in light of two key issues presented in Chap. 1, namely "corporate control" and "corporate rule." The German form of Lenin's "finance capital," which he proposed as a capital form created by uniting and knitting industrial and banking capital, and its significance are explained. Understanding the role of personnel connection systems and personnel networks established by interlocking directorates clarifies the mechanism for achieving such objectives from the perspectives of industry and banking. This chapter also discusses the significance of personnel connections between a bank and an industrial enterprise in terms of German enterprises' behavioral mode and accumulation structure.

Keywords Advisory council · Bank · Corporate control · Corporate rule · Germany Inc. · Industry–bank relationships · Personnel connection · Personnel network

This book analyzes historical changes to clarify the overall structure and functions of personnel connections formed by the interlocking directorates of members of the supervisory and managing boards of three large German banks and the system of the banks' advisory councils. In Germany, industrial enterprises and banks have established a tight and extensive network of personnel ties. This was based on their unique relationships, as determined by the universal character of "money" provided by banks and the intermediation of business transactions. The system of such personnel connections allows for coordinating various conflicts and interests between companies through information exchange and sharing rather than market competition, which is deeply concerned with Germany's specific business management and its enterprise behavioral mode. It is an important component of Germany's

T. Yamazaki, *Relationships Between Industry and Bank in Germany*,
https://doi.org/10.1007/978-981-97-4996-6_17

social economic system, known as "cooperative capitalism" (Chandler 1990), and has served as a solid foundation for German enterprises' administrative behavior.

Based on the previous chapters' analyses, this chapter first examines the historical changes in personnel connections between banks and industrial enterprises established through the interlocking directorates and the Bank's advisory council system, as well as their characteristics in Sect. 17.1. Section 17.2 then considers the implications of analyses of interlocking directorates and personnel networks from the perspective of differences and relationships between "corporate control" and "corporate rule," as introduced in Chap. 1. Section 17.3 also explains how changes in personnel ties relate to historical conditions.

Meanwhile, Sect. 17.2 examines Lenin's proposed German form of "finance capital," which is based on uniting and knitting of monopolistic capital in the industrial and banking sectors (Ленин 1962, Chap. 3). It is important to understand how interlocking directorates were used to achieve the common interests of banks and industrial enterprises in both directions, from banks to industrial enterprises and from the latter to the former, as well as the personnel network formed due to this process. This chapter analyzes the German style of "financial capital," focusing on the information flow and media system established by personnel connections and networks as a foundation for cooperation to achieve "maximization of industrial and commercial profit" through information exchange and sharing between banks and industrial enterprises.

17.1 Industry-Bank Relationships Based on the Personnel Connections and Their Characteristics: Historical View

17.1.1 Historical Changes in Interlocking Directorates and Their Characteristics

17.1.1.1 Historical Changes in Direct Interlocking Directorates and Their Characteristics

First, this subsection discusses direct and indirect interlocking directorates. This book examines personnel connections formed by the interlocking directorates of the three largest banks' board members (supervisory and management boards), including invited members on each bank's supervisory board. Until the end of World War II, interlocking directorates on the supervisory boards of other enterprises were distributed across a wide range of industries. Except for the banking industry, many interlocking relationships were formed among the various industries, with the mining and heavy and chemical industries serving as the key industrial sectors, which included the iron and steel, chemical, electrical, and machine industries. The number of companies and mandates in which board members of the companies in the insurance and electric power industries formed personnel ties with other companies was still low in the period after World War II. Interlocking directorates were established through more than two posts in representative enterprises in the major industrial sectors, and personnel ties with several companies competing in the same industrial sector were established through several mandates of the supervisory board, which was remarkable. Furthermore, there were numerous instances where interlocking directorates were established through important mandates such as chairman and vice-chairman. Such close and strong personnel connections helped the company obtain a wealth of information for its own financial business and decision-making regarding industrial enterprise policies. Large banks built a solid foundation for gathering, exchanging, and sharing information and its use. Although access to information about individual companies was only one aspect of the close relationships through the supervisory board between banks and industrial enterprises, banks had a core role as advisers for companies in securing the interests of both parties (Dahlem 2009, S. 279).

Except for the period at the beginning of the twentieth century, in terms of the number of direct interlocking directorates on the supervisory boards of other companies, Deutsche Bank tended to build the most personnel ties in terms of both companies and mandates among the three largest banks. Dresdner Bank followed, and Commerzbank had the fewest interlocking directorates of board members. When examining the types of interlocking mandates of the supervisory board, a similar pattern emerges. Deutsche Bank established the most interlocking directorates through chairman or plural posts, while the other two banks' situations differed. Otto Eglau pointed out that at least a person for supporting member of the managing board of Deutsche Bank who had interlocking mandate on the supervisory board of other industrial enterprise was organized, and materials regarding the supervisory board that reached one hundred pages were condensed to only three or four pages, and he prepared items for questioning management teams (Eglau 1990, SS. 136–137).

Regarding characteristics of each period, the number of both enterprises and mandates in which interlocking directorates were formed increased dramatically during the inflationary period following World War I, compared to those established during the period of monopolistic capitalism, and even more than those in the other periods considered in this book. During the period of inflation, banks were forced to confront the trend of industrial enterprises becoming independent of banks, and they attempted to expand personnel connections through interlocking directorates to maintain and strengthen business relations with industrial enterprises as customers. Such measurements were extremely important to banks. The Bank's efforts to expand interlocking directorates were an important countermeasure to the decrease in the level of the organized economic system of German finance capital. If financial transactions were not generated under the trend of declining industrial enterprises' dependence on banks, the personnel ties of banks with many large businesses had to be maintained in the closest way, and cooperation in the management of companies with which banks had friendly relationships was pursued through involvement in the supervisory board (Berliner Handels-Gesellschaft 1956, S. 172). This was a countermeasure to protect business relationships with industrial enterprises.

Following World War II, a system of interlocking directorates led by large banks was established on the basis of a deposit stock system that allowed banks to vote at general meetings as the secondary stock market expanded and banks cooperated. This system laid the groundwork for banks' influence over corporations, exchanging and sharing information, and coordinating interests and conflicts between banks, industrial enterprises, and corporations. As a result, in the late 1950s, when postwar Germany's industrial concentration system was established by reconcentrating large enterprises dissolved by victorious countries' occupation policies, interlocking directorates of bank members on the supervisory boards of other enterprises were developed for various industries. Banks built strong personnel ties with companies in the electric power, gas, and energy industries, as well as those in the insurance sector, indicating an increase in the importance of these industries.

However, the 1965 Corporations Law limited the number of supervisory board mandates that one person could hold (Pfeiffer 1993, SS. 158–159, 1986a, S. 164, 1986b, S. 477; Stanzick 1969, S. 72; Eglau 1990, S. 128; Der Spiegel 1965, S. 50), which influenced the conditions of interlocking directorates through the supervisory board's mandate. Consequently, there was a trend toward fewer companies with interlocking directorates and mandates. This trend was caused by large banks' careful selection of companies to build and strengthen interlocking directorate relationships, as well as the industrial sectors that the banks emphasized. Furthermore, as discussed in Sect. 17.3, the progress of mergers and acquisitions (M&As) and the decrease in the number of joint-stock companies were linked to the decrease in interlocking directorates. However, as evidenced by the increase in the number of interlocking directorates due to important positions on the supervisory board, such as the chairman's mandate to all interlocking directorates, large banks have tended to pursue interlocking directorate building structures that emphasize personnel connections.

Thus, such personnel connections remained a fundamental interlocking directorate system in postwar Germany for a long time. While a bank's interlocking directorate on the supervisory board of other enterprises spans multiple industries, large banks strengthened personnel connections with several competing companies in the same industrial sector that they regarded as important through supervisory board mandates. Such a system was important in coordinating interests and conflicts among enterprises, including banks and industrial enterprises. Until the late 1980s, no factors significantly impacted the status of interlocking directorates on other companies' supervisory boards.

When comparing the conditions at the end of the 1950s and 1960s (see Chaps. 5 and 6), the rates of interlocking directorates with chairman mandates to all interlocking directorates that Deutsche Bank built in terms of the number of enterprises and mandates increased from 43.8% to 50.3% and 35.9% to 41.8%, respectively. Similar figures for Dresdner Bank decreased slightly, from 32.1% to 30.5%, and increased slightly, from 26.4% to 26.6%, respectively. Meanwhile, those for Commerzbank decreased from 30.6% to 26.2% and from 27% to 24.5%, respectively.

Deutsche Bank's figures were higher than those of the other two banks, indicating that this bank pursued an interlocking directorate structure emphasizing the quality of the personnel connection more strongly than its competitors.

However, the picture changed when the rates of interlocking directorates formed by appointing board members from each of the three largest German banks as chairmen on the supervisory boards of other enterprises were compared to all interlocking directorates of board members from each of these banks. Deutsche Bank's number of mandates increased from 53.7% to 69%. Those for Dresdner Bank increased from 31.4% to 40.4%, whereas those for Commerzbank greatly increased from 34.4% to 63% (author's calculation based on Morr 1960; Mossner 1971). These figures show that the three largest banks emphasized the assignment of their board members, who were originally from each bank, to chairmanships on the supervisory boards of other enterprises as part of their own strategy. Despite this trend, Deutsche Bank had a stronger intention to secure chairmanships than the other two banks. With the addition of vice-chairman mandates, Deutsche Bank's dominant position becomes much clearer (Joly 1998, S. 202).

For example, at the end of the 1960s, as analyzed in Chap. 6, although the difference in the rates of interlocking directorates built through vice-chairman mandates to all interlocking directorates was not very large among the three largest banks, Deutsche Bank had a relatively high rate of interlocking directorates formed via chairman and vice-chairman posts to all interlocking directorates (57%). This emphasis on the quality of the interlocking directorates reflected the Banks' strategic intentions to build and reinforce interfirm relationships, considering the selection of objects to form personnel ties and the prioritization of many enterprises as candidates.

After the 1990s, there was a noticeable shift in the industry–bank relationship, as observed by decreased dispatches of bank representatives on the supervisory boards of other enterprises and the interlocking directorates of banks' top management (Monopolkommission 2008, S. 198; Jürgens et al 2000, p. 70; Höpner 2001, pp. 26, 50). In the latter half of the 2010s, compared to conditions at the end of the 1960s (see Chaps. 6 and 7), the number of enterprises and mandates where direct interlocking directorates were established decreased significantly. In particular, the number of enterprises and mandates with interlocking directorates established by members of Deutsche Bank's supervisory board and managing board on the supervisory boards of other enterprises decreased from 167 to 17 and 201 to 23, respectively. In the case of Commerzbank, similar figures decreased from 103 to 11 and from 110 to 13, respectively.

Personnel connections established through the two largest banks' interlocking directorates are extremely limited to a few enterprises. Personnel ties with enterprises in the heavy and chemical industries as key industrial sectors decreased dramatically, whereas those with enterprises in the banking industry as the same industry to which Deutsche Bank belonged tended to be numerous in terms of mandates. Personnel relations established through interlocking directorates by the two largest banks are extremely limited to a few enterprises and can no longer be used to coordinate interests and conflicts through informal discussions and effective measures of cooperative behavior between banks and industrial enterprises.

Given the situation of interlocking directorates in relation to the position of the supervisory board's mandate, the number of cases in which these two banks established interlocking directorates using the supervisory board chairman's mandate has significantly decreased. In the case of Deutsche Bank, the rates of interlocking directorates through chairman posts to all interlocking directorates in terms of the number of enterprises and mandates decreased from 50.3% to 17.6% and from 41.8% to 13%, respectively. The number of enterprises and mandates where Deutsche Bank established interlocking directorates through plural mandates decreased significantly, from 25 to one and 59 to seven, respectively. Similar figures for Commerzbank decreased from seven to two and fourteen to four, respectively.

17.1.1.2 Historical Changes in Indirect Interlocking Directorates and Their Characteristics

Indirect interlocking directorates among the three largest banks, or between two of them, played an important significance in developing interfirm cooperative relationships. In general, direct interlocking directorates between companies in the same industry were uncommon, whereas indirect interlocking directorates on the boards of other firms between members of plural companies that were mutually competing in the same industry but did not have a direct interlocking directorate were common (Schönwitz and Weber 1982, SS. 80–81, 103).

Indirect interlocking directorates established among the three largest banks or between two banks via direct interlocking directorates of each bank's top management organs on the supervisory boards of other enterprises were important to the strong connection between banks. Such personnel connections were important in exchanging and sharing information about various industrial departments and many companies in which banks were involved in financing and capital investment decisions. They could also be important for coordinating interests and conflicts through discussions. Therefore, indirect interlocking among banks on the same firm's supervisory board significantly impacted enterprise cooperation. This point was important in determining the characteristics of cooperative capitalism in Germany.

Indirect interlocking directorates established on the supervisory boards of other companies among Deutsche Bank, Dresdner Bank, and Commerzbank, or between two banks, played important roles in gathering, exchanging, and sharing data. Enterprises with indirect interlocking directorates were built in a variety of industrial sectors. In addition to the banking and insurance sectors, many indirect interlocking directorates were established in the mining, heavy, and chemical industries, including iron and steel, chemical, electrical, automobile, and machine industries. Indirect interlocking directorates built in multiple companies with mutually competing relationships in the same industry were characteristic of such personnel connections between banks. Some of the three largest banks' multiple mandates were typically in representative enterprises in major industries. The largest and leading enterprises in the industry concerned were numerous enterprises with interlocking directorates established through multiple mandates. In cases where some of the three largest banks that established the indirect interlocking directorates had chairman or vice-chairman mandates, this type of interlocking directorate may be more important in exchanging and sharing information and coordinating interests and conflicts between companies.

In examining the situations involving indirect interlocking directorates among the three banks on the supervisory boards of other enterprises, such a case was seen in only one company during the establishment of monopolistic capitalism, which was due to the fact that Commerzbank was not one of Germany's largest banks yet and did not belong to the six big banks in Berlin. Commerzbank was a company composed of three of the largest German banks during the periods of inflation following World War I, National Socialism, and before and after the 1965 Corporations Law, and it played an important role in the indirect interlocking directorates among these banks or between two of them. However, Commerzbank established personnel ties with fewer enterprises and mandates than Deutsche Bank and Dresdner Bank. As a result, the number of indirect interlocking directorates between Deutsche Bank and Commerzbank or Dresdner Bank and Commerzbank was lower than that between Deutsche Bank and Dresdner Bank.

To understand a bank in a leading position in an indirect interlocking relationship, examine cases in which one bank held more than two mandates on another company's supervisory board and important and influential positions such as chairman and vice-chairman. In this regard, there were numerous instances where Deutsche Bank was in the lead due to having more mandates than the other two banks combined. In general, which bank held the most important positions on supervisory boards determined a bank's dominant position in the indirect interlocking mandates among three banks or between two of them. Deutsche Bank tended to have more chairman mandates than its two rivals, which could position it as a leader in the indirect interlocking directorates.

The system underwent significant changes after the 1990s. In the latter half of the 2010s, indirect interlocking directorates were built in only three companies on the supervisory boards of other enterprises between Deutsche Bank and Commerzbank, for a total of seven mandates. In comparison to the late 1960s, the number of enterprises and mandates where Deutsche Bank and Commerzbank formed indirect interlocking directorates decreased from 14 to 3 and 35 to 7, respectively. In the banking industry, there was only one instance where Deutsche Bank and Commerzbank established indirect interlocking directorates. Only one company has cases where one or both banks had more than two mandates on another company's supervisory board (see Chaps. 6 and 7).

Until the beginning of the 1990s, indirect interlocking directorates were established between large banks through direct interlocking directorates of members of each bank's top management organs on the supervisory boards of other enterprises. This should be an important foundation for the strong connection between banks. However, they have changed dramatically, reflecting a significant decrease in the direct interlocking directorates of large banks. In the latter half of the 2010s, establishing such personnel connections relations was extremely limited to a few enterprises. It could not be an important means of coordinating interests and conflicts through informal discussions and an effective measure of cooperative behavior among banks.

In this way, personnel connection relations between banks and industrial enterprises through direct and indirect interlocking directorates as a core element have been in the process of dissolution since the 1990s, resulting in tremendous changes in the German system of "industry–bank relationships" and interfirm relationships, including those between industrial enterprises. This is very different from the situation at the end of the 1980s.

17.1.2 Historical Changes in Personnel Networks and Their Characteristics

Next, comparing personnel networks built that included second- and third-party enterprises through interlocking directorates between supervisory board members in the Nazi period, the end of the 1960s, and the latter half of the 2010s (see Part 2), densities as indicators of the cohesiveness of Deutsche Bank's network in each period were 0.004494, 0.0077138, and 0.018481, respectively. The number of enterprises in which Deutsche Bank formed interlocking directorates on the supervisory boards of other enterprises fell sharply from 254 to 65, with an additional 17. The total number of companies in this network decreased from 2702 to 702 and to 163. The Commerzbank network's densities in each period were 0.003738, 0.0078716, and 0.067779, respectively. The number of companies in which this bank established interlocking directorates decreased dramatically from 162 to 54, with an additional eight. The number of companies that comprised this network fell from 2290 to 606 and 54. Dresdner Bank had already vanished by the 2020s, and the densities of its network were 0.0038978 and 0.0085992, respectively, during two periods of National Socialism and the end of the 1960s. The number of companies for which this bank established interlocking directorates on the supervisory boards of other companies decreased from 187 to 58. The number of companies that comprise this network has decreased from 2331 to 628.

During the Nazi period, Deutsche Bank's network was denser than that of Dresdner Bank or Commerzbank. The difference in the number of lines indicating personnel ties between enterprises (Deutsche Bank's figure was 16,398 and Dresdner Bank's figure was 10,536) was greater than the difference in the number of all companies that comprised the network (Deutsche Bank's figure was 2702 and Dresdner Bank's figure was 2331), indicating a density difference between the two networks. The density figure of Deutsche Bank's network was higher than that of Commerzbank's network because the difference in the number of lines of interlocking directorates (Deutsche Bank's figure was 16,398 and Commerzbank's figure was 9891) was greater than the difference in the number of companies that comprised the network (Deutsche Bank's figure was 2702 and Commerzbank's figure was 2290).

In the late 1960s, the Dresdner Bank network had a higher density than the Deutsche Bank or Commerzbank networks. The Deutsche Bank network (702) comprised more enterprises than the Dresdner Bank network (628), which was connected with density difference. Meanwhile, Dresdner Bank's network had a higher density than Commerzbank's network. Although the number of enterprises in the Dresdner Bank (628) and Commerzbank (606) networks was nearly identical, the number of lines in the Dresdner Bank network (1693) was greater than in the Commerzbank network (1443), which was connected to the difference in density between the two networks.

Several distinct changes were observed when the personnel networks of large banks were compared before and after World War II. The number of second- and third-party enterprises before World War II was much more than that after the war. This is a common trend across the networks of the three largest banks. Numerous second-party enterprises had interlocking directorates before WWII. This was connected to the differences in the network's cohesiveness between these periods. The consolidation of enterprises did not progress as quickly before the war as it did after the war, and the fact that cartels were fundamentally legal resulted in several enterprises in the network. Cooperation led by banks between industrial enterprises under monopoly regulation by a country that regulated cartels as legal and industrial enterprises' reliance on banks determined by an underdeveloped stock market compared to the USA and the UK fundamentally led to close interfirm relationships. Before the war, personnel connections and networks formed through interlocking directorates were important means of aligning with restrictive conditions for the accumulation and reproduction structure of German capitalism defined by the narrowness of the German domestic market, difficulties in export markets, and inferiority to the USA in the fields of technique and production (Lenin 1953, S. 511).

In the latter half of the 2010s, the Commerzbank network was denser than the Deutsche Bank network. This was because the Commerzbank network consisted of significantly fewer companies. The numerical figures for the densities of these two banks' networks were higher during this period than at the end of the 1960s. Such conditions have resulted from a significant decrease in the number of enterprises that comprise each bank's network during the latter half of the 2010s.

Next, in terms of "centrality" indicating the importance of individual enterprises in the network, in this book, unlike global centrality, which means all personnel tie in the entire network and is measured by the sum distance reaching all other companies, local centralities in the networks of three largest banks were grasped due to the great importance of certain companies in the core position in the information flow and media. Companies with high network centrality typically play an important role in information gathering, exchange, and dissemination. Business relations and connections give personnel relationships with many enterprises significant meaning. For example, when a bank extends credit to an enterprise, the bank should gather information on the funds demanded by the company as the subject of the bank's financing, as well as demand from various industries for such a company and industry. Personnel ties make a significant contribution to these objectives. As a result, an enterprise that establishes personnel connections with multiple companies in various industrial sectors lays the groundwork for obtaining valuable business information.

Large representative banks have a relatively high centrality in networks of both industrial enterprises and banks, as evidenced by interlocking directorates between supervisory board members on the supervisory boards of other enterprises, including second- and third-party enterprises. Although this bank was in a decisively important position in the Deutsche Bank prewar network, some major enterprises in key industrial sectors, such as the iron and steel industry, chemical industry, electrical industry, and automobile industry, were also in a core position in terms of "centrality," as measured by an indicator called "adjacency," which means the number of enterprises in which interlocking directorates are built. Following World War II, electric power and insurance enterprises also became highly centralized, and their roles in the network expanded significantly.

This means that both banks and industrial companies played important roles in the network's information flow and media, with the bank serving as only one of the major players. In the field of information flow and media, a system was developed in which large banks and representative enterprises from major industrial sectors played mutually beneficial roles. As a result, a bank's influence on business management in various sectors, such as industrial enterprises, was not always significant. Similar conditions were observed in the network of industrial enterprises (Yamazaki 2019, Chaps. 8 and 9).

Before World War II, some companies ranked first in adjacency within the networks of the three largest banks or between two of them. Prior to World War II, four enterprises held the highest adjacency in the network of the three largest banks. In the mid-1930s, Allgemeine Electricitäts-Gesellschaft (AEG) in the electrical industry ranked first in terms of adjacency in Dresdner Bank and Commerzbank, and second in the network of Deutsche Bank. Thus, AEG held the most important position in these banks' network before World War II. Vereinigte Stahlwerke AG in the iron and steel industry and Deutsche Centralbodenkredit AG in the banking industry were ranked third and fourth in the three banks' networks, respectively. In the chemical industry, Kokswerke and Chemische Fabriken AG ranked fifth in the Commerzbank AG network and sixth in the networks of the other two banks.

Furthermore, among the three largest banks, some enterprises ranked in the top ten in terms of adjacency in two-bank networks. Only two companies were in the top ten of the Deutsche Bank and Dresdner Bank networks. Rheinische AG für Braunkohlenbergbau und Brikettfabrikation in the mining industry, and Deutsch-Atlantische Telegraphengesellschaft in other industries, ranked fifth and ninth in these two banks' networks, respectively. Daimler-Benz AG in the automobile industry ranked seventh in the Deutsche Bank and Commerzbank networks. Two enterprises were ranked in the top ten of both the Dresdner Bank and Commerzbank networks. Mitteldeutsche Stahlwerke AG, which operated in the iron and steel industry, was ranked second in these bank networks. Allianz and Stuttgarter Verein Versicherungs-AG in the insurance industry ranked sixth and seventh in the Commerzbank and Dresdner Bank networks.

Such overlapping of companies with high centralities provided the three largest banks, two of which, with the ability to obtain the same information on the supervisory boards of these leading companies, which played important roles as a uniting point of the information flow and media in the network and could promote common recognition of a management issue between banks and between a bank and an industrial enterprise in the network concerned. The sharing of recognition and understanding was an important foundation for the coordination of interests, conflicts, and cooperative behaviors among the three largest banks and between two banks and industrial enterprises.

Although AEG was at the first position measured by adjacency in the networks of Dresdner Bank and Commerzbank and at the second position in the network of Deutsche Bank during the Nazi period and was at the first position in the Dresdner Bank network at the end of the 1960s, it was not even in the upper 20 in the networks of Deutsche Bank and Commerzbank. In contrast, measured by adjacency in all networks of the three largest banks after the war, Rheinisch-Westfälisches Elektrizitätswerk AG, as an electric power firm with no mandate from the three banks' supervisory boards in the mid-1930s, prior to World War II, rose to second place in the networks of the three banks. This most representative enterprise in the electric power industry played an important role in the network's information flow and media against the backdrop of industrial development determined by the progress and expansion of electrification of family, industry, and railroads following the war.

As analyzed in Chap. 10, the postwar personnel network underwent significant changes after the 1990s. The number of enterprises in the two largest German banks' networks between supervisory board members decreased dramatically in the latter half of the 2010s when compared to the end of the 1960s. The range of industrial sectors to which these enterprises belonged was limited to a few industries, and enterprises in the heavy and chemical industries, which had been key industrial sectors in German capitalism, became scarce, with many representative enterprises disappearing. The adjacencies of enterprises with high centrality in the networks of Deutsche Bank and Commerzbank decreased. These indicate significant changes in personnel networks in "distant 2," including second- and third-party enterprises via interlocking directorates, and the system's role for information exchange and sharing between banks and industrial enterprises and between industrial enterprises. As the most representative enterprises in the banking industry, these large banks no longer play significant roles as the central link in the network's information flow and media due to personnel ties with numerous enterprises in various industrial sectors. Regarding personal connections, a significant transformation appeared in "Germany Inc." as cooperative interfirm relationships between industry and banks, as well as a reduction in the roles of large banks.

17.1.3 Functions of the Interlocking Directorate and Their Characteristics

Next, as seen in Daimler-Benz, there were cases in which personnel issues concerning the election of management board members were delegated to the interlocking chairman on the supervisory board, who was a banker. In many other cases, the board of directors requested that the chairman approve personnel issues and admissions. Such examples in Daimler-Benz prior to World War II can be found in the roles and involvements of Emil G von Stauss and Hans Rumel, Stauss's successors. In this company, various exchanges and negotiations were conducted between the interlocking chairman of the supervisory board from Deutsche Bank and individuals from this automobile enterprise, including board members. Furthermore, there were instances in which a personnel from Deutsche Bank was involved in personnel negotiations at the request of E. G. von Stauss, chairman of the supervisory board, on the basis of this bank's intentions. In many cases, the bank strongly influenced the personnel affairs of an industrial company's management board because bank representatives served on the supervisory board that provided the interconnections. This was evident in numerous instances where the company name of Deutsche Bank and the position of chairman of the supervisory board of this bank, as well as the company name of Daimler-Benz and the position of chairman of the supervisory board of this industrial enterprise, were written in an address of a document concerning personnel issues. Cases in which important personnel issues, such as managing board member election, were decided with the intention and interest of a large bank with an interlocking mandate in mind, as well as strict bank review, were typical of the role of interlocking supervisory board members, particularly the chairman.

Personnel issues involving the appointment of managing board members by the supervisory board in an industrial enterprise were important foundations for obtaining valuable information for the bank's business, including providing financing to companies and investing in other companies. By obtaining such information, a large bank can ensure a consistent collection of financing funds for companies and improve the efficiency of investments in industrial companies. This role in an industry–bank relationship was deeply related to the development and accomplishment of a bank's policy for industrial companies, and it was an important component and the foundation of cooperative capitalism in Germany (see Chap. 11).

In terms of assigning bank members to the industrial enterprise supervisory board, holding and maintaining a supervisory board mandate trumped other issues related to this behavior. Interlocking supervisory board members from banks typically possessed expertise and knowledge of financial issues, economic trends, and the industrial world, which they obtained through numerous interlocking mandates from enterprises in various industrial sectors. They also had international business experience and could provide valuable information and advice to industrial enterprises. Industrial firms had high expectations of receiving valuable information and advice on financial, industrial, and economic matters and inviting bank representatives to supervisory boards and committees within organs such as the financial and capital participation committees. This purpose on the part of industrial enterprises that accepted bankers on their supervisory boards explains why bank board members frequently held important and influential positions, such as chairman and vice-chairman. In companies where the personnel committee was established as a special inner circle within the supervisory board, bank representatives on the supervisory board of industrial enterprises played significant roles in important personnel issues, such as top management member election. In cases where the election of a specific bank representative associated with the position of such committee was successful, a large bank could secure a mandate on the supervisory board and a seat on such an important committee.

Interlocking supervisory board members from banks significantly impacted coordinating of various conflicts and interests between companies. Such functions and roles were especially important in situations where there was serious conflict and opposition between a company with an interlocking supervisory board member from a bank and another company, or when difficult business negotiations between companies were required. The former increased the room for coordination by bringing together bankers who had personnel contact points with opponents. In the latter, if there were business or personnel relationships with an enterprise as an object to be negotiated, the person in question could hold an important position and serve as a strong intermediary. As a result, company coordination could be strengthened. If an enterprise in which the bank representative served as an interlocking supervisory board member experienced a management crisis, the financial crisis was mitigated or overcome through agreement and cooperation with other financial institutions, with the assistance of loaning. Conflicts were avoided, and goals were set to rebuild the company and achieve economic development through personnel contact with key people observed in this issue, as well as gathering, exchanging, and sharing information. These functions were critical for rebuilding the company in significance and protecting the bank's interests, such as providing credit and investment. It is possible to obtain various information about various industrial sectors and use measurements to coordinate between companies on the basis of the quality of interlocking mandates, the presence of such posts in almost all economic departments, and the number of mandates.

Furthermore, as seen in efforts to promote enterprise concentration measures such as mergers, sales of unprofitable departments, withdrawal from them, and reform of organizations that enable effective business management, strict demand for restructuring of enterprises in which bank representatives served as supervisory board members, as well as participation in such rebuilding, were important roles of interlocking board members. In such cases, attempting to coordinate conflicts and interests for orbiting restructuring through involvement in personnel issues such as replacing top management personnel played an important role.

There were cases in which interlocking supervisory board members from banks with mandates on the supervisory boards of multiple enterprises in mutually competitive conditions in the same industry attempted to coordinate conflicts and interests among these enterprises. In the German automobile industry, under increasing competition and a severe depression that began in 1929, through his interlocking mandates, E. G von Stauss, who served on the supervisory boards of Daimler-Benz AG and BMW, pursued cooperative relationships such as production consignment and division of labor in terms of products (aircraft engines) as both firms' survival strategies. Stauss sought to achieve a division of labor in which Daimler-Benz AG would produce water-cooled engines and BMW would produce air-cooled engines. W. Kissel from Daimler-Benz served on the supervisory boards of BMW and F. J Popp from BMW has joined Daimler-supervisory Benz's board. These personnel connections enabled to achieve smoother coordination between them (James 2003, S. 93, 95).

As discussed in Chap. 12, indirect interlocking played an important role in coordination between companies by establishing personnel ties on the supervisory boards of other companies. Interlocking supervisory board members from Deutsche Bank and August Thyssen Hütte, who formed an indirect interlock in the Demag AG, discussed a personnel issue in Thyssen, and efforts to coordinate interests between this iron and steel enterprise and Germany's largest bank were made.

In terms of the bank's role and intention in industry–bank relationships via an interlocking supervisory board member, a representative of a large bank in the "Germany Inc." system tended to balance competition and cooperation in order to maintain long-term business relationships with industrial companies and expand the role as a house bank. The interlocking members from the bank on the supervisory boards of other companies worked to lay the groundwork for high profitability through consistent loan collection and high dividends from many companies in which the bank invested, rather than pursuing short-term interest from higher stock prices and dividends. Monitoring management execution in a company where the bank formed an interlocking directorate, as well as the bank's interest and participation in electing members of the managing board who were appropriate for the development of such management and supervisory board members who were suggested as candidates at the annual meeting, were important functions for the interlocking directorate. This also includes the bank's position as an interlocking supervisory board member in corporate governance.

The close relationships between industry and banks established through the interlocking directorate did not imply that banks exercised control over business policy and industrial enterprise management, but rather that they sought to build cooperative relationships based on mutual interests. Including cases where a company was experiencing a management crisis, the primary efforts of interlocking supervisory board members were to promote and strengthen economic relationships formed through financial transactions with industrial enterprises.

17.1.4 *Characteristics and Significance of Personnel Connection through Advisory Council System*

17.1.4.1 Structure of Personnel Connection through Advisory Council System and Their Characteristics

A bank's advisory council was also an important source of information for the bank and its member enterprises. This helped to coordinate corporate interests and conflicts, as well as those between banks and enterprises. The field and scope of information that members of an advisory council could obtain through such organizations were determined by their position on top management organs, such as an enterprise's supervisory and managing boards. Bank advisory councils were important in supplementing personnel ties based on interlocking directorates.

In many cases, central or regional advisory council members served on the supervisory board rather than the managing board. Members of the advisory council particularly served on the supervisory boards of enterprises in several key industrial sectors across Germany. In some cases, a company's advisory council member also served on a supervisory board for other member companies. In such cases, a strong personnel connection was established between the member companies of an advisory council. In several cases, top management members of each of the three major banks held interlocking mandates on the supervisory board of the central advisory council's member enterprises.

In terms of personnel connections through regional advisory councils, the composition of member companies and the conditions under which advisory council members had top management mandates reflected each district's industrial accumulation. For example, the Württemberg regional advisory council included many companies from the machine industry in a broad sense, such as the automobile industry and the metal production and processing industries. Holding of top management mandates tended to be concentrated in such industrial sectors. The Rhein-Westfalen regional advisory council had a large number of enterprises in the heavy industrial sectors, such as the iron and steel, machine, and mining industries. There were numerous holdings of the supervisory board mandates for enterprises in these industrial sectors. These examples from both regional advisory councils reflected each district's industrial accumulation characteristics. Some enterprises delegated representatives to regional advisory councils in a similar district with several banks. However, before World War II, industrial accumulation in the machine and metal industries in general in the Württemberg region was not as high as after the war, when the automobile industry expanded and developed rapidly. In the period preceding World War II, reflecting such a situation, there were differences in the depth of relationships with enterprises in key industrial sectors between this regional advisory council and the advisory council in the Rhein-Westfalen region, where industrial accumulation centered on the mining sector and the iron and steel industry had already advanced to a high level. There were also instances where advisory council members of three large banks or multiple banks held mandates from top management organs such as supervisory or managing boards of the same enterprise.

In Germany, regional advisory councils existed in some large banks prior to World War II, whereas a central advisory council was established as the core of a special committee that managed information exchange between enterprises and between banks and industrial enterprises for bank head offices. The central advisory council comprised members of representative enterprises from the major industrial sectors. Members of leading companies in key industries frequently served as chairman or vice-chairman of such organizations. In many companies Deutsche Bank established direct interlocking directorates on the supervisory boards, resulting in deep relationships between the bank and these companies. The number of cases in which Dresdner Bank or Commerzbank established interlocking directorates with member companies of their central advisory councils was lower than that of Deutsche Bank.

In some cases, people from different companies that were competing in the same industry belonged to the central advisory council. In the case of Deutsche Bank, similar cases can be observed in the iron and steel, chemical, and electrical industries. Similar cases were observed in the iron and steel, mining and distribution industries in the central advisory council of Commerzbank. In the case of Dresdner Bank, similar cases were seen in the iron and steel industry.

There were few cases in which members of the central advisory council served on the managing board, but many on the supervisory board. Deutsche Bank's central advisory council had more companies and mandates than Dresdner Bank and Commerzbank, and the industrial sectors to which such companies belonged were diverse. There were cases in which companies of the central advisory councils of Deutsche Bank and Dresdner Bank, or Dresdner Bank and Commerzbank, held positions on the same company's supervisory board. Meanwhile, none of these three banks, Deutsche Bank and Commerzbank, held a seat on the same enterprise's supervisory board.

When comparing the connection of personnel through indirect interlocking directorates and the advisory council system, the former was a measure of informal personnel connection between enterprises established due to direct interlocking directorates. In contrast, the latter was an important formal means of personnel connection between a bank and industrial enterprises on the one hand, and corporations on the other. The purpose and content of the information obtained through indirect interlocking directorates and the advisory council system were distinct. Indirect interlocking directorates between banks, established through direct interlocking on the supervisory boards of other enterprises, provide an important foundation for sharing information on industrial enterprises in which a bank finances and invests and banks' cooperative behavior over such enterprises, including interest coordination and conflict between banks. On the contrary, for banks, the advisory council system as a means of personnel connection between banks and enterprises in various industrial sectors was an important foundation for maintaining and expanding business relations with industrial enterprises, consistent credit collection, and the realization of higher efficiency in share investment. It was critical to obtain information on financing and investment conditions in industrial enterprises and market and competition conditions in various industries through an advisory council. A bank could use this data to determine the priority order of financing and investment.

Thus, both indirect interlocking directorates and a bank's advisory council system played important roles in supplementing personnel connections via direct interlocking directorates in top management entities such as the supervisory board and the board of directors. These were the important foundations of a bank's industrial policy and industrial system as a German mechanism for the development of industries and an economy dominated by large banks.

17.1.4.2 Functions of Personnel Connection through the Advisory Council System and Their Characteristics

The roles of personnel ties established through central or regional advisory councils were important. As discussed in Chap. 14, at the meetings of the Deutsche Bank regional advisory councils prior to World War II, reports on the business conditions of the branches in the advisory council's region, the entire business situation of this bank, and general situations surrounding the banking industry, including the securities market and business, were often made. Lectures on each type of theme were given. The lectures covered production and sales volumes, economic conditions, labor trends such as employment and unemployment, trade conditions, global economic conditions, and the conditions and problems of each industry. In some cases, lectures covered state policy, the influences and roles of the state on enterprises and the economy, and the effects of armament expansion and autarky under the Second Four-Year Plan, which began in 1936. Reports, lectures, and discussions, including questions and answers, were used to provide useful information for the decision-making of the advisory council's member companies, to share information and personnel contacts between banks and industrial companies, as well as between many companies in various industries, and to connect companies.

As we analyzed in Chap. 16, there were many instances in which members of Deutsche Bank's managing board presented reports on business conditions and account settlement and lectures on various topics such as the most recent economic condition, financial situation, and trend. In many cases, regional advisory councils met jointly. Such organizations provided a forum for developing close and friendly relationships between banks and industrial enterprises and active discussions, including critical examination.

Including people actively involved in the industrial world on a regional advisory council was beneficial for exchanging opinions and experiences and providing an opportunity to discuss general issues with attendees personally. Many attendees from both banks and industrial enterprises expressed their belief that the interchange through this type of organization would be an important foundation for maintaining friendly and good relationships. The regional advisory council provided the significance for active discussion, which helped to establish new personnel contacts and strengthen existing personnel ties, and expert advice was extremely valuable. The goal of this organization was to foster special relationships that would allow mutual profits for bank management and key personnel in charge of business execution in economic fields. Securing personnel ties through a regional advisory council had important implications for banks in forming personnel connections with enterprises with which banks had previously been unable to build close relationships due to relations between this enterprise and other banks, as well as companies with which banks were inferior in business relationships.

The election of members to the regional advisory council was an important issue for banks. It was widely regarded as one of the most important personnel agendas and was approved at the bank's supervisory board meeting. The branches in each region were encouraged to maintain and strengthen business relationships with enterprises, which are important customers. There were numerous cases in which members of this organization were chosen on the basis of a variety of factors, including the replacement of a predecessor with someone from the same company, the candidate's experience and expertise in a specific field, the condition of his installation in similar or other organizations of other banks, and the person's business relationships and intentions, as well as the enterprise to which he belonged. Because of the importance of members of this organization to banks, competition over electing members among banks was not uncommon.

Personnel connections through bank regional advisory councils were important in supplementing personnel connections and interfirm relationships between banks and industrial enterprises through interlocking directorates on other companies' supervisory boards and invitations from individuals outside a bank's supervisory board. Personnel connections through advisory councils have the potential to broaden relationships between banks and industrial enterprises beyond those established through supervisory board connections. Such personnel connections could also lead to closer ties with representative companies in specific regions where the bank had business interests. Such entities established by large banks were important components of cooperative capitalism in Germany.

The central advisory council's purpose was to provide advice from the bank's management to its member management, to develop close relationships with the group in the economic world, and to strengthen business relations by building the bank's friendly group. In general, members of the managing board presented reports on the bank's business situation and conditions in the financial sector, including issues of competition, as well as the general economic conditions and capital market in West Germany, lectures on issues that were considered important at the time, and discussions based on them. In the Dresdner Bank's central advisory council, personnel changes led to proposed and discussed issues [*Historisches Archiv der Commerzbank*, HAC-500/121, 18232-2000, Bd.1, Auszug aus der Niederschrift über die Gesamtvorstandssitzung am 25. Februar 1965 in Frankfurt a. M. (7.4.1965)].

Being a member of such a committee organization of leading economic figures with extensive experience allowed the provision of valuable advice and information to the bank in question and this organization. This organization helped lay the groundwork for maintaining close contact with member companies even after industrial attendants retired. The election of company members as successors fostered such close and cooperative relationships. Meetings of the central advisory council were heavily focused on reports from the supervisory board, and there were many similarities in the content of both committees, implying the significance of the personnel ties formed through such special committee organization. When an interlocking member of a large bank's supervisory board moves to the same bank's central advisory council, the personnel ties between the bank and the concerned company may be strengthened even further. Furthermore, the bank's friendly and unique relationship and contact with the concerned enterprise could be strengthened by appointing and installing an individual from the industrial company who was a member of the regional advisory council as a member of the central advisory council. As seen at Dresdner Bank, when members of the central advisory council were asked to attend the general meeting and accepted the invitation, they could play an important role equal to the interlocking supervisory board members.

Seating arrangements for meetings and meals at the central and regional advisory councils were carefully analyzed and decided. Such an effort demonstrates the significance of these organizations in developing and maintaining close relationships with enterprises that have deep cooperative relations with the bank in question, as well as clear positions in such relationships, differences in the depth of such relations among industrial enterprises, and each company's clear position for this bank.

Central and regional advisory councils exchanged and shared information, opinions, and experiences on general economic issues, while conditions in individual fields and advice on important fundamental business policy issues were developed. Such committee organizations strengthened banks' business relationships with industrial enterprises as customers and coordinated between banks and industrial companies and among industrial firms via personnel contacts and connections. In many cases, members of advisory councils were appointed by the top management entities of other enterprises in various industries, such as the supervisory board. Such personnel connections served as an important foundation for demonstrating the functions of personnel ties established through the bank advisory councils. Thus, under the extensive systems of exchanging and sharing information and coordinating interests and conflicts between companies based on supervisory board mandates, personnel connections through the advisory council supplemented personnel connections through the interlocking of supervisory board and managing board members in top management entities of other companies. Personnel connections were an important part of cooperative capitalism in Germany.

17.2 "Corporate Control" and "Corporate Rule" in Germany

17.2.1 *Differences and Relations of "Corporate Control" and "Corporate Rule"*

Section 17.1 describes historical changes in personnel connections between banks and industries and their characteristics. This section then considers the implications of the network analysis from the perspective of the differences and relationships between "corporate control" and "corporate rule," which were presented in Chap. 1. Regarding the "corporate rule" in the USA, the top management organ is a one-layer system of the board of directors, A. A. Berle and G. C. Means regarded the power to select the members of such a top management organ as "control." Berle included both "corporate control" regarding the issue of electing members of the management board and "control over business and asset of enterprises," which is concerned with the authority of decision-making of salaried managers in the concept of "corporate control" (Berle and Means 1932, pp. 69–70, 220). Despite their similarities, both concepts must be clearly distinguished. John Scott insists "corporate control must be distinguished from corporate rule" (Scott 1988, p. 34) and draws a clear distinction between them. He regards the power of determining a member of the board of directors as a top management organ in the USA as "corporate control" and control over enterprises' business and assets as "corporate rule" (Scott 1990, pp. 352–353, 371). While "'control' is a structural relationship through which particular agents have the capacity to exercise the legal powers of owners," rule is "the actual exercise of power in decision-making." In practice, the ruling group can exercise decision-making power "within the constraints set by the structure of control" (Scott 1988, p. 34).

The management board is in charge of business execution in both one-layer and two-layer systems of top management organs. In a two-layer system, such as that used in Germany, the supervisory board can participate in the decision-making process for fundamental corporate policy through discussion and approval. In this sense, corporate control is the foundation of the corporate rule. The relationship between corporate control and corporate rule becomes clear at this point. However, in terms of shareholder authority, whereas corporate control is a power that shareholders can exercise, corporate rule is not a set of rights in which stockholders can participate. Corporate control and corporate rule differ in this respect.

17.2.2 *Corporate Control in Germany and Its Characteristics*

To understand the power of electing a decision-maker in top management, we consider the term "corporate control." In the USA, the UK, and Japan, corporate control refers to the ability to determine the composition of the board of directors. Meanwhile, a German company uses a two-tiered system. Selecting the members of the supervisory board can be viewed as "control." Bank control exists in Germany because a bank has voting rights at general meetings under the deposited stock system and cooperates with other banks.

Stock deposits in banks and bank proxy holders exercising voting rights have been a long-standing practice in Germany (Schaad 1972, SS. 14–16). While G. Püttner noted that some voting rights based on deposited stocks were executed at general meetings prior to World War I (Püttner 1963, S. 29), the 1937 Stock Act limited the conditions under which banks and financial institutions could exercise deposited stock rights (Pohl 1937, SS. 371–372; Lindhardt 1958, S. 169, 171; Gottschalk 1990, S. 11; Schaad 1972, S. 17). The ratio of deposited stocks of banks and other institutions to common stocks in a total of 50 companies changed from 41 and 20% in 1931 to 43% and 24% in 1937 and 49% and 19% in 1942, respectively, and the significance of voting rights based on deposited stocks grew rather than decreased (Püttner 1963, SS. 32–33).

After World War II, for example, the attendance rates of the three largest German banks to all attendants in the general meeting in 1960 or 1961 were 53.7% in BASF, 50.7% in Bayer, 48.2% in Hoechst, 54.4% in Hoesch, 53.2% in Rheinsiche Stahlwerke, 39.8% in Siemens & Halske, and 26.6% in Daimler-Benz (DWI-Bericht 1964, SS. 10–11). In German corporations with a total amount of 545 million Deutsche Mark (DM) nominal capital (listed corporations excluding insurance companies), the ratio of deposited stocks of domestic and foreign financial institutions to all stocks was approximately 54% (292 million DM) in 1970 (Arndt 1974, S. 16). Examining the ratio of banks' voting rights in representative corporations effective in 1975, we see that AEG had 89.29%, Hoechst had 88.62%, BASF had 87.15%, Siemens had 81.02%, Bayer had 79.09%, and August Thyssen had 45.28%, all of which are quite high figures. However, the proportion of owner-held stock voting rights held by banks in these corporations was less than 1% (Monopolkommission 1978, S. 560), whereas banks exercising voting rights via the deposited stock system were significant. A 1992 survey by Baums and Fraune, who analyzed in terms of added value 24 of the 100 largest public corporations with the largest shareholding, showed that banks held an average of 84.09% of voting rights at these companies' annual meetings, whereas those held through the deposited stock system were 60.95%. Furthermore, there were 11 corporations with more than 75% of voting rights solely through deposited stocks, 18 with banks holding more than 75% of their voting rights, and 17 with more than 90% (Baums and Fraune 1995, S. 98, 103). A 1994 study conducted by J. Edwards & K. Fischer also showed that German banks, particularly the top three banks, had significant control over voting rights in corporations, primarily through proxy voting rights through the deposited stocks system (Edwards and Fischer 1994, p. 226).

When exercising voting rights through the deposited stocks system, banks could transfer voting rights deposited by customers to third parties, such as other trusted banks (Yamaguchi 1981, p 113). As a result, even the transfer of voting rights through the deposited stocks system from smaller banks to large banks increased the influence of these collaborative interbank relationships on corporations (Busse 1962, S. 65; Bundesministerium der Finanzen 1979, S. 568). According to a 1979 Gesler commission investigation into voting rights deposited by customers in 172 financial institutions, the rate of voting rights deposited to third parties reached 57% (Bundesministerium der Finanzen 1979, S. 568). Joly (1998) pointed out that because small financial institutions did not attend annual meetings, the three largest banks could collect more voting rights than those transferred to customers, and approximately 70% of voting rights represented by banks were provided to the three largest banks in this manner (Joly 1998, SS. 195–196). Thus, bank control can be observed through collaboration among banks. As discussed in Part 3, even in the case of bank control in corporate control, it should be noted that in the process of selecting bank members to be suggested as candidates for supervisory board members at other companies' general meetings, the decision was made through close exchange and negotiation with the industrial enterprises involved, and the assignment was based on business relationships.

The trend of bank control in corporate control applied to large banks themselves. Cooperative relations between banks were observed in executing voting rights at bank general meetings. For example, according to Gottschalk's study, which investigated at the total number of stocks, deposited stocks, and deposited shares owned by investment companies and their parent banks, Deutsche Bank had 47.17% of the voting rights in 1986, while the top three banks had 60.36%. Dresdner Bank's stock and deposited share percentages were 40.07% and 64.04%, respectively, whereas Commerzbank's percentages were 34.58% and 60.81%. These were strikingly high rates (Gottschalk 1988, SS. 297–298). According to Baums and Fraune's 1992 survey, Deutsche Bank had 32.07% of the voting rights, while the top three banks had 49.24% each. Dresdner Bank's percentages were 44.19% and 53.66%, whereas Commerzbank's were 18.49% and 48.27%, respectively (Baums and Fraune 1995, S. 106). The three largest banks controlled their general meetings cooperatively and effectively because they owned a large percentage of the voting stock (Böhm 1992, S 75). H. Pfeiffer emphasized that large banks were their own controllers (Pfeiffer 1986b, S. 475).

Such phenomena were already observed in the period before World War II, and Fohlin pointed out the existence of some evidence that banks strongly controlled themselves through interlocking shareholdings, effectively protecting themselves from the influence of the outside (Fohlin 2007, p. 327). A. Bol also emphasizes that in Deutsche Bank, most shareholders were represented by banks in the annual meeting from the nineteenth century to the twentieth century (Bol 2018, S. 137). Between 1870 and 1929, Deutsche Bank had no dominant stockholders at its annual meeting (Bol 2018, S. 144, 155). However, when considering the voting rights of the deposited shares, the largest representative could influence decision-making alongside the majority of 66% or 75% at the general meeting (Bol 2018, S. 156).

17.2.3 Corporate Rules in Germany and Their Characteristics

In Germany, bank control exists because a bank has voting rights at a general meeting under the deposit stock system [(1)]. However, different situations can be observed in the "corporate rule," which refers to the "control over business and asset of enterprise."

17.2.3.1 Involvement of the Supervisory Board in Corporate Rules

The supervisory board's primary functions include (1) electing and dismissing members of the board of directors, (2) approving the managing board's business policy, (3) supervising the managing board's management execution, and (4) participating in important issues concerning business principles through reservation of rights. Because of the supervisory board's powers, this organ decides the fundamental corporate policy in these four points. Banks can participate in a company's corporate governance by serving on its supervisory board.

These points are important regarding the importance of holding the chairman's mandate on the supervisory board of banks. First, there is the possibility of influencing and participating in decisions made by the managing board regarding management principles and business execution through prior discussions between the supervisory board chairmen and the managing board. Second, if such committees are established, there is the opportunity to participate in important management issues by becoming a member (or chairman) of special committee organizations within the supervisory board, such as the personnel and financial committees.

Regarding the second point, in collaboration with the supervisory board's personnel committee, the bank can develop the original plan of candidates for members of the supervisory board proposed at the annual meeting, as well as the election of members of the managing board, by interlocking bank members. In the case of a company in the rebuilding process, the chairman of the managing board's involvement in personnel issues, as the most important position in management execution, has a greater significance. Furthermore, in companies with a financial committee within the supervisory board, the opportunity to participate in the decision-making process for important financial issues and provide advice increases. For example, as seen in the cases of Bayer and AEG after World War II, in cases where these committees included the chairman and vice-chairmen of the supervisory board (see Chap. 12), the bank's involvement in these important issues could be expanded by having the mandate of chairman or vice-chairman on the supervisory board of the company in question. Even in companies without organizations such as personnel committees, there are instances where the chairman of the supervisory board takes the initiative and plays a role in the management board's personnel issues. In cases where the selection of a bank's representative on the supervisory board was combined with the appointment to such committee organizations, a large bank could hold a mandate not only on the supervisory board but also on the personnel committee. Thus, the personnel tie became more important in the relationships between industry and banks.

As analyzed in Chap. 12, Jürgen Ponto's significant involvement and role as chairman of the supervisory board of AEG in the company's rebuilding process during the 1970s, who collaborated in planning for the company's rebuilding, dismissed the chairman of the managing board, and elected people who were appropriate for rebuilding, can be considered an important case. Herrhausen from Deutsch Bank was heavily involved in the decision-making process of Daimler-Benz AG's business strategy, and he played a leading role in developing the diversification strategy during the 1980s as chairman of the automobile company's supervisory board. He was the architect of the new strategy and implemented the dismissal of the chairman of the management board and the election of a successor who was appropriate for developing the diversification strategy (Ingersoll and Brady 1987, p. 19; Wirtschaftswoche 1987, SS. 88–89; Der Spiegel 1987a, S. 100; Der Spiegel 1987b, SS. 70–71; Der Spiegel 1988a, S. 116, 1988b, S. 110, 112; Aizawa 1994, Chap. 4). These cases demonstrate the bank representative's important and important involvement and roles on the supervisory board, which differed from those of other interlocking members, including individuals from industrial enterprises.

17.2.3.2 Interlocking Directorates and Corporate Rules

Next, this subsection examines the cooperative mechanism in industry–bank relationships for "finance capital" proposed by Lenin (Ленин 1962). Analysis of capital relations, such as share investment and financing, and personnel relations, such as interlocking directorates on the supervisory board, confirms the existence of "finance capital" as a type of capital formed by combining and knitting industrial and banking capital.

Due to the depth of the business transaction relationship, personnel ties with many enterprises are important in interfirm relationships, both for banks and industrial enterprises. The more personnel connections a company establishes with companies in various industries, the greater the possibility of gathering, exchanging, and sharing useful information for its business. For example, when a bank provides loans to industrial enterprises, it is critical to obtain information on the basis of the company's capital demands as a bank customer, such as company demand. As a result, developing a diverse network of personnel can lay the groundwork for obtaining important information for a business's effective and stable growth. The significance and maintenance of a personnel network between companies is critical to achieving these objectives. In Germany, personnel ties and networks have been formed through interlocking directorates on both sides, from bank to industrial enterprise and from industrial enterprise to bank on the supervisory board.

From a corporate rule standpoint, supervisory board members were personally aligned with monopolies in the banking industry and various industrial sectors who were in charge of corporate rule at the supervisory board level under the two-layer top management organs in charge of management execution. They made decisions about the company's administration based on the personnel network formed on many company supervisory boards. Members of the supervisory board were personally united in the application of corporate rule through approval and agreement with its policy, and they served as top management on the basis of the interlocking directorates of such top management organs. Thus, a personally unified and institutionalized "finance capitalist" existed, not just one individual, but a social system consisting of a supervisory board with interlocking members.

Considering personnel networks of both bank and industrial companies from the perspective of corporate rule, a "financial capitalist" who represented the interests of both parties as an interlocking member of the supervisory board played an important role as a uniting point of flow and communication medium in the network through personnel relationships with many enterprises. As explored in Part 2, in the analysis of "centrality," which clarifies the weight of individual enterprises within the network, including second- and third-party enterprises in the category "finance capital," large representative banks tended to show relatively high centrality in networks of both industrial enterprises and banks (Yamazaki 2019). However, some major companies in key industrial sectors, such as the iron and steel industry, chemical industry, electrical industry, automobile industry, electric power industry, and insurance industry (the last two are true for the period after World War II), were also in the core position in terms of "centrality" as measured by an indicator called "adjacency," which means the number of companies with interlocking directorates. As a result, both banks and industrial enterprises played important roles in the flow of information and network media, with the bank being only one of the significant players. In this way, the "financial capitalist" as an interlocking member of the supervisory board between a bank and an industrial enterprise, serves as the primary figure of top management in the corporate rule of many companies, including banks. As a result, bank control cannot always be observed under corporate rules.

In Germany, the two-layer top management system, which includes the supervisory board and the board of directors, has helped unite and realize the interests of banks and industrial enterprises. In such a system, banks' credit and securities businesses, the development of interlocking directorates through supervisory mandates based on the voting rights of deposited stock by banks at the annual meeting, and the expansion of the interlocking directorate of an industrial enterprise due to a member of the bank's interlocking supervisory board are all extremely important.

Building a capital form is difficult because of the need to create a mechanism that balances the interests of both industry and banks without contradicting or conflicting with either party. Enterprises maximize industrial and commercial profits, whereas banks maximize interest and dividends. Interest is a cost factor for industrial companies but an income for banks. As a result, maximizing industrial and commercial profit by exchanging and sharing information between banks and industrial enterprises and promoting control of competition among enterprises through discussion is an important premise for avoiding conflict between industries and banks and maximizing interest and dividends for banks. An institution was established to realize the interests of both industry and bank through a structure of personnel connections and network based on interlocking directorates of bank to industrial enterprise and from industrial enterprise to bank on the supervisory board, as well as a system of information flow and media based on these personnel relations.

Banks, particularly house banks, play a unique role in the German corporate governance model, and these roles appear to benefit shareholders and credit providers. The interests of banks and industrial enterprises can be consistent as long as enterprises are growing, enabling an increase in value creation that allows them to pay dividends at the level of practice in the business world after paying interest on credit without the issue of liquidity. However, if this condition cannot be met, how decisions are made between the level of interest and dividends on the one hand and self-financing on the other become important. This internal conflict of interest that banks face reflects the position of the bank's representative on the supervisory board (Ipsen and Pfitzinger 2003, S. 77). Therefore, an "industrial system" established as a German mechanism for the development of the enterprise, industry, and economy through business management in the form of coordinated and united interests of the bank and industry, as well as the institution of information flow and media in the personnel network, is highly significant. The essence of "finance capital" as a capital form created by unifying and knitting industrial and banking capital and an important German characteristic are observed.

In terms of the policy of "finance capital" to maximize industrial and commercial profit and interest and dividends for banks, financial policies such as building concealed reserves played an important role in finance capital's "industrial policy" until the end of World War II. Large German banks played an important role in this policy. In the relationship between AEG and Berliner Handels-Geselslchaft, one of Germany's largest banks, financing and personnel were closely linked. Carl Fürstenberg from Berliner Handels-Gesellschaft provided valuable financial advice to Emili Rathenau from AEG (*Historisches Archiv des Deutschen Technikmuseums*, I0.2060 A.03486, Aufzeichung über die historische Entwicklung des Verhältnisses der AEG zur Deutschen Bank). Fürstenberg, who served on the AEG supervisory board, believed that strengthening self-financing through regular capital increases and creating ordinary and secret reserves were important business policy principles. This principle was also applied to AEG, determining the unique character of the company's financial policy (Berliner Handels-Gesellschaft 1956, SS. 96–97; Fürstenberg 1931, SS. 299–301). This demonstrates the bank's consideration of the profitability structure of the industrial enterprise, as well as the significant roles played by the bank's representative on the company's supervisory board.

The "One Mark Account" ("Eine Mark Konto"), a financial policy based on excessive depreciation that allows the formation of hidden reserve funds that began during the transition to monopolistic capitalism and continued in the period before World War II, also indicates a "finance capital" policy. It was implemented to ensure a consistent dividend policy. Banks played a significant role in the development of such policies (Rosendorff 1932, SS. 97–98; Prion 1931, SS. 20–21, S. 28). The capital participation system and personnel connections were important measures to transfer the method of drawing up the balance sheet of large banks to banks subordinated to them and industrial enterprises (Tsumori 1961, p. 62). For example, "one Mark account" was established in AEG and can be observed almost consistently in the period preceding World War II after 1893/1894, except for partial years of depression (Allgemeine Elektricitäts-Gesellschaft, *Geschäftsbericht*, each fiscal year; *Handbuch der deutschen Aktiengesellschaften*, each year; Heß 1958, 29–30; Rosendorff 1932, S. 98). As evidenced by Carl Fürstenberg's roles at AEG, such individuals could play important roles in cases where bank supervisory boards existed. Cases in which, in addition to the supervision of a company's business, the inspection and report of issues such as the annual account, balance sheet, and profit allocation plan, and the evaluation of assets based on the bylaw, the supervisory board was given the authority to decide on the depreciation method were common (Passow 1923, S. 4). In AEG, the chairman and first vice-chairman of the supervisory board were responsible for determining the increase of stocks issued, implementing capital increases, and executing stock issuances (*Historisches Archiv des Deutschen Technikmuseums*, I0.2060A.03055, Nummer 172 des Notariateregisters für 1915, S. 4). In such a situation, the involvement and roles of interlocking supervisory board members were greatly facilitated by policies such as "one Mark account."

These discussions show that, in an interfirm relationship in Germany, an important issue is corporate rules for making the best use of information obtained, exchanged, and shared through personnel connections between enterprises in business management at the highest levels. The style above of corporate rule based on the personnel network, in which banks and representative industrial enterprises in the major industrial sectors play an important role as knighting points in information flow and media, indicates an important characteristic of the "German finance capital." Exchanging and sharing information via networks encourages banks, industrial enterprises, and corporations within the network to recognize common management issues. This recognition lays the groundwork for enterprises to coordinate their interests and resolve conflicts. The common interests of banks and industrial enterprises were pursued by leveraging the personnel network established through interlocking directorates among supervisory board members. The significance of industrial concentration in Germany stems from personnel connections established through interlocking directorates between enterprises in both directions from bank to industrial enterprise and from industrial enterprise to bank on the supervisory board. The interlocking supervisory board members' efforts to realize the interests of banks and industrial companies while avoiding the opposition of mutual interests were aided by an information flow and media system that promoted the common recognition of a management issue between companies by exchanging and sharing information based on the interlocking directorates in both directions between the bank and the industrial company.

The condition under which interests and various conflicts between banks and industrial enterprises, as well as between enterprises, can be coordinated through discussion rather than market competition, was created and maintained by personnel connections composed of direct and indirect interlocking directorates, networks that include many second- and third-party enterprises, and bank central and regional advisory councils. Such industry–bank relationships were cooperative systems for industrial and commercial profit maximization, which served as a solid foundation for banks' important credit collection and increased share efficiency. The German enterprise behavior of emphasizing price competition avoidance in an oligopolistic market following the war was appropriate. This system determines the cooperative characteristics of German capitalism.

When considering such a system in relation to the behavior of a German enterprise, interfirm relationships based on personnel connections are an important component of business management. The characteristics of the German and European markets, which served as the primary market for German exports and emphasized product quality and functionality, influenced the development of postwar business management. Germany emphasized product differentiation based on technology, quality, and functionality and market positioning through competitiveness in Europe's relatively high share of exports aligned with high-quality goods. Under these conditions, German companies sought an appropriate business management system. A typical example can be observed in the functionality-focused production system that is supported by the German-specific method of specialized skill qualification and the vocational education system. German companies prioritized non-price competition in quality through product specialization and differentiation (Yamazaki 2024; Yamazaki 2013). Interfirm relationships based on a personnel connection system via interlocking directorates and a bank advisory council were critical foundations of German enterprise business management and postwar behavior.

17.3 Changes in Personnel Connections in Relation to Historical Context

Based on the preceding examinations in this chapter, this section attempts to understand the changes in personnel ties between banks and industries in relation to historical conditions in each period.

17.3.1 Period of Establishment of Monopolistic Capitalism

As discussed in Chap. 1, the interlocking directorates on the supervisory boards of other companies were established as a system of personnel connection in Germany during the transition to monopolistic capitalism from the end of the nineteenth century to the twentieth century. They can be regarded as a unique and distinct form of monopolistic capitalism. These personnel connections during this time were based on business relationships between banks that organically combined credit, securities, and current account businesses and industrial companies. They were extremely important as a personal guarantee of relationships between banks and industrial enterprises, strengthened through stockholding or capital participation.

The industry–bank relationship was based on financial relations, with advance financing of long-term finance performed by combining the debtor in the current calculation that occupied the majority of short-term credits at the time (2) with the issue of securities (3) was a premise of personnel ties (Kato 1973, p. 214). Debtor in current calculation based on account current credit as the essentially short-term commercial credits could acquire the characteristic of long-term capital credits by combining them with the issue of shares (Kato 1973, p.221; Tohara 1963, p. 365). Business relationships in terms of financial mechanisms between industrial enterprises and banks were built not as individual relationships in the three fields of lending, securities business, and account current business, but as the provision of long-term capital credits through the liquidation of account current credits based on industrial enterprises issuing securities and banks accepting and selling them. According to Jacob Riesser, account current business was "the strongest lever for planned industrial policy of bank" (Riesser 1971, S. 222), and combining this business with the issuance of securities was an important foundation for raising large capital by large companies and the development of a stable credit business for industrial enterprises.

In Germany, the universal banking system and the significance of relationships between industry and banks based on it were extremely important as a countermeasure to the rapid development of industries such as the heavy and chemical industries, as well as restrictive conditions such as small domestic markets and underdeveloped financial markets caused by unused money shortages, particularly the security market. However, during the period of monopolistic capitalism's establishment, based on the progress of concentration in the heavy industry, the link between industry and bank became a permanent characteristic as a system to secure monopolistic profit for both industrial enterprises and banks. This differed from phenomena observed in the periods following the 1857 crisis, when the bank's business moved from promotion to securities, such as the acceptance of public loans due to difficulties in issuing stocks, and the period of the 1873 crisis (Tohara 1963, pp. 143, 243; Ono 1956, p. 47).

Concentration of enterprises and the formation of monopolies in the heavy industry, which included the coal mining and iron and steel industries, from the end of the nineteenth century to the beginning of the twentieth century, facilitated this in the banking industry. Due to the amount of capital demands of industry subordination of regional banks to large banks in issuing of securities to collect long-term lending provided by the account current business and concentration of regional banks by large banks progressed (Tohara 1963, p. 334, regarding concentration in the banking industry during this period, see Jeidels 1905, Zweiter Abschnitt; Riesser 1971, Abschnit IV). The account current business of big banks was expanded by the concentration of regional banks, whose debtor rate in current calculation to total asset accounts was larger than that of big banks (Tohara 1963, pp. 333–334) and the importance of such businesses increased. However, financing for enterprise concentration, which became a widespread phenomenon with the formation of monopolies, was not clear enough through long-term lending based on current credit. Berlin's large banks, where large-scale securities issuance was required, enabled the collection of large amounts of capital credits provided to companies integrating the mining and iron and steel sectors by combining the current account and securities businesses. The ability of integrated enterprises in the heavy industry, such as large joint-stock companies, to raise capital could be really used by building close relationships with large banks through such a mechanism (Tohara 1963, pp. 365–366). The liquidation of funds in the form of repayment debt against a bank with subscriptions obtained through the issuance and acceptance of new stocks or bonds by banks was pursued, as well as the acquisition of promoter profit (Nagasaka 1961, p. 144. Concerning promoter profit, see Hilferding 1923, II. Abschnitt, Achtes Kapitel, 1.).

Based on such financial relationships, the ties between industry and banks established the necessity and importance of personnel connections as "the personal guarantee" for maintaining and strengthening them. Personnel connections did not create fusion but were based on economic relationships. In the expansion of the account current business as an important point in economic relations, not only the capacity of large banks to lend money, but also the ability of companies receiving credit to repay through the issue of securities was premised (Tohara 1963, pp. 375–376). During the transition to monopolistic capitalism, each large enterprise in the industry built unified relationships with many banks (Tohara 1963, pp. 367–368). As Paul Windolf emphasizes, this period was corporate networks' "take off" (Windolf 2014, pp. 72, 80).

However, the relationship between industry and banks was forced to evolve during World War I. With the outbreak of the war, a new era for banks began, and the foundation business and financial business lost their previous significance (DWI-Bericht 1961, S. 3). The most important business of banks at the time was support in war financing, so industrial financing was forced to move strongly backward (Hagemann 1931, SS. 119–120). The credit, issuing, securities, and account current business, which occupied an important position in the bank business from the shift to monopolistic capitalism until World War I, declined (Kato 1973, p. 217). Banks became estranged from corporate finance under the excess weight of war financing by credit banks, and the financial relationships between industry and banking became thin (Kato 1973, pp. 219, 222).

17.3.2 Period After World War I

17.3.2.1 Period of Inflation After World War I

During the post-World War I inflationary period, banks were forced to develop their businesses at lower mark prices. Meanwhile, the trend toward self-financing of industrial enterprises accelerated due to the enormous profits earned during the war and compensation money for lost factories in the alienated region. Industry–bank relationships greatly changed on account of the very limited scale of financing of banks and the situation that large concentration movement from 1920 to 1921 was developed without involvements and influences from banks, and independence of large corporate groups in industry on banking capital became stronger, and the development of policy of industrial enterprises for banks appeared (Duschnitzky 1927; Hagemann 1931, SS. 20–21; Lampe 2004, S. 370; Wixforth 1995, S. 510). Big corporate groups attempted to expand businesses in the banking sector (Duschnitzky 1927, SS. 227–233).

The account current business, which was important in the bank before World War I, changed dramatically. This is evident in the decrease in growth rate. The debtor in the current calculation of total asset accounts. 19 large banks' ratios decreased from 41% in 1913 to 25.1% in 1920, 30.1% in 1921, and 27.9% in 1923 (Goldschmidt 1928, S. 60). Deutsche Bank's figures for 1913, 1920, 1921, 1922, and 1923 (end of each year) (see Table 17.1) were 28.43%, 14.33%, 21.6%, 19.7%, and 42.26%, respectively. Dresdner Bank reported similar figures of 40.63%, 22.49%, 29.13%, 22.3%, and 37.95%. Commerzbank's interest rates were 38.97%, 30.33%, 32.76%, 33.1%, and 44.02%, respectively. Although the figures for these large banks in 1923 were nearly identical to or exceeded those of 1913, Deutsche Bank and Dresdner Bank's figures from 1920 to 1922 were significantly lower than those of 1913. Though the rate of the debtor in current calculation to total asset accounts significantly increased in 1923, the account current business lost characteristics such as the fixed capital credit, as seen before World War I (Kato 1973, p. 228).

During the inflationary period, banks' liquidity decreased dramatically due to an increase in securities accounts under the inactivity of stock markets after their activity until the beginning of 1922, and thus banks were forced to restrain the issuing and securities businesses (Kato 1973, p. 229). The amount of securities issued by 19 big banks increased from 750 million Gold Marks in 1920 to 1270 million Gold Marks, then decreased to 185 million Gold Mark in 1922 (Goldschmidt 1928, S. 224). The ratio of bills to total asset accounts of 19 large banks significantly decreased from 52.3% in 1920 to 2.4% in 1923 (Goldschmidt 1928, S. 60). The function of credit businesses of banks almost generally stopped due to the situation that stock issue after 1922 forced banks to take charge of roles of credit for distribution rather than bill credit (Kato 1973, p. 229).

Building and maintaining personnel connections with many enterprises in close relationships was critical for large banks during the inflationary period following World War I, as the financial relationships between industry and banks became weaker than before the war. This is consistent with a trend of decreasing industrial enterprises' independence from banks in which financial transactions did not occur. This also applied to pursuing cooperation in the management of enterprises through involvement in the supervisory boards with which banks had friendly relations (Berliner Handels-Gesellschaft 1956, S. 172). An increase in interlocking directorates was an important countermeasure for banks facing the trend of industrial enterprise independence, and it reflected the bank's policy to deal with the need to maintain and strengthen business relationships with a large number of companies as personal guarantees. At the beginning of the Weimar Republic, concentration movement in industries performed under the dominance of industrial enterprises and the financial oligarchy based on it, as personal connections made up for the organized economic system of finance capital (Matsuba 1984, p. 243). During the inflation period after World War I, supervisory board became an important committee organization for banks to gather information and acquire customers (Ziegler 2019, S. 468).

Reflecting the retreat of business relationships between industry and banks formed by organically combining credit, securities, and account current businesses with industrial enterprises, personnel connections could no longer form organic ties between both parties, and such conditions persisted during the relatively stable period that began in 1924.

17.3.2.2 Period of Relative Stability

This subsection examines the interlocking directorates in a relatively stable period in light of historical conditions. Personnel connections also increased (Hagemann 1931, SS. 79–81). Mergers of small and medium banks proceeded, and interlocking supervisory board members in acquired banks were succeeded to the banks that merged (Kominato 1970, p. 42). Furthermore, the impact of branch network expansion through bank mergers was significant, and the number of supervisory board members appointed from large Berlin banks with branches rapidly increased (Kato 1973, p. 264).

Before and after stabilization in 1923–1924, the general shortage of capital caused industrial enterprises to rely on financial institutions that had funds for lending to industrial and commercial enterprises or had intermediate access to the capital market (Hardach 1984, p. 217). The rate of bills and debtors in the current calculation to the total of asset accounts was high, and that of Berlin's big banks amounted to approximately more than 60%, and financial institutions coped with the capital demands of industrial enterprises through these two credit forms (Kato 1973, pp. 232–233). The debtor's increase rate in the current calculation was extremely high. Dresdner Bank and Commerzbank were close to the 1913 level, while Deutsche Bank exceeded it (see Table 17.1). As a result, account current credit was the most common type of bank credit extended to industrial enterprises. In the Berlin Stock Exchange, share price indicators (1924 = 100) were 25 in 1924 and 27 in 1926 and they recovered to 40 in 1927 and 37 in 1928 (Kuczynski 1963, S. 67), indicating a partial stock market recovery after 1927. Although securities issuing was developed as an axis of corporate finance, it was no longer performed as the long-term financial relationship with industrial companies by organically combining account current credit with securities issuing (Kato 1973, pp. 236–237). During this relatively stable period, only large joint-stock companies could borrow long-term debt to repay short-term bank debt (Prion 1929, SS. 42–43). Although bank credit was a prerequisite for obtaining issuing business for industrial enterprises in the past, large trust no longer relied on a high probability of bank credit. They developed self-financing through a low dividend policy and a high-rate depreciation policy, as opposed to raising funds by issuing securities under a long-term financial plan and depositing them in banks when the securities market was in good shape (Prion 1928, S. 343; Prion 1929, SS. 133–134). Although the balance of possessed securities and consortium participation in absolute terms tended to increase, their ratio to the total amount of asset accounts was low and lower than in 1913. For example, the ratios of possessed securities to the total amount of asset accounts of Deutsche Bank were 7.18%, 0.92%, and 1.2% in 1913, 1924, and 1928, respectively. Corresponding figures for Commerzbank were 5.53%, 2.39%, and 1.36% (See balance sheets of Deutsche Bank and Commerzbank of each year).

The pattern of differentiation into two poles was as follows: A few large enterprises tended to avoid current calculation credit for investment in fixed assets by liquidating bank credit through issuing securities based on domestic and foreign debentures, primarily based on foreign bonds and funds raised by self-financing (Kato 1973, p. 256). Due to the lack of bank credit before issuing securities, banks lost the large, certain, and profitable debtor, and banks' issuing business was forced to change to the mere entrusted business (Prion 1929, S. 134). Credit banks involved in issuing industrial securities tended to have characteristics of entrusted business rather than active acceptance of issuing with the aim of participation (Kato 1973, p. 250). Meanwhile, most other companies could not sufficiently liquidate existing bank credits and relied on account current credit to raise funds for fixed asset investment. Under such a differentiated corporate finance trend, the premise for business relationships between industry and banks, built by organically combining account current credit with issuing business prior to World War I, was lost. Whereas enterprises that received capital credit from banks could not strikingly issue securities and large enterprises with the capacity to issue securities oriented toward independence from capital credit provided by banks, banks were forced to restrain the acceptance of issuing securities due to their composition of funds and the condition in the capital market (Kato 1973, pp. 257–258).

Thus, industrial enterprises could not expect providing funds for rationalization by banks (Chandler 1990, p. 590), and the organic relationships between industry and bank in reality failed under the trend of stronger dependence on US banks and capital (Wixforth and Ziegler 1994, p. 113; Wixforth and Ziegler 1995, p. 260). This refers to the limitation of the organized structure of German finance capital following the establishment of monopolistic capitalism (Kato 1973, p. 258). The accumulation of "frozen" debtors in current calculations intensively expressed the limping relations between industry and bank (Kato 1973, p. 260). The trend of increasing the

Table 17.1 Ratios of debtors in the current calculation (overdrafts) to total asset accounts in Deutsche Bank, Dresdner Bank, and Commerzbank (%)

	1913	1920	1921	1922	1923	1924	1926	1928	1929
Deutsche Bank	28.43	14.33	21.60	19.70	42.26	35.66	43.08	40.63	43.42
Dresdner Bank	40.63	22.49	29.13	22.30	37.95	39.33	37.12	37.02	39.94
Commerzbank	38.97	30.33	32.76	33.10	44.02	37.84	40.52	41.72	41.76

Source This table was compiled by the author, based on the annual balance sheets of Deutsche Bank, Dresdner Bank, and Commerzbank

number of people assigned from banks as supervisory board members never indicated strengthening of the organic and stable relationships between industry and bank, but rather reflected changes in relations between both, such as the destruction of financial relations between industry and bank based on combining account current business with issuing business (Kato 1973, pp. 267–268). Characteristics of the financial business relationships between industry and bank that were the foundation for personnel connections had changed (Kato 1973, p. 263). Therefore, the characteristics and significance were forced to be different between interlocking supervisory board members assigned to many irregularly united companies and those dispatched to partial large companies, indicating a trend of independence of banks in terms of corporate finance (Kato 1973, p. 266). W. Hagemann pointed out that the total number of interlocking supervisory board members increased many times during the relatively stable period in the 1920s, but the influence of banks showed not an increasing trend but a declining tendency (Hagemann 1931, S. 82). The internationalization of capital markets led to an increase in the number of business relations and intensification of competition among banks, which weakened the influence of German banks in large industrial enterprises (Wixforth and Ziegler, 1995, p. 260). As Hagemann emphasized, it is extremely dangerous to estimate the influence of banks on industrial enterprises solely on the basis of the conditions of assignment of supervisory board members (Hagemann 1931, SS. 74–75).

17.3.3 Period of National Socialism

When compared to the inflationary period following World War I, the direct interlocking directorates of the three largest banks tended to decrease in terms of the number of enterprises and mandates. The following factors were linked to such conditions.

The crisis of big banks caused by the Great Economic Crisis that began in 1929, the temporary nationalization of banks, and the impact of bank restructuring were all important factors. The number of supervisory board positions was limited by law as a response to the bank crisis of 1930/31. The 1931 Corporations Act prohibits holding more than 20 mandates on boards (Windolf 2014, p. 73; David and Weserhuis 2014, p. 16). Economic policy toward munitions production, as well as the war economy, had an impact on personnel connections. "The trustful network" between industry managers and banks no longer had a decisive meaning in obtaining information and planning strategy and had a definite network with the people in charge of the significance of political decisions (Wixforth 2006, S. 893). Thus, changes occurred within the personnel network.

The shift of companies toward capital companies, specifically a reduction in the number of joint-stock companies or limited liability companies, could also contribute to a decrease in the number of interlocking directorates. Laws regarding the transformation of capital companies in 1934 (Gesetz über die Umwandlung von Kapitallgesellschaft and Gesetz über Steuererleichtungen bei der Umwandlung und Auflösung von Kapotalgesellschaft) allowed joint-stock companies, partnerships partly limited by shares, and limited liability companies to form unlimited or limited partnerships through financial incentives for personal companies based on a decrease or exemption of taxes such as transfer tax (e.g., company and turnover taxes) and property tax (e.g., income and corporate income taxes) to promote desirable transformation (Reichsministerium des Innern 1934, pp. 354–356, 569–572; Bergmann 1935, SS. 1–4, 8–9). The fact that the anonymity of the joint-stock company contradicted the initiative and responsibility of directors under the "Leadership principle" (*Führerprinzip*) of National Socialism provided a context to the enactment of these laws (Nishihara 1936a, pp. 117, 119, 1936b, pp. 106–107). From 1934 to 1938, 1690 joint-stock companies converted to individual proprietorships and private companies (including civil law partnerships), while 13,265 limited liability companies converted to similar forms of enterprise (Wirtschaft and Statistik 1939a, S. 75). The number of joint-stock companies (excluding companies in the Saar region and companies whose capital was not yet transformed to Reichsmark, and concerning 1939 including companies whose capital was indicated in Shiling) decreased from 9148 at the end of 1933 to 8618 at the end of 1934, 7204 at the end of 1936, 6094 at the end of 1937, 5518 at the end of 1938, and 5767 at the end of 1939. (Statustisches Reichsamt 1938, SS. 436–437, 1940, SS. 452–453; Wirtschaft und Statistik 1939a, SS. 237–238, 1939b, S. 75). The number of limited liability companies decreased from around 39,000 at the end of 1935 to 39,249 at the end of 1936, 30,454 at the end of 1937, 25,662 at the end of 1938, and 24,617 at the end of 1939 (Statistisches Reichsamt 1937, S. 426, 1938, SS. 442–443, 1940, S. 461; Wirtschaft und Statistik 1936, S. 965, 1939c, SS. 274–275). The decrease in the number of joint-stock companies and limited liability companies coincided with a decline in personnel ties based on interlocking directorates.

Ariazation's influence grew significantly after the Nazis took power in 1933. The expulsion of Jewish bankers and industrialists resulted in the departure of many people from the management and supervisory board (Windolf 2014, 73; David and Weserhuis 2014, p. 16). The Ariazation became a measurement for industrial enterprises to acquire banks, enter the banking sector, and expand their operations (Der deutsche Volkswirt 1938, S. 1996; Neumann 1942, p. 100).

Credit control had a significant impact on personnel connections. Various capital-building funds were raised through public means, and the function of bank financing was discontinued. Outside funds' role in raising long-term funds for industries declined, and bank investment credit was effectively excluded from the capital procurement process (Lurié 1947, S. 60). The state's promotion of company self-financing was also an important factor influencing personnel companies. Companies' self-financing progressed through various economic policies, such as the preferable tax system for equipment investment in 1933, reinforcing monopolies by the Constraint Cartel Law and the Dividend Restrictive Act in 1934 (Neumann 1942, pp. 240–241, 261). The Nazi state enforced company self-financing and absorbed their profits by issuing war national debts and Mefo bills and allocating such funds to necessary military goods (Yamaguchi 2006, p. 7). In some cases, the effects of a significant increase in internal financing can be observed. Self-financing was due not only to economic advancement under the Nazi state, but also to an integrated component of the superior strategy of resource control in the entire economy, combined with "monopolization of capital market by state" (Lurié 1947, S. 99). In July 1933, the Constraint Cartel Law gave state institutions the authority to refuse undesirable investment projects. It brought about the capital demands of industries, artificially causing the shortage of demand in the capital markets (Spoerer 1996, SS. 113–114). Despite the possibility of worsening capital raising in free capital markets during the 1933–1936 prohibition on securities issuance, customers in industries repaid their borrowings. As a result, banks, an important economic sector, barely functioned (Spoerer 1996, SS. 114–115). The tax laws in the first stage of the rearmament until 1936 also restrained the payment of dividends, so that self-financing became advantageous by admitting rooms of depreciation in the balance sheet for taxation, allowing the immediate depreciation of nondurable economic goods (Spoerer 1996, S. 115). These results show a significant increase in the significance of self-financing in the Third Reich (Spoerer 1996, S. 116). Government finance significantly impacted financial intermediation in the 1930s, and capital markets were reserved for government financing. Private issuance of shares and securities requires special permission (Hardach 1984, p. 233).

Furthermore, the Dividend Restrictive Act made the capital market less appealing, directing capital flow to the national bond market and limiting capital procurement in the capital market. Although this law was moderated in 1936, private companies could not access capital markets until 1939. It was abolished this year (Neumann 1942, pp. 259, 261). The prevalence of self-financing over loans in monopolistic enterprises indicated a decline in the role of bank capital as a whole. However, Neumann pointed out that the dominant position in finance capitalism shifted from the bank to the industrial enterprise, or what was to be regarded as the combined body of bank and industrial enterprise (Neumann 1942, pp. 261–262). Companies used the accumulation of unpaid dividends not only to expand equipment and capital, but also to expand their monopolistic control over other companies. Industrial enterprises expanded their power into almost all other economic activities, including the fields of banks and insurance companies (Neumann 1942, p. 264).

Under the Nazi regime, bank credits were not used to strengthen business relationships with industrial enterprises or to increase bank influence. Business relations established through loans and securities issuance were forced to deteriorate, resulting in a shift in the foundation for personnel connections through director assignment and the interlocked directorate. With it, and due to the increased importance of personnel relations with those in charge of political decisions, the importance of the interlocking directorate has diminished slightly.

17.3.4 Period Before the Enactment of the 1965 Corporations Law

The German occupation policy heavily influenced Germany following World War II. Victorious nations became a major influence on restructuring of personnel connections between enterprises. Unlike during the Third Reich occupation, the policy aimed to dismantle monopolies and promote holistic regulation, rather than relying on the state's influence through personnel connections. For the German business, US industrial policy aimed to eliminate cartels and promote an oligopolistic market based on competition, similar to that of the USA (Berghahn 1985, S 280). According to Windolf (2014, p. 74), "the decline of network density after World War II was a spillover effect of the antitrust regulation and of the deconcentration process of the 1950s."

Personnel ties played a crucial role in "cooperative capitalism," replacing cartels. The revival of the three largest banks and the reorganization of large corporate groups according to the business field occurred in the latter half of the 1950s, as did organizational restructuring of the fragmented personnel connections advanced through the subsequent personnel ties of each bank. The interlocking directorates were expanded by assigning management and supervisory board members to each of the reconcentrated banks and inviting members from other companies to join bank supervisory boards.

Restructuring personnel connections is crucial for the three largest banks to maintain strong business relationships with industrial enterprises. To maintain financial relationships with industrial enterprises, banks must secure supervisory board mandates from members of the same bank during succession elections. Inviting bank members to supervisory boards is crucial for industrial companies to maintain and strengthen business relationships. Thus, at the end of the 1950s, personnel connections were formed as a correspondence to the postwar industrial concentration unlike the prewar economic concentration, which relied on market control and giant trusts in industrial sectors seen in the prewar period, particularly in the 1920s. Bank credits have emerged as the primary form of corporate financing.

The fact that bank credit had become the major method in corporate finance with the concentration of banks in 1957 was an important factor in the backward movement of the issuance of stocks and industrial bonds (Aizawa 1988, p. 135). Business relationships between industrial enterprises and banks have strengthened, emphasizing the need to monitor enterprise management when banks provide funds. In the three largest banks, the rates of personnel connections through influential mandates, such as chairman and vice-chairman increased, and the Deutsche Bank was especially visible in the interlocking directorates thanks to the chairman posts.

17.3.5 Period After the Enactment of the 1965 Corporations Law

Later, the 1965 Corporations Law limited the number of mandates: one person could hold a supervisory board, significantly impacting the personnel connections formed due to directors being assigned to organizations' supervisory boards of other enterprises or interlocking directorates within a similar organization. Large banks tended to choose companies to assign their personnel as supervisory board members rather than accept people from other companies to serve on such boards. As a result, the number of enterprises and mandates in which interlocking directorates were formed decreased compared to the end of the 1950s; banks emphasized personnel ties to the most prominent companies in key industrial sectors. For example, emphasizing the size of enterprise concerned with close business relationships, Deutsche Bank considered six companies—Siemens & Halske1, Daimler-Benz, BASF, Vereingte Glanzstoff-Fabrik, Rheinish-Westfälisches Elektrizitätswerk AG, and Dortmund-Hörder Hüttenunion—as enterprises in which this bank absolutely maintained these mandates (Gall 2004, SS. 338–339, 342–344). Although the Dresdner Bank central advisory council was established in 1957 (Meyen 1992, S. 331), similar organizations emerged in other banks during the mid-1960s, in response to the influence of regulation by the 1965 Corporations Law. Establishing banks' central advisory council was necessary because of the need to maintain the level of personnel connection between banks and other enterprises in various important industries (Pfeiffer 1986a, S. 164, 1986b, S. 477, 1993, SS. 158–159; Stanzick 1969, S. 72; Eglau 1990, S. 128).

Other than the 1965 Corporations Law, factors affecting the decline in interlocking directorates include enterprise concentrations such as mergers and a decrease in the number of joint-stock companies. Concentrations of enterprises in the 1960s, particularly following the 1966–1967 crisis, and M&As of subsidiaries within certain corporate groups based on the same capital line as a core of concentrations in the 1950s, company concentrations and alliances between large corporate groups became prominent. As a result, much stronger and new large monopolistic groups were formed (Hahn and Tammer 1970, SS. 24–25). While until the mid-1960s, forms such as bankruptcy and acquisition of small and medium firms were at the heart of monopolistic enterprises' concentration strategy, mergers, collaboration, and joint enterprise formation among representative large corporate groups became important strategic methods in the latter half of the 1960s (Tammer and Hahn 1969, S. 7). Many purchases and capital participation in industries were directly intermediated by bank activities as receivers and sellers, with banks profiting significantly from such activities (Tammer 1969, S. 7). The number of joint-stock companies (West Germany and Berlin) decreased from 2573 at the end of the 1960s to 2537 at the end of 1965, and a further 2317 at the end of 1969 as enterprises consolidated (Statistisches Bundesamt 1961, SS. 196–197, 1966, SS. 212–213, 1970, SS. 170–171).

The postwar basic system of the interlocking directorate was established at the end of the 1960s as a result of these factors and phenomena, and it was fundamentally maintained until the end of the 1980s. Comparing personnel connections among

Germany's largest 100 enterprises in 1978, 1984, and 1990, the number of personnel ties by members of nonfinancial managing boards decreased from 145 to 127 and then to 96, but the decline was not significant. The numbers of personnel connections by members of the management boards in the financial sectors increased from 97 to 106 before falling slightly to 104. Thus, changes were almost not observed. Although personnel ties among members of the control organs increased from 527 to 600, then decreased to 437 during the same period, the decline was not very significant (Monopolkommission 2020, S. 101).

In the 1980s, the German banking system was widely considered superior to the market-based system capable of providing industries with long-term patient capital (Vitols 2003). This was because of the importance and effectiveness of monitoring other companies by banks with interlocking directorates. In the 1980s, banks were companies that frequently assigned representatives to supervisory authorities. They served on the boards of other companies and remained in a prominent position within the corporate network (Windllf 2002, p. 70).

17.3.6 Period Following the 1990s

The 1990s saw significant changes in personnel ties and networks based on interlocking directorates occurred. During the latter half of the 2010s, the numbers of enterprises and mandates where interlocking directorates were built significantly decreased in the cases of Deutsche Bank and Commerzbank. The numbers of interlocking directorates through influential posts such as chairman or vice-chairman have also dramatically declined, indicating decisive changes in personnel relationships initiated by banks. The range of industries to which companies with such personnel ties belonged was limited to narrow extent. Interlocking directorates of these banks with enterprises in the heavy and chemical industries, as former key industrial sectors, have declined significantly. Such changes reflected in the indirect interlocking directorates. These types of personnel ties between Deutsche Bank and Commerzbank can only be observed in only few cases unlike the period at the end of the 1960s. In the personnel networks built between supervisory board members to the extent of "distance 2" composed of second- and third-party enterprises, the number of enterprises composing the network has significantly decreased, and characteristic changes such as the enterprises with low adjacency and a narrow range of industry composition can be seen. In addition, large linkers or network specialists with more than ten mandates disappeared (Windolf 2014, pp. 74, 80).

Thus, a system based on interlocking directorates to gather, exchange, and share information between banks and industries has changed dramatically. Paul Windolf argued that the corporate network in the twentieth century which was a national network is no longer effective for coordination of exchange in the markets due to condition in which stable circumstances changed in the process of globalization (Windolf 2014, p. 74). In terms of personnel connections, the interfirm relationships known as "Germany Inc.," which are based on cooperative relations between industry and banks, as well as between industrial enterprises, have faced radical changes.

As a result, we will now look at the factors that determine such changes. The period after the 1990s saw significant changes due to the globalization of the economy and enterprise, internationalization of financial market and the corresponding change in conditions of company financing, the development of new financial technologies and changes in risk for banks, transformation of bank behavior, that is, shift from credit banks to investment banks, changes in laws, and the Corporate Governance Code.

The globalization of enterprises and economy and the deregulation pursued at the worldwide level and intensified competition had a significant impact on the mode of corporate behavior. Specifically, the results of globalization and deregulation of the finance affected the activities of banks (David and Weserhuis 2014, p. 20). In Germany, despite increasing capital market pressures, the market for corporate control has not developed as seen in the USA and the UK (Furch 2012, S. 65, 153, 231; Velte and Weber 2011, S. 478; Beyer 2006, S. 104; Heinze 2004, pp. 218, 226, 228, 230). A business strategy geared toward the capital market gained importance (Furch 2012, S. 132). The impact of change in the conditions of company financing with internationalization of financial market was also large. The trend of corporate finance from indirect financing to direct financing changed risks for banks. If stocks or bonds largely met the external capital demand of large companies, risks were borne not by the banks but by the shareholders or owners who lost capital during the enterprise's bankruptcy. As a result, the close cooperation with industrial enterprises had no strategic significance for pure investment banks. Furthermore, as speculative trading increased, the type of risk shifted. The benefits of internal monitoring systems were reduced as transparency was to be realized, as observed in Anglo-American systems (Beyer 2001, pp. 6–7, 9–10, 2006, pp. 102–103).

Innovation with high risk requires a provider of funds who is granted risk, and external financing becomes unsuitable for such demand as procurement of funds using equity capital (Ifrim 2007, S. 36). Unlike small and medium firms in which financing through bank credits still plays significant role, for large firms, such form of financing relatively lost importance compared with raising of capital in new market, namely securities market (Ifrim 2007, S. 39). New financial technologies became a factor changing risk for banks. The securitization and credit insurance system allowed banks to decentralize or avoid credit risks. As a result, any necessity to assign directors to the supervisory board of companies with debts no longer existed (Windolf 2014, p. 80). Moreover, the trend of diffusion of the accounting standards securing higher transparency represented by the International Accounting Standard and the US-GAAP decreased merits of internal monitoring (Beyer 2006, S. 104).

The transformation of bank behavior, such as that seen in the movement from the credit bank business as a house bank to an investment bank business, is deeply related to changes in personnel connections. The increase in the significance of M&As for the development of companies made investment banking more attractive. The essential cause was the increasing significance of M&A in corporate expansion (Beyer 2006, pp. 105–106; Furch 2012, S. 235; Plump et al. 2020, S. 560). Banks came to orient toward the high profit brought about by intermediating M&A and support hostile takeovers rather than protective behavior (Ringe 2015, p. 517; Furch 2012, S. 155; Höpner and Jackson 2001, p. 18). However, it should be noticed that even in Commerzbank, which does not maintain pursuing the first class of investment bank in the world equivalent to American banks as Deutsche Bank did and made efforts to concentrate on the traditional fields (Furch 2012, S. 231), interlocking directorates dramatically decreased. Such financial strategy as a result of change of business policy under the influence of competition and internationalization, political decisions, and company-specific factors (Beyer 2006, S. 114) led to weakening of connection between enterprises in terms of capital and personnel connections.

Furthermore, the influences of changes in laws were significant. The transformation of the law system from the standpoint of creditor protection to that of investor protection, law reforms along with the US line to promote capital market, and deregulation progressed. The European Union pursued liberalization in the financial market for each member country. It regarded stock markets as more important and had reinforced investor protection (Jackson 2005, p. 419; Schnitzler 2007, S. 229).

The reforms by three laws to promote financial market from 1990 to 1998 during the Kohl political power aimed at activating financial market (Cioffi and Höpner 2006, S. 424). The Law of Control and Transparency in the Field of Company Sector (Gesetz zur Kontrolle und Transparenz im Unternehmensbereich = KonTraG) enacted in 1998 intended to restrain strong influence of banks through voting right of deposited stocks and regulated that the number of chairman post on the supervisory board was to be calculated two when calculating the number of mandates one person could hold (Ringe 2015, p. 507). Reforms of three laws after 2000 aimed at strengthening participation and roles of shareholders (Ringe 2015, pp. 530–531). Another law passed in 1998 (Kapitalaufnahmeerleichterungsgesetz) enabled us to use the international accounting rules such as the US-GAAP and International Accounting Standard (Furch 2012, S. 152). This law was intended to defend the decline of the monitoring and superintendence functions of the chairman of the supervisory board. The tax reform in 2002 to dissolve a corporate network abolished taxation of capital gain (Beyer 2006, S. 110, 153). This law was an important factor in promoting the change in ownership relationships with other firms and brought about the sale of shares possessed by financial institutions. However, even with the decrease in the holding of banks of industrial enterprises shares, the possibility of executing the voting right via deposited stocks still remains. Therefore, even in cases where a bank sells shares of other companies, the assignment of members from the bank to the supervisory board depends on the bank's behavior. However, banks do not always intend to execute their voting right at the general meeting to assign their own member to the supervisory board of the concerned company.

Besides these hard laws, the influence of the Corporate Governance Code as the soft law was also an important moment of further promoting changes of interlocking directorates. The cord regulated the number of posts one person can hold on the supervisory boards as recommendation (Monopolkommission 2022, S. 34). It became the final strong blow bringing about the end of big linkers with more than ten mandates (Windolf 2014, p. 80).

In addition to these factors, the influence of changes in competition structure after the 1990s was also great. Regarding changes in capitalism in this period, understanding the complicated competition structure with the progress of globalization was important. After the 1990s, the competition structure has shifted from the Japan-US-Europe trilateral structure to global competition due to globalization and borderless conditions of market, economic, and industrial development in each country in the other region, including developing and emerging countries, the entry of old socialist nations in central and eastern Europe and the Soviet Union into market and productive forces, and the rise of socialist countries such as China and Vietnam. Furthermore, as seen in measures such as trade and other field and industrial policy, particularly policy aimed at bringing up key industries, state strategy and protectionist measures have made an overwhelming dominance by foreign capital in each country or region's market more difficult. Moreover, the advancement of information and communication technology tends to decrease the involvement of elements of tacit knowledge and their meaning in the use of such technology compared to technologies previously represented by technologies used in production techniques. As a result, the leveling of technological standards has occurred even between advanced countries and developing countries that have recently made inroads into capitalistic competition since the 1990s, which has become an important factor in strengthening price competition.

In considering the management problems with which global enterprises are forced to cope with market conditions, it is important to pay attention to the characteristics of the market in each region or country, determined by differences in market conditions between nations due to the level of development of the economy and industry, and as seen, for example, in liberalistic or protectionist policies, which each country adopts as the target of the market. As a result, global companies must deal with market changes flexibly, with a complex product mix that takes into account market characteristics in each region or country.

Under such conditions, even for the USA, Japan, and advanced European countries, achieving overwhelming dominance and a single victory in all or most industries and business processes and decisive expansion of dominance fields has proven difficult. As a result, even in advanced countries, industries with strong competitiveness and those without such a competitive advantage have become increasingly complex.

A similar situation can be observed in terms of company business fields and products, as well as business processes such as development, production, sales, purchasing, logistics, and customer service. There is a condition in which business fields, product fields, and business processes with a high dominance and no advantage are combined. The complexity and diversity of competition relations determined by differences in conditions to build competitive power marks a significant qualitative shift in global capitalism since the 1990s.

In this way, during the period after the 1990s, accumulation conditions have strikingly changed as well under such competition structure and business relationships between industry and bank were forced to be changed reflecting corporate behaviors in banking industry as well as various industrial sectors composed of manufacturing, distribution, and service industries. The significance of capital and personnel connections with enterprises in many industries has changed and maintaining of the close interfirm relationships built till then in itself has become difficult. Connection between such changes of competition structure at the global stage of capitalism and industry–bank relationships is an important issue to be explored afterward.

(1) Edwards and Fischer (1994) referred to German banks, specifically the three largest banks that had a substantial degree of control over equity voting rights in German corporations, and this control was primarily due to proxy votes. There was only "weak evidence of any association between the number of bank representatives on the supervisory board," and the bank supervisory board representatives were not sufficiently numerous to determine supervisory board decisions (Edwards and Fischer 1994, p. 226). However, based on the conditions of voting rights execution in annual meetings discussed in Sect. 17.2.1 and cooperative behaviors between banks in this issue, it is important to note that large banks tend to have the power to decide the composition of the company's supervisory board members.
(2) The debtor rates in the current calculation of the total number of asset accounts of 19 large banks in Germany were 41% in 1914 (Goldschmidt 1928, S. 60).
(3) The annual average amount of issuing industrial securities (stocks and bonds) measured by issue price were 159, 77, 338, 746, 357, and 840 million Mark in the 1883–1890, 1891–1894, 1895–1897, 1898–1900, 1901–1904, and 1905–1913 periods, respectively (Spiethoff 1955, Tafel 3).

References

Aizawa K (1988) Nishi Doitsu no kinyu sijyo to kozo (Financial markets in West Germany and their structure). Toyo keizai shinposya, Tokyo

Aizawa K (1994) Oshu saikyo no kinyu teikoku. Doitsu Ginko (The strongest financial empire in Europe). Nihon keizai shinbunsya, Tokyo

Arndt H (1974) *Wirtschaft und Macht.Tatsachen und Theorien*. C. H. Beck, München

Baums T, Fraune C (1995) Institutionelle Anlage und Publikumgesellschaft: Eine empirische Untersuchung. In: Die Aktiengesellschaft 40(3):97–112

Berghahn V (1985) Unternehmer und Politik in der Bundesrepublik. Schurkamp, Frankfurt am Main

Bergmann H (1935) Umwandlung, Auflösung und Löschung von Kapitalgesellschaften: Erläuterungen zu den neuen handrechtlichen und steuerrechtlicher Vorschriften. Carl Heymann, Berlin

Berle AA, Means GC (1932) The modern corporation and private property. Macmillan Press, New York

Berliner Handels-Gesellschaft (1956) Die Berliner Handels-Gesellschaft in einem Jahrehundert deutscher Wirtschaft 1856–1956. Brüder Hartmann, Berlin

Beyer J (2001) Deutschland AG a.D.: Deutsche Bank, Allianz und das Verflechtungszentrum großer deutscher Unternehmen. In: MPIfG (MaxPlanck-Institut für Gesellschaftsforschung) Working Paper 02/4, pp 1–26

Beyer J (2006) Pfadabhängigkeit. Über institutionelle Kontinuität, anfällige Stabiltät und fundamentalen Wandel. Campus, Frankfurt am Main

Böhm J (1992) Der Einfluß der Banken auf Großunternehmen. Steuer- und Wirtschaftsverlag, Hamburg

Bol A (2018) Aktionärstrukture der Deutschen Bank, 1870–1929. In: Jahrbuch für Wirtschaftsgeschichte 59(1):135–156
Bundesministerium der Finanzen (Hrsg) (1979) Bericht der Studienkommission. Grundsatzfragen der Kreditwirtschaft (Schriftenreihe des Bundesministeriums der Finanzen, Heft 28), Stollfuss, Frankfurt am Main
Busse A (1962) Depotstimmrecht der Banken. T. Gabler, Wiesbaden
Chandler A (1990) Scale and scope: the dynamics of industrial capitalis. Harvard University Press, Berkeley, Massachusetts
Cioffi HW, Höpner M (2006) Das parteipolitische Paradox des Finanzmarktkapitalismus. Aktionärsorientierte Reformen in Deutschland, Frankreich, Italien und den USA. In: Politische Vierteljahresschrift 47(3):419–440
D.W.I.-Bericht (1961) Die Deutsche Bank—Zentrum des deutschen Finanzkapitals. In: D.W.I. Bericht 12(15):1–23
Dahlem M (2009) Der Professionalisierung des Bankbetriebs.Studien zur Institutionellen Struktur Deutschen Banken im Kaiserreich 1871–1914. Klartext Verlag, Essen
David T, Weserhuis G (2014) Comparing Corporate networks in a long-term perspective. In: David T, Weserhuis G (eds) The power of corporate networks. a comparative and historical perspective. Routledge, New York, pp 1–28
Der deutsche Vokswirt (1938) Industrie als Bankier? In: Der deutsche Vokswirt 12(41):1996
Der Spiegel (1965) Ordner an der Orgel. In: Der Spiegel 19(45):49–69
Der Spiegel (1988a) Daimler/MBB: Die Niederlage des Grafen. In: Der Spiegel 42(46):116–118
Der Spiegel (1988b) Daimler-Benz: Übernimmt sich der Reise? In: Der Spiegel 42(16):108–113
Der Spiegel (1987a) Denkt weiter. In: Der Spiegel 41(18):98–101
Der Spiegel (1987b) Schwere Fehler. In: Der Spiegel 41(29):69–71
Duschnitzky Sv (1927) Das Konzern-Problem unter Berücksichtigung der Schwerindustriellen Wirtschaft im Nachkriegs-Deutschland: eine Sozialökonomischen Studie zu den Phänomenen der modernen kapitalistischen Konzentration. Kommissionsverlag der Deutschen Buchhandlung, Kaunas
DWI-Berichte (1964) Die Verschmelzung von Industrie- und Bankkapital in Westdeutschland. In: DWI-Berichte 15(21):1–24
Edwards J, Fischer K (1994) Banks, finance and investment in Germany. Cambridge University Press, Cambridge
Eglau HO (1990) Wie Gott in Frankfurt: Die Deutsche Bank und die deutsche Industrie, 3rd edn. Econ Verlag, Düsseldorf
Fohlin C (2007) Finance capitalism and Germany's rise to industrial power. Cambridge University Press, New York
Furch D (2012) Marktwirtschaften unter dem Druck globalisierter Finanzmärkte, Finanzsysteme und Corporate-Governance-Strukturen in Deutschland und Italien. Springer NV, Wiesbaden
Fürstenberg C (1931) Die Lebensgeschichte eines deutschen Bankiers, 1870–1914. Ullstein, Berlin
Gall L (2004) Der Bankier Hermann Josef Abs. Eine Biographie, C. H. Beck, München
Goldschmidt RW (1928) Das deutsche Groβbankkapital in seimer neueren Entwicklung. Emil Ebering, Berlin
Gottschalk A (1988) Der Stimmrechtseinfluβ der Banken in den Aktionärversammlungen von Groβunternehmen. In: WSI Mitteilungen 41(5):294–304
Gottschalk A (1990) Depotstimmrecht und die Macht der Banken. Die Tageszeitung 3108:11
Hagemann H (1931) Das Verhältnis der deutschen Grossbanken zur Industrie. W. Christian, Berlin
Hahn W, Tammer H (1970) Kapitalkonzentration in Westdeutschaland an der Wende zum neuen Jahrzehnt. In: D.W.I.-Berichte 21(8):21–29
Handbuch der deutschen Aktiengesellschaften (jedes Jahr)
Hardach G (1984) Banking and industry in Germany in the interwar period 1919-1939. In: J Eur Econ Hist 13(2):203–234
Heinze T (2004) Dynamics in the German system of corporate governance? Empirical findings regarding interlocking directorates. In: Econ Soc 33 (2):218–238

Heβ P (1958) AEG Energie-Profit-Verbrechen, Wirtschaft: Manuskript-Nachlass von Eberhard Koebel-Tusk. Verlag Die Wirtschaft, Berlin
Höpner M, Jackson G (2001) An emerging market for corporate control? The Mannesmann takeover and German corporate governance. In: MPIfG (MaxPlanck-Institut für Gesellschaftsforschung) Discussion Paper 01/4, pp 1–53
Höpner M (2001) Corporate governance in transition: ten empirical findings on shareholder value and industrial relations in Germany. In: MPIfG (MaxPlanck-Institut für Gesellschaftsforschung) Discussion Paper 01/5, pp 1–61
Ifrim S (2007) Erosion der Deutschland AG—Ursachen und konsequenzen Veränderter Personal- und Kapitalverflechtungen aud dem deutschen Kapitalmarkt. Examicus Verlsg, Frankfurt am Main
Ingersoll R, Brady R (1987) The banker behind the shakeup at Daimler-Benz. Deutsche Bank's Alfred Herrhausen is pushing the company his way. In: Business week 3007:19–20
Ipsen D, Pfitzinger J (2003) Krise in der Deutschland AG: Der Fall AEG. In: Streeck W, Höpner M (Hrsg) Alle Macht dem Markt? Fallstudien zur Abwicklung der Deutschland AG. Campus Verlag, Frankfurt am Main, New York, pp 60–92
Jackson G (2005) Stakeholders under pressure: corporate governance and labour management in Germany and Japan. In: Corp Gov Int Rev 13(3):419–428
James H (2003) Die Deutsche Bank im Dritten Reich. C. H. Beck, München
Jeidels O (1905) Das Verhältnis der deutschen Groβbanken zur Industrie mit besonderer Berücksichtigung der Eisenindustrie. Duncker & Humblot, Leipzig
Joly H (1998) Groβunternehmer in Deutschland. Leipziger Universitätsverlag, Leipzig, Soziologie einer industriellen Elite
Jürgens U, Naumann K, Rupp J (2000) Shareholder value in an adverse environment: the German case. In: Econ Soc 29(1):54–79
Kato E (1973) Waimaru taisei no keizai kozo (Economic structure of the Weimar system). Tokyo daigaku shuppankai, Tokyo
Kominato S (1970) Sotaiteki anteiki ni okeru Doitsu no daiginko to sangyo no shihon chikuseki (2) Relationships between large German bank and industry in the relatively stable period of capitalism and capitalistic accumulation (2). In: Shakai kagaku ronshu (J Soc Sci) 22(2):37–106
Kuczynski J (1963) Die Geschichte der lage der Arbeiter unter dem Kapitalismus. Bd.15, Akademie Verlag, Berlin
Lampe L (2004) Der Bankbetrieb in Krieg und Inflation. Deutsche Groβbanken in den Jahren 1914 bis 1923. Franz Steiner Verlag, Stuttgart
Lenin WI (1953) Bericht über das Parteiprogramm auf dem VIII. Parteitag der KPR (B). In: Ausgewählte Werke: in zwei Bänden. Bd. II, Diez Verlag, Berlin, pp 506–541
Lindhardt H (1958) Wider das Depotstimmrecht der Banken. In: Die Aktiengesellschaft 3(8):169–176
Lurié S (1947) Private investment in a controlled economy. Germany, 1933–1939. Columbia University Press, New York
Matsuba M (1984) Kinyu Shihon to Syakaika—Waimaru ki Shoki Kinyu Shihon Bunseki—(Finance capital and socialization—analysis of finance capital in the early period of the Weimar Republic—).Yuhikaku, Tokyo
Meyen HG (1992) 120 Jahre Dresdner Bank. Unternehmens-Chronik. Dresdner Bank AG, Frankfurt am Main
Monopolkommission, (1978) Fortschreitende Konzentration bei Groβunternehmen: Hauptgutachte 1976/77 (Haupugutachten der Monopolkommission; 2), 1. Aufl., Nomos-Verlagsgesellschaft, Baden-Baden
Monopolkommission (2008) Weniger Staat, mehr Wettbewerb. Gesundheitsmärkte und staatliche Behilfen in der Wettbewerbsordnung: Hauptgutachten 2006/2007 (Hauptgutachten der Monopolkommission; 17), 1. Aufl., Baden-Baden
Monopolkommission (2020) Wettbewerb 2020 (XXIII.Hauptgutachten der Monopolkommission gemäβ §44 Abs.1 Satz 1 GWB), Nomos, Wiesbaden

Monopolkommission (2022) Wettbewerb 2022 (XXIV.Hauptgutachten: Gutachten der Monopolkommission gemäβ §44 Abs.1 Satz 1 GWB), Nomos, Wiesbaden
Morr JM v (Hrsg) (1960) Adreßbuch der Direktoren und Aufsichtsräte.Jahrgang 1960, Bd. I, Nach Persönlichkeiten geordnet, Finanzverlag G.m.b.H., Berlin
Mossner G (Hrsg) (1971) Handbuch der Direktoren und Aufsichtsräte—seit 1898—, Bd. I, Nach Personen georнet, Jahrgang 1970/71, Finanz- und Korrespondenz-Verlag, Berlin
Nagasaka S (1961) Doitsu kinyu shihon no seiritsu (The birth of German finance capital). In: Takeda T (ed) Teikokusyugiron (Theory of imperialism). Tokyo daigaku shuppankaikai, Tokyo
Neumann F (1942) Behemoth: the structure and practice of national socialism. V. Hollancz, London
Nishihara K (1936a) Kabushikigaishahou ni okeru Nachisu siso (1) (Concept of National Socialism regarding corporation law, 1). In: Hogaku Kyokai Zassi (J Jurisprudence Assoc) 54(8):110–135
Nishihara K (1936b) Kabushikigaishahou ni okeru Nachisu siso (2) (Thought of National Socialism regarding corporation law, 2). In: Hogaku Kyokai Zassi (J Jurisprudence Assoc) 54(9):93–118
Ono E (1956) Doitsu kinyu shihon seiritsushiron (History of establishment of Finance capital in Germany). Yuhikaku, Tokyo
Passow R (1923) Die Bilanzen der privaten und öffentlichen Unternehmungen, 3., nue durchgesehne Aufl., Bd.II, B. G. Teubner, Leipzig
Pfeiffer H (1986a) Das Netwerk der Groβbanken. Personelle Verflechtungen mit Konzernen, Staat und ideologischen Apparaten. In: Blätter für deutsche und Internationale Politik 31(2):161–177
Pfeiffer H (1986b) Groβbanken und Finanzgruppen.Ausgewählte Ergebnisse einer Untersuchung der personellen Verflechtungen von Deutscher, Dresdner und Commerzbank. In: WSI Mitteilungen 39(7):473–481
Pfeiffer H (1993) Die Macht der Banken. Die personellen Verflechtungen der Commerzbank, der Deutschen Bank und der Dresdner Bank mit Unternehemen. Campus, Frankfurt am Main
Plumpe W, Nützenadel A, Schenk R (2020) Deutsche Bank. Die globale Hausbank 1870–2020. Propyläen, Berlin
Pohle W (1937) Das Depotstimmrecht der Banken. In: Die Bank 30(11):369–374
Prion W (1931) Selbstfinanzierung der Unternehmen. J. Springer, Berlin
Prion W (1928) Der deutsche Geld- und Kapitalmarkt seit der Stabilisierung. In: Harms B, Strukturewandlungen der deutschen Volkswirtschaft. Vorlesungen gehalten während der Herbst-Lehrgangs 1927 der Deutschen Vereinigung für Staatswissenschaftliche Fortbildung. Zweiter Band, Raimar Hobbing, Berlin
Prion W (1929) Kapital und Betries: Finanzierungsfrage der deutschen Wirtschaft. G. A. Gloeckner, Leipzig
Püttner G (1963) Das Depotstimmrecht der Banken. Duncker & Humblot, Berlin
Reichsministerium des Innern (1934) Deutsches Reichsgesetzblatt, Teil I, Jahrgang 1934, Reichsverlagsamt, Berlin
Riesser J (1971) Die deutsche Groβbanken und ihre Konzentration im Zusammenhang mit der Entwicklung der Gesamtwirtschaft in Deutschland. Vierrte verbesserte und vermehrte Auflage, Verlag. Detlev Auvermann KG, Glashutten im Taunus,
Ringe W-G (2015) Changing law and ownership patterns in Germany: corporate governance and the erosion of Deutschland AG. In: Am J Comp Law Spring 2015 63(2):493–538
Rosendorff R (1932) Was müssen die Aktionäre und Verwaltungen von neuern Aktienrecht wissen? Spaeth & Lind, Berlin, Wien
Schaad H-P (1972) Das Depotstimmrecht der Banken nach schweizerischem und deutschem Recht. Schulthess Polygraphischer Verlag, Zürich
Schnitzler W (2007) Implementierung der Anforderungen des Sarbanes-Oxle Acts in einem deutschen Groβunternehmen. In: Freidank C-C, Altes P (Hrsg) Rechnungslegung und Corporate Governance. Reporting, Steuerung und Überwachungder Unternehmen im Umbruch, Berlin, SS 225–246
Schönwitz D, Weber H-J (1982) Unternehmenskonzentration, Personelle Verflechtungen und Wettbewerb. Eine Untersuchung auf der Grundlage der hundert gröβten Konzerne der Bundesrepublik Deutschland. 1. Aufl., Nomos Verlagsgesellschaft, Baden-Baden

Scott J (1988) Entrepreneurial capital in Japan and Britain. In: Ritsumeikan keieigaku (The Ritsumeikan business review) 27(2):29–51

Scott J (1990) Corporate control and corporate rule: Britain in an international perspective. In: Brit J Soc 41(3):351–373

Spiethoff A (1955) Die Wirtschaftliche Wechsellagen: Aufschwung, Krise, Stockung. II, Lange statistische Reihen über die Merkmale der wirtschaftlichen Wechsellagen. J. C. B. Mohr, Tübingen

Spoerer M (1996) Vom Scheingewinnen zum Rüstungsboom. Die Eigenkapitalrentabilität der deutschen Industrieaktiengesellschaften 1925–1941. Franz Steiner, Stuttgart

Stanzick K-H (1969) Der ökonomische Konzentrationsproze. In: Schäfer G, Nedelmann C (Hrsg) Der CDU-Staat.Analysen zur Verfassungswriklichkeit der Bundesrepublik, Bd. I, 2. Aufl., Schurkamp, München, SS 48–79

Statistisches Bundesamt (1961) Statistisches Jahrbuch für die Bundesrepblik Deutschland 1961. W. Kohlhammer GmbH, Stuttgart, Mainz

Statistisches Bundesamt (1966) Statistisches Jahrbuch für die Bundesrepblik Deutschland 1966. W. Kohlhammer GmbH, Stuttgart, Mainz

Statistisches Bundesamt (1970) Statistisches Jahrbuch für die Bundesrepblik Deutschland 1970. W. Kohlhammer GmbH, Stuttgart, Mainz

Statistisches Reichssamt (1937) Statistisches Jahrbuch für das Deutsche Reich 1937. Verlag für Sozialpolitik, Wirtschaft und Statistik, Paul Schmidt, Berlin

Statistisches Reichsamt (1938) Statistisches Jahrbuch für das Deutsche Reich 1938. Verlag für Sozialpolitik, Wirtschaft und Statistik, Paul Schmidt, Berlin

Statistisches Reichsamt (1940) Statistisches Jahrbuch für das Deutsche Reich 1940. Verlag für Sozialpolitik, Wirtschaft und Statistik, Paul Schmidt, Berlin

Tammer H, Hahn W (1969) Eine neue Etappe monopolistischer Machtkonzentration in Westdeutschland. In: D.W.I.-Berichte 20(2):2–17

Tammer H (1969) Konzentration und Zentralisation des Kapitals in Westdeutsch-land im Jahre 1968. In: D.W.I.-Berichte 20(6):2–10

Tohara S (1963) Doitsu kinyu shihon no seiritsu katei (Establishment of Finance capital in Germany). Tokyo daigaku shuppankai, Tokyo

Tsumori T (1961) Doitsu dokusen keiseiki ni okeru jikokinyu to kessanseisaku (2) (Self-financing and policy of balancing of accounts in the period of establishment of monopolies in Germany). In: Keizai ronso (Econ Rev) 88(6):58–68

Velte P, Weber SC (2011) Outsider- und Insider-Systeme der Corporate Governance. In: Zeitschrift für Planung & Unternehmenssteuerung 21(4):473–482

Vitols S (2003) From banks to markets: the political economy of liberalization of the German and Japanese financial systems. In: Yamamura K, Streeck W (eds) The end of diversity? Prospects for German and Japanese capitalism. Cornell University Press, Ithaca, NY, pp 240–260

Windolf P (2002) Corporate networks in Europe and the United States. Oxford University Press, New York

Windolf P (2014) The corporate networks in Germany, 1896–2010. In: David T, Weserhuis F (eds) The power of corporate networks. a comparative and historical perspective. Routledge, New York, pp 66–85

Wirtschaft und Statistik (1939a) Die Aktiengesellschaften im Jahre 1938. In: Wirtschaft und Statistik 19(6):236–238

Wirtschaft und Statistik (1939b) Die Entwicklung des Unternehmensbestandes im Jahre 1938. In: Wirtschaft und Statistik 19(2):75–76

Wirtschaft und Statistik (1939c) Die Gesellschaften mit beschränkter Haftung Ende 1938. In: Wirtschaft und Statistik 19(7):273–276

Wirtschaft und Statistik (1936) Bestand der eingetragenen Unternehmungen Ende 1935. In: Wirtschaft und Statistik 16(24):965–966

Wirtschaftswoche (1987) Der Herr im Haus. In: Wirtschaftswoche 41(30):88–92

Wixforth H (1995) Banken und Schwereindustrie in der Weimarer Republik. Böhlau, Köln, Weimar, Wien
Wixforth H (2006) Expansion der Dresdner Bank in Europa. R. Oldenbourg Verlag, München
Wixforth H, Ziegler D (1994) The Niche in the universal nanking system: private bankiers within German industry,1900–1933. In: Fin Hist Rev 1(1):99–119
Wixforth H, Ziegler D (1995) Bankenmacht: universal banking and German industry in historical perspective. In: Cassis Y, Feldmann GD, Olsson U (eds) Evolution of financial institutions and markets in twentieth century Europe. Scblar Press, Aldershot, pp 247–272
Yamaguch H (1981) Nishi Doitsu ni okeru ginko to aangyo no kankei—Futatsu no Iinkai no chosa to bunseki—(Relationships between bank and industry in West Germany—investigations and analyses of two commissions—). In: Shoken keizai (JSIR J Fin Secur Mark) 135:103–131
Yamaguchi H (2006) Doitsu shoken shijyoshi kenkyu—Torihikisho no chiki tokusei to togo katei—(Study of history of German securities markets—regional characteristics and integration process of exchanges—). Hokkaido daigaku shuppannkai, Sapporo
Yamazaki T (2013) Gendai no Doitsu kigyo—Sono gurobaru chiikika to keiei tokusitsu—(Contemporary German enterprises—their global-regionalization and characteristics of business management—). Moriyama shoten, Tokyo
Yamazaki T (2019) Doitu no kigyokan kankei—Kigyokan jinteki ketugo no kozo to kino—(Inter-firm relationships in Germany—structure and functions of personnel connections between enterprises—). Moriyama shoten, Tokyo
Yamazaki T (2024) Japanese and German enterprises: Comparison of industrial concentration system and business management. Springer Nature, Singapore
Ziegler D (2019) Die Macht der Banken. Governance-Defizite deutscher Groβbanken am Beispiel der Commerzbank 1870–1932. In: Hesse J-O, Kleinschmidt C, Köster R, Schanetzky T (Hrsg) Moderner Kapitalismus. Wirtschaft- und Unternehmenshistorische Beiträge. Mohr Siebeck, Tübingen, SS 455–474
Ленин ВИ (1962) Империализм, как высшая стадия капитализма: популярный очерк. In: Полное собрание сочинений. Том 27, ос. изд-во полит. лит-ры, Москва, pp 299–426

Archival Sources

1. **Historisches Archiv der Deutschen Bank, Frankfurt am Main**

   P00033, P00034, P00035, P00036, P00037, P00038, P00039, P00040, P00041, P00042, P03247, P03248, P03250, P03251, P03253, P03254, P03259, P03262, P03328, P03500, P03525

2. **Historisches Archiv der Commerzbank, Frankfurt am Main**

   HAC-303/3, HAC-400/624, HAC-400/1814, HAC-400/1817, HAC-400/1819, HAC-400/1820, HAC-400/1821, HAC-400/1822, HAC-500/121, 1227-2000, HAC-500/121, 7902-2002, HAC-500/121, 8106-2002, HAC-500/121, 18093-2000, HAC-500/121, 18227-2000, HAC-500/121, 18232-2000, HAC-500/192, 1379-2002, HAC-500/196,12005, HAC-500/196, 120020, HAC-500/196, 120021, HAC-500/196, 120025, HAC-500/196, 120027, HAC-500/196, 120036, HAC-500/196, 120038, HAC-500/196, 120039, HAC-500/196, 120043, HAC-500/196, 12044, HAC-500/211, 107841, HAC-500/211, 107847, HAC-500/211, 108114, HAC-500/211, 109332, HAC-500/211, 109333, HAC-500/211, 120021, HAC-500/257, 108273, HAC-500/337, 447/50, HAC-500/337, 447/51, HAC-500/337, 447/52, HAC-500/337, 449/6, HAC-S3/A183, 5014-2002. MS, 5041-2002. MS

3. **Bayer Archiv, Leverlusen**

   384-1

4. **Siemens Archiv, Berlin**

   4Lr302-20

5. **thyssenkrupp Corporate Archives, Duisburg**

   A/132107, A/132108

6. **Historisches Archiv der Deutschen Technikmuseums, Berlin**

T. Yamazaki, *Relationships Between Industry and Bank in Germany*,
https://doi.org/10.1007/978-981-97-4996-6

I.2.060A.02381, I.2.060A.0995, I.2.060A.-ÜV0192, I.2.060 U438, I.2060 U439, I.2.060 U440, I.2.060 U441, I.2.060 U443, I.2.060 U444, I.2.060 U445, I.2.060 U446, I.2.060 Ü-2, 0257, I.2.060 Ü-2 4218, I.2.060 Ü-2-FA0192, I.2.060 Ü-V0425, I.2.060 Ü-V0428, I.2.060 Ü-V0430, I.2.060 Ü-V0432, I.2.060 Ü-V0438, I.2.060 Ü-V0442, I.2.060 Ü-V0443, I.1206 Ü-V0444, I.2.060 Ü-V0445, I.2.060 Ü-V0446, I.2.060V0441

7. **National Archives, Washington D.C.**

   RG59, 862A.14

8. **Bundesarchiv Berlin, Berlin**

   R8119F/34, R8119F/10913

Index

T. Yamazaki, *Relationships Between Industry and Bank in Germany*,
https://doi.org/10.1007/978-981-97-4996-6

GPSR Compliance

The European Union's (EU) General Product Safety Regulation (GPSR) is a set of rules that requires consumer products to be safe and our obligations to ensure this.

If you have any concerns about our products, you can contact us on ProductSafety@springernature.com

In case Publisher is established outside the EU, the EU authorized representative is:

Springer Nature Customer Service Center GmbH
Europaplatz 3
69115 Heidelberg, Germany

The manufacturer's authorised representative in the EU is Springer Nature Customer Service Centre GmbH, Europaplatz 3, 69115 Heidelberg, Germany. If you have any concerns regarding our products, please contact ProductSafety@springernature.com

Printed and bound by CPI Group (UK) Ltd, Croydon, CR0 4YY
01/10/2026
02225849-0018